ESTATE PLANNING

2015

Published by:
KEIR EDUCATIONAL RESOURCES
4785 Emerald Way
Middletown, OH 45044
1-800-795-5347
1-800-859-5347 FAX
E-mail customerservice@keirsuccess.com
www.keirsuccess.com

"Topic List for CFP® Certification Examination Copyright © 2011, Certified Financial Planner Board of Standards, Inc. All rights reserved. Used with permission."

"Certified Financial Planner Board of Standards, Inc. owns the marks CFP®, CERTIFIED FINANCIAL PLANNER™, and CFP (with flame logo)®, which it awards to individuals who successfully complete initial and ongoing certification requirements."

ISBN PRINT 978-1-937404-83-3
ISBN EPUB 978-1-937404-84-0

INTRODUCTION

For over 40 years, Keir Educational Resources has helped hundreds of thousands of insurance and financial professionals to obtain their professional designations. Over the last 20 years, Keir has produced supplemental study materials to help students complete the required courses at local universities and colleges in order to qualify to sit for the CFP® Certification Examination. Keir also has comprehensive review materials for the CFP® Certification Examination that have helped thousands of students to pass the CFP® Certification Examination.

While working with numerous program directors and instructors from universities and colleges across the country, Keir Educational Resources frequently receives requests for a book that can serve as the primary textbook for each course that is required by CFP Board Registered Programs. Program directors and instructors involved with these programs are frequently looking for textbooks focused specifically on the topics and learning objectives outlined by CFP Board. **Keir is pleased to offer textbooks designed specifically for each of the courses included in CFP Board Registered Programs. Keir also offers a Case Studies book that can be used in the Financial Planning Development Course that is required as of 2012.**

Keir designed this textbook using our well proven methodology of structuring each book to follow the 78 topic list provided by the CERTIFIED FINANCIAL PLANNER™ Board of Standards. We have used this methodology for over 10 years to help thousands of students pass the CFP® Certification Examination. The 78 topic list is the current basis for the CFP® Certification Examination, along with the Student-Centered Learning Objectives released by CFP Board in 2012 and updated in 2014, as the basis for student learning in Registered Programs. This textbook covers Estate Planning (Topics 53 – 73). **Since we designed this textbook to follow the CFP Board's topic list and Learning Objectives, we are confident that students and instructors will find this unique format to be the most effective way to learn the skills required of a successful financial planner. While written with CFP Board Registered Programs in mind, this Estate Planning textbook is comprehensive and flexible enough to be used in non-CFP Board programs as well.**

This textbook includes over 700 multiple choice questions and case questions to help reinforce each topic. The multiple choice questions included in this textbook cover the four cognitive levels of questions used on the CFP® Certification Examination which are: (1) Knowledge/Comprehension, (2) Application, (3) Analysis/Synthesis, and (4) Evaluation. Although there is more emphasis in the CFP® Certification Examination on higher level cognitive questions, a student needs to master lower level knowledge and comprehensive questions in order to master the application, analysis, and evaluation questions.

The CFP® Certification Examination includes comprehensive cases and mini-cases. To provide the experience of working on cases, we have included case fact patterns with multiple choice questions in the Appendix at the end of this textbook. Each of the topics contains a table identifying cases and questions covering material in that particular topic. Students should read the case in the Appendix and attempt to answer the case questions identified for that topic. The cases range from short fact patterns to full blown 5 to 10 page fact patterns. The short fact patterns are similar to mini-cases and allow students to start to build on their ability to answer case questions. The full blown case fact patterns provide the student with the same level of difficulty as the comprehensive cases on the CFP® Certification Examination.

Although most of the multiple choice questions in this textbook were written by Keir Educational Resources, some of the questions have appeared on past CFP® Certification Examinations and are reprinted here with permission.

TABLE OF CONTENTS

Title	**Page**
Estate Planning (Topics 53-73)	
Topic 53: Characteristics and Consequences of Property Titling	53.1–53.23
Topic 54: Methods of Property Transfer at Death	54.1–54.34
Topic 55: Estate Planning Documents	55.1–55.17
Topic 56: Gifting Strategies	56.1–56.40
Topic 57: Gift Tax Compliance and Tax Calculation	57.1–57.22
Topic 58: Incapacity Planning	58.1–58.16
Topic 59: Estate Tax Compliance and Tax Calculation	59.1–59.48
Topic 60: Sources for Estate Liquidity	60.1–60.17
Topic 61: Powers of Appointment	61.1–61.13
Topic 62: Types, Features, and Taxation of Trusts	62.1–62.22
Topic 63: Qualified Interest Trusts	63.1–63.12
Topic 64: Charitable Transfers	64.1–64.26
Topic 65: Use of Life Insurance in Estate Planning	65.1–65.18
Topic 66: Marital Deduction	66.1–66.21
Topic 67: Intra-Family and Other Business Transfer Techniques	67.1–67.29
Topic 68: Deferral and Minimization of Estate Taxes	68.1–68.34
Topic 69: Generation-Skipping Transfer Tax (GSTT)	69.1–69.17
Topic 70: Fiduciaries	70.1–70.8
Topic 71: Income in Respect of a Decedent (IRD)	71.1–71.5
Topic 72: Postmortem Estate Planning Techniques	72.1–72.22
Topic 73: Estate Planning for Non-traditional Relationships	73.1–73.7

TABLE OF CONTENTS, CONTINUED

<u>Title</u>	<u>Page</u>

Appendix

Bartlett Case	Appendix – 1
Marshall Case	Appendix – 9
Webster Case	Appendix – 19
Unser Case	Appendix – 30
Tingey Case	Appendix – 41
Lytle Case	Appendix – 44
Beals Case	Appendix – 50
Mocsin Case	Appendix – 63
Young Case	Appendix – 70
Borelli Case	Appendix – 81
Cunningham Case	Appendix – 93
Ferris Case	Appendix – 108
Wyatt Estate Plan	Appendix – 143
Williams Hypothetical Estate Tax Return	Appendix – 158
Gantry Hypothetical Gift Tax Return	Appendix – 163
Worthington Hypothetical Gift Tax Return with GST Tax	Appendix – 169
Johns Hypothetical Estate Tax Return with GST Tax	Appendix – 175
Selected Facts and Figures	Appendix – 181
78 Topic List	Appendix – 202
Glossary	Glossary – 1
Index	Index – 1

ESTATE PLANNING

Topics 53–73

ESTATE PLANNING

Characteristics and Consequences of Property Titling (Topic 53)

CFP Board Student-Centered Learning Objectives

(a) Compare and contrast the most common types of titling property (sole ownership, joint tenancy with rights of survivorship, tenants in common, tenants by the entirety, and community property).

(b) Recommend the appropriate property titling mechanism given the client's lifetime and estate distribution objectives, and relevant state laws.

Characteristics and Consequences of Property Titling
- A. *Community property vs. non-community property*
- B. *Sole ownership*
- C. *Joint tenancy with right of survivorship (JTWROS)*
- D. *Tenancy by the entirety*
- E. *Tenancy in common*
- F. *Trust ownership*

Community Property vs. Non-Community Property

Community property laws apply in ten states: Alaska, Arizona, California, Idaho, Louisiana, Nevada, New Mexico, Texas, Washington, and Wisconsin. In these states, community property is the ownership interest of the husband and wife in any property acquired by the couple during their marriage.

When married couples take title to property concurrently in states that follow the common law, they usually become tenants by the entirety or joint tenants with right of survivorship. We will discuss community property in more detail at the end of this Topic, after we review the common-law forms of ownership.

Sole Ownership

Sole ownership means one person holds the title to the property and has full ownership rights. For real estate, this full ownership title is referred to as a fee simple. The sole owner has complete control over the property and can sell, mortgage, or give it away during his or her lifetime without the consent of any other person. At death, the sole owner can dispose of the property by will; in the absence of a will, the property is distributed according to intestacy laws.

One of the main advantages of sole ownership is the owner's complete control over the handling and disposition of the property.

During the owner's lifetime, the property can be the subject of gifts to any person, organization, or charity. At death, the owner similarly has complete testamentary control over the property. In estate planning, sole ownership affords the most flexibility in meeting a client's objectives.

The sole owner is entitled to all income from the property, so the sole owner is also subject to the income tax on all of this income. At the owner's death, the full value of the property is included in the probate estate, as well as in the gross estate, for federal estate tax calculation. Property of the sole owner is fully subject to the claims of creditors, both during lifetime and during probate administration.

Joint Tenancy WROS

When title to property is held by two or more persons in joint tenancy with right of survivorship, each joint tenant has an equal ownership interest in the property. The ownership reflects the four unities: interest, title, time, and possession. The joint tenants acquire the same interest, in the same property, at the same time, and they take possession simultaneously.

The unique feature of joint tenancy WROS is that ownership of the property passes by operation of law to the surviving tenant(s). When a joint tenant dies, the ownership interest passes outside probate and is not subject to testamentary disposition. Nevertheless, during a joint tenant's lifetime, the interest can be sold or disposed of by converting the joint tenancy to a tenancy in common.

Property held in joint tenancy WROS will avoid the expense, delay, and publicity of probate proceedings. Property passing to the surviving joint tenant can also avoid the spouse's elective share, will contests, and claims of creditors in probate. Joint tenancy property also has the potential income tax advantage of splitting the income from the property among the joint tenants. This income-splitting can result in income tax reduction when some of the joint tenants are in lower marginal income tax brackets.

A joint tenant WROS does not have the same control over the property that a sole owner has. At death, the joint tenant has no ability to dispose of the property, and it passes by operation of law to the other joint tenant(s). During the joint tenant's lifetime, income must be split with the other joint tenants.

When persons who are not spouses sell property owned in joint tenancy WROS, each joint tenant must report a proportionate share of the gain for income tax purposes. If there are three joint tenants, for example, each must report one-third of the gain. Even when one joint tenant receives more than his or her proportionate share of the proceeds, each tenant must report the proportionate amount.

Unless the interest a joint tenant acquires is proportionate to his or her contribution to the purchase price, the creation of a joint tenancy can give rise to a taxable gift. The creation of joint tenancies between spouses, however, will not result in gift tax liability, due to the unlimited gift tax marital deduction.

For estate tax purposes, the full value of jointly held property will be included in the gross estate of the first joint tenant to die, except to the extent that the survivor can show consideration furnished for the purchase of the property. In other words, if the decedent contributed 1/3 of the purchase price, and the other joint tenants contributed 2/3, then 1/3 of the value of the jointly owned property will be included in the decedent's gross estate. When joint tenancy property is received as a gift or inheritance, only the decedent's fractional interest is included in the gross estate.

When the joint tenancy is between spouses, one-half of the value of the property is included in the decedent's gross estate, regardless of the consideration furnished by the parties for the purchase. Showing that the surviving spouse furnished the entire purchase price will not reduce the included amount below 50%.

REMEMBER: IF JOINT TENANTS ARE SPOUSES, *ONE-HALF* OF THE PROPERTY'S FAIR MARKET VALUE AT DEATH IS INCLUDED IN THE DECEDENT'S GROSS ESTATE. IF JOINT TENANTS ARE NOT SPOUSES, THE *PERCENTAGE-OF-CONTRIBUTION RULE* APPLIES.

Since one-half of spousal joint tenancy property will be included in the gross estate of the first spouse to die, there is a step-up in basis to the date-of-death value on one-half of the property. For non-spousal joint tenancy property, there is a step-up in basis equal to the amount of property included in the decedent's gross estate.

Practice Question

Which of the following statements concerning joint tenancy WROS is correct?

A. If the joint tenants are spouses, the entire value of the property may be included in the gross estate of the first to die.
B. If the joint tenants are not spouses, the entire value of the property will be included in the gross estate of the first to die.
C. If the joint tenants are spouses, the first to die does not have testamentary control over any of the property, regardless of any contribution to the purchase price.
D. If the joint tenants are not spouses, the tenant who contributed the purchase price will report the income from the property.

Answer:
If the joint tenants are spouses, the first to die does not have testamentary control over any of the property, regardless of any contribution to the purchase price. One-half of entire value of the property will be included in the gross estate of the first to die. If the joint tenants are not spouses, the entire value of the property will be included in the gross estate of the first to die only where the survivor cannot show any contribution to the purchase price. The joint tenants will report equal shares of the income.
The answer is C.

Tenancy by the Entirety

Tenancy by the entirety is joint tenancy ownership of property by spouses. The same rules generally apply to tenancy by the entirety as apply to joint tenancy WROS. When a spouse dies, the surviving spouse becomes the sole owner of the property by operation of law. For federal estate tax calculation, one-half of the value of the property will be included in the gross estate of the first spouse to die. Of course, no estate tax will be owed because the property passes to a spouse and is eligible for the marital deduction. Since only one-half of the property held in tenancy by the entirety is included in the gross estate of the first spouse to die, there is a step-up in basis to the date-of-death value for only one-half of the property.

The major difference between tenancy by the entirety and joint tenancy WROS is that any sale or transfer of the entireties property requires the consent of both spouses. Since the concurrence of both spouses is required for transfers, property held in tenancy by the entirety is not subject to the creditors of an individual spouse.

Tenancy in Common

Property is held in tenancy in common when two or more persons own an undivided, fractional interest in the property. The fractional interests may be unequal. Each co-tenant owns a portion of the property separately and can transfer that interest at any time, without the consent of the other co-tenants. Each co-tenant has testamentary control over his or her share of the property, and the fractional interest is included in the deceased owner's probate estate and in his or her gross estate.

In some states, concurrent ownership is presumed to be tenancy in common rather than joint tenancy WROS. The intent to provide for a right of survivorship must be clearly stated. Use of the words "joint tenants" alone may be deemed to be a tenancy in common. The additional words "with right of survivorship" should be stated when the intent is for the title to pass automatically to the surviving tenant(s).

The income from property owned by tenants in common will be split according to the fractional interests of the co-tenants. When property is transferred from sole ownership to tenancy in common, the income-splitting can result in income tax reduction.

Each tenant in common has control over his or her own fractional interest in the property and can sell it or give it away at any time. **Each co-tenant has full testamentary power over the interest and can dispose of the interest by will.** Since the fractional interest will be included in the deceased co-tenant's gross estate, it will receive a full step-up in basis.

When the sole owner transfers property to tenancy in common, there is a loss of control over the property. One co-tenant cannot sell, transfer, mortgage, or give away another co-tenant's interest, so the owner has given up these rights to the co-tenant. In addition, the owner loses a portion of the income that was previously received from the property. As in joint tenancy WROS, creation of the tenancy in common can give rise to a taxable gift unless each tenant in common contributed proportionately to the purchase price.

In contrast with joint tenancy WROS ownership, any property owned by a decedent as a tenant in common will be subject to probate.

<table>
<tr><td colspan="5">🔑 KEY SUMMARY 53 – 1
Property Ownership in Common-Law States</td></tr>
<tr><td></td><td>Sole Ownership (Fee Simple)</td><td>Tenancy in Common</td><td>Joint Tenancy WROS</td><td>Tenancy by the Entirety</td></tr>
<tr><td>Who can own?</td><td>Anyone, but only one</td><td>Anyone and any number</td><td>Anyone and any number</td><td>Husband and wife only</td></tr>
<tr><td>What is the ownership percentage?</td><td>100%</td><td>Can be equal or unequal, as stated in title</td><td>Equal</td><td>Equal for spouses</td></tr>
<tr><td>Is consent of others needed for a sale or gift?</td><td>No</td><td>No, but can only transfer the portion owned</td><td>Yes, but can transfer portion after converting to tenancy in common</td><td>Yes</td></tr>
<tr><td>Can an owner transfer at death?</td><td>Yes</td><td>Yes, to extent of ownership interest</td><td>No, passes by right of survivorship</td><td>No, passes by right of survivorship</td></tr>
<tr><td>Is probate required?</td><td>Yes</td><td>Yes</td><td>No</td><td>No</td></tr>
</table>

Community Property

Community property is the separate, undivided, and equal ownership interests of husband and wife in any property acquired by the couple during marriage. Property acquired with the earnings of one spouse is still deemed community property even when the title is placed in the name of only one spouse. **Unlike joint tenancy WROS and tenancy by the entirety, there is no right of survivorship in community property.** Each spouse has the right of disposition over one-half of the community property.

Separate Property

Property acquired by either spouse before marriage or by gift or inheritance during the marriage is treated as separate property. Interest earned in a separate bank account is separate property, but the earned income of either spouse during the marriage is community property. A recovery of damages for personal injuries suffered by one spouse during marriage is also separate property.

If separate property is used to acquire property, the newly acquired property is also separate property. Thus, property can be traced even when it is mixed with community property. When separate property is commingled with community property so that they become indistinguishable, however, courts will apply the presumption that property acquired during marriage is community property. For example, where a separately-owned business increases in value, resulting from efforts of one or both spouses during marriage, the increase in value is usually held to be community property.

Practice Question

Jim and Kathy Fields have been married for 15 years and live in a community-property state. Which one of the following items belonging to them is community property?

    A. A municipal bond inherited from Jim's mother
    B. A Roth IRA in Jim's name, funded by Jim's earnings
    C. A sailboat given to Kathy 5 years ago by her father
    D. A rental property purchased by Kathy before their marriage

Answer:

Property acquired during the marriage by the earnings of either spouse is community property. The Roth IRA is community property even though the money comes only from Jim's earnings. Separate property is any inheritance or gift and any property acquired before the marriage.
B is the answer.

Life Insurance in Community-Property States

Life insurance policies purchased during marriage are community property, and if the insured dies, one-half of the death benefit will be included in the insured's gross estate. If the life insurance policy was separate property but the premiums were paid during marriage with community property, the states have made different rules. In California and Washington, an apportionment rule is followed, and the portion of premiums paid from community property determines the portion of death proceeds that is community property. In Texas, Louisiana, and New Mexico, the courts follow the inception-of-title rule, and the policy remains the separate property of the original purchaser, despite the payment of premiums from community funds. The surviving spouse can receive reimbursement for the amount of premiums paid from community property but does not share in the growth of the policy's value.

Gifts of Community Property

In most community-property states, one spouse may not make a gift of community property without the other spouse's consent. Gifts of separate property, however, may occur without a spouse's consent. One-half of the value of a gift of community property is considered made by each spouse even if the spouses elect not to split gifts. Splitting gifts only applies to separate property. If separate property is converted to community property, there is a gift, but it is not subject to gift tax because of the unlimited marital deduction.

One-Half of Community Property Is Included in the Gross Estate

When a spouse domiciled in a community-property state dies, one-half of the community property is included in the decedent's estate. The decedent can make testamentary disposition of the one-half interest in the community property, so the interest can be left to children, heirs, the surviving spouse, or anyone the decedent designates by will. The one-half interest in the community property is also subject to probate.

Full Step-Up in Basis for Community Property

For federal estate tax purposes, one-half of the value of the community property is included in the gross estate, but the whole property receives a step-up in basis. **This full step-up in basis is one of the main advantages of the community-property form of ownership.**

KEY SUMMARY 53 – 2 Property Ownership in Community-Property States	Separate Property	Community Property
How is it acquired?	• Before marriage • Gift • Inheritance • Personal injury	By earnings of spouses during marriage even if only one spouse is on the title and has all the earnings
Is consent required for a sale or gift?	No	Yes
Can the owner transfer the interest at death?	Yes	Yes, one-half
Is probate required?	Yes	Yes, for one-half
Does basis receive a full step-up at death?	Yes	Yes

Quasi-Community Property

Quasi-community property exists in only five states. California, Washington, Idaho, Arizona, and Wisconsin. When a married couple moves from a common-law state to one of these community-property states, their separate property may be treated as quasi-community property. If the separate property would have been community property had the couple lived in the state at the time it was acquired, then it will be treated as quasi-community property. In general, quasi-community property is subject to the same rules as community property.

In the community-property states that have not adopted the quasi-community-property concept, separate property acquired in a common-law state remains separate property when a couple moves to the state. When a couple sells a home owned in joint tenancy WROS in a common-law state and moves to a community-property state, the sale proceeds remain separate property of the spouses. Similarly, when a couple sells a home owned as community property and moves to a common-law state, the sale proceeds remain community property.

Recommendations for the Form of Property Interest

When a high-income family member seeks income tax reduction, a transfer of title from sole ownership to joint tenancy or to tenancy in common with a family member in a lower income tax bracket may be recommended. In community-property states, a transfer of separate property to community property (by commingling separate funds with community property) may have a similar effect. Such transfers will cause the income from the property to be split among the owners, and some of the income will be taxed at a lower income tax bracket.

Joint tenancy WROS is an inexpensive way to avoid probate. In a business transaction, tenancy in common should be used, rather than joint tenancy, when several owners take title to property. Each owner then can make disposition of his or her interest either during lifetime or at death.

🔑 KEY SUMMARY 53 – 3
Comparison of Spousal Joint Tenancy WROS and Community Property

	Joint Tenancy WROS	Community Property
Subject to probate?	No	Yes
Pass to surviving spouse?	Yes	No, but it can be left by will to the spouse
Can it pass to heirs or persons other than the spouse?	No, passes by operation of law to the spouse	Yes, one-half can be left by will to heirs or others
What amount is included in the decedent's gross estate?	One-half	One-half
What amount receives a step-up in basis?	One-half	All

Trust Ownership

With trusts, ownership interests in the trust property are divided among the parties to the trust: the grantor, the trustee, and the beneficiaries. The trustee takes legal title to the trust property, but the beneficiaries are granted the right to enjoy the beneficial interest or equitable interest in the property.

Present and Future Interests

A beneficial interest may be a present interest or a future interest. If the beneficiary has the right to the immediate enjoyment and possession of the property or income, there is a present interest. If the beneficiary's right to enjoy the property is delayed to some future date or until the occurrence of a future event, it is a future interest. When a grantor establishes a trust with income payable to his or her children for their lives, the children have received a present interest of a life income.

Reversions and Remainders

The most common future interests are reversions and remainders. When a future interest is retained by the grantor or transferor, it is a reversion. A reversion gives the grantor or transferor the right to regain the property at a future time, after other interests have terminated. For example, suppose a grantor transfers a home to his sister for her life, but the home will become the grantor's property again at the sister's death, the grantor has retained a reversionary interest.

When the future interest is held by someone other than the grantor or transferor, it is a remainder interest. A remainder interest is the right to possess or enjoy property after another interest ends. For example, the grantor transfers property to his or her children for their lives and at their deaths to the grantor's grandchildren. The children have life estates, and the grandchildren have remainder interests.

A **vested remainder** cannot be forfeited. While the right to possess or enjoy the property is delayed to a time in the future, it does not depend on the occurrence of any event. For example, the grantor transfers Blackacre property to his or her son for life, and at the son's death, it will pass to the grantor's granddaughter. The granddaughter has a vested remainder interest.

A **contingent remainder** is a right that depends upon the happening of a future event. For example, a grantor conveys Blackacre property to his or her sister for her life, and at her death, to the grantor's son, if the son is living. The grantor's son has a contingent remainder interest because if he dies before the grantor's sister, he does not obtain Blackacre.

Remainderpersons and Income Beneficiaries

Transfers in trusts typically involve a division of interests between the income beneficiaries and the remainderpersons. The income beneficiaries have a right to receive income from the trust for life (life estate) or for a specified number of years (estate for years). The remainderpersons are entitled to the trust assets remaining after the death or the termination of the income interests.

APPLICATION QUESTIONS

1. When David and Jill Rooney moved from Oregon, a common-law state, to California, a community-property state, they sold the home they had owned as joint tenants WROS during the 10 years of their marriage. They used the proceeds, totaling $200,000, to buy a new home in California. At the time of the move, David owns common stock, valued at $100,000, in a brokerage account in his name, which was purchased for $40,000 from his earnings over the past 6 years. He also owns $20,000 in mutual funds that he bought for $10,000 before he was married, using his earnings. David is also one of five investors in a limited partnership valued at $100,000 (his share is $20,000). David's interest in the limited partnership was purchased with money he earned during the marriage. David and Jill own two cars in joint names, with a total value of $50,000. Jill owns $20,000 in municipal bonds in her own name that she received as a gift from her parents. If David were to die soon after the Rooneys move, what would be the total value of the property considered quasi-community property in California?

    A. $250,000
    B. $270,000
    C. $290,000
    D. $350,000
    E. $370,000

2. If Jill Rooney (in the previous question) sells the mutual funds for $25,000 and the common stock for $120,000 after David's death, what is the amount of capital gain that she should report?

    A. $0
    B. $5,000
    C. $12,500
    D. $25,000
    E. $45,000

3. Roger Allen, who lives with his wife Jean in New York, inherited a vacation home in Maine from his uncle. Roger would like to arrange for the title to the vacation home to pass to his wife at his death to avoid the expense of probate. Roger also wants to avoid any title arrangement that might allow his wife to sell or transfer the property before his death.

Which of the following forms of titling the vacation home would be most appropriate?

    A. Tenancy in common
    B. Joint tenancy WROS
    C. Tenancy by the entirety
    D. Sole ownership
    E. Quasi-community property

4. Which of the following transfers to an irrevocable trust conveys a present interest to the beneficiary?

(1) The beneficiary will receive income from the trust for 10 years, and then the trust assets will be paid to the grantor.

(2) The trust allows the grantor's spouse to live in the home for life, and at the spouse's death, it will pass to the beneficiary.

(3) The trust provides for income to be accumulated in the trust, and both income and principal are payable to the beneficiary (a minor) at age 21.

(4) The trust provides for the beneficiary to receive income for life, and at the beneficiary's death, any remaining trust assets will be paid to the Red Cross.

    A. (1) and (2) only
    B. (1) and (4) only
    C. (2) and (3) only
    D. (2) and (4) only
    E. (3) and (4) only

5. Jerry Freeman, age 65, and his wife Elizabeth, who is 55 years of age, own a shopping center property as joint tenants WROS. Jerry would like to use the property to fund a trust for his son and daughter, but Elizabeth wants the property to pass outright to their son. If no agreement can be reached, which of the following statements would be appropriate advice to give Jerry?

    A. Jerry can sever the joint tenancy and put one-half of the property in trust for the two children.

    B. Jerry can convert ownership to a tenancy in common and place one-half in trust for the daughter and give one-half outright to the son.

    C. Jerry will have to wait until he outlives Elizabeth to take any action.

    D. Jerry cannot sever the joint tenancy, but he can buy Elizabeth's share and then leave the property in trust.

    E. If Jerry paid all of the purchase price for the property, he can convert it to sole ownership at any time.

6. (Published question released February, 1999)

A tenancy by the entirety may be terminated in which of the following ways?

(1) Death, whereby the survivor takes the entire estate
(2) Mutual agreement
(3) Divorce, which converts the estate into a tenancy in common or a joint tenancy
(4) Severance, whereby one spouse transfers his or her interest to a third party without the consent of the other spouse

    A. (4) only
    B. (1) and (3) only
    C. (2) and (4) only
    D. (1), (2), and (3) only
    E. (1), (2), (3), and (4)

7. (Published question released January, 1999, updated)

Sam and Sue paid $100,000 for their home 5 years ago. Its fair market value was $150,000 when Sam died. What was Sue's basis in the home after Sam's death if the home was held as community property?

    A. $50,000
    B. $75,000
    C. $100,000
    D. $125,000
    E. $150,000

8. Steve and Jean lived in a community-property state for the 18 years they were married. Steve's will left his entire estate in trust for his children. Which of the following assets will pass to the children's trust?

(1) The securities in Steve's brokerage account, started 10 years ago with his earnings
(2) A vacation home inherited by Steve from his mother five years ago
(3) One-half of the value of the home they purchased in Steve's name 12 years ago
(4) One-half of the value of mutual funds given to Jean by her father

    A. (1) and (2) only
    B. (2) and (3) only
    C. (3) and (4) only
    D. (1), (2), (3), and (4)

9. Which of the following situations involve inappropriate titling of property?

    A. The will provides for an interest owned as tenants in common to pass to the testator's children.
    B. The estate plan called for a revocable trust to reduce probate costs on a property, so the property was titled in fee simple.
    C. The estate plan called for a will substitute to reduce probate costs on a property, so the property was titled in tenants by the entirety.
    D. The taxpayer sought income tax reduction for income-producing property by titling the property in joint tenancy with an adult child.

10. All the following are advantages of sole ownership of property, EXCEPT:

   A. Full control over the handling and management of property
   B. Full power to make testamentary disposition
   C. Full exclusion from probate at death
   D. Full step-up in basis upon death
   E. Full power to make lifetime gifts

11. All the following statements concerning the characteristics of property held in joint tenancy with right of survivorship are correct, EXCEPT:

   A. Property held in joint tenancy WROS will be included in the probate estate.
   B. Property held in joint tenancy WROS is not subject to testamentary transfer.
   C. Income from property held in joint tenancy WROS is divided equally among all joint tenants.
   D. Joint tenants WROS acquire the same interest in the same property at the same time and take possession at the same time.
   E. Property held in joint tenancy can be converted to a tenancy in common.

12. Which of the following statements concerning ownership of property by married couples is correct?

   A. The value of a gift of a joint interest with right of survivorship made by one spouse to another requires actuarial calculations to determine the value of the gift for gift tax purposes.
   B. Joint ownership with a spouse may result in the full value of the property being included in both estates if simultaneous deaths occur.
   C. Title taken in joint names is invalid without the knowledge of or notice being given to both spouses.
   D. The entire value of property held jointly by spouses with right of survivorship is includible in the estate of the last to die.
   E. Property held in joint tenancy will be subject to probate in both of the married couple's estates.

13. "A" and "B" are brother and sister. In 1992, they bought corporate stock in joint names with right of survivorship, at a cost of $5,000. "A" contributed the money. "A" died in 2000, and the stock was valued in his estate at $12,000. "B" sold the stock this year for $14,000. What is "B's" taxable gain?

   A. Zero
   B. $2,000
   C. $3,500
   D. $4,500
   E. $12,000

14. Harold Free inherited a piece of residential real estate, purchased by his uncle for $5,000 and valued in his uncle's estate at $10,000 twenty years ago. Approximately 10 years ago, Mr. Free transferred the property into joint tenancy with right of survivorship with his girlfriend. The property then had a fair market value of $25,000. Just before Mr. Free died last year, his girlfriend put an addition on the property, costing $5,000. The property was then valued at $30,000. The girlfriend sold the property this year for $35,000. What is her taxable gain?

    A. $5,000
    B. $10,000
    C. $15,000
    D. $25,000
    E. $30,000

15. In the problem in Question 14, the amount includible in Mr. Free's gross estate for federal estate tax purposes is which of the following?

    A. $5,000
    B. $10,000
    C. $15,000
    D. $25,000
    E. $30,000

16. If, in Question 14, Mr. Free had sold the property for $30,000 just before his death, but after the addition was completed, his taxable gain would have been which of the following?

    A. $7,500
    B. $10,000
    C. $12,500
    D. $15,000
    E. $20,000

17. All the following statements concerning joint ownership of property by spouses are correct, EXCEPT:

    A. The contents of safe-deposit boxes in joint names are subject to the fractional interest rule, for estate tax purposes.
    B. Unequal contributions to joint brokerage accounts give rise to no gift tax.
    C. The purchase in joint names by one spouse of Series EE savings bonds costing over $30,000 is free of gift taxes.
    D. Termination of joint ownership of property by sale results in no gift tax.
    E. One-half of the value of property owned in joint tenancy is includible in the estate of the first spouse to die.

18. Which of the following statements concerning joint tenancies are correct?

(1) Conversion of a joint tenancy to a tenancy in common, in the same proportion, gives rise to no gift tax.

(2) If property held by spouses in joint tenancy is transferred to one spouse before divorce, gift tax will be payable at the time of divorce.

(3) When the owner of an apartment building makes his two children joint tenants with him on a $1 million building, there is a gift subject to federal gift tax.

(4) A joint tenancy is a terminable interest, so the gift tax marital deduction does not apply when an owner makes his or her spouse a joint tenant of property.

    A. (1) and (2) only
    B. (1) and (3) only
    C. (2) and (3) only
    D. (2) and (4) only
    E. (3) and (4) only

19. "A" and "B" are married. They bought a farm in 1982 for $100,000 and titled it in joint names with right of survivorship. Assume that when "A" died last year, the property was worth $250,000. "B" sells the property this year for $270,000. If "A" and "B" did not use the farm as a residence, what is "B's" taxable gain?

    A. $20,000
    B. $95,000
    C. $150,000
    D. $170,000
    E. $250,000

20. Dennis Mennis owns commercial real estate with his wife as tenants by the entirety. He would like to leave the property to his daughter Emily, but his wife and daughter are not talking to one another. Mrs. Mennis wants the property to go to their son, who will also receive the family business. What problem does Dennis Mennis face as a result of the form of ownership of the property?

    A. Dennis Mennis can only sell a portion of the property without his wife's consent.

    B. The property will pass to the surviving tenant, regardless of the terms of Mennis' will.

    C. The property will not be eligible for a step-up in basis if it passes to the son under Mrs. Mennis' will.

    D. Dennis Mennis can make his daughter a joint tenant WROS without his wife's consent, but the property passing to the daughter will not be eligible for the step-up in basis if Dennis dies.

    E. Any transfer of the property into joint tenancy with his daughter will result in gift tax liability to Dennis Mennis on the entire value of the property.

21. "C" and "D" are brothers. In 1983, they purchased commercial real estate at a price of $10,000 and took ownership as tenants in common. "C" died three years ago, leaving his share of the property to "D." The property was valued at $100,000 at the date of death. "D" sold the property this year for $120,000. What is "D's" taxable gain?

    A. $20,000
    B. $45,000
    C. $65,000
    D. $75,000
    E. $110,000

22. Which of the following property interests is community property?

   A. Shares of stock inherited by one spouse from a grandparent

   B. Income earned by a husband prior to marriage

   C. Appreciation of real estate owned solely by the husband and managed by him during the marriage

   D. Income earned by a wife during marriage

   E. A gift of a vacation home to one spouse from a parent

23. All the following statements concerning community property are correct, EXCEPT:

   A. Proceeds of life insurance policies may be includible in the gross estate of a deceased in a community-property state.

   B. Proceeds of life insurance may be community property if the policy was purchased in a community-property state.

   C. Proceeds of life insurance may become separate property by assignment to the beneficiary.

   D. Proceeds of life insurance are not taxable in the gross estate of a domiciliary in a community-property state.

   E. Proceeds of life insurance may be community property if the premiums were paid with community property.

24. Peter Holmes and his wife Betty moved to a community-property state shortly after their marriage in 1973. Peter's earnings have been used to pay for the Holmes' residence, valued at $300,000, and for a vacation home, currently worth $175,000. Peter has also recently inherited $500,000 of investment securities from his uncle. Peter started a computer business about 10 years ago, and the business is worth approximately $20 million today. Peter and Betty have two children. Which of the following recommendations for Peter's estate plan is likely to be the most beneficial?

   A. Peter should place the title to the vacation home in joint names with his children to keep the home from becoming community property.

   B. Peter should leave his one-half interest in the Holmes' residence in trust for Betty for her life, with remainder to the children to keep this one-half interest out of Betty's estate.

   C. Peter should make a lifetime gift of the business interest to their children because the business is Peter's separate property.

   D. Peter should convert the investment securities inherited from his uncle from separate to community property, so the entire amount of the securities will receive a step-up in basis at his death.

   E. Peter should give the investment securities to Betty; otherwise, she will have insufficient assets to take advantage of the unified credit.

25. Which of the following statements concerning community property are correct?

(1) Property received as an inheritance or gift to one spouse during marriage is separate property.
(2) Only one-half of community property is subject to each spouse's will.
(3) All community assets are eligible to receive a step-up in basis following the death of one of the spouses.
(4) Community property is fully includible in the decedent's gross estate.

    A. (1) and (2) only
    B. (1) and (4) only
    C. (2) and (3) only
    D. (1), (2), and (3) only
    E. (1), (2), (3), and (4)

26. Which of the following statements concerning property settlements in California are correct?

(1) An asset acquired in a common-law state will retain its character as separate property when a couple moves to California.
(2) An asset acquired in a community-property state will not be treated as community property when a couple moves to California.
(3) An asset that is community property in California will be community property when the couple moves to a common-law state.
(4) One-half of quasi-community property passes to the surviving spouse, and one-half passes through probate.

    A. (1) and (2) only
    B. (1) and (3) only
    C. (2) and (3) only
    D. (2) and (4) only
    E. (3) and (4) only

27. All the following statements concerning joint tenancy and sole ownership of properties are correct, EXCEPT:

    A. Joint tenancy enables the husband or wife to have testamentary control of the property.
    B. Sole ownership of property has the least number of restrictions upon the transfer of property.
    C. Joint ownership of property places restrictions on postmortem control.
    D. A gift of property held in sole ownership requires consents from no persons other than the owner.
    E. A bequest of property owned by joint tenants is ineffective.

For practice answering case questions related to Topic 53, please answer the following questions in the cases included in the Appendix at the back of this textbook.

Case	Questions
Bartlett	1
Marshall	1, 2, and 3
Webster	
Unser	
Tingey	
Lytle	
Beals	
Mocsin	
Young	
Borelli	1
Cunningham	1
Fred and Mary Ferris	1, 2, 3, 4, and 5

ANSWERS AND EXPLANATIONS

1. E is the answer. Quasi-community property is property acquired in a common-law state that would have been treated as community property if the couple had lived in a community-property state at the time of acquisition. The couple moved from Oregon, a common-law state, to California, a community-property state which also has the concept of quasi-community property. In California, only the municipal bonds received by Jill as a gift and the mutual funds purchased by David before the marriage will be treated as separate property. The home ($200,000), the brokerage account ($100,000), the cars ($50,000), and the 1/5 interest in the limited partnership ($20,000) are all considered quasi-community property and will be treated as community property.

2. D is the answer. The quasi-community property is treated as community property, and it will receive a full step-up in basis to the date-of-death value. The common stock in the brokerage account is quasi-community property and will also receive a full step-up in basis. The mutual funds were David's separate property and, therefore, will receive a full step-up in basis, too. The date-of-death value for the stock is $100,000, so Jill's gain on this stock is $20,000. The date-of-death value for the mutual funds is $20,000, so Jill's gain on these funds is $5,000.

3. C is the answer. Tenancy by the entirety will enable Roger to include his wife in the title to the vacation home and still require her to obtain his consent before making any transfer or disposition of the property. Tenancy in common will not prevent Roger's wife from selling her interest. Joint tenancy WROS will also not prevent Roger's wife from selling her interest in the property because the joint tenancy could be severed and turned into a tenancy in common, allowing the wife's separate interest to be sold or transferred. Sole ownership in Roger's name will not avoid probate. Quasi-community property is not available in Maine.

4. B is the answer. The beneficiary who receives income from the trust for 10 years begins to enjoy the income immediately and is given a present interest to the income. There is no delay in the start of this income interest. By contrast, the beneficiary who must wait until the death of the grantor's spouse cannot make immediate use of the home and has a future interest. The beneficiary who must wait until age 21 to receive income and principal also has only a future interest. Note that Code Section 2503(c) provides that gifts to such a trust shall not be treated as gifts of a future interest for purposes of the annual exclusion. The beneficiary who has an income interest for life has an immediate life estate and a present interest.

5. A is the answer. Jerry can sever the joint tenancy, and then as a tenant in common, he can dispose of his one-half interest as he wishes. He can leave the one-half interest in trust for both children or set the trust up entirely for the daughter. He will not be able to exercise control over the entire property by converting to a tenancy in common. He cannot convert it to sole ownership even if he paid all of the purchase price. Waiting to outlive Elizabeth does not make sense because he is older by 10 years. If the property were owned in tenancy by the entirety, Jerry could not sever the interests.

6. D is the answer. A tenancy by the entirety is joint ownership WROS by spouses, but it cannot be severed by the unilateral action of one spouse. Death will end the tenancy by entirety, and the title will vest entirely in the survivor. Consent, mutual agreement, or divorce can terminate the entirety. The attempt to transfer an interest in a tenancy by the entirety without the consent of the other spouse will be ineffective.

7. E is the answer. Sam's gross estate included one-half of the home because it was community property. With community property, if part of the property was included in the gross estate, the entire property takes a new basis. So, there is a full step-up in basis to the date-of-death value. Sue's basis was the fair market value on the date of Sam's death, which was $150,000.

8. B is the answer. The brokerage account was acquired with Steve's earnings during the marriage, so it is community property, and only one-half is subject to Steve's testamentary control. The vacation home is Steve's separate property and can be left entirely to the children's trust. The home is community property, so one-half can be left to the children's trust. The mutual funds are Jean's separate property, so they are not subject to Steve's testamentary control.

9. B is the answer. If the estate plan calls for a revocable trust in order to reduce the costs of probate, the plan will only work if the interest is titled to the trust and not owned in fee simple. Fee simple property will pass through probate. A will that provides for an interest owned as tenants in common to pass to the testator's children will be effective for passing the testator's interest. If an estate plan seeks to reduce probate costs by will substitute, titling property as tenants by the entirety is an effective will substitute. A taxpayer seeking income tax reduction for income-producing property can accomplish this objective by means of a joint tenancy with a child.

10. C is the answer. The entire value of property held in sole ownership at death is included in the probate estate. Property held in sole ownership is eligible for the step-up in basis.

11. A is the answer. Property held in joint tenancy WROS will not be included in the probate estate. The property passes automatically by operation of law to the surviving joint tenant.

12. D is the answer. The "50-50" rule requires one-half of the property owned in joint names by spouses to be included in the gross estate of the first spouse to die. The property passes automatically to the surviving spouse and will be fully included in the gross estate of the spouse that is last to die. Simultaneous deaths may mean that one-half of the joint property will be included in one estate, and the other estate will include the entire value of the property.

13. B is the answer. When "A" died, the entire value of the stock was included in "A's" gross estate because "A" contributed the entire purchase price. The fractional interest rule applies because "A" and "B" are not spouses. At "A's" death, the stock was valued at $12,000, so the stock received a step-up in basis to $12,000. The sale this year for $14,000, therefore, results in a reportable long-term capital gain of $2,000.

14. A is the answer. When Mr. Free died, the entire value of the property was included in his gross estate, except for the $5,000 addition. The property is included in Free's estate under the fractional interest rule because Free contributed all of the cost, except for the addition. The girlfriend's basis, with the cost of the addition added on, is $30,000, so she has a gain of $5,000 on the sale.

15. D is the answer. The property is includible in Free's estate to the extent of his contribution. Since his girlfriend contributed only $5,000 to a property valued at $30,000, Mr. Free contributed $25,000.

16. A is the answer. When Mr. Free transferred the property into joint ownership, he made a gift of an undivided one-half interest to his girlfriend. She took his basis in the one-half interest, and he retained a $5,000 basis in his one-half interest. When the girlfriend completed the addition, in effect, she made a gift of a one-half interest in the addition, and Mr. Free's basis was increased by one-half of her expenditure. His basis, therefore, was $7,500. A sale of the property for $30,000 would mean that Mr. Free's interest, in which he had a basis of $7,500, sold for $15,000. The taxable gain would have been $7,500.

17. A is the answer. Property owned by spouses in joint tenancy is subject to an automatic one-half inclusion in the gross estate. The rule for spouses is the so called "50-50" rule, not the fractional interest rule. Gifts between spouses, such as described in B and C, do not result in gift tax, by reason of the gift tax marital deduction. Sale of jointly owned property is not a gift. A gift would only arise if one joint tenant received an excessive portion of the proceeds, and, in any event, the gift tax marital deduction would eliminate any tax liability.

18. B is the answer. If property is acquired by two joint tenants through equal contributions, each joint tenant has a one-half interest. If the joint tenants then become tenants in common, there will be no gift if each receives an interest equal to one-half of the jointly held property. If property held jointly by spouses is transferred to one spouse, the gift tax marital deduction will mean that no gift tax is payable. Transfers pursuant to a decree of divorce are also nontaxable. There is no gift tax due when one spouse makes another a joint tenant. The gift tax marital deduction applies to such gifts of joint tenancy interests to shelter them from tax. Gift tax, however, will be due when non-spousal joint tenancies are created, such as in the case of the owner making his children joint tenants of a building.

19. B is the answer. When the farm was acquired, the joint tenants had a total basis of $100,000, which was divided between them equally. When "A" died, "A's" one-half interest received a step-up in basis to the date-of-death value. At "A's" death, the property was worth $250,000, so "A's" one-half interest was worth $125,000. "B" then had a basis of $125,000 in the interest received from "A" and a basis of $50,000 in "B's" original one-half interest. "B's" new basis, therefore, is $175,000. The property is sold for $270,000, so the gain is $270,000 – $175,000 = $95,000.

20. B is the answer. Unlike property held in joint tenancy, property held as tenants by the entirety cannot be transferred in any portion without the consent of both spouses. The entirety's property passes to the survivor, the same as joint tenancy property.

21. C is the answer. "C" and "D" had an original cost basis for their interests of $5,000 each. When "C" died, his interest was worth $50,000, and the property received a step-up in basis to that value. "D's" basis, therefore, was $55,000 in the entire property. Sale of the property for $120,000, therefore, resulted in a taxable gain of $65,000.

22. D is the answer. Income earned by both spouses during the marriage is considered community property. Income earned before the marriage and assets inherited by one spouse are separate property. Appreciation of separate property remains separate property unless the other spouse's efforts contributed to the appreciation.

23. D is the answer. In community-property states, one-half of the death benefit proceeds of a policy on the insured decedent-spouse are included in the decedent's gross estate. The proceeds may become separate property by assignment to the beneficiary.

24. B is the answer. The one-half interest of each spouse in community property does not pass automatically by operation of law to the surviving spouse; rather, each spouse has testamentary control over one-half of community property. By placing Peter's one-half interest in trust, the couple can prevent this one-half interest from being taxed in Betty's estate at her death. Choice A is not correct because Peter cannot make a gift of community property. A transfer of the vacation home into joint tenancy with the children is a gift of an interest in community property. Choice C is not correct because the business is also community property. Choice D is not correct because the securities will receive a full step-up in basis in Peter's estate, anyway. The securities are Peter's separate property because Peter received them as an inheritance. While converting separate property to community property will allow a married couple to take advantage of the full step-up in basis when one spouse dies, in this case, the advantage only arises from the possibility that Betty may die first, thereby giving Peter a full step-up in basis. Moreover, since Peter only recently received the property as an inheritance, the securities already have a step-up in basis. Under community-property law, Betty is entitled to one-half of the business and one-half of the residence and vacation home. The total value of these items of property is more than the $5.43 million estate exemption available in 2015; moreover, the portability of the unified credit will mean that it is unnecessary for Betty to use her unified credit at her death because any unused credit can be used by her spouse, so choice E is also incorrect.

25. D is the answer. (4) is incorrect because only one-half of community property is includible in the decedent's gross estate. All community assets, however, are eligible to receive a full step-up in basis following the death of one of the community tenants. Only one-half of community property may be disposed of by will, and the property may pass to heirs other than a spouse.

26. E is the answer. The quasi-community-property concept in California requires assets that are separate property acquired in a common-law state to be treated as community property in California. An asset that is community property in a community-property state, such as California, will generally retain its character as community property when the couple moves to a common-law state. One-half of quasi-community property passes to the surviving spouse, and one-half passes through probate.

27. A is the answer. Upon the death of one of the owners of property owned by joint tenants with right of survivorship, the property will pass to the survivor. The joint tenant has no testamentary control over the property because the property passes by operation of law and not under a will.

Methods of Property Transfer at Death (Topic 54)

CFP Board Student-Centered Learning Objectives

(a) Describe the probate process, its advantages, disadvantages and costs.

(b) Explain the characteristics and consequences of using alternative methods of transferring property at death, including named beneficiary, trusts (revocable and irrevocable), payable on death and transfer on death designations, intestate succession, and direct transfers through titling).

(c) Select the most appropriate property transfer mechanism for a client's situation.

Methods of Property Transfer at Death
- A.   *Transfers through the probate process*
  - 1)   *Testamentary distribution*
  - 2)   *Intestate succession*
  - 3)   *Advantages and disadvantages of probate*
  - 4)   *Assets subject to probate estate*
  - 5)   *Probate avoidance strategies*
  - 6)   *Ancillary probate administration*
- B.   *Transfers by operation of law*
- C.   *Transfers through trusts*
- D.   *Transfers by contract*

Transfer at Death

At death, property owned by the deceased is transferred in one of the following four ways:

(1) **The probate process** – Any property that a person has the complete power to dispose of at death is subject to probate. The deceased's property is transferred according to the instructions of a will; or, if there is no will, the property is distributed according to the rules of the state's intestacy laws.

(2) **Operation of law** – Property owned in joint tenancy with right of survivorship (WROS) passes automatically to the other joint tenant(s). This property passes outside probate, and a will is ineffective for transferring this property.

(3) **Trusts** – Property transferred to a trust during the grantor's lifetime is actually no longer owned by the grantor and is not subject to distribution at death. Property placed in either a revocable or irrevocable (living) trust is subject to the provisions of the trust document, does not pass through probate, and is not affected by the provisions of a will.

However, **testamentary trusts created by the will are subject to probate**.

(4) **Contracts** – Life insurance contracts provide for payment by the insurance company to the designated beneficiary, so death proceeds do not pass through probate. An exception to this rule occurs when the estate is named as the beneficiary; then, the death proceeds are added to the probate estate. Pension benefits are similarly paid to the named beneficiary, outside probate. By law, qualified retirement plan benefits must be paid to the surviving spouse unless the surviving spouse has waived this right.

Practice Question

Which of the following assets are typically probate property?

    A. Assets in an irrevocable trust
    B. Assets passing to a testamentary trust
    C. Assets titled to a revocable trust
    D. Assets held by an IRA trust account

Answer:
Assets in an irrevocable or revocable living trust do not pass through probate. Assets that pass to a testamentary trust must pass through probate because they are subject to the decedent's will. The assets in an IRA trust typically pass to a designated beneficiary. The IRA assets would only pass through probate if there were no designated beneficiary or if the designated beneficiary was the decedent's estate.
The answer is B.

Testamentary Distribution

Property transferred at death either by testamentary distribution or by intestacy are subject to probate. Testamentary distribution requires probate of a will that has been executed according to state laws. The legal requirements for a will are discussed in Topic 55.

Intestacy

Intestate succession laws provide a scheme of distribution for the property of any person who dies without a will. **Any property that does not pass by operation of other laws, by contract, or by will passes to the persons specified by the intestacy statutes.** Typically, intestacy statutes distribute property to the decedent's blood relatives. If the decedent is survived by a wife and children, the surviving spouse is usually entitled to one-third of the intestate estate, and the children receive the remaining two-thirds. Under the Uniform Probate Code adopted in some states, a surviving spouse inherits the entire intestate estate even when all of the decedent's children are also descendants of the surviving spouse. State-specific information can be found at http://www.mystatewill.com/. Most states also make this information available on their website.

Intestate Distribution – If No Children Survive

If the decedent is survived by a spouse but no children, the intestacy statutes provide either that: (a) the spouse will take all of the estate; (b) the surviving spouse takes a specified dollar amount or a specified portion of the estate, with the rest going to the decedent's parents or siblings; or (c) the surviving spouse receives all the personal property but shares real property with the decedent's parents and siblings. Under the Uniform Probate Code (UPC), a surviving spouse inherits the entire intestate estate when the decedent had no surviving parent or children. The UPC also provides that when a decedent is survived by a parent and a spouse but no children, the surviving spouse receives the first $200,000, plus three-fourths of the remaining intestate estate.

Intestate Distribution – If Only Children Survive

If the decedent is survived only by children, the children share equally in the intestate estate. If the decedent is not survived by a spouse or children, intestacy statutes provide for the estate to pass to the decedent's parents. If the parents are deceased, the intestate estate is shared equally by the decedent's siblings. If the decedent is survived by no relatives, the estate escheats to the state.

Inadvertent Intestacy

Intestacy may sometimes occur inadvertently, even though a person had prepared a will. If the will does not meet the state law requirements for a valid will, the will is unenforceable, and the state's intestate succession laws will determine the distribution of the decedent's estate. A will may be found invalid because the formal requirements for execution of a will were not observed or because the testator was of unsound mind or subject to undue influence at the time he or she executed the will.

A will contest can result in the will being declared invalid, in which case, the decedent's estate must then pass under the intestate laws.

Partial Intestacy

Partial intestacy arises when a testator fails to provide directions in a will as to the disposition of a particular item of property. **Partial intestacy can be avoided by means of a residuary clause that disposes of any remaining property not specifically mentioned in the will**. Failure to include a residuary clause can cause property not mentioned in the will to pass under intestacy laws, despite the execution of a valid will.

Disadvantages of Intestacy

The major disadvantage of failing to leave a valid will and dying intestate is that the intestate succession laws are rigid and specify a distribution of estate assets that may be contrary to what the decedent wanted. If an individual wants to leave property to friends or to charity, the intestacy laws do not provide for such disposition. If a person wants the estate to pass to heirs in different proportions than what is prescribed by the intestacy laws or if the person wants specific property to pass to a particular heir, a will is necessary to make such dispositions. The state intestacy laws are not able to adapt the distribution of an intestate estate to the special needs of a family. The spouse's share is fixed, regardless of what the financial needs may actually be. Children receive equal shares, regardless of their ages, competency, needs, or abilities.

If a child is a minor, the court must appoint a guardian or conservator to supervise the child's share, and additional expenses are incurred for the fees of the guardian or conservator and for court supervision. If the estate includes real estate or business interests, intestate distribution among fractional interests may require the immediate sale of such an interest at a price below what otherwise might have been obtained. Court costs may be higher because of the need for additional court proceedings and court supervision of the distribution of the intestate estate. Death taxes may also be higher and may be imposed on heirs in a way that the decedent would not have wanted. In addition, the court will select the personal representative for the intestate estate and will probably require the representative to incur the additional expense of posting a bond.

Probate Process

"Probate" originally meant proving the validity of a will. Today, the probate process applies both to estates with wills and to intestate estates. The major feature of the probate process is judicial supervision of the decedent's estate. A court is given responsibility for overseeing the administration and distribution of the deceased owner's property until it is transferred to beneficiaries. If there are claims or disputes over the property, the court hears evidence and decides these matters.

Ancillary Probate

If a decedent dies owning real estate in a state other than the decedent's state of residence, ancillary probate is required. Ancillary probate is an additional probate proceeding that must be administered in any state in which the decedent owned real estate.

Since ancillary probate requires additional court proceedings, the costs of administration are usually higher for an estate containing out-of-state property.

How might an owner of out-of-state property avoid ancillary probate?

EXHIBIT 54 – 1
Avoiding Ancillary Probate for Out-of-State Property

Factor to Evaluate	Technique 1	Technique 2
Does the owner need income from the property or want to continue to use it?	If an owner wants income or continued use, transfer the property to a grantor trust (revocable or irrevocable) or use a deed in escrow.	If an owner does not need income or future use, consider joint tenancy WROS.
Does the owner need to reduce the size of his or her gross estate?	If an owner has charitable interests, consider a lifetime charitable gift.	If an owner wants to benefit individual donees, consider gifts outright or in trust.
Has property risen or fallen in value from the date of purchase?	If value has fallen, consider a sale for income tax loss.	If value has risen, consider an installment sale, like-kind exchange, or other sale technique.
Is the property a residence?	If an owner wants to provide a benefit to an individual donee, consider a QPRT.	Consider the sale of a principal residence due to the exclusion; $500,000 of gain is excluded for married couples.

Assets Subject to Probate

Property over which the decedent has a power to transfer to heirs at his or her death, either through the directions of the will or by intestacy, is subject to probate. Property held in sole ownership or sole proprietorship is subject to probate, and property owned in tenancy in common with others is subject to probate; however, property owned in joint tenancy with right of survivorship is not subject to probate. The joint tenancy property passes by operation of law to the survivor, so it is not part of the probate estate. The consequences of titling property in joint tenancy or tenancy in common are discussed in more detail in Topic 53.

 K Study Tip – The personal balance sheet (statement of financial position) shows the client's proportionate interest in a tenancy in common. This interest is **not** divided again to value the probate estate. A joint tenancy WROS is shown on the balance sheet in its full amount, but none of the joint tenancy interest is included in the probate estate.

Property placed in revocable or irrevocable trusts is also not subject to probate. Property that is paid to a beneficiary as a result of a contract made by the decedent is not subject to probate. Life insurance death benefits and retirement plan benefits are the most common examples of these non-probate assets.

The following summary is a review of probate and non-probate assets:

🔑 KEY SUMMARY 54 – 1
Probate and Non-Probate Assets

Assets Subject to Probate	*Non-Probate Assets*
• Property held in fee simple or sole ownership	• Property owned in joint tenancy with right of survivorship
• Property owned in tenancy in common with others	• Property owned in trust (revocable or irrevocable)
• Community property	• Government savings bonds
• Life insurance policy proceeds or retirement plan benefits when no beneficiary is named or the estate is the named beneficiary	• Deeds of title delivered in escrow
	• Property paid to a beneficiary as a result of a contract entered into by a decedent: -Life insurance death benefits -Annuity payments to survivors -Retirement plan benefits -Totten trusts -Payable-on-death accounts

---

Community Property and Probate

The decedent's share of community property is subject to probate. This share is one-half of the community property owned by the couple. Additional discussion of the characteristics of community property is found in Topic 53.

🔑 KEY SUMMARY 54 – 2
Community Property and the Probate Estate

In a community-property state, one-half of community property is included in the decedent's probate estate, and the decedent has the power to pass that one-half by will. All separate property is included in the probate estate and is subject to the decedent's will. The separate property includes:

- Gifts
- Inheritances
- Assets owned before marriage
- Court awards of personal injury damages
- Assets transmuted (converted by an agreement of the husband and wife) from community property

---

Techniques for Avoiding Probate

To avoid delay, expense, and publicity, many people seek to avoid probate of their assets. Probate can be avoided by means of techniques referred to as will substitutes. Various will substitutes commonly used by financial planners are discussed below:

(1) Joint tenancy WROS. Property held in joint tenancy with right of survivorship is an effective will substitute because jointly owned property passes to the surviving tenant(s) by operation of law. Joint tenancy property is not subject to probate and cannot be bequeathed by will. Both real and personal property may be held in joint tenancy WROS. Unlike joint tenancy WROS, property held in tenancy in common does become part of the probate estate and must be bequeathed by a decedent's will.

(2) Joint bank accounts. Bank accounts can be set up in joint tenancy by signing signature cards containing the agreement of the bank to pay the account balance to the survivor. Since the survivor becomes the owner of the account at the death of the joint tenant, there is no property to pass through probate.

During the owner's lifetime, the owner-depositor can withdraw the money at any time; consequently, there is no completed gift until the other person makes a withdrawal.

(3) Revocable living trusts. A widely recommended and publicized technique for avoiding probate is the revocable living trust. A revocable living trust is a trust established by the grantor during his or her lifetime, where the grantor retains the right to change or revoke the trust at any time before death.

Since property transferred to a trust (whether revocable or irrevocable) is no longer owned by the transferor, the transfer is effective for removing the property from the probate estate. After the grantor's death, the trust becomes irrevocable, and the trustee administers the trust and distributes the assets according to the terms of the trust document.

(4) Government savings bonds. Series "EE" and Series "HH" bonds can be issued payable to alternative payees (Payable to A or B) or to a beneficiary (Payable to A, payable on death to B). With alternative payees, each payee has an equal right to the proceeds. With the beneficiary arrangement, the primary payee (A) can replace the beneficiary at any time.

There is no completed gift until the bond is cashed. The payment to the beneficiary is outside probate and not subject to will provisions.

(5) Contract provisions taking effect at death. An individual can enter into a contract that will take effect or be enforceable by another person after the contracting party's death (typically by designating a beneficiary).

The benefits provided to survivors under such contracts avoid probate and are not subject to will provisions. Examples of these contracts are annuities, life insurance policies, and retirement plans.

(6) Deeds. A deed usually transfers an interest in real estate from the grantor to the grantee. In order for the transfer to be effective, a properly executed deed must be delivered to the grantee or to an escrow agent, with instructions for the agent to deliver it to the grantee at the grantor's death. An escrow agent is used when the grantor does not want the deed recorded during his or her lifetime. In effect, the grantor retains the appearance of being the owner during his or her lifetime and continues to receive any income from the property. If the deed is properly executed, there is a completed gift at the time the deed is delivered to the grantee or to the escrow agent, and the transfer is not subject to probate.

🔑 KEY SUMMARY 54 – 3			
How Probate and Non-Probate Property Passes			
Probate Property – passes by:	*Non-Probate Property – passes by:*		
<u>Will or Intestacy</u> Fee simple Sole proprietor Tenancy in common Partnership interest Community property	<u>Operation of Law</u> Joint tenancy WROS Tenancy by the entirety	<u>Trust</u> Revocable trust Totten trust Irrevocable trust	<u>Contract Provision</u> Life insurance Annuity Retirement plan IRA Deed in escrow Government bond payable to a beneficiary

Practice Question

Which of the following is not a technique for avoiding probate?

    A. Series EE bonds payable to a beneficiary
    B. Payable-on-death account with a child
    C. Joint tenancy WROS with a nonspouse owner
    D. Life insurance, payable to the insured's estate

Answer:
Series EE bonds payable to a beneficiary are not subject to probate, nor are payable-on-death accounts or joint tenancy property. Life insurance, payable to the insured's estate is subject to probate.
The answer is D.

Advantages of Probate

Probate provides a systematic, orderly, and judicially-supervised method of distributing a decedent's property.

Court supervision of the process assures fair treatment of the parties and proper administration of the estate.

Probate is useful to establish the title to property when disputes are anticipated. Deeds issued by a probate court can serve to document a title and remove uncertainty.

In the probate process, creditors are given notice of the estate proceedings, and after a certain time, claims that are not filed will be barred. Thus, for the heirs, probate proceedings can bring some closure to claims and disputes. In some cases, the time for filing claims in the probate proceeding is shorter than the statute of limitations on the claims. This benefit can be particularly important to professionals, such as accountants or engineers, who may face lengthy statutes of limitations on malpractice claims.

Sometimes, there is an opportunity for income tax reduction. Since the estate is a separate entity for income tax purposes, an estate that is in a lower income tax bracket than the beneficiary will afford some income tax savings during the period of administration. In 2015, however, an estate must pay income tax at the maximum 39.6% rate, with only $12,300 of income.

Disadvantages of Probate

The probate process is expensive because of court costs, attorneys' fees, and other administrative expenses. The fees are usually calculated as a percentage of the value of the probate estate, so the larger the estate, the more expensive probate becomes.

During the period of probate administration, beneficiaries are not able to obtain their inheritances. Delays in distribution and transfer of property can be a hardship for the deceased's family.

A will and the records of probate administration (including the distribution of assets) become public records, and some people prefer to avoid publicity in their affairs.

Uses of Probate Avoidance Techniques: Joint Tenancy – Inexpensive and Easy to Set Up

Advantages of joint tenancy WROS. The most widely used and least expensive of the probate avoidance techniques is joint ownership. Any type of real or personal property may be owned in joint tenancy WROS, and all property held in joint tenancy WROS passes at death outside the will and outside the probate estate.

Joint tenancy can be used with any group of heirs and is not limited to spouses. Parents can enter into joint tenancy with children; brothers and sisters may own property in joint tenancy; even friends and associates may use the joint tenancy technique. Arranging for joint ownership typically involves only the signing of a document and, often, does not require an attorney.

Income Shifting with Joint Tenancy

When the owner transfers property into joint tenancy, a pro rata share of income from the property is shifted from the owner to the new joint tenant. If the new joint tenant is in a lower marginal income tax bracket, income tax reduction will result.

Protection from Creditors

Death of a joint tenant causes an automatic transfer of the property to the surviving joint tenant by operation of law, and the survivor receives the property free of any unsecured claims against the deceased. Thus, joint tenancy is a way to provide protection against some creditors.

Loss of Control

Disadvantages of joint tenancy WROS. The downside to joint tenancy WROS is that the owner relinquishes control over the disposition of the property. When the property is placed in joint tenancy WROS, the owner no longer can bequeath it by will.

The survivor, rather than the original owner, will have complete control over the eventual disposition of the property. In addition, there is a danger of unintended consequences from joint tenancy. An individual may have intended to leave a substantial inheritance to children or other heirs, but if most of his or her property is owned in joint tenancy, the disposition in the will has no effect. The surviving tenant becomes the owner by operation of law.

Overqualification of Property for the Marital Deduction

Historically, one of the unintended consequences of joint tenancy was over-qualification of assets for the marital deduction and failure to use the applicable credit amount. If most of the assets of a married couple are in joint tenancy WROS, the assets pass by operation of law to the surviving spouse and qualify for the marital deduction. Thus, few assets pass to other heirs, and the applicable (unified) credit was wasted. However, the concern of over qualifying for the marital deduction has been largely eliminated by portability provisions, which were made a permanent part of estate tax law by the American Taxpayer Relief Act of 2012. Portability allows the decedent to leave any remaining estate tax exemption amount (up to $5.43 million in 2015) to the surviving spouse by making an election on the estate tax return. The surviving spouse will then be able to claim both the surviving spouse's $5.43 million applicable exemption amount and the amount left by a deceased spouse (up to $5.43 million). This will allow the surviving spouse to die in 2015 with up to $10.86 million of assets without owing an estate tax.

Estate Tax Impact of Joint Tenancy

Joint tenancy WROS can trigger estate tax inclusion. **At the death of the first joint tenant, the entire joint asset is included in the decedent's estate when the joint owners are not spouses unless there is proof that the surviving joint tenant(s) contributed to the purchase price**. A gift is not treated as a contribution. Thus, if Father gives Son cash so they can buy a beach house in joint tenancy, the son has made no contribution, and the entire value of the property will be included in the father's gross estate at his death. Note that for probate purposes, none of the value of the property will be included in the father's probate estate.

If the surviving joint tenant is the decedent's spouse, one-half of the joint tenancy asset will be included in the decedent's estate, regardless of the decedent's contributions to the acquisition of the asset.

Practice Question

Gerry and his wife Marcia bought a house, using some money that Marcia inherited and some of Gerry's earnings. Marcia's inheritance was $10,000, and Gerry's accumulated earnings were $20,000. They bought the house as joint tenants WROS for $120,000. At Gerry's death, the house was worth $210,000. What is the amount attributable to the house that will be included in Gerry's gross estate for federal estate tax purposes?

    A. $0
    B. $80,000
    C. $105,000
    D. $140,000
    E. $210,000

Answer:
For married taxpayers, one-half of the value of the property owned in joint tenancy is included in the gross estate, regardless of contributions. Gerry's gross estate must include one-half of the $210,000, or $105,000.
The answer is C.

Revocable Living Trusts

Advantages of a revocable living trust. For wealthy clients, a revocable living trust offers potentially significant savings on probate costs. The savings usually exceed the costs of preparing the trust document, transferring assets to the trust, and administering the trust.

If the living trust is designed to receive all of a couple's property, the savings may be greater because estates for both spouses can avoid probate.

Since clients often fail to transfer all of their property to the revocable trust, planners generally need to write a will, even though the client has a revocable trust. In such a case, the will typically contains a pour-over provision stating that the estate will be poured over into the trust. Thus, some probate costs will probably be incurred for these assets passing under the will.

Control is Maintained

The revocable living trust is a very flexible document, allowing the client to change or cancel the trust arrangement at any time before death. Thus, the client does not give up any control over the property, as occurs with joint tenancy.

Management Can Be Observed

Since a trustee is appointed during the client's lifetime, the client has an opportunity to observe the management of the trust and to decide whether the trustee is a capable administrator. The client can help the trustee learn about managing the trust assets and can give the beneficiary a chance to learn the use of the assets.

Provide for Incapacity

The living trust can also be structured to handle a client's incapacity. The client may be named as the trustee when the living trust is set up, but a successor trustee can be named to take over if the client becomes incapacitated, dies, or otherwise gives up the trustee position.

Living trusts avoid the delays and publicity of probate because trusts are not subject to the same requirements as estates. The trustee can make distributions immediately to family heirs.

Titling Assets to the Trust is Often Forgotten

Disadvantages of a revocable living trust. The revocable trust is effective only to the extent a client transfers assets to the trust. Transferring titles of assets to the trust can be inconvenient and is often overlooked.

No Income or Transfer Tax Advantages

There is no income-splitting or income tax reduction as a result of establishing a revocable trust. The trust income is taxable to the grantor under the grantor trust rules.

While no gift tax is owed on the creation of the revocable trust since there is not a completed gift, there is also no estate tax reduction. The assets transferred to the revocable trust will be included in the decedent's gross estate at the date-of-death value. **As a result, the assets will receive the benefit of a full step-up in basis at the grantor's death**.

EXHIBIT 54 – 2
Joint Tenancy WROS and Revocable Trusts – Will Substitutes Compared

	Joint Tenancy WROS	*Revocable Trust*
What property is used?	Real or personal property.	Real or personal property.
What are the effort and expense to set up?	Only requires signing a document; thus, little, if any, cost.	Attorney writes the trust document; owner changes the titles of assets to the trust; cost is moderate.
What are the gift tax consequences?	Creating JT with a nonspouse may be a taxable gift.	No completed gift is made.
What are the income tax consequences?	Income is split among joint tenants.	Income is taxed to the grantor.
What are the estate tax consequences?	Entire value is included in the gross estate unless the survivor made contributions; but, the "50-50" rule applies for spouses.	Entire value of trust assets are included in the grantor's gross estate.
How much control does the owner retain?	Owner gives up control over property and cannot bequeath it.	Owner can change trust at any time and retains control until death.
Do assets avoid probate?	Yes.	Yes.
How much step-up in basis occurs at death?	Only to the extent of inclusion in the decedent's estate; one-half for spouses.	Full step-up in basis.
Will assets qualify for the marital deduction or unified credit?	If spouse is JT, ½ qualifies for marital deduction, but no use of unified credit; if nonspouse is JT, no marital deduction, but the unified credit is used.	Trust can provide for assets to qualify for the marital deduction and/or the unified credit, depends on the trust provisions.
Are there any special problems?	Owners may forget that they cannot bequeath this property.	Owners tend to forget to change titles to the assets to place in the trust.

Estate Planning Weaknesses and Pitfalls

An estate planning weakness is any part of the client's plan that is inconsistent with the client's objectives. For example, the client may want a child who is working in the business to inherit the business property. Nevertheless, the property may be owned in joint names with a spouse or business partner, and the client will not have control over the disposition of the business. The following are some common estate planning mistakes:

- Leaving everything to the spouse and not taking advantage of the unified credit (applicable credit amount). While portability allows surviving spouses the ability to use any remaining estate tax exclusion amount from the first spouse's estate provided an election is made on the first spouse's estate tax return, it may still be best to take advantage of the unified credit in the estate of the first decedent spouse. Assets expected to appreciate greatly may be placed in a bypass trust, utilizing the decedent's unified credit, to remove the appreciation from the estate of the surviving spouse.

- Lack of liquidity, which may result in a forced sale of assets
- Failure to provide for the survival of a business by means of a buy-sell agreement
- Inappropriate ownership of life insurance
- Failure to name contingent beneficiaries and alternate fiduciaries
- Failure to avoid ancillary probate for real property located in other states
- Excessive use of joint ownership of property
- Failure to write or update a valid will
- Failure to execute durable powers of attorney
- Selection of the wrong executor
- Failure to leave separate funeral instructions

Application Questions

1. Jim Cleary transferred $200,000 of marketable securities to an irrevocable trust for the benefit of his children. He transferred his $200,000 house and his $25,000 car to a revocable trust. He has a brokerage account in which stock valued at $50,000 is held in street name. He owns a life insurance policy with a $100,000 face value. His qualified retirement plan has an account value of $300,000. Jim named his children as the beneficiaries of his life insurance policy and his retirement account. If Jim dies without a valid will, what is the value of Jim's assets that will be subject to probate?

   A. $0
   B. $50,000
   C. $100,000
   D. $150,000
   E. $300,000

2. Jane Harding, age 55, has been paying income tax at the rate of 35% and has an estate of approximately $5 million. Jane is not married and has no children. She intends to leave a portion of her estate to her two young nieces. Which of the following will substitutes will most likely enable Jane to reduce her current income taxes, as well as the future costs of probate?

   A. Joint bank account with her nieces
   B. Deed delivered to an escrow agent for commercial real estate
   C. Revocable living trust containing marketable securities
   D. Series "HH" bonds with her nieces as alternative payees
   E. Joint tenancy WROS with her nieces for corporate bonds

3. Bill Jameson, age 58, and his wife Emma, age 52, established a revocable living trust that will pay Bill and Emma income for life and distribute their assets to their children at their deaths. Bill and Emma transferred the following assets owned in joint tenancy WROS to the trust:

Residence	$175,000
Two cars	$ 50,000
Vacation home	$125,000

Bill also transferred to the trust the stock brokerage account that was in his own name, which held stocks and bonds valued at $200,000. Bill and Emma did not transfer their IRAs to the trust, and each own IRAs valued at $50,000. Bill and Emma named each other as beneficiaries of the IRAs. Bill and Emma also did not transfer to the trust a joint and survivor annuity that has an account value of $200,000. If Emma predeceases Bill and no changes are made to Bill's estate plan, what will be the amount of the assets subject to probate at Bill's death?

   A. $0
   B. $50,000
   C. $100,000
   D. $550,000
   E. $850,000

4. Jerry Harner wants to leave a cottage in the mountains to his mistress after he dies. Jerry does not want the gift to be included in his will since it will be public and will be read by his wife. Jerry also does not want his family to know about the gift during his lifetime. Which of the following will substitute techniques will be most likely to serve Jerry's needs?

    A. A deed delivered to an escrow agent
    B. Joint tenancy WROS
    C. A revocable living trust
    D. An irrevocable trust
    E. A deed placed in a bank safe-deposit box

5. Homer Bard left a will in which he established a $600,000 trust for his children and a $600,000 charitable trust, and the remainder is to pour over into a revocable trust. The revocable trust will pay income to his wife for life, and at her death, the principal will be distributed to the children. At his death, Homer left the following assets:

Residence - JT	$200,000
Common stock - H	$250,000
Municipal bonds - H	$150,000
Investment real estate - R	$200,000
Life insurance - B	$500,000

JT = Joint tenancy WROS
H = Homer is the owner
W = Homer's wife is the owner
R = Revocable trust holds the title
B = Homer is the owner and his wife is the beneficiary

What was the amount of the probate estate when Homer died?

    A. $250,000
    B. $400,000
    C. $600,000
    D. $900,000
    E. $1,100,000

6. Which of the following estate planning techniques can be used to avoid ancillary probate for a real estate investment in another state?

(1) Joint tenancy WROS
(2) Revocable living trust
(3) Irrevocable trust
(4) Deed delivered to an escrow agent
(5) Testamentary trust

A. (1) and (2) only
B. (2) and (3) only
C. (2) and (4) only
D. (1), (2), (3), and (4) only
E. (1), (2), (3), (4), and (5)

7. Herbert and Wendy Meadows own the following property interests:

Residence - JT	$250,000
Common stock - JT	$100,000
Municipal bonds - JT	$100,000
Investment real estate - H	$100,000
Vacation home - W	$150,000
Life insurance - H	$100,000

(Note that Wendy is the beneficiary of the life insurance death benefit.)

401(k) plan assets - H	$250,000
Car - H	$ 40,000
Car - W	$ 30,000

JT = Joint tenancy WROS
H = Herbert is the owner
W = Wendy is the owner

What is the amount of the probate estate if Herbert dies today?

A. $140,000
B. $450,000
C. $490,000
D. $675,000
E. $1,070,000

8. Which of the following interests is (are) subject to probate?

(1) Securities transferred to a revocable trust
(2) A house transferred to an irrevocable trust for 15 years
(3) A life annuity
(4) A joint and survivor annuity

A. (1) only
B. (1) and (4) only
C. (2) and (3) only
D. (3) and (4) only
E. None of the above

9. Peter Forth, age 65, owns a furniture business valued at $10 million, a commercial real estate investment valued at $700,000, and a $250,000 life insurance policy, for which his wife Samantha is the beneficiary. The commercial real estate investment is expected to increase in value at a rate of 11% per year. Their other assets are as follows:

Common stock - JT	$600,000
Municipal bonds - JT	$200,000
Vacation home - JT	$150,000
Motorboat - H	$ 50,000
Car - H	$ 40,000
Car - W	$ 40,000
Savings account - JT	$ 50,000
Checking account - JT	$ 30,000
Jewelry and antiques - W	$ 75,000

JT = Owned in joint tenancy
H = Owned by Peter
W = Owned by Samantha

Peter's will provides for $1,000,000 of assets to be placed in a trust that pays income to his wife for her life and the remainder to his children. The rest of the estate will pass under a residuary clause to Peter's wife. Samantha's will leaves everything to Peter, and the children are contingent beneficiaries. Which of the following weaknesses or mistakes is (are) present in the Fords' estate plan?

(1) Lack of liquidity
(2) Excessive use of joint ownership
(3) Failure to take advantage of the unified credit (applicable credit amount) to remove appreciation from taxation in their estates
(4) Excessive use of the marital deduction

    A. (1) only
    B. (1) and (2) only
    C. (2) and (3) only
    D. (3) and (4) only
    E. (1), (2), (3), and (4)

10. George and Judy Collins live in California, where George has his own business as a meeting planner. George bought a whole life policy soon after he was married, insuring his life for $100,000. The policy has a cash value of $22,000, and Judy is the designated beneficiary. The Collins also own the following assets:

Checking account - CP	$ 6,000
Savings account - CP	$ 8,000
Mutual funds - CP	$ 35,000
Common stock portfolio - CP	$ 50,000
Rental property - H	$200,000
Sole proprietorship - CP	$150,000
IRA (George's) - CP	$ 30,000
403(b) plan (Judy's) - CP	$ 80,000
Residence - CP	$200,000
BMW car - CP	$ 40,000
Jewelry - W	$ 30,000

CP = Community property
H = George's separate property
W = Judy's separate property

If George died today, what would be the approximate value of his probate estate?

    A. $719,000
    B. $610,000
    C. $510,000
    D. $444,500
    E. $200,000

11. (Published question released December, 1996)

Identify the statement(s) below that correctly characterize(s) property interests held by the decedent that, at death, pass by operation of law:

(1) If the property passes according to the operation of law, the property avoids probate.
(2) If the property passes according to the operation of law, it will <u>not</u> be included in the decedent's gross estate.
(3) Property that passes by operation of law <u>cannot</u> qualify for the marital deduction.
(4) The titling on the instrument determines who shall receive the property.

A. (1) only
B. (2), (3), and (4) only
C. (1) and (4) only
D. (1), (3), and (4) only
E. (2) and (3) only

12. In a community-property state, which of the following assets acquired during the marriage will be included in the decedent's probate estate?

A. One-half of a qualified plan at the decedent's place of work
B. An annuity with a period certain and no designated beneficiary, which was obtained in settlement of the decedent's injury claim
C. Life insurance on the decedent's life
D. The decedent's home

13. Gary Chapelle owns a duplex with his brother in joint tenancy with right of survivorship. Gary would like to pass his interest in the property to his son Bill, and Gary has provided in his will that his interest in the duplex will pass to Bill. Which of the following statements concerning the transfer of Gary's interest to his son Bill is correct?

A. Gary's interest in the duplex will pass to Bill by operation of law because the survivorship feature is a will substitute.
B. Gary's interest in the duplex will pass to his brother, but not under the will.
C. Gary's interest in the duplex will pass to Bill under Gary's will.
D. Gary's interest in the duplex will pass first to Gary's brother and then at his death, under Gary's will, to Bill.
E. Gary's interest in the duplex will pass partially by will and partially by operation of law.

14. All the following ways to transfer property to family members are considered will substitutes, EXCEPT:

A. A revocable living trust
B. An irrevocable living trust
C. A joint bank account
D. A testamentary trust
E. An IRA beneficiary designation

15. Which of the following contract provisions, effective at death, will serve as will substitutes for the designated beneficiaries?

    (1) Qualified retirement plan benefits for which the decedent named a child as the designated beneficiary

    (2) An IRA account for which the decedent named a child as the designated beneficiary

    (3) Life insurance death benefits for which the insured named a child as the designated beneficiary

    (4) A provision in a prenuptial agreement, naming a child to receive the decedent's estate and eliminating the spouse's right to any portion of the estate

    A. (1) and (2) only
    B. (2) and (3) only
    C. (3) and (4) only
    D. (2), (3), and (4) only
    E. (1), (2), (3), and (4)

16. Which of the following transfers of property are subject to probate administration?

    (1) A gift *causa mortis*
    (2) A bequest of real estate
    (3) Property passing by intestacy
    (4) An exempt-property allowance

    A. (1) and (2) only
    B. (2) and (3) only
    C. (3) and (4) only
    D. (2), (3), and (4) only
    E. (1), (2), (3), and (4)

17. Which of the following statements describes the rule applicable to the distribution of property under intestacy?

    A. Real property is distributed according to the laws of the state where the land is located, and personal property is distributed according to the laws of the state of the deceased's domicile.

    B. Real property is distributed according to the laws of the state of domicile, and personal property is distributed according to the laws of the state where the property is located.

    C. Real property and personal property are distributed according to the laws of the state where the owner died.

    D. Real property and personal property are distributed according to the laws of the state where the decedent had his or her domicile at the time of death.

    E. Real property and personal property are distributed according to the laws of the state of the property's situs.

18. Property passes through probate when held at death in all the following forms of ownership, EXCEPT:

    A. Sole ownership
    B. Tenancy in common
    C. Community property
    D. Tenants by the entirety
    E. Uniform Gifts to Minors Act

19. Carl Darwin and his second wife own their residence, valued at $3 million, as tenants by the entirety, and they own securities worth $6 million as joint tenants with right of survivorship. Darwin also owns an apartment building titled in his name alone, valued at $8.0 million. Darwin wants to leave at least half of his property to his wife, and he wants to leave property to his two children, Michael and Denise, to take advantage of the unified credit. Which of the following recommendations is most appropriate for Darwin?

   A. The apartment building should be titled to Darwin and the children as joint tenants with right of survivorship to reduce Darwin's gross estate.

   B. Darwin should title the apartment building as tenants in common with his children so that they receive a step-up in basis on their interests at his death.

   C. Darwin should transfer the securities to his children by will to avoid his wife taking a share.

   D. Darwin can make lifetime gifts of interests in the apartment building to his children, without his wife's consent, and avoid her elective share.

   E. Darwin can use the unified credit by having the children take out a life insurance policy on his life in the amount of the unified credit and give them the premiums each year.

20. All of the following characteristics of the probate procedure are common to all states, EXCEPT:

   A. Creditors have a fixed time in which to file claims against the estate. Failure to file in time will bar a claim.

   B. Probate procedures are only required if the decedent had a valid will.

   C. Wills are filed in the probate court in the county in which the decedent resided.

   D. Proof of the valid execution of a will is required in all states.

   E. A personal representative or executor is appointed by a court to administer the estate.

21. Which of the following statements concerning probate procedures is (are) correct?

   (1) The personal representative is responsible for the payment of any estate taxes and all debts of the estate and for distribution of the estate's assets, as directed by the will (or by the intestate statutes).

   (2) A final accounting by the executor or administrator is necessary.

   (3) Acceptance of a final accounting by the probate court relieves the executor or administrator of further liability.

   A. (1) only
   B. (2) only
   C. (1) and (3) only
   D. (2) and (3) only
   E. (1), (2), and (3)

22. All of the following statements concerning reasons to avoid probate are correct, EXCEPT:

   A. The probate proceedings are public, and some people do not want the details concerning their property made public.

   B. Costs of probate can be reduced if property does not pass through the probate procedure.

   C. Probate proceedings do not help to resolve title disputes, which require separate actions, anyway.

   D. The probate process can cause long delays in property being transferred to beneficiaries.

   E. Attorneys' fees for probate are often based on a percentage of the assets passing through probate administration.

23. Which of the following is (are) valid reasons for a testator to make a lifetime disposition of real property located in a state other than his or her state of residence?

   (1) The laws of the nonresident state may create problems concerning legal rights in such property and the executor's power to deal with such property.

   (2) Ancillary probate proceedings in the nonresident state will be needed, thereby increasing the expenses for settling the estate.

   (3) The payment of real estate taxes in the nonresident state may be a problem.

   A. (1) only
   B. (1) and (2) only
   C. (1) and (3) only
   D. (2) and (3) only
   E. (1), (2), and (3)

24. Which of the following property interests will pass under intestacy laws?

   (1) Specific bequests of stock to the owner's children

   (2) Real property that will pass under a residuary clause

   (3) A car owned by the decedent and spouse in joint names with right of survivorship

   (4) All property in the name of an individual who dies leaving no will

   A. (2) only
   B. (4) only
   C. (1) and (3) only
   D. (2) and (4)
   E. (3) and (4)

25. All the following are among the advantages of the probate process, EXCEPT:

   A. Assurance of fair treatment and impartial decisions regarding disputes

   B. Assurance of proper administration of estate property

   C. Avoidance of publicity because the process is conducted behind closed doors

   D. Some income is taxable in the low marginal bracket of the estate, rather than the higher bracket of some beneficiaries.

   E. After a certain period of time, creditors' claims against the decedent's property will be barred.

26. Which of the following is (are) among the advantages of the probate process?

(1) A limited time period for any creditors to file their claims
(2) The avoidance of income tax while the property is in probate
(3) A reduction in the cost of estate administration

    A. (1) only
    B. (3) only
    C. (1) and (2) only
    D. (2) and (3) only
    E. (1), (2), and (3)

27. "A" wishes to leave his Iowa farmland to his daughter from a previous marriage. "A" also wants to provide equitably for his present wife and the two children of their marriage. Under these circumstances, which of the following statements concerning will substitutes are correct?

(1) "A" could disinherit his wife of the previous marriage only by will substitutes.
(2) Joint tenancy WROS with his daughter would avoid both the costs of probate and his new wife's elective share.
(3) "A" could transfer the property before death by placing a properly executed deed in his safe-deposit box for his daughter.
(4) "A" could place the farmland in a revocable living trust, but the trust will probably not be secret from his present wife.

    A. (1) and (2) only
    B. (1) and (3) only
    C. (2) and (3) only
    D. (2) and (4) only
    E. (3) and (4) only

28. Under the circumstances of Question 27, which of the following will substitutes could be used to transfer full title to the Iowa farmland to "A's" daughter at "A's" death?

    A. The creation of a Totten trust
    B. The creation of a joint tenancy WROS
    C. A deed granting the daughter sole ownership, but stating that it takes effect only at "A's" death
    D. The creation of a tenancy in common
    E. A testamentary trust

29. All the following statements concerning will substitutes are correct, EXCEPT:

    A. Money in a joint tenancy bank account passes entirely to the survivor only if there is immediate vesting when the account is established.
    B. Revocable trusts are appropriate for passing real estate outside of probate.
    C. Totten trusts can be altered by the "trustee" withdrawing money.
    D. A will substitute passes property outside of intestacy laws.
    E. Benefits paid under an annuity contract are the result of an enforceable contract that is not subject to probate.

30. If "A" executes a valid deed to real estate to "C," a child by an earlier marriage, all the following statements concerning the rights of "B," who is presently married to "A," are correct, EXCEPT:

    A. "B" may not legally claim an interest in the real estate.

    B. If "C" does not record the deed before "A's" death, "B" will receive the property.

    C. If "A" delivers the deed to "C," then "C" becomes the owner without recording it.

    D. "C" may record the deed after "A's" death and the property will not be subject to probate.

    E. The execution and delivery of the deed is irrevocable, so "B" cannot require "C" to return the real estate.

31. Reginald Rich owns a parcel of commercial real estate worth $500,000. He has an estate valued at $3 million. He has a son, age 25, by his first marriage and two daughters by his present wife. Mr. Rich would like to see his son receive the real estate but does not want his present wife and daughters to cause a scene over the property being given to his son or left in his will. He knows his wife will check the records and will want to see his will when it is written. What will substitute can Mr. Rich use most appropriately to achieve his objective?

    A. Joint tenancy with right of survivorship with his son and daughter

    B. Tenancy in common with the son

    C. Deed in sole ownership to his son, not recorded, but delivered to an agent

    D. Revocable trust with power of appointment reserved in his will

    E. Irrevocable trust of the real estate, with his son as beneficiary

32. The requirements for the formal execution of a valid deed differ from the requirements of a valid will in all the following ways, EXCEPT:

    A. Deeds pass a present interest; wills do not.

    B. Deeds require witnesses; wills do not.

    C. Deeds must be delivered to a grantee or an agent; wills need not be so delivered.

    D. Deeds are written as irrevocable; wills are revocable.

    E. Deeds cannot be contested for undue influence; wills can be.

33. All the following forms of ownership of property will result in the transfer of property at death, without the property being subject to probate, EXCEPT:

    A. Joint tenancy between a brother and sister with right of survivorship in corporate stock

    B. Tenancy by the entireties in commercial real estate

    C. Life insurance payable to a niece

    D. Joint and survivor annuity payable to a married couple

    E. Tenancy in common by a mother and daughter in their residence

34. Which of the following statements concerning payable-on-death (POD) accounts is (are) correct?

(1) POD accounts are testamentary in nature because they take effect at death.
(2) POD accounts are included in the probate estate.
(3) POD accounts are included in the gross estate.

   A. (1) only
   B. (2) only
   C. (1) and (3) only
   D. (2) and (3) only
   E. (1), (2), and (3)

35. Which of the following contract provisions, effective at death, will serve as a will substitute?

(1) Qualified retirement plan benefits for which the decedent named a child as the designated beneficiary
(2) An IRA account for which the decedent named a child as the designated beneficiary
(3) Life insurance benefits for which the insured named a child as the designated beneficiary

   A. (1) only
   B. (3) only
   C. (1) and (3) only
   D. (2) and (3) only
   E. (1), (2), and (3)

36. Which of the following statements concerning the use of life insurance policies as will substitutes are correct?

(1) The death benefit proceeds are not included in the insured decedent's probate estate if the insured owned the policy at the time of death.
(2) The death benefit proceeds are included in the insured decedent's gross estate if the insured owned the policy at the time of death.
(3) The death benefit proceeds avoid probate even if the policy is made payable to the decedent's estate.
(4) The insured can retain the right to change the beneficiary designation until the time of death without having the policy proceeds included in the probate estate.

   A. (1) and (2) only
   B. (2) and (3) only
   C. (3) and (4) only
   D. (1), (2), and (4) only
   E. (1), (2), (3), and (4)

37. All the following statements concerning revocable trusts are correct, EXCEPT:

   A. A revocable trust may be used to pass an equitable interest in assets.
   B. A grantor may reserve a life interest or income for life.
   C. A grantor's gross estate will include the value of the trust property, whether or not he or she reserves a life interest.
   D. A revocable trust will not remove assets from probate unless the beneficiary receives a vested right to income during the grantor's lifetime.
   E. Assets must be transferred to a revocable trust before death in order for the trust to serve as an effective will substitute.

38. Property transferred to which of the following trusts avoids probate?

(1) Revocable living trust
(2) Testamentary trust
(3) Irrevocable *inter vivos* trust
(4) Spousal remainder trust

    A. (1) and (3) only
    B. (3) and (4) only
    C. (1), (2), and (4) only
    D. (1), (3), and (4) only
    E. (1), (2), (3), and (4)

For practice answering case questions related to Topic 54, please answer the following questions in the cases included in the Appendix at the back of this textbook.

Case	Questions
Bartlett	2, 3, 4, and 5
Marshall	
Webster	1 and 2
Unser	
Tingey	
Lytle	1
Beals	1
Mocsin	
Young	1
Borelli	2
Cunningham	2 and 3
Fred and Mary Ferris	6, 7, 8, 9, and 10

Answers and Explanations

1. B is the answer. The stock in the brokerage account is the only asset subject to Jim Cleary's power of disposition at his death, and it is, therefore, subject to probate. The assets transferred to the irrevocable trust and to the revocable trust avoid probate. The life insurance and qualified plan are paid to beneficiaries under contracts that Jim entered into during his lifetime. The same assets are subject to probate, whether Jim Cleary leaves a valid will or dies intestate.

2. E is the answer. If the assets are held in joint tenancy WROS, they will pass automatically to Janes' nieces by operation of law at her death, and they will avoid probate. During her lifetime, the income from property held in joint tenancy will be divided among Jane and her nieces, and thus will reduce Jane's current income taxes. This income tax reduction is not available with the other will substitutes.

3. C is the answer. The assets in the revocable trust will not be subject to probate at Bill's death because Bill does not hold title to them and the terms of the trust transfer the assets directly to the children outside of probate. Emma's IRA will have been paid to Bill, and Bill's IRA will not have an effective beneficiary designation, so they will both pass through his estate and be subject to probate. The annuity will terminate at Bill's death, and nothing remaining in the account balance will pass through the estate. Thus, the probate estate will consist only of the two IRAs, which are $50,000 each, for a total of $100,000.

4. A is the answer. A deed delivered to an escrow agent is deemed a completed gift even though it is not recorded immediately. The delivery is completed, so the gift is not testamentary in nature. It avoids publicity during the donor's lifetime because the donor (Jerry) continues to act as the sole owner. In addition, the property is not included in the will and is not subject to probate. Joint tenancy WROS is not suitable for Jerry's purposes because the title would be changed during his lifetime, and the change in title would give the other joint tenant (the mistress) an immediate ownership interest. Both revocable and irrevocable trusts would similarly require a change in title during Jerry's life to be effective. Thus, the trusts would not provide the protection needed from publicity. The safe-deposit box is not satisfactory because there would be no delivery of the deed during Jerry's lifetime. Placing a deed in the safe-deposit box would probably not be deemed irrevocable delivery because the donor could always go to the box and take it back. Thus, the gift would likely be found to be ineffective or testamentary and subject to the will and his wife's statutory right.

5. B is the answer. The property held in joint tenancy WROS and the property were titled to the revocable trust were not subject to probate. The life insurance death proceeds were also not subject to probate. The only assets subject to probate, therefore, were the common stock and the municipal bonds, for a total of $400,000. The will provisions do not affect the size of the probate estate.

6. D is the answer. Property owned in joint tenancy WROS, in a revocable trust, and in an irrevocable trust do not pass through probate, including ancillary probate. A deed delivered to an escrow agent is a completed gift, so it, too, avoids probate. A testamentary trust is created by a will, so any property passing to a testamentary trust is subject to probate.

7. A is the answer. The probate estate will include the property interests that were owned by Herbert at the time of his death and over which he had a power of disposition. Herbert could not make a disposition of the property owned in joint tenancy because that property would automatically become solely owned by his wife. The life insurance is paid directly to the beneficiary and is not paid to Herbert or to Herbert's estate. The 401(k) plan assets are payable to the surviving spouse and are not subject to probate.

The only probate assets are the investment real estate and the car owned by Herbert. The total value of these assets is $140,000.

8. E is the answer. Assets transferred to trusts are no longer under the grantor's control for disposition at death. Assets avoid probate when placed in either a revocable or irrevocable trust. An annuity is a contract with an insurance company for payments to the annuitant. If the annuity is a life annuity, no payments are owed after the annuitant's death. If the annuity is joint and survivor, the insurance company makes payment to the survivor after the annuitant's death. Payment is governed by the contract, and the annuitant makes no disposition at death. Thus, the annuity is not subject to probate. For additional information on annuities, see Topic 71 in this Estate Planning material.

9. E is the answer. Peter's estate will lack liquidity because the business interest and the commercial real estate are his largest assets, and they will have to be sold to pay expenses and taxes. While taxes will not be great, the probate costs could be substantial. The other large assets are jointly owned and will not be available to the executor to pay taxes. The life insurance will also be payable to Peter's wife and will not be available to the estate. Joint ownership of the more liquid assets is part of the problem. While portability will allow both unified credits to be used, they could be used more effectively to remove highly appreciating assets, such as the real estate, from both estates. This can be accomplished by placing the highly appreciating assets in a bypass trust upon Peter's death, allowing the transfer to be sheltered by his unified credit and removing appreciation from Samantha's estate. Since the unified credit is not used effectively, there is excessive use of the marital deduction.

10. D is the answer. The life insurance death proceeds would not be subject to probate because the insurer makes payment directly to the beneficiary under the insurance contract. The IRA and 403(b) are also not probate assets because they are payable under contract provisions. The jewelry is Judy's separate property and is not subject to George's disposition at death. The rental property is George's separate property and would be subject to probate at the full value of $200,000. The remaining assets are community property and are subject to probate to the extent of one-half of their value. The total is $444,500.

11. C is the answer. The way in which property is titled determines how it will pass at the decedent's death. If property is in joint tenancy with right of survivorship, it passes by operation of law to the joint tenant(s). The property that passes by operation of law avoids probate, which is why joint tenancy is a technique for avoiding probate. Property held in joint tenancy does not entirely avoid inclusion in the gross estate. If spouses own property in joint tenancy, one-half of the date-of-death value is included in the decedent's gross estate. The interest passing to the spouse by operation of law, such as the joint tenancy interest, will qualify for the marital deduction.

12. B is the answer. The settlement for the decedent's injury claim is separate property, so the annuity is separate property that will pass through probate. This annuity does not provide for survivorship payments, so the payments are not made to a survivor by contract. The qualified plan passes outside probate even if it contains community property. The qualified plan passes by law to the spouse or designated beneficiary. Life insurance passes by contract outside probate. Only one-half of the decedent's home will be subject to probate as community property.

13. B is the answer. Property held in joint tenancy WROS will pass to the surviving joint tenant. The property cannot be transferred by will because the joint interest passes by operation of law at death. Gary Chapelle cannot transfer his interest in the duplex by his will, and his son will not receive any interest in the duplex unless Gary's brother provides in his will for Bill to receive an interest. Note that Gary may be able to avoid this problem by selling his joint interest in the duplex and leaving the money to Bill.

14. D is the answer. A testamentary trust is not a will substitute; rather, a testamentary trust is established by will, and the assets placed in the trust pass through probate administration. A revocable trust and an irrevocable trust are both will substitutes because the assets placed in these trusts do not pass through probate. Money in a joint bank account is payable to the survivor without passing through probate; thus, a joint bank account is a will substitute.

15. D is the answer. The benefits of a qualified retirement plan pass automatically to the surviving spouse, even if the spouse is not named as the beneficiary. The beneficiary designation for IRA accounts can provide for a child to receive the benefits instead of a spouse. Life insurance benefits can also be designated for children. A prenuptial agreement can also provide that a decedent's estate will pass to a child, and the spouse can relinquish an elective share.

16. D is the answer. A bequest of real estate passed under the will is subject to probate. Property passing by intestacy is also subject to probate. An exempt-property allowance is claimed against probate property. A gift *causa mortis* passes before death and is not subject to probate.

17. A is the answer. When a person dies intestate, real property is distributed according to the laws of the state where the land is located, and personal property is distributed according to the laws of the state of the deceased's domicile.

18. D is the answer. Property held as tenants by the entirety is not included in the probate estate, whereas property held in sole ownership, tenancy in common, and one-half of community property are included in probate.

19. D is the answer. Since the apartment building is owned solely by Darwin, he can make lifetime gifts of interests in the building without his wife's consent. The basis to the children will be Darwin's basis, and at Darwin's death, there will be no step-up in basis in the interests given to the children. Darwin's wife might otherwise reduce the children's inheritance by electing her spousal share. The only asset in the estate would be the apartment building because the other property was owned jointly or by entireties. If Darwin left the apartment building to the children to take advantage of the unified credit, the elective portion would reduce the children's inheritance and reduce the estate's use of the unified credit. Titling the apartment building to Darwin and the children as joint tenants WROS would not reduce Darwin's gross estate because the entire value of the building would still be includible and would exceed the unified credit. The securities cannot be given to the children because they are held in joint names WROS with Darwin's wife. The life insurance policy purchased by Darwin's children will not be includible in Darwin's estate and will not take advantage of the unified credit.

20. B is the answer. Probate procedures apply to intestate estates, for which no will is offered, as well as to testate estates, for which a will is offered. The probate procedures are similar for both intestate and testate estates.

21. E is the answer. The executor or administrator is issued letters testamentary or letters of administration to act on behalf of the estate in collecting assets and paying debts. After a final accounting is made, the probate court discharges the personal representative of further liability.

22. C is the answer. Probate proceedings can sometimes be advantageous for establishing title to property. Once title is resolved, the executor's deed will serve as proof of legal title.

23. B is the answer. Lifetime gifts of real estate located in another state will avoid an ancillary probate in that state. In most cases, there is no problem in pursuing the ancillary probate procedure, but the laws of the state where the real estate is located may affect legal rights in the property adversely. Payment of real estate taxes should not be a problem.

24. B is the answer. Intestacy laws determine how property will be distributed when a person leaves no will or when a testator leaves a will that does not provide for disposition of certain property. A residuary clause is a way to avoid partial intestacy by making disposition of any remaining property after the distribution of specific bequests. Property held as joint tenants with right of survivorship passes to the surviving joint tenant by operation of law, not under intestacy laws.

25. C is the answer. The probate process is conducted in courts of law in a public administration, not behind closed doors.

26. A is the answer. The probate process affords a limited time for creditors to file claims against the decedent's estate. Otherwise, claims may be filed for as long as the statute of limitations on suits. Income tax savings result for the beneficiaries if they are in high tax brackets, but income tax is not completely avoided while the property is in probate. The estate must pay income tax. Estate administration costs are increased by probate.

27. D is the answer. (1) is incorrect because "A" could disinherit a wife of an earlier marriage in his will. (3) is incorrect because the deed must be transferred to the donee or to an escrow agent to be an effective lifetime gift. In (2), the joint tenancy WROS will keep the property out of "A's" probate estate, and the farm will pass directly to "A's" daughter. "A's" present wife cannot defeat this transfer by exercising her election against the will. In (4), the revocable living trust will pass the property to "A's" daughter at "A's" death. The trust must be funded during "A's" lifetime, so "A" will not be able to keep the trust a secret and may have to justify it to his present wife.

28. B is the answer. A Totten trust is a bank account in which the depositor names himself or herself the trustee for another person's benefit, but the beneficiary cannot obtain the funds deposited in the account until the depositor dies. A deed that has no effect until the grantor's death is deemed the equivalent of a will and must comply with the formalities of a will execution. Otherwise, the deed is ineffective to pass title. A tenancy in common only passes title to a portion of the property because there is no right of survivorship as there is with joint tenancy WROS.

29. A is the answer. Joint tenancy bank accounts may be of three types: joint tenancy with immediate vesting, a revocable account, or a convenience account. All of these joint accounts are will substitutes, and the survivor will receive the proceeds. A will substitute passes property outside of probate, and the property is not subject to intestacy laws.

30. B is the answer. If "A" has delivered the deed to "C," the deed may be recorded after "A's" death and still be valid against "B's" right to an elective share. The property has passed to "C" at the time the deed is executed and delivered, so the property will not be subject to probate.

31. C is the answer. The joint tenancy requires a transfer by deed that will occur during Mr. Rich's lifetime, whereas the deed in escrow will not take effect until Rich's death. The deed in escrow will not cause a scene because it will not be accessible to anyone. Even the revocable trust will have some immediate effect in transferring title to the trust, and Mr. Rich's present wife is likely to become aware of it.

32. B is the answer. Wills require the additional formalities of witnesses and a declaration that the document is intended as an individual's will. Deeds do not require witnesses or the other formalities for a will.

33. E is the answer. The mother's interest in property held as tenants in common with her daughter will be subject to testamentary disposition and will be part of the probate estate.

34. C is the answer. POD accounts are testamentary in nature and may require the formalities of execution for a will. POD accounts are not included in the probate estate, but are included in the gross estate for estate tax purposes.

35. D is the answer. The benefits of a qualified retirement plan pass automatically to the surviving spouse, even if the spouse is not named as the beneficiary. This is not true for IRA accounts and life insurance contracts.

36. D is the answer. The insured can retain any incidents of ownership, including the right to change the beneficiary designation, without the danger of the death benefit being included in the probate estate. If the insured fails to transfer all incidents of ownership at least 3 years before death, however, the death benefit will be included in the insured's gross estate. A policy payable to the estate does not avoid probate.

37. D is the answer. A revocable trust conveys a present, equitable interest in assets to its beneficiaries. The grantor may retain a life interest or a right to income for life, but the revocable trust remains an effective will substitute even without the beneficiary receiving any income during the grantor's lifetime. The entire value of the trust assets will be included in the gross estate for federal estate tax purposes, regardless of whether the grantor receives a life interest or not.

38. D is the answer. Of the choices given, only the assets transferred by will to a testamentary trust will pass through probate. Assets transferred to the other trusts will avoid probate because at the grantor's death, the trustee, not the grantor, is the legal owner.

Estate Planning Documents (Topic 55)

CFP Board Student-Centered Learning Objectives

(a) Identify and describe the components of estate planning documents, such as wills and trusts that are used to facilitate the transfer of one's assets.

(b) Explain the roles of the parties used in estate planning including executor, trustee, power of attorney, beneficiary(ies), heirs, and guardians. [See Topics 58 and 70]

(c) Recommend appropriate estate planning documents to meet a client's goals and objectives.

Estate Planning Documents
- A. Wills
  - 1) Legal requirements
  - 2) Types of wills
  - 3) Modifying or revoking a will
  - 4) Avoiding will contests
- B. Powers of attorney
- C. Trusts
- D. Marital property agreements
- E. Buy-sell agreements

Wills

The basic document of estate planning is the will. A will must be executed according to the formal requirements specified by state law. Generally, the will must be in writing and must be signed by the testator (testatrix) and witnessed by two or three competent individuals. A will is a revocable instrument that can be altered, amended, or rewritten at any time before death.

The following estate planning objectives require execution of a valid will:

- Distributing property to charities or to persons other than heirs
- Establishing a trust at death (testamentary trust)
- Allocating particular estate assets to pay debts, estate administration expenses, and taxes
- Naming guardians and custodians for minor children and for assets passing to minors
- Providing for a presumption of survival in cases of the simultaneous death of spouses

- Coordinating the use of the unified credit and marital and charitable deductions to reduce estate taxes

State laws generally prevent a person from using a will for the following purposes:

- Disinheriting a spouse
- Creating illegal conditions for inheritances
- Transferring property that passes by operation of law or trying to change an irrevocable trust

Types of Wills

A **holographic will** is a handwritten will and is valid in some states, without the formality of witnesses signing. The testator must prepare the holographic will entirely in his or her own handwriting and sign and date the will. A **nuncupative will** is an oral will spoken by the testator in the presence of the required number of witnesses and later reduced to writing. Nuncupative wills are not valid in all states.

Joint, Mutual, and Reciprocal Wills

Sometimes, spouses seek to establish a single estate plan, applicable to both of their estates, and then execute joint, mutual, or reciprocal wills. A joint will is a single will executed by two or more individuals, usually a husband and wife.

A mutual will is a will made pursuant to an agreement between individuals to dispose of property in a certain way. Reciprocal wills are written to make each testator the beneficiary of the other's estate. The use of joint, mutual, and reciprocal wills is generally inadvisable. At the death of one of the parties to a joint will, it is questionable whether a new will can be written to take into account changed circumstances.

In addition, these wills may be found to create a contract requiring the surviving spouse to make specific bequests. Any property subject to such a contract may then be disqualified from the marital deduction. Similar questions arise concerning the enforceability of mutual and reciprocal wills after one of the parties has died. The preferable approach is to allow each testator the freedom to dispose of property as seems best under the circumstances.

Common Will Provisions

A "simple" will usually leaves everything outright to a spouse or relative. Such a will contains only a few provisions, but includes a residuary clause bequeathing all of the rest and residue to the spouse or relative.

"Per stirpes" means by the root or stock. *Per stirpes* distribution under a will or trust means the property passes to the issue as

though their immediate ancestor had divided the property equally among them. For example, under *per stirpes* distribution, if a decedent's two children each had two children, the children would each receive one-half of the decedent's estate, and the grandchildren would receive nothing. If one of the decedent's children had died before the decedent, the two children of that predeceased child would share their parent's one-half interest. Thus, the two grandchildren would receive one-quarter of the estate, and the surviving child would receive one-half. *Per stirpes* is also called right of representation.

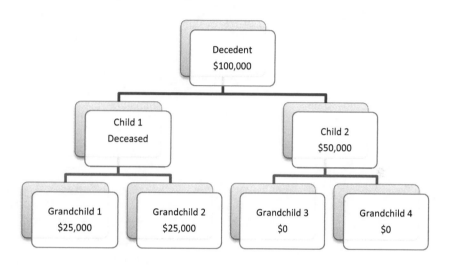

Per capita means per each person or "by the head." Per capita distribution means all issues share equally regardless of their degree of relation. Thus, if a decedent is survived by only one of two children and by four grandchildren, the one child and four grandchildren would each take a one-fifth interest.

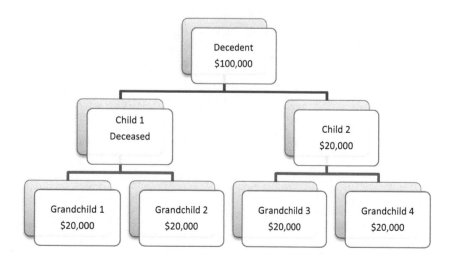

A presumption of survivorship clause determines the order of death for purposes of distributing the testator's estate in the event that the testator and a beneficiary die simultaneously, such as in a plane crash. Such a clause can save an estate expensive litigation over the validity of bequests or the availability of the marital deduction. Some states have enacted simultaneous death statutes to deal with this issue, but a testator may want to include a clause to ensure a particular order of death for his or her estate. These clauses are also sometimes called common disaster clauses or simultaneous death clauses. A survival clause requiring the heir or beneficiary to survive the decedent by a specified period of time, such as by 60 days, can have similar effect.

Modifying or Revoking a Will

A will can be modified by executing a document, called a codicil. The codicil must satisfy the same formal requirements as a will, i.e., a writing signed by the testator and witnessed. A valid codicil can change or eliminate provisions of a will without revoking the will.

A will can be revoked by destroying it or by defacing it with intent to revoke. For example, a testator may write the word "Revoked" on the face of the will. A will can also be revoked by executing a new will, and it will revoke any codicils applicable to the previous will. Generally, a person executing a new will should state that all prior wills are revoked by the new will; otherwise, any previous will may remain valid to the extent not inconsistent with the new will.

Avoiding Will Contests

A will contest is a law suit to overturn the provisions of a will. A disappointed heir can contest a will on the grounds that the will was not executed properly, the testator was not of sound mind, or the testator was under the undue influence of another individual. It is very difficult to avoid a will contest, because in most circumstances, a person cannot be prevented from filing a law suit. Nevertheless, the will contest can be rendered superfluous by means of the techniques for avoiding probate discussed in Topic 54. These will substitute techniques remove the assets from the distribution provisions of the will, so a will contest will have no effect on those assets. Where the estate owner has transferred assets to a trust, for example, the distribution of assets established by the trust is unaffected by a will contest.

A will contest may be avoided in some cases by the execution of a prenuptial agreement discussed below.

Right of Survivorship

A will is not effective for passing property owned by joint tenants with right of survivorship. Where there is a **right of survivorship**, the property passes automatically by operation of law to another person. For both real estate and personal property owned in joint tenancy with right of survivorship, the title to the property passes to the surviving joint tenant(s) at the death of the other joint tenant(s). The property held in joint tenancy with right of survivorship, therefore, can be transferred without a will. Similarly, joint bank accounts can be set up so the proceeds of the account will be paid to the survivor without passing through probate.

Living Wills

State laws in most states provide for the execution of "living wills." These living wills are really medical life-support directives and do not dispose of the owner's property. In a living will, an individual can declare his or her wishes for medical treatment and procedures in the event he or she becomes unconscious or incompetent. For example, an individual can direct physicians or family not to make use of life-support systems to prolong life when there is no hope of a recovery.

Powers of Attorney

A power of attorney is a document executed by the principal, authorizing another person to act as an agent. The principal can grant limited or general powers to the attorney-in-fact, and the power can be durable or nondurable. A power can be executed to deal with healthcare for the principal or to manage the principal's property. Additional treatment of powers of attorney is found in Topic 58.

Trusts

Trusts are created by the execution of trust documents, sometimes called trust agreements. These documents are generally not public documents and are not subject to court supervision. Trusts established during the grantor's lifetime are *inter vivos,* or living trusts; trusts established by a will at death are testamentary trusts. A revocable trust can be terminated, revoked, or changed by the grantor at any time; an irrevocable trust cannot be changed after it is established.

Trusts can be used to achieve the following objectives:

- To provide professional management (by trustees) of assets for beneficiaries
- To reduce income and estate taxes (e.g., an irrevocable trust)
- To avoid creditors and prevent the waste of assets (e.g., a spendthrift trust)

- To arrange for income to be paid to one person and the remaining assets to another
- To provide assets or income to charities
- To avoid probate

Marital Agreements

Prenuptial (or antenuptial) agreements can be entered into before marriage to establish a plan for the disposition of property (as well as children) in the event of divorce, separation, or death. These agreements must be in writing and must be signed by both parties. If the agreements are entered into willingly and with full knowledge, courts find them effective for purposes of estate disposition. If full disclosure is not made before the agreements are entered, courts will invalidate them as lacking in mutuality.

Premarital agreements can be especially useful for protecting a client's wealth when there is a disparity in the wealth of the parties or when one party has obligations from a previous marriage.

Domestic Partnership Agreements

Domestic partnership agreements are similar to prenuptial agreements but generally entered into by unmarried couples; both heterosexual and same-sex. Like a prenuptial agreement, if entered into willingly, courts find them effective for purposes of estate disposition.

When used in conjunction with a will, domestic partnership agreements can be particularly valuable in minimizing will contests from the blood relatives of the deceased.

Business Agreements

A buy-sell agreement or business continuation agreement is a contract providing for the sale and purchase of a business interest at the time the owner retires, becomes disabled, or dies. Buy-sell agreements are discussed in more detail in Topics 60 and 67 in this estate planning material.

Application Questions

1. (Published question released December, 1996)

Mr. and Mrs. Jones own 640 acres of farmland deeded as "joint tenants, *not* as tenants in common." Currently, the land has an appraised value of $3,000 per acre, and it continues to appreciate annually in value. In addition, Mr. Jones holds a $250,000 CD in his name only, and Mrs. Jones holds a $250,000 CD in her name only. Mr. and Mrs. Jones have no debts. Mrs. Jones' last will and testament provides that, "all of my assets at my death shall be divided in three equal portions among my children and my husband."

Mrs. Jones dies unexpectedly, leaving her husband and two children as her sole heirs. Which of the following statements is true?

A. The children will inherit two-thirds of Mrs. Jones' interest in the CD and her 50% interest in the farm.
B. The children will inherit two-thirds of Mrs. Jones' interest in the CD and no interest in the farm.
C. The children will inherit two-thirds of Mrs. Jones' interest in the CD and two-thirds of her 50% interest in the farm.
D. The children will inherit a statutory interest in the CD and the farm.
E. The children's share of Mrs. Jones' CD and her 50% interest in the farm are subject to probate.

2. (Published question released December, 1996)

Two weeks after Mrs. Jones death, Mr. Jones dies, and his will provides that, "I hereby give all my real property to my brother James, and I give all my personal property to my children, share and share alike." Which one of the following statements is true?

A. The children will inherit Mr. Jones' CD and his interest in the farm.
B. The children will inherit Mr. Jones' CD and none of his interest in the farm.
C. The children will inherit no interest in either Mr. Jones' CD or the farm.
D. Mr. Jones' CD is subject to probate, but Mr. Jones' farm interest is not subject to probate.
E. Neither the CD nor Mr. Jones' interest in the farm is subject to probate.

3. Sam Rivera had a buy-sell agreement for his equipment rental business that provided for his brother to buy out Sam's interest at Sam's death, according to a formula they had developed. At Sam's death, the formula required Sam's brother to buy the interest for $500,000. Sam's will leaves the business interest to his two sons, who are active in the business. Which one of the following statements is correct?

   A. The business interest will pass under the will and will be subject to probate.

   B. The business interest will not pass under the will but will be subject to probate.

   C. The business interest will be sold to Sam's brother, and the proceeds will avoid probate.

   D. The business interest will be sold to Sam's brother, and the proceeds will be subject to probate.

   E. The business interest will be sold to Sam's brother, and the proceeds will be distributed to the two sons.

4. (Published question released December, 1996)

A premarital agreement should not be considered by individuals contemplating marriage in which one of the following situations?

   A. When one or both parties are unwilling to make a full disclosure of all their income and assets to the other party

   B. When each party has significant wealth and wishes to protect his/her financial independence

   C. When there is a significant difference in the wealth of the parties

   D. When one or both parties have ongoing obligations, rights, and/or children from a previous marriage

   E. When one party is considering making a substantial gift to the other in consideration of the marriage

5. Robert Hoey has lived in Texas, a community property state, with his wife Clara for their entire marriage of 30 years. Robert has executed a will, leaving all of his assets to a trust that will pay income to Clara for life and the remainder to his children at her death. Which of the following assets will pass to the trust?

(1) Utility stock Robert inherited from his mother
(2) One-half of a business Robert started 15 years ago and built up through his efforts
(3) One-half of the settlement Clara received for personal injuries in a car accident
(4) Life insurance Robert purchased before marriage and for which he paid premiums with earned income during marriage (Clara is the beneficiary.)

   A. (1) and (2) only
   B. (1) and (4) only
   C. (2) and (3) only
   D. (2) and (4) only
   E. (1), (2), (3), and (4)

6. Alan and Lucy Long are both 45 years of age and have two children, ages 7 and 4. The Longs heard about avoiding probate by creating a revocable living trust, so they had a revocable trust prepared and transferred their $500,000 of investments to it. Alan bought a $10 million life insurance policy and transferred it to the trust. Their residence was kept in joint names. The Longs decided that with their estate plan, they did not need wills. Which of the following weaknesses or mistakes are present in the Longs' estate plan?

(1) Failure to execute valid wills
(2) Incorrectly titled assets
(3) Failure to avoid probate for both
(4) Inappropriate ownership of life insurance

   A. (1) only
   B. (1) and (2) only
   C. (3) and (4) only
   D. (1), (2), and (4) only
   E. (1), (2), (3), and (4)

7. Which of the following statements concerning a will are correct?

    (1) A will can be altered, amended, or completely rewritten at any time before a person's death.

    (2) A will cannot be rewritten but can be amended at any time by a codicil.

    (3) A will generally must be signed by the maker and usually must be witnessed by two or three people.

    (4) A will assures a testator of orderly disposition of his or her property because the will becomes effective as soon as it is signed and witnessed.

    A. (1) and (2) only
    B. (1) and (3) only
    C. (2) and (3) only
    D. (3) and (4) only
    E. (1), (2), (3), and (4)

8. Which of the following wills may be entirely handwritten and need not be witnessed, but may be effective for disposing of the testator's property?

    A. A holographic will
    B. A living will
    C. A nuncupative will
    D. A pourover will
    E. A power of attorney

9. Which of the following is (are) a single will executed by two or more individuals?

    (1) A joint will
    (2) A mutual will
    (3) A reciprocal will

    A. (1) only
    B. (2) only
    C. (1) and (2) only
    D. (2) and (3) only
    E. (1), (2), and (3)

10. Which of the following are valid reasons for avoiding the use of joint and mutual wills?

    (1) Mutual wills may be unenforceable after the first decedent dies.

    (2) Joint wills between spouses may result in loss of the marital deduction.

    (3) Joint wills cannot be changed.

    (4) These wills may not result in the disposition of property as seems best to a testator under existing circumstances.

    A. (1) and (2) only
    B. (2) and (3) only
    C. (3) and (4) only
    D. (1), (2), and (4) only
    E. (1), (2), (3), and (4)

11. Which of the following statements describe(s) characteristics of will substitutes?

(1) A will substitute transfers property outside of probate.
(2) A will substitute transfers property by intestate succession, rather than by will.
(3) A lifetime gift of property can be a will substitute.
(4) The public generally has greater access to will substitutes than to a formal will.

A. (1) only
B. (1) and (2) only
C. (1) and (3) only
D. (2) and (4) only
E. (1), (2), (3), and (4)

12. Which of the following circumstances is the LEAST likely to indicate a need to change a will?

A. Tax laws have changed since the will was last reviewed.
B. Property bequeathed to one heir has been sold.
C. Assets bequeathed to one heir have appreciated substantially in value.
D. The maker of the will has been committed and found mentally incompetent.
E. The person named as executor in the will has died.

13. All the following estate planning objectives can be accomplished by the use of a will, EXCEPT:

A. The establishment of a testamentary trust
B. The creation of a presumption of survivorship
C. The disinheritance of a spouse in a non-community-property state
D. The disinheritance of a child (except in Louisiana)
E. The expansion of investment authority for a trustee or executor

14. Which of the following estate planning objectives can be accomplished by the execution of a will?

A. To avoid the publicity and expense of probate
B. To provide for family income during the probate process
C. To bequeath all assets to children, rather than to a surviving spouse
D. To change a beneficiary designation on a life insurance policy owned by the testator
E. To bequeath qualified retirement plan assets to a charity, rather than a surviving spouse

15. All the following are considered to be valid reasons for not including funeral arrangement instructions in a will, EXCEPT:

A. The funeral arrangements usually are completed before the instructions in the will are disclosed.
B. Funeral arrangement instructions can be admitted to probate immediately and before the will.
C. Any special instructions pertaining to funeral arrangements can be given to the family or executor apart from the will.
D. The force and effect of any such instructions in a will is questionable.
E. A will is often kept in a lockbox to which the executor may not have access until the will appoints the executor to administer the estate.

16. A residuary clause would logically be included in a will for which of the following reasons?

(1) To provide a method for disposal of any portion of the estate remaining after the payment of all debts, taxes, administrative expenses, and specific bequests
(2) To prevent any portion of the remaining estate's assets from being distributed in a manner inconsistent with the testator's wishes
(3) To avoid partial intestacy with regard to particular items of property
(4) To provide for disposition of property that may be acquired after execution of the will

    A. (1) only
    B. (2) only
    C. (2) and (3) only
    D. (3) and (4) only
    E. (1), (2), (3), and (4)

17. All the following statements concerning the disinheriting of heirs by a testator are correct, EXCEPT:

A. The statutes of some states provide that the testator's children not named in the will are entitled to the share of the testator's estate they would have received had there been no will.
B. A testator can impose conditions on an heir, such as: the heir must remain unmarried in order to inherit property.
C. Pretermitted heir statutes protect children born after a will was executed so that they are not unintentionally disinherited.
D. The testator's reasons for disinheriting an heir must be lawful reasons.
E. A surviving spouse has a right to elect against a will which disinherits the spouse.

18. In which of the following circumstances might a testator be able to disinherit his or her surviving spouse?

    (1) An antenuptial agreement was executed by the spouse.

    (2) A state statute permits the surviving spouse to take a specified percentage of the estate if the percentage of the deceased's estate left to a spouse is less than the statutory share.

    (3) The spouse was the testator's second wife.

    (4) In a community-property state, the decedent left a will directing that all of the community property be placed in a trust for the decedent's children.

    A. (1) only
    B. (4) only
    C. (1) and (3) only
    D. (2) and (4) only
    E. (1), (2), (3), and (4)

For practice answering case questions related to Topic 55, please answer the following questions in the cases included in the Appendix at the back of this textbook.

Case	Questions
Bartlett	6
Marshall	4
Webster	
Unser	1
Tingey	
Lytle	2
Beals	
Mocsin	
Young	
Borelli	3
Cunningham	4 and 5
Fred and Mary Ferris	11, 12, 13, 14, and 15

Answers and Explanations

1. B is the answer. The farmland is titled in joint tenancy, so it passes by operation of law to Mr. Jones and will not pass under Mrs. Jones' will. The only asset passing under the will is the CD owned by Mrs. Jones in her own name. The will provides for the division of all assets into three portions for her two children and husband. Thus, the two children will receive two-thirds of Mrs. Jones' interest in the CD.

2. B is the answer. The CD is personal property and will pass to the children under the will provision directing that the children receive Mr. Jones' personal property. The farmland is real property and will pass to Mr. Jones' brother under the provision in the will directing that real property be given to his brother. Both the real property and the personal property will be subject to probate.

3. D is the answer. The business interest is subject to the buy-sell contract, so it will be sold to Sam's brother, and the proceeds will be paid to the estate. The sale proceeds are subject to probate, but the proceeds may or may not be distributed to the two sons. The sons were entitled to receive the business interest, but since it had to be sold, under the terms of the buy-sell contract, they will not be able to take that interest. They will only be entitled to the proceeds if the will makes a distribution to them in some other provision.

4. A is the answer. If one or both of the parties fail to make full disclosure of their income and assets, the premarital agreement can be nullified. The agreement is ineffective unless it is based on full knowledge by the parties of the relevant information on assets and income. The other situations listed in this question are examples of the need for a premarital agreement.

5. A is the answer. The utility stock is Robert's separate property because it was inherited from his mother, so he can dispose of it under his will. The business that he started during marriage is community property, and one-half is subject to his testamentary disposition. The settlement Clara received for personal injuries is her separate property, and Robert cannot dispose of this property by his will. The life insurance is payable to Clara under the beneficiary designation, so it does not pass under the will and will not go into the trust.

6. E is the answer. Wills are needed to appoint guardians for the Longs' children. Wills are also a good idea for the disposition of property that may have been omitted or for property, that is acquired later, such as inheritances. The life insurance should not be titled to the revocable trust. There is no advantage to placing it in a revocable trust. In addition, the life insurance should not be purchased by Alan. It should be purchased by Lucy or by an irrevocable trust to keep it out of Alan's gross estate for federal estate tax purposes. The Longs will avoid probate for the first to die, but the surviving spouse will own the residence outright. Unless the home is then transferred to the trust, the surviving spouse's estate will be subject to probate.

7. B is the answer. A will can be altered, amended, or completely rewritten at any time before a person's death. A will can also be amended at any time by a codicil. A will must be signed by the maker and usually must be witnessed by two or three people. A will assures a testator of the orderly disposition of his or her property, but the will is not effective until the testator is dead.

8. A is the answer. A holographic will is entirely in the handwriting of the decedent and is signed and dated by the decedent, but it need not be witnessed.

9. A is the answer. A joint will is a single document executed by two individuals. The one document serves as the will for both persons. A mutual will is signed by only one person, but there is an agreement with another person who signs another will, prepared according to their agreed plan. In reciprocal wills, the persons agree to leave property to each other. Each person signs a separate will.

10. E is the answer. Joint wills are not recommended because the property interests of the first decedent-spouse may be construed as terminal interests and thus not qualify for the marital deduction. Whether the survivor may write a new will to change the terms of a joint will is questionable. A mutual will can be changed. Finally, it is difficult to enforce an agreement for mutual wills after the death of the first party.

11. C is the answer. Property transferred by a will substitute avoids probate administration. A lifetime gift of property avoids probate, so it is a will substitute. Property that passes by intestacy or intestate succession passes through probate, so intestate succession is not a will substitute. A will is filed with the court and is available to the public, while most will substitutes are private documents.

12. D is the answer. If a person has been found mentally incompetent, a new or amended will would be subject to contest. A maker of a will who later becomes incompetent should not revoke a will made during a time when the maker was competent. The other choices are circumstances that may or may not indicate a need to change a will.

13. C is the answer. Most states provide by statute for protection of a spouse by affording a right of election or elective share, regardless of the testator's will. The surviving spouse is entitled to a specified percentage of the decedent's estate, despite any attempt to disinherit the spouse in the will. The will, however, can be used to disinherit a child when the testator states an express intention to do so. Only in Louisiana are the decedent's children entitled to a percentage of the estate, despite a will provision disinheriting them. A will may be used to create a presumption of survivorship in the event a decedent and spouse die simultaneously, as in an accident. A will can also be used to establish trusts, which are called testamentary trusts, as distinguished from living trusts set up during the owner's lifetime.

14. B is the answer. A will can make a specific bequest of living expenses for the decedent's family during the probate process. The other objectives cannot be accomplished in a will.

15. B is the answer. Funeral arrangement instructions separate from the will are not admitted to probate. The probate process is for administering and distributing the decedent's estate, according to the will. The separate instructions are given to a friend, relative, or executor, so the funeral can be arranged before the probate process begins.

16. E is the answer. A residuary clause bequeaths all property remaining after specific bequests. The debts, taxes, and administrative expenses must be paid before any distribution to legatees. A residuary clause can protect against acquisition of future property and partial intestacy for particular items of property. The residuary clause will assure that any remaining assets will be distributed as the testator wanted.

17. B is the answer. Will provisions that condition an inheritance upon a person's not marrying are against public policy and are void.

18. A is the answer. A surviving spouse who enters into an antenuptial agreement may waive the right to take the elective share of the estate. Otherwise, a surviving spouse retains a right to an elective share when disinherited. In a community-property state, a surviving spouse also has a right to an elective share of one-half of community property, but this right may be given up to obtain benefits conferred conditionally by the will.

Gifting Strategies (Topic 56)

CFP Board Student-Centered Learning Objectives

(a) Determine when gifting strategies are appropriate.

(b) Select appropriate gifting techniques or vehicles to achieve the client's goals and objectives.

Gifting Strategies
- A.   *Inter vivos gifting*
- B.   *Gift-giving techniques and strategies*
- C.   *Appropriate gift property*
- D.   *Strategies for closely held business owners*
- E.   *Gifts of present and future interests*
- F.   *Gifts to noncitizen spouses*
- G.   *Tax implications*
    - 1)   *Income*
    - 2)   *Gift*
    - 3)   *Estate*
    - 4)   *Generation-skipping transfer tax (GSTT)*

Inter Vivos Gifts

Lifetime gifts (*inter vivos* gifts) allow donors to observe donees benefiting from their largesse, and the gifts can reduce a donor's income taxes, future estate, and probate costs. By making lifetime gifts, donors can remove future appreciation of assets from their estates, and they can take advantage of the gift tax laws that allow multiple gift tax annual exclusions, exclusions for payments of tuition and medical care, and valuation discounts that might not be available for testamentary dispositions.

Planning for Gifts

An owner can consider gift giving if the owner does not need either the property or the income from it and is able to give up control over the property. The owner must be able to part with the property, both financially and emotionally.

A gift of a personal residence may be suitable if the client is planning to retire and move to Florida, but the gift would not be suitable if the residence is the client's major retirement asset. A gift will also be suitable where the owner can achieve estate planning goals, such as reduction of estate taxes or probate costs, and it may be appropriate where income tax reduction can be accomplished by shifting income to others. Charitable gifts may be suitable for achieving the donor's personal satisfaction, as well as for reducing income taxes. Even if a donor is not able to part or does not want to part completely with property, a gift may still be made, but with retained interests.

Selecting Gifts for Donees

A gift of cash may be more suitable than a gift of land if the donee has an immediate need for the money. A gift of property that is expected to appreciate in value may be more suitable than a gift that is expected to decline in value. The strategy is to pay the gift tax on the appreciating assets when the value of those assets is low, rather than paying estate taxes on the assets after the value had appreciated.

Prior to 2010, taxpayers could only gift up to $1 million of assets during their lifetime before owing a gift tax (excluding annual exclusion gifts). For 2015, the unified credit amount for both estate and gift tax purposes will shelter the transfer of $5.43 million of assets either during life or at death (or some combination of the two) before owing a gift or estate tax.

Competency

An outright gift to an incompetent person may be unsuitable, whereas a gift in trust to the same person may be suitable. A gift of an antique car to a 10-year-old boy may be unsuitable, but a gift in trust of other assets may be suitable.

Relationship

A gift to a grandchild may be unsuitable if the generation-skipping transfer (GST) tax will be imposed. (The GST tax is discussed in Topic 69.) A gift to a spouse may be suitable because of the marital deduction.

Income Tax Bracket

A gift to a child may be suitable for income tax reduction if the child is 19 years of age or older (due to the kiddie tax), but a gift to a child under age 19 or to a person with a large income may not be suitable for accomplishing this objective. As of 2008, the kiddie tax rules also apply to students under age 24.

Estate Tax Situation

A gift to a person who has a substantial estate will not accomplish estate tax reduction, whereas a gift to someone without assets may be suitable for this purpose.

Techniques for Gift Giving

There are essentially two ways to transfer property during the owner's lifetime: (1) sale, and (2) gift.

Bargain Sales

One way to make a gift is by means of a bargain sale. In a bargain sale, the owner sells an asset below fair market value, so a gift is made of the difference.

UGMA

Gifts to children may be made under the Uniform Gifts to Minors Act (UGMA) enacted in many states. Under the UGMA, the types of property that can be given to minors are restricted to securities, money, life insurance, and annuities. The transfer is made to an adult custodian for the minor, and only one custodian and one minor may be named for each UGMA account. The UGMA custodianship must end when the child reaches the age of majority.

UTMA

In some states, gifts to minors may be made under the Uniform Transfers to Minors Act (UTMA). **Unlike the UGMA, the UTMA has no restrictions on the types of property permitted to be transferred to a minor.** While the UGMA permits only lifetime gifts, the UTMA provides for both lifetime and testamentary gifts to minors. The UTMA also allows for broader investment powers to the custodian than are afforded under the UGMA. For example, a minor cannot be given real estate under the UGMA, but can under the UTMA. With the UTMA, the custodian can invest in any reasonable manner, subject only to the fiduciary responsibility of ordinary prudence.

For the UGMA and the UTMA accounts, any adult may be the custodian, not just parents. If a parent is selected as the custodian and is serving in that capacity at the time of death, the assets will be subject to inclusion in the parent's gross estate. The reason for inclusion is the retained power of the custodian-parent over the assets.

For both the UGMA and the UTMA, the transfer to the child is an irrevocable gift. The minor is deemed to have both legal and equitable title to the account assets. For both kinds of accounts, the gift is a completed gift of a present interest, which will be eligible for the gift tax annual exclusion. For both kinds of accounts, the income from the account assets is taxed to the minor.

☼ *REMEMBER: UGMAs MUST BE FUNDED WITH CASH, SECURITIES, LIFE INSURANCE, OR ANNUITIES (NOT REAL ESTATE); HOWEVER, THERE ARE NO RESTRICTIONS ON THE TYPES OF PROPERTY (INCLUDING REAL ESTATE) THAT FUND UTMAs.*

Charitable Gift Techniques

Techniques for making charitable gifts and techniques for intra-family business transfers are presented in Topics 64 and 67.

Gifts Subject to Debts

Generally, the value of a gift of property subject to indebtedness is the donor's equity in the property. Thus, if a building that is subject to a mortgage is transferred, the amount of the gift is the net value after deducting the amount of the unpaid mortgage from the building's fair market value. If the donor remains personally liable on the debt, however, the amount of the gift is the entire value of the property, without reduction for the debt.

Net Gifts

A "net gift" is similar to a gift subject to a debt because with a net gift, the donor requires the donee to pay the federal gift tax as a condition of making the gift.

A donee actually pays the gift tax, however, only after the donor's unified tax credit has been exhausted. Since the exemption equivalent is $5.43 million for gift taxes as of 2015, substantial gifts can be made as net gifts before a donee is required to pay any gift tax.

Appropriate Gift Property

To select appropriate property for gifts, the estate planner should ask the following questions:

- Is the value of the property likely to appreciate?
- What are the marginal income tax brackets of the donor and the intended donee?
- Is the property subject to any debt?
- Is the property's fair market value above, below, or equal to its cost basis?

The Most Appropriate Lifetime Gift-Giving Techniques

A lifetime transfer of cash is probably the simplest form of gift. If after receiving the gift, the donee acquires an investment asset with the cash, the donee's basis will be the actual dollar amount of the invested cash. Some income shifting occurs because the donee will receive all of the income from the investment, and the donor does not receive the income that he or she would have received by investing the same cash.

If the donee is in a lower marginal tax bracket than the donor, the transfer will result in reduced overall income taxes.

Income-Producing Property

Income shifting is more apparent in the case of lifetime transfers of income-producing property. Once the transfer is completed, the investment income from the property is included in the donee's gross income, rather than in the donor's.

Appreciated Property

Property that the owner is likely to sell in the near future should be considered for gifts to donees in lower marginal tax brackets. If the property has appreciated significantly, a gift of the property may shift capital gains to a lower tax rate, and the income will be removed from the donor's gross income.

The lifetime gift of appreciating property will also remove future appreciation from the donor's gross estate for federal estate tax purposes. The donor will not have to pay any transfer costs on the future appreciation once the gift is completed.

If the owner holds appreciated property until death, the property is included in the gross estate and receives a step-up in basis to the date-of-death value (or the alternate valuation date, six months later). If the heirs sell the property after the step-up in basis, no capital gain is reported. Thus, an owner can avoid passing taxable capital gains to heirs by keeping appreciated property in the estate until death.

Reverse Gifts – Sec. 1014(e)

Giving property with a low adjusted basis to a less wealthy donee who is likely to predecease the donor is called a "reverse gift."

Under the Internal Revenue Code, if appreciated property is given to a person within one year of his or her death and the property returns to the original donor at the donee's death, the donor must retain his or her original cost basis. In other words, the property does not receive a step-up in basis at the death of the donee. This rule prevents a property owner from giving assets to a dying family member, who will transfer the property back to the donor at death, with a step-up in basis.

Estate planners can avoid this rule by having the donee leave the property by will to the donor's child or to another person so the property receives a step-up in basis.

Life Insurance as Ideal Gifts

Property that has a low value for gift tax purposes but will have a high value at the date of death is ideal for giving away to reduce an estate. For this reason, life insurance policies are often selected for gifts.

Generally, the value of a life insurance policy for gift tax purposes is the interpolated terminal reserve (approximately its cash surrender value or replacement value), but at the death of the insured, the beneficiary is entitled to the entire death benefit tax-free. Thus, a policy with a $100,000 face value may be valued for gift tax purposes at less than $10,000, but the face amount will be paid to the beneficiary at the insured's death, and the death proceeds will be free of any estate tax. Similarly, property that is likely to appreciate is a good choice for a gift. The future appreciation will be removed from the donor's gross estate and thus avoids any gift or estate tax.

The table below shows the gift tax value of various types of life insurance. For exam purposes, the cash value of the policy is frequently substituted for the interpolated terminal reserve. However, should an exam question ask the value of a policy, and both cash value and interpolated terminal reserve appear as answer choices, the interpolated terminal reserve is the better answer. These valuations are also used to value life insurance in the gross estate when the decedent died owning a policy on the life of another.

Gift Tax Value of Life Insurance	
Type of Policy	**Value**
New (<1 year)	Gross premiums paid
Term	Unused premium
Paid-up or Single Premium	Replacement cost
Premium-Paying Cash Value Policy	Interpolated terminal reserve + unused premium + accumulated dividends – outstanding loans
Insured is Terminally Ill at Time of Gift	Death benefit

Practice Question

Alice Goodheart is contemplating making a gift of her whole life policy to her daughter on September 1st of this year. Alice paid the $2400 annual premium for her whole life policy on April 1st of this year. The interpolated terminal reserve on April 1st of this year is $30,000 and the interpolated terminal reserve on April 1st of next year is expected to be $34,000. What will be the gift tax value of the whole life policy if Alice makes the gift on September 1st of the current year?

    A. $2,400
    B. $30,000
    C. $33,067
    D. $34,000

Answer:

The gift tax value of a premium-paying whole life policy is the interpolated terminal reserve + unused premium + accumulated dividends - outstanding loans. The interpolated terminal reserve is expected to increase by $4,000 over the 12 month period from April 1st of this year to April 1st of next year. The policy is being gifted in September of this year, 5 months into the 12 month period, so 5/12 of the increase will have been earned at the time of the gift (5/12 x $4,000 = $1,667). Therefore, the interpolated terminal reserve on September 1st of this year is expected to be $30,000 + $1,667 = $31,667. The unused (unearned) premium is

the amount that was paid in advance and not yet earned by the insurance company. The annual premium is paid in April and the gift is being made in September, therefore, only 5/12 of the premium has been earned, and 7/12 of the premium is unearned. The unearned premium amount (7/12 x $2,400 = $1,400) is added to the interpolated terminal reserve to determine the gift tax value of the policy. $31,667 + $1,400 = $33,067.
The answer is C.

Property Below Basis Should Not Be Used for Gifts

If the owner's adjusted basis in property is greater than the property's current fair market value, the property generally should not be used for a lifetime transfer. IRS rules do not permit an owner to make a gift of a tax loss. In computing capital losses, the donee takes as his or her basis the lower of the fair market value or the donor's basis. Accordingly, the owner would be well-advised to sell the property that has a value below the owner's basis so the owner can take advantage of the tax loss.

Depreciated Property May Be Advantageous for Gifts

For gifts of depreciated or cost-recovery property, the donee will carry over the donor's adjusted cost basis, but the full amount of the donor's recapturable depreciation or cost recovery must also be passed on to the donee. At the time the donee sells the property, the recapture rules require that any cost recovery be added as taxable ordinary income.

The donor will have received the benefit of the depreciation deductions in reducing the donor's taxable income, and, hopefully, when the donee sells the property, the donee will pay tax on the income at a lower marginal tax bracket.

An owner may want to retain depreciated property to obtain the step-up in basis that results from including this property in the gross estate. Consequently, gifts of depreciated property should be considered with care. In addition, a donor may want to retain depreciable income property in order to continue to have the benefit of depreciation deductions for income tax purposes.

Closely Held Stock – Use Caution

Care must also be exercised in making gifts of stock in a closely held corporation. If the owner makes lifetime gifts of this stock, the owner's estate may not be able to qualify for the Sec. 303 redemption or for the Sec. 6166 installment payment of federal estate tax. At least 35% of the value of the adjusted gross estate must consist of the closely held stock to qualify for the Sec. 303 redemption or for the Sec. 6166 installment payment of estate taxes. (Sec. 303 and Sec. 6166 are discussed in Topic 72.)

EXHIBIT 56 – 1 **Selecting Gifts**	
Income-Producing Property	• Ideal gift for a donee in a low tax bracket.
Highly-Appreciated Property	• Overall, an ideal gift to a person in a lower tax bracket for lower capital gain rates. • A good gift for a person in a lower tax bracket, when the donor is likely to sell the property.
Life Insurance	• An ideal gift that will have a high value at the date of death and a low value (replacement value) for gift tax purposes.
Property Likely to Appreciate	• A good choice for gifts to remove future appreciation from the donor's estate, especially if there is concern about higher estate taxes in the future.
Closely Held Stock	• Use caution! Care must be exercised in giving stock in a closely held corporation. The estate may be disqualified from using Sec. 303 or Sec. 6166.
Out-of-State Real Property	• Gifts avoid ancillary probate.
Depreciable Property	• The donor may want to keep this property in order to take the depreciation.
Depreciated or Cost-Recovery Property	• This property may be good for using the gift – leaseback technique.
Loss Property	• Never use for gifts! Always sell the property and take the loss.

Property in Other States Is Good for Gifts

Real estate located in a state other than the owner's domicile is a good subject for gifts because by giving the property away, the owner saves his or her estate the additional expense and burden of ancillary probate in the state where the property is located. In most cases, avoiding ancillary probate will be only one factor to consider in selecting the property most appropriate for lifetime gifts.

Gifts of Present and Future Interests

Gifts of present interests are eligible for the gift tax annual exclusion, but gifts of future interests are not. The annual exclusion eliminates gift tax consequences for the first $14,000 as indexed in 2015) of present-interest gifts made in a year to each donee. A donee is given a present interest when the gift transfers immediate and unrestricted right to the possession, use, and enjoyment of the property.

A donee is given a future interest when the donee's possession, use, or enjoyment will not begin until a time in the future, after the date of the transfer. The most common example of a future-interest gift is a remainder interest. For example, the owner of $1 million of U.S. Treasury bonds sets up a trust that will pay his wife the income from the securities for life, and at her death, the property passes to their children. At the time of the creation of the trust, the children have a remainder interest in the trust.

A reversionary interest is also a future interest. If, in the above example, the trust is set up so the U.S. Treasury bonds will return to the owner upon his wife's death, the owner's interest is a reversion.

Gifts to Noncitizen Spouses

Gifts to spouses who are citizens of the U.S. qualify for the unlimited gift tax marital deduction, but gifts to noncitizen spouses do not qualify for this deduction. Instead, a special $147,000 (in 2015) annual exclusion is available.

This exclusion will apply if the transfer qualifies under both the annual exclusion rule and the marital deduction rule. In other words, the gift must be of a present interest, and it must not be a terminable interest.

Income Shifting

Gifts are not taxable income, but a gift of appreciated property can mean capital gain income to the recipient when the property is sold. The capital gain will be taxed at the donee's capital gain rate, and the future income from the asset will be taxed to the donee at his or her marginal rate for ordinary income. Lifetime gifts, therefore, can shift income from the donor's higher marginal rates to a donee's lower marginal income tax rates.

Income Taxation of Lifetime Transfers

A gift is not income to the recipient (donee). If the donee sells the gift property, however, the amount of the gain that the donee must report as income will depend upon the donee's basis.

COST BASIS OF PROPERTY RECEIVED AS A GIFT

A Donee's Basis

The general rule for the basis of gifts is that the donee will carry over the basis of the donor. While this carryover basis rule applies to most gifts, it does not apply in all cases. The carryover basis rule applies when the donee will report a *gain* on the sale of the gift property.

If the donee will report a *loss*, however, the basis is the lower of the donor's basis or the fair market value of the property on the date of the gift.

Example:

Dan received a gift from his uncle of an $80,000 property. The uncle's basis in the property was $100,000. Dan sold the property for $70,000.

Dan will report a loss, so he must use a basis that is the lower of FMV at the date of the gift or his uncle's basis. The lower figure is the FMV at the date of the gift, or $80,000, so Dan will report a loss of only $10,000.

Since the basis of gift property is determined by two different methods, the sale of gift property can result in there being no gain or loss. This result occurs when the sale is above the gift's fair market value but below the donor's basis.

Example:

Dan received a gift from his aunt of an $80,000 property. The aunt's basis was $90,000.

Dan sold the property later for $85,000. When reporting a loss, Dan must use the lower of the FMV at the date of the gift or the donor's basis. The lower figure is the FMV at the date of the gift, or $80,000. The sale was for $85,000, so there was no loss.

For determining gain, Dan will use the carryover basis from his aunt, or $90,000. The sale at $85,000 was, therefore, not a gain. Dan will report no gain and no loss.

EXHIBIT 56 – 2
Gift Basis – Two-Part Test

Gift Basis – Two-Part Test

⟵―――――――――――――――――――――――――――――――――――――⟶

Test 1:	**Test 2:**
Donor's (Carryover) Basis	**FMV at Time of Gift**
$1,000	**$800** (FMV is less than the donor's adjusted basis of $1,000.)

If the donee sells for a gain (e.g., $1,200)... Use <u>$l, 000</u> as basis.	*If the donee sells for an amount between the donor's adjusted basis and the FMV at the time of the gift (i.e., $900), the donee recognizes no gain or loss.*	**If the donee sells for a loss (e.g., $700)...** Use <u>$800</u> as basis.
GAIN	*NO GAIN OR LOSS*	*LOSS*

Exception for Gift Taxes Paid on Appreciation

The rules for basis contain one more exception for gift tax payments.

Any gift tax paid by the donor or donee will increase the donee's cost basis to the extent the gift tax is paid on any appreciation of the property.

Generally, the donee's basis in gift property is the same as the donor's basis, but it is increased for the amount of gift tax paid by the donor or donee that is attributable to the appreciation in the value of the property during the donor's holding period.

The formula for calculating the addition to basis is as follows:

$$\text{Addition to basis} = \text{Gift tax paid} \times \frac{\text{Appreciation}}{\text{Value of gift}}$$

Example:

A donor gives property with a present fair market value of $100,000, and the donor has a basis of $30,000. If the donor pays gift tax of $18,000, the donee will take the donor's basis of $30,000, plus the following addition to basis:

$$\text{Addition to basis} = \$18,000 \times \frac{\$\,70,000}{\$100,000} = \$12,600$$

The donee's basis, therefore, will be $42,600. If the donee sells the property for its fair market value, the donee will have taxable capital gains of $100,000 – $42,600 = $57,400.

Where the fair market value of a gift is below or equal to the donor's adjusted basis, any gift tax paid will not increase the donee's basis.

EXHIBIT 56 – 3
Increase to Basis for Gift Taxes Paid

Increase to Basis for Gift Taxes Paid

*Applies **ONLY** to appreciated property (the FMV is higher than the donor's adjusted basis)*

Step 1: Gift tax attributable to appreciation = $\dfrac{(\text{FMV} - \text{Donor's basis})}{(\text{FMV})} \times$ Gift tax paid

Step 2: **Donee's Basis** = Donor's carryover basis + Gift tax attributable to appreciation

Example:

Donor's adjusted basis	$10,000
FMV at time of gift	$20,000
Gift tax paid	$ 2,000

(*Step* 1): Gift tax attributable to appreciation = $\dfrac{\$10,000}{\$20,000} \times \$2,000 = \$1,000$

(*Step* 2): Donee's basis = $10,000 + $1,000 = **$11,000**

INCLUSION OF GIFTS IN THE GROSS ESTATE

Circumstances Causing Inclusion of Gifts in the Gross Estate

A lifetime gift of property will not be included in the donor's gross estate if the gift is a complete and irrevocable gift.

Lifetime gifts will be included in the gross estate if the donor has a retained interest or a reversionary interest.

In general, gifts made within three years of death are excluded from the decedent's gross estate.

The exceptions to this rule are:

- Gifts of life insurance
- Gift taxes paid on gifts given within three years of death
- Gifts of retained life estates
- Gifts of (or giving up) retained interests, such as the right to revoke a trust or gift
- Gifts of reversionary interests (transfers conditioned on the donee surviving the donor)

These gifts are included in the donor's gross estate at the property's full fair market value at the estate valuation date, i.e., the date of death or the alternate valuation date. In addition, under the gross-up rule, any gift taxes paid within three years of death are included in the gross estate, even though the gift was not included in the gross estate.

USE OF GIFTS TO REDUCE TRANSFER TAXES

Calculation and Analysis of the Effect of a Lifetime Gift Program

A wealthy person who embarks on a program of lifetime gifts can take advantage of a number of the techniques presented in this section to reduce transfer taxes.

First, the individual can take advantage of the gift tax annual exclusion, the GST annual exclusion, and gift-splitting. Gifts to minors and Crummey trusts can be designed to use the annual exclusions in advantageous ways. Over a period of several years, substantial assets can be given away, free of transfer taxes, using these annual exclusions.

Second, the individual can use the unified credit (applicable credit amount) to eliminate paying gift tax on lifetime gifts.

Third, an individual can leverage gifts by means of life insurance trusts, GRATS, GRUTs, and personal residence trusts. These trusts are discussed in Topic 62 in this estate planning material.

Fourth, the gift tax is tax-exclusive, while the estate tax is tax-inclusive, so any gift tax paid escapes additional transfer taxes unless the gift is within three years of death.

The effect of a lifetime program of gifts can also be measured in terms of income, as well as appreciation shifted to the donees.

When assets are transferred to a donee, the future appreciation will escape any transfer taxation, and the income will be taxed to the donee.

The downside to gifts is that the donee will not receive a step-up in basis, as occurs for assets that pass through an estate.

If the asset is sold, the donee will have a higher capital gains tax from a lifetime gift than from a testamentary gift.

Section 2503(b) Trusts

A Section 2503(b) trust, also called a mandatory income trust, can be used for making gifts to minors, and the gift will be eligible for the annual exclusion.

The trust is required to distribute all income each year to the minor beneficiary, but the remainder can pass to someone other than the minor. Thus, the trust consists of an income interest and a remainder.

The present value of the income interest will be a present-interest gift, eligible for the annual exclusion, and the remainder is a future-interest gift, not eligible for the annual exclusion. There are no restrictions on the kinds of property that can be transferred to a trust for a minor, and the 2503(b) trust is an irrevocable trust.

REMEMBER: THE GIFT TO THE 2503(b) TRUST IS A GIFT OF TWO INTERESTS: AN INCOME INTEREST AND A REMAINDER INTEREST. THE INCOME INTEREST IS A PRESENT INTEREST THAT QUALIFIES FOR THE GIFT TAX ANNUAL EXCLUSION. THE REMAINDER INTEREST (ASSETS LEFT IN THE TRUST WHEN THE INCOME INTEREST ENDS) IS A FUTURE INTEREST THAT DOES NOT QUALIFY FOR THE ANNUAL EXCLUSION.

Section 2503(c) Trusts

Section 2503(c) of the Internal Revenue Code provides that a gift to a minor under 21 years of age is not treated as a future-interest gift for purposes of the annual gift tax exclusion if the income and property will pass to the minor when he or she reaches age 21. Thus, a gift in trust for a minor will be eligible for the annual exclusion when the trust accumulates the income, rather than distributing it. The income accumulated in such a 2503(c) trust will be taxed annually to the trust.

Under Section 2503(c), the trust property and income may be expended for the minor's benefit before age 21.

The trust must provide that any assets in the trust will be paid to the minor's estate if the minor dies before age 21. Once the beneficiary turns 21, he or she must have a right to withdraw all accumulated income and principal.

🔑 **KEY SUMMARY 56 – 1**
Trusts for Minors Compared

	Section 2503(b) trust	Section 2503(c) trust
Can income be accumulated?	No.	Yes.
Must trust assets be distributed to the minor?	Yes, each year, income must be distributed; remaining principal can pass to any beneficiary.	No, but at age 21, the beneficiary must have a right to income and principal not used earlier for the minor's benefit.
Is the annual exclusion available for gifts to the trust?	Yes, but only for the present value of the income interest, not for the remainder.	Yes.
What property can be contributed to the trust?	No restriction.	No restriction.

Crummey Trusts

Gifts to minors will be eligible for the gift tax annual exclusion when the trust agreement includes Crummey powers. **By giving the beneficiary a noncumulative right to withdraw the annual contribution to the trust, the donor will be able to take advantage of the annual exclusion.** The beneficiary must be given reasonable notice of the withdrawal right (also known as the demand right). With a Crummey trust, a grantor may make a gift to a trust that can have many beneficiaries, including adults. The grantor will be entitled to an annual exclusion for each beneficiary given a withdrawal right.

🔔 **REMEMBER:** *THE CRUMMEY POWERS GIVE THE TRUST BENEFICIARY THE RIGHT TO WITHDRAW THE ANNUAL CONTRIBUTION TO THE TRUST. THESE POWERS ARE OFTEN LIMITED TO THE ANNUAL EXCLUSION AMOUNT OR TO THE GREATER OF $5,000 OR 5% OF THE CORPUS.*

Many estate planners draft the Crummey powers to restrict the withdrawal right to the maximum amount of the gift tax annual exclusion, so the grantor gets the benefit of the annual exclusion, but the beneficiary cannot withdraw more than that amount from the trust.

The Crummey powers may also be restricted to the greater of $5,000 or 5% of the corpus (a "5-and-5 power"), so a lapse of the power will have no gift and estate tax consequences. The 5-and-5 power is discussed in Topics 59 and 61.

Generation-Skipping Transfer Tax (GSTT)

Lifetime gifts to persons two or more generations below the transferor are subject to the generation-skipping transfer (GST) tax. The GSTT tax is treated in Topic 69.

Application Questions

1. Last year, Jeremy gave his daughter $50,000 of securities that he purchased for $100,000. This year, his daughter sold the securities for $45,000. What are the income tax consequences?

   A. The daughter will report no gain and no loss.
   B. The daughter will report a $5,000 capital loss.
   C. The daughter will report a $55,000 capital loss.
   D. The daughter will report $45,000 of ordinary income.

2. Jesse Jones has made some gifts in the past, so when he gave his son Tom an apartment building with a fair market value of $600,000, Jesse paid $10,000 in gift tax. Jesse's adjusted basis in the building was $1 million. Tom sold the building 3 years later for $1,200,000. What gain must Tom report?

   A. $190,000
   B. $195,000
   C. $200,000
   D. $590,000
   E. $600,000

3. Fred Gregory is 57 years of age, and his wife Jane is 39. They have two young children, ages 4 and 6. Fred has a gross estate estimated at $15 million and an annual income of over $180,000. Fred would like to begin some lifetime gifts that would reduce his estate and his family's overall federal income taxes. Fred is considering gifts of assets with fair market value and basis as follows:

Asset	FMV	Basis
Corporate 8% bonds	$ 50,000	$ 40,000
Common stock	$ 50,000	$ 25,000
Municipal bonds	$ 50,000	$ 42,000
Commercial real estate	$100,000	$120,000
Residential real estate	$100,000	$ 85,000

There is a $50,000 mortgage on the commercial and residential properties. After payment of the mortgage, the commercial real estate produces an annual income of $3,000 annually, and the residential real estate produces an annual income of $2,000 annually.

If Fred decides to make a gift of the common stock, which of the following techniques is the most appropriate?

   A. GRUT
   B. UGMA
   C. 2503(c) trust
   D. 2503(b) trust
   E. GRAT

4. If Fred (from Question 3) made an outright gift to one of the children of the common stock and paid gift tax of $18,500, what is the amount of capital gain that the child should report upon selling the stock later for $60,000?

 A. $10,000
 B. $16,500
 C. $25,000
 D. $25,750
 E. $35,000

5. If Fred (from Question 3) sells the common stock, which asset would be most appropriate to give as an outright gift to his children?

 A. Municipal bonds
 B. Corporate bonds
 C. Commercial real estate
 D. Cash
 E. Residential real estate

6. If Fred (from Question 3) wants to make a gift to his children of commercial real estate, which of the following gifts will qualify for the gift tax annual exclusion?

 (1) A gift to a Crummey trust
 (2) A gift to a Section 2503(b) trust
 (3) A gift to a grantor-retained annuity trust (GRAT)
 (4) A gift to a grantor-retained unitrust (GRUT)

  A. (1) only
  B. (1) and (2) only
  C. (1) and (3) only
  D. (3) and (4) only
  E. (1), (2), (3), and (4)

7. Harvey bought a property for $100,000 and took a depreciation of $20,000 before giving it to his father. The property was worth $125,000 when Harvey made the gift. Harvey paid no gift tax. Harvey's father died 8 months later, when the property was worth $130,000. Harvey inherited the property from his father. What is Harvey's basis in the property?

 A. $80,000
 B. $100,000
 C. $125,000
 D. $130,000

8. (Published question released December, 1996)

Identify the statement(s) below that correctly identify gift giving likely to result in favorable tax consequences.

 (1) An advantage of giving property with a current value that is less than its basis ("loss property") is that when the recipient sells the property, the loss is available to offset any gains.
 (2) Elderly taxpayers should give highly-appreciated, low-basis property in preference to cash.
 (3) Making net gifts is a technique for clients who do not have very much in liquid assets and who want to make taxable gifts.
 (4) The donee can depreciate his or her depreciable property based on its value for gift tax purposes.

  A. (1), (2), and (3) only
  B. (2), (3), and (4) only
  C. (1) and (4) only
  D. (1), (3), and (4) only
  E. (3) only

9. Which of the following transfers to an irrevocable trust convey a present interest to the beneficiary?

   (1) The beneficiary will receive income from the trust for 10 years, and then the trust assets will be paid to the grantor.
   (2) The trust allows the grantor's spouse to live in the home for life, and at his or her death, it will pass to the beneficiary.
   (3) The trust provides for income to be accumulated in the trust, and both income and principal are payable to the beneficiary (a minor) at age 21.
   (4) The trust provides for the beneficiary to receive income for life, and at the beneficiary's death, any remaining trust assets will be paid to the Red Cross.

   A. (1) and (2) only
   B. (1) and (4) only
   C. (2) and (3) only
   D. (2) and (4) only
   E. (3) and (4) only

The following facts should be used to answer Questions 10 – 12.

Mark Downey has established an irrevocable trust for his son Donald. Donald is entitled to the trust income annually and has been given Crummey powers. The Crummey powers must be exercised during the last 60 days of the year. Mark will contribute $28,000 annually to the trust.

10. How much can Donald demand in the first year due to his Crummey powers?

   A. $0
   B. $5,000
   C. $14,000
   D. $28,000

11. If Donald does not exercise his demand right the first year, how much can he withdraw under the Crummey powers in the second year?

   A. $10,000
   B. $14,000
   C. $28,000
   D. $56,000

12. If Donald does not exercise the Crummey powers in the first two years and Mark does not make a contribution in the third year, what amount can Donald demand under the Crummey powers in the third year?

   A. $0
   B. $14,000
   C. $28,000
   D. $56,000

13. All the following are tax-related incentives for making lifetime gifts, EXCEPT:

   A. Availability of the gift tax annual exclusion
   B. Availability of the $1 million lifetime gift tax exemption
   C. Availability of the gift tax marital deduction
   D. Removal of the amount of any gift taxes paid from the estate
   E. Appreciation of the assets given away will not be subject to gift or estate taxes.

14. "F" places $100,000 of securities in trust for his son "S." Income is to be paid annually to "S" until age 38, at which time, the corpus is to be distributed to "S," if living, and otherwise, to "S's" estate. Under these circumstances, which of the following statements concerning federal gift taxes is (are) correct?

(1) "F" has made a gift of a present interest to "S."
(2) "F" has made a gift of a future interest to "S."
(3) The value of the gift of the present interest and the value of the gift of the future interest will each be exactly $50,000, regardless of the length of time income is to be paid.

    A. (1) only
    B. (2) only
    C. (1) and (2) only
    D. (2) and (3) only
    E. (1), (2), and (3)

15. In Question 14, if "F" had authorized the trustee to pay out or accumulate income at the trustee's discretion, which of the three statements would have been correct?

    A. (1) only
    B. (2) only
    C. (3) only
    D. (1) and (2) only
    E. (2) and (3) only

16. In Question 14, if "F" had provided that "S" could withdraw corpus at any time, which of the three statements would have been correct?

    A. (1) only
    B. (2) only
    C. (3) only
    D. (1) and (2) only
    E. (2) and (3) only

17. All the following statements concerning future-interest gifts are correct, EXCEPT:

    A. The annual exclusion does not apply to future-interest gifts.
    B. A single gift can be both a present-interest and a future-interest gift.
    C. The marital deduction does not apply to a future-interest gift.
    D. A gift of a remainder interest is a future-interest gift.
    E. A gift of a reversion interest is a future-interest gift.

18. All the following statements concerning the income, estate, and gift tax consequences of a net gift are correct, EXCEPT:

A. The donor will have taxable income to the extent that the donee's payment of gift tax exceeds the donor's adjusted basis in the gift property.

B. Because the donee pays the gift tax, the donor does not use up any of his or her unified credit.

C. Gift taxes paid by the donee will reduce the amount of the taxable gift.

D. The net amount of the gift is treated as an adjusted taxable gift in the calculation of the donor's estate tax at the time of the donor's death.

E. The value of the gift property, plus any appreciation will be removed from the donor's gross estate for federal estate tax purposes.

19. All the following statements concerning the income tax consequences of a lifetime gift or a testamentary gift of property are correct, EXCEPT:

A. Lifetime gifts and bequests are not income to the recipients.

B. The donee's basis in a lifetime gift is the lesser of the donor's adjusted basis or the fair market value at the time the gift is made.

C. The basis of inherited property that has decreased in value is limited to the fair market value at the date of death.

D. The income from a lifetime gift of property is taxable income to the donee and not to the donor.

E. Both lifetime gifts and testamentary gifts are eligible for the step-up in basis.

20. Bill Farmer bought 1,000 acres of farmland for $300,000. When his oldest son married, Bill gave him 400 acres for a farm. When Bill died last year, the remaining 600 acres were divided in Bill's will between his two younger sons. The 600 acres had a fair market value at Bill's death of $600,000. Which of the following statements concerning the sons' basis in the farmland are correct assuming the executor elects to allocate as much of the basis step-up as possible?

(1) The oldest son will have a basis of $120,000 in the 400 acres.

(2) The younger sons will have a basis of $180,000 in the 600 acres.

(3) The younger sons will have a basis of $600,000 in the 600 acres.

(4) The oldest son will have a basis of $400,000 in the 400 acres.

A. (1) and (2) only
B. (1) and (3) only
C. (2) and (3) only
D. (2) and (4) only
E. (3) and (4) only

21. Danny Warbucks' mother is dying of a heart ailment and will not be leaving much of an estate. He wants to take advantage of his mother's available step-up in basis by giving her real estate that has appreciated greatly, so she can bequeath the property in her will to whomever Danny Warbucks selects. If his mother dies this year, which of the following people could receive the bequest with a step-up in basis?

(1) Danny Warbucks
(2) Danny Warbucks' wife
(3) Danny Warbucks' children
(4) Danny Warbucks' business partner

    A. (1) and (2) only
    B. (1) and (3) only
    C. (2) and (3) only
    D. (2) and (4) only
    E. (3) and (4) only

22. All the following rules are applied by the government in determining if a gift is complete for gift tax purposes, EXCEPT:

    A. There must be both a legally competent donor and a legally competent donee.
    B. The donor must have a clear intent to make a gift.
    C. The donee must be given a present interest in the gift property.
    D. The transfer must be irrevocable.
    E. The gift property or evidence of title must be delivered to the donee.

23. "D," age 67, has decided to make annual gifts to his daughter Pearl to achieve several estate planning objectives. If Mrs. "D" joins in the annual gifts, which of the following statements are correct?

(1) To reduce his estate, "D" would be wise to select assets to give away that are likely to increase in value.
(2) "D" will be required to add back into the value of his taxable estate at death his share of the taxable gifts in excess of the annual exclusions.
(3) Pearl's cost basis for all property given by "D" will be "D's" cost basis even if "D's" cost basis exceeds fair market value.
(4) Any gifts in excess of the annual exclusions will reduce "D's" unified credit, but not the unified credit for Mrs. "D."

    A. (1) and (2) only
    B. (1) and (3) only
    C. (2) and (3) only
    D. (2) and (4) only
    E. (3) and (4) only

24. "A" is in the 27% marginal federal and state income tax bracket. He acquired 400 shares of XYZ, Inc. common stock two years ago for $60,000, but the stock's current market value is $45,000. "A" plans to give 200 shares of the stock to each of his two granddaughters. Rowena is age 24 and Susan is age 12. Under these circumstances, all the following statements are correct, EXCEPT:

A. If "A" makes the gifts to the children, he will lose the tax benefit of the $15,000 loss available if he sold the stock.

B. "A" can use the annual exclusion for both stock gifts.

C. If the grandchildren sell the stock immediately after receiving the stock, they both may take a loss based on "A's" cost basis.

D. If Rowena keeps her stock, any dividends will be taxable at her marginal income tax bracket or at the dividend tax rate, if lower.

E. If Susan keeps her stock, any dividends in excess of $2,100 (2015) will be taxable at her parents' marginal income tax bracket or at the dividend tax rate if lower.

25. All the following statements concerning the factors to consider in selecting an appropriate subject of a gift are correct, EXCEPT:

A. Property that is likely to appreciate is good gift property.

B. Life insurance is appropriate gift property.

C. The donor's cost basis should be below or equal to the market value of the gift property because the income tax law forbids the recognition of a capital loss if the corpus has a cost basis above its present fair market value.

D. Property with a low cost basis, relative to its current market value, may be poor gift property.

E. The income tax bracket of the donor and donee are unimportant in considering gifts since gifts are income-tax-free to donees.

26. All the following statements concerning the tax implications of a gift made to a person who dies within one year of receiving the gift are correct, EXCEPT:

A. If the property is willed back to the original donor, such property is denied the usual stepped-up basis for valuing property transferred to a designated heir.

B. The beneficiary of the deceased's will can be in receipt of capital gains, even if he or she sells the property on the date of the testator's death.

C. If the decedent wills the property to someone other than the original owner or his or her spouse, the transferee can benefit from the available step up in basis.

D. If the original donor is the spouse of the decedent-donee, a testamentary disposition to the decedent's children will prevent realization of the benefits of the stepped-up basis.

E. The technique of a reverse gift seeks to obtain a step-up in basis through gifts of property to someone who will die before the donor.

27. Reginald Rice, age 72, is in poor health and suffering from heart disease. He is expected to live 12 to 24 months. Reginald has an estate of approximately $15 million and would like to reduce his anticipated estate taxes. Reginald Rice's only surviving family is a son Ben. Reginald has a paid-up life insurance policy; a portfolio of utility stocks that have appreciated slightly but produce a steady income; a beach house in New Jersey that is worth approximately $175,000, which is the price Reginald paid for it; a duplex in Staten Island worth approximately $180,000, purchased 15 years ago for $80,000; and Reginald's residence in New York, which has grown in value since Reginald purchased it 22 years ago and is now worth approximately $250,000.

Which property would be most appropriate for a lifetime gift to Reginald's son?

A. The paid-up life insurance policy
B. The beach house in New Jersey
C. The residence in New York
D. The duplex in Staten Island
E. The portfolio of utility stocks

28. Why is a life insurance policy often a good item to give away?

   A. Because if given more than two years before death, it escapes gift taxation

   B. Because when placed in an irrevocable trust, it always qualifies for the annual exclusion

   C. Because it has a low value for gift tax purposes and a high value for estate tax purposes

   D. Because in one's older years, and particularly after retirement, one really has no need for life insurance

   E. Because gifts of life insurance policies are more likely to be eligible for the annual exclusion than other gifts

29. All the following are provisions of the Uniform Gift to Minors Act with which the parties must comply, EXCEPT:

   A. All states permit the gift property to be almost any type of investment asset, including securities and real estate.

   B. An adult custodian must be the transferee of the property.

   C. Legal title is vested in the minor.

   D. The custodianship must terminate when the child reaches age 21.

   E. A separate custodial account is required for each minor, so custodial accounts cannot be joint accounts.

30. Which of the following statements correctly identify significant differences between the UGMA and UTMA?

  (1) The UGMA places no restrictions on types of property that may be transferred, whereas the UTMA places restrictions.

  (2) The UGMA permits only lifetime transfers, whereas the UTMA permits both lifetime and testamentary transfers to a minor.

  (3) The UGMA allows the custodian only limited investment powers, whereas the UTMA allows any reasonable investment.

  (4) Lifetime gifts under the UGMA are eligible for the annual exclusion, whereas lifetime gifts under the UTMA are not.

   A. (1) and (2) only
   B. (1) and (3) only
   C. (2) and (3) only
   D. (2) and (4) only
   E. (3) and (4) only

31. Which of the following statements concerning the estate tax treatment of assets held in a custodial account under either a UGMA or a UTMA is (are) correct?

(1) If the donor parent-custodian dies before the minor reaches age 21, the custodial assets are caught in the gross estate of the donor parent.

(2) If the minor dies before age 21, the custodial assets are caught in the gross estate of the minor.

(3) The parent can remove the custodial property from the parent's gross estate by naming the parent's brother as custodian.

    A. (1) only
    B. (2) only
    C. (1) and (3) only
    D. (2) and (3) only
    E. (1), (2), and (3)

32. Which of the following statements concerning the income tax treatment of a 2503(c) trust are correct?

(1) Income that is accumulated by the trust is taxable annually to the trust.

(2) The transfer of property to the trust results in a taxable gift by the donor.

(3) Property in the trust will be included in the gross estate of a minor, whether he or she dies before or after age 21.

(4) The income of the trust above $2,100 (in 2015) is taxed to a minor under age 19 (24 if a student) at the parents' marginal income tax rate.

    A. (1) and (2) only
    B. (1) and (3) only
    C. (2) and (4) only
    D. (1), (2), and (3) only
    E. (1), (2), (3), and (4)

33. All the following statements concerning the tax characteristics of a 2503(b) trust are correct, EXCEPT:

    A. The gift of the right to future income is a gift of a future interest.

    B. The gift of the corpus (as distinct from the gift of the income) does not qualify for the annual exclusion.

    C. The corpus will be excluded from the gross estate of the donor.

    D. The corpus will be excluded from the gross estate of the income beneficiary if the income interest terminates at the beneficiary's death.

    E. The income from the trust is taxable to the beneficiary each year.

34. All the following statements concerning the use of 2503(b) and 2503(c) trusts (both with a minor as the beneficiary) are correct, EXCEPT:

    A. Under a 2503(b) trust, income must be distributed annually to the minor beneficiary.

    B. Under a 2503(c) trust, income can be accumulated, provided all such accumulated income is made available to the beneficiary by age 21.

    C. Under a 2503(b) trust, the trust corpus must pass to the minor beneficiary by age 21.

    D. Under a 2503(b) trust, the trust income may be payable to the trust beneficiary for his or her lifetime.

    E. Under a 2503(c) trust, the income and principal may be used for the benefit of the minor each year.

35. All the following statements concerning the 2503(c) trust are correct, EXCEPT:

   A. Almost any type of property may be placed in the trust, including real estate.

   B. The trustee may be given very broad, almost unlimited investment powers.

   C. The trust income must be distributed at least annually.

   D. The trust corpus must be available to the beneficiary at age 21 if he or she asks for the corpus.

   E. The grantor can provide that the trust will continue beyond the time the minor reaches age 21.

36. Which of the following statements most accurately describes the rights conveyed to a minor under the terms of a trust that give the minor a so-called "Crummey" power?

   A. The right to withdraw the corpus at any time during minority

   B. The right to accumulate trust income to age 21 and the right to receive these funds as a distribution of corpus

   C. The right to withdraw limited amounts of the trust corpus for a limited time after a contribution is made to the trust

   D. The right to withdraw the trust's income for the calendar year without a guardian's approval

   E. The right to request principal and income of a trust for a specified period each year after reaching age 21

37. A grantor recently created a trust giving a minor the rights associated with the so-called Crummey power. The donor can take advantage of the gift tax annual exclusion under which of the following conditions?

   (1) The minor failed to exercise his or her right during the limited time period.

   (2) A formal guardian for the minor was never appointed.

   (3) The minor was not told he or she had the Crummey power.

   (4) The donor made only one contribution to the trust during the year, and this was on December 30th.

   A. (1) and (2) only

   B. (1) and (3) only

   C. (2) and (3) only

   D. (3) and (4) only

   E. (1), (2), (3), and (4)

38. All the following statements concerning "net gifts" are correct, EXCEPT:

   A. If the gift tax paid by the donee exceeds the donor's cost basis, the donor is in receipt of taxable income.

   B. Only the net amount of the gift will be considered as an adjusted taxable gift in the estate tax computation.

   C. The gift tax paid by the donee can be credited against the donor's estate taxes.

   D. The unified tax credit is not available for net gifts.

   E. Any gift tax paid by the donee on appreciation of the gift property will increase the donee's cost basis.

39. Which of the following statements concerning "net gifts" is (are) correct?

(1) Such gifts always require the donee to pay gift tax.
(2) Because of the substantial exemption equivalent now available, the donee may pay no tax.
(3) If the gift is one of a present interest, the annual exclusion is available.

    A. (1) only
    B. (1) and (2) only
    C. (1) and (3) only
    D. (2) and (3) only
    E. (1), (2), and (3)

40. All the following statements concerning the income tax consequences of lifetime gifts to an individual (noncharitable) are correct, EXCEPT:

    A. Dividends and interest from the assets given away will be taxed to the donee.
    B. The donee's basis in the gift property is the fair market value on the date of the transfer or the donor's basis, whichever is less, which is adjusted for any gift tax paid.
    C. The donee receives a step-up in basis to the date-of-death value for capital gains tax purposes.
    D. Overall income tax savings may be achieved by transferring appreciated property to a donee in a lower marginal tax bracket than the donor.
    E. When a donee sells appreciated property received as a gift, the capital gains tax is imposed at the donee's marginal tax rate unless the donee is under age 18.

41. All the following statements concerning the income tax consequences of a lifetime gift to a minor under the UGMA or UTMA are correct, EXCEPT:

    A. For a donee, age 20 who works full-time as a marketing assistant, any capital gain from the sale of the asset will be taxed at the parents' marginal income tax bracket.
    B. The minor's basis will be the lesser of the fair market value or the donor's adjusted basis, with adjustment for gift taxes paid.
    C. For a minor under the age of 19 (24 if a student), any interest income up to $1,050 (in 2015) is tax-free, and the next $1,050 (in 2015) is taxed at the child's marginal tax rate.
    D. For a minor under the age of 19 (24 if a student), any capital gains in excess of $2,100 (in 2015) in any year will be taxed to the minor at the parents' marginal income tax bracket.
    E. The income tax consequences to a minor are the same, whether the gift is under the UGMA or UTMA.

42. Which of the following property interests would be the most appropriate for a lifetime gift to a minor, age 8?

    A. A portfolio of growth stocks
    B. Depreciable real estate
    C. Securities that have declined in value
    D. Fixed-income securities
    E. Corporate bonds

43. Harold and Helen Ford would like to help provide a fund for the education of their grandson Peter, age 16. The Fords and Peter's parents are in the 27% marginal federal and state income tax bracket, and they would like to minimize income taxes. Helen and Harold would like to be certain that the money is used for their grandson's education and that he does not obtain the money or assets in the fund for purposes other than his education, at least until he is able to handle the money responsibly. Helen and Harold would like to minimize any estate and gift taxes, as well. They have made no prior gifts and have a gross estate of approximately $10 million. Which of the following techniques would you recommend that the Fords use to make a lifetime transfer for the benefit of their grandson?

A. An outright gift to their grandson under the Uniform Gift to Minors Act, naming a parent as the custodian
B. A 2503(c) trust for their grandson
C. A 2503(b) trust for their grandson, with the corpus not payable to the grandson until he reaches age 35 or older
D. A Crummey trust for their grandson
E. A Clifford trust for their grandson

44. All the following statements concerning the gift and estate tax consequences of a lifetime gift to a minor under the UGMA or UTMA are correct, EXCEPT:

A. Gifts to minors under the UGMA or UTMA qualify for the gift tax annual exclusion.
B. A gift to a minor under the UGMA or UTMA is a completed gift of a present interest.
C. Lifetime gifts will reduce the probate estate and the gross estate for federal estate tax purposes.
D. Gifts to minors that incur no gift tax, due to use of the unified credit, are not considered adjusted taxable gifts for calculation of the donor's estate taxes.
E. The gift and estate consequences of a gift under the UGMA and of a gift under the UTMA are the same.

45. All the following statements concerning the income, estate, and gift tax consequences of a gift to a 2503(b) trust for a minor are correct, EXCEPT:

A. The trust income is payable to the minor beneficiary annually and is taxed to the minor.
B. The trust is a separate tax entity, but the trust pays no income tax because all income is distributed to the minor.
C. The value of the gift for gift tax purposes is only the present value of the income interest.
D. Assets transferred to the trust are not includible in the donor's gross estate for federal estate tax purposes if the donor is not the trustee.
E. If the minor is under age 18, the income is taxed to the minor at his or her parents' marginal income tax rate and not to the trust.

46. All the following statements concerning the income, estate, and gift tax consequences of a gift to a 2503(c) trust for a minor are correct, EXCEPT:

    A. The trust can provide that a minor will not be able to obtain principal until age 35, or the principal can be distributed according to the grantor's will.

    B. A gift of securities or real estate to a 2503(c) trust for a minor can qualify for the gift tax annual exclusion.

    C. The trust principal and income can be invaded for the benefit of the minor before age 21.

    D. Assets transferred to the trust are not includible in the donor's gross estate for federal estate tax purposes if the donor is not the trustee.

    E. Gift-splitting is permitted with regard to gifts made for a minor to a 2503(c) trust.

47. All the following statements concerning the income, estate, and gift tax consequences of a gift to a Crummey trust for a minor are correct, EXCEPT:

    A. If the trust beneficiary exercises the power to receive funds from the trust, the beneficiary must report income.

    B. To the extent the beneficiary could request distributions from the trust, the beneficiary has taxable income, even if the funds are not actually requested or distributed.

    C. The amount contributed annually to a Crummey trust qualifies for the gift tax annual exclusion.

    D. The amount contributed to the trust that is eligible for the annual exclusion is excluded from the calculation of the donor's estate taxes.

    E. The addition of the annual premium payments for a life insurance policy held by the trust are eligible for the gift tax annual exclusion.

48. A transfer to an irrevocable trust involves a gift, and, in general, the annual exclusion is not available except for gifts of present interest. All the following statements concerning this rule are correct, EXCEPT:

A. The annual exclusion applies to a gift of an income interest if the trust requires income to be distributed annually.

B. The annual exclusion applies to a gift of an income interest where the trust holds stock in a dividend-paying corporation controlled by the grantor, and where the trust must distribute its income annually.

C. The annual exclusion applies to a gift of an income interest, even if the trustee can distribute or accumulate income at his or her discretion, if the beneficiary is a minor.

D. The annual exclusion applies to the gift of an income interest in non-dividend-paying stock if the beneficiary has the right to sell the stock and purchase income-producing securities.

E. The annual exclusion does not apply to the present value of a remainder interest in trust even if the trustee may accumulate income.

49. Douglas Wye created a trust for his daughter Jill and transferred stock in a closely held corporation to the trust. The stock does not pay dividends, but has been appreciating greatly. The trust provides that income from the trust is payable to Jill for her life. If Jill predeceases Douglas Wye, the trust assets return to Douglas. The value of Douglas' interest in the trust assets is greater than 5%. Which of the following statements concerning this trust are correct?

(1) The gift of stock in trust for Jill does not qualify for the annual gift tax exclusion.

(2) If Douglas dies before Jill, the value of all the trust's assets is includible in his gross estate.

(3) If the trust provided that the trustee could sell the stock, the gift of stock in trust would qualify for the annual exclusion.

(4) If the trust sells the stock within a year after Douglas transfers the stock to the trust, the capital gain is taxed at Douglas' marginal tax rate on his individual tax return.

A. (1) and (2) only
B. (2) and (3) only
C. (3) and (4) only
D. (1), (2), and (3) only
E. (1), (3), and (4) only

50. Assume that non-income-producing property is placed in a trust. The donor can obtain the benefits of the gift tax annual exclusion by using which of the following approaches?

(1) Giving the income beneficiary a so-called "Crummey" power to withdraw income or principal in a specific amount, up to the amount of the annual exclusion
(2) Giving the income beneficiary a right to withdraw principal annually
(3) Giving the income beneficiary a right to withdraw the greater of: (a) the annual addition to the trust, or (b) the greater of $5,000 or 5% of the trust assets
(4) Placing the assets in a 2503(c) trust for a minor

    A. (1) and (2) only
    B. (2) and (3) only
    C. (2) and (4) only
    D. (3) and (4) only
    E. (1), (2), (3), and (4)

51. All the following statements concerning the use of a Crummey trust are correct, EXCEPT:

A. It permits a donor to contribute annually up to the gift tax annual exclusion amount to a trust and exclude the gift for gift tax purposes.
B. The trust beneficiary may have the right to withdraw annually the lesser of the amount of the annual contribution or the greater of $5,000 or 5% of the principal amount of the trust.
C. Only gifts to the trust of a present interest qualify for the annual exclusion.
D. The use of a Crummey trust is only possible when life insurance is the property held by the trust.
E. The withdrawal right can convert what would have been a future interest to a present interest.

For practice answering case questions related to Topic 56, please answer the following questions in the cases included in the Appendix at the back of this textbook.

Case	Questions
Bartlett	7
Marshall	
Webster	3, 4, 5, and 6
Unser	2
Tingey	
Lytle	3
Beals	
Mocsin	1, 2, 3, and 4
Young	
Borelli	4
Cunningham	
Fred and Mary Ferris	16, 17, 18, 19, and 20

Answers and Explanations

1. B is the answer. Since Jeremy's daughter is reporting a loss, her basis is the lower of the FMV or the donor's carryover basis. In this case, the FMV is only $50,000, so this is the basis to use to calculate the loss. The loss is only $5,000. Note that this question does not ask about the amount of capital loss that can be used to reduce ordinary income. The maximum capital loss that can be deducted against ordinary income is $3,000.

2. C is the answer. Since Tom has a gain on the sale, he must use the carryover basis of $1 million from the donor. The basis is not adjusted for the gift tax paid because the gift was made at a fair market value below the donor's adjusted basis. The basis for Tom in the apartment building is $1 million. The sale for $1.2 million will mean a reportable capital gain of $200,000.

3. B is the answer. The GRAT and GRUT are not required for these gifts because the annual exclusion with gift-splitting will shelter $56,000 each year. The accumulation in the 2503(c) trust will be subject to income taxation at the trust level, which is a compressed rate schedule. The transfer will qualify for the annual exclusion, and the assets will be removed from Fred's estate. While the 2503(c) trust may provide the estate tax reduction that Fred is seeking, it does not provide the best income tax savings. The 2503(b) trust requires distribution of income to the minor, which will be subject to kiddie tax (the first $1,000 of unearned income is tax free as a standard deduction, the next $1,000 is taxed at the child rate, and any income over $2,000 is taxed at the parent rate). The transfer will qualify for the annual exclusion, and the assets will be removed from Fred's estate. A UGMA gift will also be taxed under kiddie tax rules for income tax purposes. The transfer will qualify for the annual exclusion, and the assets will be removed from Fred's estate if Fred is not the custodian. The choice, then, is between the 2503(b) trust and the UGMA. Based on the rather low amount of the gift, the UGMA is the better choice due to ease and low cost to establish.

4. D is the answer. The basis for the stock must be increased by the amount of gift tax paid that is attributable to the appreciation during the donor's holding period. The appreciation of the common stock was $25,000, and the value of the gift was $50,000, so the addition to basis is:

$$\frac{\$25,000}{\$50,000} \text{ x } \$18,500 = \$9,250$$

The basis is then $25,000 + $9,250 = $34,250. The capital gain is then $60,000 − $34,250 = $25,750.

5. B is the answer. The municipal bonds would not reduce Fred's income taxes. The residential real estate would probably generate depreciation deductions that would help to reduce Fred's income. The commercial real estate might not be a good choice for a gift because it could produce a tax loss for Fred if it were sold. This loss would be eliminated if it were given to the children. Cash does not produce much income, so the corporate bonds would likely produce the best reduction of income taxes.

6. B is the answer. A gift to a Crummey trust and to a Section 2503(b) trust will qualify for the gift tax annual exclusion because the children receive a present interest. The GRAT and GRUT involve a transfer of a remainder interest to the children, and this gift is a future interest, which does not qualify for the annual exclusion.

7. A is the answer. Harvey inherited the property from the donee (his father) within one year of the gift, so Harvey must retain his original adjusted basis of $80,000. This gift is a "reverse gift," so there is no step-up in basis.

8. E is the answer. A net gift requires the donee to pay any gift taxes that are owed. A client who wants to make taxable gifts (after exhausting the unified credit) can give property as a net gift, and the donee will pay the tax. Thus, the client lacking liquidity can make the gift without further exacerbating his or her liquidity problem. Property with a value below its cost basis should not be used for gifts because the loss cannot be passed on to the donee. The donee's cost basis will be the current value. The donor should sell the property, take the loss, and give the proceeds to the donee. Highly-appreciated property is not a good choice for gifts by elderly taxpayers because the donees will have to pay capital gains on the property, based on the donor's basis. If the elderly taxpayer retains the property until the time of death, it will receive a stepped-up basis when it passes through the estate. A donee uses the donor's basis for purposes of depreciation, not the gift tax value.

9. B is the answer. The beneficiary who receives income from the trust for 10 years begins to enjoy the income immediately and is given a present interest to the income. There is no delay in the start of this income interest. By contrast, the beneficiary who must wait until the death of the grantor's spouse cannot make immediate use of the home and has a future interest. The beneficiary who must wait until age 21 to receive income and principal also has only a future interest. Note that Code Sec. 2503(c) provides that gifts to such a trust shall not be treated as gifts of a future interest for purposes of the annual exclusion. The beneficiary who has an income interest for life has an immediate life estate and a present interest.

10. D is the answer. Under the Crummey powers, Donald can demand the amount of the annual contribution. Unless the powers are restricted to the annual exclusion or a "5-or-5" power, the Crummey powers permit withdrawal of the annual contribution to the trust. The annual contribution is $28,000, so that amount can be withdrawn. If the powers were limited to the lesser of the annual contribution or the annual exclusion, then Donald could only demand $14,000. Note that he also receives the income from the trust.

11. C is the answer. The Crummey powers are noncumulative, so Donald can only demand the amount of the contribution made in that second year.

12. A is the answer. If no contribution is made to the trust for the year, then the beneficiary cannot withdraw any amount under the Crummey powers. The Crummey powers allow a withdrawal only of an annual contribution.

13. B is the answer. The lifetime taxable gift exemption is $5.43 million in 2015. By giving away assets, the donor will reduce income derived from the assets, and this reduction in income can result in income tax savings. The amount of gift taxes paid is removed from the estate if the donor lives more than three years after making the gift.

14. C is the answer. The present interest given to "S" includes the present value of the future income stream that will be paid annually to "S." The future interest of the remainder corpus to be distributed in the event of "S's" death is a very small portion of the gift.

15. B is the answer. If enjoyment of a gift depends on the exercise of a trustee's discretion, the gift is of a future interest. In this case, the trustee has discretion to pay out or accumulate income, so "S" receives a distribution only if the trustee decides to pay out income. The gift, therefore, is of a future interest.

16. A is the answer. If "S" can withdraw corpus at any time, he has an unrestricted right to enjoy all of the property immediately, so it is a gift of a present interest.

17. C is the answer. While the annual exclusion applies only to gifts of a present interest, the marital deduction applies to gifts of present and future interests. The marital deduction is only unavailable for a gift of a terminable interest.

18. B is the answer. With net gifts, a donor must exhaust the unified credit before any taxes are paid by the donee.

19. E is the answer. Only testamentary gifts are eligible for a step-up in basis to the fair market value at the date of death However, if the fair market value is less than the basis at date of death, then the basis will be limited to fair market value at date of death.

20. B is the answer. The oldest son will carry over the basis of the donor, Bill Farmer. Bill's basis was $300 per acre, or $120,000 for the 400 acres. The younger sons will get a step-up in basis because they are receiving the property through Bill's estate. The basis for their testamentary gifts will be $600,000 for the 600 acres.

21. E is the answer. If the property is returned to Warbucks or his spouse, he will not receive a step-up in basis. If the property is bequeathed to Danny Warbucks' children or to his business partner, there will be a step-up in basis.

22. C is the answer. C is not a correct statement because a completed gift can be either a gift of a present interest or a gift of a future interest. A, B, D, and E are valid rules applied in determining whether a gift is a completed gift.

23. A is the answer. Appreciating assets make excellent choices for gifts because the appreciation is removed from the gross estate. The gifts in excess of the annual exclusion will reduce "D's" unified credit, but due to gift-splitting, Mrs. "D's" unified credit will also be reduced. The amount of adjusted taxable gifts must be added to the taxable estate in computing the tentative tax base for the federal estate tax. "D" cannot give away a tax loss, so the basis must be the lower of the fair market value or "D's" cost basis.

24. C is the answer. A loss may not be transferred by gift. A, B, D, and E are correct statements.

25. E is the answer. Income-splitting may be achieved by giving income-producing property to a family member 19 years of age or older (24 if he or she is a student) who has a lower marginal income tax bracket. Property that is likely to appreciate is usually ideal for gifts. Life insurance is appropriate for gifts because it has a low present value but a high appreciation potential. Property that has already appreciated may not be appropriate for gifts because the donee takes over the donor's cost basis. On the other hand, a beneficiary receiving the property at the owner's death will receive a stepped-up basis.

26. D is the answer. D is not a correct statement. If the decedent-spouse-donee makes a testamentary disposition of the property to one of the decedent's children, the property is eligible for a stepped-up basis at death. The property does not go back to the donor-spouse, so the stepped-up basis is retained. A, B, C, and E are correct statements.

27. B is the answer. The beach house in New Jersey is located in a state other than Reginald Rice's state of residence. Reginald can save the costs of ancillary probate, as well as reduce his estate, by making a gift of the beach house. The beach house is not depreciable property like the duplex, so there is no advantage to retaining it in the estate to get a step-up in basis. Moreover, the beach house has not appreciated in the way the residence and the duplex have appreciated. The life insurance policy is not a good subject for a gift at this point in time because if Reginald does not live three years, the death proceeds will be includible in his estate. The portfolio of utility stocks produces a steady income, which Reginald still needs.

28. C is the answer. A large dollar amount is removed from the gross estate, but only a low value is given, and, therefore, the federal gift tax will be small.

29. A is the answer. In many states, real estate may not be among the items of property gifted. B, C, D, and E are correct statements.

30. C is the answer. UGMA in most states restricts investments to securities, money, and life insurance and annuity contracts. The UTMA has no restrictions on the types of property that can be transferred to a minor. The UGMA permits only lifetime transfers, while the UTMA permits both lifetime and testamentary transfers. The UTMA affords wider investment powers than the UGMA. Gifts to both the UGMA and UTMA are eligible for the annual exclusion.

31. E is the answer. All three statements are correct, as the parent's estate will include the custodial accounts if the parent dies before the child reaches age 21. The child's estate will also include these accounts if the child dies before age 21. The custodial accounts can be removed from the parent's estate by naming someone else as the guardian.

32. D is the answer. The income from the 2503(c) trust is taxed to the trust and is accumulated. It is not distributed to the minor, so it is not taxed to the minor, and the kiddie tax rules do not apply. The transfer to the trust is a taxable gift, although the annual exclusion can reduce the amount of the gift. The trust property will be included in the minor's gross estate if he or she dies before the trust assets are distributed.

33. A is the answer. Under the Tax Code, the gift of the right to future income is a gift of a present interest, and the beneficiary's interest is the present value of that future income. B, C, and D are correct statements.

34. C is the answer. Under a 2503(c) trust (but not under a 2503(b) trust), the trust corpus must be available to the minor beneficiary by age 21. A, B, D, and E are correct statements.

35. C is the answer. The 2503(c) trust is an accumulation trust, so income need not be distributed; rather, income may be accumulated.

36. C is the answer. A Crummey power is the noncumulative right of a trust beneficiary to withdraw annually the lesser of the annual exclusion, the amount of the annual contribution, or the greater of $5,000 or 5% of the trust corpus. The beneficiary must have reasonable time to make the withdrawal and reasonable notice of the existence of the withdrawal right after the donor has made the contribution to the trust.

37. A is the answer. (3) would be a failure to give reasonable notice. (4) would be failure to provide the beneficiary with reasonable time. Thus, (3) and (4) would not permit the donor to take advantage of the gift tax annual exclusion. (1) and (2) would not prevent the donor from taking advantage of the gift tax annual exclusion. If the donor places property in the trust, it will still qualify as a gift of a present interest, despite the failures suggested by items (1) and (2).

38. D is the answer. D is not a correct statement because the donor's unified tax credit must be used in computing the donee's gift tax liability. A, B, C, and E are correct statements.

39. D is the answer. (1) is not a correct statement because a "net gift" results in a gift tax payable by the donee only after the donor's unified tax credit has been exhausted. With the $5.43 million exemption equivalent available to the donor, substantial taxable gifts can be made as "net gifts" before the donee will be required to pay any gift tax. (2) and (3) are correct statements.

40. C is the answer. The donee's basis in the gift property is the fair market value on the date of the transfer or the donor's basis, whichever is less, which is adjusted for any gift tax paid. The donee's basis is not given a step-up in basis to the date-of-death value because the donee is receiving a lifetime gift.

41. A is the answer. For a donee 19 years of age or older (24 if a student), the income from an asset given to the donee and any capital gains on the sale of the asset are taxed to the donee at the donee's own marginal tax rate. Thus, it may be advantageous for a minor to hold an asset until reaching age 19 (24 if a student) before selling and taking a capital gain.

42. A is the answer. The portfolio of growth stocks can be retained until the minor reaches age 18 and is taxed at his or her own marginal tax rate. The depreciable real estate usually should be retained by the donor because the depreciation deductions can reduce his or her income, and then, if passed to the minor as a testamentary gift, the depreciable real estate will receive a step-up in basis. The securities that have declined in value should not be given to the minor because the owner could sell them first and take the loss as a deduction. Fixed-income securities are not as appropriate as a growth stock portfolio because the income is taxed to the minor at the parents' marginal tax bracket. With the growth stocks, the capital gain can be deferred until the child reaches age 21 and then will be taxed at a lower rate.

43. C is the answer. If the Fords establish a 2503(b) trust, the income from the trust assets is not accumulated in the trust and is taxable to their grandson. For the first two years, the trust distributions will be taxed at the parents' marginal rate, but after Peter reaches age 18, he will be able to pay income taxes at his own marginal rate. Thus, in only two years, Peter will have a lower tax rate, and if the income is payable to him, the income taxes will be lower. Under the 2503(b) trust, the assets can be held in the trust until any age whereas under a 2503(c) trust, the assets must be made available to the beneficiary at age 21. The 2503(b) trust, therefore, provides greater protection for the assets from Peter's possible misuse. Since income is accumulated in the 2503(c) trust and is taxable to the trust, the taxes will probably be higher for the 2503(c) trust than under the 2503(b) trust. The Crummey trust will enable Peter to obtain the annual contributions made by the Fords to the trust if he so requests. While it is unlikely that he would request the contributions, the 2503(b) trust prevents any such possibility. The gift to the 2503(b) trust qualifies for the annual exclusion only to the extent of the income interest, so the gift of the remainder interest will be a taxable gift. The remainder interest can be made smaller by making the income interest longer in duration. Moreover, the Fords can offset the amount of this gift tax by using their unified credit. While use of the unified credit is a disadvantage of the 2503(b) trust, the Fords may not need to worry about exhausting their unified credit.

44. D is the answer. Gifts to minors that incur no gift taxes due to use of the unified credit, are still considered adjusted taxable gifts for calculation of the donor's estate taxes. The adjusted gifts must be added to the taxable estate to determine the estate tax liability.

45. C is the answer. The value of the gift for gift tax purposes is the fair market value of the assets placed in the trust. The amount of the gift that qualifies for the annual exclusion is only the present value of the income interest payable to the minor.

46. A is the answer. The assets of the trust must be made available to the beneficiary at age 21, so the trust agreement cannot require the assets to be held to age 35. The trust agreement can provide that the trust will continue if the beneficiary does not exercise the right to withdraw the assets at age 21. The donor cannot retain control over the disposition of the assets of a 2503(c) trust by will after his or her death.

47. B is the answer. The beneficiary will have taxable income only to the extent that income from the trust is actually distributed to the beneficiary.

48. B is the answer. Generally, a gift to a trust does not qualify for the annual gift tax exclusion unless the trust is structured to give the beneficiary an immediate right to the use and enjoyment of the trust property. This can be accomplished in several ways. One is by the provision of an annual income stream to the beneficiary. Another, specifically applicable to minors, is the 2503(c) trust, which permits the trustee to accumulate income for the beneficiary during minority (under the age of 21), provided the trust corpus, including the accumulated income, is made available to the beneficiary upon attainment of age 21. Still another means of qualifying transfers to the trust for the gift tax exclusion – and an approach that is applicable particularly to trusts funded with non-income-producing property – is by giving the beneficiary the right to require the sale of trust property to provide an income stream. There would be no present interest for the beneficiary, and, therefore, no gift tax exclusion, if the grantor could control the production of income for the trust by controlling the dividend payment (or nonpayment) of the securities used to fund the trust.

49. D is the answer. The gift of stock in trust for Jill does not qualify for the annual gift tax exclusion because the stock is non-income-producing property. If the trust provided that the trustee could sell the stock, the gift of stock in trust would qualify for the annual exclusion. If Douglas dies before Jill, the value of all the trust's assets is includible in his gross estate. The reversionary interest that Douglas has in the trust is greater than 5%, so the trust assets are includible in his gross estate. If the trustee sells the stock within a year after Douglas transfers the stock to the trust, the capital gain is taxed to the trust at the grantor's marginal tax rate.

50. E is the answer. The incorporation of a Crummey provision in the trust agreement enables periodic transfers of property to the trust to qualify for the annual gift tax exclusion. The Crummey provision is an annual withdrawal right of the amount transferred to the trust each year. This withdrawal power can be limited in some trust documents to the greater of $5,000 or 5% of the trust corpus. As contained in the answer to the preceding question, the right of the beneficiary to make annual withdrawals from principal is considered to be a present interest and thus qualifies transfers to the trust for the annual gift tax exclusion. Assets transferred to a 2503(c) trust for a minor also qualify for the annual exclusion.

51. D is the answer. The use of a Crummey trust is permitted for any kind of property. The important point is that the $5,000 or 5% withdrawal right must be available to the donee, so that the gift tax annual exclusion will be available to the donor.

Gift Tax Compliance and Tax Calculation (Topic 57)

CFP Board Student-Centered Learning Objectives

(a) Calculate the gift tax consequences of lifetime transfers to individuals and charities and recommend when filing a gift tax return is necessary.

(b) Calculate the income tax consequences of lifetime transfers to individuals and charities.

(c) Calculate the estate tax consequences of lifetime transfers to individuals and charities.

Gift Tax Compliance and Tax Calculation
- A.   *Gift tax filing requirements*
- B.   *Calculation*
  - 1)   *Annual exclusion*
  - 2)   *Applicable credit amount*
  - 3)   *Gift-splitting*
  - 4)   *Prior taxable gifts*
  - 5)   *Education and medical exclusions*
  - 6)   *Marital and charitable deductions*
  - 7)   *Tax liability*

Gift Tax Filing Requirements

Federal gift tax returns must be filed for any calendar year in which a taxpayer has made total gifts of a present interest to any one person, exceeding the annual exclusion. The gift tax return must be filed even though no gift tax is due. A gift tax return must also be filed for any gift of a future interest, regardless of the amount.

A gift tax return must be filed for any year in which a couple elects to split gifts if the total gift is greater than the annual exclusion. There is no joint filing of gift tax returns, so each spouse must file a separate return.

No gift tax return is required for gifts to a spouse that qualify for the marital deduction. No gift tax return is required for charitable contributions unless there is a transfer of a partial interest, such as a remainder interest in a personal residence.

Filing Form 709

The U.S. Gift Tax Return Form 709 must be filed on or before April 15 of the year following the calendar year in which the gift was made. The donor is responsible for filing the return. If the donor dies, the executor will generally file both the gift tax and any estate tax return. If the estate tax return must be filed before April

15, then the gift tax return must also be filed at the same time as the estate tax return. The taxpayer can request a 6-month extension of time to file.

Overview

Transfer taxes are imposed on the gratuitous transfer of property, either during a person's lifetime or at death. There are three federal transfer taxes: gift tax, estate tax, and generation-skipping transfer (GST) tax.

Unified System

Since 1977, the federal gift and estate taxes have been made into a unified system. Under this unified system, taxes on lifetime gifts are imposed at the same rate as the taxes on property left to heirs in an estate. Progressive rates from 18% to 55% applied to both of these taxes and were set forth in a unified estate and gift tax table.

2001 and 2010 Tax Act Changes

The Economic Growth and Tax Relief Reconciliation Act enacted in 2001 reduced the estate and gift tax rates for the years 2002 through 2009. In 2002, the highest rate for the estate and gift tax and also the generation-skipping transfer tax were 50%. In addition, the estate tax and gift tax was no longer a unified system. The estate tax and generation-skipping transfer tax were originally repealed in 2010, but the gift tax stayed in place at the highest individual income tax rate of 35% with a $1 million applicable exclusion amount for the gift tax. The 2010 Tax Act retroactively reinstated the estate tax for 2010 at 35% with a $5 million applicable exclusion amount for the years 2010 through 2012 (indexed for inflation starting in 2012 which increased the amount to $5.12 million). However, taxpayers who died during 2010 had the option to avoid estate taxes by electing the 2010 estate tax repeal rules which includes the carryover basis rules plus the $1.3 million in the step up in basis of assets passing to any heir plus the additional $3.0 million of basis step up for assets passing outright to a surviving spouse. The 2010 Tax Act also reunified the estate and gift tax with the $5.12 million exemption amount in 2012. The American Taxpayer Relief Act of 2012 signed into law in January 2013 set the applicable exclusion to be indexed for inflation each year and made portability permanent. For 2015, the applicable exclusion for both gift and estate tax, as indexed for inflation, is $5.43 million.

Year	Estate Exemption	Gift Exemption
2002-2003	$1 million	$1 million
2004-2005	$1.5 million	$1 million
2006-2008	$2 million	$1 million
2009	$3.5 million	$1 million
2010	$5 million*	$1 million
2011	$5 million	$5 million
2012	$5.12 million	$5.12 million
2013	$5.25 million	$5.25 million
2014	$5.34 million	$5.34 million
2015	$5.43 million	$5.43 million

* Assuming the executor did not elect to remain under the 2010 estate tax repeal with carryover basis rules

Current Gift and Estate Tax System – Prior Taxable Gifts

Under the current unified system, differences in tax rates between the gift and estate taxes were eliminated, and the system provides for calculation of the taxes by adding gifts and estate transfers. The gift tax is calculated by adding the value of all taxable gifts made since 1932 to the amount of taxable gifts made in the current year, and the estate tax is calculated by adding the value of all adjusted taxable gifts made since 1976 to the taxable estate.

This manner of calculating the gift and estate taxes means that these taxes are cumulative.

Differences between Gift and Estate Taxes

Despite their being unified, certain differences have existed between the federal gift and estate taxes.

First, the **gift tax annual exclusion** allows a person to make gifts of a present interest up to $14,000 (in 2015) per donee, without gift tax consequences.

Second, **gift-splitting** with a spouse is permitted under gift tax rules, but not under estate tax rules. Under gift-splitting, the annual exclusion is, in effect, enlarged to $28,000 (in 2015) per donee for married persons.

Third, the **gift tax is tax-exclusive**, while the estate tax is tax-inclusive. Under gift tax rules, the money used to pay the gift tax is not added to the taxable gift in calculating gift tax liability. In contrast, the estate tax rules require calculation of the value of all assets in the estate and then impose the tax, so tax is paid on the money used to pay the estate tax.

Fourth, a **step-up in basis** occurs for transfers at death, but not for lifetime gifts. In the case of a gift, the donee who sells the asset must generally calculate capital gains by carrying over the donor's adjusted basis. In contrast, an heir's basis in inherited property will not be the donor's adjusted basis, but will be the fair market value on the date of death (or six months later, if the executor elects the alternate valuation date).

Gifts Subject to Tax

A gift is a transfer of a property interest for less than adequate and full consideration in money or money's worth. A gift occurs whenever there is a gratuitous transfer or benefit conferred on another, regardless of the means or device employed. A bargain sale in which property is sold below market value will involve both a sale and a gift. Property transferred in recognition of past benefits or for friendship or affection is not a transfer for money or money's worth and is a gift.

Exemptions:
(1) Tuition Payments
(2) Medical Care
Payments –
Sec. 2503

Two kinds of "qualified transfers" are excluded from treatment as gifts under the Internal Revenue Code. "Qualified transfers" include:

(1) Payment of tuition (not room and board) directly to an educational institution for the education or training of a person
(2) Payment directly to any provider of medical care on behalf of a person

🔔 **REMEMBER:** *PAYMENTS ARE "QUALIFIED TRANSFERS" ONLY IF MADE DIRECTLY TO THE EDUCATIONAL INSTITUTIONS OR MEDICAL PROVIDERS AND NOT TO THE PERSONS WHO WILL BENEFIT.*

Political Contributions

The gift tax rules also do not apply to contributions to political organizations. (**Editor's Note:** Income tax law does not treat a political contribution as a charitable contribution; therefore, there is no income tax deduction for political contributions. This means that political contributions have no gift tax or income tax consequences.)

Reducing Gifts to Taxable Gifts

In the calculation of gift tax, the gift tax rates are applied only to "taxable gifts." The taxable gift is determined by making certain reductions in the total value of the gift. The reductions allowed under the gift tax laws are:

(1) Gift-splitting
(2) The annual exclusion
(3) The marital deduction
(4) The charitable deduction

Gift-Splitting –
Sec. 2513

For married donors, gift-splitting reduces the amount of a donor's taxable gift because one-half of the gift is treated as if made by the donor's spouse. The spouse must consent to gift-splitting, and a federal gift tax return must be filed, reflecting the election to split gifts. If any gift is split in a tax year, all gifts made by the spouses (except to each other) during that tax year must be treated as split gifts, including both present- and future-interest gifts. Because gift tax rates are progressive (larger gifts are taxed at higher rates), gift-splitting can help to reduce gift taxes by keeping the taxpayer in lower brackets.

The Annual Exclusion – Sec. 2503

The annual exclusion is $14,000 (in 2015) per year but can be used with any number of donees. This annual exclusion amount will be indexed for inflation, but indexing will only increase the exclusion in increments of $1,000. With gift-splitting, a married couple can make use of $28,000 (in 2015) in annual exclusions per donee. **The annual exclusion only applies, however, to a gift of present interest.** Future-interest gifts, such as remainder and reversion interests, will not qualify for the annual exclusion.

Gifts of Life Insurance

When a life insurance policy is given outright to a donee, the gift will qualify for the annual exclusion. A gift in trust of life insurance, however, will generally not qualify because the beneficiaries are given only a future interest. The reason is that the trust will not make payments to the beneficiaries until the insured dies because the policy does not pay a death benefit until that time. Thus, the beneficiaries must survive the insured to receive an interest under the trust, and their interest may be enjoyed in the future.

Crummey Powers

The gift of a life insurance policy in trust can be made a present-interest gift by the addition of Crummey powers to the trust agreement.

With Crummey powers, the beneficiaries have an immediate right to withdraw a portion of the assets placed in the trust. Since the beneficiaries have a right to take immediate possession of these assets, the gift confers a present interest. Both the gift of the life policy and any later gifts of annual premiums, then, are eligible for the annual exclusion.

With gifts in trust, the donor may use the annual exclusion for each beneficiary of the trust. The annual exclusion is available even for contingent beneficiaries with remote interests if they have Crummey powers.

Indirect Gift

An unexpected gift may arise in connection with the beneficiary designation for a life insurance policy when the owner of the life insurance policy is different from the person insured by the policy.

In this case, if the owner of the life insurance policy names someone other than himself or herself as the beneficiary, there is a gift at the time the death benefit is paid. Thus, if a wife owns a policy on her husband and names a child as beneficiary, there is a gift to the child when the death benefit is paid.

Gifts to Minors

Even though minors in most states cannot take legal title to property, an outright gift to a minor will generally qualify as a present-interest gift, so the annual exclusion is available. Gifts made under a state's Uniform Gifts to Minors Act or Uniform Transfers to Minors Act qualify for the annual exclusion. Additional ways to make gifts to minors, provide supervision over the assets, and still qualify for the annual exclusion are the Section 2503(b) trust and the Section 2503(c) trust. (See, Topic 62 in this estate planning material for more information.)

🔑 KEY SUMMARY 57 – 1 Crummey Powers	
What are Crummey powers?	Crummey powers are a general power over the annual contributions to a trust, a noncumulative right to withdraw the annual addition to the trust; the powers are often limited to the annual exclusion amount or to the greater of $5,000 or 5% of the assets subject to the power.
Why are Crummey powers used?	A future interest can be changed to a present interest, qualifying for the annual exclusion.
What are the gift tax consequences?	The annual contribution to a trust will be eligible for the gift tax annual exclusion. Downside: If Crummey powers are not exercised, there is a gift to remainderpersons when the lapse is more than the greater of $5,000 or 5% of the value of the trust assets.
What are the estate tax consequences?	The assets subject to Crummey powers that are unexercised at death are included in the gross estate, but none of the other trust assets are included.
With Crummey powers, how many annual exclusion gifts can be claimed?	The IRS allows annual exclusions for every person who holds a beneficial interest in the trust, but the IRS has been unsuccessful in opposing annual exclusions for contingent beneficiaries.
When are Crummey powers used?	Crummey powers are used in irrevocable life insurance trusts, trusts for minors, and, sometimes, other trusts.
What special rules apply?	Actual notice of Crummey powers must be given to the beneficiary with a reasonable period (at least 30 days) to exercise the powers.
Can Crummey powers be exercised if there is no contribution in that year?	Crummey powers are noncumulative, so if there is no contribution, there is nothing for the holder of the powers to appoint, even if the trust has other assets.
Can Crummey powers be exercised in later years?	After the year ends, Crummey powers lapse for that contribution; the holder must wait for a new contribution.

Gifts of Non-Income-Producing Property

If a donor makes gifts of non-income-producing property, the gifts will be eligible for the annual exclusion when the property is given outright to donees. If the same property is placed in trust for beneficiaries, however, the donor will not be able to use the annual exclusion. The reason is that for non-income-producing property, the present value of the income interest cannot be determined. The gift in trust of non-income-producing property can qualify for the annual exclusion if the trustee is given authority to sell the assets and purchase income-producing property.

The Marital Deduction – Sec. 2523

Gifts of property to a spouse (including a same-sex spouse, as indicated by the Supreme Court's 2013 ruling regarding the Defense of Marriage Act) are not taxable gifts. Due to the gift tax marital deduction, a donor can give an unlimited amount of property to a spouse, free of gift tax. A gift qualifies for the marital deduction if it meets the following requirements:

- The donee must be a U.S. citizen.
- The gift must be made to a spouse during marriage.
- The gift must not be of a terminable interest. A terminable interest is a property interest that will cease under some specified condition. For example, a life estate is a terminable interest because the life tenant's interest ends at death. There is an exception to the terminable-interest rule for qualified terminable-interest property (QTIP).

The Charitable Deduction – Sec. 2522

Gifts to qualified charities are not taxable gifts. Due to the gift tax charitable deduction, a donor can give an unlimited amount of property to charity, without gift tax consequences. A gift qualifies for the charitable deduction if the donor gives his or her entire interest in the asset. A gift of a partial interest qualifies for the charitable deduction when the donor uses one of the following techniques:

- Charitable remainder annuity trust or unitrust
- Charitable lead trust or unitrust
- Pooled-income fund
- Qualified conservation easement
- Remainder interest in a personal residence or farm
- Undivided portion of the donor's entire interest

These techniques will be discussed more fully in Topic 64 in this Estate Planning material.

Unified Credit or Applicable Credit Amount – Sec. 2505

The unified credit offsets the gift tax that would otherwise be owed on lifetime taxable gifts. **The credit must be used each year that a person makes taxable gifts until the unified credit is used up.** The Internal Revenue Code now refers to the unified credit as the "applicable credit amount" because the amount of the credit changes over the years. In 1997, the credit was $192,800, and a taxpayer could give the exemption equivalent of $600,000 in assets, free of federal gift tax. The exemption equivalent is now referred to in the Code as the "applicable exclusion amount." The applicable credit amount and the applicable exclusion amount are increasing each year according to the following schedule:

Year	Estate Tax Applicable Credit	Estate Applicable Exclusion	Highest Estate Tax Rate
1987-1997	192,800	600,000	55%
1998	202,050	625,000	55%
1999	211,300	650,000	55%
2000	220,550	675,000	55%
2001	220,550	675,000	55%
2002	345,800	1,000,000	50%
2003	345,800	1,000,000	49%
2004	555,800	1,500,000	48%
2005	555,800	1,500,000	47%
2006	780,800	2,000,000	46%
2007	780,800	2,000,000	45%
2008	780,800	2,000,000	45%
2009	1,455,800	3,500,000	45%
2010-2011	1,730,800	5,000,000	35%
2012	1,772,800	5,120,000	35%
2013	2,045,800	5,250,000	40%
2014	2,081,800	5,340,000	40%
2015	2,117,800	5,430,000	40%

The maximum gift tax rate will be the same as the maximum estate tax rate each year. The gift tax was not repealed and was equal to the highest individual income tax rate of 35% in 2010 with a $1 million applicable exclusion amount. The applicable gift tax credit amount remained at $345,800 from 2002 through 2009. The amount of the applicable gift tax credit dropped to $330,800 in 2010 since the highest gift tax rate dropped from 45% to 35%. For 2012, the top gift tax rate remained at 35%, but the applicable exclusion amount increased to $5.12 million (the same amount for estate tax purposes). As a result, the applicable credit amount increased to $1,772,800 for 2012. The American Taxpayer Relief Act of 2012 signed into law in January 2013 set the applicable exclusion to index for inflation each year, with a top tax rate of 40%. In 2015, the applicable exclusion is $5.43 million, with a top tax rate of 40%, and a resulting applicable credit amount of $2,117,800.

If, for example, a taxpayer made a gift of $1 million in 2010, the taxpayer would be entitled to an additional credit amount and could make additional taxable gifts of $4.43 million this year without the payment of gift tax.

Calculation of Gift Tax – Sec. 2502

To calculate the gift tax, the total value of all taxable gifts made since 1932 must be added to the total value of taxable gifts made in the current year. The progressive gift tax rates are applied to the total lifetime taxable gifts to compute a total gift tax liability. The gift tax paid in prior years is then subtracted from the total to arrive at the gift tax owed for the current year.

If applicable credit amounts remain unused, they must be used before any gift tax is paid. The calculation of the gift tax requires the following steps:

1. Value all gifts and compute the total value of gifts for the current year (qualified transfers are excluded).
2. Split gifts between spouses when gift-splitting is elected.
3. Subtract the annual exclusion per donee for gifts of present interests.
4. Subtract the marital deduction, if applicable.
5. Subtract the charitable deduction, if applicable.
6. Add all taxable gifts made since 1932. (The gift tax is cumulative.)
7. Apply the appropriate rate from the unified schedule of estate and gift tax rates to the total of all taxable gifts made since 1932, including gifts in the current year.
8. Subtract the gift tax on taxable gifts made in prior years, but calculate the tax on these gifts at current rates.
9. Reduce the gift tax payable by the amount of the available unified credit. (Use of the donor's applicable credit amount is mandatory for lifetime gifts.)

The 2015 estate and gift tax table is in the back of this book.

Tax Liability

The donor is primarily liable for payment of the gift tax, but if the donor fails to pay the tax, the donee becomes liable.

Paying the Gift Tax – Net Gifts

The donor may require the donee to pay the gift tax, and, in this case, the gift tax payable reduces the amount of the gift. The gift is then called a net gift, and the value of the net gift is reduced by the amount of the gift tax payable.

🔑 KEY SUMMARY 57 – 2	
What Techniques Reduce Gift Taxes?	
Technique	*Result*
Gift-splitting	The value of the gift is split with the consenting spouse.
Annual exclusion	$14,000 (in 2015) per donee can be given each year, without gift tax consequences, or $28,000 (in 2015) per donee by a married couple who split gifts.
Unified credit	No gift tax is payable until the taxpayer's unified credit is exhausted.
Qualified transfers	These transfers are not taxable gifts: – Tuition payments to an educational institution – Payment to a provider of medical care
Gifts to a spouse	The marital deduction eliminates the gift tax.
Gifts to charity	The charitable deduction eliminates the gift tax.
Bargain sales	Sale is below the FMV, and the gift is only the difference; income taxes are reduced, too.
Net gifts	Requiring the donee to pay the gift taxes reduces the amount of the gift.
Partial-interest gifts (GRATs, GRUTs, QPRTs, etc.)	Assets can be transferred at reduced gift tax values, due to the grantor's retained interests.
Valuation discounts (See, Topic 68.)	Family limited partnership interests and stock in closely held corporations can be transferred at discounts for lack of marketability and minority interest.
Gifts of life insurance	A small premium can be leveraged into a substantial death benefit.
Trusts	Gifts to Crummey trusts, 2503(b) trusts, and 2503(c) trusts for minors are eligible for the gift tax annual exclusion.

Application Questions

1. During the current year, Randy Lippincott made gratuitous transfers to the following persons:

Donee	Gift	Value
George Lippincott (son)	Boat	$45,000
Julie Lippincott (daughter)	Car	$35,000
Harry Lippincott (grandson)	Trip	$ 5,000
Harry Lippincott (grandson)	Tuition	$12,000
Jean Harrison (fiancé)	Ring	$50,000
Lionel Lippincott (father)	Medical Bills	$60,000

If Randy Lippincott did not split gifts, what is the amount of his taxable gifts for the year?

A. $52,000
B. $88,000
C. $137,000
D. $142,000
E. $207,000

2. In 1998, Tony gave his wife a new car that cost $45,000 and gave land valued at $180,000 to each of his two children. Tony has been married since 1959 and has filed gift tax returns with elections to split gifts with his wife. What is Tony's remaining applicable credit amount available for gift tax purposes in 2015? (**Note:** The annual gift tax exclusion was $10,000 when Tony made the above gifts.)

A. $42,000
B. $84,000
C. $2,075,800
D. $2,117,800

3. If Joe Hinton makes gifts to each of his two children of ranch land valued at $250,000 per gift, and if his wife consents to split gifts, what amount of gift tax will Joe need to pay with his gift tax return if this is the first time he has made taxable gifts?

A. $0
B. $31,240
C. $62,480
D. $70,800
E. $138,120

4. In the current year, Sally Marrow gave gifts of $41,000 each to her mother, her daughter, her husband, and her college. Marrow also created a trust that will pay income to her daughter for life and the remainder to her son. The present value of the income interest is $150,000, and the remainder interest has a present value of $40,000. If Sally and her husband elect to split gifts but make no other special elections, what is the total amount of taxable gifts that Sally must report on a gift tax return?

    A. $80,000
    B. $94,000
    C. $108,000
    D. $136,000
    E. $272,000

5. Phillip Carter was advised to set up a trust with Crummey powers to which he would transfer his life insurance policy. After Phillip's death, the trust would pay income for life to his two children, and after their deaths, the remaining assets would go to his two grandchildren. Phillip is married and will split gifts with his wife. What is the maximum value of the policy that Phillip can transfer to the trust this year without gift tax consequences?

    A. $0
    B. $28,000
    C. $56,000
    D. $84,000
    E. $112,000

6. Which of the following transfers will result in a taxable gift for federal gift tax purposes?

    A. Melissa Parker transfers a $14,000 plot of undeveloped land to a trust for her daughter.
    B. Robert Garcia transfers $14,000 of corporate bonds to a Section 2503(c) trust for his minor daughter.
    C. Sam Waters, a widower, sends a payment of $15,000 to his grandson's college for tuition.
    D. Jill Clayborn contributes $14,000 to a Crummey trust for the premium on a whole life policy held by the trust.
    E. Marcia Clarkson, who is divorced, pays $20,000 to the hospital for her mother's medical bills.

7. (Published question released February, 1999; updated)

Assuming neither person has used any of his/her unified credit, what is the maximum amount a married couple can give to a single, third-party donee in 2015 without paying federal gift tax?

    A. $28,000
    B. $1,014,000
    C. $5,430,000
    D. $5,444,000
    E. $10,888,000

8. (Published question released November, 1994; updated)

Which of the following gifts constitute a taxable gift?

(1) $25,000 to the donor's adult child
(2) $14,000 to a friend
(3) $35,000 paid to a friend for medical expenses
(4) $15,000 to a college to cover a friend's tuition

    A. (1), (2), and (3) only
    B. (1) and (3) only
    C. (2) and (4) only
    D. (4) only
    E. (1), (2), (3), and (4)

9. (Published question released December, 1996)

Your client owns a whole life insurance policy with a death benefit of $200,000 on the life of his spouse. The policy has a cash value of $13,500, and the dividends are used to purchase additional paid-up life insurance. Their son is the named beneficiary. If the spouse were to die today, which of the following is true?

    A. The client continues to own the policy for the benefit of the son.
    B. A taxable gift of the life insurance proceeds has been made from the client to the son.
    C. The client receives an amount equal to the cash value, and the son receives the remainder of the life insurance proceeds tax-free.
    D. The son must be at least 14 years old in order to collect the proceeds.
    E. The client receives the proceeds of the life insurance policy but must hold them in a life insurance trust for the benefit of his son.

10. In 2015, what is the maximum gift tax exemption that can be used to offset gift tax liability?

    A. $14,000
    B. $28,000
    C. $1 million
    D. $5.43 million
    E. An unlimited amount

11. Which of the following statements best describes the "exemption equivalent" for 2015?

    A. All lifetime gifts are taxed at 40%.
    B. A donor may give $14,000 per person tax-free to as many donees as the donor wishes.
    C. Each individual can make lifetime transfers or testamentary bequests of $5.43 million in 2015 without payment of estate or gift taxes.
    D. Both estate and gift tax rates are progressive.
    E. A donor may give unlimited amounts of assets to a spouse free of gift tax or estate tax.

12. In the current year, "S," a widower, age 65, made the following gifts: (a) $84,000 of listed securities to his son, (b) $19,000 cash to his daughter, (c) $6,000 to his granddaughter, and (d) $20,000 to his church. What is the amount of "S's" taxable gifts?

    A. $63,000
    B. $75,000
    C. $80,000
    D. $86,000
    E. $99,000

13. In Question 12, assume that "S" was remarried when he made the four gifts. What would be the value of the taxable gifts made by "S" and his wife, if she joined in the gifts?

    A. Zero
    B. $41,000
    C. $56,000
    D. $68,000
    E. $98,000

14. In 2015, Mrs. "X" wishes to give each of their four children a substantial amount of cash. What is the total amount of the gift tax annual exclusion available if Mr. "X" consents to the gifts but, for financial reasons, is unable to participate personally?

    A. $14,000
    B. $28,000
    C. $56,000
    D. $112,000
    E. $140,000

15. All the following statements concerning gift-splitting are correct, EXCEPT:

    A. Gift-splitting is available for present-interest and future-interest gifts.
    B. Gift-splitting is a right of a married donor, and the consent of the donor's spouse is not necessary.
    C. If one gift is split in a year, all gifts must be split for that year.
    D. Gift-splitting is not necessary if all gifts made by a donor are present-interest gifts under $14,000.
    E. A federal gift tax return must be filed if gifts are split.

16. All the following qualify for the federal gift tax annual exclusion, EXCEPT:

    A. The absolute assignment of a life insurance policy to one's child
    B. A gift of stock to a Sec. 2503(c) trust for a child
    C. A minor's right to the corpus of a Sec. 2503(b) trust at age 21
    D. An outright gift of non-income-producing property to a child
    E. A gift of a life insurance policy to a Crummey trust

17. David Berry put $5.5 million into a trust for his two children, and he bought a vacation home that he put in joint names with his two children. The vacation home was valued at $240,000. David and his wife have agreed to split gifts. Assuming no prior gifts, what is the approximate amount of David's gift tax liability?

    A. $0
    B. $51,000
    C. $70,000
    D. $79,000
    E. $601,000

18. Earlier this year, Edgar Othman gave his nieces and nephews gifts that exhausted his applicable credit amount. This year, Edgar also gave his wife a boat that cost $150,000, and to each of his three children, Edgar gave securities valued at $220,000. Edgar split gifts with his wife. Which of the following amounts is closest to Edgar's gift tax liability for this year?

    A. $54,200
    B. $101,850
    C. $115,200
    D. $141,900
    E. $432,650

19. .Last year, Ms. Evers made a gift to her son of a vacation home, valued at $250,000. What is Ms. Evers' applicable unified credit amount available this year? (Hint: The annual exclusion was $14,000 last year.)

    A. $0
    B. $66,320
    C. $1,845,800
    D. $2,051,480
    E. $2,117,800

20. Based on the facts of the previous question, what is the amount of gift tax that Ms. Evers would be required to pay if she made a gift of a $364,000 home to her daughter this year?

    A. $0
    B. $104,800
    C. $140,000
    D. $187,620
    E. $192,800

21. For which of the following gratuitous transfers must a gift tax return be filed?

    A. A contribution to a political organization
    B. The payment of another person's legal fees
    C. The payment of another person's hospital bills
    D. A payment of educational tuition for another person
    E. A gift to a spouse of non-income-producing securities, valued at $50,000

22. A gift tax return must be filed for all the following gifts, EXCEPT:

   A. The grantor creates an *inter vivos* trust with a terminable life-income interest payable to the spouse, and a QTIP election is made.

   B. A wife makes a gift of a $25,000 car to her son, and her spouse consents to gift-splitting.

   C. A grantor of a trust gives a remainder interest to his son, and the remainder interest has a present value of $8,000.

   D. A gift of $100,000 in cash is made from a wife to her husband.

   E. A gift of a life insurance policy is made to a trust, with no Crummey powers.

23. Which of the following statements concerning the filing of gift tax returns are correct?

   (1) If spouses agree to split gifts, they must file a joint gift tax return.

   (2) The recipient of a gift is responsible for filing the gift tax return.

   (3) The recipient of a gift is liable for the gift tax if the donor does not pay the tax.

   (4) Generally, the gift tax return must be filed on or before April 15 of the year following the calendar year in which the gift was made.

     A. (1) and (2) only
     B. (1) and (3) only
     C. (2) and (3) only
     D. (2) and (4) only
     E. (3) and (4) only

24. In 2015, Richard Poore gave gifts of $30,000 each to his church, his wife, his son, and his mother. Poore also created a trust for his wife with a life-income interest, valued at $175,000, and his daughter is to receive the remainder interest valued at $7,000. What is the total amount of the annual exclusions used by Richard Poore?

   A. $14,000
   B. $42,000
   C. $56,000
   D. $63,000
   E. $70,000

For practice answering case questions related to Topic 57, please answer the following questions in the cases included in the Appendix at the back of this textbook.

Case	Questions
Bartlett	
Marshall	5
Webster	7 and 8
Unser	
Tingey	
Lytle	
Beals	
Mocsin	
Young	2
Borelli	5 and 6
Cunningham	6, 7, 8, and 9
Fred and Mary Ferris	21, 22, 23, 24, and 25

Answers and Explanations

1. C is the answer. The value of the gifts must be reduced by the annual exclusion for each donee. The taxable gift to George is reduced by the $14,000 annual exclusion to $31,000, the gift to Julie is reduced to $21,000, the gifts to Harry (which total $17,000) are reduced to $3,000, the gift to Jean is reduced to $36,000, and the gift to Lionel is reduced to $46,000. The total is $137,000. None of the gifts qualify for the marital or charitable deductions. The payment to Harry for tuition is not a qualified transfer because it was not made to an educational institution. The payment to Lionel for medical bills is not a qualified transfer because the money was not paid directly to the medical care providers.

2. C is the answer. The two gifts of land are split, and the $10,000 annual exclusion in effect in 1998 applies to both, so the taxable gift is $80,000 for each child. The gift to Tony's wife is not taxable due to the marital deduction. The total taxable gifts are $160,000. The tax on this amount of taxable gifts is $42,000 ($38,800 + 32% x ($160,000 − $150,000) = $42,000). The applicable credit for gift tax purposes is $2,117,800 for 2015, so the remaining applicable credit amount is $2,117,800 − $42,000 = $2,075,800.

Editor's Note: The tax calculation above is based off the gift tax table in the back of this book.

Ignoring the gift to his wife, the gift tax returns would report the gifts as follows:

	Tony's Gift Tax Return	Wife's Gift Tax Return
Gift to Child #1	$180,000	$0
Gift to Child #2	$180,000	$0
Total gifts before gift-splitting	$360,000	$0
Gift-splitting	($180,000)	$180,000
Total gifts after gift-splitting	$180,000	$180,000
Less annual gift tax exclusions	($20,000)	($20,000)
Taxable gifts	$160,000	$160,000

3. A is the answer. The gifts of ranch land will be split, and the annual exclusion will reduce them to $111,000 each. The total gifts for the current year will be $222,000 on Joe's gift tax return. Since Joe has not gifted above $5.43 million in 2015, he will not owe any gift taxes. Note that Joe's wife will also have to file a gift tax return due to the gift-splitting.

The gift tax returns would report the gifts as follows:

	Joe's Gift Tax Return	Wife's Gift Tax Return
Gift to Child #1	$250,000	$0
Gift to Child #2	$250,000	$0
Total gifts before gift-splitting	$500,000	$0
Gift-splitting	($250,000)	$250,000
Total gifts after gift-splitting	$250,000	$250,000
Less annual gift tax exclusions	($28,000)	($28,000)
Taxable gifts	$222,000	$222,000

4. C is the answer. The gifts of $41,000 each to Sally's husband and college are not taxable gifts, due to the marital and charitable deductions. The gifts to her mother and daughter will be split, and the annual exclusion will reduce the taxable gift to $6,500 each. The total of these two taxable gifts is $13,000. The $150,000 gift in trust for the daughter will be split with her husband ($75,000 each) but will not be offset by an annual exclusion, as she also gave her daughter $41,000 this year. The remainder interest to the son is a future-interest gift, so the annual exclusion does not apply. The gift will be split with Morrow's husband, so the gift by Morrow is $20,000. The total of the taxable gifts is $6,500 + $6,500 + $75,000 + $20,000 = $108,000.

5. E is the answer. The trust contains Crummey powers, so a gift to the trust is a present-interest gift. Phillip can take advantage of the gift tax annual exclusion for each beneficiary of the trust. Since there are four beneficiaries (two children and two grandchildren), Phillip can give $14,000 for each beneficiary, without gift tax consequences. Phillip can split gifts with his wife, so the total that can be transferred to the trust without gift tax consequences is $112,000.

6. A is the answer. The undeveloped land is non-income-producing, so the transfer to the trust is a future-interest gift that will not qualify for the annual exclusion. The entire amount of the transfer to the trust will be a taxable gift. Transfers to a Section 2503(c) trust for a minor qualify for the annual exclusion. The tuition payments and payment of medical bills are "qualified transfers" and are excluded from treatment as gifts. The contribution of cash to a Crummey trust for paying life insurance premiums is a present-interest gift because the beneficiaries can withdraw the amount contributed. Thus, it qualifies for the annual exclusion.

7. E is the answer. Each person is entitled to a unified credit in 2015 that will allow gifts of $5,430,000 without payment of federal gift tax. Each person can also make use of the annual exclusion. Thus, a gift to a single third person can total $5,430,000 + $5,430,000 + $14,000 + $14,000 = $10,888,000.

8. B is the answer. The gift of $25,000 to the donor's adult child is a taxable gift because it exceeds the annual exclusion, which is currently $14,000 per donee. The gift of $35,000 to a friend for medical expenses is also a taxable gift because the money was given to the friend and not paid directly to the hospital or other provider of medical services. If the payment were made directly to a medical provider, it would be a qualified transfer and not be subject to gift tax. The payment to a college for a friend's tuition is a qualified transfer, which is not subject to gift tax.

9. B is the answer. A is incorrect because when the client's spouse dies, all values belong to his son. C is incorrect for the same reason. D is incorrect, though the insurer may require that an adult give a receipt for the proceeds on behalf of the son. E is incorrect because the son owns the proceeds when the spouse dies.

10. D is the answer. The gift tax exemption equivalent in 2015 is $5.43 million, which is the maximum value of assets that can be transferred tax-free.

11. C is the answer. The 2012 Tax Act increased the exemption amount to $5.43 million for both estate and gift taxes in 2015.

12. B is the answer. After deducting the $14,000 annual exclusion available for each donee, "S's" taxable gifts include $70,000 of the listed securities given to his son, and $5,000 of the cash given to his daughter. The gift to the church is eligible for the charitable deduction. None of the $6,000 gift to his granddaughter is taxable. The total is $75,000.

13. C is the answer. If "S" and his wife split gifts, they can give each donee up to $28,000 tax-free. Only the gift of securities to "S's" son exceeds $28,000, so after deducting the annual exclusion, the taxable gift is $56,000.

14. D is the answer. Mr. and Mrs. "X" can split their gift and give $28,000 to each of the four children. The total of their gifts, therefore, is $112,000. Gift-splitting requires the consent of the donor's spouse, but only his or her consent is required. The donor can give the entire amount of the gift, and the spouse need only consent to splitting the gift for tax purposes.

15. B is the answer. Gift-splitting requires the consent of a donor's spouse, but only consent is required. The donor may give the entire amount of the gift, and the spouse need only consent to the splitting of the gift for tax purposes.

16. C is the answer. The outright gift of life insurance will qualify for the annual exclusion, but an assignment of life insurance to a trust does not qualify. The gift of life insurance in trust is a gift of a future interest in most cases because the beneficiaries do not have an immediate right to possession or enjoyment of the policy values in the trust. Similarly, an outright gift of non-income-producing property will qualify for the annual exclusion, but a gift in trust of non-income-producing property will not qualify. The gift of stock to a Sec. 2503(c) trust is a gift of a present interest only to the extent of the income interest, but the minor's right to the corpus of a Sec. 2503(b) trust is a future interest, not eligible for the annual exclusion.

17. A is the answer. The $5.5 million placed in trust is subject to gift tax, but this gift is split with David's wife. David's gift is $2,750,000. The vacation home is a gift to each of the children of one-third of the value of the home. The total gift is $160,000, but it is split with David's wife. The gift on David's gift tax return will be $80,000. The total gifts on David's return, therefore, are $2,830,000. The $14,000 annual exclusion will reduce these gifts to $2,802,000 because there are two donees receiving the gifts. The gift tax on this amount is $0 because the exemption amount is $5.43 million in 2015.

18. C is the answer. Each of the three children will receive a gift of $220,000, so the total is $660,000. The gifts are split with Edgar's wife, so Edgar's gifts are $330,000. He can use three annual exclusions of $14,000, so the taxable gifts are $288,000. Since he already used up his applicable credit amount with the gifts to the nieces and nephews, he will owe 40% on all taxable gifts. Thus, he will owe $115,200 (40% x $288,000). The gift to Edgar's wife is not a taxable gift, due to the marital deduction.

19. D is the answer. The $250,000 gift made in 2014 is reduced by the $14,000 annual exclusion leaving $236,000 as a taxable gift. The gift tax due on this amount is $38,800 + 0.32 x ($236,000 – $150,000) = $66,320. This amount is subtracted from the unified credit of $2,117,800 in 2015 available for gift tax purposes. The result is $2,117,800 – $66,320 = $2,051,480. **Editor's Note:** The estate and gift tax table is included in the back of the textbook.

20. A is the answer. Ms Evers has made taxable gifts of $236,000 from last year and $350,000 from this year after subtracting the $14,000 annual exclusion available in 2014 and the $14,000 annual exclusion available in 2015. Thus, her total taxable gifts are $586,000. Since she has not given more than $5.43 million of taxable gifts, she does not owe a gift tax due to the gift tax applicable credit amount.

21. B is the answer. A contribution to a political organization and payment of another person's hospital bills, medical bills, or educational tuition are not considered gifts, and no return is required for these payments. A payment of another person's legal fees is a gift for which a tax return is required.

22. D is the answer. A donor is not required to file a gift tax return for gifts to a spouse, regardless of the amount. If a QTIP election is required, however, a gift tax return must be filed. For a future interest in any amount, a gift tax return must be filed, so a gift tax return must be filed for the gift of a remainder interest, even though it is valued at only $8,000. A gift tax return must be filed if spouses elect to split gifts.

23. E is the answer. There is no such thing as joint gift tax return. A spouse splitting gifts must file his or her own return. The donor, not the recipient, of a gift is responsible for filing the gift tax return. The recipient of a gift is liable for the gift tax if the donor does not pay the tax. Generally, the gift tax return must be filed on or before April 15 of the year following the calendar year in which the gift was made.

24. C is the answer. Richard Poore has made present-interest gifts to four donees: his church, his wife, his son, and his mother. A $14,000 annual exclusion is available for each of these gifts, so the total is $56,000. The gift to his daughter is a future-interest gift that does not qualify for the annual exclusion.

Incapacity Planning (Topic 58)

CFP Board Student-Centered Learning Objectives

(a) Identify the risks and costs of incapacity.

(b) Develop a strategy for managing incapacity.

Incapacity Planning
- A.   *Definition of incapacity*
- B.   *Risks and Costs of Incapacity*
- C.   *Powers of attorney*
  - 1)   *For health care decisions*
  - 2)   *For asset management*
  - 3)   *Durable feature*
  - 4)   *Springing power*
  - 5)   *General or limited powers*
- D.   *Advance medical directives (e.g., living wills)*
- E.   *Guardianship and conservatorship*
- F.   *Revocable living trust*
- G.   *Medicaid planning*
- H.   *Special-needs trust*
- I.   *Long-term care insurance*

Definition of Incapacity

Incapacity means a person cannot manage his or her own affairs due to a physical, mental, or legal obstacle. Most incapacity planning focuses on the physical and mental disabilities that come with aging. A minor child is subject to legal incapacity, regardless of his or her abilities. A person who is incapacitated physically is usually able to participate in making decisions about his or her affairs and is not incompetent for executing legal documents. A person who is mentally incompetent, however, cannot enter into legally binding transactions and cannot execute documents for incapacity planning.

There are two main concerns that must be addressed when a person becomes incapacitated, whether from age or illness:

(1) Management of the incapacitated person's property
(2) Management of the incapacitated person's life, that is, decisions regarding medical care and personal affairs

There are four common techniques used to manage an incapacitated person's property: guardianship (conservatorship), power of attorney, trusts, and joint ownership.

All legal documents, including wills, trusts, powers of attorney, and advance medical directives require that the individual signing the document have the mental capacity to comprehend the significance of the document he or she is signing; therefore, it is imperative that planning be done in advance.

The Cost of Incapacity

There are financial, physical, and emotional costs involved with incapacity. Some costs of incapacity are direct, such as lost income from the incapacitated individual, lost income of a primary caregiver no longer able to work, and increased expenses of medical bills. Other costs may be indirect, such as lost time for growth in the retirement portfolio when health issues force early retirement, reduced Social Security benefits due to loss of high-income years, and lost benefits from insurance policies that lapse because the incapacitated person forgot to pay the bill. Seniors with diminishing mental capacity also frequently become prey to scam artists or even unscrupulous family members. Emotional costs include feelings of depression or worry about becoming a burden to family members. Proper planning can relieve many of these costs.

Guardianship

A guardian or conservator may be appointed either on a voluntary or involuntary basis. When a person has become incompetent, the person usually cannot consent to a guardian, so a state court appoints the guardian to protect the ward. Appointment of a guardian by a state court usually requires evidence and findings of incompetence, that is, inability to manage one's own affairs. (The Uniform Probate Code adopted in about one-third of the states refers to a guardianship for an incompetent person's property as a conservatorship.)

The court may give the guardian general or limited power to make decisions for the ward. A limited guardianship means the guardian may manage only a portion of the incapacitated person's property. A guardian who arranges only for the personal care of the incompetent is called a guardian of the person. More traditionally, a guardian is appointed to manage the entire estate of the incompetent and also to manage the person. A plenary guardianship provides for the guardian to manage both the estate and personal affairs.

A guardian may be appointed for a minor when both parents are dead or incapacitated or when parental rights have otherwise been terminated. The guardian will have essentially the powers of a parent for the minor's care and education. **An important part of a parent's estate planning is executing a will in which a guardian will be appointed for a minor in the event that both parents are deceased**.

Powers of Guardians

A guardian or conservator generally has all the powers over the ward's estate that the ward could exercise, except the power to make a will.

Given the wide powers to act concerning the incompetent person's estate and affairs, there is a potential for abuse. Accordingly, court supervision is required and can be very expensive, burdensome, and time-consuming. Guardians and conservators are required to make reports and file accountings, and they may be required to furnish a bond. The guardianship arrangement is generally inflexible, and the ward is deprived of virtually all rights. For these reasons, many people choose to seek alternatives to guardianship, in advance of the possibility of incompetency. The following alternative techniques are often pursued to avoid a guardianship and its difficulties.

Power of Attorney

A power of attorney is a legal document authorizing another person to act as one's agent or attorney. The person executing the power must have legal capacity and is called the principal; the person appointed by the power is the attorney-in-fact. The principal can appoint the attorney-in-fact to act as agent in a particular transaction, in a series of transactions, or in a broad range of transactions, including any transaction the principal could perform, except making a will.

Special Power

A special or limited power grants the attorney-in-fact power to act only for a specified period of time or in only one transaction or one series of transactions. For example, it is very common for a person to use a power of attorney to enable another person to complete a real estate purchase or sale in the principal's absence. The power terminates when the real estate transaction is completed.

General Nondurable Power

In a nondurable power, the agent is usually given restricted rights, and the power ends when the principal becomes incompetent. The agent acts on the principal's behalf but does not take ownership of any property. Since the power ends at the time the principal becomes incompetent, it does not help much with planning for incompetency. In addition, the power of attorney will only work if an institution or other person involved in a transaction will accept it.

Durable Power

Most financial planners recommend to their clients that they execute a durable power of attorney. This durable power may apply to the principal's property interests or to health care decisions. These two types of durable powers are usually executed separately.

Durable Power for Property

The durable power of attorney for property is recognized by statute in every state.

The durable power continues indefinitely, even after the principal becomes incompetent or incapacitated.

The durable power, like any other power, ends with the death of the principal, so the attorney-in-fact cannot engage in transactions for the estate. During the principal's lifetime, the acts by the attorney-in-fact are binding upon both the principal and any third parties who accept the power and proceed with the transaction.

The durable power is effective both during the time the principal is legally competent and when he or she becomes incompetent.

With a broadly drafted durable power, the attorney-in-fact can act to the same extent as the principal could act, including the power to make gifts, to create trusts, to buy and sell property, and to elect gift-splitting. The major advantage of the durable power of attorney is that it avoids the expense of guardians and the legal fees of court supervision over the principal's estate. The affairs of the principal are not made public in court proceedings, and title remains in the principal.

One potential drawback of the durable power is that the agent generally has no duty to act under the power, and third parties are under no obligation to accept the power as valid. Some planners have also tried to create a duty on the agent to act by making the power a bilateral contract signed by the attorney-in-fact, who also receives compensation. To enhance acceptance by third parties, some planners include a provision authorizing the attorney-in-fact to bring suit against a third party who refuses to accept it. Another technique to gain acceptance is for the client to take the power to banks, brokerage firms, insurance companies, and others to show its validity while he or she is still competent. Some states have enacted penalties for third parties who refuse to rely on these powers.

A second potential problem with the durable power is the risk that the attorney-in-fact may die first, and the principal's property subject to the power will then be included in the gross estate of the attorney-in-fact. This misfortune could occur if the attorney-in-fact is found to hold a general power of appointment over the principal's property. One way to avoid this problem is to prohibit the attorney-in-fact from making gifts to himself or herself; another way is to limit the gifts to an ascertainable standard.

Another risk of the durable power is the potential for misuse. Sometimes, attorneys-in-fact may use the power in ways that are adverse to the client's interests.

While the principal may have a right to bring legal action for such abuses, claims are rarely made since attorneys-in-fact are often family members.

Springing Power

A springing power is a durable power that is activated only when a person becomes incapacitated or incompetent. The power must specify the standard for incompetency or incapacity that will cause the power to spring into effect. In addition, the power should specify who is to make the determination of incapacity.

Not all states recognize the springing power, and, as with other powers, third parties are not required to recognize its validity.

Durable Power for Health Care

Durable powers of attorney for health care are always springing powers. These powers are recognized in nearly all states, and many states have preprinted forms of the powers prepared by the state medical association. The power appoints a person to make medical decisions for the incapacitated principal, such as the decision to withdraw life-support systems. The power should also authorize the attorney-in-fact for health care decisions to have access to medical records, to grant releases to medical personnel, to pay (or refuse payment) for treatment, and to give or withhold consent for treatment.

Since the durable power actually names a person or persons to make the important health care decisions and can apply to a broader range of medical conditions, it can be more effective than a living will. Some planners have clients execute both living wills and durable powers for health care. Powers of attorney for health care are also sometimes referred to as "Health Care Proxies".

Medical and Personal Decisions

Many decisions required for incompetents involve the management of personal affairs. In order to manage an incompetent person's personal care decisions, similar methods to those just discussed can be used. The same guardian who is appointed to manage the property of an incompetent may be appointed to manage the incompetent's personal affairs. Personal and medical care decisions may also be accomplished through durable powers of attorney. In particular, the durable power of attorney can be used to appoint a person to act as the agent for a person's medical decisions. While a guardian generally cannot make decisions to withhold or to withdraw life support or to refuse medical treatment, a durable power of attorney can be written to specify conditions under which an agent will be able to make these decisions.

> ☞ *K Study Tip* – **A power of attorney *cannot* be given to the attorney-in-fact to execute a living will or to execute/revoke a testamentary will.**

Advance Medical Directives – Living Wills

In states that have enacted "living will" statutes, a person can state his or her wishes concerning the use of life-sustaining medical treatment. These laws allow a person to give directions to be allowed to die without pursuit of futile medical treatment to prolong existence.

A person may execute a living will specifying the conditions and circumstances for withholding medical treatment or feeding tubes. Living will statutes may also provide for naming a person to make medical decisions when the patient is in a terminal condition.

In the absence of a living will statute, one must look to state court decisions concerning a patient's right to refuse medical treatment. These court decisions identify the sources that may be considered as evidence of the incompetent patient's wishes relating to life-support treatment. If there are no relevant court decisions in the state, the law of informed consent generally prohibits medical treatment without the patient's consent.

Trusts

Several types of trusts may be used in planning for incompetency. We will discuss the revocable trust, the special-needs trust, the supplemental trust, and the Medicaid trust.

Funded Revocable Trusts

A revocable living trust may be either funded or unfunded. If the revocable trust is funded, the grantor transfers assets to the trust during his or her lifetime. The grantor can also write provisions that specify management by the trustee in the event of the grantor's incompetence. The grantor has more control over what happens to his or her property by virtue of being able to write the provisions of the trust document.

The main drawback of the revocable living trust is the expense of attorney fees and costs of transferring titles of assets.

An advantage of the trust is that a trustee's authority to act in managing assets will be recognized and can be enforced, while a durable power of attorney may not be recognized. Another advantage of the revocable trust is that it continues after death, whereas, the power of attorney ends at the principal's death.

The funded revocable trust is a grantor trust, so income is taxed to the grantor. There is no completed gift, so there are no gift tax consequences. The assets in the trust will escape probate but are included in the grantor's gross estate.

Unfunded Revocable Trusts – Standby Trusts

An unfunded revocable trust is also called a standby trust. The grantor establishes the trust but does not transfer assets to it. In addition, the grantor executes a durable power of attorney or springing durable power of attorney so that when the grantor becomes incompetent, the attorney-in-fact can transfer the assets to the trust. The trustee then manages the assets for the grantor.

Special-Needs Trusts

A special-needs trust is an irrevocable trust set up by a grantor for an elderly parent, a child, or others. The trustee usually is given discretion over distributions of income so that the trustee can take into consideration the special needs of beneficiaries. Since the beneficiary cannot compel distributions, the trust assets are not considered resources available to the beneficiary that could reduce assistance from public authorities. The trust can also include spendthrift and other provisions that prevent public authorities from recovering from the trust for benefits previously provided to the beneficiary.

Medicaid Trust

A Medicaid trust is an irrevocable trust that pays income only to the grantor and may also provide for additional invasion of the principal for special needs. The purpose of the Medicaid trust is to remove assets from the control of the grantor so that he or she becomes eligible for Medicaid assistance without expending his or her assets to the poverty level. In this way, the grantor retains more of the benefits of assets.

The Revenue Reconciliation Act of 1993 has removed much of the advantage of these trusts by requiring that the assets in trusts created by the Medicaid applicant or spouse be treated as assets of the applicant.

Joint Ownership Convenience Account

A simple but effective way to handle the finances of the incapacitated is to use a joint bank account, known as a convenience account. The account should be designated as a convenience account and not as joint ownership with right of survivorship. The account is established simply by placing another name on the incapacitated owner's account for the convenience of paying bills. Usually, a close relative or a child's name is added to the account. This cosigner can make deposits and withdrawals for the benefit of the incompetent person. As long as the funds are used solely for the benefit of the incompetent person, the interest income from the account is still taxed to the owner, and the assets will be included in the gross estate of the original owner.

Long-Term Care Insurance

Long-term care insurance can help protect assets, lifestyle, and dignity. The rising cost of long-term care is a significant threat to financial well-being, while the disability that causes the need for care may be a significant threat to quality of life. Long-term care insurance provides financial assistance with the cost of caring for an incapacitated insured, thereby allowing financial assets to remain available for other goals. LTCI can also ensure that care can be provided in the most desirable location (home or institution) without the need for family members to make major lifestyle adjustments in order to provide care for the incapacitated individual.

EXHIBIT 58 – 1
Incapacity Planning Techniques

	Durable Power	*Living Will*	*Revocable Trust*
When is it effective?	Immediately or springing; continues after incompetency; ends at death	Only for a terminal condition, and only effective after incompetency	Immediately if funded; or after incompetency, if it is a standby trust; can continue after death
Can it be used for estate planning after incompetency?	Yes, if the attorney-in-fact is given broad powers, e.g., to make gifts	No	No, provisions cannot be changed after incompetency
Is it useful for health care decisions?	Yes, it can authorize health care decisions	Yes, but only for terminal conditions	No, the trustee makes decisions on property only
What potential drawbacks exist?	Third parties may not be required to accept it, and the attorney-in-fact is not required to act	Requires a terminal condition	Attorney fees and title transfer costs will be incurred

Application Questions

1. Joe Dunstan has been a widower for 5 years and does not have contact with his children. He would like to have someone ready to handle his affairs during his upcoming heart surgery. Assuming state law recognizes their validity, which of the following powers of attorney should be recommended to Joe Dunstan?

    A. Nondurable power of attorney with immediate powers

    B. Durable power of attorney with immediate powers

    C. Durable power of attorney with springing powers

    D. Nondurable power of attorney with springing powers

2. Joyce Rivera, who is 45 years of age, is planning to leave the country on a sabbatical for two years. Joyce owns real estate and closely held business interests in the U.S. Joyce is unmarried and would like to have her brother ready to handle her business interests while she is away. Assuming state law recognizes their validity, which of the following techniques is (are) options a CFP® certificant should recommend to Joyce Rivera?

    (1) Durable power of attorney
    (2) Revocable living trust
    (3) Standby trust
    (4) Joint convenience account

        A. (1) only
        B. (2) only
        C. (1) and (3) only
        D. (2) and (4) only
        E. (1), (2), (3), and (4)

3. (Published question released December, 1996)

Doris Jenkins is a 71-year-old widow with a son and daughter, ages 43 and 45, and six grandchildren. Doris has an estate currently worth $572,000, which includes her home, worth $250,000, and a life insurance policy on her life with a face value of $160,000. Her children are named as primary beneficiaries. Doris recently suffered a severe stroke that left her paralyzed on her right side. She is home from the hospital, but her health will continue to decline, and she will need to go into a nursing home within one year. The only estate planning she has done to date is to write a will in 1989, which left all her assets to her children equally. Of the following estate planning considerations, which is (are) appropriate for Doris at this time?

    (1) Transfer ownership of her home to her children so it will not be counted as a resource should she have to go into a nursing home and apply for Medicaid.

    (2) Execute a durable general power of attorney and a durable power of attorney for health care.

    (3) Place all of her assets in an irrevocable family trust, with her children as beneficiaries.

    (4) Start a gifting program, transferring assets up to the annual exclusion amount to each of her children and grandchildren.

        A. (1), (2), (3), and (4)
        B. (2) and (3) only
        C. (1) and (4) only
        D. (4) only
        E. (2) only

4. After John Kane developed Alzheimer's disease, his wife died, leaving her substantial estate to John. John's children would like to avoid estate taxes by taking advantage of her unified credit. Which of the following documents executed by John when he was competent would enable the children to accomplish their objective?

    A. A nondurable power of attorney
    B. A durable power of attorney
    C. Both a nondurable and a durable power of attorney
    D. A living will
    E. None of the above

5. All the following statements concerning a power of attorney are correct, EXCEPT:

    A. A power of attorney can be used by the authorized person to transfer real estate.
    B. A power of attorney is not effective if the person signing is mentally incompetent at the time of signing.
    C. A special power of attorney authorizes only a specific transaction.
    D. A power of attorney cannot be used if a person is physically incapacitated even though mentally competent.
    E. A power of attorney cannot be used after death to dispose of property omitted from a will.

6. In many instances, a standby trust can be more advantageous from the grantor's point of view than the granting of a power of attorney or a durable family power of attorney. All the following statements concerning standby trusts are correct, EXCEPT:

    A. They can be arranged to come into effect upon the grantor's physical disability.
    B. They can be arranged to come into effect upon the grantor's mental disability.
    C. They can be arranged to come into effect if the grantor is away on a trip.
    D. They are irrevocable, so the grantor obtains income tax advantages during any disability.
    E. They can be unfunded trusts until the grantor sustains a disability.

7. All the following are methods used to handle the affairs of an incompetent person, EXCEPT:

    A. Guardianship
    B. Written instructions
    C. Power of attorney
    D. Trust
    E. Living will

8. Which of the following instruments and techniques would provide effective planning for medical decisions that may accompany a terminal illness?

    (1) A living will
    (2) A nondurable power of attorney
    (3) A living trust
    (4) A guardian
    (5) A durable power of attorney

    A. (1) only
    B. (3) and (5) only
    C. (2) and (3) only
    D. (4) only
    E. (1) and (5) only

9. All the following are powers of attorney, EXCEPT:

    A. Absolute power
    B. Nondurable power
    C. Durable power
    D. Springing power
    E. Springing durable power

10. All the following statements concerning durable powers of attorney are correct, EXCEPT:

    A. If the attorney-in-fact uses the principal's property contrary to the best interests of the principal, the attorney-in-fact can be held liable.
    B. The attorney-in-fact can continue to exercise the power during the principal's incapacity, incompetence, or death.
    C. The durable power can be used by the attorney-in-fact before the principal has become incompetent or incapacitated.
    D. Since failure to act does not create any liability, an attorney-in-fact can simply decide not to exercise the durable power and do nothing.
    E. Generally, a bank or brokerage firm is under no obligation to accept a durable power or to follow the instructions of an attorney-in-fact.

11. Which of the following statements concerning a durable power of attorney is (are) correct?

    (1) It ceases to function after an incapacitated person gets well.
    (2) It is used to render health decisions for the principal.
    (3) The attorney-in-fact may make gifts of the principal's property.
    (4) Third parties who have had dealings with the principal must accept the acts of the attorney-in-fact under a valid durable power.

    A. (1) only
    B. (1) and (2) only
    C. (2) and (3) only
    D. (3) and (4) only
    E. (1), (2), (3), and (4)

12. Which of the following statements concerning living trusts are correct?

    (1) They are legal trust instruments in all but nine states.

    (2) The trustee holds title to the assets and manages the assets for the beneficiaries.

    (3) Living trusts must be revocable, just as testamentary trusts must be irrevocable.

    (4) Living trusts are not effective in making decisions concerning medical treatment or the use of life-support systems.

      A. (1) and (2) only
      B. (1) and (3) only
      C. (2) and (3) only
      D. (2) and (4) only
      E. (3) and (4) only

For practice answering case questions related to Topic 58, please answer the following questions in the cases included in the Appendix at the back of this textbook.

Case	Questions
Bartlett	
Marshall	
Webster	
Unser	
Tingey	
Lytle	4
Beals	
Mocsin	
Young	
Borelli	7
Cunningham	10 and 11
Fred and Mary Ferris	26, 27, 28, 29, and 30

Answers and Explanations

1. C is the answer. A durable power of attorney appears to be the most prudent approach for Joe Dunstan. The durable power is necessary to survive any incapacity or incompetency, but the power will not be needed until the time of the surgery. By including a springing power, Joe will avoid the problem of someone exercising the power before the time it is needed.

2. E is the answer. All of these techniques should be recommended to Joyce Rivera and discussed with her, but she will probably not want to use all of them. For example, she might elect to use only the revocable trust. She might use only the durable power of attorney. She could use the durable power of attorney in conjunction with the standby trust. She could set up a joint convenience account and handle many problems through it until she needs a standby trust or revocable living trust. Each of these techniques could offer her some advantages and do not necessarily exclude use of some or all of the others.

3. E is the answer. Under Medicaid rules, a person is ineligible for public assistance for up to 60 months after a transfer for less than full value. As a result, transferring ownership of her home to children is not recommended because of the 5-year look-back. Likewise, placing all of her assets in an irrevocable family trust with her children as beneficiaries will leave Doris with no assets to pay for nursing home care, in addition to being subject to the 5-year look-back rule. Executing a durable general power of attorney and a durable power of attorney for health care are appropriate. These powers will help with decision making concerning assets and health care in the event Doris becomes incapacitated. The durable powers remain effective after any incapacity that would prevent Doris from participating in these decisions.

A gifting program is not appropriate because Doris' estate will not be subject to estate tax. Her estate is less than the applicable exemption amount, so she does not need to reduce it to avoid taxes. She is more likely to need the assets herself for her health care. A gifting program might be considered in connection with Medicaid planning.

4. B is the answer. The durable power of attorney will remain effective after John becomes incompetent. The durable power can be used by the attorney-in-fact to file a disclaimer so that enough assets pass to the children to take advantage of the unified credit.

5. D is the answer. One of the most common uses of the power of attorney is for the client who is physically incapacitated but still mentally competent. The power of attorney cannot be used if the client is mentally incompetent at the time of signing. A power of attorney can be used in real estate transactions.

6. D is the answer. In normal usage, standby trusts are set up to become effective when there is a temporary interruption in the grantor's ability to manage his or her financial affairs. Standby trusts are usually revocable in nature and, whether revocable or irrevocable, provide no income tax or estate tax benefits for the grantor. If desired, the standby trust can be arranged to become irrevocable in the event of the grantor's permanent disability.

7 B is the answer; B is an incorrect example. A, C, D, and E are all examples of methods of handling an incompetent person's affairs.

8. E is the answer. Planning for medical decisions may be done by use of a living will or a durable power of attorney. In states with living will statutes, the directions given in a living will can eliminate the need for futile medical treatment in terminal cases. Durable powers of attorney will also be effective for this purpose since these powers survive incompetence of the principal. Nondurable powers do not survive incompetence and, therefore, are not as useful. A guardian will usually not be able to make the decisions to terminate or withdraw treatment, and planning usually tries to avoid the expense and inconvenience of a guardian.

9. A is the answer because it is an incorrect statement. B, C, D, and E are examples of powers of attorney.

10. B is the answer. A durable power is effective only until the death of the principal. Like all powers of attorney, it terminates at the principal's death. The durable power, however, is important because it continues to be valid and effective during the principal's incapacity and incompetence.

11. C is the answer. (1) is an incorrect statement. The unique provision of a durable power is that is does not cease to function when the person is incompetent and will remain effective when the person recovers. The attorney-in-fact may be given very broad powers under a durable power, including the power to make gifts. Third parties are not required to accept the power of attorney or the acts of the attorney-in-fact.

12. D is the answer. (1) is an incorrect statement. Living trusts are permitted in all states. The trustee takes title to property placed in trust, unlike the guardian and attorney-in-fact, who do not take title. Accordingly, a trustee can usually manage assets more effectively than a guardian or attorney-in-fact under a power of attorney. Living trusts may be revocable or irrevocable. Testamentary trusts cannot be revocable. Living trusts are not effective for making decisions on medical treatment, so living wills or powers of attorney are prepared for these problems.

Estate Tax Compliance and Tax Calculation (Topic 59)

CFP Board Student-Centered Learning Objectives

(a) Describe the basic components of estate tax preparation including related deductions, exemptions, credits, and tax rates.

(b) Explain the relationship between the federal gift and estate tax laws.

(c) Estimate federal and state estate (inheritance) tax liabilities.

(d) Outline the consequences and calculate the costs of non-compliance with estate tax rules.

Estate Tax Compliance and Tax Calculation
  - A.   *Estate tax filing requirements*
  - B.   *The gross estate*
    - 1)   *Inclusions*
    - 2)   *Exclusions*
  - C.   *Deductions*
  - D.   *Adjusted gross estate*
  - E.   *Deductions from the adjusted gross estate*
  - F.   *Taxable estate*
  - G.   *Adjusted taxable gifts*
  - H.   *Tentative tax base*
  - I.   *Tentative tax calculation*
  - J.   *Credits*
    - 1)   *Gift tax payable*
    - 2)   *Applicable credit amount*
    - 3)   *Prior transfer credit*

2010 Tax Act Retroactively Reinstated the Estate Tax As of 2010

The 2010 Tax Act signed by President Obama on December 17, 2010 extended the 2001 Tax Act signed by President Bush, but also retroactively reinstated the estate and generation skipping transfer (GST) tax for 2010. However, taxpayers who died during 2010 had the option of:

1. Being subject to the estate tax with a top 35% tax rate, a $5 million exemption, and step-up in basis to fair market value at date of death, or
2. Staying with the 2010 estate tax repeal rules which allowed them to avoid the estate tax, but required the carryover basis rules. The executor was only able to increase the carryover basis by $1.3 million plus an additional $3 million for assets passing directly to the surviving spouse (assets not placed in a marital deduction trust). If a taxpayer

died with more than $1.3 million ($4.3 million if there is a surviving spouse) of appreciation in the estate, the heirs received the assets with a carryover basis from the deceased taxpayer (limited to fair market value at time of death).

Although the GST tax was retroactively reinstated for 2010, the GST tax rate was zero percent with a $5 million exemption amount. As a result, no GST tax was due for 2010.

For 2011 and 2012, the estate, GST and gift tax was reunified with a $5 million exemption amount with a top tax rate of 35% (indexed for inflation starting in 2012 to $5.12 million). This means taxpayers had the option to make lifetime gifts up to $5.12 million in 2012 rather than having to wait until death in order to have full access to the exemption available for estate tax purposes.

The 2010 Tax Act also created a new portability feature between spouses for the exemption from estate taxes for taxpayers who die after 2010 and before 2013. If the first spouse to die did not use up the entire $5.12 million exemption amount in 2012, the executor could make an election on the first spouse's estate tax return to allow the surviving spouse to claim any remaining portion of the first spouse's $5.12 million exemption.

The 2010 Tax Act only provided for these new estate, GST and gift tax rules through December 31, 2012, however the American Taxpayer Relief Act of 2012, signed into law in early 2013, made portability permanent and extended the $5 million exemption set in 2011 (indexed for inflation each year). For 2015, the indexed exemption amount is $5.43 million.

The portability feature only applies to the estate tax exemption amount and not the GST exemption. In addition, the portability feature only applies to the exemption of the last deceased spouse if the surviving spouse has survived more than one spouse.

Estate Tax Filing Requirements – Sec. 6018

The U.S. Estate Tax Return, Form 706, must be filed if the decedent's taxable estate, plus adjusted taxable gifts, exceeds the applicable exemption equivalent. The return is due 9 months after the decedent's date of death. The executor is responsible for filing the return and is personally liable for paying the federal estate tax. The executor can request a six-month extension by filing Form 4768. The extension is only an extension of the time to file the return and is not an extension of time to pay the tax.

A decedent can direct what property interests will bear the taxes. If the will states that the residue will bear the taxes, then the specific bequests will not be reduced by estate and inheritance taxes. In the absence of directions in the will, each property interest will bear its own proportion of the death taxes.

The Federal Gross Estate – Sec. 2031

To calculate federal estate taxes, step one is to add the value of all assets included in the gross estate. In general, the gross estate consists of all property a person owned or over which the person held a general power of appointment at the time of death. Certain additional property interests must be added to the gross estate, even though these interests were not actually owned at the time of death.

Property Interests Included in the Gross Estate

The Internal Revenue Code specifies that the gross estate includes the following property interests:

1. Property owned by the deceased or in which the deceased had an ownership interest at death (Sec. 2033)
2. Property subject to the deceased's general power of appointment (Sec. 2041)
3. Proceeds of life insurance policies on the life of the deceased, payable to the deceased's estate, or in which the deceased had any incidents of ownership (Sec. 2042)
4. Property held in joint tenancy with right of survivorship (Sec. 2040)
5. The survivorship interest of joint and survivor annuities (Sec. 2039)
6. Dower or curtesy interests (Sec. 2034)
7. Gifts of certain property made within three years of death, such as gifts of life insurance on the deceased's life and gift taxes paid within three years of death (Sec. 2035)
8. Retained interests and gifts of property over which the deceased retained control of the income (Sec. 2036)
9. Gifts over which the deceased retained the power to alter, amend, or revoke (Sec. 2038)
10. Reversionary interests or gifts, where enjoyment of the property is conditioned on the donee surviving the deceased (Sec. 2037)

These ten categories of property are described more fully below.

Owned Property – Sec. 2033

All real and personal property, tangible and intangible, in which the deceased had an ownership interest, wherever located, within the U.S. or foreign countries, must be included in the gross estate and is subject to estate tax.

If the deceased owned an interest as a tenant in common, the value of the deceased's proportionate share is included in the gross estate. The deceased's share of community property is also included.

Loan obligations and notes, such as installment notes owed to the deceased, and income earned but not yet paid (called income in respect of a decedent, or IRD), are also included in the gross estate.

General Power of Appointment – Sec. 2041

If a decedent held a general power of appointment over property at the time of death, the assets subject to the general power are included in the decedent's gross estate. A general power can be exercised in favor of the holder, the holder's estate, the holder's creditors, or the creditors of the holder's estate. Assets subject to a limited or special power of appointment are not included in the gross estate. (Powers of appointment are discussed in more detail in Topic 61.)

"5-and-5 Power"

If the decedent held a power to appoint annually the greater of $5,000 or 5% of a trust principal, the holder's gross estate will include the greater of $5,000 or 5% of the trust assets. The amount included will be reduced to the extent this "5-and-5 power" was exercised in the year of death.

Life Insurance – Sec. 2042

If at the time of death, the decedent owned a life insurance policy on his or her own life, the death benefit will be included in the decedent's gross estate. The death benefit is also included if the decedent had any incidents of ownership in a life insurance policy on his or her life. Rights that establish *incidents of ownership* include the following:

- The right to name or change the beneficiary
- The right to surrender the policy for its cash value
- The right to borrow against the policy cash values
- The right to pledge the policy as collateral for a loan
- The right to assign the policy or to assign any of these named rights
- The right to revoke any assignment of the policy

Since the three-year rule applies to life insurance, the death benefit is included in the gross estate if the decedent gave up incidents of ownership within three years of death.

🔑 **KEY SUMMARY 59 – 1**
Life Insurance Death Benefits Included in the Decedent's Gross Estate

- Decedent held some incident of ownership at death.
- Decedent gave up incidents of ownership within three years of death (e.g., by gift of a life policy).
- The death benefit is payable to the decedent's estate or executor.
- The death benefit is available to the decedent's estate.
- The insured is a controlling owner of the business that owns the policy, and the insured has named the beneficiary.

Policies on Another Person

If at the time of death, the decedent owned a life insurance policy on the life of another person, the replacement cost of the policy is included in the decedent's gross estate. The three-year rule does not apply to a policy on another's life.

Proceeds Payable to the Executor or Estate Is Included

If a policy is payable to the executor or to the decedent's estate, the proceeds are included in the gross estate, even though the decedent had no incident of ownership in the policy at the time of death.

"50-50 Rule" – Sec. 2040

If the decedent held title to property in joint tenancy with right of survivorship with a spouse, or in tenancy by the entirety, one-half of the value of the property is included in the decedent's gross estate. This "50-50 rule" applies, regardless of the contribution of the spouses to the purchase price.

Contribution Rule

If the decedent owned property in joint tenancy WROS with persons other than the spouse, the entire value of the jointly held property is included in the decedent's gross estate, except to the extent the survivor can show contribution to the acquisition costs. If a survivor can show the property was purchased entirely with funds provided by the survivor, none of the value of the jointly owned property will be included in the decedent's gross estate.

Practice Question

Zach Peabody bought a cabin in the mountains with his son Phillip. They each paid one-half of the $70,000 purchase price. They took title in joint tenancy WROS but kept no other records of the transaction. When Zach died, the cabin was worth $80,000.

How much of the value of the cabin will be included in Zach's gross estate?

    A. $0
    B. $35,000
    C. $40,000
    D. $80,000

Answer:
At Zach's death, his son will not be able to show any contribution because he has no records. The full value at the date of death will be included in Zach's gross estate. The amount included will be $80,000.
The answer is D.

Joint and Survivor Annuity – Sec. 2039

If at death, the decedent owned an annuity that will pay a survivorship benefit to a named beneficiary, **the present value of the future payments that will be made under the contract to**

the beneficiary will be included in the decedent's gross estate. This rule also applies to pension and retirement plans that provide for a survivorship benefit.

To the extent the survivor contributed to the purchase price of the annuity, a portion of the value of the income interest will not be included in the decedent's gross estate. Thus, if the decedent contributed 2/3 of the purchase price, then 2/3 of the survivor's income interest will be included in the decedent's gross estate.

> ☞ *K Study Tip* – **This *estate tax rule* determining the amount of the survivor's annuity income interest included in the gross estate should not be confused with the *income tax rule* that determines the amount of each annuity payment included in the gross income.**

Contributions by an employer arising out of the decedent's employment are treated as contributions by the decedent.

Dower and Curtesy – Sec. 2034

Dower is a widow's right to a life estate in a portion of her deceased husband's real estate. Curtesy is a widower's right to a life estate in his deceased wife's real estate.

Many states have replaced these rights with statutory rights for surviving spouses. Dower, curtesy, or other statutory rights are included in the gross estate.

Transfers within Three Years of Death – Sec. 2035

Generally, gifts made within three years of death are not included in the gross estate. The following transfers are exceptions to this rule and are included in the gross estate if made within three years of death:

- Transfer of a retained life estate
- Transfer of a retained power to alter, amend, or revoke
- Transfer of life insurance on the deceased's own life
- Transfer of a retained reversionary interest with a 5% or greater probability of reversion
- Transfer that the transferee can enjoy or possess only at the deceased's death

Gross-Up Rule

Under the "gross-up rule," gift taxes paid by the decedent on gifts made within three years of death are also included in the decedent's gross estate.

🔑 **KEY SUMMARY 59 – 2**
3-Year Rule: Gifts Made Within Three Years of Death

Gift	Included in Gross Estate
Outright lifetime gift	No
Life insurance	Yes
Revocable trust made irrevocable	Yes
Retained life estate	Yes
Gift taxes paid on gifts	Yes

Retained Life Interests – Sec. 2036

If a decedent made a gratuitous lifetime transfer of property but retained the right to income from the property or retained the right to possess or enjoy the property for life, then the value of the property is included in the decedent's gross estate. Similarly, if the decedent retained for life a right to designate who would enjoy, possess, or receive the income from the property, it will be included in the gross estate. In addition, if the decedent retained such a right for a period that did not, in fact, end before the decedent's death, the property is included. Further, if the decedent gave up or transferred these retained rights within three years of death, the property is still included in the decedent's gross estate.

Retained interests usually arise in connection with a transfer to a trust. For example, a father places his vacation home in a trust for his daughter but retains the right to use the home for life. At the father's death, the value of the home will be included in his gross estate. If the father named himself trustee and retained only the right to designate who would enjoy the property, the value of the home would still be included in his gross estate.

🔔 *REMEMBER: IF THE DECEDENT RETAINED ANY RIGHTS OVER LIFETIME TRANSFERS, THE FULL VALUE OF THE PROPERTY IS INCLUDED IN THE GROSS ESTATE. IN ADDITION, IF THE DECEDENT GAVE UP OR TRANSFERRED THESE RETAINED RIGHTS WITHIN THREE YEARS OF DEATH, THE PROPERTY IS STILL INCLUDED IN THE DECEDENT'S GROSS ESTATE.*

Reciprocal Trusts

The reciprocal trusts doctrine arose from the application of the Code Section on retained life interests.

If a brother establishes a trust that pays income for life to his sister and then to her children, and his sister establishes a trust that pays income for life to her brother and then to his children, the IRS will seek to include the assets of the brother's trust in his gross estate, based on the implied understanding between the brother and sister. In effect, each transferor has a retained life estate.

Inclusion in the gross estate occurs only when the life estate was retained at the time a decedent made a gift. If the life estate is received by gift or bequest from another person, it will not be included in the decedent's gross estate. Thus, if a son was given a life estate in a vacation home by his mother, the value of the home will not be included in the son's gross estate.

Power to Amend, Alter, or Revoke – Sec. 2038

If the decedent made a lifetime gift of property but retained the power to alter, amend, revoke, or terminate the gift, the value of the property will be included in the decedent's gross estate. Due to this rule, property transferred to a revocable trust is included in the grantor's gross estate.

Even if the power must be exercised with others or the power is only to change the time at which a beneficiary will be able to enjoy or receive an interest, the value of the property will be included in the decedent's gross estate. Moreover, the capacity in which the decedent retained a power does not matter. If any power to amend, alter, or revoke a trust are reserved to the trustee, and the decedent names himself or herself trustee or reserves the right to name a new trustee, then the trust assets are included in the decedent's gross estate. Further, if the decedent gave up or transferred these retained rights within three years of death, the property is still included in the decedent's gross estate.

If the power to alter, amend, revoke, or terminate is subject to an ascertainable standard, the property subject to the power is not included in the decedent's gross estate. For example, if a father places assets in trust for his daughter and retains the right to invade for his daughter's benefit, but only for health, maintenance, support, or education, the power is subject to an ascertainable standard and will not be included in the father's estate.

Gifts *Causa Mortis*

A gift *causa mortis* is a revocable gift because the donor makes the gift when he or she thinks his or her own death may be imminent and expects to receive the gift back in the event of recovery. The gift *causa mortis* is retained by the person to whom the deceased gave it, but it is still included in the decedent's gross estate.

Reversionary Interests – Sec. 2037

Transfers that become effective at death are included in the decedent's gross estate if the decedent's reversionary interest at the date of death is actuarially computed to exceed 5% of the value of the property. For example, a son transferred his house to a trust for his mother for her lifetime, and at her death, it is to pass to his brother; but, if his brother is not living, the house is to return to the son. The son, therefore, can receive the house only if he survives his brother, so the son has a reversionary interest. If this reversion is actuarially computed to be worth more than 5% of the value of the house (there is a greater than 5% chance of the son outliving his brother), then the reversionary interest is included in the son's gross estate if he dies before his brother. Further, if the son gave up or transferred the reversion within three years of death, the property is still included in his gross estate.

Adjusted Gross Estate – Secs. 2053, 2054, and 2058

The adjusted gross estate is actually not calculated on the U.S. Estate Tax Return, Form 706, but is calculated in the course of determining other exclusions, credits, and benefits under the estate tax laws. The deductions that are subtracted from the gross estate to compute the adjusted gross estate are also deducted in computing the taxable estate. The deductions subtracted to compute the adjusted gross estate are:

(1) Funeral expenses
(2) Estate administration expenses
(3) Debts, taxes, and medical expenses
(4) Mortgages and liens
(5) Casualty and theft losses

Debts of the decedent that are deductible include unpaid income taxes, medical bills, costs of the decedent's last illness, and any outstanding loans. Loan guarantees and cosigned loans are not deductible unless the estate will be required to pay the loan. Mortgage debt is deductible to the extent the mortgaged property was included in the gross estate. If one-half of the value of a residence is included in the gross estate, then one-half of the mortgage debt on the residence can be deducted. Casualty and theft losses are deductible if they occurred during the administration of the estate and were not covered by insurance.

Editor's Note: State death taxes are also deductible in calculating the taxable estate. However, the deduction is typically taken *from* the adjusted gross estate, rather than *for* the adjusted gross estate. This treatment was due to the fact that the Section 303 redemption and Section 6166 installment payment of taxes (discussed in Topic 60) define the adjusted gross estate without the state death tax deduction. As a result, executors deducted the state death tax deduction from the adjusted gross estate. This treatment is similar to the marital deduction and charitable deduction, which are also deducted from the adjusted gross estate.

The Taxable Estate

The taxable estate is computed by subtracting from the gross estate the same deductions subtracted to compute the adjusted gross estate, as well as the state death taxes, marital, and charitable deductions.

State Death Taxes Deduction – Sec. 2058

The state death taxes deduction equals the amount of state death taxes paid to a state on property included in the decedent's gross estate.

Prior to 2005, an estate was entitled to a credit for state death taxes that was the lesser of: (1) the tax actually paid to the state, or (2) the maximum credit shown in an IRS table. The Tax Act of 2001 reduced the state death tax credit by 25% in 2002, by 50% in 2003, by 75% in 2004, and the credit was repealed in 2005. An estate tax deduction for state death taxes replaced the credit, starting in 2005.

The Marital Deduction – Sec. 2056

The marital deduction is unlimited in amount and applies to any property passing to the surviving spouse, whether by will, intestacy, or operation of law. **To qualify, the property must be included in the decedent's gross estate, must pass at the decedent's death to a surviving spouse, and must not be a nondeductible terminable interest.**

Terminable Interest

A terminable interest is an interest in property that will end by reason of a lapse of time or due to the occurrence of a specified event. A life estate is a terminable interest because the interest ends when the life tenant dies. The life estate passes to another person, without being included in the life tenant's gross estate. Thus, the surviving spouse who is a life tenant cannot direct to whom the property will pass, and the terminable interest passes to someone, without passing through the surviving spouse's estate.

A terminable interest is deductible only when the decedent's executor files a QTIP election. This election means the property will be included in the surviving spouse's gross estate, rather than the decedent's taxable estate.

A life estate will qualify for the marital deduction if the life tenant has been given a general power of appointment. In this case, the interest passes through the life tenant's estate and is included in his or her gross estate.

Charitable Deduction – Sec. 2055

Any bequest or transfer by the decedent to a "qualified charity" may be deducted from the gross estate. **Since the charitable deduction is unlimited in amount, an entire estate can pass to charity.** The charitable deduction is only limited by the net value of the property included in the gross estate and by the requirement that the property must pass to a qualified charity. Political organizations do not qualify for the deduction.

Adjusted Taxable Gifts

Adjusted taxable gifts are taxable gifts given after 1976.

To calculate the taxable gift, the total gift is first reduced by the annual exclusion. The annual exclusion is subtracted from gifts to spouses and charities, and then after the annual exclusion is subtracted, the marital and charitable deductions are subtracted. Any gift amount in excess of the annual exclusion that is not passing to charity or to a spouse will then be a taxable gift.

Example: If a donor gives a property to his son, his wife, and his church, the only taxable gift is the portion going to his son that is in excess of the annual exclusion.

Tentative Tax Base – Sec. 2001

A decedent's adjusted taxable gifts are added to the taxable estate to compute the tentative tax base. Gifts that have already been included in the gross estate, such as a gift with a retained life estate, are not added to the tentative tax base.

Tentative Tax Calculation

The tentative estate tax is computed by applying the unified rate schedule for estate and gift taxes to the tentative tax base. The addition of adjusted taxable gifts is what makes lifetime and testamentary gifts cumulative, and it makes the estate and gift taxes into a unified system. Obviously, the result of adding adjusted taxable gifts has been to push estates into higher marginal tax rates.

Subtract Gift Taxes Payable for Gifts after 1976

When the gift taxes on gifts made by the decedent after 1976 have exceeded the applicable credit amount, an amount is subtracted from the tentative tax for these gift taxes. Note that the gift taxes are recalculated, using the rate schedule for gifts that is in effect at the time of the decedent's death. Thus, the amount subtracted is not the actual gift taxes paid, but the amount of gift taxes that would be payable if the decedent had made the gifts on the day of death.

Credit for Tax Paid on Gifts before 1977

The credit for gift tax paid applies only to gifts of property made before 1977, and the credit is only available when the property is included in the decedent's gross estate. This situation arises when the decedent has set up a trust with a retained life interest and paid gift tax on the remainder interest. Due to the retained life interest, the trust assets are included in the decedent's gross estate. The credit is for the gift taxes actually paid.

Unified Credit – Sec. 2010

The unified credit (or applicable credit amount, as it is also called under the Code) reduces the tentative estate tax dollar-for-dollar. As a reminder, the unified credit amount for estate and gift taxes covers the first $5.43 million of assets in 2015.

Even if the decedent exhausted the credit on the first $5.43 million of assets during his or her lifetime by making gifts, the entire credit is used in calculating the net estate tax on Form 706 because adjusted taxable gifts are added back to the tax base under the unified system.

☞ *K Study Tip* – **The unified tax credit on the first $5.43 million of assets in 2015 may be fully used by one taxpayer either for lifetime gifts or for bequests at death, but it is not used twice. Adjusted taxable gifts are added back to calculate the taxable estate (increasing the taxpayer's taxable base), and the entire unified credit is subtracted from the tentative estate tax. Therefore, the credit on the first $5.43 million of assets is actually used to reduce tax liability (gift or estate) only once.**

An example of this study tip follows:

===

Example:

Tim made lifetime taxable gifts of $1 million and paid no gift tax, due to the unified credit (applicable credit amount). He died in 2015, when the applicable exclusion amount was $5.43 million. His taxable estate was $8 million.

	Taxable estate	$8,000,000
[Plus]	Adjusted taxable gifts	1,000,000
	Tentative tax base	$9,000,000
	Tentative tax	3,545,800
[Minus]	Unified credit	2,117,800
	Net estate tax	$1,428,000

While Tim used the unified credit to eliminate the gift tax on lifetime gifts, those gifts were added back to his tentative tax base in the estate tax calculation. The unified credit was subtracted from the tentative tax to determine the net estate tax due.

===

Practice Question

Which of the following statements concerning an estate's use of the unified credit (applicable credit amount) are correct?

(1) The credit is a maximum of $5.43 million in 2015.
(2) If the maximum unified credit was used against lifetime gifts, no credit will be subtracted from the tentative estate tax.
(3) The credit available to an estate is reduced by the amount of credit applied to taxable lifetime gifts.
(4) The unified credit can be preserved for use by the estate by electing not to use it against gift tax liability.
(5) If an individual does not use the unified credit, it cannot be transferred to children for their use.

    A. (1) and (3)
    B. (3) and (5)
    C. (2) and (4)
    D. (2) and (5)

Answer:
The maximum unified credit for an estate in 2015 is $2,117,800. It can be used to offset the estate tax where the decedent did not use the credit against lifetime gifts. If the unified credit was exhausted by lifetime gifts, the adjusted taxable gifts will be added back to the estate, and additional credit can be subtracted from the tentative estate tax. The unified credit must be used against lifetime taxable gifts. Use of the unified credit is not optional. It cannot be preserved for use by the estate by electing not to use it against gift tax liability. If an individual does not use the unified credit, it can only be transferred to the surviving spouse.
The answer is B.

Credit for Tax on Prior Transfers – Sec. 2013

If property has been subject to tax in an estate within 10 years before or two years after the decedent's death, a credit for tax on prior transfers is available. The credit is reduced 20% for each 2 years the transferor's death preceded the decedent's death, up to 10 years. The credit is also limited to the smaller of: (1) the amount of the federal estate tax attributable to the transferred property in the transferor's estate, or (2) the amount of federal estate tax attributable to the transferred property in the decedent's estate.

If a gift is brought back into a decedent's estate, such as for a retained interest, the gift taxes paid are a credit against the tentative estate tax.

The Cost of Non-Compliance

While the federal estate tax ultimately applies to only about 2 of every 1,000 people who die each year, the amount of taxes paid by those who do fall subject to the tax can be quite high.

The federal estate tax return, Form 706, is due, along with payment, 9 months from date of death. The penalty for late filing is 5% per month up to 25% unless reasonable cause is shown. While a 6-month extension to file is available, this does not extend the time for payment. The penalty for late payment is 1/2 of 1% per month up to a maximum of 25%.

When underpayment of estate taxes is attributable to valuation understatements, Section 6662 provides a 20% penalty for the underpayment of estate tax that exceeds $5,000. A valuation understatement occurs when the value of property reported on Form 706 is 65% or less of the actual value of the property.

The penalty will increase to 40% if there is a gross valuation understatement in which any property on the return is valued at 40% or less of the value determined to be correct.

State Death Taxes

While the federal estate tax applies to only about 2% of the population due to the large exemption amount, the impact of state death taxes may apply to a much larger number of estates.

There is no uniformity among the 50 states and District of Columbia regarding death taxes. Some states have no death taxes, some states impose an estate tax, and some states impose an inheritance tax. In 2015, two states (Maryland and New Jersey) collect both estate taxes and inheritance taxes. In 2015, there are 4 states that collect an inheritance tax only, and 13 states and the District of Columbia collect an estate tax only.

Like the federal estate tax, a state estate tax is a tax on the decedent's right to transfer property, and is assessed to the estate regardless of who is named as the beneficiary. Many states have exemption amounts far below the federal exemption level, so while the estate may be below the exemption amount for federal taxes, the state estate tax can be a significant amount.

An inheritance tax is a tax on the beneficiary's right to receive property and the amount of tax is often based on the degree of relationship of the beneficiary. For example, there may be no inheritance tax if the spouse is the beneficiary, a small amount of tax if a child is the beneficiary, and a larger percentage of tax for other beneficiaries.

The differences among the state death taxes can have a significant impact on a client's estate plan and on the amount of taxes that must be paid at death. For clients who spend equal time in multiple states each year, establishing domicile will be of utmost importance. For example, a client with an estate of $5.43 million would pay no estate tax at the federal level in 2015. If the client were a resident of Florida, where there is no state death tax, his total death taxes would be $0. If the same client, however, were a resident of a state that imposes an estate tax, the tax impact could be as high as several hundred thousand dollars.

State death tax laws tend to change frequently. Some states have passed laws that increase the exemption amount part way through the year, and some states are gradually working toward appeal (Tennessee has an estate tax in 2015, but it is repealed starting in 2016, for example), so planners will need to check for updates on a regular basis and work with a qualified estate attorney.

Federal Estate Tax Calculation Summary

The following exhibit summarizes the steps in the calculation of the federal estate tax:

EXHIBIT 59 – 1
Estate Tax Calculation

STEP 1

Add   10 categories of property interests

(1) **Gross Estate**   _____

STEP 2   *Subtract*   (a) Funeral and administration expenses
                              (b) Debts, medical expenses, and taxes
                              (c) Mortgages and liens
                              (d) Casualty and theft losses

(2) **Adjusted Gross Estate**   _____

STEP 3   *Subtract*   (a) State death taxes
                              (b) Marital deduction
                              (c) Charitable deduction

(3) **Taxable Estate**   _____

STEP 4

Add   Adjusted taxable gifts (post-1976)

(4) **Tentative Tax Base**   _____

STEP 5

Multiply   Unified gift and estate tax table rates

(5) **Tentative Tax**   _____

STEP 6

Subtract   Gift taxes payable on post-1976 gifts

(6) **Gross Estate Tax** (before credits)   _____

STEP 7

Subtract   (a) Applicable credit amount (unified credit)
                              (b) Credit for foreign death taxes
                              (c) Credit for gift tax for pre-1977 gifts
                              (d) Credit for tax on prior transfers

(7) **Net Estate Tax**   _____

Application Questions

1. Homer Bard left a will in which he established a $600,000 trust for his children and a $600,000 charitable trust, and the remainder was to pour over into a revocable trust set up by Homer. The revocable trust is to pay income to his wife for life, and at her death, the principal is to be distributed to their children. At his death, Homer left the following assets:

Residence - JT	$200,000
Common stock - H	$250,000
Municipal bonds - H	$150,000
Investment real estate - R	$200,000
Life insurance - H	$500,000
Mutual funds - W	$100,000

JT = Joint tenancy WROS
H = Homer is the owner
W = Homer's wife is the owner
R = Revocable trust holds the title

What is the amount of his gross estate if Homer dies today?

A. $400,000
B. $600,000
C. $700,000
D. $1,200,000
E. $1,300,000

2. George and Judy Collins live in California, where George has his own business as a meeting planner. George bought a whole life policy soon after he was married, insuring his life for $100,000. The policy has a cash value of $22,000, and Judy is the designated beneficiary. The Collins also own the following assets:

Checking account - CP	$ 6,000
Savings account - CP	$ 8,000
Mutual funds - CP	$ 35,000
Common stock portfolio - CP	$ 50,000
Rental property - H	$200,000
Sole proprietorship - CP	$150,000
IRA (George's) - CP	$ 30,000
403(b) plan (Judy's) - CP	$ 80,000
Residence - CP	$200,000
BMW car - CP	$ 40,000
Jewelry - W	$ 30,000

CP = Community property
H = George's separate property
W = Judy's separate property

If George died today, what would be the approximate value of his gross estate?

A. $435,000
B. $505,000
C. $550,000
D. $610,000
E. $720,000

3. Herbert and Wendy Meadows own the following property interests:

Residence - JT	$250,000
Common stock - JT	$100,000
Municipal bonds - JT	$100,000
Investment real estate - H	$100,000
Vacation home - W	$150,000
Life insurance - H	$100,000
401(k) plan assets - H	$250,000
Car - H	$ 40,000
Car - W	$ 30,000

Note that Wendy is the beneficiary of the life insurance death benefit.

JT = Joint tenancy WROS
H = Herbert is the owner
W = Wendy is the owner

What is the amount of his gross estate if Herbert dies today?

A. $450,000
B. $490,000
C. $675,000
D. $715,000
E. $1,070,000

4. Peter Forth, age 65, owns a furniture business valued at $4 million, a commercial real estate investment valued at $700,000, and a $250,000 life insurance policy for which his wife Samantha is the beneficiary. His other assets are as follows:

Common stock - JT	$600,000
Municipal bonds - JT	$200,000
Vacation home - JT	$150,000
Motorboat - H	$ 50,000
Car - H	$ 40,000
Savings account - JT	$ 50,000
Checking account - JT	$ 30,000

JT = Owned in joint tenancy
H = Owned by Peter

Peter's will provides for $700,000 of assets to be placed in a trust that pays income to Samantha for her life and the remainder to his children. The rest of the estate will pass under a residuary clause to Samantha, who is a U.S. citizen.

If Peter dies today and the executor files no special election, what is the amount of the marital deduction for which Peter's estate will qualify?

A. $4,855,000
B. $5,440,000
C. $5,555,000
D. $5,855,000
E. $6,070,000

5. James Kent's gross estate is $3 million, and his assets are titled to a revocable living trust, except for his principal residence, which he owned in tenancy by the entirety with his wife. The residence is valued at $200,000. The revocable trust will pay income to his wife for her life, and she is given a power to appoint any remaining property to their children at her death. James had funeral expenses of $20,000, a mortgage on the residence of $80,000, an outstanding personal loan of $50,000, and a loan that he guaranteed for his brother's business in the amount of $100,000. The brother's business is still making payments on this loan. Estate administration expenses are expected to be $50,000. James' estate paid $10,000 in state death taxes.

What is the amount of the deductions that James Kent's estate will be able to take in computing the taxable estate if James dies today?

A. $230,000
B. $270,000
C. $330,000
D. $370,000
E. $3,000,000

6. Which of the following values will be included in the decedent's gross estate?

(1) A $100,000 life insurance policy was transferred to an irrevocable trust two years before the decedent's death.
(2) A $300,000 life insurance policy was transferred to a revocable trust four years before the decedent's death.
(3) Two years before her death, the decedent gave her daughter $50,000, which was used to buy a $500,000 life insurance policy on the decedent's life.
(4) Two years before her death, the decedent exercised a general power of appointment over trust assets, in which she was the life beneficiary, to make a gift to her children of $50,000.

A. (1) and (2) only
B. (1) and (3) only
C. (2) and (3) only
D. (2) and (4) only
E. (3) and (4) only

7. In 2002, Mary Horter, a widow, made a gift to her daughter of a vacation home valued at $260,000, and she gave $50,000 to a local orphanage. In 2004, she gave $90,000 of securities to her daughter and $40,000 to the Red Cross. In 2005, Mary established an irrevocable trust that was to pay income to Mary for 12 years, and any remaining assets would be paid to her daughter. The assets transferred to the trust were valued at $300,000, and the remainder interest was valued at $60,000. Mary died unexpectedly and left a taxable estate of $4.5 million. The trust assets were valued at Mary's death at $400,000. (**Editor's Note:** the annual gift tax exclusion was $11,000 at the time of these gifts.)

What is the amount that will be added to the taxable estate to compute the tentative tax base for Mary's estate?

    A. $260,000
    B. $328,000
    C. $390,000
    D. $630,000
    E. $730,000

8. At age 65, "X" will receive from his employer $500 per month for ten years. Mrs. "X" is to receive any residual payments if "X" dies before ten years have passed. "X" dies after receiving five payments. Under which of the following circumstances would the death benefit payable to "X's" widow be included in "X's" gross estate for federal estate tax purposes?

    (1) "X" had agreed to forfeit all benefits if he failed to comply with the employer's request for consulting services during the ten years he was to receive benefits.
    (2) "X" made no commitment of any kind as to the services he would perform.
    (3) Prior to his retirement, "X" agreed to accept the greater security provided by a pure life annuity for his benefit payments.

    A. (1) only
    B. (2) only
    C. (1) and (2) only
    D. (1) and (3) only
    E. (1), (2), and (3)

9. (Published question released November, 1994; updated)

A decedent who died this year had made substantial lifetime gifts such that her estate is in the 40% marginal bracket. In her will, she made a bequest of $100,000 to her adult son, with no special arrangements or allocations for the payment of estate taxes. The balance of her estate goes to her husband. How much of this bequest will the son actually receive, assuming there are no other bequests to him from her estate?

A. $60,000 because estate taxes of $40,000 would be charged against the bequest.
B. $65,600 because the $14,000 per beneficiary exclusion reduces the taxable amount.
C. $86,000 because the $14,000 per beneficiary exclusion applies even for adult children.
D. $100,000 because the estate tax will be paid from the residual estate.
E. The amount cannot be determined unless it is known whether a QTIP election was made.

10. (Published question released November, 1994; updated)

Which of the following circumstances would definitely cause the date-of-death value of gifted property to be included in the donor's gross estate?

(1) The donor retains a life estate in the gift property.
(2) The donor retains the power to revoke or amend the gift.
(3) The donor gives more than $14,000 to one donee in one year.
(4) The donor dies within three years of the date of the gift.

A. (1), (2), and (3) only
B. (1) and (2) only
C. (2) and (4) only
D. (3) and (4) only
E. (1), (2), (3), and (4)

11. (Published question released November, 1994)

Jack and Jill Jones, age 65, have decided that in order to best pay their $3,000,000 federal estate tax bill, they will purchase a second-to-die insurance policy. In order to keep the proceeds out of their estate, they were advised to create an irrevocable life insurance trust. Jack and Jill applied for the insurance, and the policy was issued to them. An irrevocable trust was drafted. The policy was transferred into the irrevocable trust, and 90 days later, both Jack and Jill were killed in a plane crash.

The Internal Revenue Service wants to include the insurance in the estate for tax purposes. Which statement is (are) correct?

   (1) The insurance will be included in the estate because the trust was drafted after the insurance was approved.
   (2) The insurance will be included in the estate because the premiums were a gift from the insured.
   (3) The insurance will be included in the estate because the insureds transferred the policy within three years of death.
   (4) The Internal Revenue Service is wrong – the insurance will *not* be included in the estate.

   A. (1), (2), and (3) only
   B. (1) only
   C. (2) and (3) only
   D. (3) only
   E. (4) only

12. (Published question released December, 1996)

Which of the following is a deduction from the gross estate used in calculating the adjusted gross estate?

   A. Costs associated with maintaining the estate assets
   B. Nontaxable gifts made within three years of death
   C. Federal estate tax marital deduction
   D. Property inherited from others

13. (Published question released December, 1996)

Which of the following gifts made two years before the donor's death will be included in the gross estate at the full date-of-death value?

   (1) A gift of $50,000 cash, which is split equally between a son and daughter-in-law
   (2) A gift in which the donor retains an income interest for life
   (3) The donor's residence, transferred into joint tenancy with his daughter
   (4) Stock worth $30,000 that is given to a friend
   (5) A life insurance policy (cash value of $5,000) that is transferred by the deceased to an irrevocable trust

   A. (1), (2), and (3) only
   B. (1) and (4) only
   C. (1), (2), and (5) only
   D. (3), (4), and (5) only
   E. (2), (3), and (5) only

14. (Published questions released December, 1996, updated)

Jack, who had never married, died last year. Two years before his death, he paid gift tax of $15,000 as a result of making the following gifts (these were the only gifts he made that year, and the annual gift tax exclusion was $12,000):

- Stock worth $40,000 to Mickey
- A $300,000 (proceeds value) life insurance policy on his life to Molly (The policy was worth $5,000 at the time of transfer.)

At Jack's death, the stock had increased in value to $70,000, and the life insurance company paid the $300,000 to Molly.

How much will Jack's gross estate be increased as a result of the two gifts he made?

A. $15,000
B. $60,000
C. $315,000
D. $355,000

Use the information given in Question 14 to answer the next two questions:

15. Jack's adjusted taxable gifts will be:

A. $0
B. $28,000
C. $40,000
D. $370,000

16. If the two gifts had been made four years before Jack's death, by how much would his gross estate have been increased?

A. $0
B. $15,000
C. $30,000
D. $300,000

17. Michelle died this year with $3 million of stock in a large publicly traded company and $500,000 in cash. Michelle bought the stock 6 years ago for $1 million. Michelle's will provides that her daughter Melinda inherits the stock at her death. What will be Melinda's basis?

A. $1,000,000
B. $1,300,000
C. $2,300,000
D. $3,000,000

18. Jason died this year with $4 million of stock in a closely held family business. Jason inherited the stock from his mother 10 years ago. The stock was worth $3 million at the time his mother died. His mother's basis was $2 million. Jason's will provides that his wife Amy will inherit this asset. What would be Amy's basis in the asset?

    A. $3,000,000
    B. $3,300,000
    C. $4,000,000
    D. $7,300,000

19. Owen bought his California home at the peak of the real estate market for $2 million. At the time of his death this year, the value of the home was $1.5 million. Owen left the home to his daughter Lisa who lives in Tennessee. If Lisa waits four years for the housing market to recover and is able to sell the home for $2.25 million, what is the amount of her gain?

    A. $0
    B. $250,000
    C. $500,000
    D. $750,000

20. Mario and Carrie live in a community-property state. They bought their home for $800,000 in 1998. Carrie died during this year when their home was worth $2 million. Carrie's will provides that all of her assets pass to Mario. What will be Mario's basis?

    A. $800,000
    B. $1,000,000
    C. $1,400,000
    D. $2,000,000

21. Mike and Beth live in a common law state. They bought their home for $800,000 in 1998. Mike died during this year when their home was worth $2 million. Mike's will provides that all of his assets pass to Beth. What will be Beth's basis?

    A. $800,000
    B. $1,000,000
    C. $1,400,000
    D. $2,000,000

22. Which of the following statements concerning estimation of the size of a client's estate is (are) correct?

    (1) An individual's estate consists of his or her real estate and interests in real property only.
    (2) The gross estate includes all property owned by a person at the time of death, except property held in joint names.
    (3) The gross estate is defined by the federal estate tax laws and consists of all property interests owned by the decedent, including life insurance death benefits paid to a named beneficiary.
    (4) The probate estate includes all property owned by the decedent, including property held in joint tenancy.

    A. (1) only
    B. (3) only
    C. (3) and (4) only
    D. (1), (2), and (4) only
    E. (1), (2), (3), and (4)

23. All the following statements concerning property includible in a decedent's gross estate are correct, EXCEPT:

A. Dividends on corporate stock owned by the decedent will be includible in his or her gross estate only if he or she was alive on the date the dividends were paid.

B. Property transferred to a revocable trust four years before death will be includible in the deceased's gross estate.

C. The decedent's estate includes all property that he or she was entitled to receive at the time of death.

D. Gift taxes paid on a lifetime gift made two years prior to death are includible in the deceased's gross estate.

E. Even minor household items like old furniture are includible in the gross estate.

24. All the following items will be included in "M's" gross estate at his death, EXCEPT:

A. Municipal bonds exempt from federal income taxes

B. One-half the value of the residence he owns in joint tenancy with Mrs. "M"

C. The right to the income for his lifetime, derived from a Kansas wheat farm willed to "M" by his father

D. A general power of appointment over trust property

E. A $100,000 life insurance policy owned by "M" and payable to his wife under a lump-sum settlement arrangement

25. Knowing death was imminent, "X," a widower, gave $5,000 to each of his four children only a few months before his death. What dollar value would be included in "X's" gross estate for these gifts made in contemplation of death?

A. Zero
B. $5,000
C. $7,000
D. $13,000
E. $20,000

26. "R" purchased a twenty-payment whole life policy over 20 years ago, designating Mrs. "R" as the lump-sum revocable beneficiary. Under which of the following circumstances will the policy proceeds be included in "R's" gross estate at his death?

(1) Because of "R's" disability, Mrs. "R" paid all the premiums out of her earned income.

(2) "R" assigned the policy to Mrs. "R" four years prior to death, hoping to reduce his estate taxes.

(3) "R" transferred the policy to a Crummey trust a year before his death, and Mrs. "R" is the income beneficiary of the trust for her lifetime.

A. (1) only
B. (2) only
C. (1) and (3) only
D. (2) and (3) only
E. (1), (2), and (3)

27. "H" gave $30,000 in cash to his son two years ago, a $50,000 life insurance policy to his sister one year ago, and $6,000 in cash to his wife five years ago. He made no other lifetime gifts. "H" died yesterday. Under these circumstances, which of the gifts would be included in "H's" gross estate?

A. $20,000 of the gift to his son
B. The $30,000 gift to his son
C. The life insurance gift to his sister
D. The gift to his son and the life insurance gift to his sister
E. None of the gifts

28. "A" transferred a $100,000 whole life policy on "A's" life to his wife two years before his death. The cash value was $3,000. Which of the following statements is correct?

A. The policy is not includible in "A's" gross estate since the value of the gift did not exceed the annual exclusion.
B. The policy is includible in "A's" gross estate at $100,000 because a gift of a life insurance policy within three years of death is includible at the value of the benefit paid.
C. The policy is includible in "A's" gross estate at $3,000, the amount of the gift.
D. The policy is includible in "A's" gross estate at $3,000 plus the present value of the interest earnings for two years.
E. The policy is not includible in "A's" gross estate because the gift qualified for the marital gift and estate tax deductions.

29. Which of the following statements concerning revocable transfers is correct?

A. If "X" gives up the power to revoke a trust four years before his death, the property will be includible in his gross estate.
B. Powers of revocation must be exercised in order to include the property in the deceased's gross estate.
C. If a decedent had the power to revoke a trust but was mentally incompetent for two years before his death, the trust property would not be included in the decedent's gross estate.
D. If a trustee who was not the grantor has the power to revoke, the trust property will be excluded from the trustee's gross estate.
E. If a person places all of his or her assets in a revocable living trust, the trust assets will escape probate and will not be includible in the gross estate.

30. "X," a widower, made a cash gift to his son of $1,000,000 two years before he died and paid a $350,000 gift tax. What is included in his gross estate?

A. $175,000
B. $350,000
C. $1,000,000
D. $1,350,000
E. Nothing

31. "X" gave his son property valued at $1,000,000 and paid a $350,000 gift tax. "X's" cost basis is $700,000. The value of the property is the same as it was on the date of the gift. Under these circumstances, all the following statements are correct, EXCEPT:

A. If "X" dies six months after the gift, the $350,000 gift tax will be includible in "X's" gross estate.
B. If "X" dies six months after the gift, the $1,000,000 gift will not be included in "X's" gross estate.
C. If "X" was married at the time of the gift, he could have saved tax dollars by gift-splitting.
D. If "X" survives the date of the gift by more than three years, the $350,000 gift tax will still be included in "X's" gross estate.
E. The cost basis for the gift is of no significance in determining what is includible in the donor's gross estate.

32. Which of the following is (are) among the incidents of ownership that will cause inclusion of a life insurance policy in the insured's gross estate if possessed by the insured at the time of death?

(1) The right to change the beneficiary
(2) The right to surrender the policy for its cash value
(3) The right to obtain a policy loan

A. (1) only
B. (2) only
C. (1) and (2) only
D. (2) and (3) only
E. (1), (2), and (3)

33. "R," age 70, placed $100,000 of securities in an irrevocable trust to provide a lifetime income for his sister, age 60. For purely sentimental reasons, "R" provided that the securities were to be returned to him if his sister failed to survive him. As expected, "R" died several years before his sister. Why might the IRS include the value of the securities in "R's" gross estate?

A. Because "R" lived beyond his life expectancy
B. Because "R's" reversionary interest is valued at greater than 5%
C. Because of the present value of the income in respect of a decedent
D. Because "R" had the right to specify who would possess or enjoy the income from the securities
E. Because "R" did not use a revocable living trust

34. "G," age 91, created an irrevocable trust for his daughter and placed income-producing securities in the trust. In which of the following circumstances would the full value of the trust corpus be included in "G's" gross estate at his death?

(1) "G" retained the right to change the trust beneficiary.
(2) "G" retained the right to the trust's income for his lifetime.
(3) "G" selected his own bank to be trustee, but retained no control over the trustee.

A. (1) only
B. (2) only
C. (1) and (2) only
D. (2) and (3) only
E. (1), (2), and (3)

35. By the terms of his will, "K" gave his wife the right to live in their home until her death. "K's" daughter by a former marriage is to have the property upon Mrs. "K's" death. Under these circumstances, which of the following statements is correct?

A. The property will be included in Mrs. "K's" gross estate.
B. The property will be excluded from "K's" gross estate.
C. Mrs. "K" has a contingency interest in the property.
D. Mrs. "K" has a terminable interest in the home.
E. Mrs. "K" has a retained interest in the home.

36. "K" has funded a trust with $300,000 of listed common stocks. "K's" three children are to share equally in the trust income for their lifetimes. Any corpus remaining at the death of the three children is to go to their issue per stirpes. "K" retained the right to terminate the trust at any time. Under these circumstances, which of the following statements is (are) correct?

(1) If "K" should die today, none of the corpus would be included in his gross estate.
(2) If any one of the three children should die today, none of the corpus would be included in his or her gross estate.
(3) "K" may take an annual exclusion for each of the children and their issue.

A. (1) only
B. (2) only
C. (1) and (2) only
D. (2) and (3) only
E. (1), (2), and (3)

37. In her will Mary left an apartment house to her husband Fred in trust, with income payable to Fred for life. The terms of the trust provided that Fred could appoint the property in his will to any of their five children. Under these circumstances, which of the following statements are correct?

(1) Fred has a general power of appointment.
(2) The value of the apartment will be included in Fred's gross estate.
(3) The value of the apartment will not be includible in Fred's gross estate.
(4) If Fred could appoint only according to an ascertainable standard, there would be no change in whether the property would be includible in his gross estate.

A. (1) and (2) only
B. (1) and (3) only
C. (2) and (3) only
D. (2) and (4) only
E. (3) and (4) only

38. Over the last twenty-year period, Mr. and Mrs. "A" bought and paid for their home exclusively out of "A's" earnings. They own the fully paid for home now as joint tenants with right of survivorship. They did not treat Mr. "A's" payments as a gift to Mrs. "A." If $130,000 is the value of the home, which of the following statements is correct? (Assume this is a non-community-property state.)

    A. If Mrs. "A" dies first, $130,000 would be included in her gross estate if it could not be shown that "A" contributed to the purchase price.

    B. If Mr. "A" dies first, only $65,000 would be included in his gross estate.

    C. At the moment of death, Mr. "A" will be considered to have made a taxable gift of $65,000 to Mrs. "A."

    D. Since Mr. "A" paid for the house, its full value will be included in his estate, regardless of who dies first.

    E. If Mrs. "A" dies first, none of the value of the home would be includible in her gross estate.

39. Bill Jones and his brother, both unmarried, purchased an apartment house in joint tenancy with right of survivorship. Bill paid the entire purchase price of $200,000. His brother managed the apartment. At Bill's death, the apartment was valued at $400,000. Under these circumstances, what is includible in Bill's gross estate?

    A. Zero
    B. $100,000
    C. $200,000
    D. $300,000
    E. $400,000

40. In Question 39, if Bill's brother dies first, what is includible in the brother's estate?

    A. Zero
    B. $100,000
    C. $200,000
    D. $300,000
    E. $400,000

41. All the following are deductions from the gross estate in computing the federal estate tax if the taxpayer dies when there is an estate tax, EXCEPT:

    A. The value of real estate located in Mexico but owned by the deceased, who is a U.S. citizen

    B. Funeral expenses

    C. Fees paid by the executor for investment advice

    D. Outright bequests to the spouse

    E. A note representing bank debt

42. It would be possible for an estate owner to die in a year when there is an estate tax and avoid having to pay any estate tax if he or she implemented which of the following?

(1) Left all of his or her property to a qualified charity

(2) Left all of his or her property to his or her spouse

(3) Made annual gifts during the remainder of his or her lifetime that were precisely equal to the gift tax annual exclusion and that, in the aggregate, reduced his or her estate below $5.43 million

(4) Transferred his or her entire estate to a revocable living trust

    A. (1) and (2) only
    B. (1) and (3) only
    C. (2) and (4) only
    D. (1), (2), and (3) only
    E. (1), (2), (3), and (4)

43. Which of the following statements concerning the estate tax charitable deduction is correct?

    A. The deduction is limited to 30% of AGI.
    B. The deduction is limited to 50% of AGI.
    C. The deduction is available for estate tax purposes but not for gift tax purposes.
    D. The amount excluded is a maximum of $1 million (2015).
    E. The deduction amount is unlimited.

44. Which of the following statements concerning "adjusted taxable gifts" is (are) correct?

(1) The dollar amount is added to the determined value of the deceased's taxable estate.

(2) The dollar amount is the value of all gifts the deceased made after 1976, plus any gift taxes paid on those gifts.

(3) The dollar amount is less than it otherwise would be because the annual exclusion may be used for any gifts of present interests made after 1976.

    A. (1) only
    B. (1) and (2) only
    C. (1) and (3) only
    D. (2) and (3) only
    E. (1), (2), and (3)

45. Which of the following are credits to be used against the federal estate tax for all years when there is an estate tax?

(1) Unified credit

(2) Credit for tax on prior transfers

(3) Credit for gift taxes

(4) Foreign estate tax credit

    A. (1) and (2) only
    B. (2) and (3) only
    C. (1), (2), and (3) only
    D. (2), (3), and (4) only
    E. (1), (2), (3), and (4)

46. "S" has a gross estate of $1,000,000. His funeral costs are $6,000. He leaves $10,000 to his church and $4,000 to his college. The mortgage balance on the home he owns by entirety with his wife is $100,000. The home is valued at $400,000. He has miscellaneous debts of $5,000. His executor's fee and estate administration expenses are estimated to be $30,000. He leaves $200,000 to his wife. What is the value of his adjusted gross estate?

    A. $200,000
    B. $645,000
    C. $859,000
    D. $895,000
    E. $909,000

47. In Question 46, what is the total amount deductible by using both the marital deduction and the charitable deduction?

    A. $200,000
    B. $214,000
    C. $264,000
    D. $364,000
    E. $909,000

48. In Question 46, what is the dollar value of the taxable estate?

    A. $200,000
    B. $214,000
    C. $264,000
    D. $545,000
    E. $909,000

49. In Question 46, assume that "S's" executor determines the value of "S's" adjusted taxable gifts to equal $80,000. What is the tentative tax base for "S's" estate?

    A. $465,000
    B. $545,000
    C. $625,000
    D. $989,000
    E. $1,080,000

50. When an individual dies, which of the following statements concerning the filing of the federal estate tax return is (are) correct?

(1) The federal estate tax return is due nine months after the decedent's date of death.
(2) The executor is personally liable for the federal estate tax.
(3) If there is no executor for the estate, persons in possession of the decedent's property must file an estate tax return.

    A. (1) only
    B. (2) only
    C. (1) and (3) only
    D. (2) and (3) only
    E. (1), (2), and (3)

51. Which of the following estates for a decedent who dies in 2015 must the executor file a federal estate tax return?

(1) The gross estate is valued at $6,250,000.
(2) The decedent made adjusted taxable gifts during the years 2005 through 2009 of $1,500,000, and the gross estate is valued at $4.5 million.
(3) The gross estate is valued at $3,750,000.
(4) The decedent transferred his entire estate, consisting of assets valued at $7 million, to a revocable living trust.

A. (1) only
B. (2) only
C. (1) and (2) only
D. (1), (2), and (4) only
E. (1), (2), (3), and (4)

52. At the time of George Jansen's death, he and his wife Phoebe owned their home as tenants by the entirety. The home was valued at $400,000. Phoebe owned a life insurance policy that she purchased on George's life and for which she paid the premiums. The policy paid her a $100,000 death benefit. George owned a policy on his life that paid Phoebe $100,000, as well. George also owned a small duplex with his son in joint tenancy WROS. George bought the duplex for $100,000 and contributed all of the purchase price. The duplex was valued at the date of his death at $150,000. Based on these facts, what is the value of George Jansen's gross estate?

A. $250,000
B. $450,000
C. $550,000
D. $700,000
E. $750,000

53. All the following statements concerning gift and estate taxes are correct, EXCEPT:

A. The gift tax is 75% of the estate tax.
B. There is a single unified tax rate schedule that can be applied to "lifetime" and "deathtime" gifts.
C. Gift taxes and estate taxes can be levied on the same property.
D. Generally, the estate tax imposed at death is found by adding to the taxable estate any taxable gifts made during one's lifetime.

54. All the following statements concerning allowable charitable deductions from estates at death are correct, EXCEPT:

A. The deduction is allowable if the contribution is made in accordance with the terms of a life insurance policy.
B. The deduction is only allowable if the contribution is made by the executor.
C. The deduction is allowable if the contribution is made in accordance with the terms of a will.
D. The deduction is allowable if the contribution is includible in the decedent's gross estate but was actually made by the decedent prior to death.
E. The deduction is allowable if the contribution is made to a qualified public charity.

55. Very often, a major objective in the establishment of a living trust is the removal of property from the grantor's estate. In establishing the trust agreement, care must be taken to avoid retention of powers which would defeat accomplishment of the objective. Which of the following powers will result in the trust assets being included in the grantor's gross estate?

    A. Retention of a general power of appointment
    B. Retention of the right to use trust income for the benefit of a dependent minor, provided that the grantor does not do so
    C. Retention of a right to change the amount of income that will pass to a beneficiary
    D. Retention of a life interest in the trust
    E. All of the above

56. Which of the following are among the exceptions to the general rule that property given within three years of death is excluded from the donor's gross estate for federal estate tax purposes?

    (1) Life insurance
    (2) Gift taxes paid on the value of a gift
    (3) Farmland gifted to a son or daughter
    (4) A gift of securities in trust with a retained life income

    A. (1) and (2) only
    B. (2) and (3) only
    C. (3) and (4) only
    D. (1), (2), and (3) only
    E. (1), (2), and (4) only

57. Which of the following statements concerning the "gross-up" rule is (are) correct?

    (1) Income taxes paid in the year of death are includible in the deceased's gross estate.
    (2) Gift taxes paid in the year of death are included in the deceased's gross estate.
    (3) Life insurance given in the year prior to the year of death is excluded from the deceased's gross estate.

    A. (1) only
    B. (2) only
    C. (1) and (2) only
    D. (2) and (3) only
    E. (1), (2), and (3)

58. Which of the following items would be included in a decedent's gross estate for federal estate tax purposes?

    (1) A gift of life insurance made four years before the decedent's death
    (2) Gift taxes paid for a gift of securities made two years before the decedent's death
    (3) A gift of life insurance made two years before the decedent's death

    A. (1) only
    B. (3) only
    C. (1) and (2) only
    D. (2) and (3) only
    E. (1), (2), and (3)

59. "D" and "E," a married couple, make a gift of their vacation home to their children but reserve the right to use the property during their lifetimes. Under these circumstances, which of the following statements is (are) correct?

(1) The property will be included in the donors' gross estates at their deaths.
(2) The gift tax annual exclusion is not available to "D" and "E."
(3) The unified tax credit is available to "D" and "E."

    A. (1) only
    B. (1) and (2) only
    C. (1) and (3) only
    D. (2) and (3) only
    E. (1), (2), and (3)

60. All the following statements concerning the estate and gift tax consequences of a lifetime gift of securities made to an individual (noncharitable) are correct, EXCEPT:

A. After the gift is made, the future appreciation of the value of the asset will not be subject to the gift or estate tax.

B. To the extent the fair market value of the securities on the date of the transfer exceeds the annual exclusion, the transfer is a taxable gift that will be offset by the donor's unified credit.

C. A lifetime gift in excess of the annual exclusion is a taxable gift that will be taken into account as an adjusted taxable gift in calculating estate taxes.

D. A lifetime gift is includible in the donor's gross estate for federal estate tax purposes if the gift was made within three years of the donor's death.

E. Dividends and interest paid by the securities after the date of the gift will be taxable income to the individual receiving the gift and not to the donor.

61. Which of the following rights retained by a donor who gifts property during his or her lifetime will result in the inclusion of such property in the gross estate of the donor-decedent?

(1) The right to the property's income for the donor's lifetime
(2) The right to revoke the transfer in case of financial need
(3) The right to a reversionary interest where the probability of reversion is less than 5%
(4) The right to trust income for the donor's support and maintenance

A. (1) only
B. (1) and (2) only
C. (2) and (3) only
D. (3) and (4) only
E. (1), (2), and (4) only

62. Which of the following statements concerning a property's step-up in basis are correct?

(1) No step-up occurs for property passing to a surviving spouse who was a joint tenant WROS.
(2) A partial step-up occurs at death for property held as tenants in common.
(3) No step-up occurs for property transferred by deed before death.
(4) No step-up occurs when property is obtained by inheritance.

A. (1) and (2) only
B. (1) and (4) only
C. (2) and (3) only
D. (2) and (4) only
E. (3) and (4) only

63. All the following statements concerning the marital and charitable deductions are correct, EXCEPT:

A. The marital deduction permits a taxpayer to leave an entire estate to a spouse tax-free.
B. A taxpayer may make tax-free lifetime gifts up to a maximum of $5.43 million to a spouse or a charity.
C. At death, a taxpayer may leave any size estate or any portion of an estate to a qualified charity, free of federal estate taxes.
D. The charitable deduction is available under both the gift tax and estate tax rules.
E. The marital deduction is available under both the gift tax and estate tax rules.

64. All the following statements describe characteristics of the estate and gift tax system, EXCEPT:

A. The exemption equivalent may be used by a donor or by the estate.
B. The annual exclusion may be used by a donor or by the estate.
C. The marital deduction may be used by a donor or by the estate.
D. The tax rate for taxable gifts is the same as the tax rate for taxable estates.
E. A decedent's adjusted taxable gifts are used in the calculation of estate taxes.

65. All the following statements concerning the estate and gift tax system are correct, EXCEPT:

    A. The annual exclusion is cumulative and is available for lifetime gifts or testamentary gifts.

    B. The gift tax exemption amount is $5.43 million this year.

    C. An unlimited charitable deduction is available under both the gift and estate tax rules.

    D. An unlimited marital deduction is available under both the gift and estate tax rules.

66. All of the following statements concerning the system of estate and gift taxation are correct, EXCEPT:

    A. Lifetime gifts are taxed at a flat rate of 45% in 2015.

    B. A taxpayer can make lifetime taxable gifts of up to $5.43 million without incurring gift taxes.

    C. An estate of $200 million can pass tax-free to the decedent's spouse.

    D. Annual exclusion gifts are not added to the taxable estate as an adjusted taxable gift in computing the estate tax.

67. Which of the following statements concerning differences between the estate and gift tax rules is (are) correct?

    (1) Gift-splitting is permitted with lifetime gifts, but not with testamentary bequests.

    (2) The annual exclusion is available to reduce taxable lifetime gifts, but not with testamentary bequests.

    (3) The estate tax is tax-exclusive, while the gift tax is tax-inclusive.

    A. (1) only
    B. (1) and (2) only
    C. (1) and (3) only
    D. (2) and (3) only
    E. (1), (2), and (3)

68. Alan died during 2015 with $2 million of stock in a large publicly traded company and $1 million in cash. Alan bought the stock 6 years ago for $500,000. Alan's will provides that his son Barry inherits the stock at his death. What will be Barry's basis in the stock?

    A. $500,000
    B. $1,300,000
    C. $1,800,000
    D. $2,000,000

69. Carly died during this year with $5 million of stock in a closely held family business. Carly inherited the stock from her mother 10 years ago. The stock was worth $1 million at the time her mother died. Her mother's basis was $500,000. Carly's will provides that her husband David will inherit this asset. What would be David's basis in the asset?

    A. $4,000,000
    B. $4,800,000
    C. $5,000,000
    D. $5,300,000

70. Eric bought his California home at the peak of the real estate market for $1 million. At the time of his death this year, the value of the home was $750,000. Eric left the home to his daughter Emily who lives in South Carolina. If Emily waits four years for the housing market to recover and is able to sell the home for $1.1 million, what is the amount of her gain?

    A. $0
    B. $100,000
    C. $250,000
    D. $350,000

71. Frank and Gina live in a community property state. They bought their home for $600,000 in 1990. Gina died this year when their home was worth $1.4 million. Gina's will provides that all of her assets pass to Frank. What will be Frank's basis in the home?

    A. $600,000
    B. $1,000,000
    C. $1,300,000
    D. $1,400,000

72. Henry and Jennifer live in a common law state. They bought their home for $600,000 in 1990. Henry died this year when their home was worth $1.4 million. Henry's will provides that all of his assets pass to Jennifer. What will be Jennifer's basis in the home?

    A. $700,000
    B. $1,000,000
    C. $1,300,000
    D. $1,400,000

For practice answering case questions related to Topic 59, please answer the following questions in the cases included in the Appendix at the back of this textbook.

Case	Questions
Bartlett	8, 9, 10, and 11
Marshall	6 and 7
Webster	9, 10, and 11
Unser	3 and 4
Tingey	
Lytle	
Beals	2 and 3
Mocsin	
Young	3
Borelli	8, 9, 10, 11, and 12
Cunningham	12 and 13
Fred and Mary Ferris	31, 32, 33, 34, and 35

Answers and Explanations

1. D is the answer. The gross estate will include one-half of the value of the residence which is held in joint tenancy by spouses. The gross estate will also include the entire value of the assets individually owned by Homer. These assets are the common stock and municipal bonds. Since Homer owned the life insurance, the proceeds of the policy are included in his gross estate. The investment real estate is held by a revocable trust, so it is included in Homer's gross estate by reason of the retained power to revoke the trust. The mutual funds owned by Homer's wife are not included in Homer's gross estate. Note that the provisions of Homer's will do not have any effect on the gross estate.

2. C is the answer. The gross estate will include one-half of the community property and all of George's separate property. George's gross estate will include the following values:

Life insurance	$ 50,000
Checking account	$ 3,000
Savings account	$ 4,000
Mutual funds	$ 17,500
Common stock portfolio	$ 25,000
Rental property	$200,000
Sole proprietorship	$ 75,000
IRA (George's)	$ 15,000
403(b) plan (Judy's)	$ 40,000
Residence	$100,000
BMW car	$ 20,000
Total	$549,500

3. D is the answer. The gross estate will include one-half of the property that Herbert owns jointly with Wendy and all of the property that Herbert owns individually. All of the life insurance will be included in Herbert's gross estate. The total is as follows:

Residence - JT	$125,000
Common stock - JT	$ 50,000
Municipal bonds - JT	$ 50,000
Investment real estate - H	$100,000
Life insurance - H	$100,000
401(k) plan assets - H	$250,000
Car - H	$ 40,000
Total	$715,000

4. A is the answer. One-half of the jointly owned property is included in the gross estate and will pass by operation of law to Peter's spouse, so it qualifies for the marital deduction. The life insurance will be paid to Peter's wife and will qualify for the marital deduction. All of the individually-owned assets, including the $4 million business interest, the $700,000 real estate investment, the car, and the boat will be included in Peter's gross estate and will pass under the residuary clause to Peter's wife Samantha, except for the $700,000 going to the trust. The

$700,000 of assets passing to the trust set up under the will do not qualify for the marital deduction because Samantha is given only a life interest, which is a terminable interest. The total marital deduction, therefore, is $4,855,000. The total is as follows:

Furniture business	$4,000,000
Real estate	$700,000
Life insurance	$250,000
Common stock	$300,000
Muni bonds	$100,000
Vacation home	$75,000
Motorboat	$50,000
Car	$40,000
Savings account	$25,000
Checking	$15,000
Total	$5,555,000
Less amount going to trust	($700,000)
Total	$4,855,000

5. A is the answer. The estate will be able to take a deduction for the funeral expenses ($20,000), one-half of the mortgage on the residence ($40,000), the personal loan ($50,000), administration expenses of $50,000, and the $10,000 in state death taxes. The loan guarantee is not deductible because the estate has not been required to make payments. One-half of the residence is included in the gross estate and passes by operation of law to James Kent's wife, so it qualifies for the marital deduction. However, the mortgage on the residence has already reduced the value of this interest, so the additional deduction for the interest passing to James Kent's wife will be reduced to $60,000. The assets in the revocable trust will not be subject to a general power of appointment because James Kent's wife has only a limited power at death to appoint the assets to their children. Thus, these assets in the trust do not qualify for the marital deduction. The total amount of deductions is $230,000.

6. A is the answer. The three-year rule applies to transfers of life insurance policies, so the policy transferred to an irrevocable trust within three years of death will be included in the gross estate. The life insurance in the revocable trust will be included in the gross estate, regardless of when it was transferred to the trust because the decedent retained a right to revoke the transfer. The gift of $50,000 to the decedent's daughter is not included in the gross estate because outright gifts are not subject to the three-year rule. The donee was free to use the money to buy insurance or any other investment. The exercise of the general power of appointment is also not subject to the three-year rule, so this gift is not included.

7. B is the answer. The adjusted taxable gifts must be added to the taxable estate in calculating the tentative tax base. The adjusted taxable gifts are reduced by the amount of the $11,000 annual exclusion and by the marital and charitable deductions. There are no reductions for the marital deduction since Mary was a widow. The taxable gifts are $249,000 in 2002, and $79,000 in 2004, for a total of $328,000. The assets transferred to the trust will be included in Mary's gross estate because she retained an income interest that had not ended when she died. Since it is already included in the gross estate, this gift will not be added as an adjusted taxable gift.

8. C is the answer. The death benefit payable to Mrs. "X" would be includible in "X's" gross estate under the circumstances of both (1) and (2). Since there is an agreement to pay the $500 a month, it makes no difference whether "X" had a forfeitable or a nonforfeitable right to the $500 a month at the time of his death. (3) provides Mrs. "X" with no residual benefit after "X's" death. A pure life annuity results in the termination of benefits at "X's" death.

9. A is the answer. In the absence of a will provision allocating the payment of estate taxes, each bequest will generally bear its own portion of the estate taxes. Since the decedent made no allocation in her will for the estate taxes, the bequest to her son will be subject to taxes at the same rate as the estate. If 40% of the estate is paid in taxes, the bequest will be reduced by 40%. The son will then receive only $60,000 of the $100,000 bequest. Annual exclusions only apply to gift tax transfers and not to estate tax transfers.

10. B is the answer. If the donor retains a life estate in the gift property, the value of the property is includible in the gross estate under Code Sec. 2036. If the donor retains the power to revoke or amend the gift, it is a revocable transfer, includible under Code Sec. 2038. A completed gift made during the donor's lifetime is not includible in the gross estate even if it is valued at more than $14,000 and even if it is given within three years of death.

11. D is the answer. The life insurance policy will be included in at least one of the estates because the life insurance was transferred within three years of death. This question demonstrates the advisability of having a trust apply for and purchase life insurance. If the trust had always owned the policy, the three-year rule would not have come into play. The policy would not have been included in either estate if the trust had applied for and obtained the policy and then paid the premiums. The trust would have been the only owner of the policy. Even though life insurance premiums are a gift from an insured to a trust, the trust is the owner of the policy, so the policy cannot be included in the insured's estate. Note that this fact situation also presents the need for a simultaneous-death clause in wills. Many states have statutes dealing with simultaneous deaths, but it is advisable to have clients deal with it in their wills.

12. A is the answer. The adjusted gross estate is calculated by subtracting from the gross estate the deductions for: (1) funeral expenses, (2) estate administration expenses, (3) debts, and (4) casualty and theft losses. The costs associated with maintaining the estate assets are estate administration expenses. The federal estate tax marital deduction is subtracted from the adjusted gross estate in calculating the taxable estate. There is a credit against the tentative tax for any estate tax paid on property inherited from others within the past ten years.

13. E is the answer. The completed gift of $50,000 to both the donor's son and daughter-in-law will not be included in the donor's gross estate. The stock worth $30,000 given to a friend is similarly a completed gift and will not be includible. A gift in which the donor retains a life income interest will be includible because the gross estate includes any retained life interests. The residence is includible because the donor contributed the entire cost of the property. For a joint tenancy with a person who is not a spouse, the contributions of the parties determine how much will be includible. The death proceeds of a life insurance policy transferred within 3 years of death will be includible in the gross estate.

14. C is the answer. Since the life insurance policy was given away within three years of death, the policy proceeds of $300,000 will be includible in Jack's gross estate. Under the gross-up rule, the gift taxes paid within three years of death are also includible in the gross estate, so the $15,000 that Jack paid in gift taxes will be includible. The completed gift of the stock will not be included in Jack's gross estate. The total is $315,000.

15. B is the answer. Since the policy proceeds are includible in Jack's gross estate, the policy is not an adjusted taxable gift. The only adjusted taxable gift is the gift of stock. The gift value is $40,000, and this amount is reduced for the $12,000 annual exclusion in effect at the time, so the adjusted taxable gift will be $28,000.

16. A is the answer. If the stock and the life insurance policy had been given away four years before death, the gift tax paid and the policy proceeds would not have been includible in the gross estate. The three-year limit applies to the life insurance and to the gift tax under the gross-up rule. Neither of these gifts would have been brought back into the gross estate.

17. D is the answer. Michelle's basis will be equal to the $3 million fair market value at date of death.

18. C is the answer. Amy's basis will be equal to the $4 million fair market value at date of death.

19. D is the answer. Lisa's basis will be the $1.5 million fair market value at death which means her gain will be $750,000. Unlike assets that have declined in value at the time of the gift, the estate tax basis rules do not allow the heir to use the higher carryover basis if the asset is ultimately sold for a gain. The inherited asset basis will be stepped down to fair market value at date of death.

20. D is the answer. Since Mario and Carrie live in a community-property state, it is possible to step-up the entire property to fair market value at death.

21. C is the answer. Since Mike and Beth live in a common law property state, the executor can only step-up Mike's portion of the property. This $1,000,000 of basis is then added to Beth $400,000 of basis for a total basis of $1,400,000.

22. B is the answer. An individual's estate consists of all property interests, including real and personal property. The gross estate is defined by the federal estate tax laws and includes joint tenancy property and life insurance death benefits paid on a policy owned by the decedent. The probate estate includes all property owned by the decedent at the time of death that passes by will. Thus, the probate estate does not include joint tenancy property or life insurance death benefits.

23. A is the answer. Dividends will be included in a decedent's gross estate if the dividends were declared before the date of death, even if the dividends were unpaid. Property transferred to a revocable trust is included in the gross estate because the grantor retains a right to alter, amend, or revoke the trust and the gift. Gift taxes paid within three years of death are included in the gross estate under the "gross-up" rule.

24. C is the answer. A decedent's gross estate does not include the value of property in which the decedent received only a life estate. The right to income for life from a property is a life estate and is not includible in the gross estate. The gross estate will include trust property over which the decedent had a general power of appointment and one-half of the property held in joint tenancy by spouses.

25. A is the answer. Generally, gifts made in contemplation of death are not included in the gross estate. Moreover, the annual exclusion would apply to gifts of less than $14,000 per donee.

26. C is the answer. In (1), "R" has retained the incidents of ownership in the life insurance policy, so the policy proceeds will be included in his gross estate, even though Mrs. "R" paid the premiums. In (2), "R" assigned the policy to Mrs. "R" and gave up all incidents of ownership more than three years before his death, so the policy proceeds will not be includible in his gross estate. In (3), the incidents of ownership were given up less than three years before death, so the policy proceeds will be includible in "R's" gross estate.

27. C is the answer. The general rule is that gifts made within three years of death are not included in the gross estate. One exception is for life insurance policies. Thus, the life insurance policy given to the sister would be includible in "H's" gross estate.

28. B is the answer. A gift of a life insurance policy within three years of death is included in the decedent's gross estate at the value of the death benefit. Assets that qualify for the estate tax marital deduction are still includible in the gross estate.

29. D is the answer. A revocable transfer will be included in the transferor's gross estate, but when a trustee who was not the transferor is given a power to terminate the trust, the trust assets are not includible in the trustee's gross estate. A power of revocation need not be exercised to have the property included in the transferor's gross estate, and the transferor need not have the capacity to exercise the power at the time of death. A power of revocation released within three years of death will not prevent inclusion of the asset in the gross estate. Assets placed in a revocable living trust will escape probate, but they are includible in the grantor's gross estate.

30. B is the answer. Under the gross-up rule, gift taxes paid within three years of death are included in the decedent's gross estate. The gift itself is not includible, but the gift tax is includible.

31. D is the answer. If a donor survives three years after making a taxable gift, the gift tax will not be includible in the gross estate; within three years, the gift tax is includible in the gross estate.

32. E is the answer. If any of these three incidents of ownership are possessed by an insured at the time of death, the policy proceeds will be includible in the gross estate.

33. B is the answer. The trust provision that the securities would return to "R" in the event his sister predeceased him is a reversionary interest. If the reversionary interest is actuarially valued in excess of 5% at "R's" death, the entire $100,000 of securities will be included in "R's" estate.

34. C is the answer. In (1) and (2), "G" has retained interests that require the full value of the trust corpus to be included in "G's" gross estate. The right to determine who will enjoy the property and the right to receive income are retained interests that require the full value to be included. The selection of a trustee is not a retained interest.

35. D is the answer. "K" has bequeathed a life estate in the home to Mrs. "K," so Mrs. "K's" interest terminates at her death. The home will be included in "K's" gross estate, but not in Mrs. "K's" gross estate.

36. B is the answer. "K" has retained a power to revoke the trust, so the entire value of the trust would be includible in his gross estate. Each of the children received only a life interest under the trust, so none of the trust assets would be includible in the children's gross estates. No annual exclusions are available because the gift is revocable. Moreover, the children's issue have only a future interest, so no annual exclusion would be available for them, either.

37. E is the answer. Fred was given a limited power of appointment because he could appoint the property only to the five children and not to himself, his estate, his creditors, or his estate's creditors. The value of the apartment will not be included in his gross estate because Fred does not have a general power of appointment.

38. B is the answer. One-half of the value of property owned jointly by spouses is included in the gross estate of the first to die. This rule also applies to property acquired out of only one spouse's earnings.

39. E is the answer. With noncharitable joint tenants with right of survivorship, the entire value of the jointly owned property is included in the gross estate of the first decedent unless the surviving joint tenants can prove their financial contribution to the purchase. In this case, Bill paid the purchase price, so the entire value of the building at his death is included in his gross estate.

40. A is the answer. If Bill can establish that he paid the entire purchase price, none of the value of the apartment building is includible in his brother's estate.

41. A is the answer. Funeral and administrative expenses, debts, and casualty losses are deductible from the gross estate in arriving at the adjusted gross estate. The amount of bequests to a spouse is deductible in computing the taxable estate. There is no deduction for assets located outside the U.S.

42. D is the answer. If all of a decedent's property was bequeathed to a spouse or charity, the marital and charitable deductions reduce the gross estate to zero. In 2015, a decedent can transfer the exemption equivalent of $5.43 million tax-free. Property transferred to a revocable trust is includible in the decedent's gross estate and does not avoid estate tax.

43. E is the answer. AGI limits apply to the income charitable deduction. The estate and gift tax charitable deduction is unlimited.

44. C is the answer. Adjusted taxable gifts include neither the amount of the gift taxes paid nor the amount of the annual exclusion used by a decedent.

45. E is the answer. All of these credits reduce the estate tax on a dollar-for-dollar basis.

46. E is the answer.

Gross estate	$1,000,000
Less funeral costs	6,000
Less administrative costs	30,000
Less debts (one-half of mortgage and miscellaneous debts)	55,000
Adjusted gross estate	$909,000

47. D is the answer. The marital deduction will include one-half of the home owned as tenants by the entirety. Since the interest passing to "S's" wife is reduced by one-half of the mortgage, the value of the interest is reduced by $50,000, to only $150,000. The bequest of $200,000 will also qualify for the marital deduction. The charitable deduction will include the $10,000 bequest to the church and the $4,000 bequest to the decedent's college. The total is $364,000.

48. D is the answer.

Adjusted gross estate	$909,000
Less marital deduction	350,000
Less charitable deduction	14,000
Taxable estate	$545,000

49. C is the answer.

Taxable estate	$545,000
Plus adjusted taxable gifts	80,000
Tentative tax base	$625,000

50. E is the answer. The federal estate tax return is due nine months after the decedent's date of death. The executor is personally liable for the federal estate tax. If there is no executor for the estate, persons in possession of the decedent's property must file an estate tax return.

51. D is the answer. A federal estate tax return for a decedent dying in 2015 must be filed if the decedent's gross estate is more than $5.43 million or if the adjusted taxable gifts made by the decedent after 1976, plus the gross estate, total more than $5.43 million. Assets held by a revocable trust will be includible in the gross estate, so a federal estate tax return must be filed for a decedent who transferred an estate of $7 million to a revocable trust.

52. B is the answer. The gross estate includes the death proceeds from life insurance policies owned by the decedent at the time of death, but not policies on the decedent's life owned by others. Thus, the proceeds from the policy owned by Phoebe are not included. One-half of the value of the home owned by the spouses as tenants by the entirety is includible in George's gross estate, and all of the value of the duplex owned jointly with his son is includible because George contributed all of the purchase price. The duplex is includible at the date-of-death value. The gross estate, therefore, is $450,000.

53. A is the answer. Under the estate and gift tax system, the same tax rates are used for computing estate taxes and gift taxes. The same property may be subject to both estate tax and gift tax when a donor makes a gift and retains a life interest.

54. B is the answer. A charitable contribution made from an estate at death constitutes a qualifying deduction from the estate assets if made in accordance with the decedent's directions. It does not matter whether the contribution is in the form of a life insurance policy, a testamentary bequest, or a gift from the estate, so long as it was made or directed to be made by the decedent and not some other party, such as a beneficiary or a trustee acting on his or her own initiative.

55. E is the answer. Most powers retained by a grantor will result in the assets of the trust being included in the grantor's gross estate. The powers that can be retained for income tax purposes are not the same powers that can be retained for estate tax purposes. For example, retention of the power to use trust income for the benefit of a dependent minor will result in the assets being included in the grantor's gross estate for federal estate tax purposes, even if the grantor did not exercise the right. For income tax purposes, retention of the same power will not result in the trust income being included in gross income.

56. E is the answer. Farmland gifted prior to death is excluded from the deceased's gross estate. Life insurance and gift taxes are both included in the gross estate when the gift takes place within three years of death. A gift of a retained life estate is also an exception.

57. B is the answer. (2) is the substance and essence of the "gross-up" rule, except that gift taxes for gifts made within three years before death are also includible in the gross estate. (1) and (3) are not correct statements and, obviously, have nothing to do with the gross-up rule.

58. D is the answer. The gift in (1) would be excluded from the decedent's gross estate because the gift of the life insurance was made more than three years prior to death. The gift in (2) would be included in the decedent's gross estate because the decedent made the gift less than three years ago. The gift in (3) would be included in the decedent's gross estate because three years have not passed since the life insurance was gifted.

59. E is the answer. All three statements are correct. "D" and "E" have retained a life estate, so the entire value of the property will be includible in their gross estates. The gift tax annual exclusion is not available because the gift is of a future interest, not a present interest. The unified credit is available for future interests.

60. D is the answer. A lifetime gift of securities would not be included in the donor's gross estate for federal estate tax purposes even if the gift was made within three years of death. A gift is only includible when made within three years of death if there was a retained interest, a reversionary interest, a life estate, or the gift was of life insurance. Gift taxes on gifts within three years of death are includible under the gross-up rule.

61. E is the answer. (3) does not result in the inclusion of the property in the gross estate of the donor-decedent because the probability of reversion to the donor is less than 5%. Both (1) and (2) are rights which when retained by the donor will result in the inclusion of such property in the gross estate of the donor-decedent. The retention of a life interest, even though subject to an ascertainable standard, is a retained right that makes trust assets includible in the donor's gross estate.

62. C is the answer. For property held in a spousal joint tenancy WROS or as tenants by the entirety, there is a step-up in basis on the one-half interest held by the decedent. A step-up also occurs for the interest of a decedent who held property as a tenant in common. The donee who receives property during the donor's lifetime takes the donor's basis, and there is no step-up at the donor's death. A step-up generally occurs for property inherited from a decedent.

63. B is the answer. The charitable and marital deductions are unlimited, so there is no maximum amount that may be given tax-free to charity or to a spouse. Under the unified tax system, these deductions are available to reduce both estate and gift taxes.

64. B is the answer. The annual exclusion applies only to lifetime gifts and not to testamentary transfers. The other statements are characteristics of the estate and gift tax system.

65. A is the answer. The annual exclusion is available only with respect to lifetime gifts and is not cumulative. If an annual exclusion is not used in any given year, it cannot be used in subsequent years and is not carried over to the estate.

66. A is the answer. Lifetime gifts are taxed on a progress tax table with the highest rate being 40% in the year 2015. A taxpayer can make lifetime taxable gifts up to $5.43 million without incurring gift taxes. An estate of $200 million (or any other size) can pass tax-free to the decedent's spouse due to the unlimited marital deduction. A gift that qualifies for the annual exclusion is not added to the taxable estate as an adjusted taxable gift in computing the estate tax. Only the taxable gifts are added to the taxable estate.

67. B is the answer. Gift-splitting is permitted with lifetime gifts, but not with testamentary bequests. The annual exclusion is available to reduce taxable lifetime gifts, but not testamentary bequests. The estate tax is tax-inclusive, while the gift tax is tax-exclusive.

68. D is the answer. Barry's basis will be $2 million which is the fair market value at the date of death.

69. C is the answer. David's basis will be the $5 million fair market value at the date of death.

70 D is the answer. The estate tax rules limit the basis to the fair market value at the time of death. As a result, Emily's basis will be limited to $750,000 which means her gain will be $350,000. Unlike assets that have declined in value at the time of the gift, the estate tax basis rules do not allow the heir to use the higher carryover basis if the asset is ultimately sold for a gain. The inherited asset basis will be stepped down to fair market value at date of death.

71. D is the answer. Since Frank and Gina live in a community property state, it is possible to step-up the entire property to fair market value at death. As a result, Frank's basis would be $1.4 million.

72. B is the answer. Since Henry and Jennifer live in a common law property state, the basis can only be stepped-up to fair market value at death on Henry's portion of the property. This $700,000 of basis is then added to Jennifer $300,000 of basis for a total basis of $1 million.

Sources for Estate Liquidity (Topic 60)

CFP Board Student-Centered Learning Objectives

(a) Determine the need for estate liquidity.

(b) Develop a cash flow plan for maintaining a client's estate from date of death to final distribution including the payment of tax liabilities.

Sources for Estate Liquidity
   A.   *Sale of assets*
   B.   *Life insurance*
   C.   *Loan*

Estate Liquidity Defined

An estate has adequate liquidity when the executor can convert assets in the estate into cash within the time required to meet the estate's obligations. These obligations include federal estate taxes, state death taxes, income taxes, mortgage debt, and other debts and claims against the deceased.

When a financial planner is reviewing an estate plan, it is important to check whether there will be sufficient liquid assets to pay immediate liabilities. The planner and client should list the obligations that the client's estate will have to pay in a short period of time after the client's death. The assets which can be readily converted into cash should then be listed. Assets which are very liquid are life insurance proceeds, checking and savings accounts, money market funds, CDs, and U.S. government securities. While corporate securities that are listed for trading on exchanges have relatively high liquidity, the stock of closely held corporations and other business interests are often not very liquid. Residential and commercial real estate usually take a period of time to sell and are not very liquid.

Sale of Assets

Following the death of the owner, the sale of assets is often required to provide adequate liquidity. The sacrifice of value required to make a sale in a short period of time is often the most troubling aspect of illiquid estates. Forced liquidation of assets is one of the major causes of estate shrinkage.

Reduction in the value of assets after the owner's death may be a cause of lack of liquidity for an estate. When the decedent is no longer around, the services that built the business assets are no longer provided, and the business assets may become less valuable.

Improving Estate Liquidity

Planning in advance of the owner's death is obviously important for improving the estate's liquidity. Estate liquidity is improved by any action that will reduce estate taxes or probate costs. For example, estate taxes may be reduced by removing assets through gifts; by transferring assets to irrevocable trusts; by using the charitable, marital, and other deductions; and by making use of the unified credit and other credits. Probate costs can be reduced by using any of the will substitute techniques, such as revocable trusts and joint tenancy WROS, or by disposing of real estate in other states.

Estate liquidity can also be improved by adding liquid assets to the estate, such as by the purchase of life insurance, or by selling illiquid assets, such as real estate or closely held business interests.

EXHIBIT 60 – 1
Techniques for Improving Estate Liquidity

Reducing Cash Needs of the Estate	*Increasing Cash Available to the Estate*

• Reduce gross estate:
  - Lifetime gifts
  - Special-use valuation
  - Valuation discounts
	• Sale of illiquid assets
	• Buy-sell agreements for business interests
	• Sec. 303 redemption of closely held stock

• Reduce taxable estate:
  - Marital deduction
  - Charitable deduction
	• Life insurance

• Reduce estate tax payment: - Installment tax payments	• IRA and retirement plan benefits available to the estate

• Reduce probate and administration costs:
  - Living trust
  - Will substitutes
  - Avoid ancillary probate
  - Postmortem elections and actions
	• Loans
	• Irrevocable life insurance trust (trustee can make loans to the estate or buy assets)

Techniques for Closely Held Business Interests

Special techniques have been developed for business owners to deal with estate liquidity problems. These techniques include:

(1) Buy-sell agreements
(2) Installment payment of taxes (Sec. 6166)
(3) A stock redemption to pay taxes and expenses (Sec. 303)

(4) Special-use valuation (Sec. 2032A)

Buy-Sell Agreements

Buy-sell agreements are contracts for the purchase and sale of a business interest in the event of the owner's death, disability, or retirement. With such an agreement in place before the owner's death, the estate will receive cash proceeds from the sale of the business interest, instead of an illiquid closely held business interest.

The agreement establishes a price or pricing formula for the business interest, and if the agreement is written properly, this agreed price will serve as the valuation of the business interest for federal estate tax purposes.

Agreements Provide Estate Valuation

For the agreed price in the buy-sell agreement to serve as the estate tax valuation, the agreement must conform to the requirements of Internal Revenue Code, Sec. 2703 (Chapter 14). This Section requires:

- The agreement must be a bona fide business arrangement.
- The agreement must not be a device to transfer the property to members of the decedent's family for less than full and adequate consideration.
- The terms of the agreement must be comparable to similar arrangements entered into by persons in an arm's-length transaction.

An agreement that specifies a formula for the agreed price or that requires an appraisal and is updated regularly will generally satisfy the IRS. A genuine plan for succession and transfer of the business will generally meet these rules.

Types of Buy-Sell Agreements

The most common types of buy-sell agreements are: (1) entity-purchase agreements, in which the business entity contracts with the owners; and (2) cross-purchase agreements, in which the individual owners contract among themselves.

Entity-Purchase Agreement

An entity-purchase agreement provides for the corporation or partnership to buy the owner's interest, and the owner commits to selling. The agreement may apply not only in the circumstance of the owner's death, but also to disability and retirement.

In an insured plan, the business entity will purchase life insurance on the owner, so the entity will have death proceeds with which to buy the business interest at the owner's death. While the business interest will be included in the decedent's estate, the insurance death benefit will not be. If the agreement covers disability, a disability buyout policy is usually added.

If the agreement covers retirement, the entity can use the cash value of the life insurance policy to buy the business interest at the owner's retirement. Premiums for this life insurance are not deductible by the entity.

Avoiding Dividend Treatment – Sec. 302

In drafting an entity agreement, an owner will want to avoid having the purchase treated as a payment of dividends. This danger arises in stock-redemption agreements if less than the entire amount of stock owned by the decedent is sold. If a complete redemption of the stockholder's interest occurs, the transaction will be treated as a sale, rather than as a dividend.

Attribution Rules

A complete redemption is not easily accomplished under the tax laws, due to the constructive ownership or attribution rules. For example, under the attribution rules, even if the owner's spouse owns no stock, the stock owned by other family members will be attributed to the spouse. Moreover, if the spouse is a beneficiary of the estate, the stock of the family members will also be attributed to the estate. Thus, even if the corporation redeemed all the stock in the deceased's estate, the transaction would only be a partial redemption, due to the attribution rules.

The 10-year waiver rule is an exception to the attribution rules that allows for the treatment of a complete redemption as a sale, rather than as a dividend. The rule requires that a stockholder's entire interest be redeemed and that the stockholder agrees not to acquire any interest for 10 years.

Cross-Purchase Agreement

In a cross-purchase agreement, the stockholders or partners contract to buy each others' interests, in the event of death, disability, or retirement. Each owner contracts for his or her estate to sell the business interest, and each owner promises to buy the interests of the other owners. An owner buys the interests of another owner at the latter's death.

Insured Cross-Purchase Agreement

With a cross-purchase agreement, the stockholders or partners are usually obligated to buy life insurance on each other in an amount sufficient to buy a portion of the others' interests. The death proceeds are used to purchase the deceased's interest. Life insurance assures the parties that the money will be available at the required time to buy the deceased's interest. The agreement may provide for a trustee to collect premiums from each party to ensure that the premiums are paid. As with the entity agreement, the premiums are not deductible.

Under a cross-purchase agreement, the surviving owners will typically buy the life insurance policies owned by the decedent on the other owners. At the time of their deaths, part of the proceeds from these policies may be subject to income tax under the transfer-for-value rule of the IRC, Sec. 101.

First-Offer Provision

Typically, both an entity agreement and a cross-purchase agreement contain a "first-offer" requirement, which obligates the stockholders or partners to offer their business interests to other owners before offering it to outsiders. This provision should apply at all times, even before the occurrence of death, disability, or retirement. If the buy-sell agreement has a wait-and-see provision, the surviving owners will have the first offer to buy the shares under a cross-purchase agreement. If the surviving owners decline, then the corporation has the option to implement a redemption. The wait-and-see approach could also be used in conjunction with a Section 303 stock redemption, in which case the entity would first purchase the shares being redeemed under the Section 303 redemption, then the surviving owners would be offered the remaining shares under a cross-purchase agreement.

Comparison of Agreements

The cross-purchase agreement is a more equitable approach than the entity agreement when there is a substantial difference in the ages and ownership interests of the parties. Under an entity agreement, an older owner with a larger interest will be subsidizing the younger owners because the older owner will, in effect, be paying more of the premiums out of his or her share of the profits in order to help the other owners buy the interest.

The premiums are higher on older insureds, and the amount of insurance required is greater, so more of the premiums will be spent on the coverage needed to buy the older owner's larger interest.

If the ages and ownership interests are approximately equal, the entity agreement will probably be preferable because there will be fewer insurance policies.

Since the entity is not involved in the cross-purchase agreement, there is no danger that a stock purchase will result in dividend treatment.

Under the entity approach, the purchase of the decedent's interest does not change a surviving owner's income tax basis in the stock or partnership interest. With a cross-purchase agreement, the purchase of the decedent's interest adds to the tax basis for each surviving owner. Thus, if the owners expect to sell their interests before they die, the capital gain will be less from a cross-purchase agreement than from the entity approach.

Additional details of buy-sell agreements are presented in Topic 21 of Keir's Insurance Planning textbook.

🔑 **KEY SUMMARY 60 – 1**
Comparison of Entity and Cross-Purchase Buy-Sell Agreements

Entity Buy-Sell Agreement	Cross-Purchase Buy-Sell Agreement
Business entity contracts with the owners.	Owners contract among themselves.
Business entity buys life and disability insurance on the owners. Premiums are not deductible.	Owners buy life and disability insurance on one another. Premiums are not deductible.
Dividend treatment is a danger if a complete redemption or waiver is not obtained.	No danger of dividend treatment.
Surviving owners' income tax basis does not change.	Purchase of the decedent's interest increases the income tax basis for the surviving owners.
If ages and ownership interests are nearly the same, the entity agreement is preferred because fewer insurance policies are required.	If ages and ownership interests differ, the cross-purchase agreement is more equitable because premiums will be higher on older, larger owners.

Installment Payment – Sec. 6166

Sec. 6166 permits an estate to pay federal estate taxes in installments if it meets the following requirements:

- **35% or more of the value of the decedent's adjusted gross estate (excluding the state death tax deduction, if applicable) consists of a closely held business interest.** The closely held business may be a sole proprietorship, a partnership in which the decedent owned at least 20% of the capital interest or which had 15 or fewer partners, or a corporation in which the decedent owned at least 20% of the voting stock or which had 15 or fewer shareholders.
- Several closely held business interests in which the decedent had a 20% interest can be aggregated to meet the 35% requirement. The closely held interest must have actively carried on a trade or business interest at the time of the decedent's death.

If the estate qualifies, it may make the payment of tax attributable to the closely held business interest in 10 equal installments.

The first installment must be made within five years after the estate tax return is due. While tax is deferred on the first $1 million (indexed for inflation to $1,470,000 in 2015) of a closely held business interest, the interest rate is only 2%. If the closely held interest is greater than that amount, the remaining tax is subject to an interest rate that is 45% of the usual underpayment rate. If the estate makes use of the lower interest rates, the interest is not deductible.

*REMEMBER: SEC. 6166 IS A TOOL USED TO **ENHANCE ESTATE LIQUIDITY**. IT IS AVAILABLE TO ESTATES CONTAINING INTERESTS IN A BROAD RANGE OF BUSINESS ENTITIES (PARTNERSHIPS, CORPORATIONS, AND SOLE PROPRIETORSHIPS), WHILE SEC. 303 CAN ONLY BE USED WHEN THE ESTATE CONTAINS STOCK OF A CLOSELY HELD CORPORATION.*

Sec. 303 Redemption

If a closely held corporation is 35% of the decedent's adjusted gross estate (excluding the state death tax deduction if applicable), the estate may also qualify for a Sec. 303 redemption. Under Sec. 303, stock may be redeemed equal to the total amount of all estate taxes, inheritance taxes, estate administration expenses, and funeral expenses.

The redemption proceeds will be treated as a sale, rather than as a dividend.

Note that even though the tax rates on capital gains and dividends are now the same, there is still an advantage to a redemption being treated as a sale because the adjusted basis for the stock will generally be equal to its sale price due to the step-up in basis to the date-of-death value. As a result, little or no capital gains tax will actually be owed.

🔑 KEY SUMMARY 60 – 2
Rules for Sec. 303 Stock Redemption

Sec. 303 stock redemption is a tool used to enhance the liquidity of the decedent's estate by converting a limited amount of stock into cash. The following conditions must be met to use Sec. 303:

- Stock in a **closely held corporation** is more than 35% of the decedent's **adjusted gross estate**.
- The amount of stock redeemed **cannot be more than** the estate's total amount of estate taxes, inheritance taxes, and administration expenses.

The redemption proceeds will not qualify if they are used to pay estate debts. Any beneficiary who will bear the tax burden may take advantage of Sec. 303, but if a bequest will not bear any taxes, the beneficiary cannot make use of Sec. 303.

🔔 *REMEMBER: IF THERE ARE NO ESTATE TAX LIABILITY AND NO ADMINISTRATION EXPENSES, SEC. 303 CANNOT BE USED BY THE ESTATE.*

Special-Use Valuation – Sec. 2032A

Sec. 2032A allows an executor to elect to value qualifying real property on the basis of its actual use, rather than at its fair market value, based on the highest and best use.

The maximum reduction in value is $1,100,000 in 2015. The requirements for this special-use valuation are described in Topic 72.

Note that with the percentage tests required for the installment payment of taxes (Sec. 6166, Sec. 303 redemption, and special-use valuation), the adjusted gross estate is specially defined to include gifts made within three years of death.

🔔 *REMEMBER: SEC. 2032A SPECIAL-USE VALUATION CAN **ONLY** BE USED WHEN THERE IS **REAL PROPERTY** IN THE GROSS ESTATE.*

Practice Question

John Kelly was the founder of the Kelly Masonry Works, which was worth $6 million when he died this year. His gross estate was worth $7.2 million, and his adjusted gross estate was $6.75 million. The estate tax owed was $300,000. The family is planning to continue operating the business. Which of the following techniques would be most helpful to the executor in enhancing liquidity for the John Kelly estate?

A. Sec. 303 redemption
B. Installment payment under Sec. 6166
C. Special-use valuation under Sec. 2032A
D. Buy-sell agreement

Answer:
The facts of this question do not reveal that the business was a corporation, so the Sec. 303 redemption may not be available. The facts also do not reveal that the estate owns real estate. The buy-sell agreement is inconsistent with the family's plan to continue the business. Moreover, a buy-sell agreement is useful when it is arranged during the owner's lifetime, not after death. The installment payment of the estate tax under Sec. 6166 is available to the estate because any business form can make use of it. The estate will qualify because the business is more than 35% of the value of the adjusted gross estate.
The answer is B.

Life Insurance

Life insurance is an important technique for liquidity planning. Uses of life insurance, including liquidity planning, are treated in Topic 65.

Loan

An estate can provide liquidity by pledging assets as collateral for loans. The executor will typically have the power to borrow money and to mortgage or pledge property as collateral. The executor must, however, be careful to manage the estate assets according to fiduciary standards and principles.

Creation of an irrevocable life insurance trust is one technique for providing liquidity to an estate through loans. The life insurance trust is set up so the trustee is specifically authorized, but not directed, to make loans to the estate. After the insured's death, the trust will receive life insurance death benefits that will not be included in the decedent's estate and will not be subject to the estate tax. The trustee can then lend the proceeds to the estate to provide liquidity.

Cash Flow Plan for Estate Liquidity

The process of maintaining an estate from date of death to final distribution may require a number of various outflows. The personal representative of the estate is responsible for resolving all outstanding obligations of the estate and transferring property to the intended beneficiaries. He or she will need to establish estate accounts and gather assets, value assets, file the will with the probate court, send out notice to creditors, pay debts of the estate, pay administrative costs of the estate, and file and pay numerous tax returns, among other responsibilities.

Cash outflows during the administration process may include the following:

- Funeral expenses
- Payments to help maintain the family
- Court fees to probate the will and cost of issuance of Letters Testamentary
- Attorney fees
- Accountant fees
- Costs to preserve, protect, and maintain property
- Fees for appraisal and valuation of estate assets
- Fees for advertising the existence of the estate notifying interested parties
- Payment of debts of the decedent
- Payment of taxes
- Payment of final medical expenses
- Distribution of bequests

Also see Topic 72 for a discussion of installment payment of estate taxes under Section 6166 and Stock Redemption to pay certain estate expenses under Section 303.

Application Questions

1. Edgar Hadley, age 59, is the president of Ajax Computer Software Company, which is valued at $25 million. Edgar is one of the five founders and owns 28% of the stock of the corporation. Edgar's home is owned with his wife in tenancy by the entirety and is valued at $300,000. Edgar owns common stock mutual funds in an IRA valued at $75,000, and his wife is the beneficiary. He also has a brokerage account in joint names with his wife, containing common stock and corporate bonds valued at $100,000. Edgar also owns a beach house valued at $200,000 and a boat worth $50,000. The family cars are owned jointly with his wife and are worth $50,000 each. Edgar and his wife have two children, ages 17 and 15. Edgar's will leaves his entire estate to his wife, and his wife's will leaves everything to him.

Which of the following techniques can be useful to Edgar Hadley in connection with his current estate plan (assume he expects to live for at least 5 more years)?

(1) Cross-purchase buy-sell agreement
(2) Installment payment of estate taxes
(3) Sec. 303 redemption
(4) Special-use valuation

    A. (1) only
    B. (1) and (2) only
    C. (2) and (3) only
    D. (2), (3), and (4) only
    E. (1), (2), (3), and (4)

2. If Edgar Hadley (from Question 1) bought a whole life insurance policy and arranged for an enforceable stock-redemption agreement at Ajax, which of the following techniques would then be applicable to his estate planning?

    A. Irrevocable life insurance trust
    B. Installment payment of the estate tax
    C. Sec. 303 redemption
    D. All of the above

3. If Edgar Hadley (from Question 1) and the other founders of Ajax negotiate over a buy-sell agreement, which of the following statements concerning the selection of an appropriate agreement will be correct?

    A. If Edgar is the oldest and holds the most shares, he will prefer an entity-redemption agreement.
    B. If Edgar is the youngest and holds the most shares, he will prefer an entity-redemption agreement.
    C. If Edgar is the oldest and holds the most shares, the other founders will most likely prefer a cross-purchase agreement.
    D. If Edgar is the oldest and holds the most shares, the cross-purchase agreement will be more equitable than an entity agreement.
    E. If Edgar is the oldest and holds the most shares, the entity agreement will be more equitable and easier to administer than a cross-purchase agreement.

4. If Edgar Hadley (from Question 1) arranged for a buy-sell agreement for his Ajax stock, which of the following statements are correct?

(1) Under a cross-purchase agreement, the life insurance benefit paid at Edgar's death will be included in his gross estate.

(2) The life insurance policies Edgar purchases on the other shareholders will be included in his gross estate.

(3) If the purchase price for Edgar's shares under a cross-purchase agreement does not represent fair market value, the estate will have to arrange a different valuation for federal estate tax purposes.

(4) Edgar's estate will pay a larger capital gain tax with a stock-redemption agreement than with a cross-purchase agreement.

   A. (1) and (2) only
   B. (1) and (3) only
   C. (2) and (3) only
   D. (3) and (4) only
   E. (1), (2), (3), and (4)

5. (Published question released February, 1999)

Which of the following statements concerning the choice of an entity versus a cross-purchase partnership buy-sell agreement funded with insurance is false?

A. The use of existing insurance to fund the agreement causes a transfer-for-value problem if an entity agreement is selected, but does not cause this problem if a cross-purchase approach is used.

B. A cross-purchase agreement should be selected if the surviving partners expect to sell their interests during their lifetimes.

C. An entity approach may solve the affordability problem if one partner is significantly older than the others.

D. An entity agreement becomes more desirable as the number of partners included in the agreement increases.

6. Two accountants, Gary and Nancy, are equal stockholders in an accounting practice incorporated as a personal-service corporation. Their annual gross billings are $850,000. They have a cross-purchase agreement that values the business according to a formula. Under the formula, the business is currently valued at $1.5 million, including $250,000 of goodwill. They each own life insurance policies on the life of the other stockholder, in the face amount of $650,000. If Gary dies first, what amount will be included in his estate, related to the business?

A. $425,000
B. $625,000
C. $650,000
D. $750,000

7. All the following statements concerning an insured buy-sell (business-continuation) agreement are correct, EXCEPT:

A. Under the cross-purchase agreement, the stockholders buy life insurance on each others' lives.

B. Under the redemption agreement, the corporation itself can be the premium payer, beneficiary, and policyowner.

C. Under the redemption agreement, the value of the business interest, but not the life insurance proceeds, is included in the deceased's gross estate.

D. Under the redemption plan, the premiums paid by the corporation are considered paid on behalf of the stockholders and thus are taxable income to the respective stockholders.

E. Under a cross-purchase agreement, the parties can agree to buy from the deceased's estate the remaining life insurance policies on the lives of surviving shareholders.

8. Which of the following statements concerning the parties to the stock buy-sell agreement are correct?

(1) A trustee must be a party to the cross-purchase agreement.

(2) Under a stock-redemption plan, the corporation is a party to the agreement.

(3) The proceeds of a policy owned by a surviving shareholder on the life of a deceased shareholder are not includible in the deceased's gross estate.

(4) Under a cross-purchase agreement, the owner of each life insurance policy names his or her estate as the beneficiary.

A. (1) and (2) only
B. (1) and (3) only
C. (2) and (3) only
D. (2) and (4) only
E. (3) and (4) only

9. A stockholder had paid $20,000 in net premiums over several years to insure the life of another stockholder under a corporate cross-purchase buy-sell agreement. The insured stockholder died, and the $100,000 proceeds were used by the surviving stockholder to purchase the deceased stockholder's interest. The book value of the deceased's stock was $140,000 at the date of death. If the surviving stockholder's cost basis was $80,000 for the original stock interest, what would the cost basis be in both interests after the acquisition of the deceased's stock interest?

A. $100,000
B. $140,000
C. $160,000
D. $180,000
E. $220,000

10. All the following statements concerning the use of an insured corporate cross-purchase buy-sell agreement are correct, EXCEPT:

  A. The value of any life insurance policies the deceased owned on the lives of the other stockholders will be included in his or her gross estate.
  B. The buyout will not involve dividend distributions to the deceased's estate or to his or her family.
  C. It is preferred over the redemption-type agreement when the stockholders are all in a higher tax bracket than the corporation.
  D. The surviving stockholders get an increase in their basis for income tax purposes.
  E. It produces greater equity of results than a redemption-type agreement when there is a significant difference in the ages of the stockholders and in their percentages of stock ownership.

11. All the following provisions are usually included in an insured stock cross-purchase buy-sell agreement, EXCEPT:

  A. A provision giving each surviving stockholder an option to buy a proportionate part of a deceased's stock
  B. A provision establishing the purchase price to be paid for the stock of a deceased stockholder
  C. A provision committing each stockholder to buy and maintain life insurance on the other stockholders
  D. A provision permitting each surviving stockholder to buy from the estate of a deceased stockholder the life insurance the deceased's estate owns on the life of each surviving stockholder
  E. A provision prohibiting stockholders from transferring their stock without first offering it to the other parties to the agreement

For practice answering case questions related to Topic 60, please answer the following questions in the cases included in the Appendix at the back of this textbook.

Case	Questions
Bartlett	
Marshall	
Webster	
Unser	5
Tingey	
Lytle	5
Beals	4 and 5
Mocsin	
Young	
Borelli	13
Cunningham	14
Fred and Mary Ferris	36, 37, 38, 39, and 40

Answers and Explanations

1. A is the answer. The cross-purchase buy-sell agreement is appropriate for obtaining the full value from the business asset for the benefit of his wife. The agreement will assure Edgar's wife that the stock in the software company will be sold at his death for the value that it should bring, based on a formula or appraisal specified in advance. The remaining techniques are not relevant to Edgar's estate because all of the assets will pass to his wife. The marital deduction will eliminate any estate tax. If the estate were not passing entirely to Edgar's wife, the other techniques would be appropriate, except for the special-use valuation. The special-use valuation is not appropriate because the real estate is not used for farming or in a closely held business.

2. A is the answer. An irrevocable life insurance trust will still be useful in keeping life insurance out of his estate and in providing additional assets for liquidity or to pay estate taxes. The stock-redemption agreement will result in sale of the stock, so the estate will no longer qualify for the installment payment of the estate tax or the Sec. 303 redemption.

3. D is the answer. If Edgar is the largest and oldest shareholder, he will not want an entity-redemption agreement because the insurance policy on his life will be the most expensive, and the premiums will come largely from his share of the profits. If Edgar is the largest and oldest shareholder, the equitable approach is a cross-purchase agreement, in which each shareholder will own life policies on the other shareholders. The cross-purchase agreement will mean more life insurance policies because each shareholder has to buy life insurance on four other shareholders. The entity agreement is easier to administer and will be less expensive for the other founders because a smaller part of the premiums will be paid from their profits.

4. C is the answer. The life insurance policies purchased on other founders will be an asset that must be included in Edgar's gross estate, but they are included at their replacement costs (the interpolated terminal reserve value plus the unearned premium). If the purchase price does not represent fair market value, the IRS can ignore the buy-sell agreement, and the estate will have to obtain a valuation of the shares. There is generally no capital gain when stock is sold under a buy-sell agreement due to the step-up in basis at the owner's death. The death benefit will not be included in Edgar's estate because he has no incidents of ownership. The proceeds from the sale of the shares will be included.

5. A is the answer. The use of existing insurance will not cause a transfer-for-value problem in an entity agreement because the partnership will not have to buy additional insurance to fund the agreement. There is no transfer that is subject to the rule. The entity approach can help make the buy-sell agreement more affordable because the entity will pay the premiums, instead of the individual partners. If one partner is much older than the others, the younger owners may find the premiums for insurance on his or her life to be expensive. An entity agreement becomes more desirable as the number of partners increases because the number of policies required is much lower than with a cross-purchase agreement. With a cross-purchase agreement, the number of policies required is $n(n-1)$, where n is the number of partners, but the number of policies to fund an entity agreement is only n. The basis for ownership shares will increase when a cross-purchase agreement is used and the surviving owners buy the decedent's interest. This increase in basis does not occur with an entity agreement. For this reason, a cross-purchase agreement may be preferred if the owners expect to resell their interests before death, when they would receive a step-up in basis.

6. D is the answer. One-half of the value of the business will be included in Gary's gross estate, based on the formula valuation of the business. The cross-purchase agreement was a bona fide business arrangement and will be used to fix the value of the business. Gary is a one-half owner, so one-half of the value will be included. The amount of the life insurance insuring Gary's life will not determine what is included in his gross estate because Gary did not have incidents of ownership over the policy on his life. Note that the replacement value of the life insurance policy owned by Gary on Nancy will be included in Gary's gross estate, but the facts did not give a value for that policy.

7. D is the answer. Under the redemption plan, the premiums paid by the corporation are paid with after-tax dollars, but the premiums are not taxable income to the corporation's shareholders. A, B, C, and E are correct statements.

8. C is the answer. A trustee is usually not a party to the cross-purchase agreement. Under a stock-redemption plan, the corporation is a party to the agreement. The proceeds of a policy owned by a surviving shareholder on the life of a deceased shareholder are not includible in the deceased's gross estate. Under a cross-purchase agreement, the shareholders take out insurance policies on each other and name themselves the beneficiaries of the policies they own. When a shareholder dies, each of the other shareholders will receive the death proceeds under the policies purchased on the deceased shareholder. The surviving shareholders will then have sufficient funds to purchase the deceased's interest.

9. D is the answer. The surviving stockholder's new cost basis will be the old cost basis of $80,000, increased by the $100,000 life insurance death proceeds used to pay for the deceased stockholder's stock.

10. C is the answer. C is an incorrect statement because the redemption agreement is preferred when the stockholders are all in a higher tax bracket than the corporation. This is so because the corporation pays the premium with after-tax dollars; this is better than paying out salaries to the stockholders, to be taxed at their high tax bracket, and then having them pay the premiums with after-tax dollars. A, B, D, and E are correct statements.

11. A is the answer. A is a trick item. Each surviving stockholder does not have to have an option to buy any of the stock owned by a deceased stockholder because the buy-sell agreement already spells out the number of shares that each stockholder can and must buy of a deceased stockholder's stock. Each stockholder owns life insurance on each other stockholder that is adequate to pay for the deceased's stock. It is mandatory that the surviving stockholders buy the specific number of shares from the deceased's estate. It is not a matter of having an option to buy. It is a requirement. B, C, D, and E are provisions usually included in a cross-purchase agreement.

Powers of Appointment (Topic 61)

CFP Board Student-Centered Learning Objectives

(a) Identify and describe the most common forms of transferring powers to others during life including Power of Attorney, Health Care Power of Attorney, Living Will, Healthcare Proxy, Do Not Resuscitate Orders. [See Topic 58]

(b) Evaluate the most common forms of lifetime powers of appointment and ensure compliance with client's goals and objectives.

(c) Recommend the use of power of appointment to direct distribution of assets to alternative recipients when appropriate.

> *Powers of Appointment*
> A. *Use and purpose*
> B. *General and special (limited) powers*
>   1) *5-and-5 power*
>   2) *Crummey powers*
>   3) *Distributions for an ascertainable standard*
>   4) *Lapse of power*
> C. *Tax implications*

Power of Appointment – Sec. 2514

A power of appointment is the right or authority given to another to designate who shall possess or enjoy certain property. The grantor or creator of the power is called the donor, and the person given the power is the donee or holder. The persons who are to receive the property subject to the power are called the beneficiaries or appointees. When the donee designates a person (or persons) to receive the property, the power has been exercised. A power of appointment can be created by a trust, a will, or other document.

A power of appointment is a way to provide flexibility in an estate plan because decisions over the disposition of property can be delayed and delegated to other persons. The donor can choose the property that will be subject to the power and may even select a class of beneficiaries, but the final decision is left to another time, when needs and worthiness may be more apparent.

No special words are needed to create a power of appointment. The power does not even have to be called a power of appointment. **The trust or will may provide that a person has a right to invade principal or consume trust assets or make gifts of**

property. Any similar words authorizing a person to act with regard to the property will be sufficient.

General Power

With a general power of appointment, the holder can exercise the power in favor of anyone, including the holder himself or herself. Under the federal estate tax laws, a general power can be exercised in favor of the holder, the holder's creditors, the holder's estate, or the creditors of the holder's estate. A power that is not subject to or limited by the Internal Revenue Code's definition of an ascertainable standard is also a general power.

> *REMEMBER: HOLDING A GENERAL POWER OF APPOINTMENT IS CONSIDERED THE SAME AS "OWNING" THE PROPERTY.*

Special or Limited Power

A special or limited power of appointment restricts the persons in whose favor the power may be exercised. The donor of the power designates the persons or class of persons to whom the property may be appointed, and these designated persons may not be the holder, the holder's creditors, the holder's estate, or the creditors of the holder's estate.

Ascertainable Standard

A power is also limited if it can be exercised only in accordance with an **ascertainable standard**. For example, a grantor may establish a trust that permits her son to consume trust income and principal for his **"health, maintenance, education, and support."** This power is subject to an ascertainable standard. The following powers to invade principal also contain ascertainable standards:

- For support in the holder's accustomed manner of living
- For support in reasonable comfort
- For the holder's education
- For all medical expenses, including convalescence
- For maintenance in reasonable health and reasonable comfort

A power that can be exercised for the holder's comfort, welfare, or happiness is not subject to an ascertainable standard and is a general power.

A power that can be exercised only with consent of the grantor is a special power, and a power that can be exercised only in conjunction with a person having a substantial adverse interest in the property is also a special power.

🔑 KEY SUMMARY 61 – 1
Powers of Appointment

General Power	*Special Power*

Can be exercised in favor of:
    - Holder
    - Holder's creditors
    - Holder's estate
    - Creditors of holder's estate
 AND:
   is <u>not</u> subject to an ascertainable standard
	Cannot be exercised in favor of:
	    - Holder, holder's creditors, holder's estate, and creditors of holder's estate
	 BUT:
	 Can be exercised:
	    - Only with consent of the creator
	    - Only with consent of a person having an adverse interest in the property
	 OR:
	   Is subject to an ascertainable standard

Assets subject to a general power at death are included in the holder's gross estate.	Assets subject to a special power at death are <u>not</u> included in the holder's gross estate.
The exercise or release of a general power will be a gift. A lapse of a general power <u>over</u> $5,000 or 5% of the value of assets is a gift.	Lapse or release is <u>not</u> a gift.

Release or Lapse of a Power –
Sec. 2514(e)

During a holder's lifetime, a general power of appointment can be exercised in favor of a beneficiary, or it can be released. When a power is exercised in favor of a beneficiary, a gift has been made to that person. Similarly, a release of a power is deemed a gift because the property passes to a different person. For gift tax purposes, the release of the power is treated the same as the exercise of the power.

If the holder fails to exercise the power and the power lapses or terminates, the IRS deems that, in effect, a gift has been made. Often, the gift has been made to the person who will receive the remainder interest. Lapses are subject to gift tax to the extent the value of the property not appointed was in excess of $5,000 or 5% of the total value of the property subject to the power.

A power of appointment may be exercisable by means of a will, and, sometimes, a grantor establishes a trust that provides for the beneficiaries to make disposition of the trust assets by means of a will. If a person is a holder of such a power at death, the value of the trust property will be included in his or her gross estate.

"5-and-5 Power"

Under the Tax Code, the lapse of a general power of appointment does not give rise to a gift, up to the greater of $5,000 or 5% of the value of the property. To take advantage of this provision, estate planners have devised the "5-and-5 power." With the "5-and-5 power," the beneficiary has a right annually to appoint the greater of $5,000 or 5% of the trust assets. Since a holder of a general power can appoint to himself or herself, the beneficiary can obtain from the trust each year a payment that is at least $5,000. Moreover, the power is made noncumulative, so when it is not exercised for a given year, it lapses for that year. Thus, failure to exercise this power in any year will not result in gift tax consequences.

In addition, if the power has not been exercised in the year of death, the beneficiary's gross estate will only include the greater of $5,000 or 5% of the property and not all of the trust assets. Thus, the "5-and-5 power" can provide additional money for a beneficiary, while avoiding adverse estate and gift tax consequences.

Estate and Gift Tax Consequences

If a person dies with a general power of appointment over property, the value of the property is included in the holder's gross estate. The release of a general power during the holder's lifetime can trigger gift tax consequences. The exercise of a general power in favor of the holder will not be a gift, but exercise of the power in favor of a third party will have gift tax consequences.

If a person dies with a special or limited power of appointment, the property is not included in the holder's gross estate. The exercise, lapse, or release of a special power will have no gift or estate tax consequences.

Application Questions

1. Howard Jensen has a substantial estate that he would like to see used to provide for his children after his wife's death. The Jensens have a young child with a medical condition, and the child may be unable to provide his or her own support in later life. Howard also has another child who is expected to go to college in 10 years. Which of the following powers could provide flexibility in Howard's estate plan in providing for the needs of the children?

    A. A general power of appointment
    B. A special power of appointment
    C. Both a general and a special power of appointment
    D. Neither a general nor a special power of appointment

2. Bill Hart's will leaves his estate to a trust that will pay income to his wife for life and the remainder to their children. Bill's wife can withdraw additional amounts for reasonable medical expenses for herself and for the children. She can also withdraw up to 10% of the trust assets or $10,000 each year. Which of the following statements concerning this trust are correct?

    (1) The withdrawal right for medical expenses is a special power.
    (2) The withdrawal right of 10% of the trust assets or $10,000 is a general power.
    (3) Failure to withdraw money from the trust for medical expenses will not result in a taxable gift.
    (4) Failure to withdraw 10% of the trust assets or $10,000 each year will result in a taxable gift.

    A. (1) and (2) only
    B. (1) and (3) only
    C. (2) and (3) only
    D. (2) and (4) only
    E. (1), (2), (3), and (4)

3. Which of the following powers to withdraw from the assets of a trust are general powers?

    (1) The holder has the right to withdraw to maintain his or her welfare and comfort.
    (2) The holder has the right to withdraw with the consent of the grantor.
    (3) The holder has the right to withdraw with the consent of a non-adverse party.
    (4) The holder has the right to appoint the property to any of his or her children.

    A. (1) and (2) only
    B. (1) and (3) only
    C. (2) and (3) only
    D. (2) and (4) only
    E. (3) and (4) only

4. Assets from which of the following trusts will be included in the decedent's gross estate?

    A. Decedent held a power to determine which of the decedent's children would inherit assets of the trust.
    B. Decedent held a power to withdraw amounts as needed from the trust and to name an heir but did not name an heir to this power.
    C. Decedent executed a lifetime written release of a general power of appointment over assets in the trust.
    D. Decedent was entitled to the income from the trust for life and had a 5-and-5 power that was exercised in the year of death.

5. Which of the following statements best describes the difference between a general power of appointment and a special power of appointment?

   A. The former permits exercise of the power only in favor of family members.

   B. The former permits exercise of the power in favor of anyone, including the holder of the power.

   C. The latter permits exercise of the power only in favor of creditors of the holder of the power.

   D. The latter permits exercise of the power in favor of anyone, including the holder of the power.

   E. The latter permits exercise of the power in favor of the holder's estate.

6. Which of the following is a general power of appointment for federal estate tax purposes?

   A. Power exercisable in favor of the holder for support in the holder's accustomed manner of living

   B. Power exercisable only in the favor of creditors of the holder's estate

   C. Power exercisable in favor of the holder for the holder's health, maintenance, and support

   D. Power exercisable in favor of the holder, only with the consent of the power's creator

   E. Power exercisable in favor of the holder for support in reasonable comfort

7. Which of the following is a general power of appointment for federal estate tax purposes?

   A. Power exercisable only in favor of the holder's children

   B. Power exercisable in favor of the holder for the holder's happiness and well-being

   C. Power exercisable in favor of the holder for the holder's health, education, maintenance, and support

   D. Power exercisable in favor of the holder for all medical expenses, including expenses of convalescence

   E. Power exercisable in favor of any of the holder's siblings

8. Which of the following statements concerning powers of appointment is (are) correct?

   (1) A power to appoint to oneself the annual contributions to a trust is a general power.

   (2) A power to appoint to oneself the lesser of $5,000 or 5% of the assets of a trust is a special power of appointment.

   (3) Failure to exercise a power to appoint up to 10% of the trust assets to the grantor's children will not result in a taxable gift.

   (4) Failure to exercise a power to appoint to oneself 5% of the trust assets will not result in a taxable gift.

   A. (1) only

   B. (1) and (2) only

   C. (2) and (3) only

   D. (1), (3), and (4) only

   E. (1), (2), (3), and (4)

9. All the following are special powers of appointment, EXCEPT:

A. Power exercisable in favor of the holder for the holder's comfort
B. Power exercisable in favor of the holder for the holder's maintenance in reasonable health and reasonable comfort
C. Power exercisable only with the consent of a person who has interests adverse to the holder
D. Power exercisable in favor of the holder for the holder's education, including graduate or professional school
E. Power exercisable in favor of the holder for the holder's maintenance and support

10. Which of the following may result in a gift for federal gift tax purposes?

(1) Exercise of a general power of appointment
(2) Exercise of a special power of appointment
(3) Lapse of a general power of appointment
(4) Release of a general power of appointment

A. (1) and (2) only
B. (2) and (3) only
C. (1), (2), and (3) only
D. (1), (3), and (4) only
E. (1), (2), (3), and (4)

11. Which of the following will result in a gift for federal gift tax purposes?

(1) Lapse of a general power
(2) Release of a special power
(3) Disclaimer of a general power
(4) Disclaimer of a special power

A. (1) only
B. (1) and (2) only
C. (2) and (3) only
D. (3) and (4) only
E. (1), (2), (3), and (4)

12. All the following statements concerning powers of appointment are correct, EXCEPT:

A. If Harry gives $10,000 in trust with income to his son Joe for life, with the right to withdraw principal only for college tuition bills, the $10,000 will be included in Joe's gross estate.
B. A power exercisable in favor of the holder's creditors will be included in the holder's gross estate.
C. A power exercisable by a decedent only with the consent of the grantor of a trust will be excluded from the decedent's gross estate.
D. If "A" places $100,000 in trust for "B" but limits "B's" right of withdrawal to $5,000 or 5% of the aggregate value of the property each year, the total value of the remaining trust corpus will be excluded from "B's" estate at his or her death.
E. If Harry has a power to appoint principal and income from a trust for his own health, maintenance, and support, he does not have a general power of appointment.

13. Which of the following statements concerning powers of invasion are correct?

(1) A five-and-five power may be added to a nonmarital trust, without the trust assets being includible in the surviving spouse's gross estate.

(2) A five-and-five power may be added to a QTIP trust.

(3) The surviving spouse may be given the power to invade the entire corpus of a marital trust.

(4) The surviving spouse need not be given a power to invade principal under a power-of-appointment trust.

    A. (1) and (2) only
    B. (1) and (4) only
    C. (2) and (3) only
    D. (3) and (4) only
    E. (1), (2), (3), and (4)

14. George Foster has created an irrevocable trust with $2 million worth of rental properties. The trust provides that the income from the assets will be paid annually to George's wife Margery. At Margery's death, the assets will pass to George's four children, according to whatever plan of distribution Margery directs in her will. Which of the following statements concerning the Foster trust is (are) correct?

(1) Margery has a power of appointment over the trust assets.

(2) Margery has a general power of appointment.

(3) The four children are the donees of the power of appointment.

(4) George is the holder of the power of appointment.

    A. (1) only
    B. (2) and (3) only
    C. (3) and (4) only
    D. (1), (2), and (3) only
    E. (1), (2), (3), and (4)

For Matching Questions 15-19, you should select the power of appointment that will be appropriate for the scenario. If both the general and special power can be used, then your choice should be C. If neither a general nor a special power can be used, then you should choose D.

15. Which of the following powers of appointment could be used by the holder to appoint funds held by another entity?

    A. A general power only
    B. A special power only
    C. Both a special and a general power
    D. Neither a special nor a general power

16. For which of the following powers of appointment would a holder's release of the power mean that there was a gift for federal gift tax purposes?

    A. A general power only
    B. A special power only
    C. Both a special and a general power
    D. Neither a special nor a general power

17. For which of the following powers of appointment held at death would the assets subject to the power be includible in the holder's gross estate?

    A. A general power only
    B. A special power only
    C. Both a special and a general power
    D. Neither a special nor a general power

18. Which of the following powers of appointment is the power to appoint to oneself the lesser of $5,000 or 5% of the assets held by a trust?

    A. A general power only
    B. A special power only
    C. Both a special and a general power
    D. Neither a special nor a general power

19. A power to appoint trust assets to oneself that can be exercised only with the consent of an adverse party is which of the following powers of appointment?

    A. A general power only
    B. A special power only
    C. Both a special and a general power
    D. Neither a special nor a general power

For practice answering case questions related to Topic 61, please answer the following questions in the cases included in the Appendix at the back of this textbook.

Case	Questions
Bartlett	
Marshall	
Webster	
Unser	6
Tingey	
Lytle	
Beals	
Mocsin	
Young	
Borelli	14
Cunningham	
Fred and Mary Ferris	41, 42, 43, 44, and 45

Answers and Explanations

1. C is the answer. Both a general and a special power of appointment can be used to provide flexibility in an estate plan and would help with providing the flexibility needed for the Jensen family. If Howard gave his wife a general power of appointment, she could appoint property to anyone, including herself and her children. If Howard gave his wife only a limited (special) power of appointment to appoint property to the two children, it would still provide substantial flexibility in the estate plan.

2. E is the answer. The withdrawal right for medical expenses is a special power because the power is limited by an ascertainable standard. The right to withdraw 10% or $10,000 is a general power because the assets can be appointed to the holder and are not limited by any standard. The withdrawal right of 10% or $10,000 exceeds the amount of a "5-and-5 power" and, therefore, will give rise to a taxable gift when there is a lapse. Failure to exercise a general power is a lapse that results in a taxable gift when it exceeds the $5,000 or 5% limit. The lapse of a special power is not a taxable gift.

3. B is the answer. The right to withdraw assets in order to maintain the holder's welfare and comfort is not an ascertainable standard, so the power is a general one. A right to withdraw with the consent of the grantor or an adverse party is a special power. If the holder has a power that can be exercised with a non-adverse party, then it is a general power. A right to appoint property to the holder's children is a special power because the persons to whom the property can be appointed do not include the holder, the holder's estate, the holder's creditors, or creditors of the holder's estate.

4. B is the answer. The decedent's power to withdraw amounts as needed from the trust was a general power of appointment, and this power over the assets of the trust meant that the assets would be included in the decedent's gross estate. The fact that the decedent did not name an heir to this power does not affect its inclusion in the gross estate. The power to determine which of the decedent's children would inherit assets of the trust is a special power, so the assets are not included in the gross estate. The lifetime written release of a general power of appointment is a lifetime gift, so the assets are not included in the gross estate. If the decedent had a right to the income from the trust and had a 5-and-5 power that was exercised in the year of death, the trust assets are not included in the gross estate. The right to the income is not a power over the trust principal. The right to the income and a 5-and-5 power are typically given to the surviving spouse in the nonmarital trust, and the trust assets are not included in the spouse's gross estate.

5. B is the answer. A general power of appointment can be exercised in favor of anyone, including the holder, the holder's estate, the creditors of the holder, or creditors of the holder's estate. A special power is a limited power.

6. B is the answer. A power exercisable in favor of the creditors of the holder's estate is a general power of appointment. The other powers are special powers of appointment.

7. B is the answer. A power that can be exercised in favor of the holder for the holder's happiness and well-being is a general power of appointment. There is no ascertainable standard or limitation on the power because any expenditure would be justifiable.

8. D is the answer. A power to appoint trust assets to oneself is a general power of appointment, even if the power is limited to only the annual contributions of additional assets. The power to appoint the annual additions to a trust is often called a "Crummey" power because of the decision in the Crummey case involving such a power. When the power is limited to $5,000 or 5% of the assets of the trust, it is still a general power. A power to appoint trust assets to the grantor's children is a special power, and the lapse of a special power is not a release of a power that is subject to gift tax. The failure to exercise the power, therefore, does not give rise to gift tax liability. The failure to exercise a general power of appointment is a lapse or release that is subject to gift tax. The Code, however, exempts a release or lapse of a power that is limited to $5,000 or 5% of the value of the trust assets. The failure to exercise this power does not result in gift tax consequences.

9. A is the answer. A power exercisable in favor of the holder for the holder's comfort is a general power of appointment. Comfort is too indefinite to provide an ascertainable standard or limitation on expenditures.

10. D is the answer. The exercise, release, or lapse of a general power of appointment will result in a completed gift that may be subject to gift tax. The exercise, release, or lapse of a special power of appointment is not subject to gift tax, except in special situations.

11. A is the answer. The disclaimer of a general or special power does not result in a taxable gift.

12. A is the answer. A general power can be exercised in favor of the holder, the holder's estate, the holder's creditors, or the creditors of the holder's estate. A limited power of appointment can be exercised by the holder only with the consent of the creator, for only a limited class of beneficiaries, or only for specific purposes. The right to withdraw for college tuition bills is a specific purpose with an ascertainable standard, so the power is not unlimited. Thus, Joe's power is limited, and the trust assets will not be included in Joe's gross estate.

13. E is the answer. The five-and-five power permits invasion of principal to the extent of $5,000 or 5% annually. The power is not cumulative and is lost for any year in which it is not exercised. The five-and-five power is used with nonmarital and QTIP trusts. Under the marital or power-of-appointment trust, the surviving spouse may, but need not, be given a power to invade corpus during his or her lifetime.

14. A is the answer. Margery has a power of appointment over the trust assets because she can make disposition of the grantor's (George's) property in her will. Margery has a special power of appointment because she can appoint the assets only to specified persons and not to herself or to her estate. Margery is the sole donee or holder of the power of appointment, and the four children are the remainderpersons. George is the grantor and not the holder of the power of appointment.

15. C is the answer. Powers of appointment give the holder the right to appoint property or funds in the hands of another entity, such as a trust. Both a special and a general power of appointment give the holder such power.

16. A is the answer. A release of a general power results in a gift for federal gift tax purposes, but a release of a special power does not.

17. A is the answer. Assets subject to a special power of appointment are not includible in the decedent's gross estate, but assets subject to a general power are includible.

18. A is the answer. The power to appoint to oneself, to one's estate, to one's creditors, or to creditor's of one's estate is a general power. In this case, the power to appoint to oneself is a general power over 5% or $5,000 of the trust assets.

19. B is the answer. A power that can only be exercised in conjunction with an adverse party is a special or limited power of appointment.

Types, Features, and Taxation of Trusts (Topic 62)

CFP Board Student-Centered Learning Objectives

(a) Define and describe the uses of the four types of trusts including revocable, irrevocable, living and testamentary trusts.

(b) Describe the basic components of charitable and non-charitable trusts including identifying the parties to a trust, and the operating terms of a trust.

(c) Identify the basic income tax consequences of a trust including deductions, exemptions, credits, tax rates and penalties for non-compliance.

(d) Explain the income tax implications of trust income and distributions to beneficiaries.

Types, Features, and Taxation of Trusts
- A. *Classification*
  - 1) *Simple and complex*
  - 2) *Revocable and irrevocable*
  - 3) *Inter vivos and testamentary*
- B. *Types and basic provisions*
  - 1) *Totten trust*
  - 2) *Spendthrift trust*
  - 3) *Bypass trust*
  - 4) *Marital trust*
  - 5) *Qualified terminable-interest property (QTIP) trust*
  - 6) *Pour-over trust*
  - 7) *§2503(b) trust*
  - 8) *§2503(c) trust*
  - 9) *Sprinkling provision*
- C. *Trust beneficiaries: income and remainder*
- D. *Rule against perpetuities*
- E. *Estate and gift taxation*
- F. *Income taxation of trusts*

Trust Features

To establish a trust, a grantor transfers property to a trustee, who will administer the property for the benefit of the beneficiaries. The trust is created by means of a document, such as a will or a trust agreement, and this document gives directions for the trustee to follow in administering the trust property. State laws define a trustee's powers and duties, but additional powers and duties can be specified by the grantor in the trust document.

The trustee acts as a fiduciary and must act for the benefit of the beneficiaries. The trustee takes legal title, and each beneficiary has an equitable interest.

A trust requires three parties: a grantor, a trustee, and a beneficiary. Nevertheless, a trust may be established in which one person plays all three roles. State law requires that a trust be funded, which means some property must go into the trust when the grantor creates it. Trusts may be created with trust principal or trust corpus of only a nominal amount, such as $10, to satisfy the minimum legal requirement. The grantor may plan to transfer additional assets to the trust later. Trusts containing only a nominal amount are sometimes called unfunded trusts because they are really only an empty container for later use. A trust to which the grantor has transferred assets is called a funded trust.

Revocable and Irrevocable Trusts

Trusts can be either revocable or irrevocable. **A revocable trust provides that the trust can be revoked or changed by the grantor at any time. A revocable trust must be a living, or *inter vivos,* trust because the grantor must be alive in order to exercise the power to revoke or amend the trust.** After a grantor's death, a revocable trust becomes irrevocable because no one has the power to revoke it.

***Inter Vivos* and Testamentary Trusts**

An irrevocable trust may be living or testamentary, i.e., created during the grantor's lifetime or at his or her death by means of the grantor's will. **With an irrevocable trust, the grantor retains no right or power to change the trust and gives up control over the trust property permanently.** A revocable trust can be made into an irrevocable trust during the grantor's lifetime if the grantor gives up the power to revoke or if the grantor becomes incompetent so that the power cannot be exercised.

 K Study Tip – **Estate taxes are paid when property passes to a testamentary trust, and no additional estate taxes are due even if corpus is held for several generations. Income taxes will be due as income is distributed from the trust over time.**

Uses of Revocable Trusts

Revocable trusts are typically used to avoid probate and the costs, delays, and publicity that accompany the probate process. Because a trustee administers the assets, a revocable trust can provide professional management and administration of the assets. In addition, the trust can provide income for a surviving spouse, without being subjected to estate taxes a second time. **The assets of a revocable trust, however, are included in the**

grantor's gross estate for federal estate tax purposes, so there is really no estate tax benefit to a revocable trust.

Uses of Irrevocable Trusts

Irrevocable trusts are typically used to reduce estate taxes and, sometimes, to reduce income taxes. Since the grantor gives up all control over the trust assets, the assets are not included in the grantor's gross estate, and the income from the assets is taxed to the trust (or to its beneficiaries). Unlike the revocable trust, a transfer to an irrevocable trust is considered a completed gift, so there is a potential gift tax liability.

EXHIBIT 62 – 1
Revocable and Irrevocable Trusts

	Revocable Trusts	*Irrevocable Trusts*
Assets avoid probate?	Yes	Yes
Gift tax applies?	No, not a completed gift	Yes, is a completed gift
Estate tax avoidance?	No	Yes, unless an exception applies
Income taxed to the grantor?	Yes	No, is taxed to the trust unless the grantor trust rules apply
Owner retains control over assets in trust?	Yes	No

Totten Trust

A Totten trust is a bank account set up in the name of the depositor, which is in trust for a named beneficiary. The depositor retains the bank account passbook and can withdraw the money in the account at any time, so there is no completed gift. The beneficiary does not obtain possession until after the depositor's death. The account is essentially a revocable trust.

Bypass Trust

The "bypass trust" is also called a credit-shelter trust, nonmarital trust, family trust, or "B" trust. The bypass trust is set up by will to receive assets that will take advantage of the applicable credit amount under the estate tax laws (which is the equivalent of $5.43 million in 2015). This trust must be drafted so that the assets will not qualify for the marital deduction. Typically, the trust is created to provide an income for the surviving spouse and the remainder to the decedent's children.

Since portability has been made permanent, a bypass trust is not needed to save estate taxes if both spouses are expected to die with combined estates, including appreciation of assets, below $10.86 million. The bypass trust will remain useful for transferring highly appreciating assets at the death of the first spouse to remove the appreciation from the estate of the surviving spouse. See Topic 59 in this Estate Planning material for more information.

Marital Trust

A marital trust is set up to avoid estate tax by qualifying the assets for the marital deduction. The trust typically qualifies for the marital deduction because the surviving spouse is given a general power of appointment over the assets.

QTIP Trust

A QTIP trust, also called a "C" trust, requires an election by the executor for QTIP treatment. The assets escape estate tax in the decedent's estate by qualifying for the marital deduction, but are taxable in the surviving spouse's estate. Even though the QTIP trust qualifies for the marital deduction, the decedent can direct who will inherit the assets after the surviving spouse.

Pour-Over Trust

A pour-over trust is a trust established to receive assets that will "pour over" from different sources. It may be revocable or irrevocable. A pour-over trust can be useful for receiving and distributing an individual's non-probate assets, such as employee benefits, IRA benefits, and life insurance proceeds. A pour-over trust may be set up to hold real property situated in different states so that the property will not be subject to ancillary probate in those states.

A pour-over trust may be set up during a grantor's lifetime, with the plan that it will also receive assets from the grantor's estate that will be specified by will. A will provision stating that assets shall pour over to a trust will not be effective, however, unless the trust was in existence at the time the will was written.

Spendthrift Trust

A trust containing spendthrift provisions will prevent a beneficiary's creditors from obtaining trust assets, so the beneficiary is protected from his or her own "spendthrift" propensities. The trust provision may prohibit a beneficiary from assigning his or her interest in the trust corpus and income, so that the beneficiary will not be able to borrow against the anticipated payments or spend them in advance.

Asset Protection Trust

In most U.S. jurisdictions, a grantor cannot protect his or her own assets from creditors by transferring them to a trust and then still receive benefits from the trust, so a trust formed under foreign law may be required to obtain asset protection. A trust formed under foreign law may also benefit from the refusal of foreign courts to recognize judgments entered in U.S. courts.

Recently, a few states (such as Alaska, Delaware, Nevada, Ohio, Tennessee, and Rhode Island) have adopted trust laws that more closely follow the asset protection laws of foreign jurisdictions. Thus, a domestic trust with asset protection is now a possibility. Rules and protections vary among the states, so planners will need to work with a knowledgeable attorney to accomplish the asset protection objectives.

Support Trust

A support trust provides income to beneficiaries in discharging the grantor's legal obligation to provide them with support. Support trusts are usually used as part of the terms of a property settlement in a marriage dissolution. The trust usually pays income to the parent having custody of the children and terminates when the youngest child reaches majority.

Standby Trust

A standby trust does not become operational and is essentially unfunded (except for the nominal amount placed in it to make it a valid trust) until the grantor becomes disabled or incapacitated. The trustee is then authorized to use trust assets for the needs of the grantor. The primary benefit of the standby trust is to provide management expertise for the grantor's assets, in the event the grantor is unable to manage them. A standby trust might also be used when a grantor takes an extended absence from the U.S.

Rule Against Perpetuities

The rule against perpetuities limits a noncharitable trust essentially to a maximum duration of 21 years and 9 months beyond the life span of any persons alive at the time the trust was created. If a trust has a beneficiary that is a charity, the trust can have a perpetual duration; otherwise, a trust is limited by the rule against perpetuities. The rule is intended to prevent removal of property from the stream of commerce for long periods of time.

Dynasty Trust

A dynasty trust is an irrevocable trust that postpones vesting and continues as long as is permitted under state law. The dynasty trust is similar to a generation-skipping trust and often makes use of a life insurance policy to provide benefits for grandchildren. It is designed to avoid federal estate and generation-skipping transfer taxes by taking advantage of the $5.34 million GST exemption in 2015. (GST is discussed in more detail in Topic 69.) The duration of a dynasty trust is limited by the rule against perpetuities, but a few states such as Alaska, Arizona, Delaware, Idaho, Illinois, Maryland, North Dakota, South Dakota, and Wisconsin have no state rule against perpetuities. In these states, the trust can be established with a perpetual duration, and trust assets can escape federal transfer taxes indefinitely. Many other states have set the maximum duration of trusts at 250 to 1,000 years. Dynasty trusts may also contain provisions protecting assets from an heir's creditors and from becoming marital property in a divorce.

Sec. 2503(b) Trust and Sec. 2503(c) Trust

The Sec. 2503(b) trust and the Sec. 2503(c) trust are used for making gifts to minors and are discussed in Topic 56.

Discretionary and Sprinkling Provisions

A *discretionary provision* gives the trustee the authority to decide whether to distribute or not distribute income or corpus to beneficiaries. The trustee may make distributions or accumulate the income for later distribution. This discretion adds flexibility to the trust.

A *sprinkling or spray provision* allows the trustee to allocate income and, sometimes, corpus among the trust beneficiaries, according to their needs, abilities, or talents. In this way, a trustee will have discretion to provide for the unique needs of a beneficiary who may have a health impairment, uncertain employment, or a special talent. This provision also provides flexibility to a trust.

Trusts often provide for beneficiaries to have powers to invade the principal, to withdraw corpus, or to appoint assets. These *powers of appointment* have been discussed in an earlier section.

Trust Beneficiaries: Income and Remainder

Under a trust, beneficiaries can be given income interests or remainder interests. An income interest entitles the beneficiary to receive the income, such as interest, dividends, and rents, currently earned by the assets. The beneficiary with an income interest does not have a right to direct who will inherit the assets.

A remainder interest entitles the beneficiary to the assets after the income interest terminates. The beneficiary with a remainder interest receives nothing until the income interest terminates but will become the full owner and can then direct who will inherit the assets.

Gift Tax Rules for Trusts

Transfers to revocable trusts are not completed gifts, so there are no gift tax consequences for a transfer to a revocable trust. Transfers to irrevocable trusts are completed gifts, so the grantor is responsible for any gift tax liability.

With gifts in trust, a grantor may take advantage of gift-splitting, the gift tax annual exclusion, the GST annual exclusion, and the unified credit.

A grantor can make use of the gift tax annual exclusion to the extent that the gift passes a present interest to the donee. Trust documents often provide for contingent beneficiaries, who may have an interest only after other interests terminate. These future interests such as remainders are generally not eligible for the annual exclusion. The use of Crummey powers can overcome this problem. Crummey powers give the beneficiary a noncumulative right to withdraw the annual addition to a trust. This withdrawal right is usually granted for only a limited time, such as 30 days. By virtue of this power, a beneficiary is deemed to have a present interest in the trust assets. A trust can provide for several beneficiaries and contingent beneficiaries to have such demand powers, and the grantor will be able to take an annual exclusion for each such beneficiary and contingent beneficiary. Thus, Crummey trusts are useful devices for reducing the gift tax consequences of a gift in trust.

Gifts to Section 2503(b) and Section 2503(c) trusts will also qualify for the gift tax annual exclusion. These trusts are used for gifts to minors and are discussed more fully in Topic 56.

Estate Taxation of Trusts

Assets that a grantor transfers to a revocable trust will generally be included in the grantor's gross estate for federal estate tax purposes. As a general rule, assets transferred to an irrevocable trust will not be included in the grantor's gross estate, but there are some important exceptions. The following transfers to irrevocable trusts will be included in the grantor's gross estate:

- The grantor retains a life income or life estate.
- The grantor retains a reversionary interest.
- The grantor has a general power of appointment to direct to whom the assets will pass.
- The grantor dies within 3 years of transferring life insurance policies to the trust.
- The grantor transfers life insurance policies to the irrevocable trust and retains incidents of ownership, such as naming himself or herself trustee.
- The grantor retains an interest in the trust property, such as the right to pledge it for loans.

Recommendation of Appropriate Trust

To avoid probate, a grantor may make use of either the revocable or the irrevocable trust. Since assets are transferred to a trust, there is no testamentary power of disposition over the trust assets, whether revocable or irrevocable. Changes can be made to a revocable trust, whereas the irrevocable trust cannot be changed.

To reduce federal estate taxes, the irrevocable trust is recommended because assets transferred to the irrevocable trust are not included in the grantor's gross estate.

The main exception is life insurance, which must be transferred more than three years before the grantor's death to escape inclusion in the gross estate. Revocable trusts provide no estate tax reduction.

Some income shifting and income tax reduction can be accomplished by means of irrevocable trusts, but this benefit has been reduced by the steep tax rates applied to trusts.

Income Taxation of Trusts

Trusts and estates must file a return if they have more than $600 in gross income for the tax year. Also, a trust must file a return if it has any taxable income for the year.

A taxable trust files a Form 1041 to report income and distributions to beneficiaries. Estates use the same form. The due date for Form 1041 is the 15th day of the fourth month following the end of the entity's tax year. An automatic 6-month extension is available.

Trusts must use a calendar year unless they are tax-exempt, charitable, or a grantor trust. Estates may choose to use either a calendar or a fiscal year.

Tax Treatment of Distributions to Beneficiaries

The income of a trust or estate is taxed to the beneficiaries if it is distributed, and it is taxed to the trust if it is retained. Beneficiaries are also taxed on the amount that is required to be distributed even if it is not actually distributed. The income in the hands of the beneficiaries retains the same character it had in the hands of the trust or estate. Capital gains and interest income required to be distributed to beneficiaries are taxed as capital gains and interest, respectively, to the beneficiaries.

Rate Structure

Income retained and taxable to the trust or estate will be subject to the following tax brackets:

Tax Rates for Estates & Trusts

Tax Rate	2015 Taxable Income
15%	$0 – $2,500
25%	$2,501 – $5,900
28%	$5,901 – $9,050
33%	$9,051 – $12,300
39.6%	Over $12,300

The tax brackets for trusts and estates are very compact, and a trust will reach the highest tax rate with very little income. It is, therefore, difficult to create a significant reduction in overall taxes by transferring assets to a trust from a high-income client. Even if multiple trusts are formed, the income from all trusts will be added together before applying the tax rates if the grantor and the beneficiaries are substantially the same. However, one grantor could set up many trusts with different beneficiaries, and these trusts would be taxed separately, even if the trust assets were kept in one fund.

Grantor Trusts – Secs. 671-678

Under income tax laws, when a grantor creates a trust and retains certain powers or control over the trust, the trust is considered a grantor trust, and the trust income will be taxed to the grantor. An irrevocable trust that violates the grantor trust rules is sometimes called a defective or tainted trust. A trust may be set up as an intentionally defective trust so that trust income will be taxed to the grantor. The grantor may want to report the income if he or she will be in a lower tax bracket than the trust. Even though the income will be taxed to the grantor, the transfer to the trust may still be a completed gift for gift tax purposes and may remove the assets from the grantor's gross estate.

 ***K Study Tip* – The grantor trust rules are income tax rules and require the grantor to report trust income as though the grantor still owned the trust assets. These rules are not estate tax rules and do not require inclusion of trust assets in the grantor's gross estate.**

The following powers, if held by a grantor, will make a trust a grantor trust:

- The trust income is paid to the grantor or to his or her spouse.
- The trust income may be payable to the grantor or his or her spouse.
- The trust income is accumulated for future distribution to the grantor or his or her spouse.
- The trust income is or may be used to purchase life insurance on the grantor or his or her spouse.
- The trust income is or may be used to discharge a legal obligation of the grantor or the grantor's family, except where the income may be, but is not, used for the support of dependents.
- The trust principal or corpus will return to the grantor or spouse; in other words, the grantor retains a reversionary interest. A trust is not considered reversionary if the grantor's interest is 5% or less at the time the trust is funded. Thus, based on IRS tables and current interest rates, the trust will be reversionary unless it has a duration of approximately 43 years. However, if the grantor's reversionary interest exceeds 5%, income tax liability arises.

- The grantor retains the power to revoke or amend the trust.
- The grantor can dispose of income or corpus at less than full value.
- The grantor can borrow from the trust without adequate security or interest.
- The grantor retains the right, without the consent of an adverse party, to alter the beneficial enjoyment of the trust property or its income. There are several exceptions to this general rule. For example, a trust will not be subject to grantor trust taxation if it allows the grantor, as trustee, to sprinkle or to accumulate income or if the trustee can invade corpus for beneficiaries where the power of invasion is limited by a definite or ascertainable standard.

A trust that allows the grantor, a spouse, or a third party any of the above rights or powers will generally be taxed as a grantor trust. The third party granted such rights or powers will be treated as the owner.

If the purpose of setting up a trust is to have its income taxed separately from the grantor, then these provisions must be carefully considered in drafting the trust document. Grantor trusts do not report income and deductions on Form 1041; rather, all income and deductions are reported on the grantor's Form 1040.

Simple Trusts – Sec. 642(b)

For tax purposes, there are two distinct types of trusts described in the IRC. **Simple trusts are required to distribute all of their current accounting income to beneficiaries**. A simple trust cannot make charitable contributions and cannot make distributions in excess of current accounting income (no principal). These trusts can take as deductions most of those deductions allowed for individuals. Investment expenses incurred specifically for the trust's operation are deductible, without being subject to the 2% of AGI floor. A simple trust has a standard deduction of zero and a personal exemption of $300.

Complex Trusts

Complex trusts can accumulate income, make charitable contributions, and distribute principal to beneficiaries. Complex trusts also have a standard deduction of zero and are allowed the same deductions as simple trusts, except that the personal exemption amount is only $100, and the deduction for distributions is calculated differently.

Revocable and Irrevocable Trusts

Trusts can be either revocable or irrevocable. A revocable trust provides that the trust can be revoked or changed by the grantor at any time. A revocable trust must be a living, or inter vivos, trust because the grantor must be alive in order to exercise the power to revoke or amend the trust. After a grantor's death, a revocable trust becomes irrevocable because no one has the power to revoke it.

Trust Accounting Income

A trust's accounting income includes interest, dividends, rents, royalties, and other items. Capital gains may also be included in the income of the trust if allowed by state laws. As states adopt prudent investor statutes, which consider a total return approach to investing, capital gains are seen as a greater portion of the return on assets. Thus, more of the capital gains may be allocated to income, rather than to the corpus of the trust. The fiduciary will then allocate expense items to the sources of income, including depreciation and amortization allowed for individuals. The allocation of some items will be set out in local law, while others will be governed by the trust document. Where the trust document departs significantly from local statute, it will be ignored by the IRS.

Trust Taxable Income

A trust's taxable income is determined by taking accounting income and subtracting a trust's deductions for distributions. The trust can also take other deductions allowed by Regulation that are not subtracted from the accounting income, including the personal exemption previously described.

Distributable Net Income (DNI)

A trust's deduction for distributions cannot exceed its distributable net income (DNI). DNI includes capital gains, to the extent included in accounting income, and ignores capital losses, unless used to offset capital gains. DNI also includes tax-exempt income. However, the income distribution deduction (IDD) does not include any tax-exempt income, as the tax-exempt income is not part of the trust's taxable income. Likewise, the IDD does not include capital gains, as capital gains are typically taxed to the trust. When multiple items of income are received and distributed by a complex trust, the items distributed are governed by the trust document (i.e., interest and dividends are all distributed, but rental income is retained) or by multiplying each income item included in the DNI by a ratio calculated by dividing the actual distribution by the DNI. A complex trust can deduct actual distributions made, up to 65 days after the end of the trust's tax year, subject to the DNI ceiling.

The DNI is also the ceiling for the amount to be included in the income of the beneficiaries. Thus, the amount included in a beneficiary's income is the lesser of the allocation of DNI or the amount required to be distributed by the trust document. For example, if a trust has DNI of $5,000 and distributes $6,000, the first $5,000 is taxable income to the beneficiary, and the remaining $1,000 is a tax-free distribution of corpus.

A trust avoids double taxation on DNI because there is a deduction for any income that is actually distributed to beneficiaries. If a trust is required to distribute income to a beneficiary, the beneficiary must report the taxable income. The trust files a return, reporting the income that it retains, and the beneficiary files a tax return, reporting the income received or payable from the trust. The beneficiary will pay income tax based on his or her individual income tax rates.

Application Questions

1. Paul Grant does not want to transfer assets and property titles to a trust during his lifetime, but he would like to have a trust to administer assets for his grandchildren after his death. His assets consist mainly of life insurance proceeds, 401(k) plan benefits, and IRA accounts. The total of his assets is estimated to be less than $650,000. Which of the following trusts would be appropriate to recommend to Paul Grant?

    A. An irrevocable life insurance trust
    B. A revocable living trust
    C. A generation-skipping trust
    D. A Section 2503(c) trust
    E. A pour-over trust

2. Bernice Sinkler became angry at her children, so she executed a will, leaving $1 to each child. The remainder of her estate will pass to a trust which will pay income at least annually to her grandchildren until the youngest reaches age 21. The amount of income payable to each grandchild will be determined by the trustee. At the time the youngest grandchild turns 21, any principal and income remaining in the trust will be distributed to the grandchildren equally.

Which of the following statements concerning this trust are correct?

(1) If Bernice Sinkler's children predecease her and she has two grandchildren at the time of her death, the trust will be a simple trust.
(2) If Bernice Sinkler's children have not had any children at the time of her death, the trust will be invalid under the rule against perpetuities.
(3) If Bernice Sinkler has only one grandchild at the time of her death, the trust will be a revocable trust.
(4) If Bernice Sinkler's children are alive at the time of her death, the income beneficiaries and the remainder beneficiaries of the trust will be different persons.

    A. (1) and (2) only
    B. (1) and (3) only
    C. (2) and (3) only
    D. (3) and (4) only
    E. (1), (2), (3), and (4)

3. Victor Carmel established an irrevocable trust to which he transferred a vacation home that was located in another state. Victor provided that during the existence of the trust, anyone in his family could use the home upon consent of the trustee. Victor also contributed some marketable securities to the trust for maintenance and upkeep on the home. The trust is to terminate upon his wife's death, and the home is to be distributed to his children equally.

Which of the following statements concerning this trust are correct?

    (1) At Victor's death, the value of the vacation home will not be subject to inclusion in his gross estate.
    (2) Victor is an income beneficiary, and his wife is a remainder beneficiary of the trust.
    (3) In the year the vacation home is transferred to the trust, Victor is considered to have made taxable gifts for federal gift tax purposes.
    (4) Victor's trust is a complex trust.

    A. (1) and (2) only
    B. (1) and (3) only
    C. (2) and (3) only
    D. (3) and (4) only
    E. (1), (2), (3), and (4)

4. (Published question released December, 1996)

Which one of the following goals can be accomplished using a "pour-over" provision in a will?

    A. Transfer of assets from an estate into a trust created prior to the "pour-over" provision
    B. Minimization of estate taxes, resulting from the assets owned prior to the existence of the "pour-over" provision
    C. Transfer of assets from an estate to the estate of another person who died within the past three years
    D. Reduction of probate expenses during administration

5. Which of the following trusts is (are) complex trusts?

    (1) A revocable living trust
    (2) A 2503(b) trust
    (3) A 2503(c) trust
    (4) A QTIP trust

    A. (1) and (2) only
    B. (2) and (3) only
    C. (3) only
    D. (3) and (4) only

6. Which of the following pairs of trusts will allow the grantor to retain control during his or her lifetime but allow the assets to avoid probate at death?

    A. Sprinkle trust and irrevocable trust
    B. Pour-over trust and marital trust
    C. Bypass trust and standby trust
    D. Totten trust and revocable trust

7. Income from which of the following trusts will be taxed to the grantor?

(1) Revocable living trust
(2) Spousal remainder trust
(3) Irrevocable *inter vivos* trust
(4) Support trust

    A. (1) and (2) only
    B. (2) and (3) only
    C. (3) and (4) only
    D. (1), (2), and (4) only
    E. (1), (3), and (4) only

8. Which of the following statements concerning the taxation of estate and trust income are correct?

(1) Trusts are entitled to a personal exemption, but estates are not.
(2) Trusts and estates are both entitled to a standard deduction.
(3) For income in the range of $5,000 to $100,000, income taxes are lower for married individuals than for estates and trusts.
(4) The personal exemption for individuals is higher than the personal exemption for trusts.

    A. (1) and (2) only
    B. (1) and (3) only
    C. (1) and (4) only
    D. (2) and (3) only
    E. (3) and (4) only

9. Which of the following statements concerning trustees are correct?

(1) A trustee holds the legal title to the assets placed in the trust.
(2) The grantor may be the trustee for the trust.
(3) The trustee's obligation is to administer the trust assets for the grantor's benefit.
(4) The trustee is a fiduciary and has an equitable or beneficial right to the trust assets.

    A. (1) and (2) only
    B. (1) and (3) only
    C. (2) and (3) only
    D. (3) and (4) only
    E. (1), (2), (3), and (4)

10. Reginald Fortescue has created an irrevocable trust in which he has placed securities, valued at $1 million. His wife Jeanette will receive the income from the trust for her lifetime, and at her death, the trust assets will be divided between their son George and their daughter Mary. Which of the following statements concerning the Fortescue trust is (are) correct?

(1) George has a remainder interest in the trust.
(2) Mary has a reversionary interest in the trust.
(3) Jeanette has a life interest in the trust.
(4) Reginald has a reversionary interest in the trust.

    A. (1) only
    B. (4) only
    C. (1) and (3) only
    D. (2) and (3) only
    E. (3) and (4) only

11. Which of the following statements concerning revocable and irrevocable trusts are correct?

(1) An irrevocable trust may convey both a present interest and a future interest to the income or assets placed in the trust.
(2) A revocable trust may convey only a future interest to the income or assets in the trust.
(3) A revocable trust is not a completed gift because the assets can be taken back.
(4) An irrevocable trust can be either a testamentary trust or a living trust.

    A. (1) and (2) only
    B. (2) and (3) only
    C. (2) and (4) only
    D. (1), (3), and (4) only
    E. (1), (2), (3), and (4)

12. All the following statements concerning revocable living trusts are correct, EXCEPT:

    A. The trust becomes irrevocable upon the grantor's death.
    B. The trust enables a going business to continue without interruption.
    C. The trust provides first-generation estate tax advantages.
    D. The creation of the trust gives rise to no gift tax liability.
    E. When a grantor revokes the trust, there is no gift tax liability.

13. Which of the following objectives is LEAST likely to be achievable by means of an irrevocable *inter vivos* trust?

    A. To provide professional management of assets for beneficiaries unable to handle financial affairs
    B. To reduce income taxes
    C. To apportion death taxes among a person's heirs
    D. To provide income or assets for a charity
    E. To reduce federal estate taxes

14. Which of the following statements are correct for both revocable and irrevocable living trusts?

(1) Grantors can provide a life income for a primary beneficiary and avoid federal estate tax at the death of that beneficiary.
(2) The life-income beneficiaries can be given a right to obtain principal, in addition to the income of the trust.
(3) The assets transferred to the trust will avoid probate.
(4) The grantor can reduce income and estate tax liability.

    A. (1) and (2) only
    B. (1) and (3) only
    C. (2) and (3) only
    D. (3) and (4) only
    E. (1), (2), and (3) only

15. An irrevocable trust has certain advantages not provided by a revocable trust. Which of the following are advantages of the irrevocable trust over the revocable trust?

(1) Avoidance of probate
(2) Removal of assets from the gross estate
(3) Use of the annual exclusion
(4) Retention of control during the grantor's lifetime

    A. (1) and (2) only
    B. (1) and (3) only
    C. (2) and (3) only
    D. (2) and (4) only
    E. (3) and (4) only

16. Securities transferred to which of the following trusts will be included at the time of the grantor's death in the grantor's gross estate for federal estate tax purposes?

(1) Revocable living trust
(2) Testamentary trust
(3) Irrevocable *inter vivos* trust
(4) Funded revocable trust

    A. (1) and (2) only
    B. (3) and (4) only
    C. (1), (2), and (4) only
    D. (1), (3), and (4) only
    E. (1), (2), (3), and (4)

17. For an individual whose estate assets will consist largely of life insurance death proceeds, benefits from a qualified retirement plan, and benefits from a Keogh plan, which of the following trusts would probably be the most appropriate?

    A. Support trust
    B. Testamentary trust
    C. Pourover trust
    D. Generation-skipping trust
    E. Dynasty trust

18. All the following statements concerning the legal limitations placed on the duration of trusts are correct, EXCEPT:

    A. Such limitations are designed to return property to the stream of commerce.
    B. The common-law rule against perpetuities is still liberal enough to permit a trust to exist for 150 years.
    C. The rule against perpetuities does not apply to trusts whose beneficiaries are qualified charitable organizations.
    D. Trusts established for noncharitable beneficiaries must contain provisions providing a measure of time for the life of the trust.
    E. A state that does not have a rule against perpetuities is recommended for the situs of dynasty trusts.

19. Barbara Boyd set up an irrevocable trust for her two sons Dale and Peter and transferred dividend-paying stock to the trust. Barbara retained the power to decide when trust income and principal could be distributed to the two beneficiaries. Which of the following statements is correct?

    A. The income from the trust will be included in Barbara's gross income.

    B. The income from the trust will be taxed to Dale and Peter.

    C. The income from the trust will be reported by the trust, and tax paid at the trust rates.

    D. The income will be reported partly by Barbara, Peter, and Dale, according to the distributions.

For practice answering case questions related to Topic 62, please answer the following questions in the cases included in the Appendix at the back of this textbook.

Case	Questions
Bartlett	12
Marshall	
Webster	12 and 13
Unser	7 and 8
Tingey	1
Lytle	
Beals	
Mocsin	
Young	
Borelli	15
Cunningham	15
Fred and Mary Ferris	46, 47, 48, 49, and 50

Answers and Explanations

1. E is the answer. The pour-over trust will provide a receptacle for Paul's non-probate assets and allow for administration of the assets for his grandchildren. A life insurance trust is not required because Paul's gross estate is within the amount that will be sheltered by the applicable credit amount. A revocable trust is not required because Paul's assets are not subject to probate. A generation-skipping trust is not required because the assets Paul is transferring will not exceed the GST exemption. A Sec. 2503(c) trust is not appropriate because Paul is not making a lifetime gift.

2. A is the answer. The Sinkler trust is a simple trust because it will distribute all the income each year, it will not distribute principal, and it will not make charitable distributions. If no grandchildren are alive when Bernice dies, the trust will be invalid under the rule against perpetuities. The duration of the trust must be based on a life in being, not on someone who is unborn. If a grandchild is alive at the time of her death, the trust is valid and irrevocable because no one will have the power to revoke it. Since the grandchildren will receive the income from the trust and the remainder, the income beneficiaries and remainder beneficiaries are the same persons.

3. D is the answer. Victor has retained a right to use the home because he is a member of the family who can use it, so he has a retained interest, and the home will be subject to inclusion in his gross estate. The transfer of the home to the irrevocable trust is also a completed gift, so it is a taxable gift. Victor's wife is not a remainder beneficiary because the remainder will pass to the children. The trust is a complex trust because income will not be distributed.

4. A is the answer. A "pour-over" provision in a will provides for estate assets to be transferred to a trust. The trust must have been established before the will provision was written. The pour-over provision does not minimize estate taxes because the assets still pass through the estate. The pour-over provision does not reduce probate expenses during administration because the estate is still subject to probate.

5. C is the answer. The 2503(c) trust accumulates income, while the 2503(b) trust is required to distribute income each year, so the 2503(c) trust is a complex trust. The revocable living trust is not treated as a separate tax entity because the income is taxed to the grantor. The QTIP trust is a simple trust because all income is required to be distributed annually to the spouse.

6. D is the answer. The Totten trust is a bank account over which the depositor retains control during his or her lifetime and then passes to the beneficiary without probate. A revocable trust also passes outside probate, and the grantor retains the right to revoke and take back the assets.

7. D is the answer. The grantor trust rules require the income from a trust to be taxed to the grantor where the grantor retains the power to revoke the trust (revocable living trust), where the trust income may be payable to the grantor or to the grantor's spouse (spousal remainder trust), and where the trust income is used to discharge the obligation of the grantor (support trust). The income from an irrevocable *inter vivos* trust is not taxed to the grantor.

8. E is the answer. Trusts and estates are entitled to personal exemptions, but the amount of the exemption for estates is $600 and for simple trusts is $300. Trusts and estates are not entitled to the standard deduction. Income taxes are generally lower for individuals than for trusts and estates. The tax rates go up sooner and faster for trusts and estates. For example, in 2015, the tax rate for trusts and estates is 25% for income above $2,500; but for married individuals, the 25% bracket begins at $74,900. The personal exemption for individuals is $4,000 in 2015, and for simple trusts, it is $300.

9. A is the answer. A trustee holds the legal title to the assets placed in the trust. The grantor may be the trustee for the trust. The trustee's obligation is to administer the trust assets for the benefit of the beneficiaries, not for the grantor's benefit. The trustee is a fiduciary and must act for the benefit of the beneficiaries; but the beneficiary, not the trustee, has an equitable or beneficial right to the trust assets.

10. C is the answer. George has a remainder interest in the trust because his interest does not become operative until after the termination of his mother's life interest. A reversionary interest is a right the grantor retains to recover the property, so Mary has a remainder interest, not a reversionary interest. Jeanette has a life interest in the trust because she will receive the income for life. Reginald has not retained a reversionary interest in the trust.

11. D is the answer. An irrevocable trust may convey both a present interest and a future interest in the income or assets placed in the trust. A revocable trust also may convey a present interest as well as a future interest in the income or assets in the trust. A revocable trust is not a completed gift because the assets can be taken back. Both testamentary trusts and living trusts can be irrevocable.

12. C is the answer. Upon the death of the grantor of a revocable trust, the trust becomes irrevocable, inasmuch as the right to revoke expires with the grantor's death. The trust then continues after the grantor's death in irrevocable form, thereby enabling the continuation of a going business. The creation of the revocable trust does not incur any gift tax liability, inasmuch as the grantor is considered to be the owner of the trust corpus. Upon the grantor's death, the trust corpus is treated as being a part of his or her estate and, therefore, subject to estate tax. (Although subject to tax, there will not be any tax to pay if the amount of the estate is no greater than the decedent's exemption equivalent.)

13. C is the answer. A will is generally the appropriate place to apportion death taxes among the heirs receiving bequests under the will. Any directions concerning payment of death taxes in a trust would probably be ineffective as to heirs receiving bequests. The irrevocable *inter vivos* trust is established during the grantor's lifetime and can be used to reduce income taxes by directing that income be payable to beneficiaries other than the grantor. The trust can also be used to provide professional management of assets and to provide for charitable activities.

14. E is the answer. Trusts can be arranged to provide, upon the grantor's death, a life-interest income to a designated party, and, upon that party's death, the corpus passes to another individual or individuals. Very often, the trust is funded with an amount equivalent to the grantor's exemption equivalent. Upon the death of the party designated to receive the life-interest income, there is no estate tax liability, inasmuch as that party received only the income and not the corpus of the trust. Trusts can also be arranged so that the life-interest recipient can also receive principal, as well as the life interest. One means of doing this is by the use of a marital trust and a disclaimer trust. To illustrate, a husband-grantor creates a marital trust for the benefit of his wife and a disclaimer trust for her use. She can then, upon his death, file a "qualified disclaimer" over a part of the property she would otherwise have received from her husband's estate via the marital trust. This is usually done to assure taking full advantage of the deceased's unified estate and gift tax exemption. The survivor-wife then retains the life interest in the income of the disclaimer trust. Another means of enabling a life-interest beneficiary to obtain principal is to authorize the trustee, at his or her discretion, to invade the trust corpus in order to provide adequate funds for the health, education, or well-being of the life-interest recipient. Assets transferred both to revocable and irrevocable trusts will avoid probate, but only irrevocable trusts will reduce income and estate tax liability. The income from a revocable trust is taxable to the grantor under the grantor trust income tax rules.

15. C is the answer. Both revocable and irrevocable trusts avoid probate, which is considered a major advantage of both trust forms. The revocable trust, however, does not provide any benefit with regard to income or estate tax benefits. Revocable trusts, because of the right to revoke, are grantor trusts, and the income from these trusts is taxable to the grantor, and the trust property remains in the grantor's estate.

16. C is the answer. Assets placed in a revocable trust, funded or unfunded, are includible in the grantor's gross estate for federal estate tax purposes. An irrevocable *inter vivos* trust will remove property from the gross estate, except in a few situations.

17. C is the answer. Pourover trusts are particularly well suited to receiving liquid assets from almost any source: qualified retirement plans, Keogh plans, IRAs, life insurance proceeds, gifts, testamentary proceeds, etc. Except for the testamentary proceeds, the other properties mentioned all avoid probate. The terms of the pourover trust then specify how the trust income and corpus shall be distributed. The pourover trust can be revocable or irrevocable, with the attendant advantages/disadvantages.

18. B is the answer. All trusts except those that have charitable organizations as their beneficiaries must have life spans capable of being measured. The limit imposed on noncharitable trusts is a maximum of 21 years and 9 months beyond the life span of any persons alive at the time the trust is created. The purpose of the rule against perpetuities is to return trust property to the mainstream of commerce, and any trusts structured to exist longer than the beneficiary's life span plus 21 years and 9 months are invalid right from the start. States that do not have a rule against perpetuities are recommended for the situs of dynasty trusts because the trusts can avoid transfer taxes for generations.

19. A is the answer. Since Barbara retained the power to decide the beneficial enjoyment of the trust income and principal, the trust is a grantor trust, and the income is taxable to her.

Qualified Interest Trusts (Topic 63)

CFP Board Student-Centered Learning Objectives

(a) Determine when a qualified interest trust is needed.
   i. Qualified Terminable Interest Trust. [See Topic 66]
   ii. Qualified Domestic Interest Trust. [See Topic 66]

(b) Develop a qualified interest trust strategy (bypass trust, A-B trust). [See Topics 62 and 66 for marital and bypass trusts]

(c) Explain how and why QTIP property is a terminable-interest rule exception. [See Topic 66]

Qualified Interest Trusts
- *A.   Grantor-retained annuity trusts (GRATs)*
- *B.   Grantor-retained unitrusts (GRUTs)*
- *C.   Qualified personal residence trusts (QPRTs or House-GRITS)*
- *D.   Valuation of qualified interests*

Introduction

With a retained-interest trust, a grantor places assets in an irrevocable trust and retains an interest for a period of time. At the end of the period, the remaining assets in the trust will pass to a named beneficiary, such as a family member. If the trust and the retained interest comply with certain Tax Code rules, the trust will be eligible for estate and gift tax advantages. The Tax Code rules are found in Chapter 14 of the Tax Code, especially Section 2702. The qualified interest trusts are the GRAT, GRUT, and QPRT.

We begin the discussion with the GRIT, which is a grantor-retained income trust and generally does not qualify for special tax benefits under the Chapter 14 rules. There are, however, some interesting exceptions to this rule.

Grantor-Retained Income Trust (GRIT)

If a grantor transfers assets to a trust that will pay income to the grantor for life or for a specified number of years, the trust is a grantor-retained income trust, or GRIT. When the trust terminates, the assets in the trust will typically pass to an individual beneficiary, such as a child or grandchild. The grantor makes a gift of only the remainder, which is a future interest, and the grantor retains the income interest.

Chapter 14 of the Internal Revenue Code generally requires grantor-retained interests to be valued at zero. These valuation rules have greatly reduced the popularity of GRITs because the value of the gift is the entire value of the assets placed in the trust.

Moreover, the gift is a future interest, so the annual exclusion is not available. Chapter 14 rules are discussed in Topic 68 under estate freezes.

> ☼ *REMEMBER: THE GRIT IS SELDOM USED BECAUSE THERE IS NO REDUCTION IN THE VALUE OF THE GIFT FOR THE GRANTOR'S RETAINED INCOME INTEREST. THE ENTIRE VALUE OF THE ASSETS PLACED IN THE TRUST IS A TAXABLE GIFT.*

Nonfamily GRITs

A GRIT is subject to the Chapter 14 rules of valuation when the grantor or an applicable family member retains an interest and when an interest is transferred to a member of the transferor's family. If a GRIT is created in which the trust corpus will pass to a nonfamily member, the Chapter 14 valuation rules will not apply. Thus, a GRIT with a remainder interest that will pass to a nonfamily member is still a viable gift technique.

Example:

Jan Forstenza transferred $1 million into a trust for her son Fred and $1 million into a trust for her close friend Nicole. Jan retained the income from the trusts for 14 years. Both trusts are GRITs due to the grantor-retained income interest.

The trust for the son will be a taxable gift of $1 million because the value of the retained income interest will be zero. The gift is a future interest, so Jan cannot take the annual exclusion.

With the trust for her friend Nicole, the value of the retained income interest will not be valued at zero, so the gift will be reduced substantially. The gift to the friend might be a taxable gift of only $400,000.

Qualified Personal Residence Trust (QPRT) – Sec. 2702

A qualified personal residence trust (QPRT) is an exception to the Chapter 14 rules of valuation. **With a QPRT, the grantor transfers a personal residence to an irrevocable trust and retains the right to live in the property for a term of years. At the end of the term of years, the trust beneficiary receives full title to the residence**.

In valuing the transfer to the trust, the gift will be the remainder interest, and the remainder is valued by subtracting the term interest retained by the grantor.

The term interest is valued using the monthly published interest rate, which is 120% of the federal midterm interest rate, and IRS tables. As interest rates decline, the present value of the retained interest drops, so the value of the gift increases. Thus, when interest rates are low, a QPRT will be less advantageous.

If the grantor survives the term of the trust, the residence will be entirely removed from the grantor's gross estate. If the grantor does not survive the term, the fair market value of the residence will be included in the grantor's estate, but the adjusted taxable gift is then reduced to zero.

Although there is little downside from an estate and gift tax perspective to setting up a QPRT, complexities can arise after the term of the trust has past and the grantor no longer retains the right to live in the property. For example, if a mother transfers her house into a QPRT for the benefit of her son and desires to continue living in the house once the term is up, she must pay a fair market value rental rate to him or risk creating a gift tax issue. Furthermore, the son is now the sole owner of the property and has the right to sell the house at anytime, potentially forcing his mother to relocate against her wishes. For these reasons it is important that family members understand the implications of the QPRT and agree on how they will handle the living arrangements post-term.

☞ *K Study Tip* – **QPRTs generally will be recommended for wealthy individuals who have homes that are over $500,000 in FMV. The grantor should be reasonably healthy and have a longer life expectancy than the term of the trust. The grantor and the beneficiaries should be in agreement on the grantor's living arrangements after the term of the trust. The benefits of the QPRT are only achieved if the grantor survives the term of the trust.**

A QPRT can hold only one residence.

Personal property such as furniture may not be transferred to the trust, but cash sufficient to pay the mortgage for six months can be contributed.

Practice Question

Ken bought a house for $300,000 and transferred it to a QPRT that was to continue for a term of 12 years. At the time the QPRT was created, the house was worth $500,000. Ken died 10 years later, when the house was worth $700,000. What amount is included for the house in Ken's gross estate?

    A. $0
    B. $50,000
    C. $500,000
    D. $700,000

Answer:
Since Ken did not outlive the term of the QPRT, the entire value of the house on his date of death is included in his gross estate. The house will be included at the value of $700,000.
The answer is D.

Tangible Personal Property Trusts

Another exception to the Chapter 14 rules for valuation is a transfer in trust of certain tangible personal property. The kinds of property that can be transferred are non-wasting assets for which no depreciation deduction is allowed. For example, artwork could be transferred to a trust, and the grantor might retain use of the work for 12 years. The retained interest must be valued according to the amount for which the term interest (enjoyment of the artwork for 12 years) could be sold to an unrelated third party. The difficulty of proving this use value makes these trusts somewhat unappealing.

Qualified Interests

**GRAT –
Sec. 2702(b)**

Chapter 14 provides special rules for valuation when the grantor retains a "qualified interest."

One such "qualified interest" is a right to receive fixed amounts, payable at least annually – or, an annuity.

If a grantor transfers assets to an irrevocable trust and retains a right to an annuity for a stated number of years, the trust is a grantor-retained annuity trust (GRAT).

For example, the grantor may transfer assets to a trust and retain a right to receive annually a payment of 6% of the initial fair market value of the trust assets.

For a GRAT, the IRS Section 7520 tables are used to calculate the present value of the annuity, and this amount is subtracted from the total value of the assets transferred to the trust to calculate the value of the remainder interest. Thus, the value of the gift, which is the remainder interest, can be relatively low for gift tax purposes. The IRS takes the position that the gift value cannot be reduced to zero, although recent court cases have held otherwise.

Example:

Nancy established a 12-year GRAT with securities valued at $300,000. If the IRS Section 7520 interest rate is 6.0%, the remainder factor is 0.496969, so the gift consisting of the remainder interest will be (0.496969 x $300,000) = $149,091.

**GRUT –
Sec. 2702(b)**

Another "qualified interest" is a right to receive annual payments of a fixed percentage of the trust assets, determined annually – or, a unitrust interest.

For example, the grantor may transfer assets to a trust and retain a right to receive annually 6% of the fair market value of the trust assets, as determined each year.

This trust is a grantor-retained unitrust or GRUT and will produce a reduced valuation of the remainder interest for gift tax purposes.

**GRATs and GRUTs –
Surviving the Term**

With GRATs and GRUTs, the assets placed in trust will pass to the remainderperson at the expiration of the term of the grantor's retained annuity or unitrust interest. If the grantor survives the term, therefore, the entire value of the assets will pass free of federal estate tax to the remainderperson, and the grantor has reported only a small taxable gift. The assets will not, however, receive a step-up in basis at the grantor's death.

Not Surviving the Term

If the grantor does not survive the term of a GRAT or GRUT, the value of the trust assets will be included in the grantor's gross estate.

GRATs vs. GRUTs

A GRAT will accomplish more wealth transfer than a GRUT if the assets are expected to appreciate because the payments to the grantor from the GRUT will increase as the assets appreciate. These increased payments return more assets to the grantor's gross estate. If the grantor needs to be assured of a fixed flow of income, the GRAT is a better choice.

The GRAT requires valuation of assets only once – at the time the property is transferred to the trust – whereas a GRUT requires valuation each year. So, property that is expensive to value should be placed in a GRAT, and only property easily valued should be placed in a GRUT.

Appreciating assets, such as dividend-paying common stocks and growth stocks, are better choices for GRATs than fixed-income assets, such as bonds.

A GRUT accomplishes more wealth transfer when the assets are not expected to perform well because the payments vary and do not exhaust as much of the trust corpus. The GRUT is a better choice when the grantor wants some inflation protection by means of increased payments as the assets appreciate. A GRUT is required if the grantor wants to add assets to the trust later.

🔑 KEY SUMMARY 63 – 1
Table of Grantor-Retained Interest Trusts

	GRAT	*GRUT*	*QPRT*
What is the grantor's retained interest?	Fixed % of the *initial* value of the assets for a term of years	Fixed % of assets as valued *annually* for a term of years	Use of a personal residence retained for a term of years
What is the value of the gift?	Remainder interest after deducting the value of the retained <u>annuity</u>	Remainder interest after deducting the value of the retained <u>unitrust</u>	Remainder interest after deducting the value of the retained <u>use</u> interest
Can the annual exclusion be used?	No, remainder is a future interest.	No, remainder is a future interest.	No, remainder is a future interest.
If the grantor survives the term of the trust, will his or her gross estate include trust assets?	No; but if the grantor dies during the term, trust assets are fully included.	No; but if the grantor dies during the term, trust assets are fully included.	No; but if the grantor dies during the term, trust assets are fully included.

Application Questions

1. Which of the following statements concerning the advantages of the GRAT and GRUT are correct?

(1) A GRAT is better than a GRUT for wealth transfer when the assets are expected to appreciate.

(2) A GRAT is better than a GRUT when additional assets will be added to the trust.

(3) A GRUT is better than a GRAT when inflation protection is desired by the grantor.

(4) A GRUT is better than a GRAT when the assets are difficult to value, such as real estate.

    A. (1) and (2) only
    B. (1) and (3) only
    C. (2) and (3) only
    D. (2) and (4) only
    E. (1), (2), (3), and (4)

2. (Published question released December, 1996)

A correct statement regarding the use of a grantor-retained annuity trust (GRAT) as an estate planning technique is that such a strategy:

    A. Is appropriate only if the remainder beneficiary is the grantor's spouse

    B. Saves estate taxes only if the grantor lives beyond the trust term

    C. Guarantees that the trust property will receive a stepped-up basis at the grantor's death

    D. Is generally inappropriate if the trust corpus consists of income-producing assets

3. Which of the following statements concerning QPRTs are correct?

(1) With a QPRT, the gift is not eligible for the gift tax annual exclusion.

(2) A QPRT can hold any number of residences but no personal property.

(3) A QPRT should be established for a term of years and not for the grantor's life.

(4) With a QPRT, the value of the gift is computed as an annuity, using the Sec. 7520 rate of interest.

    A. (1) and (2) only
    B. (1) and (3) only
    C. (2) and (4) only
    D. (1), (2), (3), and (4)

4. Jennifer Downes is 65 years of age and is a widow. She has assets that total approximately $5 million, including real estate worth $1 million that produces no income and a large home valued at $600,000. She has previously used her unified credit (applicable credit amount). She is considering estate planning and gifts for her children. Which of the following techniques would be the most appropriate for her?

    A. QPRT
    B. GRIT
    C. GRAT
    D. GRUT

5. Which of the following statements concerning a personal residence trust is correct?

   A. A taxpayer may have only one personal residence trust.

   B. A taxpayer may transfer furniture and mortgages on residential property to a personal residence trust.

   C. The right to live in a home transferred to a personal residence trust is valued at zero for federal gift tax purposes.

   D. If the grantor dies before the trust terminates, part of the value of the trust assets will be includible in the grantor's gross estate.

   E. At the end of the term of the trust, ownership of the personal residence returns to the grantor.

6. All the following statements concerning a grantor-retained income trust (GRIT) are correct, EXCEPT:

   A. The trust must be irrevocable.

   B. Money or property is transferred to the trust, and the grantor retains the right to the trust income for a fixed period.

   C. If the grantor lives beyond the specified number of years, there is no additional transfer tax.

   D. Since the remainder of the trust passes to the beneficiaries, the gift tax annual exclusion is available to the donor.

   E. For gift tax purposes, the value of the gift is equal to the entire value of the property transferred to the trust and is not reduced for the value of the grantor's retained income interest.

7. Carol wants to gift some assets to her son Dan in 5 years. She is willing to put the assets in a trust today if she can maintain an income stream that will be adjusted for the growth of the assets. Which type of trust should Carol establish to accomplish her goal?

   A. GRAT

   B. GRIT

   C. GRUT

   D. QPRT

8. Sue wants to gift some assets to her son Chris in 10 years. She is willing to put the assets in a trust today if she can maintain an income stream during the term of the trust, while saving all of the appreciation for Chris. Which type of trust should Sue establish to accomplish her goal?

   A. GRAT

   B. GRIT

   C. GRUT

   D. QPRT

9. Ron established a GRAT, a GRIT, and a GRUT for the benefit of his daughter Beth. Which of these trusts qualify for the annual gift tax exclusion?

   A. GRAT and GRUT only

   B. GRIT only

   C. All three – GRAT, GRIT, and GRUT

   D. None of the above

10. Assume that the named grantor is considering the use of a GRIT, GRAT, GRUT, or QPRT.

You should select the choice that will best accomplish the grantor's objective.

Robert Hall, age 62, has no children and wants to pass his estate to his nephew, with a minimum of transfer taxes. He is considering a gift in trust of stock in the S corporation that he owns and operates. Robert would like to receive income from the stock for at least 12 years. The corporation is an auto parts distributor, and the nephew works in the business. The stock is worth approximately $1 million and is expected to appreciate.

    A. GRAT
    B. GRUT
    C. GRIT
    D. QPRT

For practice answering case questions related to Topic 63, please answer the following questions in the cases included in the Appendix at the back of this textbook.

Case	Questions
Bartlett	
Marshall	
Webster	
Unser	
Tingey	
Lytle	6
Beals	
Mocsin	
Young	
Borelli	16
Cunningham	16
Fred and Mary Ferris	51, 52, 53, 54, and 55

Answers and Explanations

1. B is the answer. A GRAT is better than a GRUT for wealth transfer when the assets are expected to appreciate. The GRAT payments are fixed, while the GRUT payments will increase as assets appreciate. As a result, more assets return to the grantor by way of the increased payments. A GRUT is required when additional assets will be added to the trust. A GRUT is better than a GRAT when inflation protection is desired by the grantor because the payments vary according to appreciation of the trust assets. A GRAT is better than a GRUT when the assets are difficult to value, such as real estate, because the GRUT requires annual valuation, and the GRAT requires valuation only at the time of the initial creation of the trust. Annual valuation will be expensive for assets such as real estate.

2. B is the answer. Generally, a grantor-retained annuity trust (GRAT) will save estate taxes only if the grantor survives the trust term because the trust assets are includible in the grantor's gross estate as long as the grantor has a retained interest in the trust. Once the trust term ends, the assets of the trust are removed from the grantor's estate. A GRAT is not appropriate if the remainder beneficiary will be the grantor's spouse because the assets could be given to the spouse outright without any payment of gift tax, due to the marital deduction. There is no reason to set up a GRAT to accomplish a transfer to a spouse. The trust assets that pass from a GRAT to the remainder beneficiary do not receive a stepped-up basis because the assets were not held by the grantor at death. Generally, a GRAT should be set up with income-producing assets because the trust needs income to pay the grantor the retained annuity.

3. B is the answer. With a QPRT, the gift is not eligible for the gift tax annual exclusion. A QPRT can hold one personal residence and no personal property. A QPRT should be established for a term of years and not for the grantor's life. If the trust is established for the grantor's life, the value of the property in the trust will be included in the grantor's gross estate at the grantor's death. The estate tax benefit of the QPRT will, therefore, be lost. With a QPRT, the value of the gift is the remainder interest, rather than the use interest. The remainder is computed by subtracting the value of the use interest, using the Sec. 7520 rate of interest.

4. A is the answer. The residence can be transferred to a QPRT, and the gift will be substantially discounted, based on the number of years of the retained term interest. Jennifer has a sufficient life expectancy at age 65 to take advantage of the QPRT and outlive the term of years. The benefits will be obtained if she outlives the term of years of the trust. The other real estate will not be a good prospect for the GRAT or GRUT because the property is non-income-producing. A GRIT will provide no gift tax or income tax benefits.

5. D is the answer. A personal residence trust is created for a term of years, and if the grantor of a personal residence trust dies before the end of the term of years, the value of the trust assets will be includible in the grantor's gross estate because the grantor has a retained interest. If the grantor lives beyond the term of years, the trust assets will be entirely removed from the grantor's gross estate. A taxpayer may have two personal residence trusts, but furniture and other personal property may not be transferred to the trust. The residence may be transferred with a mortgage, but mortgages on other properties may not be placed in the trust. The retained right to live in the home is not valued at zero.

6. D is the answer. The gift to the remainderperson is a gift of a future interest; therefore, the gift tax annual exclusion is not available. A, B, C, and E are correct statements.

7. C is the answer. Carol will want to use the GRUT (grantor-retained unitrust), as her unitrust payment will be adjusted for the growth of the assets during the 5-year term. The GRAT payments would be fixed based on the initial value of the trust. The GRIT payments would only be the actual income earned on the trust each year. The GRIT would also be a complete gift of her interest at the time Carol funded the trust. The QPRT is used with a home and does not generate an income stream.

8. A is the answer. Sue will want to use the GRAT (grantor-retained annuity trust), as GRAT payments would be fixed based on the initial value of the trust. As a result, the appreciation will pass to her son Chris. If she used the GRUT, her annual unitrust payments would be adjusted for the growth of the trust assets. The GRIT payments would only be the actual income earned on the trust each year. The GRIT would also be a complete gift of her interest at the time Carol funded the trust. The QPRT is used with a home and does not generate an income stream.

9. D is the answer. The GRAT, GRIT, and GRUT are all future-interest gifts. As a result, they do not qualify for the annual gift tax exclusion.

10. C is the answer. The nonfamily GRIT is another exception to the rule. Since the nephew is not a family member under Sec. 2702, a gift in trust will be subject to valuation, using the Sec. 7520 rate of interest. The grantor's retained interest will not be valued at zero, so the gift tax value will be reduced. The S corporation stock can be given to a Qualified Subchapter S Trust. The GRIT offers greater flexibility than the GRAT or GRUT because the trust is only obligated to pay out whatever income it receives from the S corporation stock. The GRAT or GRUT may provide for annuity payments that exceed the income distributions on the S corporation stock in a given year, and then the trust will have to distribute stock back to the grantor. If the annuity payments are less than the distributions, the grantor will still have to pay income tax on the amounts accumulated in the trust. Assuming the same rate of interest for the GRIT as the rate of annuity payout for a GRAT or GRUT, the GRIT will have a lower gift tax value.

Charitable Transfers (Topic 64)

CFP Board Student-Centered Learning Objectives

(a) Explain the options for transferring assets to qualified charities, including current, deferred, remainder, income and insurance gifts or bequests.

(b) Select the charitable transfer vehicle appropriate to the client based on current income needs, future gifting plans, estate distribution plans, and estate tax implications.

(c) Calculate the effect of charitable gifting on income tax liabilities.

Charitable Transfers
- A.   *Outright gifts*
- B.   *Charitable remainder trusts*
  - *1)   Unitrusts (CRUTs)*
  - *2)   Annuity trusts (CRATs)*
- C.   *Charitable lead trusts*
  - *1)   Unitrusts (CLUTs)*
  - *2)   Annuity trusts (CLATs)*
- D.   *Charitable gift annuities*
- E.   *Pooled-income funds*
- F.   *Private foundations*
- G.   *Donor-advised funds*
- H.   *Estate and gift taxation*

Outright Gifts

An outright gift to charity is a transfer of assets in which the donor retains no interest or control. The donor simply makes a gift of cash or property, and the charity has free use of the property for its charitable purposes. If the gift is a lifetime gift, the donor is entitled not only to the gift tax charitable deduction (after the annual exclusion), but also to an income tax deduction.

Charitable Deduction – Secs. 2055 and 2522

As with the marital deduction, there is no limit on the value of assets eligible for the gift and estate tax charitable deductions. An unlimited amount of property can be transferred to qualified charities during a person's lifetime or at death, without incurring federal transfer taxes. A lifetime gift to charity has the advantage of providing an income tax deduction, as well as removing the property from the taxpayer's gross estate. There is no income tax deduction for a testamentary bequest to charity.

Income Tax Deduction and Public Charities – Sec. 170

For gifts to public charities, a taxpayer's income tax deduction is limited to 50% of the taxpayer's adjusted gross income (AGI). If the gift is of long-term capital gain property, the deduction is limited to 30% of AGI. A taxpayer can make a special election to have this 30% increased to 50% of AGI, provided the gift is reduced from its fair market value to the taxpayer's adjusted basis.

Income Tax Deductions with Private Charities

For gifts to private foundations or private charities, the taxpayer's income tax deduction is limited to the lesser of 30% of AGI or 50% of AGI minus the deduction taken for gifts to public charities. If the gift consists of long-term capital gain property, the deduction is limited to 20% of AGI. Gifts in excess of the limits can be carried forward for 5 years, but cannot be carried back.

Private Foundation

A private foundation is a charity set up by an individual, by a family, or sometimes by a business. The private foundation differs from the public charity in that the public does not provide most of the foundation's financial support, and the donor can retain control over the organization. The foundation must be set up for charitable, religious, scientific, literary, or educational purposes.

A wealthy individual or family may set up a private foundation not only to obtain the income and estate tax benefits from charitable gifts, but also to accomplish specific charitable goals and to focus charitable activities in a particular area. For example, the foundation may be set up to provide scholarships for talented musicians or artists. The donor makes contributions to the foundation and takes the deductions as described above. The foundation distributes the money to school scholarship funds or sometimes makes grants through its own scholarship program.

Foundations are tax-exempt, but they are subject to a 2% excise tax on investment income. A private foundation must distribute its investment income by the end of the year following the year in which the income is earned.

The amount of distributions must be at least 5% of the assets. Failure to make sufficient distributions can result in a 15% tax on the income.

A private foundation cannot hold more than 20% of the stock of a private corporation. Foundations also are prohibited from engaging in transactions with the donor or the donor's family, except that the foundation can pay family members a reasonable salary and expenses for services.

🔑 KEY SUMMARY 64 – 1
Limits on Individual Income Tax Deductions for Charitable Contributions

Gifts	Limit if to Public Charity	Limit if to Private Charity
Cash and ordinary income property	50% of AGI	30% of AGI
Long-term capital gain property	30% of AGI OR 50% with the election to value at the cost basis	20% of AGI

Selecting Property for Outright Gifts to Charity

Generally, a gift of property that has declined in value is not advantageous. The owner would do better to sell the property, deduct the loss from income, and give the money obtained from the sale to the charity. The taxpayer then will have both the charitable deduction equal to the fair market value of the property and the deduction for the capital loss.

Life Insurance

A gift of life insurance is advantageous because the relatively small gifts in the form of premiums result in a much larger gift when the charity receives the death benefit later. If an existing policy is transferred to a charity, the deduction is the lesser of the donor's cost or the replacement cost of the policy. The donor may take current income tax deductions when additional contributions of premiums are made.

Future Interests

In general, gifts to charity of future interests are not deductible for federal income tax purposes until all rights and possession have been transferred to the charitable organization.

Charitable Deduction Planning

Most charitable deduction planning involves a transfer of a partial interest. In other words, the owner of the assets plans to transfer an asset to a charity, which will also confer benefits, such as an income stream on another beneficiary who is not a charity. The general rule is that gifts of partial interest will not qualify as deductible contributions; nevertheless, such transfers of partial interests to charities can still result in a charitable deduction if approved techniques are followed. The first group of approved techniques – charitable trusts – are effective both as lifetime and testamentary gifts, but only lifetime gifts qualify for income tax charitable deductions.

CRAT – Sec. 664

A charitable remainder annuity trust (CRAT) is established by transferring money and/or securities to a trust which will provide an annual income stream to a noncharitable beneficiary. The beneficiary may receive this income for a period not to exceed 20 years or for life, and the remainder goes to the designated charity. **The annuity payable to the noncharitable beneficiary must provide for an annual payment of at least 5% of the initial value of the property placed in trust,** and the annual payment must be made from the trust income and/or principal.

The noncharitable beneficiary must be a living person when the trust is established, and the trust must be irrevocable. The annual income of the trust is taxable to the income beneficiary.

Charitable Deduction

For income tax purposes, the charitable deduction available with a CRAT is calculated using the same tables that are used in valuing annuities. If a CRAT is set up by a 65-year-old grantor with $100,000 in cash, and the trust provides for a 5% annual payment to the grantor for life, the value of the retained income interest is calculated using the IRS tables for the present worth of an annuity.

For an assumed rate of 8.6%, the table shows an annuity factor for a 65-year-old to be 8.1614. This annuity factor is multiplied by the $5,000 annual payment, to give a retained income interest of $40,807. The remainder interest, therefore, is the total value of the trust assets, less the retained income interest, which comes to $59,193. This is the amount of the charitable deduction.

If the income from the trust assets of a CRAT is insufficient to pay the 5% annual income to the grantor, the trust principal must be invaded to pay the promised annuity payment.

CRUT – Sec. 664

The feature which distinguishes the charitable remainder **unitrust** (CRUT) from the charitable remainder **annuity** trust (CRAT) is in how the amount of the annual income to the noncharitable beneficiary is specified. Income payments from the unitrust must be at least 5% of the annual value of the trust property. Thus, payments from the **unitrust** will vary with changes in the value of the unitrust's portfolio, whereas the payments from the **annuity** trust will be the same amount each year. If the income from the assets in the CRUT is not sufficient to make the 5% annual payment, invasion of the trust principal is permitted. Note that with a CRUT, the trust may provide for invasion of the principal, but it is not required. With a CRUT, the trust may also have a "make-up" provision, allowing payment from one year's income to make up for inadequate income in another year.

> ☞ **K Study Tip** – With a CRUT, the percentage of assets to be paid is *fixed*, but the actual payments are *variable* because the assets are revalued annually.

50% Rule

Two additional requirements apply to CRATs and CRUTs. First, for a CRAT, the annuity payment for any year cannot be greater than 50% of the initial fair market value of the trust assets; and for a CRUT, the percentage of assets required to be distributed annually cannot be greater than 50%.

10% Rule

Second, the value of any remainder interest that goes to the charity under a CRAT or CRUT must be at least 10% of the net fair market value of the assets on the date they are contributed to the trust.

These requirements apply to charitable remainder trusts created after July 28, 1997, and are intended to make certain that a minimum amount of assets will actually pass to the charity after the trust ends.

Comparison of CRATs and CRUTs

The annuity trust is easier to administer than the unitrust because there is no need to revalue the annuity trust assets each year in order to determine the amount of the annual income payment. Once the annuity trust is funded, the annual payments are a fixed, constant amount. For both the annuity trust and the unitrust, the donor may take a charitable deduction equal to the present value of the remainder interest passing to the charity in the future. A larger current income tax deduction may be provided by the annuity trust than by the unitrust because of differences in the way the value of the remainder interests are calculated.

Inflation Protection with CRUTs

For the annuity trust, inflation is a concern, inasmuch as the fixed annual payment from the annuity trust loses purchasing power as inflation progresses. Presumably, the value of the unitrust portfolio will increase with inflation, so payments based on a percentage of its annually revalued assets will increase from year to year.

In actuality, there is no reason that the income generated by an annuity trust should be less than that of a unitrust. Income production for either trust is, on a practical basis, related to the trust objectives and the trustee's management skills.

A potential disadvantage of the annuity trust is that an unfavorable invasion of the trust principal may occur if the fixed annuity payments are greater than the trust income. Another disadvantage is that assets cannot be added to the annuity trust in subsequent years; whereas, additional contributions to a unitrust are permitted.

Pooled-Income Fund

The pooled-income fund has many of the same characteristics as the aforementioned remainder-interest trusts (annuity and unitrust), but it differs in that **the fund is created (or has already been created) by the public charity. The donor transfers property to the charitable organization, and the property is then commingled in the trust with the property transferred by other donors**. A lifetime interest must be retained for the noncharitable beneficiary, and the annual payment to the beneficiary is a pro rata share of the trust income. If the income from trust assets is insufficient to make annual payments, the trust assets may not be invaded to make up the deficiency. While the CRAT and CRUT can invest in tax-exempt securities, the pooled-income fund cannot.

The transfer by the donor is irrevocable, as with all other remainder interest arrangements. The value of the gift for tax purposes is, again, the value of the remainder interest, but this value is calculated using slightly different IRS factors, giving it a current charitable deduction that is somewhat less than those of the annuity trust and the unitrust.

The unlimited charitable deduction applies to any interests passing to a qualified charity, so no gift tax is owed when a CRAT, a CRUT, or a pooled-income fund is created unless the income beneficiary is someone other than the donor. Similarly, no federal estate tax is owed at the donor's death since the remainder interest passes to the charity and qualifies for the charitable deduction.

┌───┐
🔑 **KEY SUMMARY 64 – 2**
  Charitable Remainder Trusts
└───┘

	CRAT	*CRUT*	*Pooled-Income Fund*
What income is paid to the noncharitable beneficiary?	Annuity pays at least 5% (but no more than 50%) of the *initial* FMV of assets annually, for up to 20 years or life.	Unitrust pays at least 5% (but no more than 50%) of the *annual* FMV of assets, for up to 20 years or life.	Trust pays a pro rata share of income earned by commingled trust assets.
Is principal invaded if trust income is not sufficient?	Yes, principal must be invaded.	Invasion can be provided, or may have make-up provision.	No, only income earned by the trust is paid.
Can the grantor add assets later?	No	Yes	Yes
Should real estate be contributed?	Yes, only one valuation is required.	No, valuation is required annually.	Yes
What is the amount of the income tax deduction?	FMV less present value of the retained annuity interest.	FMV less present value of the retained unitrust interest.	FMV less present value of the retained income interest.
What is the important feature for planning purposes?	Guaranteed annual income for life, like a fixed annuity.	Income is inflation protected like a variable annuity.	Donor does not have costs to set up and maintain a trust.
Can the remainder be payable to *any* charity or is the donor limited to a *specific* charity?	Payable to *any* charity. (Donor can select one or more charities.)	Payable to *any* charity. (Donor can select one or more charities.)	Payable to a *specific* charity. (Charity setting up the fund is the only charity benefited.)

Remainder Interests

The gift of a remainder interest in a taxpayer's personal residence or farm is another means of obtaining a current charitable income tax deduction for the gift of a partial interest. **In this case, the taxpayer gives the property to the charity but retains a lifetime right of occupancy for himself or herself, his or her spouse, and/or another third-party noncharitable beneficiary.** The value of the allowable deduction at the time of the gift is the fair market value of the residence or farm, which is reduced by an actuarial discount since the gift is postponed.

Charitable Lead Trusts (CLATs and CLUTs)

The charitable lead trust differs radically from the charitable remainder trusts in that the donor in the charitable lead trust gives away an income stream and receives a remainder interest. The donor places income-producing property in a reversionary trust and directs that the trust income be transferred to a designated charity for a period of time or for the life or lives of designated individuals. At the end of this "lead" time, the property reverts back to the donor or to some other noncharitable beneficiary. The trust is a grantor trust, and the annual income is taxable to the donor.

The benefit the donor receives is a very large income tax deduction in the year that the trust is funded because the value of the deduction is the present value of the total anticipated income during the lead period, when the charity receives the income. The charitable lead trust can also be established by a testamentary bequest, and the benefit received is a reduction in the value of the estate in the amount of the actuarial value of the income stream directed to the charity.

The charitable lead annuity trust (CLAT) makes annuity payments to the charity that are at least 5% of the initial fair market value of the trust assets. The charitable lead unitrust makes payments to the charity of at least 5% of the fair market value of the trust assets as recomputed each year.

EXHIBIT 64 – 1 **Comparison of Charitable Remainder Trusts and Charitable Lead Trusts**		
	Charitable Remainder Trust	*Charitable Lead Trust*
What is the gift to charity?	Remainder interest (at least 10% of the trust value)	Income interest
How is the charitable deduction figured?	FMV of trust assets less PV of retained income interest	PV of income interest
What are the planning opportunities?	Grantor receives annuity or unitrust income and takes a deduction for remainder interest	If grantor has other wealth, a large deduction is obtained when interest rates are low; remainder reverts to grantor or goes to a noncharitable beneficiary.

Charitable Gift Annuity

Charitable organizations offer donors the opportunity to buy annuities from the charity and make a charitable gift at the same time. The donor is buying a fixed annuity rather than a variable income flow under a pooled-income fund. The donor will often pay more than the value of the annuity, so there is a charitable contribution, as well as the purchase of an annuity.

Bargain Sale – Sec. 1011

In a bargain sale, long-term capital gain property is usually sold to a charity at a price less than its fair market value. The owner will recognize capital gain, but the amount of the gain is reduced. In computing the gain, the owner allocates his or her basis, both to the part of the property that is a gift and to the part of the property that is a sale. The percentage of the owner's basis that is assigned to the gift is the amount of appreciation divided by the property's fair market value. The basis assigned to the sale is the original basis minus the amount assigned to the gift. The owner's long-term capital gain is the sale price to the charity minus that portion of the basis assigned to the sale. The deductible value of the gift is the benefit to the charity, i.e., the fair market value of the property minus the selling price of the property to the charity.

Example:

Don bought stock for $10,000, and it is worth $16,000 at the time he sells it to a charity for $10,000. Don's charitable deduction is $6,000 ($16,000 – $10,000). Don's basis allocated to the sale is calculated as:

$$\frac{\text{Cost}}{\text{FMV}} \times \text{Selling price} = \frac{\$10,000}{\$16,000} \times \$10,000 = \$6,250$$

Don's taxable gain is the selling price less this calculated basis – $10,000 – $6,250 = $3,750.

Wealth Replacement Trust

A wealth replacement trust is a funded or unfunded life insurance trust, usually with Crummey powers that provide death benefits to the grantor's family or other heirs. The trust can be established in connection with a charitable gift to avoid depriving the donor's family of an inheritance.

The donor may make a charitable gift of an asset, such as a parcel of land, and take charitable deductions against his or her income. The tax savings may be used to make annual contributions to the life insurance trust to pay for the premiums on the policy on the donor's life. The death proceeds will, in effect, replace the value of the property given to charity, so the donor's family will receive an inheritance, free of income, estate, and gift taxes.

Donor-Advised Fund

If a donor wants to donate funds to charitable causes but has not yet selected the specific charities, the taxpayer can contribute the funds to a donor-advised fund set up with a charity or brokerage firm. Later, the taxpayer can identify charities, to which the manager of the fund will make grants in amounts, specified by the donor. Nevertheless, the taxpayer can claim the income tax charitable deduction in the year of the contributions. As a result,

the donor-advised fund provides the taxpayer with the up-front charitable deduction and the ability to spread charitable gifts over many years and over several different charities.

The manager of the donor-advised fund typically collects an account management fee. This fee is normally less than the costs associated with establishing and maintaining a private foundation.

Estate and Gift Taxation

For purposes of the gift and estate tax charitable deductions, there is no difference between public and private charities. The unlimited gift tax and estate tax charitable deductions are also available whether the gift is a present interest or a future interest.

Conservation Easement – Sec. 170

An income tax charitable deduction is available for an irrevocable transfer of a qualified real property interest for conservation purposes. The interest transferred may be a restriction on the use of the land, instead of the owner's entire interest. A restriction on use, or easement, may be granted for preservation of open space, protection of a natural habitat, preservation of outdoor recreational areas, or preservation of historic land or structures. For estate tax purposes, up to 50% of the value of the land subject to a testamentary bequest of a conservation easement may be excluded from the gross estate, up to a maximum of $500,000 in 2014.

Editor's Note: As of the time of printing, it is unclear whether the estate tax exclusion of 50% (increased from 40%) of the value of the conservation easement will be extended to 2015. An update will be posted to the Keir web site if the increased exclusion amount is extended.

Application Questions

1. Louis Langbut is 69 years of age and his wife Edy is 67. They have no children and would like to make a substantial contribution to the Children's Hospital. They currently have a six-figure income and need the continued reassurance of a fixed income that will be paid for the remainder of their lifetimes. Their life expectancies are about 11½ years and 16 years, respectively.

Which of the following charitable transfers would be most appropriate for the Langbuts?

   A. An outright charitable gift
   B. A charitable remainder annuity trust
   C. A charitable remainder unitrust
   D. A charitable pooled-income fund
   E. A charitable lead trust

2. Charles Trap owns a parcel of undeveloped real estate in the mountains of New York. The land is worth $500,000, and he purchased it for $100,000. Charles is in the 30% income tax bracket. Charles would like to make a charitable contribution of the land to a public land trust, but he does not want to give away his children's inheritance. Which of the following techniques for charitable transfers would be most appropriate for Charles Trap?

   A. A charitable lead trust
   B. A charitable annuity trust
   C. An outright charitable gift and a life insurance trust
   D. A charitable remainder interest
   E. A charitable pooled-income fund

3. Which of the following statements comparing CRATs and CRUTs are correct?

   (1) After it is created, additional assets can be added to a CRAT, but not to a CRUT.
   (2) Greater inflation protection is provided with a CRUT than with a CRAT.
   (3) When income is low, a CRAT must provide for invasion of principal, but a CRUT need not do so.
   (4) The minimum annual payment to a noncharitable beneficiary from a CRAT or CRUT must be 10% of its assets.

   A. (1) and (2) only
   B. (1) and (4) only
   C. (2) and (3) only
   D. (2) and (4) only
   E. (1), (2), (3), and (4)

4. Ken Moser is 66 years of age and has substantial assets that he wants to give to several charities after his death. During his life, Ken would like to have income from the assets that will continue to grow, to offset inflation. Ken is interested in the possibility of obtaining an income tax deduction during his lifetime for the charitable gifts. Which of the following charitable techniques would be most appropriate for Ken?

   A. A charitable lead trust
   B. A charitable annuity trust
   C. A charitable unitrust
   D. A charitable pooled-income fund

5. Gregory Harris, age 63, owns all of the stock of Harris Company, a successful clothing store which he started 20 years ago. Gregory is divorced and has two children by his former wife. The two children are not involved in the clothing store business, and they have shown no interest in coming into the business. Gregory would like to provide funding for a building at a local university and would like to use his stock in the Harris Company for this purpose. He would like to handle the matter in a way that will provide immediate benefit to the university, save taxes, and not deprive his children of an inheritance.

Which of the following statements concerning the use of charitable transfer techniques by Gregory Harris are correct?

(1) A gift to the university's pooled income fund of Harris Company stock would provide immediate benefit to the university.
(2) A charitable lead trust has no limit on the term of years.
(3) A bargain sale would result in capital gains tax on the appreciation in Gregory's shares and no charitable deduction.
(4) A remainder-interest gift would not result in any benefit to the university until Gregory's death.

    A. (1) and (2) only
    B. (1) and (4) only
    C. (2) and (3) only
    D. (2) and (4) only
    E. (1), (2), (3), and (4)

6. Which one of the following charitable transfer techniques would most likely be appropriate for Gregory Harris (in the previous question) to accomplish his objectives?

    A. A charitable lead trust
    B. A pooled-income fund
    C. A charitable remainder annuity trust
    D. A charitable remainder unitrust
    E. A remainder-interest gift

7. Cindy Taylor is 65 years of age and has adjusted gross income this year of $100,000. Her income will probably stay about the same for the foreseeable future. She would like to make a gift to her church that will afford the maximum reduction in her income taxes for this year.

Which one of the following property choices would be most appropriate for a gift to the church?

    A. Raw land, held long-term, valued at $30,000, with a basis of $45,000
    B. Stock, held long-term, valued at $30,000, with a basis of $18,000
    C. An antique car, held long-term, valued at $30,000, with a basis of $15,000
    D. A life insurance policy with a face value of $50,000, premiums paid of $15,000, with a replacement cost of $25,000

(Published Matching Questions released February, 1999)

Matching Questions

Match the charitable trusts listed below with the corresponding descriptions in the questions that follow.

A. Charitable remainder annuity trust (CRAT)
B. Charitable remainder unitrust (CRUT)
C. Both A and B
D. Neither A nor B

_____ 8. Income tax advantage, life income

_____ 9. Estate tax advantage, income from the trust is variable

_____ 10. Income tax advantage, income from the trust is a sum certain

_____ 11. Estate tax advantage, immediate income to the charity

12. Current charitable deductions are allowable for gifts of future interests when the gifts are made by means of a charitable remainder trust or by a pooled-income fund. Which of the following statements concerning the requirements to be met by charitable remainder trusts to qualify for the charitable deduction is (are) correct?

(1) The gift of a future interest must be irrevocable.
(2) The trust must pay the donor or other noncharitable beneficiary a minimum annual income specified at the time the property is transferred to the trust.
(3) The trust must be for the benefit of an individual or individuals living at the time the property is transferred to the trust.
(4) The interests of the noncharitable beneficiaries must be for a term of years not exceeding 20 years or a lifetime interest.

A. (1) only
B. (1) and (2) only
C. (2) and (3) only
D. (3) and (4) only
E. (1), (2), (3), and (4)

13. Which of the following statements correctly describe or characterize a trust that is designated to be a charitable remainder annuity trust?

(1) The donor transfers cash or securities to the trust, and, upon the termination of the trust, the remainder goes to the designated charity or charities.
(2) A fixed amount of the initial value of the trust must be payable to the noncharitable beneficiary.
(3) The specified amount must be paid to the noncharitable beneficiary annually out of income and/or principal.
(4) The annuity must provide for payments of not less than 5% of the initial fair market value of the property placed in trust.

    A. (1) and (2) only
    B. (2) and (3) only
    C. (3) and (4) only
    D. (1), (2), and (3) only
    E. (1), (2), (3), and (4)

14. A taxpayer wishes to donate his farm to a qualified charitable organization and not have it included in his or her taxable estate. The taxpayer also wishes to provide a noncharitable beneficiary with a life interest in the farm. In which of the following circumstances would the property be excluded from his or her taxable estate for federal estate tax purposes?

(1) Transfer by means of appropriate provisions in his or her will
(2) Transfer by means of a charitable remainder trust
(3) Transfer by deed, of a life estate to a noncharitable beneficiary and the remainder to a qualified charity

    A. (1) only
    B. (2) only
    C. (1) and (2) only
    D. (2) and (3) only
    E. (1), (2), and (3)

15. In contrast to the charitable remainder trust, the charitable lead trust receives an income interest from the donor, instead of a remainder interest. Which of the following statements concerning the advantages of the charitable lead trust, created for a period of ten years or less, is (are) correct?

(1) It provides a large current deduction that will be advantageous to the taxpayer who has an unusually high-income year.
(2) It provides for reversion of the principal to the taxpayer or other designated beneficiary.
(3) It provides for a substantial reduction in income taxes for the taxpayer by shifting the tax liability to the trust.

    A. (1) only
    B. (2) only
    C. (3) only
    D. (1) and (2) only
    E. (1) and (3) only

16. Which of the following factors is the critical or deciding characteristic that indicates that a trust should be classified as a charitable remainder unitrust, rather than a charitable remainder annuity trust?

A. The amount of income specified for the noncharitable income beneficiary must be paid annually out of income and/or principal.
B. A fixed percentage of the fair market value of the principal, as revalued annually, must be payable to the noncharitable beneficiary.
C. The amount payable to the noncharitable beneficiary must be at least 5% of the fair market value of the property initially transferred to the trust.
D. The trust must be irrevocable and not subject to a power by the donor, the trustee, or the beneficiary to alter or amend the trust.
E. The trust must be set up by the charity and accept property transferred by different donors for administration.

17. The annuity payment for any year for a CRAT cannot be greater than what amount?

A. 5% of the initial fair market value of the trust's assets
B. 10% of the initial fair market value of the trust's assets
C. 25% of the initial fair market value of the trust's assets
D. 30% of the initial fair market value of the trust's assets
E. 50% of the initial fair market value of the trust's assets

18. Which of the following statements concerning CRATs and CRUTs are correct?

(1) The value of the remainder interest passing to a charity must be at least 10% of the net fair market value of assets contributed to a CRAT.

(2) If interest rates decline, CRUTs created several years ago may become disqualified from failure to pass a sufficient remainder interest to a charity.

(3) The requirement that a CRUT pass sufficient assets to charity does not apply to a CRUT created by will before July 29, 1997.

(4) The percentage of assets that is required to be distributed annually from a CRUT can be greater than 50% because of the option of a "make-up" provision.

A. (1) and (2) only
B. (1) and (3) only
C. (2) and (3) only
D. (3) and (4) only
E. (1), (2), (3), and (4)

19. Which of the following statements concerning the advantages of the charitable remainder annuity trust over the charitable remainder unitrust are correct?

(1) The annuity trust is easier to administer.

(2) The annuity trust provides greater inflation protection.

(3) The annuity trust may provide a larger current income tax deduction.

(4) The annuity trust may provide a smaller value for the remainder interest.

A. (1) and (2) only
B. (1) and (3) only
C. (2) and (3) only
D. (2) and (4) only
E. (3) and (4) only

20. Certain potential disadvantages pertain to the charitable remainder annuity trust, as compared to the charitable remainder unitrust. These potential disadvantages include all the following, EXCEPT:

A. Inflation is more likely to cause a loss in purchasing power for the noncharitable income beneficiary of the annuity trust.

B. The fixed-dollar amount payable annually to the noncharitable annuity beneficiary may cause a disadvantageous invasion of the trust principal.

C. Investment income for the annuity trust may be substantially lower because of limitations as to the properties in which the trust can invest.

D. Additional contributions cannot be made in subsequent years to the annuity trust.

E. Income from the unitrust may increase from year to year, but will not increase for the annuity trust.

21. Which of the following values indicates the current deduction for the gift of a future interest in income-producing property to a qualified organization by means of a charitable remainder trust or pooled-income fund?

A. The present value of the ultimate gift to the charity

B. The fair market value of the property as of the date the trust is established, providing for irrevocable transfer of the property to the charity

C. The fair market value of the property as in B., minus 40% of the long-term capital appreciation

D. The fair market value of the property as in B., minus the present value of the income payments to be made to the donor or other designated noncharitable beneficiary

E. The present value of the projected annual income payments to be made to the income beneficiary

22. A pooled-income fund is a trust created and maintained by a public charity, rather than a private donor. All the following statements concerning the features of a pooled-income trust are correct, EXCEPT:

A. The donor must contribute an irrevocable remainder interest to the charity which maintains the trust.

B. The property transferred by the donor is commingled (pooled) with the gifts from all the other donors.

C. The fund has the right to invest in any type of security it wishes.

D. Each noncharitable income beneficiary must receive a pro rata share of the fund's income annually.

E. The trust principal may not be invaded to make up a deficiency in income for payments to the income beneficiaries.

23. Margery McCage, age 62, has inherited the family home, with 25 acres of land in a desirable suburban area. The land is very valuable, and several developers have offered to purchase the land for over $1 million. Margery has an adequate income from a portfolio of income securities, and she does not want to sell the land. She would like to make a contribution of the land to a charity in a way that would benefit her the most and still permit her to live on the land for the rest of her life. Which of the following charitable gift techniques should you recommend to Margery McCage?

    A. A charitable lead trust
    B. A charitable remainder annuity trust
    C. An outright gift to charity
    D. A remainder interest in her residence
    E. A pooled-income fund

24. The charitable lead trust can also be used to effect significant estate tax savings by a testamentary transfer, whereby a defined income stream is bequeathed to a qualifying charity for a specified number of years. All the following statements concerning testamentary charitable lead trusts are correct, EXCEPT:

    A. The donor cannot specify a noncharitable beneficiary or beneficiaries as the ultimate recipient of the trust corpus.
    B. The beneficiaries designated by the donor can also be named as trustees.
    C. The transfer of the property to the trust must be irrevocable.
    D. The donor's estate will have little or no estate tax liability for the property transferred to the trust.
    E. The trust income can be directed to a charity for a period of time or even for the lifetime of the decedent's child, with the remainder to be paid to the decedent's grandchild.

25. All the following statements concerning the income, estate, and gift tax consequences of a lifetime gift of securities to a qualified public charity are correct, EXCEPT:

A. The gift tax charitable deduction is limited to 50% of fair market value in the current year.

B. The charitable deduction against income in the current year is limited to 30% of adjusted gross income.

C. Any disallowed charitable income tax deduction can be carried forward five years until the full fair market value of the gift property has been deducted.

D. The deduction against income in the current year can be 50% of AGI if the donor elects to use the adjusted cost basis, instead of fair market value, as the amount of the charitable deduction.

E. The value of the lifetime gift of securities plus any future appreciation is removed from the donor's gross estate.

26. All the following statements concerning the income, estate, and gift tax consequences of a charitable gift of a remainder interest in a personal residence or farm are correct, EXCEPT:

A. The current income tax charitable deduction is equal to the present value of the remainder interest computed from actuarial tables.

B. The donor of the farm or personal residence must recognize a portion of any capital gain in the year of the gift.

C. The remainder interest passing to charity qualifies for the gift tax charitable deduction, but not the annual exclusion.

D. The personal residence or farm is includible in the donor's gross estate for federal estate tax purposes.

E. The residence will pass outside probate and avoid the costs associated with probate.

27. All the following statements concerning the income, estate, and gift tax consequences of a gift to a charitable remainder annuity trust (CRAT) for a qualified public charity are correct, EXCEPT:

A. The income tax charitable deduction is equal to the present value of the charity's remainder interest.

B. The amount of the life-income interest payable to the donor will be treated as an adjusted taxable gift for calculation of the estate tax.

C. If the life income is payable to the donor, rather than to a third party, there is no gift tax due on the transfer of assets.

D. If the life income is payable to the donor, the entire fair market value of the assets in the CRAT is included in the donor's gross estate for federal estate tax purposes.

E. The unlimited estate tax charitable deduction means no estate tax is owed by the donor's estate on the assets transferred to the trust.

For practice answering case questions related to Topic 64, please answer the following questions in the cases included in the Appendix at the back of this textbook.

Case	Questions
Bartlett	
Marshall	
Webster	
Unser	9, 10, 11, and 12
Tingey	
Lytle	
Beals	
Mocsin	
Young	4
Borelli	17
Cunningham	17
Fred and Mary Ferris	56, 57, 58, 59, and 60

Answers and Explanations

1. B is the answer. Only the charitable remainder annuity trust offers a fixed payment to the Langbuts during their lifetimes in the form of an annuity. The remainder is a charitable contribution, and the Langbuts can take a deduction against their income in the year the gift is made.

2. C is the answer. A life insurance trust or wealth replacement trust would provide for the inheritance by using the tax reduction from the charitable gift to fund the life insurance premiums. Since the land is not income-producing, the wealth replacement trust will work better than a charitable lead trust. The charitable lead trust gives a charity a right to an income for a term of years or for the grantor's life, and the remainder passes to the noncharitable beneficiary. The other alternatives will result in remainder gifts to a charity, so the children would have no inheritance.

3. C is the answer. After it is created, additional assets can be added to a CRUT, but not to a CRAT. Greater inflation protection is provided with a CRUT than with a CRAT because the payments from a CRUT will vary with the appreciation of its assets. The payments from a CRAT are fixed. When income is low, a CRAT must provide for invasion of principal, but a CRUT need not do so. The present value of the remainder interest that will go to charity from the CRAT or the CRUT must be 10% of the net fair market value of their assets when contributed. The payment from a CRAT to a noncharitable beneficiary must be at least 5% of the value of the assets contributed, and the payment from a CRUT to a noncharitable beneficiary must be at least 5% of the value of the assets, as revalued annually.

4. C is the answer. Ken has several charities that he wants to benefit, and he needs an income stream that will adjust for inflation. The CRUT will allow for more than one charity, or Ken can name several charities and allow the trustee to allocate the distributions among them. The income stream will adjust for inflation. The income stream from the CRAT is fixed and does not change when there is inflation. The pooled-income fund will adjust for inflation, but it will be set up by one charity and will benefit only that charity. The charitable lead trust provides income to the charity rather than to the donor, so Ken does not want to use that technique.

5. D is the answer. A charitable lead trust has no limit on the term of years. This term may or may not be sufficient for the charitable gift that Gregory wants to make. A remainder-interest gift does not benefit the university until Gregory's death, but Gregory can take an immediate charitable deduction for the value of the remainder interest. A bargain sale results in capital gains on a portion of the appreciation and a charitable deduction. A pooled-income fund would not provide a benefit to the university until Gregory's death.

6. A is the answer. A charitable lead trust will provide an immediate income stream to the university, save income taxes because of the large charitable deduction in the year of the gift, and preserve the asset for Gregory's children in a remainder interest. The other alternatives do not result in an immediate benefit to the university because they provide remainder interests.

7. B is the answer. The church is a public charity, so the maximum deduction for Cindy is 30% of her AGI of $100,000. The gift of stock will allow Cindy Taylor to take a charitable deduction of $30,000. This amount is larger than the deduction that can be taken with the other gifts, except for the raw land. The raw land will not be a good choice for a gift because it has declined in value, and Cindy can get a deduction for the loss by selling it. The deduction for a gift of the life insurance policy would be $15,000 because the 50% of AGI limit applies to valuation using premiums paid (cost). The maximum deduction for the antique car is also her basis of $15,000.

8. C is the answer. Both the charitable remainder annuity trust (CRAT) and the charitable remainder unitrust (CRUT) can provide a life income to the grantor and a deduction for the charitable contribution by remainder interest.

9. B is the answer. Both the CRAT and CRUT can provide an estate tax advantage. If the trusts are testamentary, the estate will be able to take a charitable deduction against estate taxes. Only the CRUT provides an income that is variable. The income from the CRAT is a fixed annuity and will not vary.

10. A is the answer. Both the CRAT and CRUT will provide charitable deductions that can reduce income taxes, but only the CRAT provides a fixed income that is a sum certain.

11. D is the answer. Both the CRAT and CRUT can provide an estate tax advantage, but neither of them provides immediate income to the charity. These trusts are both remainder trusts, which provide an interest to the charity after the life income terminates. The life income is paid to a beneficiary who is not a charity.

12. E is the answer. Additionally, and obviously, the trust must be irrevocable. Additionally, but not obviously, the noncharitable income beneficiary or beneficiaries must be living at the time the trust is established, and the term of the trust cannot be for more than 20 years or a lifetime interest. (A pooled-income fund must be a lifetime interest.) The value of the trust as a deduction is the present value of the ultimate gift (the remainder interest) to the exempt organization, which would be quite limited if the trust were to last for 50 or 60 years.

13. E is the answer. A charitable remainder annuity trust is established by transferring money and/or securities to a trust that will provide an annual income stream for a noncharitable beneficiary. Upon the termination of this beneficiary's interest, which must be for a period not exceeding 20 years or a life estate, the remainder goes to the designated beneficiary. The annuity payable to the noncharitable beneficiary must provide for annual payments of at least 5% of the initial value of the property placed in trust and are to be paid from the trust income and/or principal. The noncharitable beneficiary must be a living person when the trust is established, and the trust must be irrevocable.

14. E is the answer. Any irrevocable transfer of property by a taxpayer, provided he or she retains no interest in or control of the property, will remove the property from the taxpayer's estate. This can be done by a direct gift, by a will, by a trust arrangement, or by a deed, as long as it is directed by the taxpayer. A transfer by a will removes the property from the taxpayer's taxable estate upon his or her death. A transfer by a charitable remainder trust (with a life interest retained for a noncharitable beneficiary or beneficiaries) removes the property from the taxpayer's estate when the trust is funded.

15. D is the answer. The charitable lead trust differs radically from the remainder trust in that the donor in the charitable lead trust gives away an income stream and receives a remainder interest. More exactly, the donor places income-producing property in a reversionary trust and directs that the trust income be transferred to a designated charity for a period of time. At the end of this "lead" time, the property reverts to the donor or to some other noncharitable beneficiary. The trust is a grantor trust. The annual income is taxable to the donor, and the donor derives no income tax benefit. The benefit the donor receives is a very large income tax deduction in the year that the trust is funded, the value of the deduction being the present value of the total anticipated income during the lead period when the charity receives the income.

16. B is the answer. The feature which distinguishes the charitable remainder unitrust from the charitable remainder annuity trust is the manner in which the amount of the annual income to the noncharitable beneficiary is specified. Income payments from the unitrust must be at least 5% of the total value of the trust assets, as revalued annually, whereas the annuity trust payments are at least 5% of the initial value of the property placed in trust. From this, it can be seen that the payments from the annuity trust will be the same amount each year, whereas payments from the unitrust will vary with changes in the value of the unitrust's portfolio.

17. E is the answer. The Taxpayer Relief Act of 1997 required CRATs to limit the annuity payment for any year to 50% or less of the initial fair market value of the trust's assets. The minimum annual payment is 5% of the fair market value of the assets. For CRUTs, the percentage of assets required to be distributed annually cannot be greater than 50%.

18. B is the answer. The value of the remainder interest passing to a charity must be at least 10% of the net fair market value of the assets contributed to a CRAT. CRUTs created several years ago will not become disqualified from failure to pass a sufficient remainder interest to a charity. The percentage of assets that is required to be distributed annually from a CRUT cannot be greater than 50%. The option of a "make-up" provision allows for income from one year to be used to make up a deficiency in another year. This provision cannot change the maximum that can be required to be distributed annually. The requirement that a CRUT pass sufficient assets to charity does not apply to CRUTs created by will or revocable trust before July 29, 1997.

19. B is the answer. The annuity trust is easier to administer than the unitrust because there is no need to revalue the trust assets each year in order to determine the amount of the annual income payment. Once the annuity trust is funded, the annual payments are a fixed, constant amount. A larger current income tax deduction may be provided by the annuity trust because of differences in the way the value of the remainder interest is calculated. (This value, for the annuity trust, is determined by applying factors specified by the IRS to the value of the property transferred to give the value of the annuity. The value of the annuity is then subtracted from the value of the property transferred to give the value of the remainder interest. For the unitrust, the value of the remainder interest is determined directly by multiplying the value of the property transferred by a factor also prescribed by the IRS.) The remainder interest is equivalent to the allowable current income tax deduction. With a higher remainder interest from the annuity trust calculation, a higher current income tax deduction is obtained.

20. C is the answer. Advantages of the annuity trust, as compared to the unitrust, are discussed in the answer to the previous question (easier to administer, possibly higher current income tax deduction). However, there may well be disadvantages. Inflation is a possible concern, inasmuch as the fixed annual payment from the annuity trust loses purchasing power as inflation increases. Presumably, the value of the unitrust portfolio would increase with inflation, and the payments based on a percentage of the annually revalued assets would, therefore, increase from year to year. Another potential disadvantage of the annuity trust is that an unfavorable invasion of the trust principal may occur, inasmuch as the fixed annuity payments may be greater than the trust income. Still another disadvantage is that additional payments cannot be made to the annuity trust in subsequent years, and this restriction is, very likely, because the annuity payments from the trust are based on a single valuation date, namely, the day the trust is funded. Additional contributions to a unitrust are permitted. In contrast to these disadvantages, there is no reason that the income generated by an annuity trust should be less than that of the unitrust. Income production for either trust is, on a practical basis, related to the trust objectives and management skills.

21. A is the answer. A donor may deduct the present value of the remainder interest that will ultimately pass to the qualified charity under a charitable remainder trust or pooled-income fund.

22. C is the answer. The pooled-income fund has many of the same characteristics as the aforementioned remainder interest trusts (annuity and unitrust), but the trust is created (or has already been created) by the public charity. The donor transfers property to the charitable organization, which is then commingled in the trust with the property transferred by the other donors. Other significant differences are that a lifetime interest must be retained for the noncharitable beneficiary, and the annual payment to the beneficiary is a pro rata share of the trust income. The transfer by the donor is irrevocable, as with all other remainder interest arrangements. The trust is not permitted to invest in tax-exempt securities.

23. D is the answer. The gift of the remainder interest in the personal residence with the 25 acres of valuable land would produce a large charitable deduction that would reduce Margery McCage's income taxes. Margery would still be able to live on the property for her lifetime, so the gift would have little effect on her lifestyle. The land could not be transferred to a charitable remainder annuity trust, nor to a charitable lead trust. While Margery could transfer her securities to a charitable remainder annuity trust, the land would seem to be a better choice because the residence is not producing any income. By making the charitable gift of the residence, Margery will at least obtain the charitable deduction that will reduce her taxes.

24. A is the answer. The charitable lead trust can also be used to provide substantial estate tax savings. To accomplish this, a fixed amount of the annual income produced by the property placed in trust by the decedent is directed to the charity for a specified number of years. The donor obviously retains no direct reversionary interest in the property, but, at the end of the specified period of time, ownership of the property and the income from the property are transferred to the noncharitable beneficiary or beneficiaries designated by the donor. The benefit provided by this bequest is an estate tax deduction equivalent to the actuarial value of the income stream directed to the charity. The magnitude of the deduction can be surprisingly large, depending upon the annual amount of income directed to the charity and the period of time during which the charity will receive this income.

25. A is the answer. The gift tax charitable deduction is unlimited. The other statements concerning the income tax consequences of a charitable contribution are correct.

26. B is the answer. The donor is not required to recognize any gain at the time of the gift to charity of a remainder interest in a personal residence or farm.

27. B is the answer. The life-income interest retained by the donor is not a taxable gift. Moreover, the unlimited gift tax charitable deduction means that the gift of the remainder interest to charity will not be taxable for gift tax purposes and will not be an adjusted taxable gift for estate tax calculation purposes.

Use of Life Insurance in Estate Planning (Topic 65)

CFP Board Student-Centered Learning Objectives

(a) Explain the ways in which life insurance can be used in estate planning.
    i. Estate liquidity including debt payoff
    ii. Estate protection
    iii. Estate creation (Wealth accumulation)
    iv. Charitable gifting
    v. Business buy-sell

(b) Explain how different types of insurance can be used for different estate planning purposes.

(c) Explain how insurance ownership strategies can be used in estate planning.
    i. Explain incidents of ownership and their ramifications.

(d) Explain how the naming of beneficiaries can be used.

(e) Explain how a life insurance trust can be used and the provisions of such a trust.

Use of Life Insurance in Estate Planning
    A.   Incidents of ownership
    B.   Ownership and beneficiary considerations
    C.   Irrevocable life insurance trust (ILIT)
    D.   Estate and gift taxation

Introduction

Life insurance is a relatively inexpensive way to leverage assets to achieve estate liquidity. A comparatively small premium can generate large death proceeds for an estate. The death proceeds are made available just when they are needed: shortly after the insured's death. Moreover, with careful planning, the insurance proceeds may even be kept out of the decedent's gross estate, while providing important liquidity to the estate and its heirs.

Incidents of Ownership

Incidents of ownership for a life insurance policy are the rights that the owner can exercise over the policy, which include the following:

- The right to name or change the beneficiary
- The right to surrender the policy for its cash value
- The right to borrow against the policy cash values
- The right to pledge the policy as collateral for a loan
- The right to assign the policy or to assign any of these named rights

- The right to revoke any assignment of the policy

If at the time of death, the decedent had any incidents of ownership in a life insurance policy on the decedent's own life, the death benefit will be included in the decedent's gross estate. Since the three-year rule applies to life insurance, the death benefit will be included in the gross estate when the decedent gave up incidents of ownership within three years of death.

Ownership and Beneficiary Considerations

An application for a life insurance policy may be made by the person who will be insured or by anyone who has an insurable interest in the person being insured. Once a policy has been issued, however, the policy can be transferred, assigned, or sold to any other person or entity. For example, life insurance policies can be transferred to trusts or sold to viatical settlement providers.

The right to name a beneficiary is an incident of ownership, but like all rights of ownership, it can be given away. When a person is named as an irrevocable beneficiary, the right to change the beneficiary has been given up. The owner can name primary and contingent beneficiaries, so that if the primary beneficiary has predeceased the insured, the death benefit will be paid to the contingent beneficiary.

Uses of Specific Life Insurance

Survivorship Life

Survivorship life insurance, also called joint and survivor life insurance or joint and last-to-die insurance, insures two or more people and pays the death benefit when the last insured dies. Typically, survivorship life is used to insure a husband and wife, a parent and child, or business associates. Survivorship life is particularly useful to married couples who plan to take maximum advantage of the marital deduction, thereby deferring federal estate taxes until the death of the surviving spouse. The death proceeds are then obtained when the estate taxes will be owed at the second spouse's death. Survivorship life can also be useful when one insured is older or is a highly-rated risk. Premiums for these second-to-die policies are generally less than the cost of premiums on two separate policies.

First-to-Die Insurance

First-to-die life insurance insures more than one life and pays a death benefit when the first insured dies. A first-to-die policy can be useful for funding a buy-sell agreement so that the parties do not have to purchase so many policies. First-to-die life can also be effective for providing the funds to pay estate taxes when a couple wants to transfer appreciating assets to other family members at the time the first spouse dies. Premiums on a first-to-die policy are generally more than what either of the insured persons would pay for a life policy, but less than the cost of two separate policies.

Key Person Life Insurance

Key person life insurance is a policy purchased by a business on the life of an important or "key" employee. The business owns the policy and is named as the beneficiary. The premiums are not income-tax-deductible, and the build-up of cash value in the policy may affect the corporation's alternative minimum tax (AMT). The death benefit will be received free of income tax and is not included in the key employee's gross estate. Typically, a business uses the death proceeds to help pay for hiring and/or training a replacement or to offset lower profits that result.

Split-Dollar Life Insurance

Under a split-dollar life insurance plan, the employer and employee typically share the premium cost of a whole life insurance policy. Usually, the employer pays the portion of the premium that represents the annual increase in the policy's cash value, and the employee pays the portion that is pure protection (Table 2001). The employer gets back the amount it pays in premiums at the time the death benefit is paid or when the policy is surrendered for its cash value. The protection for employees is obtained at a reduced cost, but the amount of protection to employees decreases as an employer's cash value increases.

Group Term Life Insurance

When an employer pays the premiums for group term insurance for its employees, the premiums are fully deductible as a business expense. The premiums are not taxable income to the employees, except to the extent the premiums pay for coverage in excess of $50,000. Death proceeds will be included in the employees' gross estates because the employees can name beneficiaries and, therefore, they hold incidents of ownership. An incident of ownership can be removed by an irrevocable assignment, and the death proceeds will not be included in the employee's gross estate if this assignment occurs more than three years before death. The assignment is a gift and is valued at the lesser of the employer's premium payments or the IRS Table I value.

🔑 KEY SUMMARY 65 – 1
Life Insurance

Type	Use
First-to-die life insurance	To insure buy-sell agreements
Second-to-die or survivorship life insurance	To pay estate taxes at the death of the surviving spouse
Key person life insurance	To provide a business with cash to replace an important employee
Split-dollar life insurance	To provide an employee benefit for selected executives
Group term life insurance	To provide a tax-free benefit for a group of employees

---

Life Insurance Trusts

Life insurance trusts are simply trusts established to hold the titles to life insurance policies. The trust may apply for the insurance, or the grantor may transfer one or more life insurance policies to the trust. Life insurance trusts are many and varied and can be used with many different estate planning techniques. Life insurance trusts can be created by a lifetime gift or by a will.

Life insurance trusts are sometimes categorized as funded or unfunded. An unfunded life insurance trust simply holds the life insurance policy, without any additional assets to pay the premiums, and the grantor makes additional contributions annually to pay the premiums. A funded trust holds additional assets that will provide the money to pay premiums each year.

For income tax purposes, a funded life insurance trust will generally be treated as a grantor trust because trust income is used to pay for life insurance on the life of the grantor or the grantor's spouse. As a result, the trust income is taxed to the grantor under the grantor trust rules. For this reason, life insurance trusts are typically set up as unfunded trusts, and the grantor makes annual contributions in the amount of the annual premiums. The grantor will then have no income to report from the trust.

Life insurance trusts can be revocable, but they are usually irrevocable so as to keep the life insurance proceeds out of the insured's gross estate. The revocable life insurance trust has the advantage of flexibility because the grantor can change both the provisions and the trustee at any time. The disadvantages are that the income from trust assets is taxable to the grantor, and the death proceeds will be included in the grantor's gross estate.

Irrevocable Life Insurance Trust

An irrevocable life insurance trust, funded by the grantor during his or her lifetime, can have the following advantages:

- Federal estate taxes and state death taxes can be reduced because life insurance proceeds are not included in the grantor's gross estate.
- With Crummey powers, annual contributions to the trust qualify for the gift tax annual exclusion.
- Income tax savings may arise. The investment income on trust assets is taxable to the trust unless it is used to pay the premiums on the life insurance of the grantor or his or her spouse.
- The costs and publicity of probate can be avoided. The insured can leverage the transfer of wealth because comparatively small premium payments produce large death benefits.
- Estate liquidity can be helped if the trustee is given the discretion to buy estate assets or to lend to the estate. (However, the death proceeds will be included in the insured's gross estate if the trustee is directed to pay estate expenses.)

REMEMBER: THE TRUSTEE OF A LIFE INSURANCE TRUST MAY BE GIVEN DISCRETION TO BUY ESTATE ASSETS OR TO LEND TO THE ESTATE, BUT DIRECTING THE TRUSTEE TO PAY ESTATE TAXES WILL CAUSE THE INCLUSION OF THE AMOUNT PAID IN THE GROSS ESTATE.

Loss of Control

The major disadvantage of the irrevocable life insurance trust is that the grantor gives up control over the life insurance policy and any assets transferred to the trust. The assignment of the policy to the trust will mean that the beneficiaries of the life insurance and of the trust are irrevocably named, and the grantor cannot change them. The transfer to the trust is a gift, but, usually, the gift tax value is relatively modest.

Ownership

The complete and irrevocable assignment of a life insurance policy to a trust or to a beneficiary will remove the death proceeds from the insured's estate when the assignment was made more than three years before the insured's death.

To avoid the three-year rule, the irrevocable trust can apply for a new policy on the insured's life. In this case, the trustee is the applicant and owner of the policy, so the insured-grantor of the trust has no incidents of ownership in the policy.

Beneficiary Designations

If the insured is the owner, and the insured's spouse is the designated beneficiary of a life policy, the death proceeds will be included in the decedent's gross estate, but the marital deduction will eliminate any estate tax. The spouse is provided with money, but the proceeds may not be available to the estate for its liquidity needs.

If the estate is the beneficiary, the proceeds will be included in the gross estate, and the proceeds will be subject to probate and to the claims of the decedent's creditors. In this case, the estate will be provided with liquidity.

If an irrevocable trust is the owner and beneficiary, the proceeds are not included in the insured's gross estate. The trustee can be given discretion to loan to or buy assets from the estate to provide liquidity. The proceeds will not be subject to probate or to the claims of creditors.

Settlement Options

Life insurance settlement options provide a means of protecting the death benefit from the danger of being squandered by a beneficiary who is a poor manager of money. If a trust is the beneficiary, the trust provisions will provide ample guidance for distributions and protection of the trust assets from the beneficiary's profligacy. In this case, the trust will elect a lump-sum payment. Otherwise, a beneficiary may be better served by the election of an annuity, an installment payout, or an interest-only option. With the annuity and the installment payout, the insurance company will make payments to the beneficiary at regular intervals, and these payments will consist of both nontaxable life insurance proceeds and taxable interest.

Gift and Estate Taxation of Life Insurance

The gift and estate taxation of life insurance is in Topics 56, 57, and 59.

Life Insurance Techniques

The purchase of life insurance is an important technique not only for estate liquidity, but also to accomplish a multitude of other estate objectives.

Life insurance may be used effectively for making gifts to individuals or to charities, especially since a policy has a relatively low cost in premiums and a low gift tax value when given as a gift but becomes a large sum when the death benefit is paid.

Life insurance can be used for wealth replacement and is useful in connection with charitable gifts. When an individual wants to make a gift to benefit a charity but also wants to provide for heirs, the individual can accomplish both objectives by combining the gift with the purchase of life insurance.

The individual will make a lifetime charitable gift, which will, in turn, produce an income tax reduction. The savings in income taxes can be used to buy life insurance to provide for the heirs. Thus, an individual might give an artwork to charity, take a charitable deduction for the contribution, and buy a life insurance policy to provide wealth replacement for his or her heirs.

An important technique in estate planning is the removal of life insurance from the gross estate. This technique is not required where the gross estate will be sheltered by the unified credit or by a marital or charitable deduction. For large estates, however, effectively removing life insurance from the insured's ownership will reduce federal estate taxes and state death taxes.

Application Questions

1. Edgar Hadley, age 59, is the president of Ajax Computer Software Company, which is valued at $15 million. Edgar is one of the five founders and owns 28% of the stock of the corporation. Edgar's home is owned with his wife in tenancy by the entirety and is valued at $300,000. Edgar owns common stock mutual funds in an IRA valued at $75,000, and his wife is the beneficiary. He also has a brokerage account in joint names with his wife, containing common stock and corporate bonds valued at $100,000. Edgar also owns a beach house valued at $200,000 and a boat worth $50,000. The family cars are owned jointly with his wife and are worth $50,000 each. Edgar and his wife have two children, ages 17 and 15. Edgar's will leaves his entire estate to his wife, and his wife's will leaves everything to him.

If the Hadleys expect to not be able to sell the stock in Ajax within several years after Edgar's death, which of the following life insurance policies and settlement options would provide the insurance death proceeds at the time the estate taxes will be owed?

   A. Ordinary whole life on Edgar, with a lump-sum payment
   B. Survivorship life with a lump-sum payment
   C. First-to-die life with a life annuity option
   D. First-to-die life with a lump-sum payment
   E. Ordinary whole life on Edgar's wife with a lump-sum payment

2. If Edgar Hadley (from the previous question) decides to add liquidity to his estate by buying a whole life insurance policy, how should the purchase be arranged to reduce estate taxes?

   A. Edgar's wife should apply for the policy, pay the premiums, and name herself as the beneficiary.
   B. Edgar should apply for the policy, pay the premiums, and name himself as the beneficiary.
   C. Edgar should apply for the policy and transfer it to an irrevocable trust and name his wife as the beneficiary.
   D. Edgar should apply for the policy, transfer it to a revocable trust, and name the trust as the beneficiary.
   E. An irrevocable trust should be created, and the trust should apply for the policy, pay the premiums, and name the trust as beneficiary.

3. (Published question released February, 1999)

The best life insurance policy for the payment of federal estate taxes for a 50-year-old couple with illiquid assets is:

   A. An individual whole life policy on each spouse on a cross-ownership basis
   B. A joint first-to-die life insurance policy, owned jointly
   C. A joint last-to-die life insurance policy, owned by the spouse with the larger estate
   D. A joint and last-to-die life insurance policy, owned by the spouse with the smaller estate
   E. A joint and last-to-die life insurance policy, owned by an irrevocable trust

4. (Published question released February, 1999)

John and Mary Meyers have a combined estate of $900,000, including a $250,000 life insurance policy on John's life. The Meyers have two children. John prefers that Mary receive the income from the policy if he dies but wants the proceeds to go to his children after her subsequent death. John and Mary have recently executed wills that contain unified credit trusts. What is the best beneficiary designation for John's life insurance policy?

A. His wife Mary
B. His two children
C. A charitable remainder trust
D. His testamentary trust

5. (Published question released December, 1996, updated)

Harold used his own funds to create an irrevocable life insurance trust five years before his death. The trustee purchased a single-premium life insurance policy at that time. Harold and Ruth were married. Harold was the insured. The insurance proceeds were paid to the trustee after Harold died. Ruth died at the end of this year, and the trust terminated and went to their children by right of representation. Assuming a properly drafted irrevocable trust document, which statement(s) is (are) true?

(1) The proceeds will not be taxed as part of Harold's estate.
(2) The trust will not be subject to probate.
(3) The proceeds will not be taxed as part of Ruth's estate.
(4) The trust will not direct the trustee to pay estate taxes.

A. (1), (2), and (3) only
B. (1) and (3) only
C. (2) and (4) only
D. (4) only
E. (1), (2), (3), and (4)

6. All the following statements concerning the income, estate, and gift tax consequences of a gift of life insurance to a qualified public charity are correct, EXCEPT:

A. The income tax deduction is the lesser of the amount of premium payments or the cash value.

B. The value of the gift for gift tax purposes is the replacement cost.

C. A gift to charity of a life insurance policy within three years of the donor's death is not includible in the donor's gross estate for federal estate tax purposes.

D. No gift tax liability arises as a result of the gift, due to the unlimited gift tax charitable deduction.

E. After the life insurance policy has been given to charity, any additional premium payments are deductible charitable contributions.

7. John purchases a life insurance policy on the life of Mary. John is the owner, and Bill is designated the revocable beneficiary. Under these circumstances, which of the following statements is (are) correct?

(1) John is deemed to have made a gift to Bill each time he pays a premium.

(2) When Mary dies, John is deemed to have made a gift to Bill equal to the policy proceeds.

(3) If John dies before Mary, the policy will be includible in his gross estate at the policy's interpolated terminal reserve value, plus unearned premium.

A. (1) only
B. (1) and (2) only
C. (1) and (3) only
D. (2) and (3) only
E. (1), (2), and (3)

8. Under which of the following circumstances would the death proceeds of a life insurance policy be included in the gross estate of the deceased for federal estate tax purposes?

(1) The deceased gave a policy on the deceased's life to his brother five years ago and retained only the right to change the policy's beneficiary designation.

(2) The death proceeds of a policy on the life of "X" are payable to "X's" estate, but the policy is owned by "X's" brother.

(3) The deceased ("X") gave the policy on his life to his sister (the designated beneficiary) four years ago, and "X" agreed to pay all future premiums.

(4) The deceased assigned a policy on his life to his wife two years before his death, and she paid the premiums after the assignment.

A. (1) only
B. (1) and (2) only
C. (1) and (4) only
D. (2) and (3) only
E. (1), (2), and (4) only

9. It is often desirable to keep life insurance death proceeds out of the insured's estate for tax reasons. Which of the following describe(s) a necessary condition for keeping the proceeds out of the insured's gross estate?

(1) The insured must surrender all incidents of ownership.
(2) The transfer of incidents of ownership must occur more than three years prior to death.
(3) The insured cannot continue to pay premiums on the policy.
(4) The policy must be transferred to an irrevocable trust.

    A. (1) only
    B. (2) only
    C. (1) and (2) only
    D. (1), (2), and (3) only
    E. (1), (2), (3), and (4)

10. Life insurance death proceeds would be includible in the insured's gross estate in all the following circumstances, EXCEPT:

    A. The policy is owned by the insured's wife, and proceeds are payable to the insured's estate.
    B. The proceeds are payable to the insured's wife, but the insured retained the right to change the beneficiary designation.
    C. The insured assigned the policy to his wife two years before his death.
    D. The insured assigned the policy to his wife six years ago but retained the right to pay premiums.
    E. The insured irrevocably assigned the policy to his wife four years ago but retained the right to pledge the policy for a loan.

11. Which of the following statements concerning the tax treatment of life insurance is (are) correct?

(1) Where a policyowner elects to receive benefits under a settlement option, the money so received is fully taxable as current income.
(2) Premiums for personally owned life insurance are not deductible for income tax purposes, except under special circumstances, such as when premiums are part of a court-ordered alimony payment.
(3) Where a policyowner elects installment payout of death proceeds, one-half of the annual payout will be taxable income.

    A. (1) only
    B. (2) only
    C. (1) and (2) only
    D. (2) and (3) only
    E. (1), (2), and (3)

12. All the following statements concerning the tax treatment of life insurance are correct, EXCEPT:

    A. The law allows an employer to purchase up to $50,000 of group term life insurance on employees, without income tax consequences for the employees.

    B. A Crummey trust is designed to obtain an annual gift tax exclusion for premiums paid on life insurance held in trust.

    C. Gifts of life insurance made more than three years prior to death can be effective in reducing the insured's gross estate.

    D. Without Crummey powers, the death benefit received by a life insurance trust will be includible in the insured's gross estate.

    E. If the beneficiary of a life insurance policy elects the interest-only option, the entire payment to the beneficiary will be taxable income.

13. All the following statements concerning "split-dollar" life insurance are correct, EXCEPT:

    A. It provides a slowly rising death benefit to the key employee's beneficiaries.

    B. It can provide extra incentive for key employees.

    C. The firm usually receives the cash value as a death benefit.

    D. The firm and the employee share (split) the responsibility for the premium payments.

    E. Participants can be selected on an arbitrary or discriminatory basis.

14. All the following statements concerning key individual life insurance are correct, EXCEPT:

    A. Proceeds can be used to offset reduced profits and/or pay for an employee's replacement.

    B. Proceeds payable to a personal beneficiary of a controlling stockholder who is the insured will be includible in the gross estate of the insured.

    C. Premiums are deductible by the corporation as a prudent business expense.

    D. Proceeds, when received, are free of income tax.

    E. The firm is usually the owner, premium payer, and beneficiary.

15. All the following statements concerning group life insurance are correct, EXCEPT:

    A. The business firm is usually the premium payer, even if the plan is contributory.

    B. Group life premiums are fully deductible by the firm as a business expense.

    C. Proceeds are normally includible in the insured's (employee's) gross estate.

    D. Employer-paid premiums are never taxed as income to the employee.

    E. By an absolute assignment of all incidents of ownership, proceeds can be removed from the insured employee's gross estate with, at worst, minor gift tax consequences.

16. All the following statements concerning the use of irrevocable life insurance trusts are correct, EXCEPT:

A. If it is a grantor trust, any income earned on the trust's property will be taxed to the trust creator.
B. A funded trust provides increased assurance that premiums will be paid annually as they come due.
C. The best income tax benefits are available when the policy is on the life of the grantor.
D. If the trust is unfunded, and a Crummey provision is not included in the trust agreement, the payment of future premiums will be a gift of a future interest.
E. If the trustee invests in tax-free securities, a funded life insurance trust will have little income tax significance for the grantor.

17. A life insurance trust is often named the beneficiary of the life insurance policies it holds for which of the following reasons?

(1) It can provide greater flexibility than is available under insurance settlement options.
(2) It can eliminate a second estate tax upon the death of the beneficiaries.
(3) It can incorporate special limitations and restrictions on the funds designed to be paid to specific beneficiaries.

    A. (1) only
    B. (1) and (2) only
    C. (1) and (3) only
    D. (2) and (3) only
    E. (1), (2), and (3)

18. All the following statements concerning the payment of life insurance death proceeds to a revocable personal insurance trust are correct, EXCEPT:

A. The death proceeds will avoid probate.
B. The trust may be used as a pourover device for the residuary estate.
C. The death proceeds are excluded from the deceased's gross estate.
D. Such a trust may be used to unify control over the deceased's property.
E. The death proceeds will be distributed according to the grantor's provisions in the trust, rather than the insured's will.

19. All the following statements concerning the use of funded irrevocable life insurance trusts are correct, EXCEPT:

A. The income earned on the trust property is taxable to the trust creator if the income is used to pay premiums on a life insurance policy on the life of the creator.
B. The cash value of a policy on the life of the trust creator's daughter is excluded from the creator's gross estate for federal estate tax purposes.
C. The creation and funding of the trust have no gift tax implications.
D. The creator loses control over both the funding property and the life insurance policy.
E. If the trust applies for and is the owner of the life insurance, the death proceeds will not be includible in the insured's gross estate.

20. John Carver established an irrevocable life insurance trust that was funded with marketable securities and that applied for a policy on Carver's life. The trust was named as the beneficiary of the policy, and Carver's bank was named trustee. The trust provides that at Carver's death, the trust principal and income are to be paid to Carver's nieces. Under these circumstances, which of the following statements is (are) correct?

(1) The trust income is taxable to Carver.
(2) The trust income is taxable to the trust during Carver's lifetime.
(3) The life insurance death proceeds will be includible in Carver's gross estate for federal estate tax purposes.
(4) Carver can retain the right to change the trustee, without affecting the estate tax consequences of the trust.

   A. (1) only
   B. (1) and (3) only
   C. (2) and (3) only
   D. (2) and (4) only
   E. (3) and (4) only

21. Which of the following statements concerning the use of an unfunded irrevocable life insurance trust that is the designated owner of a life insurance policy on the life of the creator are correct?

(1) The life insurance death proceeds are not includible in the gross estate of the trust creator.
(2) The annual premiums can be paid with before-tax dollars supplied by the trust creator.
(3) Each payment of premiums is an additional gift, subject to federal gift tax.
(4) The payment of premiums on the life insurance is not eligible for the annual exclusion.

   A. (1) and (2) only
   B. (1) and (3) only
   C. (2) and (3) only
   D. (2) and (4) only
   E. (3) and (4) only

For practice answering case questions related to Topic 65, please answer the following questions in the cases included in the Appendix at the back of this textbook.

Case	Questions
Bartlett	
Marshall	8, 9, and 10
Webster	
Unser	
Tingey	
Lytle	
Beals	
Mocsin	
Young	
Borelli	18
Cunningham	18
Fred and Mary Ferris	61, 62, 63, 64, and 65

Answers and Explanations

1. B is the answer. If Edgar dies first, his estate will not owe any taxes, due to the marital deduction. The same will be true if Edgar's wife dies first. The need for life insurance is to provide liquidity at the time of the second spouse's death. The survivorship life policy will provide the death benefit at the time the surviving spouse dies, so the money will be available for the estate taxes that will be due at that time. The ordinary life policy on Edgar will provide the death proceeds at his death, and the ordinary life policy on his wife will provide the death proceeds at her death. There is no way to be certain whose death will occur first, and the survivorship policy will provide death proceeds at the time the assets are subject to estate tax, regardless of who dies first.

2. E is the answer. To keep the death proceeds of the life insurance out of Edgar's estate, as well as his wife's estate, the policy should be applied for, owned, and paid for by an irrevocable trust. The trust should provide that the trustee can loan money to Edgar's estate or buy assets from his estate to provide added liquidity. If Edgar's wife owns the policy and is named the beneficiary, the proceeds will be kept from Edgar's estate unless she dies first. Even if Edgar dies first, the death proceeds will be included in her gross estate at her death unless they have been consumed or given away. Transferring the life insurance policy to a revocable trust will not remove the proceeds from Edgar's gross estate.

3. E is the answer. The joint and last-to-die life insurance policy will provide liquidity when it is most needed at the death of the last spouse. The irrevocable trust can be used to keep the death proceeds out of both estates so that the federal estate taxes will not be increased. The trustee can be authorized to buy illiquid assets from the estate so that the estate will gain the liquidity that it needs. Cross-ownership of whole life policies will not remove the proceeds from the gross estate of the last spouse to die. A first-to-die policy will provide the death proceeds before they are actually needed because the marital deduction will eliminate any estate taxes at the first death.

4. D is the answer. If the testamentary trust (or John's estate) is designated as the beneficiary, the death proceeds will be available to fund the unified credit trust, which will provide income to Mary and then will be distributed to their children after Mary's death. The other alternatives do not achieve these objectives.

5. E is the answer. Since the life insurance policy is owned by the irrevocable trust, the policy proceeds will not be included in Harold's gross estate. Similarly, the trust property is not subject to probate because it was not owned by Harold at the time of his death. The trust property is also not included in Ruth's gross estate because she had no incidents of ownership at the time of her death. A properly drafted irrevocable trust will not direct the trustee to pay estate taxes because such a provision means that any trust assets used to pay the estate's taxes will be included in the gross estate.

6. C is the answer. A gift of life insurance within three years of death is includible in the gross estate for federal estate tax purposes, but the unlimited charitable deduction applies, so there is no estate tax liability for the gift.

7. D is the answer. (1) is not a correct statement. No gift is made to Bill when John pays a premium. Bill is a revocable beneficiary. Bill has no ownership right to the policy. (2) is a correct statement. If John does not change the beneficiary designation (which he could do at any time), John will have made a gift to Bill in the amount of the death proceeds when Mary dies.

8. E is the answer. (1) and (2) are circumstances under which the death proceeds would be includible in the gross estate of the deceased. In (1), the deceased retained an incident of ownership. In (2), the death proceeds are payable to the deceased's estate. In (3), the death proceeds would be excludible from the deceased's gross estate because the gift was made more than three years prior to death, and the decedent retained no incidents of ownership. Agreeing to pay future premiums is not the retention of any incident of ownership. The gift to the deceased's spouse is includible because it was assigned less than three years before death. The estate tax marital deduction will eliminate the tax, but it is still includible in the gross estate.

9. C is the answer. Paying premiums for a policy transferred to another person is a gift, but such premium payments are not incidents of ownership. To remove the proceeds from the gross estate, the insured must give up all incidents of ownership at least three years before death. A life insurance policy can be removed from the insured's gross estate by means of a transfer to an irrevocable trust, but an outright gift more than three years before death will also accomplish this purpose.

10. D is the answer. Where the insured assigned the policy more than three years before death and retained the right to pay premiums, the death proceeds would not be includible in the insured's gross estate. The right to pay premiums is not an incident of ownership. Where the proceeds of a policy are payable to the insured's estate, the proceeds are includible in the insured's gross estate, even though the policy is owned by the insured's spouse. If the insured retained incidents of ownership, such as the right to change the beneficiary or the right to pledge the policy for a loan, the proceeds are includible in the insured's gross estate. Any assignment or release of ownership rights within three years of death would mean the proceeds would be includible in the insured's gross estate.

11. B is the answer. (1) is not a correct statement. Only the interest element or the investment income paid under a settlement option is taxable income. The return of the policyowner's cost basis is a return of capital and is not taxable income. Statement (3) is not correct because the installments will consist of interest and death proceeds in varying proportions.

12. D is the answer. Crummey powers are needed in a life insurance trust to assure the donor of the annual exclusion for each contribution to the trust. Crummey powers will not affect inclusion in the insured's gross estate. Inclusion depends on incidents of ownership within the three years before death.

13. A is the answer. A is not a correct statement because as time elapses, the employer has a larger and larger claim on the policy's death benefit because of the accumulation value of the premiums paid by the employer. This means the death proceeds remaining for the employee's beneficiary become less and less. B, C, D, and E are correct statements.

14. C is the answer. C is not a correct statement because premiums paid for key person life insurance are not deductible by the corporation. A, B, D, and E are correct statements.

15. D is the answer. Premiums paid on group term life insurance in excess of $50,000 of coverage are taxable income for the employee. Also, if the coverage develops cash values for the employee, this means taxable income for the employee. A, B, C, and E are correct statements.

16. C is the answer. C is an incorrect statement. When the policy is on the life of the creator or grantor of the trust, the trust income is taxable to the grantor. Thus, no tax advantage results. A, B, and D are correct statements.

17. E is the answer. All three statements are correct.

18. C is the answer. Since the trust is revocable, the death proceeds will be includible in the gross estate of the deceased. Up to the moment of death, the deceased could have done anything he or she wanted to do with the death proceeds. Therefore, the death proceeds are caught in the gross estate of the deceased. A, B, D, and E are correct statements.

19. C is the answer. C is an incorrect statement. Any funds placed in an irrevocable trust mean a completed gift, equal to the amount of funds. A, B, D, and E are correct statements.

20. A is the answer. The irrevocable life insurance trust is a grantor trust because the trust pays the premiums on life insurance on the grantor's life. The income from a grantor trust is taxable to the grantor, so Carver will be taxed on the trust's income. Since Carver was not the owner of the life insurance policy and held no incidents of ownership, the death proceeds will not be includible in Carver's gross estate. However, if Carver retained the right to change the trustee, the trust assets would be includible in his gross estate.

21. B is the answer. If the unfunded life insurance trust is the owner of the life insurance, then the death proceeds will not be includible in the insured-grantor's estate. The annual premiums can be paid with after-tax, not before-tax, dollars supplied by the trust creator. Each payment of premiums is an additional gift, subject to federal gift tax. The premiums are eligible for the annual exclusion.

Marital Deduction (Topic 66)

CFP Board Student-Centered Learning Objectives

(a) Describe the appropriate use of the marital deduction in estate planning including for both domestic and international spouses.

(b) Explain the relationship between the marital deduction and the qualified interest Trust.

Marital Deduction
- A. Requirements
- B. Qualifying transfers
- C. Terminable-interest rule and exceptions
- D. Qualified domestic trust (QDOT)

Marital Deduction Requirements – Secs. 2056, 2523, and 2106

For federal gift tax purposes, the marital deduction is an amount subtracted from the total value of a gift of property to calculate the amount of the taxable gift. For federal estate tax purposes, the marital deduction is an amount subtracted from the gross estate (or adjusted gross estate) to calculate the taxable estate. The deduction in each case is based on the value of the property transferred gratuitously to a spouse.

For the gift tax marital deduction, the transfer must be made under the following conditions:

- The property must be transferred solely to the donor's legal spouse.
- The spouse must be a U.S. citizen (or the transfer must be to a QDOT).
- The transfer must vest full title, enjoyment, and control in the spouse – in other words, virtual outright ownership; or, the transfer must qualify for treatment as qualified terminable-interest property (QTIP).

For the estate tax marital deduction, the bequest must meet the above conditions, and the property must also have been included in the decedent's gross estate. The estate tax marital deduction is also available to the estate of a person who is not a citizen when the assets will pass to a spouse who is a citizen.

In June of 2013, the Supreme Court struck down section 3 of the Defense of Marriage Act (DOMA), which required same-sex spouses to be treated as unmarried for purposes of federal law. This ruling has significant impact on estate planning for same-sex couples. Prior to the ruling, same-sex couples who were married in states whose laws allowed these marriages were unable to claim an unlimited marital deduction for estate and gift tax purposes at the federal level. These couples will now be permitted the same tax treatment as heterosexual couples, including the ability to qualify for the unlimited marital deduction and to elect portability of unused exemption amounts. It should be noted, however, that while the court ruling does change tax treatment for same-sex married couples, it does not change the tax treatment of domestic partnerships or civil unions. Persons in domestic partnerships and civil unions will continue to be treated as unmarried at the federal level.

Marital Deduction is Unlimited in Amount

An unlimited marital deduction is available under both the gift tax rules and the estate tax rules so that any amount and value of assets can pass tax-free to a spouse, either by gift or in the spouse's estate. Because property qualifying for the marital deduction is not taxed either as a gift or in the estate of the first spouse to die, the marital deduction can be an important means of estate tax deferral.

Qualifying Transfers

Virtually any kind of property can be transferred to a spouse in a way that will meet the above requirements for the marital deduction. Some of the ways to make qualifying transfers are discussed as follows:

Outright Bequests

Outright bequests of property to a spouse will qualify for the marital deduction, and such bequests are generally preferable to the creation of trusts when the estate is not large.

Outright bequests avoid the expenses of setting up and maintaining trusts and paying the trustees, and bequests make the assets immediately and completely available to the surviving spouse and family. The surviving spouse will have complete freedom to use the property as needed, and he or she has complete control in managing the assets. Outright bequests are also recommended where the estate consists of non-income-producing property.

Joint Tenancy Property

Joint tenancy property qualifies for the marital deduction to the extent of one-half of the value of such property. Each joint tenant spouse is deemed to have a one-half interest in joint tenancy property, regardless of the parties' contributions to the purchase price. The same rule applies to property owned in tenancy by the entirety. The one-half interest belonging to the surviving spouse escapes estate tax until the death of the surviving spouse, at which time, the value of the entire property is subject to estate tax.

Life Insurance

Life insurance proceeds qualify for the marital deduction when the proceeds are payable to the surviving spouse, either in a lump sum or under an installment option. Even when proceeds are payable under the life-income option and the surviving spouse has no right of withdrawal, the proceeds still qualify for the marital deduction.

Life Estates

Where a person makes a gift of a life estate to a spouse, the donor-spouse is not entitled to a marital deduction for gift tax purposes, and the executor of the decedent's estate cannot claim a marital deduction on the federal estate tax return.

The life estate is a terminable interest that does not qualify for the marital deduction for either gift or estate tax purposes. The gift of a life estate to a spouse will be a taxable gift. Since the life estate does not qualify for the estate tax marital deduction, the value of the testamentary bequest will be subject to estate tax in the decedent's estate and will not be taxed again in the surviving spouse's estate at the time of his or her later death.

Marital Trusts

For married clients with large estates, marital and nonmarital trusts are a significant part of estate planning.

Effective uses of trusts can reduce estate and gift taxes, while providing a certain amount of flexibility to an estate plan. There are essentially three different kinds of trusts that qualify for the marital deduction, including:

(a) The power-of-appointment trust
(b) The QTIP trust
(c) The estate trust

Power-of-Appointment Trust (Marital or "A" Trust)

A power-of-appointment trust takes its name from the general power of appointment which may be granted to a spouse in order to dispose of trust assets in favor of the other spouse or his or her estate.

A power-of-appointment trust, also called a marital trust or "A" trust, will qualify for the estate tax marital deduction if it meets the following requirements:

- The surviving spouse must be entitled to all the income generated by the trust assets at least annually; thus, accumulation is not permitted. Therefore, the power-of-appointment trust is a *simple trust*.
- The surviving spouse must be granted a general power of appointment over the trust assets, but the trust may provide that the power is exercisable during lifetime, only at death, or both.

- The surviving spouse must be given a general power of appointment that can be exercised in favor of the other spouse or that spouse's estate.
- The surviving spouse must be able to exercise the power under all circumstances, i.e., the power cannot be forfeited by remarriage, etc.

A power-of-appointment trust established during a grantor's lifetime can provide a secure income for the surviving spouse and protect his or her assets from creditors, who cannot attach the trust assets. The trust assets also avoid probate.

☼ *REMEMBER: WITH A POWER-OF-APPOINTMENT TRUST, THE SURVIVING SPOUSE HAS A GENERAL POWER OF APPOINTMENT AND, THEREFORE, HAS CONTROL OF THE **ENTIRE** TRUST PROPERTY AFTER THE GRANTOR'S DEATH.*

QTIP Trust
("C" or "Q" Trust)

The qualified terminable-interest property (QTIP) trust is also called the "current income trust" or the "C" trust and sometimes just the "Q" trust. Property placed in a QTIP trust will qualify for the marital deduction if all trust income is payable to the surviving spouse at least annually.

The surviving spouse can be given a right to invade corpus to the extent permitted by a "5-and-5 power." Even though the surviving spouse is given this power of invasion, the grantor-spouse can direct the disposition of the remainder interest. Consequently, a power of appointment need not be granted to the surviving spouse under the QTIP trust.

A unique aspect of the QTIP trust is the delegation to the executor of the decision regarding how much of the decedent's property will be placed in the trust. The executor can elect to qualify more property for the marital deduction by including more assets in the QTIP trust, or the executor can direct property away from the QTIP trust to take advantage of the unified credit. For example, the will might include reduce-to-zero language instructing the executor to claim QTIP treatment for the amount of assets needed to reduce the estate tax to zero. Thus, the executor can do some estate planning to avoid estate taxes, even after the death of the grantor. Nevertheless, the executor's election that particular assets be included in the QTIP trust means these assets will be included in the gross estate of the surviving spouse.

Estate Trusts

The estate trust differs from the power-of-appointment trust and from the QTIP trust in that the estate trust agreement need not specify that income be paid annually to the surviving spouse. The trust agreement may authorize accumulation of income, and the trustee may be authorized to distribute income and principal to the surviving spouse. The surviving spouse, however, has no right to demand distributions, as under a power of appointment or under a "5-and-5 power." At the death of the surviving spouse, the principal and accumulated income in the trust must be paid to the surviving spouse's estate; consequently, the surviving spouse makes testamentary disposition of the principal and accumulated income.

The estate trust is seldom used. Its unique advantage is only that the assets qualify for the marital deduction, without payments of income to the spouse being mandatory. The estate trust may be sensible for obtaining trust management where the trust assets are not likely to appreciate in value significantly during the surviving spouse's remaining years. An estate trust may also be used to hold non-income-producing property.

EXHIBIT 66 – 1 **Marital Deduction**	
Property Interest	*Qualify for marital deduction?*
Outright bequest to spouse	Yes
Joint tenancy WROS with spouse	Yes (one-half)
Tenancy in common	Yes, to the extent of the decedents' interest, if left by will or passing by law to spouse
Community property	Yes, if left by will to the spouse

Life insurance death benefit	Yes, if payable as a lump sum:
	  - Installment option
	  - Life income
	
	No, if interest only

Life estate	No
QTIP	Yes
Terminable interest	No
Power-of-appointment trust	Yes
General power of appointment	Yes
Special power of appointment	No
Qualified Domestic Trust (QDOT)	Yes

Terminable Interests

Generally, terminable interests do not qualify for the marital deduction. A terminable interest is an interest in property that will end or fail by reason of a lapse of time or due to the occurrence of a specified event. For example, if a spouse is given only a life estate in property, the interest is terminable because it ends when the spouse dies, and, therefore, the property is not included in his or her estate. Exceptions to the terminable-interest rule include the following interests:

- A lifetime-income interest with a general power of appointment over the property
- Property that is subject to a condition that the spouse survive the decedent by a period not to exceed six months
- Life insurance proceeds payable under installment options and life annuities if the surviving spouse has a power of appointment over the proceeds
- Qualified terminable-interest property, or QTIP property
- A life-income interest from a charitable remainder trust

QTIP

For a property transfer to receive QTIP treatment, the following two conditions apply:

- An irrevocable election must be made by the donor-spouse of QTIP treatment for gift tax purposes; or, the deceased spouse's executor must make the election for estate tax purposes.
- The donee spouse (surviving spouse) must receive a "qualified income interest" for life.

A "qualified income interest" is defined as follows:

- The donee spouse must be entitled to receive all the income from the property; i.e., the distribution of income is mandatory, accumulation is not permitted, and only a spouse can receive the income; no other beneficiaries are permitted.
- Income must be paid at least annually.
- No one may be given a power to appoint any portion of the property to any person other than the surviving spouse.
- The value of the property is taxable in the surviving spouse's gross estate for federal estate tax purposes at the death of the surviving spouse.

Estate Planning for Noncitizen Residents

Persons who are U.S. citizens but are residents of other countries and persons who are not U.S. citizens but are residents of the U.S. at death are subject to federal estate tax law. Special federal estate and gift tax rules apply to real estate and tangible personal property situated in the U.S. when the owners are not U.S. citizens and not residents of the U.S.

Marital Deduction Lost for Noncitizens	If property passes to a spouse who is a U.S. citizen, the estate is entitled to the marital deduction to reduce the estate taxes. If property passes to a spouse who is not a U.S. citizen, the marital deduction is lost. However, if the spouse becomes a U.S. citizen prior to filing the estate tax return, the estate can claim the marital deduction.
Qualified Domestic Trust (QDOT) – Sec. 2056A	In some special situations, the marital deduction will be allowed for estate assets passing to a noncitizen spouse if that property passes through a trust known as a qualified domestic trust (QDOT). The noncitizen spouse must be the only beneficiary of this trust. The QDOT is a trust and is subject to U.S. laws, so whenever a trustee distributes principal from the trust, estate taxes must be withheld to pay to the U.S. Treasury. The U.S. Treasury is given the right to collect taxes at the second spouse's death, no matter where the spouse is living. This prevents a surviving spouse from taking a marital deduction and then leaving the country to avoid estate taxes. In order to qualify for the marital deduction, the property passing to the QDOT trust for the noncitizen spouse must also meet the other rules for the marital deduction, such as the terminable-interest rule.
Gift Tax Marital Deduction – Sec. 2523(i)	Lifetime gifts to a noncitizen spouse will not qualify for the unlimited gift tax marital deduction. Instead, a special annual exclusion is available. The amount of the exclusion is indexed for inflation and has increased to $147,000 in 2015.
	This exclusion will apply if the transfer qualifies under both the annual exclusion rule and the marital deduction rule. In other words, the gift must be of a present interest, and it must not be a terminable interest.
Estates of Nonresidents, Not Citizens – Secs. 2101 and 2108	Special tax provisions apply to gifts and estates of nonresident spouses who are not citizens of the U.S. A nonresident alien may not claim the unified credit (applicable credit amount) with regard to lifetime gifts. The annual exclusion is available to nonresident aliens, but gift-splitting is not. The estate of a nonresident alien cannot use the charitable deduction unless the transfer is for use in the U.S. or is made to a U.S. entity. The unified credit for a nonresident alien's estate is limited to $13,000 (the tax on transfers of $60,000) unless the amount is changed by treaty.

Application Questions

1. Which of the following estates can take a marital deduction for a decedent's U.S. assets which are passing to a spouse who is a U.S. citizen?

(1) The decedent is a U.S. citizen who resides in a foreign country.
(2) The decedent is a citizen of a foreign country and resides in the U.S.
(3) The decedent is a citizen and resident of a foreign country.
(4) The decedent has dual citizenship in the U.S. and a foreign country and resides in U.S.

    A. (1) only
    B. (1) and (4) only
    C. (2) and (4) only
    D. (4) only
    E. (1), (2), (3), and (4)

2. Homer Bard left a will in which he established a $600,000 trust for his children and a $400,000 charitable trust, and the remainder was to pour over into a revocable trust. The revocable trust is to pay income to his wife for her life, and at her death, the principal is to be distributed to the children. At his death, Homer left the following assets:

Residence – JT	$250,000
Common stock – H	$350,000
Municipal bonds – H	$250,000
Investment real estate – H	$400,000
Life insurance – R	$600,000

JT = Joint tenancy WROS
H = Homer is the owner
W = Homer's wife is the owner
R = Revocable trust holds the title

What is the amount of the marital deduction that can be claimed by Homer Bard's estate?

    A. $0
    B. $125,000
    C. $250,000
    D. $400,000
    E. $600,000

3. Which of the following provisions can be added to a QTIP trust and have the trust assets still qualify for the marital deduction?

    (1) A "5-and-5" withdrawal right
    (2) A general power of appointment
    (3) A special power of appointment
    (4) Accumulation of income
    (5) Sprinkle powers

    A. (1) and (2) only
    B. (1), (2), and (3) only
    C. (1) and (5) only
    D. (2), (4), and (5) only
    E. (1), (2), (3), (4), and (5)

4. (Published question released December, 1996)

To qualify for the marital deduction, qualified terminable-interest property (QTIP) must meet which of the following conditions?

    (1) The surviving spouse must have a general power to appoint the property.
    (2) All of the income must be paid out either to the surviving spouse or to the children of the decedent and the surviving spouse.
    (3) The executor must make the QTIP election.
    (4) The surviving spouse must be entitled to make lifetime gifts to family members, directly from the QTIP.

    A. (1) and (2) only
    B. (1) and (3) only
    C. (2) and (4) only
    D. (3) only
    E. (1), (2), (3), and (4)

5. Which of the following bequests will qualify for the marital deduction?

    (1) The decedent's will leaves $600,000 to a trust that will pay income to the surviving spouse and then will be distributed according to the directions of the second spouse's will, at his or her death.
    (2) The decedent's will leaves the residue, consisting of $600,000, to a trust that will pay income to the surviving spouse for life and then will be distributed to the decedent's children in portions specified by the spouse.
    (3) The decedent's will leaves $650,000 to a trust that gives the trustee the discretion to accumulate or pay income to the surviving spouse for life and then distribute the remainder to their children.
    (4) The decedent's will leaves $650,000 to a trust that will pay income to the surviving spouse for life, and the spouse can appoint all the trust assets during his or her lifetime.

    A. (1) and (2) only
    B. (1) and (4) only
    C. (2) and (3) only
    D. (2) and (4) only
    E. (1), (2), (3), and (4)

6. George and Judy Collins live in California, where George has his own business as a meeting planner. George bought a whole life policy soon after he was married, insuring his life for $100,000. The policy has a cash value of $22,000, and Judy is the designated beneficiary. The Collins also own the following assets:

Checking account – CP	$ 6,000
Savings account – CP	$ 8,000
Mutual funds – CP	$ 35,000
Common stock portfolio – CP	$ 50,000
Rental property – H	$200,000
Sole proprietorship – CP	$150,000
IRA (George's) – CP	$ 50,000
403(b) plan (Judy's) – CP	$ 80,000
Residence – CP	$200,000
BMW car – CP	$ 40,000
Jewelry – W	$ 30,000

CP = Community property
H = George's separate property
W = Judy's separate property

Judy is the beneficiary of George's IRA, and George is the beneficiary of Judy's 403(b) plan. George's will leaves the applicable exemption equivalent to a bypass trust and the remainder to a marital trust.

If George died today, what would be the approximate value of the marital deduction that his estate could claim?

A. $0
B. $50,000
C. $75,000
D. $100,000
E. $300,000

7. (Published question released December, 1996)

Which of the following statements about the marital deduction is (are) true?

(1) The marital deduction has the effect of treating the husband and wife as one economic unit, for gift and estate taxes.
(2) Property that qualifies for the marital deduction is excluded from the surviving spouse's estate.
(3) Qualifying all of the decedent's property for the marital deduction may result in more estate tax being paid.
(4) A qualified domestic trust is used to provide for the spouse when there has been a second marriage.

A. (1), (2), and (3) only
B. (2) and (4) only
C. (1), (3), and (4) only
D. (1) and (3) only
E. (2) only

8. Trish Lane is a U.S. citizen, married to William Lane, a British citizen, and they live in Florida. Trish will have a gross estate of $3 million. Trish's will leaves her entire estate outright to William. If she dies today, which of the following statements is (are) correct?

(1) Her estate will not qualify for the marital deduction.
(2) Her estate will not qualify for the unified credit.
(3) Her estate will qualify for the marital deduction and unified credit if William becomes a citizen before the estate tax return is filed.
(4) Her estate will qualify for the marital deduction if her assets are transferred to a QDOT created after her death.

   A. (3) only
   B. (1), (2), and (3) only
   C. (1), (3), and (4) only
   D. (1), (2), (3), and (4)

9. In which of the following circumstances would a qualified domestic trust (QDOT) be required for the surviving spouse to claim the estate tax marital deduction?

(1) The decedent was a U.S. citizen, and the surviving spouse is a nonresident alien.
(2) The decedent was a U.S. citizen, and the surviving spouse is a resident alien.
(3) The decedent was a resident alien, and the surviving spouse is a U.S. citizen.
(4) The decedent was a nonresident alien, and the surviving spouse is a nonresident U.S. citizen.

   A. (1) and (2) only
   B. (1) and (3) only
   C. (2) and (3) only
   D (2) and (4) only
   E. (3) and (4) only

10. All the following statements describe a prerequisite for a transfer of property qualifying for the gift tax marital deduction, EXCEPT:

   A. The spouse to whom the property is transferred is a citizen of the U.S.
   B. The property transferred is includible in the donor's gross estate.
   C. The transfer conveys full control and enjoyment of the property to the spouse.
   D. The transfer qualifies for treatment as qualified terminable-interest property.
   E. The transfer must be to the donor's legal spouse, as recognized in the state in which the marriage occurred.

 800-795-5347

11. Which of the following statements concerning the estate tax marital deduction are correct?

(1) A bequest of property to a spouse who is not a U.S. citizen will not qualify for the marital deduction.

(2) Only one-half of the value of property held in joint tenancy WROS with a spouse at the time of the spouse's death qualifies for the marital deduction.

(3) If one-half of community property is bequeathed to a spouse, the estate receives a marital deduction equal to the full value of the community property.

(4) Property bequeathed to the decedent's spouse and children in joint tenancy WROS will qualify for the marital deduction.

    A. (1) and (2) only
    B. (1) and (4) only
    C. (2) and (3) only
    D. (2) and (4) only
    E. (1), (2), and (4) only

12. Lance Corporal and his wife Constance have one daughter, June. Lance and Constance own their family home as tenants by the entirety. Lance has executed a will in which he gives Constance a life estate in their vacation home, and the property will belong to June after Constance's death. The will also makes a bequest of Lance's IBM stock to Constance, and the will establishes a testamentary trust under which the income from the trust is to be paid to Constance for her life, to the extent determined by the trustee, at the trustee's discretion. The trustee is also given discretion to invade principal for such amounts as the trustee shall determine in the event of emergencies. The trust corpus will be paid to June at the time of Constance's death.

Based on this set of facts, which of the following interests will qualify, in part or in whole, for the estate tax marital deduction?

(1) The testamentary trust
(2) The family home
(3) The life estate in the vacation home
(4) The bequest of IBM stock

    A. (1) and (2) only
    B. (1) and (4) only
    C. (2) and (3) only
    D. (2) and (4) only
    E. (3) and (4) only

13. Based on the facts in the preceding question, which of the following statements is (are) correct?

(1) If Lance owned the IBM stock in joint tenancy WROS with June, only one-half of the value of the stock would qualify for the marital deduction.

(2) If Constance were given the right to income and to invade corpus for whatever amounts she desired, the full amount of the trust would qualify for the marital deduction.

(3) If Constance were given the right to consume and invade trust income and principal for her own health, maintenance, and support, the full amount of the trust would qualify for the marital deduction.

(4) If Constance were given the power with June to direct to whom the trust corpus would pass at Constance's death, the full amount of the trust would qualify for the marital deduction.

A. (1) only
B. (2) only
C. (1) and (3) only
D. (2) and (3) only
E. (3) and (4) only

14. All the following transfers qualify for a marital deduction, EXCEPT:

A. The grantor of an *inter vivos* irrevocable trust specified that her husband was to receive a life income from the trust assets, and the remainder would go to her children.

B. At the time of the creation of a charitable remainder trust, the grantor gave a life interest in the trust assets to his wife.

C. The decedent provided in his will for his wife to receive a life income from his estate assets, and his wife was given a general power of appointment over the property.

D. The decedent's will provided that if his wife died within six months of his death, the residuary would pass to his children and not to her or to her estate.

E. The decedent's will provided for a QTIP trust, and the executor filed a QTIP election.

15. All the following are appropriate techniques that assure that property left to a surviving spouse will qualify for the marital deduction, EXCEPT:

A. Use of a power-of-appointment trust

B. Use of a current income bequest or a QTIP trust

C. Use of a QTIP trust

D. Use of a trust to provide a life income for a spouse, with the corpus to go to the surviving spouse's grandchildren

E. Use of a current income trust or a "C" trust

16. David Castor is terminally ill and expected to die next year. He projects a gross estate valued at $6.5 million. David will be survived by his wife Jean and two children, Gregory and Susan. David's estate will include:

- A residence owned in joint tenancy WROS with his wife, valued at $380,000
- Stock, worth $500,000, owned in joint tenancy WROS with his wife
- Municipal bonds, worth $200,000, owned in joint tenancy WROS with each of his children
- A life insurance policy owned by David, with a death benefit of $100,000 payable to Jean under a life-income option.

Jean also owned a whole life policy on David's life that will pay her death proceeds of $100,000. Jean purchased the policy and made all of the premium payments.

Based upon the facts of David Castor's projected estate, what interests will qualify for the marital deduction?

(1) One-half of the value of the residence
(2) The entire value of the stock
(3) The entire value of the municipal bonds
(4) All of the death benefits paid to Jean under the two insurance policies

    A. (1) only
    B. (1) and (3) only
    C. (2) and (3) only
    D. (2) and (4) only
    E. (3) and (4) only

17. All the following statements concerning the facts of the David Castor estate in the preceding question is correct, EXCEPT:

A. If the death proceeds of the life insurance policy owned by David are payable to Gregory and Susan, these proceeds would not qualify for the marital deduction.
B. If the policy owned by Jean had been transferred by David to Jean a year before David's death, the death benefit from the policy would qualify for the marital deduction.
C. If Gregory and Susan could prove that half of the money used to purchase the municipal bonds was provided by them, then one-half of the value of the bonds would qualify for the marital deduction.
D. If David and Jean owned their residence as tenants in common, and David bequeathed his interest in the residence to Gregory, no part of the residence would qualify for the marital deduction.
E. One-half of the value of the stock would qualify for the marital deduction.

18. James Best died this year, leaving a gross estate valued at $7.5 million. James was survived by his wife Bernice. James and Bernice had no children, but they were fond of their two nieces Sandy and Victoria. In his will, James established three trusts. The first trust is to receive $600,000 of assets from James' estate, and the income from these assets is payable to Bernice for her lifetime. At her death, the remainder is to be divided equally between Sandy and Victoria.

The second trust is to receive one-half of the residue of James' estate. The trustee is empowered to pay the income from the trust assets to Bernice, Sandy, and Victoria, according to their needs, as determined at the discretion of the trustee. The trustee may invade principal to maintain the standard of living to which Bernice has become accustomed. At Bernice's death, the trust assets will pass to Sandy and Victoria in amounts that Bernice shall determine.

The third trust is to receive the remaining one-half of the residue. All income from the trust is payable to Bernice at least annually, and at her death, the remainder is to be divided equally between Sandy and Victoria. The executor for James' estate has elected to treat this trust as qualified terminable-interest property.

Which of the trusts created by James Best qualified for the marital deduction?

A. The first trust only
B. The second trust only
C. The third trust only
D. The second and third trusts only
E. The first and third trusts only

19. All the following statements concerning the estate of James Best, as described in the preceding question, are correct, EXCEPT:

A. The property in the first trust would qualify for the marital deduction if Bernice could appoint the property to her estate.

B. The property in the second trust would qualify for the marital deduction if the trustee were provided with an ascertainable standard that would limit the trustee's discretion in distributing income.

C. The property in the third trust would not qualify for the marital deduction if the income were payable to Bernice only for such time as she did not remarry.

D. The property in the third trust would not qualify for the marital deduction if Bernice were given a power to appoint the property to Sandy or Victoria.

E. The property in the first trust would not qualify for the marital deduction if Bernice were given a testamentary power to appoint the property between Sandy and Victoria.

20. A QTIP trust may be used to qualify property for the marital deduction. All the following statements concerning the requirements that must be met for an effective QTIP trust are correct, EXCEPT:

    A. All of the income must be paid to the surviving spouse, at least annually.

    B. The surviving spouse may be authorized to invade the trust corpus.

    C. The trust corpus may pass directly to the children of the marriage upon the death of the second spouse.

    D. The surviving spouse must be given a general power of appointment over the principal at the time of death.

    E. The executor may decide how much of the decedent's property will be placed in the QTIP trust.

21. A combination of a nonmarital trust and a QTIP trust would logically be recommended to a client in all the following circumstances, EXCEPT:

    A. The client wants to control who will receive the assets after his or her spouse's death.

    B. The client wants to provide an income for his or her spouse for life.

    C. The client has confidence in his or her spouse's ability to manage finances.

    D. The client wants to reduce estate taxes by taking advantage of both the unified credit and the marital deduction.

    E. The client wants to defer estate taxes until the time of his or her spouse's death.

22. A trust that ensures the payment of federal estate taxes (for years when the estate tax exists) is called a:

    A. Tax trust
    B. QTIP trust
    C. Qualified relations trust
    D. Qualified domestic trust
    E. Craven trust

23. Which of the following property transfers at death are subject to U.S. estate tax?

    (1) A nonresident U.S. citizen leaves his or her estate to U.S. citizens who are residents of foreign countries.

    (2) A foreign citizen who resides in a foreign country leaves foreign real estate to a U.S. citizen.

    (3) A nonresident citizen of a foreign country leaves property in the U.S. to foreign citizens.

    (4) A U.S. citizen leaves foreign real estate to nonresident foreign citizens.

    A. (1) and (2) only
    B. (1) and (3) only
    C. (2) and (4) only
    D. (1), (3), and (4) only
    E. (1), (2), (3), and (4)

For practice answering case questions related to Topic 66, please answer the following questions in the cases included in the Appendix at the back of this textbook.

Case	Questions
Bartlett	13
Marshall	11
Webster	
Unser	
Tingey	
Lytle	
Beals	
Mocsin	
Young	
Borelli	
Cunningham	19
Fred and Mary Ferris	66, 67, 68, 69, and 70

Answers and Explanations

1. E is the answer. If the spouse to whom the assets pass is a U.S. citizen, the marital deduction is available. The estate tax marital deduction is also provided for the estates of residents who are not citizens and for estates of nonresidents who are not citizens. Note that only U.S. assets will be subject to estate tax even when a noncitizen is not a resident of the U.S.

2. B is the answer. The only interest that qualifies for the marital deduction is the joint interest in the residence. One-half of the value of the residence is included in the gross estate and passes to Homer's wife, by operation of law. The one-half interest is valued at $125,000. The life insurance proceeds will be paid to the revocable trust and will not qualify for the marital deduction because Homer's wife is given only a life estate, which is a terminable interest. In order for the revocable trust to qualify for the marital deduction, the executor would need to make a QTIP election. However, this election was not included in the fact pattern.

3. B is the answer. The QTIP trust can give the surviving spouse a general power of appointment or a special power of appointment at death, and it can give a power of appointment during life, as long as the property can be appointed only to the surviving spouse. Consequently, a QTIP trust can give the surviving spouse a right of invasion of the principal, such as a "5-and-5" withdrawal right. The income from a QTIP trust must be distributed at least annually to the spouse, so a provision for the accumulation of income and for sprinkle powers will disqualify the trust as a QTIP.

4. D is the answer. The QTIP election must be made by the executor. To qualify for the marital deduction, the income must be payable to the surviving spouse for life and to no other person. During the surviving spouse's lifetime, the property cannot be appointed to anyone other than the surviving spouse. The surviving spouse need not be given a general power of appointment.

5. B is the answer. Property passing to a spouse will qualify for the marital deduction if the spouse is given a life estate and a general power of appointment which is exercisable during life or at death. In (1) and (4), the surviving spouse is given a life estate and a general power of appointment. In (2), the spouse is given a limited power of appointment because the property can be appointed only to the children. In (3), the bequest is not a life estate that qualifies for the marital deduction because the income is not all payable to the spouse. Since the trustee can accumulate income, all of the income from the property is not paid to the surviving spouse. This bequest is also not an estate trust because the accumulated income and principal are not paid to the surviving spouse's estate. Furthermore, the spouse does not control the disposition of the assets.

6. C is the answer. One-half of the life insurance is community property and is included in the gross estate. Since it is paid to Judy as the beneficiary, it will qualify for the marital deduction. The IRA is also paid to Judy, so one-half of this community property is also included in the gross estate and qualifies for the marital deduction. The total value of the remaining assets subject to George's testamentary control is less than the applicable exemption equivalent for estate tax purposes of $5.43 million in 2015, so these assets are bequeathed to the bypass trust and do not qualify for the marital deduction.

7. D is the answer. The marital deduction allows a married couple to transfer assets from one spouse to the other, without payment of any gift or estate taxes, so they are treated effectively as a single economic unit. Property that qualifies for the marital deduction passes to the surviving spouse and will be includible in the estate of the surviving spouse. If all of the property in a decedent's estate is qualified for the marital deduction, then the decedent has failed to take advantage of the unified credit. If the surviving spouse has an estate that is greater than the unified credit, estate taxes will be due on the excess. By not qualifying as much property for the marital deduction and making more use of the unified credit in the first estate, the total taxes for both estates may be reduced. A qualified domestic trust is used for a spouse who is not a citizen of the United States and is generally not used for a second marriage.

8. C is the answer. Since William Lane is not a U.S. citizen, the property passing to him will not qualify for the marital deduction. The estate will be able to take the unified credit. However, the estate will be able to take the marital deduction if William becomes a U.S. citizen before the estate tax return is filed or if a QDOT is set up. The QDOT can be established after Trish's death and still qualify for the marital deduction.

9. A is the answer. If the surviving spouse is a U.S. citizen, the assets passing to the spouse will qualify for the marital deduction without a QDOT. Thus, no QDOT is required in (3) and (4) because the surviving spouse is a U.S. citizen. The surviving spouses in (1) and (2) are a nonresident and a resident alien, so the marital deduction will not be available unless the QDOT is established in these choices. The QDOT ensures that the resident or nonresident alien does not leave the country with the estate assets, which could prevent the U.S. Treasury from receiving the estate taxes due on the alien's estate.

10. B is the answer. For gift tax purposes, the property given to a spouse does not need to be includible in the gross estate. The gross estate is a concept used in the estate tax rules.

11. A is the answer. A bequest of property to a spouse who is not a U.S. citizen will not qualify for the marital deduction. Only one-half of property held in joint tenancy WROS with a spouse at the time of the spouse's death qualifies for the marital deduction because only one-half is included in the gross estate, and only property included in the gross estate is eligible for the marital deduction. If one-half of community property is bequeathed to a spouse, the estate receives a marital deduction equal to only one-half of the community property. Property bequeathed to the decedent's spouse and children in joint tenancy WROS will not qualify for the marital deduction because the property must be transferred solely to the decedent's spouse.

12. D is the answer. The bequest of IBM stock, an outright bequest, and one-half of the family home, which passes outside the will, will qualify for the marital deduction. The life estate in the vacation home will not qualify because Constance is given only a life estate, with no power of appointment. Her life estate is only a terminable interest. The testamentary trust will not qualify for the marital deduction because the income payable to Constance is subject to the discretion of the trustee, and the remainder is not paid to her estate, nor is she given a power of appointment over the corpus.

13. B is the answer. If Lance owned the IBM stock in joint tenancy WROS with June, then none of the value of the stock would qualify for the marital deduction because June is not a spouse. If

Constance were given the right to income and to invade corpus for whatever amounts she desired, the full amount of the trust would qualify for the marital deduction because Constance would have a general power of appointment over the trust. If Constance were given the right to consume and invade trust income and principal for her own health, maintenance, and support, the trust would not qualify for the marital deduction because Constance would have only a special power of appointment. If Constance were given the power with June to direct to whom the trust corpus would pass at Constance's death, the trust, again, would not qualify for the marital deduction. A power exercisable only in conjunction with a person having a substantial adverse interest in the property is a special power. June has an adverse interest because she is the remainderperson.

14. A is the answer. A life-income interest in the income from a trust is a terminable interest that will not qualify for the marital deduction. The other transfers are all exceptions to the terminable-interest rule.

15. D is the answer. A trust that provides income for life to the spouse and the corpus to the grandchildren is a nonmarital trust or bypass trust. The life-income interest is a terminable interest, so the property is taxed in the estate of the first spouse to die. The power-of-appointment trust, the QTIP trust, and the estate trust qualify for the marital deduction.

16. A is the answer. One-half of the value of the residence owned in joint tenancy will be includible in David's gross estate and will qualify for the marital deduction. Only one-half of the stock will also qualify, and none of the municipal bonds will qualify because these bonds pass to the children. The entire value of the bonds will be includible in the gross estate. Only the life insurance death benefit paid on the policy owned by David will be included in the gross estate and will qualify for the marital deduction.

17. C is the answer. By showing contribution of the purchase price, the children could avoid having one-half of the value of the municipal bonds included in David's gross estate, but the bonds would still not be eligible for the marital deduction because the assets pass to persons other than the spouse.

18. C is the answer. Only the third trust qualifies for the marital deduction because the executor has elected QTIP treatment, and Bernice receives a "qualified income interest." The first trust provides only a life income to Bernice, and she has no power of appointment over the principal. The second trust provides for income to be shared with the nieces, and the payment of income is discretionary, so this trust does not qualify for the marital deduction.

19. B is the answer. The second trust would still not qualify for the marital deduction. The standard of maintaining Bernice's accustomed standard of living is considered an ascertainable standard, so there is really no change of any significance described in B. The problem remains that the trust distributes income to beneficiaries who are not a spouse.

20. D is the answer. The surviving spouse may be given a limited power, such as the right to distribute the remaining assets of the trust among the children of the marriage.

21. C is the answer. The combination of a nonmarital trust and a QTIP trust would be more appropriate for a client who wants to retain control over the assets after death and does not have confidence in his or her spouse's ability to manage assets. The trusts provide an income stream for the surviving spouse, but the surviving spouse is given no control over the disposition of assets at death.

22. D is the answer. A function of a QDOT is to allow the U.S. Treasury to collect estate taxes. This is not a factor in other types of trusts.

23. D is the answer. Decedents who are U.S. citizens or U.S. residents at the time of death must file federal estate tax returns. Decedents who are not citizens and not residents will be required to file estate tax returns only in connection with property owned in the U.S.

Intra-Family and Other Business Transfer Techniques (Topic 67)

CFP Board Student-Centered Learning Objectives

(a) Recommend appropriate business transfer techniques such as:
- i. Buy/sell agreements
  1. Cross purchase agreements
  2. Repurchase/Entity agreements
- ii. Grantor Trust
  1. Retained Interest Trust
     - a. GRITs, GRATs, GRUTs
     - b. PRT, QPRT
  2. Intentionally Defective Grantor Trusts
- iii. Family Limited Partnerships or Family LLCs
- iv. Private Annuity

Intra-Family and Other Business Transfer Techniques

- A. *Characteristics*
- B. *Techniques*
  - 1) *Buy-sell agreement*
  - 2) *Installment note*
  - 3) *Self-canceling installment note (SCIN)*
  - 4) *Private annuity*
  - 5) *Transfers in trust*
  - 6) *Intra-family loan*
  - 7) *Bargain sale*
  - 8) *Gift- or sale-leaseback*
  - 9) *Intentionally defective grantor trust*
  - 10) *Family limited partnership (FLP) or limited liability company (LLC)*
- C. *Federal income, gift, estate, and generation-skipping transfer tax implications*

Intra-Family Transfer

An intra-family transfer of a closely held business interest is usually designed to achieve family tax savings by shifting income and capital gains to family members in lower tax brackets, by spreading income and capital gains over a period of years, and by reducing the size of an estate. While income shifting and estate reduction may be accomplished through outright gifts, a closely held business interest presents additional planning considerations for the financial planner.

Buy-Sell Agreement

Buy-sell agreements arrange sales of family-owned business interests such as stock in a closely held corporation or partnership interests. Planning for the death, disability, or retirement of a family member and for the orderly transfer of a business to other family members can prevent disruption and substantial loss of value to the business interest. A buy-sell agreement funded with life and disability income insurance can provide a source of funds for purchase of the business interests held by family members. Additional treatment of buy-sell agreements is found in Topics 60 and 68.

Installment Sales – Sec. 453

Installment sales provide for payment of the purchase price over a period of years. The advantage to the seller is that the capital gain on the sale is not realized until the payments are received, and each installment payment is part return of capital and part capital gain. Thus, the capital gain is spread over several tax years, and tax liability is deferred for a portion of the gain. An installment sale may also have advantages for estate tax purposes because the seller may remove an appreciating asset from his or her estate and substitute fixed installment payments. The advantage to the buyer is that the entire purchase price is not required immediately, and the buyer has a period of years to pay the balance.

A taxpayer does not need to make any filing with the IRS to obtain installment sale treatment; rather, installment sale treatment is automatic. In addition, for installment sale treatment, the IRS does not require that any of the installment payments be made in the year of the sale. Installment sale treatment is not available, however, for securities publicly traded on an established market or for depreciated property transferred to a controlled entity. If an installment sale triggers recapture of depreciation or investment tax credits, this recapture must all be recognized in the year of the sale.

🔑 KEY SUMMARY 67 – 1
Installment Sales

- Installment sales are appropriate vehicles when the property owner is **seeking income, security, and income tax deferral.**
- Capital gain on the sale is spread over several years, deferring tax liability over that period.
- The present value of remaining payments is included in the deceased seller's estate.
- The payments to the seller are secured by the property sold.
- If an installment sale triggers recapture of depreciation, this recapture must be recognized in the year of the sale.

Income Tax Consequences of Forgiveness of Note

If an installment sale is part of a family transaction, a seller may decide at a later date to forgive one or more of the installment payments, or the seller may cancel the note entirely. If the holder of the installment note forgives a payment or cancels the note, the holder is deemed to have been paid in full for income tax purposes. The maturity date for future payments is accelerated, and the seller is in receipt of taxable income, measured by the difference between his or her cost basis and the fair market value of the installment payments forgiven. If the installment buyer and seller are "related persons," the minimum fair market value is the face value of the note.

Whether a holder makes a gift of a note or cancels it, the income tax consequences are the same, and the holder has made a taxable gift equal to the fair market value of the remaining payments due and any forgiven accrued interest. For lifetime gifts of installment notes, the annual exclusion is available to reduce gift taxes. Thus, gift taxes may be minimized by forgiving, canceling, or making gifts of installments in the amount of the annual exclusion.

Unpaid Installments at the Owner's Death

If any installments have not been paid at the death of the holder of the installment note, the holder's gross estate will include the present value of the unpaid note. If an installment note is forgiven in the holder's will, the debt is considered to be paid to the estate, and the estate must report any gain and accrued interest on the note as taxable income.

Resale Rules – Sec. 453(e)

If the buyer and seller in an installment sale are related parties, special rules apply to any resale of the property. Generally, these rules provide that the original seller's gain will be accelerated if a related party resells within two years of the installment sale. Thus, a seller could be forced to pay tax on all the gain from the installment sale before the installment payments are made. Related parties include brothers, sisters, spouses, ancestors, lineal descendants, and certain entities.

Self-Canceling Installment Note (SCIN)

An installment note is an obligation to pay specified amounts at particular time intervals. With a self-canceling installment note, the obligation is canceled upon the happening of an event, usually the death of the person holding the note (the obligee). **Since the debt under an SCIN may be canceled before all installments are paid, the note is not worth as much as other installment notes of the same face value. Thus, the buyer must pay an additional principal amount or pay a higher rate of interest to avoid having the IRS find that a gift was made.** A higher principal amount may be based on the probability of the holder's death before completion of the payments, and the IRS tables may be used to compute this probability of death.

The SCIN is typically used in a family sale of assets, such as real estate, and the seller becomes the holder of the self-canceling note.

The holder may make a bequest of the note to the obligor in his or her will, and the note, by its terms, will provide for cancellation at the holder's death.

If there is not a matching bequest in the decedent-obligee's will, this forgiveness of indebtedness may create income to the obligor.

The value of the installments canceled at the note holder's death has been held not to be includible in the holder's gross estate. The decedent's estate, however, must report the remaining gain and accrued interest on the installment transaction as income in respect of a decedent. As a result, the estate will incur a substantial capital gain and not include any asset related to the note. Since the note is not included in the estate, there is no income tax deduction for the portion of estate tax attributable to the note. While the SCIN may result in greater income tax liability, the technique may still be used with wealthy clients, whose estate tax rates will exceed their marginal income tax rates.

 KEY SUMMARY 67 – 2
Self-Canceling Installment Notes

- An owner can accept an SCIN in a sale of assets when **seeking an income stream, income tax deferral, and estate tax reduction.**
- The buyer can depreciate assets based on the purchase price.
- The buyer (obligor) can deduct the interest paid on the SCIN installment sale (unlike a private annuity).
- The value of the installments canceled at the note holder's death is not included in the gross estate.

Private Annuity

When an annuity is used as payment for property, the annuity will provide for payments over a specified period of time, based upon factors, such as the health and life expectancy of the annuitant and the fair market value of the property exchanged. Neither party may be in the business of funding or financing annuities, nor may the promise to pay the annuity be secured. Thus, a private annuity is an annuity that is offered by a person or entity, other than an insurance company. The annuity is typically offered by a private party who purchases a business interest or property, and the purchaser makes the periodic payments of the annuity contract in exchange for the business interest.

🔑 KEY SUMMARY 67 – 3
Private Annuities

- Private annuities are appropriate vehicles for a sale when the property owner is **seeking an income stream, income tax deferral, and estate tax reduction.**
- The property is transferred to the recipient for a promise (payments are not secured).
- No value of the private annuity is included in the owner's estate (estate taxes are avoided).
- There is no depreciation recapture under a private annuity
- Annuity interest paid is not deductible.

Income Tax Treatment

For income tax purposes, each payment to the annuitant is treated as part tax-free return of capital (return of cost basis), part capital gain, and part ordinary income (annual interest). After the annuitant passes his or her life expectancy, additional payments are ordinary income because all cost basis has been recovered.

The annuity contract usually provides for payments to be made for the life of the annuitant, so the annuitant can spread any capital gain from the sale of the business interest over several years, in much the same way as with an installment sale. Unlike an installment sale, none of the annuity payment is deductible interest expense for the obligor.

The obligor's promise to make annuity payments must be unsecured, so an annuity should be accepted for a business interest only where the private party is in a sufficiently strong financial position to give the seller reasonable assurance of receiving the annuity payments. If the annuity is secured by the property sold, it will be subject to income tax as a commercial annuity and may be included in the annuitant's gross estate under Sec. 2036.

A private annuity may be attractive to an older person with a large estate, who would like to remove the future appreciation of a business interest from the estate and wants to reduce current income taxes by spreading the capital gain over several tax years. The main advantages of the private annuity are the smaller payments that will be required if the seller has a shorter than average life expectancy and the exclusion from the gross estate of any value attributable to the annuity. The main disadvantages are that the buyer cannot take a deduction for interest expense, the seller's payments are not secured, and the buyer may pay more for the business interest if the seller lives a long time.

Editor's Note: The Treasury Department issued proposed regulations that will impact private annuities transactions dated after October 18, 2006. Under the proposed regulations, the seller will have to recognize the entire capital gain in the year of the transaction rather than recognizing part of the capital gain with each annuity payment. As a result, private annuities might not be as popular in the future.

Joint and Survivor Annuity vs. Single Life

Under a single life annuity, the periodic payments cease when the annuitant dies. Under a joint and last survivor annuity, the periodic payments continue until the death of the last survivor. A single life annuity will provide a larger monthly benefit payment than will a joint and last survivor annuity because there is a lower probability of survival for one life than for two. At the death of the single life annuitant, the deceased's estate will include no amount attributable to the annuity. With the joint and survivor annuity, however, if the first to die was the sole owner of the transferred property, the present value of the future payments to the survivor will be included in the gross estate of the transferor-annuitant. Nevertheless, if the annuitants were married, the marital deduction will eliminate any estate tax liability.

Transfers in Trust

The transfer in trust of assets such as business interests can provide management of these assets for family members who are unable or unwilling to manage them. A life insurance trust may be established during lifetime to buy a business interest after the owner's death. Trusts can provide additional benefits by way of reduction in estate and probate costs as discussed. See Topics 53, 54, and 62.

Intentionally Defective Grantor Trust

In some cases, trusts are created which are intended to be defective under the grantor trust rules in order for the trust income to be taxed to the grantor, rather than to the trust and trust beneficiaries. The income tax rates for a trust are steep so that there may be income tax savings by having the income attributed to the grantor.

The trust document is written so the grantor is given a power over the trust that is impermissible under the grantor trust rules. For example, the grantor is given the power to remove trust assets and substitute other assets of equal value. When the trust is created, the grantor contributes assets sufficient to make a down payment on the purchase of a business interest. The grantor can then sell a business interest to the trust in return for the down payment and an installment note. This transfer is not a gift, so no gift tax is owed. Since the trust violates the grantor trust rules, the grantor reports income received by the trust, and the beneficiaries receive the income free of tax. In addition, since the grantor is deemed the owner of the trust for income tax purposes, the gain on the installment sale is not recognized since the grantor cannot create capital gain by selling something to himself or herself. Thus, additional assets are transferred to the beneficiaries without transfer costs or income tax costs. The trust is irrevocable, so the assets are also not included in the grantor's gross estate.

Intra-Family Loan

Loans to family members are transfers for consideration and can be helpful in arranging business transactions and transfers. For example, a loan can be made to younger family members to buy assets expected to appreciate. The loan should bear a market rate of interest; otherwise, the IRS will impute income to the lender and the amount of interest that should have been paid by the borrower will be deemed a gift.

Loans can be advantageous when there is a large differential between the rates for borrowing and the rates for returns on loans or other investments.

If a family member is willing to lend the money for purchase of a home, there can be substantial savings on mortgage application fees, points, and related costs.

Bargain Sales

A "bargain sale" means that property is sold below its market value. If the transfer of property is for less than full and adequate consideration in money or the equivalent money value of property, there is a gift of the difference. If there are no exigent circumstances which require the transfer or sale at the liquidation value, the IRS will deem the difference between the fair market value and the transfer price to be a gift.

Sale-Leaseback

A sale-leaseback is a transaction in which one party sells property to another and then leases it back from the purchaser. The selling party obtains cash that it needs, for example, for operations, without losing the use of the property, and, at the same time, is able to deduct the monthly lease payments in computing its income taxes. These deductions for lease payments also make the sale-leaseback transaction attractive for family members.

A family member in a high marginal tax bracket may sell equipment or other property to a family member in a lower bracket and make monthly lease payments that will be deductible for income tax purposes. Unfortunately, if the property has been depreciated by the seller, capital gains tax may be due on the sale, but the buyer will acquire a basis equal to the selling price and may depreciate the property for a second time. Sometimes, the sale of the property may be to a trust, which then leases the property back to the seller and distributes the income to family members. Sale of property that is likely to appreciate in value may also reduce future estate taxes.

Gift-Leaseback

The gift-leaseback is an intra-family business transfer device which involves a gift of property used in the donor's business to another family member. The donor frequently gives the property to a trust, and the donor leases the property back from the trust, thereby acquiring an income tax deduction for the cost of leasing the property from the trust.

The leaseback provides a stream of income that can be distributed by the trust to a family member in a lower marginal tax bracket, as well as providing valuable income tax deductions to the donor. **The gift asset is also removed from the donor's gross estate.**

A gift-leaseback is essentially the same transaction as a sale-leaseback, except that the asset is given to another person rather than being sold. The gift-leaseback is almost always a transaction among family members. The donor receives no cash for the asset, and gift and GST taxes may be due.

> *REMEMBER: WITH THE GIFT-LEASEBACK TECHNIQUE, THE FAMILY MEMBER-DONOR MAKES GIFTS OF **FULLY DEPRECIATED ASSETS** TO A LOWER BRACKET RELATIVE (OR TO A TRUST) AND THEN LEASES THE ASSET BACK FOR BUSINESS USE. IT IS NOT USUALLY ADVISABLE TO EMPLOY THIS TECHNIQUE FOR GIFTS TO CHILDREN UNDER THE AGE OF 18 DUE TO THE "KIDDIE TAX."*

Remainder Interest Transaction (RIT)

A remainder interest transaction (RIT) involves splitting a life estate in property from the remainder interest, and selling the remainder interest, usually to the owner's children.

The children will then obtain full ownership of the property at the termination of the life estate when the parents die.

Prior to the implementation of Chapter 14 rules, remainder interest transactions were used by parents and children to remove property from the parents' gross estate and transfer it to the children. With a RIT, the children buy the remainder interest at its present value, which is only a fraction of the property's current value. For example, if the parent is 58 years of age, the children would pay approximately 23% of the property's current value to acquire the remainder interest.

The financial burden of the acquisition may be reduced further by arranging for the children to buy the remainder interest in an installment sale or by using a private annuity. The parents then receive a monthly cash flow from the children's installment or annuity payments, they retain a life interest or life income in the property, and they remove the property from their probate estate.

Split-Interest Purchase (SPLIT)

In a split-interest purchase, two parties purchase an asset. One party (usually a parent) purchases a life estate, and the second party (usually a child or grandchild) purchases a remainder interest in the same property. The transaction is designed to accomplish the same goals as an RIT.

The life interest purchased by the parent gives the parent the right to receive the income from the property or the right to use, to possess, and to enjoy the property itself, for as long as the parent-life tenant lives. The purchaser of the remainder interest receives the property that is left when the first party's life interest terminates, which, by definition, is at death.

Each party to the SPLIT pays the actuarial value of the interest purchased. Depending on the age of the parent, the child may pay only 25% of the purchase price, while the parent pays 75%. At the parent's death, the child acquires absolute title to the property, and no federal gift or estate taxes are due on the property.

Chapter 14 Rules for RITs and SPLITs

Chapter 14 of the Internal Revenue Code, Secs. 2701-2704 has severely curtailed the use of RITs and SPLITs because the retained life interest purchased by the parent is deemed a retained "term" interest. Consequently, the retained interest is valued at zero. In the case of a RIT, the IRS argues that the parent makes a gift to the children of the retained life interest, and the value of the gift is the fair market value of the property, less the amount paid by the children. In the case of a SPLIT, the parent has a reportable gift to the extent that the fair market value of the property purchased exceeds the amount contributed by the child toward the purchase price.

Interestingly, the estate tax treatment of RITs and SPLITs is different. Since the RIT involves a retained life interest, the entire value of the asset on the date of death is includible in the decedent's gross estate.

The SPLIT, however, does not involve a retained life interest because the interests were purchased simultaneously, so nothing is includible in the gross estate.

Family Limited Partnership (FLP)

Instead of operating in the corporate form with family members as stockholders, the owner of a business may prefer a partnership in which family members are partners. Partnerships are not subject to certain tax rules that afflict corporations, such as the accumulated earnings tax and personal holding company rules.

With a family limited partnership, parents may transfer limited partnership interests to their children and retain general partnership interests. As in any limited partnership, the general partner is entitled to manage the partnership business, while the limited partners are precluded from participation in management; therefore, the parents retain control of the family limited partnership by retaining the general partnership interests.

The ability of parents to retain control over the business while passing much of the value to younger family members makes family partnerships attractive. Gifts of family limited partnership interests are advantageous because discounts for lack of marketability and minority interests are available to reduce the gift tax value of limited partnership interests. These discounts mean substantial reduction from the value of the underlying business assets, thereby saving transfer costs. Another advantage of the family limited partnership is that limited partnership interests may provide some protection against creditors. Also, the family partnership is more likely to stay intact when there are failed marriages among the owner's children because the business assets themselves are not under the control of the children.

Gifts of Partnership Interests at Discounted Values

Lifetime gifts of limited partnership units over a period of years may transfer substantial values. In this way, parents may make use of their gift tax annual exclusions and unified credits, and the future appreciation of the value of the partnership is removed from the parents' estates. If restrictions are placed on the limited partnership interests, substantial discounts may also be obtained for gift tax and estate tax valuations. For example, the limited partnership shares may be transferred to the owner's children with an appraised value that reflects a lack-of-marketability discount of 30% and a minority interest discount of 25%. Together, these discounts can reduce the value of the limited partnership interests by at least 35% of the underlying assets. The family limited partnership can also be designed to avoid any valuation problems under IRC, Secs. 2701-2704 (Chapter 14).

Income Shifting

The limited partnership interests may carry most of the value of the partnership, and the interests are entitled to partnership distributions of income to the extent of their value. For a business owner with adult children, the income shifting will result in reduced income taxes. Partnership interests passing to minor children should generally be placed in trust. The reduction in taxes from income shifting to young children will be minimal due to the "kiddie tax" imposed on the unearned income of minors under the age of 19 (24 if a student).

Gifts

When gifts of family partnership interests are planned, the owner must keep in mind that a gift will be effective only when the capital invested in the business is a material income-producing factor. In other words, if the partnership income is largely derived from the services of the owner, the transfer will be viewed as an attempt to evade income taxes by transferring earned income. In addition, the donor-partner must be paid reasonable compensation for his or her services to the partnership. For these reasons, a personal-service partnership is not a good candidate for a family partnership.

When gifts are made, the share of partnership income attributable to a donee's interest cannot be proportionately greater than the income attributed to the donor's interest. If, for example, the donor's interest is a 10% general partnership interest, and the donees receive 90% in limited partnership interests, the donees are entitled to 90% of the partnership net income.

Family limited partnerships are generally not recommended unless the owners have a net worth of approximately $3 million or higher. Setting up the family limited partnership requires attorneys' fees and appraisal fees for the limited partnership interests. Appraisal fees are also required at the time gifts are made of limited partnership interests.

Preparation of partnership returns and K-1s also require some accounting fees.

> ### 🔑 KEY SUMMARY 67 – 4
> ### Advantages of Family Limited Partnerships
>
> - With a family limited partnership, the owner can make **gifts of limited partnership interests to family members to reduce estate and income taxes,** and the owners can **retain general partnership interests to maintain control over the property or business.**
> - Future appreciation of the property or business is transferred out of the owners' estates.
> - The owners make use of the annual exclusions and the unified credit.
> - General partners (usually the parents) may choose to be paid for their services to the partnership.
> - If restrictions are placed on the limited partnership interests, substantial discounts may be obtained for gift tax and estate tax valuations.

Family Limited Liability Company (LLC)

A family LLC can be set up to obtain similar advantages as those obtained with the family limited partnership. The senior family members may be named the managing members of the LLC, and the other family members may or may not be involved in management. Similar discounts can be obtained for gifts of membership interests in the LLC, and benefits of income shifting are also obtainable.

Partnership Capital Freeze

The partnership capital freeze is a technique requiring restructuring of a partnership into at least two kinds of interests. The original owner may retain one interest which carries with it the control of the partnership or a preferred right to the distributions of income. The other interest, then, might carry rights to future appreciation and would be transferred to other family members.

The partnership freeze guarantees the general partner control of the business and a stream of income for a stated period of time.

Owners of a minority share of the partnership are provided the opportunity to work within the business and to receive a percentage of the income after the preferred interest has first been satisfied.

Under Chapter 14 of the Code, if the owner-transferor and applicable family members control the partnership, then the retained partnership interest will be valued at zero unless it is entitled to receive "qualified payments." If the retained interest is valued at zero, then the value of the gift to family members will be the full value of the original owner's partnership interest.

Preferred Stock Recapitalization

A preferred stock recapitalization is a rearrangement of a corporation's capital structure, typically involving an exchange of voting common stock for preferred stock, nonvoting common stock, and voting common stock of equal value. Generally, there is no gain or loss recognized on such an exchange of stock in a recapitalization. The stockholder can then make gifts of the common stock and thereby remove future appreciation of the stock from the business owner's estate, while allowing the business owner to retain control of the corporation.

As a result of Chapter 14 of the Code, the value of the gift of common stock following a recapitalization is likely to be the full value of the corporation because the preferred stock will be valued at zero. This retained interest is valued at zero if the owner does not have a right to "qualified payments." Obviously, the owner has a substantial interest in seeing that the recapitalization is carried out so that the preferred stock carries with it rights to "qualified payments." Generally, a recapitalization will not make sense unless such "qualified payments" are provided. Even when "qualified payments" are required, the common stock must still carry a value of at least 10% of the entire business.

🔑 KEY SUMMARY 67 – 5
Advantages of Preferred Stock Recapitalizations

The advantages of using the preferred stock recapitalization transfer technique are:

- Gifts of common stock will have reduced value for gift tax purposes.
- The donor removes future appreciation of the business from his/her estate. The appreciation accrues to the common stock (the value of the preferred stock is based on the "qualified payments").
- The preferred stock's cumulative dividends are "qualified payments" to the donor.
- The donor receives an income stream as a preferred stockholder.

Incorporation

A corporation may be organized for the purpose of receiving highly-appreciated assets that the owner transfers to the new corporation in exchange for stock in the new company. The transfer of assets to the company is a tax-free exchange if the transferor receives 80% or more of the voting stock and 80% of each class of stock.

Usually, the stock received by the transferor is divided between voting common and nonvoting common shares, so that the owner may make gifts of the nonvoting common shares to family members and remove future appreciation of the stock from the owner's gross estate. Since the owner retains the voting stock, the owner retains control over both the company and the transferred assets. The owner's basis in the company stock is the same as the owner's basis in the appreciated assets transferred to the new company.

The main reason for incorporation is for estate and gift tax savings. These savings can occur for two reasons:

- The owner may make gifts of stock in the company, thereby taking advantage of the annual exclusion and unified credits and removing any future appreciation in the assets from his or her estate.
- The owner or estate may obtain discounts in valuing the stock of the company, which may be less marketable than the underlying assets.

Personal Holding Company Rules

When an owner incorporates and transfers assets to the new corporation, the owner generally wants to avoid treatment as a personal holding company due to the separate personal holding company tax. This tax is in addition to the usual corporate income tax and is equal to 20% of the company's undistributed income.

A personal holding company is defined by two tests. The stock ownership test requires that 50% or more – in value – of the outstanding stock be owned by not more than five individuals during the last half of the taxable year. The income test requires that at least 60% of the adjusted ordinary gross income be personal holding company income, such as dividends, interest, rents, and amounts received for certain personal services.

A company will frequently be formed as an S corporation to avoid the double taxation on corporation income, which is taxed at both the corporate and individual levels, and to avoid the personal holding company rules.

S Corporation

An S corporation is a corporation that has made an election to have its income, deductions, capital gains and losses, charitable contributions, and credits passed through to its shareholders. To a great extent, an S corporation is treated for tax purposes like a partnership; however, the S corporation retains some features of a corporation, such as limited liability of the shareholders.

To receive S treatment, the corporation must file an election with the IRS.

An S corporation must be a domestic corporation with no more than 100 shareholders, and the shareholders must be individuals, estates, and only specific statutorily-defined trusts. Family members can elect to be treated as one shareholder for purposes of determining the number of shareholders. While S corporations cannot have corporate shareholders, an S corporation may have 80% owned (or more) C corporation subsidiaries or wholly-owned S corporation subsidiaries. Shareholders of the S corporation may not be nonresident aliens. An S corporation may have only one class of stock.

The S corporation election may be attractive for a closely held family business because income is taxed only once, not twice, as with a C corporation. The corporate alternative minimum tax (AMT) and the tax on unreasonable accumulations of income do not apply to the S corporation. An S corporation may have passive income, but the S election may be terminated if more than 25% of its gross receipts for 3 consecutive years are passive investment income.

Gifts of shares may be made to younger family members over the years to take advantage of the annual exclusion, and such gifts will also result in shifting income into lower tax brackets.

While an S corporation may have only one class of common stock, IRS regulations have permitted S corporations to issue both voting and nonvoting stock. Both kinds of stock, however, must have the same rights with regard to distributions and liquidation. An owner may make gifts of S corporation nonvoting stock and retain control by holding on to the voting stock. This gift giving will not result in any freezing of the owner's interest, but will remove some of the value of the S corporation from the owner's estate. Since S corporations may have only one class of stock, freeze techniques have limited applicability. The business owner who gives S corporation stock will retain an interest that is the same as the transferred interest, so Chapter 14 valuation rules do not apply.

EXHIBIT 67 – 1 Sale Techniques for Closely Held Business	
Bargain sale	Sale below FMV reduces capital gain, and the asset is removed from seller's gross estate.
Installment sale	Capital gain is spread over several years, and the asset is removed from the owner's estate.
Self-canceling installment note (SCIN)	Unpaid installments are not included in the holder's gross estate.
Private annuity	Gain is spread over several years, the asset is removed from the estate, and a life income can be provided.
Sale-leaseback	Lease payments are deductible, and the buyer can depreciate the property again.
Defective trust	Business interest sold to the trust avoids gift or estate tax plus income taxes on the installment sale, and the trust income is taxable to the grantor but distributed to the beneficiaries without gift tax

Transfer of Family Business Interests		
Transfer of ownership during life-time		
	Gift	• GRAT/GRUT – estate freeze • FLP/FLLC – discounts/control • CRAT/CRUT – charitable deduction • CLAT/CLUT – charitable deduction, estate freeze • Preferred stock recapitalization – estate freeze
	Sale	• Installment • SCIN – seller in poor health/avoid gross estate • Private Annuity – seller in poor health/avoid gross estate • IDGT – estate freeze/income tax to grantor • Bargain Sale • Buy/Sell
Transfer of ownership at death		
	Bequest	• Section 2032A – current use valuation • Section 6166 – installment payment of estate taxes • CLAT/CLUT – charitable deduction, estate freeze • Bypass trust – estate freeze
	Sale	• Buy/Sell • Sale to ILIT (**note:** trust established during lifetime, business ownership sold to trust at death)
	Redemption at death	• Section 303 – income tax savings

Application Questions

1. Peter Jordan owns all of the common stock of Jordan Auto Parts, Inc., which is valued at $1.8 million. Peter is age 60 and has two sons, but only one is active in the business. Peter would like to reduce his involvement in the company and arrange for a transfer to the son who is active in the business. Peter would like to have some income from the business, he wants to preserve his unified credit for later use, and he would like to reduce his estate taxes.

Which of the following transactions would be the most appropriate for Peter Jordan?

    A. A cross-purchase buy-sell agreement for Peter's stock

    B. A remainder interest transaction for Peter's stock

    C. Sale-leaseback of equipment owned by the company

    D. An installment purchase of Peter's stock

    E. A preferred stock recapitalization, after which, Peter will retain the voting common stock and preferred stock and give his son the nonvoting stock

2. Sally Hargrove is 58 years of age and operates a ranch that she inherited from her husband. The ranch business is valued at $4.2 million, and the land is worth $2.5 million. The equipment used in the business produces taxable income of over $200,000 annually. Sally Hargrove is in the 35% income tax bracket. Hargrove feels she does not need all of the income and would like to transfer assets to her son Paul, who works on the ranch and is in the 25% income tax bracket. She would like to make the transfer so that she does not give up management and control over the business or assets yet.

Which of the following business transfers to her son is most appropriate for Sally Hargrove?

    A. An installment sale of the business equipment to Paul

    B. A gift-leaseback of equipment with Paul

    C. A sale-leaseback of equipment with Paul

    D. A family limited partnership with Paul

    E. A bargain sale of equipment to Paul

3. Howard Edison owns $1 million of Florida commercial real estate and $2 million of Idaho undeveloped land. He also has a portfolio of marketable securities valued at $2 million. Howard is considering placing these assets in a personal holding company (PHC) that will issue voting and nonvoting common stock. Howard can then make gifts of the nonvoting shares to his two children. Which of the following statements concerning this intra-family transfer is correct?

(1) If real estate is transferred to the PHC, discounts can be obtained to reduce the value of the gifts of nonvoting stock.

(2) If marketable securities are transferred to the PHC, discounts will not be available to reduce the value of the gifts of nonvoting stock.

(3) Gifts of nonvoting shares of the PHC will give rise to valuation problems under the Chapter 14 rules, due to the retained interest of the voting shares.

(4) An election by the PHC to be taxed as an S corporation is likely to reduce income taxes.

A. (1) and (3) only
B. (1) and (4) only
C. (2) and (3) only
D. (2) and (4) only
E. (1), (2), (3), and (4)

4. Michael Deans is 62 years of age and owns and operates several restaurants under his solely-owned corporation. Michael sold 500 shares of stock in the corporation to his daughter Joan in exchange for an annuity. The annuity will pay him $10,000 per month for his lifetime. Which one of the following statements is correct concerning the estate and gift tax consequences of this transfer?

A. When Michael dies, the payments made to him during the three years before his death will be included in his gross estate.

B. If the number of shares sold is a majority of the stock in Michael's corporation, the retained interest will be valued at zero.

C. The estate tax consequences of this transfer would be no different if Michael were paid in cash and notes.

D. When Michael dies, the value of the business will be included in his estate, due to his retained life income.

E. If all of Michael's shares are exchanged for the annuity, the value of the restaurant business will be entirely removed from his gross estate.

5. Which of the following statements concerning the estate and gift tax consequences of an installment sale are correct?

(1) Unpaid installments at the owner's death must be included in the owner's gross estate.
(2) Unpaid installments forgiven in the owner's will are not included in the owner's gross estate.
(3) The estate must pay income tax on installments that are forgiven in the owner's will.
(4) Unpaid installments forgiven during the owner's lifetime do not qualify for the annual exclusion.

    A. (1) and (3) only
    B. (1) and (4) only
    C. (2) and (3) only
    D. (2) and (4) only
    E. (1), (2), (3), and (4)

6. (Published question released February, 1999, updated)

Which of the following statements about S corporations is true?

    A. S corporation status is automatic if there are fewer than 100 shareholders.
    B. S corporations are prohibited from having more than one class of stock.
    C. S corporations are prohibited from earning passive income.
    D. S corporations may have nonresident aliens as shareholders.

7. (Published question released February, 1999)

Grantor, who is not married, has established a trust, naming a bank as trustee. Pursuant to the terms of the trust document, Grantor is to receive all of the income generated by the trust assets during his life. Grantor may withdraw assets from the trust or place additional assets into it. The assets placed into the trust consist of Grantor's mutual fund portfolio, his personal residence, a rental property located in another state, and two installment notes held by Grantor. Upon Grantor's death, all of the assets remaining in the trust are to be distributed to Grantor's two children.

Which of the following statements is (are) correct?

(1) Upon the transfer of the installment notes to the trust, any deferred gain will be recognized as taxable income.
(2) After the transfer, the income from the mutual funds will be reported on Grantor's tax return.
(3) Upon the transfer of the rental property to the trust, all excess prior years' depreciation will be recaptured.
(4) After the transfer, the exclusion from capital gain remains available for the principal residence.

    A. (4) only
    B. (1) and (3) only
    C. (2) and (4) only
    D. (1), (2), and (3) only
    E. (1), (2), (3), and (4)

8. (Published question released February, 1999)

Upon Grantor's death (from the previous question), the assets remaining in the trust will:

(1) Be included in Grantor's taxable estate
(2) Be subjected to the probate process
(3) Receive a new basis, except for the installment notes
(4) Be distributed as directed by Grantor's will

    A. (4) only
    B. (1) and (3) only
    C. (1), (2), and (3) only
    D. (1), (2), (3), and (4)

9. All the following statements concerning bargain sales to charitable organizations are correct, EXCEPT:

    A. A primary purpose is to minimize the out-of-pocket cost for a gift of long-term appreciated property.
    B. The principal tax savings feature of the bargain sale is that the seller pays no capital gains tax on the sale.
    C. The cost to the charity of the property purchased is usually the seller's cost basis.
    D. The seller has a taxable gain on the transaction, but only on his or her pro rata share of the appreciation.
    E. The deductible gift is the fair market value of the property minus the selling price to the charity.

10. Ten months ago, Thirley Semple sold her motel complex to her son for its $2 million appraised value. The son paid no cash, but signed an installment obligation for the full purchase price to be paid over the next ten years. Under these circumstances, which of the following statements is (are) correct?

(1) The present value of the notes must be included in Thirley's gross estate at her death.
(2) If Thirley included a will provision canceling the notes, the value of the notes would be excluded from her gross estate.
(3) If Thirley cancelled the notes one month before her death, she would have eliminated any tax on her capital gains that would otherwise have been required in the future.

    A. (1) only
    B. (1) and (2) only
    C. (1) and (3) only
    D. (2) and (3) only
    E. (1), (2), and (3)

11. All the following statements concerning disposition of an installment obligation are correct, EXCEPT:

A. If an installment seller dies, holding an installment obligation from the buyer, the gain is reportable in the year each installment is received, the same as if the seller had lived.

B. The seller's death triggers an acceleration of the seller's gain.

C. If the seller makes a bequest of the obligation, or if his or her estate cancels the buyer's debt, gain is recognized by the estate to the extent that the amount of the obligation exceeds the seller's cost basis for the obligation.

D. Acceleration of the seller's gain can be triggered by either a will bequest or a lifetime cancellation.

E. The cancellation of the note by the seller means a gift by the seller to the buyer and an acceleration of income for the seller.

12. All the following statements concerning a "second disposition" of farmland sold initially under an installment sale arrangement are correct, EXCEPT:

A. If the second disposition occurs 18 months after the first sale, the first seller's gain will be accelerated.

B. If the second disposition occurs more than two years after the first sale, the resale rules do not apply.

C. If the second seller is a cousin of the first seller, the resale rules do not apply.

D. If the second disposition occurs within one year of the first sale, the full amount received by the second seller (who is the first seller's son) is taxable income for the first seller.

E. The resale rules will affect only the income tax treatment of the installment sale and not when payments are due under the installment note.

13. All the following statements concerning purchase of a business property with a private annuity are correct, EXCEPT:

A. Persons selling capital gain property can spread out recognition and realization of such gains over several years.

B. The property disposed of should be pledged to secure the future annuity payments.

C. An annuity can be helpful in reducing federal estate taxes.

D. Each annuity payment is partially a tax-free return of capital, partially ordinary income, and partially realization of capital gain.

E. The person who has purchased a property by giving a private annuity cannot deduct any of the annuity payments from income.

14. Which of the following statements concerning the treatment of private annuities for federal estate tax purposes is (are) correct?

(1) At the date of death, a single-life annuity has no value for federal estate tax purposes.
(2) At the date of death, a joint-and-last-survivor annuity has a value in the estate of the deceased, regardless of who supplied the consideration for the annuity.
(3) The federal estate tax marital deduction may be used to reduce the gross estate of a deceased spouse, to the extent of any joint annuity values caught in the estate of the first spouse to die.

A. (1) only
B. (1) and (2) only
C. (1) and (3) only
D. (2) and (3) only
E. (1), (2), and (3)

15. All the following statements concerning a family partnership are correct, EXCEPT:

A. It permits shifting income from high brackets to low brackets.
B. A professional partnership is frequently set up as a family partnership.
C. It can be helpful in "freezing" the value of a wealthy person's estate assets.
D. The family partnership can be formed as a limited partnership with the parents serving as the general partners in control of management.
E. Gifts to children of family partnership interests are eligible for substantial discounts in computing the gift tax value, due to lack of marketability.

16. All the following are among the requirements for a valid family partnership, EXCEPT:

A. A donee of a partnership interest must have real control over his or her interest.
B. A donee of a 50% interest can be paid 60% of the entity's profit when the donor-partner receives only 40% of the profit for his or her 50% interest.
C. Capital must be a material income-producing factor.
D. The donor must be paid reasonable compensation for any personal services he or she provides the partnership.
E. If donees receive limited partnership interests equal to 80% of the value of the partnership, they are entitled to 80% of the partnership income.

17. A sale-leaseback has which of the following tax advantages?

(1) It can remove property from the seller's estate for federal estate tax purposes.
(2) Fully depreciated property may be sold, and the buyer's cost basis is his or her purchase price.
(3) Fully depreciated property can be depreciated a second time by the second owner.
(4) If the lease is for business equipment, the seller can deduct lease payments as a business expense in computing income taxes.

A. (1) and (2) only
B. (1) and (3) only
C. (2) and (3) only
D. (3) and (4) only
E. (1), (2), (3), and (4)

18. John and Robin Parker have just married and are in the 27% marginal federal and state income tax bracket. Robin's father is in the construction business as a sole proprietor. He has three pieces of earth-moving equipment that are fully depreciated and that he proposes to give to John and Robin and then lease the equipment back from them. Under these circumstances, which of the following statements is (are) correct?

(1) The donor can deduct the annual lease payments as a business expense.
(2) John and Robin can deduct the annual depreciation, based on the fair market value of the equipment.
(3) The transfer will be treated as a gift of a present interest, and the annual gift tax exclusion will be available.

    A. (1) only
    B. (1) and (2) only
    C. (1) and (3) only
    D. (2) and (3) only
    E. (1), (2), and (3)

For practice answering case questions related to Topic 67, please answer the following questions in the cases included in the Appendix at the back of this textbook.

Case	Questions
Bartlett	
Marshall	12
Webster	
Unser	
Tingey	2
Lytle	
Beals	
Mocsin	
Young	
Borelli	
Cunningham	20
Fred and Mary Ferris	71, 72, 73, 74, and 75

Answers and Explanations

1. D is the answer. An installment purchase would involve no gift tax consequences and would transfer the company to the son who is active in the business. The value of the company would be effectively frozen for estate tax purposes. Peter would have income from the company in the form of installment payments. A cross-purchase agreement would not transfer any interest until Peter's death and would not reduce his involvement in the company. A sale-leaseback of equipment would not transfer the company or reduce Peter's involvement. The remainder interest transaction would probably involve a gift under the Chapter 14 Rules of the Code. The preferred stock recapitalization would mean a gift of nonvoting stock, which would carry at least 10% of the value of the company, so Peter would have to use his unified credit.

2. D is the answer. A family limited partnership will enable Sally Hargrove to retain control over the business and transfer limited partnership interests to her son Paul. The income shifting will save on federal income taxes, and the gifts can be made at a discount to the value of the underlying assets. The other alternatives involve giving up control over the assets and do not suit Sally's objective as well.

3. B is the answer. Discounts have been obtained for personal holding companies to which real estate and marketable securities have been transferred. The Chapter 14 rules will apply to a personal holding company that issues common and preferred stock, but when both issues are common stock (voting common and nonvoting common), there is not a Chapter 14 problem. Election of subchapter S status will mean that income is passed through, so income will not be subject to double taxation, and the tax on undistributed income of a personal holding company can be avoided.

4. E is the answer. The value of the restaurant business will be entirely removed from Michael's gross estate because Michael has sold all of his stock to his daughter. The life annuity will not be included in his estate, but the unconsumed portion of any annuity payments already received will be included. The payments within three years of death are not included in their entirety. If the value of the stock is equal to the discounted value of the annuity, there is no gift. The estate tax consequences of a sale for cash or notes are different from an annuity because with a sale, all of the proceeds are available immediately to the estate. If the death occurs after only a few years, the gross estate will include all of the unconsumed proceeds. If an annuity is received, and the annuitant receives only a few payments, nothing additional of value goes to the gross estate from the life annuity. Thus, if cash is paid, the gross estate will be much larger.

5. A is the answer. Unpaid installments at the owner's death must be included in the owner's gross estate. Unpaid installments forgiven in the owner's will are still included in the owner's gross estate. The estate must pay income tax on installments that are forgiven in the owner's will. Unpaid installments forgiven during the owner's lifetime will qualify for the annual exclusion.

6. B is the answer. S corporations are prohibited from having more than one class of stock, but they can have voting and nonvoting shares. S corporations can have no more than 100 shareholders, but S corporation status is not automatic; it must be elected. Nonresident aliens are not approved shareholders for S corporations.

7. C is the answer. The trust created by Grantor is a grantor trust, so income will be taxed to Grantor. The income from the mutual funds as well as other income is reported by Grantor on Grantor's income tax return. The transfer to the trust is not a taxable event and does not require recognition of gain or recapture of depreciation. Thus, the transfer of the installment notes is a gift of the notes, and the deferred gain will continue to be deferred until paid. The depreciation on the rental property is not recaptured; rather, the trust will carry over the donor's adjusted basis. The exclusion of gain from the sale of a principal residence requires ownership and use of the property as the principal residence for periods aggregating 2 years or more during the 5-year period ending on the date of sale. Thus, the exclusion would seem to apply for a period of time after the transfer to the trust.

8. B is the answer. Grantor may withdraw assets from the trust, so it is, in effect, a revocable trust. Consequently, the assets will be included in Grantor's gross estate. Because the assets are titled to the revocable trust, they will not be subject to probate. Since the assets in the trust will be included in Grantor's gross estate, the assets will receive a step-up in basis to the date-of-death value when Grantor dies. The installment notes do not receive a step-up in basis because they are income in respect of the decedent. The assets in the trust will be distributed according to the provisions of the trust, not the will.

9. B is the answer. The primary purpose of a bargain sale to a charitable organization is to minimize the cost of a gift of long-term appreciated property. To accomplish this, the owner of the long-term appreciated property, in most cases, sells the property to the charity at the same price as his or her basis. The owner then has a capital gain on the property, inasmuch as a portion of this basis is a gift to the charity, and the remainder is a sale. The percentage of basis assigned to the gift is the amount of appreciation, divided by the property's fair market value. The basis assigned to the sale is the original basis minus the amount assigned to the gift. The long-term capital gain is the original basis minus that portion of the basis assigned to the sale. An example should help. Property with a basis of $40,000 and a fair market value (FMV) of $100,000 is sold to the charity for $40,000. The total benefit to the charity is $60,000, and this is the amount of the owner's gift to charity. The percentage of the $40,000 basis assigned to the gift is the gain ($60,000) divided by the FMV ($100,000), or 60%. The basis for the gift, therefore, is 60% of $40,000 = $24,000. The portion assigned to the sale is the remainder of the basis, $16,000 ($40,000 – $24,000, which is the same as 40% of $40,000). The owner received $40,000 from the sale; his or her basis in the sale portion is $16,000; his or her capital gain is then $24,000. At a 20% tax rate, his or her tax liability for this gain amounts to $4,800 (20% of $24,000). The owner has made a gift of $60,000 and deducts this amount from gross income for a tax saving (assuming the owner is in the 28% income tax bracket) of $16,800 (28% of $60,000). His or her long-term capital gain tax liability was $4,800, and, therefore, his or her net tax saving is $12,000 ($16,800 – $4,800). This tax saving plus the $40,000 in sale proceeds gives a total return of $52,000. If the entire $100,000 property had been given to the charity, the tax saving (net proceeds) would have been $28,000 (28% of $100,000). If he or she had sold the property for $100,000, the tax liability would have been $12,000 (20% of the $60,000 capital gain), and the return would then be $88,000 ($100,000 – $12,000). This somewhat complicated set of numbers can be summarized as follows:

	SALES AT FMV	BARGAIN SALE TO CHARITY	GIFT OF SALE PROCEEDS TO CHARITY
Benefit to Charity	$0	$60,000	$100,000
Net Proceeds to Owner	$88,000	$52,000	$ 28,000
Cost of Charitable Gift	–	$36,000*	$ 60,000**
Dollar Cost Per Dollar Donated	–	$ 0.60	$ 0.60

> * $88,000 potential return – $52,000 actual return
> ** $88,200 potential return – $28,000 actual return

As can be seen, the out-of-pocket cost of the bargain sale is less than the cost of the outright gift and is in direct proportion to the amount of the charitable gift.

10. A is the answer. (1) is the only correct statement. (2) is not correct. A cancellation by the decedent's will is considered to be a transfer of the obligation by the decedent's estate, and the deceased's estate must report the accelerated gain. (3) is not correct because the installment obligation rules cannot be avoided by cancelling the obligation during one's lifetime.

11. B is the answer. Death of the seller does not trigger an acceleration of the seller's gain. The surviving heir would report the installment payments in the same way that the decedent would have reported the installment payments. A, C, D, and E are correct statements.

12. D is the answer. The full amount received by the second seller is not taxable income for the first seller. There is a limit on the amount the first seller must report as taxable income. A, B, and C are correct statements.

13. B is the answer. The annuity payments should be unsecured. A, C, and D are correct statements.

14. C is the answer. (2) is not a correct statement. Only at the death of the joint annuitant who was the owner of the property transferred will there be value caught in the gross estate of the deceased. The value will be the value of the future payments to the survivor. (1) and (3) are correct statements.

15. B is the answer. B is an incorrect statement because capital must be a material income-producing factor. If professional services are an important factor, obviously, the business must have a professional practitioner who is active in the business. A fifteen-year-old child is not likely to meet this essential requirement. A, C, D, and E are correct statements.

16. B is the answer. One of the primary requirements for a valid family partnership is that the share of income attributable to the donee's interest cannot be proportionately greater than that attributable to the donor's interest. Thus, in this situation, the share of income attributable to the donee's interest cannot be greater than 50%. A, C, D, and E are correct statements.

17. E is the answer. All four statements are correct.

18. C is the answer. (2) is not a correct statement. John and Robin cannot deduct any depreciation. They have a zero cost basis. (1) and (3) are correct statements.

Deferral and Minimization of Estate Taxes (Topic 68)

CFP Board Student-Centered Learning Objectives

(a) Recommend a plan that minimizes both income and estate taxes within the context of a client's goals and objectives.

A. Deferral and Minimization of Estate Taxes
1. *Exclusion of property from the gross estate*
2. *Lifetime gifting strategies*
3. *Marital deduction and bypass trust planning*
4. *Inter vivos and testamentary charitable gifts*

B. Valuation Issues
1. *Estate freezes*
   - A) *Corporate and partnership recapitalizations (§ 2701)*
   - B) *Transfers in trust*
2. *Valuation discounts for business interests*
   - A) *Minority discounts*
   - B) *Marketability discounts*
   - C) *Blockage discounts*
   - D) *Key person discounts*
3. *Valuation techniques and the federal gross estate*

Overview

To reduce taxes for an estate, a planner can: (1) reduce the size of the gross estate, (2) increase deductions, and (3) make use of as many credits as possible. Increasing deductions requires planning to make use mainly of the marital and charitable deductions. Making full use of credits, especially the unified credit, is the aim of bypass planning.

Exclusion of Property from the Gross Estate

The statutory provisions discussed in Topic 59 specify what must be included in the gross estate, and, in general, the gross estate must include all property over which the decedent possessed an interest. Certain property interests are excluded. The gross estate will not include a life estate, and it will not include any value attributable to a life annuity. Lifetime gifts of property interests will also not be included unless the decedent held a retained interest, or the property is subject to the 3-year rule. Estate taxes can be reduced by removing property from the gross estate by means of gifts and by transfers to irrevocable trusts.

Lifetime Gift Strategies

A wealthy individual can reduce his or her estate by undertaking a strategy of lifetime gifts. Gifts of present interests in the amount of the annual exclusion can be made to any number of donees, without gift tax consequences. Over the course of many years, a person can give away substantial sums by making gifts every year in the amount of the annual exclusion.

Gifts in excess of the annual exclusion will also be eligible for the unified credit (applicable credit amount). An individual can take greater advantage of the unified credit by making lifetime gifts of assets that will increase in value. If an individual makes gifts of appreciating assets, the appreciation will be removed from the gross estate without any gift or estate tax consequences.

Lifetime gifts can also take advantage of valuation discounts so that assets are transferred at reduced tax costs. The valuation discounts are discussed at the end of this topic.

Marital Deduction and Bypass Trust Planning

An entire estate can be bequeathed to a spouse and qualify for the marital deduction so that there is no estate tax. If the entire estate qualifies for the marital deduction, the estate will not use the unified credit. Estate plans often make use of a combination of marital and bypass trusts to take advantage of both the marital deduction and the unified credit.

Bypass Planning – the Unified Credit: Now Portable To Surviving Spouse

For most clients, the applicable credit amount is the key to estate tax reduction. Every individual is entitled to a credit in 2015 of $2,117,800 against estate tax liability; therefore, an individual is able to transfer up to $5.43 million of property in 2015 without paying estate tax. Assets placed in a power-of-appointment, a QTIP, or an estate trust will qualify for the marital deduction, but to take advantage of the unified credit, a testator should provide for a nonmarital trust. Virtually every estate plan should be designed to take advantage of the unified credit.

The 2010 Tax Act created a portability feature between spouses for the exemption from estate taxes. The portability feature was made permanent by the American Taxpayer Relief Act of 2012. If the first spouse to die does not use up the entire $5.43 million exemption amount in 2015, the executor can make an election on the first spouse's estate tax return to allow the surviving spouse to claim any remaining portion of the first spouse's $5.43 million exemption. This portability feature only applies to the $5.43 million estate tax exemption amount and not the $5.43 million GST exemption amount. In addition, the portability feature only applies to the $5.43 million exemption of the most recently deceased spouse if the surviving spouse has survived more than one spouse.

Bypass or Credit – Shelter Trusts ("B" or Family Trust)

The nonmarital trust is also called a "bypass trust," a "credit-shelter trust," a "family trust," or a "B" trust. The amount of property transferred to the nonmarital trust is usually just enough of the estate to take full advantage of the exemption equivalent, so no estate tax liability will be incurred on these assets. The nonmarital trust can be drafted to provide income from the trust assets to the spouse, to family members, or to other persons, and there is no requirement that income be distributed annually. The spouse can also be given a "5-and-5 power," but the remainder interest must pass to persons other than the spouse to avoid being included in the spouse's estate.

Two of the ways to draft a trust so that it does not qualify for the marital deduction are to: (1) make the distribution of income discretionary, or (2) make the spouse one, among several, income beneficiaries.

The spouse must not be given a general power of appointment over trust property (beyond a "5-and-5 power").

If the executor does not make the election for a QTIP trust, the trust will function as a bypass trust. Making the election does not change any of the provisions of the trust, only the tax consequences.

🔔 *REMEMBER: AFTER THE DEATH OF THE SURVIVING SPOUSE, THE MARITAL, NONMARITAL AND QTIP TRUST ASSETS PASS TO THE REMAINDER BENEFICIARY. THE SURVIVING SPOUSE HAS COMPLETE CONTROL OVER WHO WILL RECEIVE THE ASSETS FROM A MARITAL TRUST UNDER THE GENERAL POWER OF APPOINTMENT. THE SURVIVING SPOUSE HAS NO CONTROL (OR ONLY LIMITED CONTROL) OVER WHO WILL RECEIVE THE ASSETS FROM A NONMARITAL OR QTIP TRUST, AS THE DECEDENT WHO SET UP THE TRUST HAS CONTROL UNDER THE TRUST TERMS.*

Formula Approach to Bypass Planning

The nonmarital trust or bypass trust is generally used to take advantage of the unified credit to remove appreciation from the estate of the surviving spouse and to avoid overqualifying assets for the marital deduction. Estate planners frequently use a formula approach by which a testator's assets are placed in "A," "B," and "C" (or "Q") trusts. The nonmarital trust is funded with assets equal to the exemption equivalent, and an estate planner will typically want to specify that highly appreciating assets are contributed to the nonmarital trust so the future appreciation will pass to the family's children without additional estate tax. The remaining assets of the estate are divided, in any desired proportion between an "A" and a QTIP trust. Assets transferred to the nonmarital trust are not taxed in the decedent's estate or in the surviving spouse's estate; and assets placed in the marital trust are not taxed until the death of the surviving spouse. The assets in the estate of the first spouse to die, therefore, may pass without payment of any estate tax.

The trusts established to take advantage of the unified credit are usually testamentary trusts, but revocable lifetime trusts can also contain provisions for use of the applicable credit amount. For example, a revocable trust that provides for income to the surviving spouse and the remainder to the children is a non-marital trust, making use of the applicable credit amount.

Although the $5.43 million exemption is portable between spouses, high net worth taxpayers should still utilize a bypass trust at the first spouse's death rather than leaving their unused exemption to the surviving spouse. If the surviving spouse remarries and outlives a second spouse, the portability feature only applies to the last deceased spouse. This means any of the original spouse's $5.43 million exemption amount left to the surviving spouse would be lost. Use of the exemption upon the death of the first spouse also has the advantage of removing subsequent appreciation from the surviving spouse's estate.

Example:

Diane died during 2014 with an $8.34 million estate after a long battle with cancer. Diane's will provided that the maximum amount that can transfer free of estate taxes goes to her Bypass trust ($5.34 million in 2014) and the remainder goes to the QTIP trust to reduce the estate tax liability to zero. While her surviving husband Tom is alive, the trustee of the Bypass trust can make discretionary distributions to Tom and their two kids Sarah and Jill. At Tom's death the remaining Bypass assets will be divided equally between Sarah and Jill. Under the terms of the QTIP trust, Tom will receive the income annually from this trust. When Tom dies, the QTIP assets will be included in Tom's estate, but all remaining assets after paying any estate taxes on the QTIP assets will be distributed equally between Sarah and Jill.

Diane told Tom that she hoped he would remarry after she passed away. However, she did not want his second wife (or any of her kids or their kids) to inherit any of Diane's assets. Tom married Barbie in early 2015, but unfortunately Tom died a few months later from a heart attack.

The following diagram illustrates how Diane's assets passed at her death and then at Tom's subsequent death.

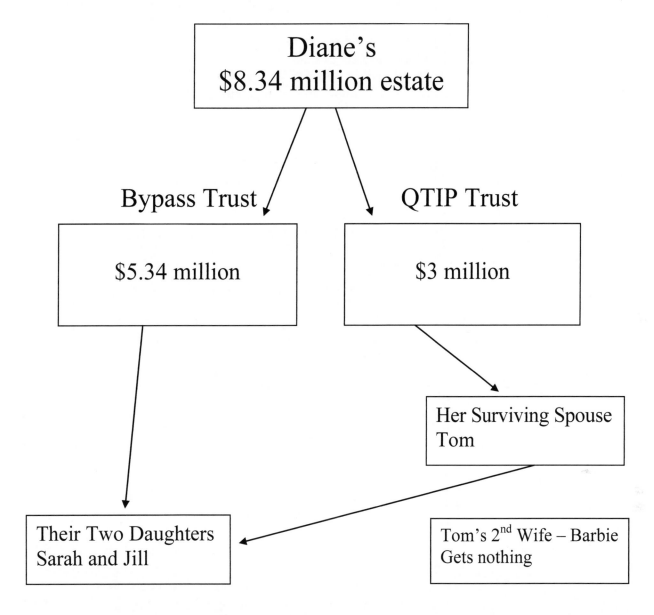

Estate Equalization with Nonmarital Trusts

Prior to 2006, married couples who had large combined estates, could save some estate taxes by funding the nonmarital trust with more than the exemption equivalent. The aim was to keep the estates approximately equal in size, thereby keeping both estates in lower marginal estate tax brackets. Because the estate and gift tax rates are graduated and progressive, the total tax liability for both estates was reduced by equalizing the estates and keeping each smaller. However, this benefit is largely eliminated for 2015 as each estate has a $5.43 million portable unified credit equivalent and starts paying estate tax at the highest marginal rate of 40%.

Estate equalization is still accomplished by placing a larger portion of the first spouse's estate in a nonmarital trust. Depending upon the size of the surviving spouse's estate, the testator may decide to bequeath one-half or more of the estate to the nonmarital trust to avoid having the assets taxed in the surviving spouse's estate. If the assets appreciate, the appreciation will avoid estate taxes that otherwise would be required when held in the surviving spouse's estate. The income from the nonmarital trust can still be paid annually to the surviving spouse, without the trust property later being included in the surviving spouse's gross estate.

The total amount of estate taxes on the two estates will be less than if the first spouse had qualified more of the estate for the marital deduction.

 REMEMBER: EQUALIZING ESTATES INVOLVES CONSIDERING THE ESTATE TAX CONSEQUENCES AT THE DEATH OF BOTH HUSBAND AND WIFE. THE MAIN GOAL IS TO MINIMIZE THE COMBINED ESTATE TAXES. EQUALIZATION IS PROBABLY NOT REQUIRED UNLESS THE COMBINED ESTATES EXCEED TWO UNIFIED CREDIT EQUIVALENTS.

KEY SUMMARY 68 – 1
Key Trusts for Estate Planning

- A Marital ("A") trust avoids estate tax because the trust assets qualify for the marital deduction. The surviving spouse is given control over all assets through a general power of appointment. The assets will later pass to a beneficiary selected by the surviving spouse.

- A nonmarital ("B") trust avoids estate tax by using the unified credit exemption. The decedent can leave the income from trust assets to the surviving spouse or split the income stream between the spouse and other persons. The decedent can direct who will receive the trust assets after the death of the surviving spouse, so the decedent can exercise a high degree of postmortem control.

- A QTIP trust ("C") qualifies for the marital deduction and the decedent can specify who will receive the trust property after the surviving spouse dies; however, only the surviving spouse may receive the income stream from a QTIP.

- The QTIP, nonmarital, and life insurance trusts can allow distributions subject to HEMS (Health, Education, Maintenance, and Support) and have 5-and-5 powers.

Inter vivos and Testamentary Charitable Gifts

Inter vivos and testamentary gifts to charity can reduce an individual's taxable estate and estate taxes. Charitable transfers are discussed in Topic 64.

VALUATION ISSUES

Date of Transfer

For federal gift tax purposes, gifts are valued as of the date on which the property is transferred irrevocably.

Date of Death and Alternate Valuation Date – Sec. 2032

For federal estate tax purposes, property is valued on the date of death. If, however, the executor makes an election to use the alternate valuation date, the property will be valued as of six months after the date of death.

The following rules apply to the election of the alternate valuation date:

- The alternate valuation date may be elected only when the result will be an overall reduction in the estate tax liability. Thus, if the decedent's business interests have declined in value due to his or her death, electing the alternate valuation date can save estate taxes. Where the entire estate will pass to a U.S. citizen spouse, and no estate tax will be due, the alternate valuation date may not be elected.
- The alternate valuation date may not be elected for assets that normally decline in value over time, such as annuities. These assets are valued at the date of death.
- If the alternate valuation date is elected and assets are sold between the date of death and the alternate valuation date, then the sale price must be used.

Fair Market Value

The general rule in the valuation of assets for federal transfer taxes is that property interests are taxed at their fair market value on the date of the transfer. **Fair market value is defined as the price that a willing buyer would pay a willing seller when both had reasonable knowledge of the relevant facts of the transaction, and neither was under any compulsion to buy or to sell.** Thus, household property and personal effects are valued according to what a willing buyer would pay a willing seller for those items.

Publicly Held Stock

For publicly traded stock, the fair market value is the mean between the highest and lowest quoted selling prices on the valuation date.

If the stock did not trade on the valuation date, IRS regulations require the use of the means between the high and low on the nearest trading dates, before and after the valuation date, and these mean prices are weighted. Under this approach, a mean price is calculated for each of the trading dates before and after the valuation date. To weight these mean prices, each mean price is multiplied by a fraction, that is: one, minus the number of days from the valuation date, divided by the total number of trading days both before and after the valuation date.

Example:

Samantha gifted stock to her son on August 10, but there were no stock trades that day. The mean price for trades on August 8 was $10 per share, and on August 13, the mean price was $11 per share. Since August 8 is 2 days before the valuation date, and August 13 is 3 days after the trade, the total number of days used for weighting is 5. The weighted price is:

$$\$10 \times \left(1 - \frac{2 \text{ days}}{5 \text{ days total}}\right) = \$10 \times \left(\frac{3}{5}\right) = \$6$$

$$\$11 \times \left(1 - \frac{3 \text{ days}}{5 \text{ days total}}\right) = \$11 \times \left(\frac{2}{5}\right) = \$4.40$$

The valuation of the stock gift is $6 + $4.40 = $10.40.

Blockage Discount

For a large holding of publicly traded stock, a blockage discount may be available in valuing the stock. A discount is applied on the theory that the large block cannot be traded without affecting the market price. This discount is recognized only with publicly traded stock, and not closely held stock. The blockage discount typically ranges between one and five percent.

Closely Held Stock

When the stock of a corporation is held by only a few shareholders, such as in a family business, valuing the stock is difficult. Since there is little trading and no organized market to look to for a market price on the closely held stock, many factors must be considered. Among the factors are the following:

- The nature of the business and the history of the enterprise
- The outlook for the general economy and for the specific industry in which the company operates
- The book value for the stock
- The earning capacity of the company
- The company's dividend-paying capacity
- Goodwill

- Any recent sales of the stock and the size of the block of stock being valued
- The fair market value of the stock of comparable companies in the same or similar business, whose stock is publicly traded

Minority Discount

In a closely held corporation, a minority shareholder is generally unable to influence corporate policy; compel dividend distributions; or force a corporate sale, liquidation, or merger. As a result, the minority stock interest typically has reduced marketability, except to the controlling shareholder. The minority discount has been recognized by the IRS and the courts, and the IRS will allow it even when the stock is held entirely by family members.

The reverse of the minority discount is the control premium. If a fractional interest in a closely held corporation is a controlling interest, the stock may actually be worth more than its proportional share of the business due to the control that the shareholder may exercise over certain decisions affecting the corporation.

Lack-of-Marketability Discount

A lack-of-marketability discount may be allowed for both minority and controlling interests in a closely held corporation or partnership. Closely held stock and partnership interests can be difficult to sell. There may be added costs of selling the stock to the public. The cost of taking a stock public can be 25% of the selling price. Thus, the lack-of-marketability discount may be from 15% to 50%. Depending on the circumstances, a combined minority discount and lack-of-marketability discount can be 30% to 40%.

Key Personnel Discount

The loss of a founding owner or other key person can have enormous adverse effects on a business. The key person may have been the source of much of the firm's goodwill or may have been crucial in important business connections. A discount may be available for this loss of earning power in the business; the percentage of the discount will vary, depending upon the seriousness of the loss or losses to the business.

EXHIBIT 68 – 1
Valuation Discounts

Discount	Asset	Reason
Minority discount	Closely held business	Minority shareholders cannot influence corporate decisions
Blockage discount	Publicly traded stock	A large holding for sale would affect price
Marketability discount	Closely held business	No established market exists
Key person discount	Closely held or public companies	Decedent was critical to business
Co-ownership discount	Real estate	Co-owners refuse to buy or sell

Pegging Value with Buy-Sell Agreements

For a closely held corporation, a mandatory buy-sell agreement, or purchase-option agreement, that definitely fixes the price for stock shares will serve to "peg" their market value for federal estate tax purposes. Valuation of the shares is then not required. For a buy-sell agreement to fix the value of stock in a closely held corporation, the following rules must be observed:

- The agreement must be a bona fide business arrangement.
- The terms must be comparable to similar arrangements entered into by persons in arm's-length transactions.
- The agreement must not be a device to transfer property to members of the decedent's family for less than full and adequate consideration in money or money's worth.

These tests are presumed to be satisfied if the parties are not family members.

Different kinds of agreements have been effective in meeting these requirements. Reciprocal options among stockholders can be exercised at a specified price for a fixed period, whether during lifetime or at death. Mandatory buy-sell agreements require stockholders (or the corporation) to buy interests at a predetermined price or according to a predetermined formula during the stockholder's lifetime, and they bind the executor to sell after the stockholder's death.

While buy-sell agreements and similar restrictive agreements can peg the value of closely held shares for estate tax purposes, they are not conclusive for gift tax valuations.

Bond Valuation

The fair market value of publicly traded bonds is the mean between the highest and lowest quoted selling prices on the valuation date.

If bonds are not traded on the valuation date, the weighted average of the means on the nearest trading dates before and after the trade is used.

If there is no active market, then the bonds are valued using all relevant factors, as those affecting closely held stock (detailed earlier in this Topic).

Series EE bonds are valued at their redemption prices. These bonds are not negotiable or transferable, and the only ascertainable value is the amount for which the Treasury will redeem them.

Mutual Funds

Mutual funds are valued at their redemption price on the valuation date.

Life Insurance Policies

For estate tax purposes, the value of a life insurance policy that is includible in the gross estate is the amount the beneficiary receives. This valuation approach applies to whole life, term life, group insurance, and accidental death insurance. If a settlement option has been elected, the amount payable as a lump sum is the value includible in the gross estate.

For a policy that is a gift during the owner's lifetime or that is owned by the decedent at the time of his or her death on the life of another person, the replacement value is used, which is determined according to the following rules:

- For a new policy, the value is the gross premium paid.
- For a paid-up or single-premium policy, the value is the single premium the insurer would charge for a comparable contract of equal face value on the life of a person who was the same age as the insured on the transfer date (or, for estates, the date of death of the policy owner).
- For an established whole life policy in the premium-paying stage, the value is computed by adding the unearned portion of the last premium to the interpolated terminal reserve.
- For a term policy, the value is the unused premium.

Annuities

Commercial annuities are valued at the price the issuing company would issue for a comparable contract. If the annuity was not issued by a company that regularly issues annuities, it is treated as a private annuity. The value of a private annuity is the present value of the future payments required under the contract.

Term Interests, Life Estates, and Remainders

The basic principle in determining the fair market value for term interests, life estates, and remainders is to compute their present value, using IRS tables. The IRS tables are prepared, based on an interest rate that is 120% of the applicable federal midterm rate. This rate is published monthly and is an average market yield for U.S. obligations for the month. Tables are also prepared for two-life remainder factors, which would be used, for example, when two people are given life estates in the same trust.

Real Estate

Real estate is deemed unique, so fair market value is often a matter of differing opinions. A real estate appraisal from a professional appraiser is required for gift and estate valuations.

The factors that affect valuation of land are its location, size, shape, condition, and defects; the physical quality of the land; the adequacy of improvements made; the design, age, and condition of existing buildings; the actual and intended uses and the suitability of the property for its intended use; zoning restrictions; income produced by the property; the costs of needed improvements or building replacements; and the prices of comparable properties in the area.

Co-Ownership Discount

For real estate, the IRS and courts have recognized a discount in cases where there are uncooperative co-owners who refuse to buy the decedent's interest from the decedent's estate and who refuse to sell their interests. Since marketability is affected, a discount in the value of the real property may be allowed.

Qualified Conservation Easement

An income tax charitable deduction is available for an irrevocable transfer of a qualified real property interest for conservation purposes. The interest transferred may be a restriction on the use of the land, instead of the owner's entire interest. A restriction on use, or easement, may be granted for preservation of open space, protection of a natural habitat, preservation of outdoor recreational areas, or preservation of historic land or structures. For estate tax purposes, up to 50% of the value of the land subject to a testamentary bequest of a conservation easement may be excluded from the gross estate, up to a maximum of $500,000 in 2014. **Editor's Note:** As of the time of printing, it is unclear whether the estate tax exclusion of 50% (increased from 40%) of the value of the conservation easement will be extended to 2015.

Special-Use Valuation – Sec. 2032A

An exception to the general rule of valuing assets at their fair market value is the special-use (or current-use) valuation defined in Internal Revenue Code, Section 2032A. **Special-use valuation applies to real estate used in a closely held business or for farming**. An executor makes the election of special-use valuation for an estate when calculating the federal estate taxes, so this rule is not applicable to lifetime gifts. If the election is made, and an estate qualifies for special-use valuation, the real estate will be valued at its actual or current use, rather than at its fair market value. **This lower valuation generally reduces the estate taxes**. In 2015, the maximum reduction permitted through special-use valuation is $1,100,000. The maximum reduction is indexed for inflation in multiples of $10,000.

The following rules apply to special-use valuation:

- On the date of the decedent's death, the real estate must be used as a farm or in a closely held business.
- The business or farming operation ("qualified property") must be at least 50% of the gross estate after the deduction of any secured debt and mortgages.
- The real estate must be at least 25% of the gross estate after the deduction of any secured debt and mortgages.
- The real estate must pass to a member of the decedent's immediate family, lineal descendants, ancestors, cousins, daughters-in-law, or sons-in-law ("qualified heirs").
- The decedent must have owned the land and been a material participant in the operation of the farm or business for 5 of the past 8 years. Operation by another family member can be added to the decedent's time of operation.

To remain eligible for the tax benefits from the special-use valuation, the heirs must continue to use the land in the same farming operation or closely held business over a period of the next 10 years. If the land is sold or the use changes within the 10 years, there will be a recapture of estate taxes.

Practice Question

Janet Brown has a legal practice in Seattle and has just inherited a farm from her parents, who lived near Spokane, Washington. Brown would like to lease the farm to tenant farmers in the area and keep the farm for when she retires in about 15 years. The farmland is valued at $2 million when being used as a farm, but a developer will pay $3.5 million. Which of the following statements concerning the treatment of the farmland in the Brown estate is correct?

A. The estate should value the land at $2 million, less the reduction of $1,100,000 for the special-use valuation.
B. The estate can value the land at $2 million under the special-use valuation.
C. The estate should value the land at $3.5 million, less $1,100,000 due to the reduction for the special-use valuation.
D. The estate should value the land at $3.5 million because Jane Brown's use will not be eligible for special-use valuation.

Answer:
The highest and best use of the land determines the market value, so the land has a market value of $3.5 million. The special-use valuation will allow a reduction of up to $1,100,000 in 2015, so the land will be valued at $3.5 million less $1,100,000. Unfortunately, the special-use valuation will not work because Janet Brown will not be participating in operating the farm. The farmland must be valued at $3.5 million.
The answer is D.

Estate Freezes

Chapter 14 (Secs. 2701-2704) alters the fair market value principle as it applies to estate freeze techniques. With an estate freeze, an owner seeks to avoid estate taxes by fixing the value of estate assets at their current levels. The owner accomplishes a "freeze" by transferring the appreciation rights to another individual during his or her lifetime.

Preferred Stock Recapitalization

An example of an estate freeze is a preferred stock recapitalization, in which a closely held corporation exchanges its common stock for a combination of newly issued common and preferred stock. The owner of the new common and preferred stocks can then make gifts of the common stock to family members, while retaining the preferred stock. The common stock will hold most of the appreciation rights, which will then be removed from the owner's estate, and the owner can receive income, in the form of dividends, on the preferred stock. This dividend income is often the owner's retirement income after relinquishing the control of the business to other family members.

Subtraction Method

In a recapitalization of a closely held corporation, IRS rules generally provide for the common stock to be valued by means of a subtraction method.

In the past, the preferred stock was first valued, based on a calculation of the present value of the stream of dividends that the owner was expected to receive, and this value was subtracted from the total value of the company, to arrive at a value for the common stock. By making the preferred dividend sufficiently large, the owner was able to make the present value of the preferred stock carry most of the value of the business, and the common stock was reduced to a minimal value, for gift tax purposes. In addition, the preferred stock might have been given liquidation preferences, conversion rights, or put and call options, that would further enhance the value of the preferred stock and reduce the gift tax value of the common stock.

Under this planned recapitalization, the future appreciation of the company would have accrued to the benefit of the common stockholders and would have been kept out of the original owner's estate.

Moreover, in the future, the business might have omitted some preferred dividends, thereby, enhancing the value of the common stock and further reducing the owner's estate.

Chapter 14 Valuation – Retained Interests Valued at Zero – Secs. 2701-2704

The basic approach of Chapter 14 is to deal with estate freezes by changing the approach to the valuation of retained interests. When there is a gift to family members of the stock of a controlled corporation, and the donor retains an interest, the general rule now under Chapter 14 is that the retained interest will be valued at zero. Consequently, in a recapitalization, the common stock will carry the full fair market value of the business, just as it had before the recapitalization. Gifts of the common stock will then have substantial gift tax consequences.

Under the Chapter 14 rules, there are several exceptions to the general rule, requiring zero valuation for retained interests:

- The donor has a right to "qualified payments." "Qualified payments" are dividends payable on a periodic basis on the cumulative preferred stock (or comparable payments under a partnership interest) to the extent the dividends (or payments) are determined at a fixed rate. The rate can be fixed in relation to a market rate of interest, such as the Treasury-bill rate.

- The stock retained or given away is publicly traded.
- The retained interest is the same class as the transferred interest, i.e., common stock is given to family members, and the original owner retains common stock.
- The retained interest has proportionately the same rights as the transferred interest, i.e., preferred and common stock are given away, and the original owner retains preferred and common stock.
- The retained interest is the common stock, and the preferred stock is given to family members (a "reverse freeze").

If one of these exceptions applies, the retained interest is not valued at zero; rather, the fair market value will be used under the subtraction method.

Control Interests

When an owner retains rights to the distributions from a business, Chapter 14 will apply if applicable family members had control of the business immediately before the transfer. Control is 50% or more ownership of the stock or partnership interests. In determining control, attribution rules require that ownership interests of all applicable family members be aggregated. Applicable family members include the transferor's spouse, ancestors of the transferor or transferor's spouse, and the spouse of an ancestor. Chapter 14 rules also apply, regardless of control, when the retained interest is a liquidation, put, call, or conversion right.

10% Minimum Value for Common Stock

When there is a gift of common stock, and the owner holds on to an "applicable retained interest," the common stock must be given a value of at least 10% of the value of the business.

This rule assures at least a minimum value for the common stock, regardless of the value of the retained interest.

Omitted Dividends Added to Estate or Gift

Because qualified payments require dividends on cumulative preferred stock, any omitted dividends are legal obligations that remain an asset of the owner and will be added to the owner's gross estate at death. If the owner gives the retained interest away during his or her lifetime, any omitted dividends will be added to the value of the gift.

Transfers in Trust with Retained Interests – Sec. 2702

Since trusts have often been used for estate freezes, special rules under Chapter 14 apply to transfers in trust for family members with a grantor-retained interest.

The general rule is that where a grantor makes a gift in trust for family members and retains an interest in the trust, the retained interest will be valued at zero.

As a result of this rule, the grantor-retained income trust (GRIT) has been virtually eliminated as an estate freeze technique.

The exceptions are the following qualified interests:

(1) GRAT – A grantor-retained annuity trust provides for the grantor to receive fixed payments annually.
(2) GRUT – A grantor-retained unitrust provides for the grantor to receive payments that are a fixed percentage of the trust's assets, determined annually.
(3) QPRT – A personal residence trust provides for the grantor to retain the use of the residence for a term of years, with a remainder to a beneficiary.
(4) Tangible personal property trust – The grantor retains an interest for a term of years in a tangible property, such as artwork, whose value as a remainder interest is not affected by the exercise of the retained rights.

With these qualified interests, the remainder-interest gifts will be valued for gift tax purposes, using traditional valuation rules. These rules require valuation by finding 120% of the applicable federal midterm rate for the month and looking up the remainder factors in IRC, Sec. 7520 tables.

Application Questions

1. (Published question released February, 1999, updated)

What is the appropriate standard estate planning strategy for married couples to minimize taxes over two deaths if they both expect to live for at least 5 years?

A. Bequeath the entire estate to a trust, giving the surviving spouse a general power of appointment.
B. Bequeath the applicable exclusion amount to a qualified terminable-interest property trust (QTIP) and the balance to the surviving spouse.
C. Bequeath the applicable exclusion amount to a bypass trust to take advantage of the unified credit at the first death.
D. Bequeath the applicable exclusion amount to the surviving spouse and the balance to the children.

2. Herbert and Wendy Meadows are 66 years of age and have two children, ages 21 and 19. The Meadows own the following property interests:

Residence – JT	$1,500,000
Common stock – JT	$5,500,000
Municipal bonds – JT	$2,000,000
Investment real estate – H	$ 750,000
Vacation home – W	$ 500,000
Life insurance – H	$ 500,000
401(k) plan assets – H	$ 750,000
Car – H	$ 40,000
Car – W	$ 30,000

(Note that Wendy is the beneficiary of the life insurance death benefit of $2,000,000.)

JT = Joint tenancy WROS
H = Herbert is the owner
W = Wendy is the owner

Which of the following steps would provide the most estate tax reduction for the Meadows on their combined estate assuming they both expect to live to be at least 75 years old?

A. They should transfer the life insurance to an irrevocable trust.
B. They should leave their estates to a power-of-appointment trust.
C. Their wills should create a family bypass trust in the amount of the exemption equivalent and a QTIP trust for the residue.
D. They should change the ownership of some jointly owned assets and make use of their unified credits.

3. James Keats, age 72, remarried 10 years ago after divorcing his first wife. James had four children with his first wife. James will leave an estate of $8 million and would like to provide for his current wife, who has an estate of about $1 million. His second wife has one child by her first marriage. James would like the assets in his estate to go to his children, after his wife's death. He would also like to accomplish these objectives with the least amount of estate taxes.

Which of the following estate planning techniques will accomplish James Keats' objectives?

    A. An estate trust

    B. Shifting ownership of some of his assets to his current wife to equalize their estates

    C. A family bypass trust and a QTIP trust

    D. ABC trusts

    E. A power-of-appointment trust

4. (Published question released December, 1996)

While deciding whether to equalize the estates at the death of the first spouse or to defer estate taxes until the death of the surviving spouse, it is important to consider:

    (1) The age and health of the surviving spouse

    (2) Whether the combined estates exceed two unified credit equivalents

    (3) Whether the surviving spouse wants to make gifts to the children

    (4) Whether the estates have substantial appreciation potential

    A. (1), (2), and (3) only

    B. (3) only

    C. (2) and (4) only

    D. (1), (2), and (4) only

    E. (1), (2), (3), and (4)

5. Martin and Cary Forbisher were married 20 years ago and have lived in a community-property state for their entire marriage. They have two children. Martin inherited $7.5 million of stock in a closely held business from his father. The business is expected to grow at a rate of 10% annually through the foreseeable future. He also owns $620,000 of Fidelity Magellan Mutual Fund that he received as a gift from his mother. Martin and Cary own $1.2 million of community property. Cary owns $900,000 of real estate that she inherited from her parents.

Which of the following estate plans for Martin will allocate assets to testamentary trusts so as to minimize the estate taxes for the Forbishers assuming Martin dies today?

A. Trust "A" $600,000; Trust "B" $620,000; Trust "C" $7.5 million

B. Trust "A" $500,000; Trust "B" $5.43 million; Trust "C" $2.79 million

C. Trust "A" $1,320,000; Trust "B" $3.7 million; Trust "C" $3.7 million

D. Trust "A" $7.5 million; Trust "B" $600,000; Trust "C" $620,000

6. Harry Tweed, a widower, wants to make a gift to his daughter of assets that will be eligible for a discount in the valuation of the property for gift tax. Which of the following property interests will most likely be valued using a discount?

A. Real estate used in a farming business, held in sole ownership by Harry

B. A commercial annuity

C. 1,000 shares of AT&T stock

D. $300,000 of EXXON corporate bonds

E. 100 shares of Tweed Company common stock – a total of 500 shares are outstanding

7. Michael Luscomb, who retired three years before he died, left an estate valued in excess of $13 million when he died at the end of this year. Luscomb's assets include the following values:

- $40,000 in certificates of deposit
- $150,000 of common stock in a family business (100 shares)
- $600,000 in a commercial building declining in value, due to changes in the neighborhood
- $80,000 of common stock in a cable company that is publicly traded on the New York Stock Exchange (1,000 shares)
- $300,000 in life insurance

Which of the following actions or techniques by the executor would most likely reduce the values in Michael Luscomb's estate?

A. Special-use valuation
B. Key personnel discount
C. Co-ownership discount
D. Blockage discount
E. Alternate valuation date

8. Fred Hitchings is the founder of the Metal Fasteners Company and owns all of its stock. Fred wants to make a gift to his son of 200 shares, out of a total of the 1,000 shares of stock in the company. The company is valued at $3 million. Which of the following techniques would be likely to apply to the valuation of this gift?

(1) Control premium
(2) Minority discount
(3) Marketability discount
(4) Key personnel discount

A. (1) only
B. (2) and (3) only
C. (1) and (4) only
D. (2), (3), and (4) only
E. (1), (2), (3), and (4)

9. Sally Boyer's husband died 6 years ago and left her a printing company, Boyer Printing Co., which is worth $1 million. He left her a farm which could be sold for $2 million to a developer, but which Sally operates as a farm. As an operating farm, the farm business is worth $1.5 million; the land itself is worth $1 million. Sally's husband left her publicly traded stock worth $600,000, and Sally has accumulated $300,000 in publicly traded corporate bonds. Sally, who is 70 years of age and in excellent health, would like to make gifts to her son and daughter but still needs income to maintain her lifestyle. Which of the following recommendations would be most effective for obtaining valuation discounts and reducing gift and estate tax consequences?

A. Place the stock of Boyer Printing Co. in a trust for her children and retain a life income.

B. Place the farm in a trust for her children and retain a life income.

C. Place the publicly traded stock and bonds in a trust for the children and retain a right to income for 12 years.

D. Place the publicly traded stock in a trust for her children and retain a fixed annuity interest for 12 years.

E. Place the farm in a trust for the children and retain a fixed annuity interest for 12 years.

10. Scott Hughes is considering a recapitalization of his wholly owned corporation, Hughes Stool Company, so that he can make gifts of stock to his children. If the corporation issues new common and preferred stock, which of the following techniques would allow Scott to reduce the value of the gifts of stock to his children?

(1) Scott could give the preferred stock to his children and retain the common stock.

(2) Scott could give the children the common stock and retain the cumulative preferred, which is entitled to a dividend that is 8% of earnings.

(3) Scott could give proportional amounts of common and preferred stock to his children.

(4) Scott could give the common stock and retain an option to repurchase it at a reduced price.

A. (1) and (2) only
B. (1) and (3) only
C. (2) and (3) only
D. (3) and (4) only
E. (1), (2), (3), and (4)

11. Which of the following factors influence(s) the selection of an appropriate estate planning technique for a client's estate?

    (1) The liquidity and marketability of the property

    (2) The effect of the client's death on the value of the property

    (3) The difficulty in valuing the property

    (4) Whether the property has appreciated or depreciated in value

    A. (1) only
    B. (1) and (2) only
    C. (2) and (3) only
    D. (3) and (4) only
    E. (1), (2), (3), and (4)

12. Dan Cartright's will provides for the typical "A-B" trusts as follows:

- $5 million in a marital trust for his wife Susan
- $1 million in a nonmarital trust for his children Adam and Jean

Cartright owns his residence valued at $750,000 with his wife as tenants by the entirety, and he owns a life insurance policy, payable to his wife in the amount of $2 million. Stock in joint names WROS is valued at $8,300,000. Dan also has a brokerage account in his own name with a current FMV of $6,800,000.

If Cartright wants to take full advantage of his exemption equivalent at his death, which of the following recommendations would be most appropriate for Cartright?

    A. Cartright should place the entire estate in an estate trust.

    B. Cartright should increase the assets in the nonmarital trust.

    C. Cartright should make full use of the marital deduction by eliminating the nonmarital trust.

    D. Cartright should replace the marital trust with a power-of-appointment trust and a QTIP trust.

    E. Cartright should replace the marital trust with a QTIP trust and give his wife a 5-and-5 power.

13. Peter Lane, age 69, has a gross estate of $7.5 million, and his wife Margaret, age 65, has an estate of $8.2 million. Peter owns $2 million worth of shares in a family corporation. The shares are not expected to appreciate greatly and are unlikely to pay dividends. Peter expects to live for at least five years. Peter wants a portion of his estate to pass to his daughter Jane, from a prior marriage. Peter would like the remainder of his estate to pass to Margaret, even though she does not need the income or principal. Margaret is in the top marginal income tax bracket and is expected to remain in the top bracket for the foreseeable future. Peter would like Margaret to have the right to additional income in the event she needs the income, and Peter would like Margaret to decide on the eventual disposition of his estate at the time of her death. Peter wants to avoid estate taxes to the extent that he can do so.

Which of the following recommendations is most appropriate for Peter Lane's will?

A. Peter should make an outright bequest of assets to Jane and bequeath the residue to Margaret.
B. Peter should provide for a power-of-appointment trust for Margaret and a QTIP trust.
C. Peter should provide for a marital estate trust and a bypass trust.
D. Peter should provide for a marital "A" trust and a nonmarital "B" trust.
E. Peter should make an outright bequest to Jane and provide for a bypass trust for the remainder of this estate.

14. All the following statements concerning recommendations for the Peter Lane estate described in Question 13, are correct, EXCEPT:

A. If Margaret had no substantial income and would need the income from the assets in Peter's estate, a power-of-appointment trust or QTIP trust would be more appropriate than an estate trust.
B. If Peter wanted to direct to whom the assets in his estate would pass at Margaret's death, a QTIP trust would be more appropriate than an estate trust.
C. Peter could reduce overall estate taxes by directing that more than the exemption equivalent be transferred to a bypass trust.
D. If Margaret had no assets of her own, Peter could reduce overall estate taxes by making a gift of some assets to Margaret, so she could make use of the unified credit.

15. John Carson, age 70, has a gross estate valued at $14 million. John married Joan eight years ago. Joan has assets valued at $200,000. John has two children from a previous marriage whom he would like to inherit a substantial part of his estate. John would like to provide for Joan with a sufficient amount of income to ensure that she is comfortable. John does not want the assets to pass to Joan so that she might make bad investments or squander the money. John would also like to avoid estate taxes if possible.

Which of the following recommendations for the will of John Carson would be most appropriate?

A. Carson should establish a bypass trust in the amount of the exemption equivalent; any additional amounts that Carson wants to go to his children should be placed in a QTIP trust, and the remainder should go into an "A" trust.
B. Carson should establish an estate trust and a bypass trust.
C. Carson should establish a power-of-appointment trust in the amount of the exemption equivalent and a QTIP trust for the residue.
D. Carson should establish an "A" trust and a "B" trust in equal amounts.
E. Carson should establish a bypass trust in the amount of the exemption equivalent and a QTIP trust for the remainder, giving Joan a 5-and 5-power and a testamentary power of appointment under both trusts.

16. Which of the following would suggest limiting the use of the marital deduction?

(1) The surviving spouse is in poor health.
(2) The surviving spouse has substantial wealth in his or her own name.
(3) The expected decedent has assets expected to appreciate greatly.

A. (1) only
B. (1) and (2) only
C. (1) and (3) only
D. (2) and (3) only
E. (1), (2), and (3)

17. How is fair market value generally described for property interests?

A. Fair market value is the generally prevailing price in the market on the day a seller sells.
B. Fair market value is the price a willing buyer would pay a willing seller, where both were free of compulsion and equally aware of the relevant facts of the transaction.
C. Fair market value is the price agreed upon by a buyer and seller for a particular property interest.
D. Fair market value is the price between a buyer's bid and a seller's asking price on any day the property is available for sale and the buyer is ready to tender the purchase price.
E. Fair market value is the average of the offering price and the bid price.

18. Adam Baker owns a nursery business that represents 65% of his total assets. The land on which the business operates was valued at $4.5 million, and the nursery business was valued at $1.5 million. Baker wanted to avoid estate taxes, so he made gifts of some of the land to his two children. Baker also took out a mortgage on some of the land so that he could make gifts of cash, as well. If Baker continues to make these lifetime gifts, which of the following effects will this course of action most likely have on his estate?

A. The estate will be reduced to the same extent as by placing the same assets in joint tenancy.

B. The estate may not be eligible for special-use valuation.

C. The estate may not be eligible for an alternative valuation date.

D. The estate may be able to take advantage of the co-ownership discount.

E. The estate will lose the benefit of the annual exclusions and unified credit that it otherwise would have had.

19. Sam McBuck has an estate of $10 million and would like to leave it to his nephews. The property in Sam's estate includes the following assets:

- An apartment building in downtown New York that Sam owns with three partners, each of whom wants to buy Sam's interest
- 500 shares of MegaSounds, Inc., which represents a one-third interest in this closely held corporation
- 5,000 shares of General Motors stock
- A joint and last survivor annuity with each of his three nephews; each annuity pays Sam $6,000 per month and will pay each nephew $4,000 per month after Sam's death

At Sam's death, which of the following valuation methods is most likely to reduce the value of his gross estate?

A. The alternative valuation date, because the annuities are declining in value with each passing month

B. The blockage discount, because the sale of the General Motors stock is likely to depress the price

C. The lack-of-marketability discount, because of the partial interest in the apartment building

D. The minority discount, because Sam owns less than a controlling interest in MegaSounds, Inc.

E. Special-use valuation, because Sam's nephews will be material participants in operating the apartment buildings

20. The estate of Charles Darnell includes the following assets:

- 3,000 shares of common stock, a controlling interest in Darnell, Inc., a closely held corporation founded by the decedent and its largest sales producer
- 500 shares of publicly traded stock in a computer company that has grown rapidly but has had reversals since just before decedent's death
- An apartment building in a relatively stable area
- A life insurance policy on the life of the decedent
- U.S. Treasury bonds that will mature in 5 years and have been declining in value due to rising interest rates

All the following valuation techniques may apply to the Darnell estate, EXCEPT:

A. The alternate valuation date
B. The key personnel discount
C. The lack-of-marketability discount
D. The blockage discount
E. The face value

21. All the following statements concerning discounts that are sometimes permitted in valuing common stocks for federal estate tax purposes are correct, EXCEPT:

A. The minority interest discount is logical because of the limited power of the owners of such shares.
B. The key personnel discount is logical because the value of a business can be expected to decline upon the death of a key person.
C. A lack-of-marketability discount is logical because compliance with SEC rules may add costs and delay disposal of closely held stock.
D. The co-ownership discount is logical when an uncooperative surviving co-tenant shares ownership of securities.
E. The lack-of-marketability discount generally applies to closely held stock and not stock traded on exchanges.

22. Which of the following statements concerning the valuation of estate assets for federal estate tax purposes is (are) correct?

(1) The fair market value on the date of death is used most frequently.
(2) The alternate valuation date would reduce the taxable estate if stock prices increased substantially, following the security owner's death.
(3) The alternate valuation date is used only when estate taxes will be reduced.

A. (1) only
B. (1) and (2) only
C. (1) and (3) only
D. (2) and (3) only
E. (1), (2), and (3)

23. For federal estate tax purposes, what is the proper method for valuing publicly traded shares of stock?

    A. The closing price on the date of death

    B. The highest price at which shares sold on the date of death

    C. The lowest price at which shares sold on the date of death

    D. The mean between the highest and lowest quoted selling price on the date of death

    E. The par value

24. Which of the following statements concerning discounts that are sometimes permitted in valuing common stocks for federal estate tax purposes is (are) correct?

    (1) A minority interest discount is logical because of the limited demand for such an interest in a closely held company.

    (2) The blockage discount is usually accepted more readily by the IRS than other requests for discounts because of its economic logic.

    (3) A co-ownership discount is accepted for closely held stock, but not for publicly traded stock.

    A. (1) only

    B. (1) and (2) only

    C. (1) and (3) only

    D. (2) and (3) only

    E. (1), (2), and (3)

For practice answering case questions related to Topic 68, please answer the following questions in the cases included in the Appendix at the back of this textbook.

Case	Questions
Bartlett	
Marshall	13 and 14
Webster	14 and 15
Unser	
Tingey	3
Lytle	
Beals	
Mocsin	5
Young	
Borelli	19 and 20
Cunningham	21 and 22
Fred and Mary Ferris	76, 77, 78, 79, and 80

Answers and Explanations

1. C is the answer. The standard estate planning strategy for married couples is to make the most efficient use of both unified credits by means of a bypass trust or other bypass planning. Enough assets should be bequeathed to the bypass trust to take full advantage of the applicable exclusion amount. The other alternatives result in overqualifying property for the marital deduction.

Editor's Note: This released question was written prior to portability provisions allowing the surviving spouse to utilize any remaining unified credit from the first decedent-spouse's estate. A more likely question in years where portability is available would be for the bypass trust to be created to receive highly-appreciating assets equal to the credit equivalent at the death of the first decedent-spouse in order to remove appreciation from the estate of the surviving spouse, thus reducing total taxation in both estates.

2. A is the answer. The Meadows currently have combined assets of $13,070,000. Transferring the $2,000,000 life insurance to an ILIT will reduce the combined estates below their combined unified credits of $10.86 million, resulting in no estate tax. Since they expect to live at least 9 years to the age of 75, Herbert will outlive the 3 years required to remove the death benefit from his estate. Leaving the assets to a power of appointment trust (answer choice B) will result in all assets being included in the surviving spouse's estate. While the portability provision will allow the surviving spouse to receive a $10.86 million exemption, the total estate of the surviving spouse will be greater than that amount. Answer choice C will have the same result. Answer choice D is not correct because portability allows both unified credits to be used by the surviving spouse.

3. C is the answer. The family bypass trust can be set up to provide a life income to James Keats' wife, and the remainder will pass to the children of his first marriage. These assets will make use of the unified credit. The remaining assets will be left in the QTIP trust to provide for James Keats' wife and will be taxed in her estate. The assets remaining at her death in the QTIP trust can also pass to the children of his first marriage. The estate trust and power-of-appointment trust will give James' wife a power to dispose of assets in her estate, so they will not be appropriate. The ABC trusts will result in some assets passing to a marital trust, so James' wife will have a power of disposition over them. Shifting assets to his current wife will give her control over disposition of the assets at her death so this strategy will not be appropriate and is unnecessary due to portability.

4. E is the answer. The decision to equalize estates requires consideration of the age and health of the spouses because the surviving spouse will need more assets if he or she is expected to live a long time after the death of the first spouse. Equalization is probably not required unless the combined estates exceed two unified credit equivalents because estates of that size can pass free of estate taxes anyway. If the surviving spouse wants to make gifts to the children, then the assets can pass to the surviving spouse free of estate taxes, due to the marital deduction, and the surviving spouse can make use of the annual exclusions to make gifts free of gift tax. Thus, there is no reason to equalize estates and pay estate tax on the first estate. If the estates have substantial appreciation potential, the clients will need to consider the advantages of deferring taxes and investing the money that otherwise would be paid in taxes or, in the alternative, paying tax now and getting the future appreciation out of the estate.

5. B is the answer. The estate taxes for the Forbishers will be minimized by making use of the maximum unified credit (applicable credit amount) that Martin has available for the highly appreciating assets. For 2015, the maximum credit amount will allow Martin to pass $5.43 million without estate taxes. This amount of highly appreciating assets should be directed to pass to a bypass or "B" trust to remove the appreciation from Cary's estate. The only choice for answers in which the full $5.43 million is passing to a "B" trust is choice B. Note that no estate tax will be owed at Martin's death under any of the estate planning choices for allocations presented here. The use of "A" and "C" trusts, however, will mean that the assets are included in Cary's estate and will increase her estate taxes. If Martin uses the maximum unified credit, the Forbishers will reduce their overall estate taxes.

6. E is the answer. A minority interest discount may be available with the 100 shares of Tweed Company since it appears to be a closely held corporation. No co-ownership discount is likely to be available for the real estate because Tweed is the sole owner of the farming business. The AT&T stock is publicly traded, and 1,000 shares would not be a sufficient block to qualify for the blockage discount. The bonds also would probably not qualify for a discount.

7. E is the answer. By making the election to use the alternate valuation date, the executor can value the commercial building six months after the date of death, to obtain a reduced valuation. Special-use valuation would not result in a reduced valuation because the current use is probably its highest use. The blockage discount is not available for the stock in the cable company because 1,000 shares in a New York Stock Exchange company would not affect the price significantly.

8. B is the answer. A gift of 200 shares, out of the 1,000 total outstanding shares, is a minority interest, so a minority discount would be likely to apply. The marketability discount would also apply to this closely held business. The key personnel discount would probably not apply to this gift because there is no reason to expect a loss of a key person. A control premium would not be likely since the 200 shares will not provide control.

9. D is the answer. If the stock is placed in a GRAT, the gift value will be reduced, due to the retained annuity interest. Sally will have the income for 12 years and will then be able to qualify the farm for special-use valuation when she dies because the farmland will be more than 25% of her gross estate, and the farm business will be more than 50% of the gross estate. Placing the farm in trust would prevent the election of the special-use valuation in her estate. For gift tax purposes, the farm would be valued at its highest and best use, not as farmland. Thus, the discount for the retained annuity would be offset by the increased valuation of the farmland at its development value. Placing the stock and bonds in trust with a retained income for 12 years is a GRIT, so the gift value will not be discounted, due to the retained interest being valued at zero. Placing the Boyer Printing Company stock in trust with a retained life income would make the gift value the full value of the company, and the stock would most likely also be included in Sally's gross estate at her death.

10. B is the answer. The gift of preferred stock with retention of the common stock is a reverse freeze and would enable Scott to avoid the consequences of Chapter 14 of the Code. The gift of preferred stock would be valued according to the calculation of the present value of the stream of payments. A gift of proportional amounts of common and preferred stock is an exception to the Chapter 14 rules, so the retained interest would not be valued at zero. Thus, Scott would be able to reduce the gift value, using the subtraction method of valuation. The cumulative preferred stock that would pay 8% of earnings would not be a retained interest, entitled to qualified payments because the 8% dividend is not a fixed rate. The dividend would depend on the level of earnings of the company. The option to repurchase the common stock would be treated as having no value, and the preferred stock given a zero value, thus the common stock would carry all of the value of the company.

11. E is the answer. The selection of estate planning techniques depends on various factors, including the marketability and liquidity of the property in the client's estate, the difficulty in valuing the property, and the effect of the client's death on the value of the property. Closely held business interests are difficult to value, and this fact usually leads to the selection of a technique such as a buy-sell agreement or trust. Property that has depreciated may be more appropriate for sale during the owner's lifetime to obtain income tax deductions, and appreciated property may be more appropriate for testamentary disposition to obtain a step-up in basis for income tax purposes.

12. B is the answer. Cartright can take advantage of the exemption equivalent by increasing the assets going into the nonmarital trust. In 2014, he will have the ability to transfer $5.34 million before owing estate taxes. With only $1 million of his assets going into the bypass trust, his wife is left with an estate that is already in excess of her combined exclusion plus the remainder of his (under portability rules). Estate taxation of any appreciation in assets transferred to the bypass trust can be eliminated by increasing the allocation of Cartright's assets into the trust. The recommendation in D is not appropriate because the power-of-appointment trust and QTIP trust will only qualify more property for the marital deduction and not take full advantage of the exemption equivalent.

13. C is the answer. The bypass trust will reduce the estate taxes on the estates of Peter and Margaret by taking advantage of the unified credit. Taxes will also be deferred on the remainder of the estate, which passes to the estate trust. The estate trust is not required to pay income to the surviving spouse as is the power-of-appointment trust, so the trustee can retain the non-income producing stock. The surviving spouse must be given the power to appoint the accumulated income and principal of the trust at death. The estate trust allows income to accumulate during Margaret's lifetime if she does not need the income. Margaret can determine the eventual disposition of the estate by exercising her power under the estate trust. By providing for the bypass trust and the estate trust, Peter's estate plan will take advantage of the unified credit.

14. D is the answer. If Margaret had no assets of her own, the combined estates of Peter and Margaret would be below $10.86 million. Peter could utilize an A trust and a QTIP trust to provide income and a portion of his assets for Margaret with the remainder to pass to his daughter. If Peter's executor elects portability on his estate tax return, Margaret would be able to use the combined exemptions of $10.86 million to reduce the tax to zero. He would not need to make lifetime gifts to Margaret. Peter could also make use of a bypass trust that would take advantage of the unified credit. The bypass trust could pay income to his wife, and she could be given a 5-and-5 power.

15. A is the answer. John Carson wants the children to receive a substantial portion of his estate, so the QTIP trust can be used to provide the income to his wife and the remainder to his children.

The power-of-appointment, or "A," trust, must allow the wife control over who will inherit the assets in the trust, so this trust must be funded with the amount of assets over which John wants to give his wife testamentary control. The bypass trust will take advantage of the unified credit, provide a life income to his wife, and then pass to his children. While John could place equal amounts of assets in "A" and "B" trusts to try to equalize estates and reduce taxes, the assets in the "A" trust must be subject to his wife's testamentary control. If John wants to be certain that the assets pass to the children, the QTIP trust will allow him to accomplish this goal and defer estate taxes until his wife's death. The bypass trust will not be effective for using the exemption equivalent if Carson's wife is given a testamentary power of appointment.

16. E is the answer. If the surviving spouse is unlikely to live long due to poor health, the property passing to such spouse will be subject to estate tax, without the surviving spouse really having any need or benefit from the assets. If the property does not pass to the spouse, the assets may pass at a lower estate tax rate or may be sheltered from tax by use of the exemption equivalent in the estate of the first spouse to die. If a surviving spouse has substantial wealth, additional assets may be taxed at a higher estate tax rate at his or her subsequent death and will provide little benefit to the surviving spouse.

17. B is the answer. Fair market value is defined as the price that a willing buyer would pay a willing seller in a transaction in which neither was under any compulsion to buy or to sell and both had reasonable knowledge of the relevant facts.

18. B is the answer. The gifts of land and the mortgages will reduce the value of the land for purposes of qualifying for special-use valuation. The value of the qualified real estate after the deduction of mortgages must be at least 25% of the gross estate. A is not correct because joint tenancy with the children would result in inclusion of the full value of the property in Baker's estate. C is incorrect because the alternative valuation date may be elected, regardless of the size or assets in the estate. The co-ownership discount is not generally available where the parties are close relations. Moreover, the land in the estate is likely to pass to the children, too. Estates are not able to use the annual exclusion, but lifetime gifts are eligible for this annual exclusion to reduce the value of a gift subject to tax. Use of the unified credit during a taxpayer's lifetime will reduce the amount of unified credit remaining for the estate.

19. D is the answer. A minority shareholder in a closely held corporation sometimes qualifies for a minority discount because a minority interest is unable to influence corporate policy, to compel dividend distributions, or other actions. The alternate valuation date will not be helpful because the annuities will be valued as of the date of death, even with an election of the alternate valuation date. The lack-of-marketability discount applies to a controlling interest in a closely held corporation. The co-ownership discount applies to real estate where the co-owners refuse to buy from or sell to the estate. In this case, the partners want to buy Sam's interest. The blockage discount is not likely to apply because General Motors stock is traded publicly and is widely held. The amount of Sam's holding is not large enough to depress the market significantly.

20. D is the answer. The blockage discount applies only to stock traded on a public exchange. The amount of stock owned by Darnell in the computer company, the only publicly traded stock in the estate, would not qualify for a blockage discount. For life insurance on the decedent's life, the includible amount is the face value.

21. D is the answer. The co-ownership discount is not generally applied to the valuation of closely held stock. This discount applies to the valuation of real estate. A discount for minority interests is not appropriate in valuing all closely held corporations, but the limited influence and control of the minority stockholder can cause a loss of marketability and reduce the value of the minority interest. The key personnel discount is appropriate in valuing closely held stock because the death of a key person can cause a decline in business and in profitability, which can affect the value of the company's stock. A lack-of-marketability discount may be allowed due to costs of SEC filings to have the stock listed on an exchange.

22. C is the answer. (1) and (3) are correct statements. (2) is incorrect because it is used when values decline.

23. D is the answer. For publicly traded stock, the value is the mean between the highest and lowest quoted selling prices on the date of death.

24. A is the answer. The blockage discount is not often accepted by the IRS and applies only to stock listed on an exchange. The co-ownership discount has been applied to real estate and not to stock.

Generation-Skipping Transfer Tax (GSTT) (Topic 69)

CFP Board Student-Centered Learning Objectives

(a) Explain the workings of the Generation Skipping Transfer Tax as well as all applicable terminology.

(b) Identify the situations that trigger the generation skipping transfer tax and the strategies that help avoid the tax.

(c) Calculate and explain the GSTT exemption and what the inclusion ratio is and what impact it has on future distributions/terminations and how a Generation Skipping Trust works.

(d) Explain the use of the Qualified Terminable Interest Trust.

Generation-Skipping Transfer Tax (GSTT)
- A. Identify transfers subject to the GSTT
  - 1) Direct skips
  - 2) Taxable distributions
  - 3) Taxable terminations
- B. Exemptions and exclusions from the GSTT
  - 1) The GSTT exemption
  - 2) Qualifying annual exclusion gifts and direct transfers

---

Overview

In the past, wealthy persons whose children had substantial assets often sought to transfer assets in trust to their grandchildren to avoid having estate taxes imposed on the assets in their children's estates. The assets skipped one round of estate tax. The generation-skipping transfer tax was intended to close this loophole and to ensure that the transfer of wealth was effectively taxed in each generation.

Generation-Skipping Transfer Tax (GSTT) – Secs. 2601 and 2641

The generation-skipping transfer tax (GSTT) is imposed on transfers to persons at least two or more generations younger than the owner. Transfers, both during the owner's lifetime and at death, are subject to the GSTT. The tax is imposed at the maximum federal estate tax rate of 40% in 2015 and is in addition to any gift or estate tax that is owed.

GSTT Exemption – Sec. 2631

Under the GSTT, each person is entitled to an exemption in 2015 of $5.43 million of generation-skipping transfers. While portability allows a surviving spouse to utilize any remaining exemption from the most recently deceased spouse for estate tax purposes, portability does not apply to the GSTT.

Reverse QTIP Election

In general, assets subject to estate tax in a surviving spouse's estate can only be allocated the surviving spouse's GSTT exemption. The GSTT exemption of a deceased spouse is not available to a surviving spouse. An exception is made for a QTIP trust. If a deceased spouse set up a QTIP trust at death, the executor of the deceased spouse's estate can make an election, so the decedent spouse will be considered the transferor for GSTT purposes. This election is called the "reverse QTIP election."

Gift-Splitting – Sec. 2652

If a couple splits gifts for gift tax purposes, the gifts are treated as split for GSTT purposes.

GSTT Annual Exclusion – Sec. 2642(c)

Outright lifetime gifts (under $14,000 in 2015) that qualify for the gift tax annual exclusion are not subject to the generation-skipping transfer tax. A gift in trust, however, will only qualify for the annual exclusion under the GSTT if the trust meets two requirements:

- During the beneficiary's life, no distribution will be made to any person other than the beneficiary.
- At the beneficiary's death, the trust assets will be included in the beneficiary's gross estate.

As a result of these requirements, a separate generation-skipping trust will be set up for each beneficiary. Crummey trusts and Sec. 2503(c) trusts can generally be set up by grandparents for grandchildren to take advantage of both the gift tax annual exclusion and the GSTT annual exclusion.

Exempt Gifts

Payments for tuition and medical expenses that are qualified transfers under the gift tax rules are exempt from the GST tax.

Direct Skip – Two or More Generations Below the Donor – Sec. 2612

The transfer of assets to a person two generations younger than the donor or a transfer to a trust for the benefit of such a person is a direct-skip transfer. In a direct skip, the first generation below the donor (or grantor) is the skipped generation, and the person who receives the assets and who is two generations below the donor is the skip-person.

If all the beneficiaries of a trust are skip-persons, then the transfer of assets in trust is a direct skip. Conversely, if any beneficiary of a trust is not a skip-person, then the transfer in trust is not a direct skip. Thus, a trust that will pay income for life to the grantor's son and then to the grandson is not a direct skip because the grantor's son is not a skip-person.

When parties are related, it is generally easy to determine when a person is two generations younger. The normal lines of descent are followed, so grandchildren, grandnephews, and grandnieces are all two generations below the donor. A donor's spouse is always assigned to the same generation as the donor. **When the donor is not related to the donee, generations must be determined by ages. If the donee is 37½ years younger than the donor, the donee is treated as two generations below the donor.**

☞ *K Study Tip* – **When the donor and beneficiary are relatives, the generations between them determine who is a "skip-person." When the donor and beneficiary are not relatives, the difference in their ages determines who is a skip-person.**

A direct skip is subject to gift or estate tax, as well as the GST tax. For a direct-skip gift, the GST tax is generally paid by the transferor or by the estate, so the beneficiary receives the full amount of the gift or testamentary bequest. If the direct skip is from an estate, the GST tax is paid by the executor of the estate. Depending on the terms of the will, a beneficiary may or may not receive the full amount of the bequest.

Taxable Distribution

A payment from a trust to a skip-person or skip-beneficiary is a taxable distribution. For example, a payment of trust income to the grantor's son and grandson means there is a taxable distribution to the grandson. The GST tax will be imposed at the time of the distribution even when the trust distribution is not subject to estate or gift taxes. The tax can be paid from the assets being transferred or by the skip-person. **The beneficiary, rather than the donor, is ultimately responsible for paying the GST tax on a taxable distribution.**

Taxable Termination

Taxable distributions and taxable terminations are sometimes referred to as indirect skips. Indirect skips are not eligible for the gift tax annual exclusion. **A taxable termination is the passing of all interest in a trust to skip-persons. The termination may occur due to a lapse of time, the release of a power, the death of other persons who had an interest, or for some other reason**. For example, the grantor establishes a trust that pays income to his wife for life, and then at her death, the remaining assets are to be distributed to the grantor's grandson. When the grantor's wife dies, there is a taxable termination, and the transfer of the remainder assets to the grandson is subject to the GST tax.

REMEMBER: *DONORS MAY USE THE GSTT EXEMPTION FOR TAXABLE TERMINATIONS, TAXABLE DISTRIBUTIONS, AND DIRECT SKIPS; HOWEVER, THE ANNUAL EXCLUSION **CAN ONLY BE APPLIED** TO DIRECT SKIPS. INDIRECT SKIPS ARE NOT ELIGIBLE FOR THE ANNUAL EXCLUSION.*

KEY SUMMARY 69 – 1
Generation-Skipping Transfers

Type	Description	GST tax paid by
Taxable distribution	A trust makes a payment to a skip-person	Trust or Skip-Person
Taxable termination	All interest in a trust passes to skip-persons	Trust
Direct skip	Assets pass to a skip-person: - Two or more generations below donor, if related - 37.5 years younger than donor, if unrelated	Donor

Predeceased Parent Exception – Sec. 2651

The predeceased parent exception applies when the parent who is descended from the grantor is dead. The grandchild is then not deemed a skip-person, and the GST tax will not apply. This exception applies to direct skips, taxable terminations, and taxable distributions. In the case of taxable terminations and taxable distributions, the parent must have died before the trust was created.

Valuation Date

For a direct skip, the valuation date for the GST tax depends upon whether the transfer is a lifetime gift or a testamentary transfer.

For a lifetime gift, the gift tax valuation date is used, and for a testamentary transfer, the estate tax valuation date is used. The valuation of a taxable distribution or taxable termination will be on the date it occurs.

Filing the Return – Sec. 2603

The GST tax is reported on the U.S. Gift Tax Return, Form 709, U.S. Estate Tax Return, Form 706, Form 706GS(D), or Form 706GS(T). The donor should file the Form 709, pay any gift and GST tax due, and allocate any GSTT exemption. The executor should file the Form 706 and pay any estate and GST taxes owed. The beneficiary files the Form 706GS(D) and pays the tax for a distribution, and the trustee must file the Form 706GS(T) and pay the tax for a termination.

Calculation of the GSTT – Sec. 2642

If a lifetime gift is subject to the GST tax, the calculation of the tax and application of the GSTT exemption is accomplished by means of an inclusion ratio. First, the rules for splitting gifts and subtracting the annual exclusion will reduce the gift. Second, the amount of GSTT exemption allocated to the gift is divided by the value of the taxable gift. The fraction is subtracted from 1, to determine the inclusion ratio. This ratio is then multiplied by the 40% GST tax rate and by the taxable amount of the gift in 2015.

$$\text{Inclusion ratio} = 1 - \frac{\text{GSTT exemption allocated}}{\text{Value of taxable gift}}$$

$$\text{GST tax} = \text{Inclusion ratio} \times \text{Tax rate} \times \text{Value of taxable transfer}$$

Note that the value of the gift is reduced by any debts, mortgages, expenses, federal estate and state death taxes, and charitable deductions for the property.

For the estate tax return, the calculation is easier because there is no annual exclusion or gift-splitting, and the inclusion ratio method is not used. The exemption is simply subtracted from the taxable transfer, and the GST tax rate is applied. Deductible items such as mortgages on the property, administration expenses, and taxes will reduce the amount subject to tax.

🔑 **KEY SUMMARY 69 – 2** **Reducing Generation-Skipping Taxes**	
Gift-splitting	Gifts split for gift tax are split for GST
Annual exclusion	Outright gifts to skip-persons qualify for the same annual exclusion as for gift taxes; trusts must meet special rules
GSTT exemption	$5.43 million in 2015
Exempt gifts	Qualified transfers to educational institutions for tuition and to medical providers for medical expenses are exempt
Reverse QTIP election	The deceased spouse is treated as the transferor of the QTIP trust, so the GST exemption can be allocated to the trust.

Automatic Allocation of GSTT Exemption

The GSTT exemption will be automatically allocated to most trusts for the benefit of children and grandchildren. However, the client has the option not to elect out of this automatic allocation of GSTT exemption at the time the gift tax return is filed. Clients who are planning on making direct gifts to grandchildren (equal to or greater than the $5.43 million GSTT exemption amount in 2015) might want to elect out of the automatic allocation on trusts for the benefit of children and grandchildren.

If the GSTT exemption is allocated at the time the transfer is made to fund the trust, the amount of GSTT exemption allocated will be the fair market value of the assets transferred (up to the $5.43 million GSTT exemption available in 2015). If the GSTT exemption is allocated at a later date, the amount of GSTT exemption allocated will be the fair market value of the trust assets on the date of the allocation (up to the $5.43 million GSTT exemption available in 2015). The risk of waiting to allocate the GSTT exemption is the potential increase in asset value and accumulated income. This could cause the client to allocate more GSTT exemption at this later date compared to the initial value of the assets when the client funded the trust.

Editor's Note: For purposes of the exam, you should assume all GSTT exemption will be automatically allocated to any trust that includes a child and a grandchild as potential beneficiaries. The detailed rules about which trusts would not trip the automatic allocation are beyond the scope of the exam.

Planning For Large Transfers to Trusts

If a client establishes a trust for the benefit of a child and grandchild and plans to fund the trust with more than the remaining GST exemption amount ($5.43 million in 2015), the client should create two separate trusts. The first trust would be funded with an amount equal to the remaining GST exemption. The second trust would be funded with all remaining assets.

Example:

James wants to transfer $8.43 million to a trust for the benefit of his son Eli and his newborn granddaughter Kate. While Eli is alive the trustee can make discretionary distributions to Eli and Kate. At Eli's death, the trustee will continue to make discretionary distributions to Kate until the corpus is distributed on Kate's 55th birthday. James will allocate his $5.43 million GST exemption to the trust.

If James funds one trust, the inclusion ratio will be $1 - \$5.43M/\$8.43M = 0.36$. As a result, 36% of all distributions to Kate while Eli is alive will be subject to GST tax (taxable distribution). When Eli dies, 36% of the trust assets will be subject to GST tax (taxable termination). The GST tax will be assessed not only on the original $8.43 million contributed, but also any future appreciation or accumulated income prior to Eli's death.

If James funded one trust with $5.43 million, the inclusion ratio would be zero (1 – $5.43M/$5.43M). Any distributions to Kate while Eli is alive should be made from this trust since it would not trip GST tax. Likewise, no GST tax would be due on the first trust when Eli dies.

The second trust would be funded with the remaining $3 million. This second trust would have an inclusion ration of 1.0 as no GST exemption would be allocated to the trust. Any distributions to Eli should be made from this trust as all remaining trust assets in this second trust will be subject to GST at Eli's death (taxable termination).

Both trusts would be for the benefit of Eli and Kate. If Eli depletes the second trust, the trustee of the first trust would then start making discretionary distributions to Eli. This would eliminate any GST tax liability as only the second trust was subject to GST tax. However, if Kate depletes the first trust, any discretionary distributions made by the trustee of the second trust would be subject to GST tax (taxable distribution). Any remaining trust assets in the second trust would also be subject to GST tax when Eli dies (taxable termination). As mentioned above, the amounts subject to GST tax includes not only the original amounts funded in the trust but also any future appreciation or accumulated income prior to Eli's death.

Application Questions

1. Phil Harris set up a Crummey trust for his granddaughter. He transferred to the trust a $200,000 life insurance policy with a cash value of $30,000 and marketable securities with a fair market value of $40,000. The trust provides that distributions may be made for the granddaughter's support and education, and no distributions may be made to anyone other than the granddaughter. At the granddaughter's death, the trust will be distributed to her issue as she directs.

Which of the following statements concerning the generation-skipping transfer tax liability for this transfer are correct (assume the GST tax existed at the time of all transfers and at the time of death)?

(1) The transfer will qualify for the GSTT annual exclusion.
(2) The transfer will be subject to GST tax if Harris has already used up his GST exemption.
(3) If GST tax is paid on the transfer, additional GST tax will not be owed when the granddaughter dies.
(4) Gifts to the trust in future years of $14,000 cash will qualify for the GSTT annual exclusion.

    A. (1) and (2) only
    B. (1) and (3) only
    C. (2) and (3) only
    D. (3) and (4) only
    E. (1), (2), (3), and (4)

2. When Judy Ludwig died in 1998, she left an estate of $4 million after federal estate and state death taxes. Under Judy's will, the assets were left in trust for her son Mark, and the trustee could make distributions of income to Mark or his issue. At Mark's death, any remaining principal and income was to go to his issue. Judy's executor allocated $1 million GSTT exemption to this trust which is the entire amount Judy had available at her death. In 2015, the trustee made a distribution of $200,000 to Mark's son Peter, while Mark was still alive; the trust was worth $5 million when Mark died in late 2015.

Which of the following statements is correct concerning the consequences of the trust distribution of $200,000 to Peter?

    A. The distribution is not subject to a GST tax.
    B. The distribution is subject to a GST tax of $16,000.
    C. The distribution is subject to a GST tax of $40,000.
    D. The distribution is subject to a GST tax of $60,000.
    E. The distribution is subject to a GST tax of $80,000.

3. For the Ludwig trust (in the previous question), what are the GST tax consequences at the time of Mark's death?

    A. There is no GST tax owed when Mark dies.
    B. When Mark dies, the GST tax is $1,200,000 in addition to estate tax.
    C. When Mark dies, the GST tax is $1,500,000.
    D. When Mark dies, the GST tax is $1,500,000, in addition to estate tax.
    E. When Mark dies, the GST tax is $2,000,000.

4. For the Ludwig trust, what are the GST tax consequences of the transfer by Judy Ludwig to the trust at her death?

    A. There is no GST tax owed when the trust is created at Judy's death.
    B. When the trust is created, the GST tax is $300,000.
    C. When the trust is created, the GST tax is $400,000.
    D. When the trust is created, the GST tax is $1,050,000.
    E. When the trust is created, the GST tax is $1,600,000.

5. (Published question released December, 1996; updated)

Which statement(s) is (are) correct regarding the generation-skipping transfer tax (GSTT) for the year 2015?

    (1) The GSTT is a flat tax.
    (2) Each person will be permitted a $5.43 million exemption in 2015 against generation-skipping transfers.
    (3) The GSTT does not apply because it was repealed.
    (4) The GSTT is designed to prevent taxpayers from avoiding estate taxes as wealth transfers from generation to generation.

    A. (1), (2), and (4) only
    B. (2) and (4) only
    C. (3) only
    D. (1) and (4) only
    E. (2) and (3) only

6. All the following statements concerning the generation-skipping transfer tax are correct when the GST tax applies, EXCEPT:

    A. The tax applies to a lifetime gift or testamentary transfer from a grandparent directly to a grandchild.
    B. A taxpayer avoids the tax by transferring property into a trust for the life of the taxpayer's child, with the remainder to the grandchildren.
    C. Outright gifts qualifying for the gift tax annual exclusion are not subject to the tax.
    D. Payment of educational or medical expenses for a grandchild are not subject to the tax.

7. All the following statements concerning direct-skips involving generation-skipping transfers are correct, EXCEPT:

    A. A direct-skip transfer occurs when title to property is transferred from an individual to a beneficiary who is two or more generations below the transferor.
    B. Direct-skips may occur only by means of an *inter vivos* gift; testamentary dispositions are not direct-skips.
    C. If the transferor's only child is dead at the time of the transfer, the transfer to a grandchild will be considered a transfer to a child of the transferor, and no generation-skipping tax is assessed.
    D. If all beneficiaries of a trust are the grantor's grandchildren, then the gift in trust is a direct-skip transfer.

8. All the following statements concerning generation-skipping transfers are correct when the GST tax applies, EXCEPT:

   A. The generation-skipping transfer tax will be triggered if a trustee makes a distribution of income or corpus to a skip-beneficiary.

   B. A skip-beneficiary is a person who is one or more generations younger than the transferor's generation.

   C. A taxable distribution is a distribution to a skip-beneficiary that is not otherwise subject to estate or gift taxes.

   D. A taxable termination, subject to the GST tax can occur when a trust for a grantor's child ends at the child's death, and the assets pass to the grandchildren.

9. Which of the following statements concerning the generation-skipping transfer tax are correct?

   A. The tax is in addition to any estate or gift tax that is due on the transfer.

   B. The tax is a flat rate of 55% in 2015.

   C. The tax is imposed on the beneficiary in a direct-skip, so the residual estate of the transferor is not reduced by the amount of the tax.

   D. If a gift qualifies for the gift tax annual exclusion, it will also qualify for the GSTT annual exclusion.

10. Which of the following statements concerning the generation-skipping transfer tax are correct when the GST tax applies?

   (1) For a lifetime direct-skip, the GST tax is calculated and reported on the federal gift tax return, Form 709.

   (2) For a testamentary direct-skip, the GST tax is calculated and reported on the federal estate tax return, Form 706.

   (3) The rules for splitting gifts between spouses apply to the GST tax on lifetime direct-skip gifts.

   (4) The annual exclusion applies to the calculation of the GST tax on a lifetime direct-skip.

   A. (1) and (2) only
   B. (1) and (4) only
   C. (2) and (3) only
   D. (3) and (4) only
   E. (1), (2), (3), and (4)

11. All the following statements concerning the application of the generation-skipping transfer tax to testamentary direct-skip transfers for 2015 are correct, EXCEPT:

   A. No annual exclusion or gift-splitting applies to testamentary direct-skip transfers.
   B. A $5.43 million exemption will be available to each decedent to the extent that the exemption has not been used for lifetime generation-skipping transfers.
   C. The executor is responsible for filing the federal estate tax return, Form 706, to report the generation-skipping transfer tax.
   D. The federal estate tax is not imposed where the generation-skipping transfer tax is applicable.
   E. The unified credit cannot be used to offset the generation-skipping transfer tax.

12. Which of the following statements concerning the generation-skipping transfer (GST) tax are correct for a GST transfer in 2015?

   (1) Unused GST exemption must be claimed when a taxpayer makes a transfer to a skip-person.
   (2) The GST exemption can be used during the transferor's lifetime or at death and is $5.43 million per taxpayer.
   (3) The GST exemption is automatically allocated to direct-skips during the taxpayer's lifetime.
   (4) The GST annual exclusion and the GST exemption cannot be used to reduce the GST tax on the same direct-skip transfer.

   A. (1) and (2) only
   B. (1) and (3) only
   C. (2) and (3) only
   D. (3) and (4) only
   E. (1), (2), (3), and (4)

13. Which of the following statements concerning the generation-skipping transfer tax (GSTT) is (are) correct?

   (1) A direct-skip transfer is always subject to estate or gift tax in addition to the GSTT.
   (2) A taxable distribution is usually not subject to gift or estate taxes, even though it is subject to the GSTT.
   (3) A taxable termination is never subject to both the GSTT and the gift or estate tax.

   A. (1) only
   B. (2) only
   C. (1) and (2) only
   D. (2) and (3) only
   E. (1), (2), and (3)

14. Harry Carmichael wants to place $10 million in a trust that will pay income to Carmichael's son during his lifetime and then to his grandson for his lifetime. The trust assets will pass under the grandson's will at the grandson's death. Which of the following statements about this set of facts is (are) correct?

(1) The transfer of assets to the trust is a direct-skip transfer and may be subject to both gift tax and generation-skipping transfer tax.
(2) At the time trust income is distributed to the grandson, the distributions may be subject to the generation-skipping transfer tax, but not the gift tax.
(3) When Carmichael's son dies, the trustee may be required to pay the generation-skipping transfer tax on the trust's assets because of the taxable termination.

A. (1) only
B. (2) only
C. (1) and (3) only
D. (2) and (3) only
E. (1), (2), and (3)

15. In which of the following situations does the predeceased parent exception apply, so no generation-skipping transfer tax will be owed?

(1) The grantor placed $6 million in trust for his son's three children, but his son is no longer living, and the grandchildren live with their mother.
(2) The decedent left $6 million in his will to his grandson, and the decedent had two living children, neither of whom was the parent of the grandson.
(3) The grantor's only son had already died when he transferred $6 million to two separate trusts for his two grandnieces, whose parents were dead and another $2 million to a trust for his grandson.
(4) The decedent had no children and left $6 million to his nephew, even though the decedent's brother was still alive but had stopped communicating with the decedent.

A. (1) and (2) only
B. (1) and (4) only
C. (1), (2), and (4) only
D. (1), (3), and (4) only
E. (1), (2), (3), and (4)

16. A testamentary gift by a grandparent to a grandchild in 2015 that is subject to the generation-skipping transfer tax is taxed at what rate?

A. 0%
B. 15%
C. 35%
D. 40%
E. 50%

17. All the following statements concerning the generation-skipping transfer tax rules are correct if the GST tax applies, EXCEPT:

A. No generation-skipping transfer tax (GSTT) is levied unless either the life-income beneficiary or the remainderperson are two or more generations younger than the grantor.

B. The GSTT seeks to impose the same tax that would have been collected if the property had passed first to the owner's child before passing to the grandchildren.

C. When a grantor's child dies after possessing a life interest, the estate of the next generation beneficiary is liable for the GSTT.

D. Upon the death of the grantor, the GSTT rules still apply when the trust bypasses the grantor's living son or daughter and names the son's or daughter's child as the beneficiary.

E. If assets from a trust are included in the gross estate of the grantor's child, there will be no GSTT imposed when the income or principal passes to the grandchild.

18. Which of the following exemptions or credits is provided in the generation-skipping transfer tax rules for a GST transfer that occurs during 2015?

A. A $1 million exemption for each transfer from the grantor to his or her grandchildren in a direct-skip

B. A $250,000 exemption per child of the grantor

C. A $5.43 million exemption per transferor for all transfers

D. A $5.43 million unified credit for lifetime or testamentary transfers

E. None of the above

For practice answering case questions related to Topic 69, please answer the following questions in the cases included in the Appendix at the back of this textbook.

Case	Questions
Bartlett	
Marshall	
Webster	
Unser	
Tingey	
Lytle	
Beals	
Mocsin	
Young	
Borelli	21 and 22
Cunningham	
Fred and Mary Ferris	81, 82, 83, 84, and 85

Answers and Explanations

1. C is the answer. The transfer to the trust does not qualify for the GSTT annual exclusion because the granddaughter does not have a general power of appointment, so the assets will not be included in her gross estate. The transfer will be subject to the GST tax if Harris has no remaining GST exemption. The transfer is a direct skip since the granddaughter is two generations below the grantor. If GST tax is paid at the time of the transfer, no GST tax will be owed on the granddaughter's death because there is no generation-skipping transfer at that time.

2. D is the answer. The distribution from the trust to Peter is a taxable distribution because Peter is a skip-person. The GSTT exemption was allocated to the trust when it was created, so the inclusion ratio is calculated as follows:

$$\text{Inclusion ratio} = 1 - \frac{\text{Allocated exemption}}{\text{Value of transfer}}$$

$$= 1 - \frac{\$1\text{ million}}{\$4\text{ million}} = .75$$

The amount of the tax (at 40% in 2015) is then calculated using this ratio:

$$(.75) \times (.40) \times (\$200,000) = \$60,000$$

3. C is the answer. When Mark dies, there is a taxable termination because all of the non-skip-persons with interests in the trust have died. Peter is a skip-person, and the trust assets will pass to him from his grandmother. The inclusion ratio is used again to compute the GST tax:

$$\text{GST tax} = .75 \times .40 \times \$5,000,000 = \$1,500,000$$

There is no estate tax owed because the trust assets are not included in Mark's estate.

4. A is the answer. The trust is created for Judy's son, who is a non-skip-person, as well as for Mark's issue who are skip-persons. No GST tax is imposed since there are non-skip-persons with interests in the trust.

5. A is the answer. The GSTT is a flat tax, imposed at the highest estate tax rate of 40% in 2015. In 2015, each taxpayer will have a $5.43 million exemption under the GSTT.

6. B is the answer. The generation-skipping transfer tax applies to direct-skips, which are gifts from grandparents to grandchildren. The GST tax also applies to trust distributions or remainder interests that pass to skip-beneficiaries.

7. B is the answer. A direct-skip may occur by means of either an *inter vivos* gift or a testamentary disposition. A gift in trust is also a direct-skip when all beneficiaries of the trust are skip-persons. Grandchildren are skip-persons because they are two generations below the grandparent. If the transferor's only child is dead at the time of a transfer to grandchildren, the transfer is not subject to the GST tax.

8. B is the answer. B is not a correct statement. A skip-beneficiary is two or more generations younger than the transferor's generation, not merely one or more generations younger. A, C, and D are correct statements.

9. A is the answer. In a direct-skip, the tax is paid by the transferor or by the estate, so the beneficiary receives the full amount of the gift or testamentary transfer, and the residual estate is reduced by the amount of the tax. Outright lifetime gifts that qualify for the gift tax annual exclusion also qualify for the GSTT annual exclusion. Gifts in trust, however, may qualify for the gift tax annual exclusion and not qualify for the GSTT annual exclusion. In order for the gift in trust to qualify for the GSTT annual exclusion, the trust must provide that it will make no distribution to any person other than the beneficiary, during the beneficiary's lifetime. In addition, at the beneficiary's death, the trust assets must be includible in the beneficiary's gross estate. In 2015, the tax rate is the highest estate and gift tax rate at 40%.

10. E is the answer. A lifetime gift that is a direct-skip is reported on the federal gift tax return, Form 709, and the GST tax is calculated on this form. For a direct-skip that is a testamentary gift, the GST tax is calculated and reported on the federal estate tax return, Form 706. The rules for splitting gifts between spouses and for the annual exclusion apply to the GST tax if it is a lifetime gift.

11. D is the answer. The generation-skipping transfer tax is imposed in addition to the federal estate tax.

12. C is the answer. The GST exemption need not be allocated to a transfer to a skip-person, but the Tax Code provides for the GST exemption to be automatically allocated to lifetime direct-skips. This automatic allocation can be changed by filing an election setting forth a different allocation. The GST exemption is currently $5.43 million in 2015. The GST annual exclusion and the GST exemption can be used to reduce the GST tax on the same direct-skip transfer.

13. C is the answer. A direct-skip is a transfer to a skip-person where the transfer is subject to estate or gift tax. A taxable distribution from a trust is not generally subject to estate or gift taxes. A taxable termination can be a release of a power, which could be a gift subject to gift or estate tax.

14. D is the answer. The transfer to the trust is not a direct-skip because Carmichael's son is a beneficiary, so all beneficiaries are not skip-persons. When trust income is distributed to the grandson, it will be a taxable distribution under the GSTT, but there is no gift subject to the gift tax at that time. When Carmichael's son dies, the only remaining beneficiary is the grandson. The grandson is a skip-person, so there is a taxable termination, and the trustee must pay the GST tax.

15. A is the answer. The predeceased parent exception applies to transfers to a grandchild where the parent who is a lineal descendant of the transferor has died. The transfer in (1) is not subject to the GST tax because the grandchildren's father is the lineal descendant of the grantor and is deceased. The grandson who received the $6 million in (2) also has no living parent descended from the decedent, so the GST tax will not apply. The transfer to the two grandnieces will be subject to GST tax because the grantor has a lineal descendant who is alive. Transfers to collateral heirs, such as the grandnieces, qualify for the predeceased parent exception, except when a lineal descendant is alive. Since the grandson is a lineal descendant, the GST tax will be applied. In (4), the bequest to the nephew is not a generation-skipping transfer because the nephew is just one generation below the transferor.

16. D is the answer. For a testamentary direct-skip, the GST tax in 2015 is 40%.

17. C is the answer. The purpose of the generation-skipping transfer tax (GSTT) is to exact a tax essentially the same as the estate tax that would have been levied if the property had passed directly to the beneficiary, instead of just a life interest. A realistic example is the case of a father creating a trust where his son receives a life interest in the trust income, and, upon his death, the trust property goes to the son's son (the grantor's grandson). In this example, the GSTT is levied at the time of the son's death in an amount similar to what the estate tax would have been if the grantor's son had been the beneficiary of the entire trust and not just the life interest. For the GSTT to come into play, two generations younger than that of the grantor must be involved, for example, grantor to son to grandson. The GSTT also applies where there is a "direct-skip," for example, grantor to grandchild, provided the lineal parent of the grandchild is still alive. If the grandchild's parent who is the offspring of the grantor is deceased, the GSTT is not levied. A good question at this point concerns the entity liable for payment of the GSTT. Unless specified otherwise in the trust agreement, the GSTT is to be charged against the property being transferred.

18. C is the answer. TRA '86 provided some significant exemptions to the basic GSTT rule. An important one, which expired on Dec. 31, 1989, provided a $2,000,000 exemption for each transfer by the grantor to a grandchild. This applied only to direct-skips (grantor to grandchild) and not to other beneficiaries. A second exception, whose provisions have also been eliminated, provided for an exemption of $250,000 for each child of the grantor. A grantor with one child had a total allowable exemption of $250,000; one with 7 children had a total exemption of $1,750,000. The number of grandchildren was immaterial. In place of these exemptions, the current provision for 2015 is a $5.43 million exemption per grantor for all of his or her generation-skipping transfers.

Fiduciaries (Topic 70)

CFP Board Student-Centered Learning Objectives

(a) Define fiduciary duties and identify the parties that would be subject to it.

> *Fiduciaries*
>   *A.   Types of fiduciaries*
>   *1)   Executor/Personal representative*
>   *2)   Trustee*
>   *3)   Guardian*
>   *B.   Duties of fiduciaries*
>   *C.   Breach of fiduciary duties*

Types of Fiduciaries

A fiduciary is a person in a position of trust and confidence who is required to act for the benefit and best interests of another person. An executor or personal representative of an estate has a duty to act in the best interests of the beneficiaries of the estate. A trustee must act in the best interests of the trust beneficiaries. Guardians are appointed to act in the best interests of the person who is their ward.

Fiduciaries are required to manage property under their supervision according to the state laws setting fiduciary standards, but additional powers or duties can be given to a trustee or executor by the trust document or will. For example, a trustee can be authorized to retain a closely held business interest even though state laws concerning prudent investments would require the trustee to sell the interest and reinvest in less risky investments.

Fiduciary Duties

Generally, a fiduciary owes the following duties to beneficiaries:

- Duty to act for the benefit of beneficiaries in regard to matters within the scope of the fiduciary relationship
- Duty not to delegate acts that can be performed by the fiduciary
- Duty to make full disclosure of all facts in any transaction with the beneficiary; any transaction must be fair to the beneficiary, or it can be set aside
- Duty not to engage in any self-dealing at the expense of the beneficiaries and duty to be loyal to beneficiaries
- Duty to preserve property and to make it productive
- Duty to invest property prudently according to state laws that may consist of a prudent-person rule, legal-list statute, or Uniform Prudent Investor Act

- Duty to be impartial toward beneficiaries so as not to favor income beneficiaries over remainder beneficiaries

Duties of the Executor   The executor or personal representative is appointed by a court to gather the decedent's assets, resolve claims and disputes against the estate, invest assets during the period of administration, prepare an accounting of the estate assets, and make distributions to the beneficiaries according to the will or intestacy laws.

Duties of the Trustee   A trustee is named in a trust document to manage trust assets during the continued existence of the trust. The trustee invests the property, collects income, and makes distributions to the beneficiaries, according to the directions of the trust provisions.

Duties of the Guardian   A guardian is appointed by a court to manage the property of an incompetent person during the period of incompetency. A guardian may be appointed as the guardian of the person or of the property of the person, or ward. A guardian for a minor child is often named in a will, and courts will generally honor a parent's selection of the guardian named in this way. The guardian of property administers these assets and makes payments from the assets for the benefit of the ward. A guardian of the person often provides food, clothing, and shelter for a minor ward.

Selecting the Executor   A will should name an executor to manage the decedent's estate during the probate process. A good executor is selected on the basis of the following characteristics:

(1) **Understanding and sensitivity**. The preferred executor is a person who will provide concerned personal attention to the financial and psychological needs of the beneficiaries. The beneficiary receiving the largest share of the estate, a good friend, or a relative is usually a good choice for executor.

(2) **Competence**. The executor must be able to make use of professional assistance but also be able to make decisions affecting the estate and the beneficiaries. The executor must be qualified under the laws of the state where probate will occur.

(3) **Experience**. In larger estates, having an experienced executor is more important. A corporate executor may be preferable to an individual executor because the corporate executor is likely to have experience with administering an estate. In addition, an executor experienced in investments and business, who is also familiar with the testator's investments and business, is important.

(4) **Knowledge of the decedent's assets and business**. The executor must locate, gather, and safeguard the assets of the estate, so familiarity with the decedent's business and the location and value of the decedent's various assets is important.

(5) **Ability and willingness to serve**. The executor takes on a tremendous responsibility, including potential liability to the beneficiaries for any breach of fiduciary duties, in the handling of the estate. The executor may spend a great amount of time in administering the estate and fulfilling his or her duties.

(6) **Integrity, loyalty, and absence of conflict of interest**. The executor is a fiduciary, and the beneficiaries rely on the executor to act fairly and in the interests of the beneficiaries.

(7) **Proximity**. Geographical proximity to the decedent's major assets and to the residences of the major beneficiaries is usually advantageous.

Fees

An executor is entitled to reasonable compensation for his or her services. Compensation for the executor is a consideration in the selection of the appropriate executor.

Often, family members will serve as executors for no fee. Inadequate compensation, however, may lead to inattention to estate affairs and to costly mistakes. Excessive compensation may lead to disputes with beneficiaries and a reduction of their inheritances.

Corporate vs. Individual Trustee

For both testamentary and *inter vivos* trusts, selection of the trustee is an important matter. A corporate trustee is advantageous due to his or her greater experience and competence with administering trusts, for accounting and record-keeping capabilities, and because he or she will provide greater financial backing and security for the trust.

An individual trustee is sometimes preferable because of the individual's greater knowledge of the beneficiaries, keener sensitivity to beneficiaries' needs, and greater knowledge of the grantor's business or of the particular assets placed in the trust. The individual trustee may also serve for a lower fee than a corporate trustee. Sometimes, an individual and a corporate trustee are selected as co-trustees in order to try to get some of the benefits of both kinds of trustee.

Breach of Fiduciary Duties

A fiduciary who breaches a duty to beneficiaries may be held personally liable for any loss to the beneficiaries. Trustees can be held liable for failing to invest assets in ways that would produce more income for the income beneficiaries. Fiduciaries can also be held liable for self-dealing and for personal use of the assets entrusted to their care and management.

An individual fiduciary can be held liable for failure to exercise the same skill and care that a person of ordinary prudence would exercise in handling his or her own affairs. A professional or corporate trustee will be held to a higher standard because of its expertise.

Some breaches of fiduciary duty are remedied by civil suit and will require the assistance of an attorney. For example, if a client's brother is the executor for their mother's estate and the client suspects that the estate is being mismanaged, the client will need to consult an attorney concerning a suit for damages. If the client's brother is stealing from the estate, then the police and district attorney should be contacted.

Uniform Fiduciary Access to Digital Assets Act (UFADAA)

As the world becomes increasingly digital, estate fiduciaries have run into problems with attempting to access online accounts and digital assets. The problems arise due to privacy laws (the Electronic Communications Privacy Act and the Computer Fraud and Abuse Act), and the strict "terms of use" agreements imposed by many internet service providers disallowing any transferability or right of survivorship. Some agreements specifically state that upon receipt of a copy of the death certificate, the account will be permanently deleted. Imagine the emotional impact on the family of a teen who committed suicide when they are told that all of the teen's photos and journal that were stored online will be lost forever. In addition to this kind of unnecessary trauma, the path for fiduciaries to overcome these strict rules has been laden with obstacles including the expense and time required to obtain a court order.

On July 16, 2014 the Uniform Fiduciary Access to Digital Assets Act (UFADAA) was approved by the Uniform Law Commission. Once adapted by the states (perhaps with some modifications from state-to-state), the act will provide fiduciaries (such as estate representatives, guardians or conservators for protected individuals, agents acting under a power of attorney, and trustees) with the power to access, control, and provide for disposition of digital assets in order to fulfill their fiduciary obligations. The account holder's privacy choices may be outlined in a document such as a will or a trust, allowing some accounts to remain private at the account holder direction.

Financial planners will want to monitor legislative action in states where they work for the new law (or a variation of it). The fiduciary's job will be made easier if clients are instructed to keep track of digital accounts (including emails, texts, photos, videos, music files, and financial account information), the email associated with each account (in case passwords need to be reset), username for each account, and online password manager information. As with all legal issues, the planner will need to work closely with an attorney.

Application Questions

1. In which of the following circumstances will a corporate executor be preferable to an individual?

    A. The individual executor lives across the country from the beneficiaries and from the place of probate.

    B. The individual executor was a close friend of the decedent and his family.

    C. The decedent's estate is not large or complicated.

    D. A will contest is expected by persons who were omitted from the will.

2. Which of the following statements concerning executors and trustees is correct?

    A. Executors are subject to fiduciary duties, but trustees are not.

    B. Fees for corporate executors are deductible, but fees for individuals are not.

    C. Corporate trustees are subject to the same standard as individual trustees.

    D. An executor must report transactions for the estate to a court, but a trustee does not report to a court.

3. The trustee, in accordance with the terms of the trust agreement, will have certain specific powers and duties. The general powers which a trustee will have include all the following, EXCEPT:

    A. The power to make payment to a beneficiary

    B. The power to receive additional assets into the trust

    C. The power to vary the division of trust income among the beneficiaries

    D. The power to manage the trust property in a manner which is advantageous to the trust

    E. The power to sell or hold investments

4. The position of trustee is an important one and imposes considerable responsibility upon the individual as the trustee. In this regard, the duties of a trustee include all the following, EXCEPT:

    A. Loyalty in the administration of his or her duties to the grantor and to the beneficiaries, without difference or distinction

    B. Impartiality in the distribution of income and/or corpus among the designated beneficiaries

    C. Maintaining items of trust property clearly separated and earmarked from his or her own properties

    D. Preserving the trust's property, using the ordinary care and diligence as a prudent individual would be expected to do

    E. Administering the trust property to keep it productive

For practice answering case questions related to Topic 70, please answer the following questions in the cases included in the Appendix at the back of this textbook.

Case	Questions
Bartlett	
Marshall	
Webster	
Unser	
Tingey	
Lytle	
Beals	
Mocsin	
Young	
Borelli	23
Cunningham	23
Fred and Mary Ferris	86, 87, 88, 89, and 90

Answers and Explanations

1. A is the answer. A corporate executor will be preferable when the executor is far away from the beneficiaries and the place of probate because the executor will have difficulty managing the estate from a distance. The corporate executor will be better able to handle the probate and administration of the estate assets. A will contest will delay administration of the estate, so the corporate and individual executors will both be unable to proceed.

2. D is the answer. An executor reports to the probate court, but a trustee does not report to a court. A trust is not supervised to the same extent as an estate. For this reason, a trust is much more private than probate. Both executors and trustees are subject to fiduciary duties. Fees for executors are deductible for both corporate and individual trustees. Corporate trustees are usually held to a higher standard than individual trustees due to their professional experience serving as a trustee.

3. C is the answer. The trustee can be empowered to do many things, which may include distributing trust income and corpus among the beneficiaries as he or she sees fit. This is a specifically assigned power, in contrast to his or her general powers. While a trustee's general powers enable him or her to do many things, these general powers do not include varying distributions among beneficiaries at his or her own discretion. A trust that provides discretion for a trustee to vary the distributions of income is a special kind of trust called a sprinkle trust.

4. A is the answer. The role of trustee carries with it certain requirements and duties which, in general, must be carried out in accordance with the "prudent person" rule. Additionally, the trustee must be impartial with regard to the beneficiaries, must do a proper job of maintaining records concerning the trust property and its location and identification, and must keep trust property separated from his or her own assets. While the trustee has an initial responsibility to the grantor when the trust is established, that responsibility and loyalty shift to the beneficiaries upon the transfer of assets from the grantor to the trustee.

Income in Respect of a Decedent (IRD) (Topic 71)

CFP Board Student-Centered Learning Objectives

(a) Define Income in Respect of Decedent.

(b) Identify the most common types of income that may be classified as IRD including pay, interest, dividends and business income.

(c) Describe the tax consequences for both the decedent and heir/beneficiary for income included in a decedent's gross estate and/or final income tax return.

Income in Respect of a Decedent (IRD)
A.	*Assets qualifying as IRD*
B.	*Calculation for IRD deduction*
C.	*Income tax treatment*

Income in Respect of a Decedent – Sec. 691

Income in respect of a decedent (IRD) is income a decedent was entitled to be paid, but did not receive before his or her death. The income was not reported for the taxable year ending with the date of death, so it must be reported by the recipient.

Assets Qualifying as IRD

IRD includes dividends declared, but not received, commissions earned but not paid, rents and royalties owed but not yet paid, partnership income of a deceased partner, S corporation income of a deceased shareholder, continuing payments from an annuity (such as a period-certain annuity), and the unpaid debt on an installment note.

Retirement Assets

One of the most common IRD assets is the money a decedent has accumulated in an IRA or a qualified retirement plan. These retirement benefits are included in the decedent's gross estate, and are subject to income tax when distributed to heirs.

Income Tax Treatment

If IRD is included in the decedent's gross estate, it is subject to estate taxes, and the recipient is entitled to an income tax deduction for the estate taxes attributable to the IRD. IRD assets do not receive a step-up in basis.

Calculation

The income tax deduction for the estate taxes attributable to the IRD is a miscellaneous deduction, but it is not subject to the 2% threshold. This deduction may reduce the heir's income tax but will not eliminate it. As a result, the combined estate and income taxes make retirement benefits inefficient means for providing an inheritance.

Example:

Jim Moore received $50,000 from his uncle's IRA after his uncle died this year. The IRA was included in the uncle's gross estate, and the estate tax at 40% was $20,000. The estate tax will be a miscellaneous deduction for Jim. If Jim is in the 33% federal income tax bracket and he itemizes, the income tax result will be as follows:

IRD amount	$50,000
Deduction for estate taxes	20,000
Taxable income	30,000
Tax rate	.33
Income tax owed on IRD	$ 9,900

Note that the total of the estate tax and the income tax on the IRD is $20,000 plus $9,900, or $29,900.

If a retired person has a choice between consuming the retirement benefit or consuming other assets, it will often be advantageous to take distributions from retirement plans and leave other assets for inheritances. In this way, the inherited assets avoid the double taxation of estate and income taxes.

🔑 KEY SUMMARY 71 – 1
Income In Respect of a Decedent (IRD) – Use It Before You Lose It

IRD is included in the owner's gross estate.

- Beneficiary must pay income taxes on IRD.
- Deduction for estate taxes on IRD reduces, but does not eliminate, income tax.
- Beneficiary does not receive a step-up in basis for IRD assets.
- Retirement assets are the most common example of IRD.
- Retirement assets are reduced by both estate and income taxes.

Therefore, consume retirement assets (IRD) first and use other assets for inheritances.

Application Questions

1. Which of the following statements concerning IRD is (are) correct?

    (1) The deduction for the estate tax attributable to IRD will eliminate the income tax.
    (2) A beneficiary does not receive a step-up in basis for IRD.
    (3) IRD is subject to estate tax or income tax, but not both.

    A. (2) only
    B. (1) and (2) only
    C. (2) and (3) only
    D. (3) only

2. Following the owner's death, all of the following items are treated as IRD, EXCEPT:

    A. Unpaid installment note payments
    B. Future payments from a life annuity
    C. The remaining IRA account balances
    D. Undistributed partnership income

3. Justin anticipates inheriting his mother's 401(k) plan at her death as she is currently terminally ill. All of the following statements regarding this inherited account are correct, EXCEPT:

    A. Justin will have to pay income taxes on all distributions from the account.
    B. Justin's mother's gross estate included the account in her gross estate.
    C. Justin's basis in the account is equal to the fair market value of the account at his mother's death.
    D. Justin can claim a deduction related to the estate taxes paid on the account.

4. Which of the following assets are treated as IRD assets at the owner's death?

    A. Roth IRA account established 10 years before the owner died
    B. Beach house purchased 10 years before the owner died
    C. Big Mac Corporate stock received as a gift 10 years before the owner died
    D. Remaining installment notes from the sale of a business 10 years before the owner died

For practice answering case questions related to Topic 71, please answer the following questions in the cases included in the Appendix at the back of this textbook.

Case	Questions
Bartlett	
Marshall	
Webster	
Unser	
Tingey	
Lytle	
Beals	
Mocsin	
Young	
Borelli	24
Cunningham	24
Fred and Mary Ferris	91, 92, 93, 94, and 95

Answers and Explanations

1. A is the answer. A beneficiary who receives IRD does not receive a step-up in basis. The IRD is subject to estate tax in the decedent's estate, and the beneficiary must pay income tax on the IRD. The income tax deduction for the estate tax paid on IRD in the decedent's estate will reduce but will not eliminate income tax on the IRD.

2. B is the answer. A life annuity ends at the death of the annuitant, so there are no more payments and thus no IRD. Retirement assets, such as IRA accounts, are common examples of IRD. Unpaid installments under a note and undistributed partnership income are also IRD.

3. C is the answer. The retirement account is an IRD (income in respect of a decedent) asset. As a result, Justin does not receive a step-up in basis at his mother's death. A is a correct statement as Justin will have to include the entire distribution in his income. B and D are correct statements, as the retirement account will be included in his mother's estate, and Justin can claim an income tax deduction related to the estate taxes on this IRD asset.

4. D is the answer. The remaining installment notes will be treated as IRD assets when the owner dies. The Roth IRA is not treated as an IRD asset, as the distributions will be income-tax-free under the Roth IRA rules. The beach house and the Big Mac Corporate stock will not be treated as IRD assets, as they qualify for the step-up in basis at the account owner's death.

Postmortem Estate Planning Techniques (Topic 72)

CFP Board Student-Centered Learning Objectives

(a) Describe when an executor should elect to value estate assets using the alternative valuation date.

(b) Outline the rules that must be followed in order to use a qualified disclaimer estate planning strategy.

(c) Describe other forms of postmortem planning, including estate tax installment payments, stock redemptions for tax payments, special-use valuations, and elections against a will.

(d) Explain how and why QTIP property is a terminable-interest rule exception.

Postmortem Estate Planning Techniques
- A. *Alternate valuation date*
- B. *Qualified disclaimer*
- C. *Deferral of estate tax (§ 6166)*
- D. *Corporate stock redemption (§ 303)*
- E. *Special-use valuation (§ 2032A)*

Postmortem Planning Defined

Postmortem planning refers to the techniques used in arranging for the disposition of property after the owner's death to minimize taxes or to achieve other objectives. Postmortem planning usually involves completing the estate plan developed during the deceased's lifetime, but this planning may require modifications of the original plan.

Alternate Valuation Date – Sec. 2032

On the federal estate tax return, the executor may elect to value estate assets as of the decedent's date of death or as of the alternate valuation date, which is six months after the date of death. The election of the alternate valuation date is simply a way to reduce the size of the taxable estate, due to events occurring after the date of death.

When assets decline in value after the date of death, the alternate valuation date may be the more advantageous choice for the estate.

Whichever date is selected, the same date must be used in valuing all estate assets. Thus, if some assets appreciate and some assets decline in value after the date of death, the election of alternate valuation is permitted only when it results in a reduction in the total value of the decedent's gross estate and a reduction in the estate tax liability.

If the entire estate passes to the surviving spouse and there is no estate tax liability, due to the availability of the marital deduction, the alternate valuation date cannot be elected. For this reason, a surviving spouse may decide to disclaim a portion of an inheritance so the estate will have a tax liability. By use of the alternate valuation date, the executor can then reduce this liability to zero, and the children or other heirs can receive an inheritance without the estate incurring any tax liability. If assets are disposed of during the six months following death, they are valued as of the date of such disposition.

🔑 **KEY SUMMARY 72 – 1**
Alternate Valuation Date

In order for the executor to use the alternate valuation date, the following conditions must be met:

- It must be used in valuing all of the estate assets.
- It cannot be used with assets that will, by their very nature, decrease with the passage of time, e.g., annuities.
- By filing the election, the total federal estate tax liability must be reduced.
- Using the alternate valuation date must cause the total value of the gross estate to be reduced.

Qualified Disclaimer – Sec. 2518

One way to modify the original estate plan is by means of a disclaimer. A disclaimer is a formal refusal of a bequest of property from a decedent. Normally, such a refusal is a taxable gift; however, by satisfying the Internal Revenue Code requirements for a "qualified disclaimer," an estate beneficiary may avoid receipt of the property bequeathed by the deceased and, thereby, avoid any gift tax. A "qualified disclaimer" must meet the following requirements:

(1) The disclaimer must be irrevocable and unqualified.
(2) The disclaimer must be in writing.
(3) The disclaimer must be delivered to the grantor or to the grantor's legal representative within nine months of the date of the transfer or within nine months of a minor heir's turning 21 years of age.
(4) The disclaiming person must not receive any benefit from the property disclaimed and must not have any control over the disposition of the property after disclaiming it (although the person disclaiming the property may know who will receive it if there is a contingent beneficiary or disclaimer clause in the will).

A disclaimer may be made of an undivided fraction or percentage of each interest owned, extending over the entire term of the interest. A disclaimer can be for part of a beneficiary's interest in a trust or for a specific portion or dollar amount of a gift or inheritance. With property owned in joint tenancy WROS, the surviving joint tenant can disclaim the interest that passes by right of survivorship. A surviving spouse can disclaim the survivor's benefits under a qualified pension or profit-sharing plan. A beneficiary of a life insurance policy can disclaim the death benefit.

Practice Question

Which of the following interests can be disclaimed?

(1) The beneficiary's right to the death benefit from a life insurance policy
(2) The joint tenant's survivorship interest in real estate
(3) A beneficiary's income interest under a testamentary trust
(4) A remainder interest under an irrevocable living trust

    A. (1) and (2) only
    B. (1) and (4) only
    C. (2) and (3) only
    D. (1), (2), (3), and (4)

Answer:
All of these interests may be disclaimed by filing a qualified disclaimer.
The answer is D.

Using a Disclaimer to Reduce Estate Taxes

A "qualified disclaimer" may be used to reduce estate taxes. For example, if a decedent's child disclaims a bequest, the property may then pass to the surviving spouse under the residuary clause in the decedent's will. The transfer will then be eligible for the marital deduction, and no estate tax will be due on the transfer. Similarly, a surviving spouse may elect to disclaim a bequest in order to reduce the amount of property qualifying for the marital deduction and to take advantage of the unified credit. Such a disclaimer can reduce the estate tax that will be owed when the surviving spouse dies and thus reduce overall estate taxes on both estates.

Disclaimer Trusts

Some estate planners recommend the use of a "disclaimer trust." A disclaimer trust is an irrevocable trust created under the terms of a will. **The will provides that if a surviving spouse disclaims a bequest, the property will be transferred to the trust, and**

income from the trust will be paid to the surviving spouse at specified intervals.

The surviving spouse cannot retain any right to invade corpus and at the surviving spouse's death, the trust assets will pass to a beneficiary named by the decedent spouse.

Under a disclaimer trust, the surviving spouse has only a life interest, so the assets will not be included in his or her gross estate. In addition, the trust assets will not qualify for the marital deduction, so the decedent's estate will make greater use of the unified estate tax credit.

Disclaimer of Joint Interest

Some states recognize a disclaimer of the survivorship interest. This disclaimer is made by a surviving joint tenant after the death of the other joint tenant. If state law permits such a disclaimer, the disclaimer will also be valid for federal estate tax purposes, assuming it meets the requirements for a qualified disclaimer under the IRS rules. In the absence of state law, the IRS will recognize a disclaimer of a joint tenancy survivorship interest only if the disclaimer is made within nine months of the transfer creating the interest.

Installment Payment of Estate Taxes

Under Sec. 6166, a qualifying estate may postpone the payment of tax attributable to a closely held business interest and pay in 10 equal installments. The first installment of principal and interest must be paid within five years and nine months of the decedent's death.

The installments may be paid over ten years and are due annually within one year of the last installment. In addition, a portion of the deferred tax bears interest at only 2% per annum. This interest rate applies to the first $1,470,000 (in 2015), of a closely held business interest that is subject to estate tax. Above the $1,470,000 (in 2015), the interest rate on deferred taxes is 45% of the usual underpayment rate. The interest paid cannot be deducted by the estate.

Sec. 303 Redemption

Under Sec. 303 of the Internal Revenue Code, stock may be redeemed from an estate equal to the total amount of all estate taxes, inheritances taxes, estate administration costs, and funeral expenses, and the proceeds of the redemption will not be treated as a dividend.

Special-Use Valuation – Sec. 2032A

An executor may elect to value "qualifying" real property on the basis of its actual use, instead of on the basis of its highest and best use. The election of special-use valuation may be desirable in the case of farmland that is worth $25,000 per acre to a real estate developer, but only $5,000 per acre to a farmer. The maximum reduction of the decedent's gross estate permitted by the special-use valuation election is $1,100,000 in 2015. See Topic 68 for additional details regarding special use valuation.

**QTIP Election –
Sec. 2056**

Another postmortem planning technique that may reduce federal estate taxes is the executor's election of a QTIP treatment. By filing the QTIP election, the executor may qualify property for the marital deduction even though the property would not otherwise qualify. Ordinarily, to qualify property for the estate tax marital deduction, property must be left to the surviving spouse under conditions that avoid the terminable-interest rule. The qualifying life-income property, known as QTIP property, however, is an exception to the terminable-interest rule.

If the executor elects the QTIP treatment, the executor preserves the marital deduction for the estate of the first spouse to die even though the surviving spouse has a terminable interest in the property that provides a life income. **The executor's election statement must promise that the QTIP property will be included in the surviving spouse's gross estate**.

The executor's decision to elect a QTIP treatment is sometimes a difficult one. If the surviving spouse has a sizeable estate, adding more assets to this estate will only increase taxes due at the death of the surviving spouse. To assist the executor in making the decision, a testator may want to include a provision in the will, authorizing the executor to make the QTIP election. The testator may also want to grant the executor immunity from legal liability, in the event the election is subsequently found to be adverse to the interests of the surviving spouse or other heirs.

**Election Against
the Will**

In most states, a surviving spouse is permitted to make an election against the will. Elective-share laws protect the surviving spouse against the possibility of being disinherited by the provisions of the decedent's will.

A surviving spouse can obtain the statutory share without contesting the decedent's will and without court proceedings. This election can be used to qualify more property for the marital deduction.

EXHIBIT 72 – 1	
Postmortem Actions to Reduce Estate Taxes	
Technique	*Effect*
QTIP election	Preserves the marital deduction
Election against the will	Qualifies property for the marital deduction
Alternate valuation date	Reduces the taxable estate
Special-use valuation	Reduces the gross estate
Sec. 303 redemption	Stock is redeemed equal to: - Taxes - Administration costs - Funeral expenses
Installment payment	Estate taxes paid over 14 years, 9 months
Qualified disclaimer	Can take advantage of the unified credit **OR** Can increase the marital deduction

A Will Contest

A will contest is litigation brought by family members, relatives, or heirs who believe the deceased's will is invalid. Arguments for invalidating the will must be presented to a court of law. If the will is held to be invalid, the will provisions are set aside, and the decedent's assets are distributed according to state intestacy laws. Distribution according to intestacy laws may or may not be in conformity with the decedent's estate plan and may or may not result in estate tax savings.

Family Settlement Agreements

Family settlement agreements may be used to redistribute the assets of a decedent's estate without court proceedings. This plan of distribution may be different from the testator's wishes as contained in the will.

After all family members and heirs agree to the distribution of assets, however, the plan is submitted to a probate court for approval. A probate court will generally approve the plan if it is fair to the parties involved.

Homestead Allowance

The homestead allowance provides statutory protection of the family residence from the claims of creditors. The family homestead is preserved for the surviving spouse and the children, regardless of will provisions. The definition of homestead and the amount of land that will be included in this allowance vary from state to state.

Exempt Property Award

An exempt property award is a statutory allowance of specific property in a decedent's estate, such as the car, furniture, clothes, books, and similar items of personal property, up to a certain dollar limit. The exempt property is protected from the claims of creditors, and the property is preserved for the spouse and minor children, regardless of any will provisions. Both the homestead allowance and the exempt property awards are in addition to any statutory share that the surviving spouse may be entitled to elect against the will. Thus, these allowances can increase the portion of a decedent's estate passing to the spouse and children.

Filing a Joint Return

To save income taxes, the deceased's personal representative may file a joint income tax return with the surviving spouse for the year of death. Filing a joint return will usually result in lower taxes than filing two separate returns. Since the surviving spouse's tax year continues beyond the death of the first spouse, the remainder of the tax year can be used to realize gains or losses and to accelerate or postpone income in order to minimize income taxes on the joint return.

Medical Expense Deduction

For unreimbursed medical expenses incurred before the deceased's death, the deceased's personal representative has the option of claiming the expenses as medical expense deductions on the decedent's final federal income tax return or as an estate tax deduction. In order to claim the final medical expenses as an income tax deduction, the personal representative must file a waiver of the right to claim the medical expenses as an estate tax deduction.

If the estate will use the unified credit and marital deduction to eliminate any estate tax liability, no tax benefit will be achieved by deducting the medical expenses on the estate tax return. For federal income tax purposes, medical expenses are only deductible to the extent that the expenses exceed 10% of a taxpayer's adjusted gross income.

Deduction of Estate Administration Expenses

Certain estate administration expenses may be deducted either on the Federal Estate Tax Return, Form 706, or on the estate's income tax return on Form 1041, but not on both returns. The double deduction rule requires the executor to elect on which return the deduction will be taken.

The personal representative may decide to deduct the expenses on the estate's income tax return if use of the marital deduction or unified credit has eliminated the estate's tax liability.

Otherwise, in electing whether to deduct the expenses on the estate tax return or on the estate income tax return, the personal representative should consider the relative marginal tax brackets to achieve the lowest overall tax liability.

Since income distributions are deductible on the estate income tax return and must be reported by the beneficiaries on their income tax returns, the personal representative may also need to consider the relative tax liability of the estate and the beneficiaries. In addition, an executor must consider that using the expense deduction to reduce the estate's income taxes may increase estate tax liability. If estate taxes are paid out of the residuary estate, the effect will be to favor the life-income beneficiary over the remainderperson. Some state courts require the life-income beneficiaries to reimburse the remainderpersons in these circumstances.

If the personal representative elects to deduct the administration expenses on the estate's income tax return, Form 1041, the representative must file a waiver of the right to use the deduction on the estate tax return.

The personal representative cannot change the election later and request the deduction on the estate tax return. On the other hand, if the personal representative initially elects to deduct the expenses on the estate tax return, Form 706, the representative may later elect an income tax deduction if the deduction on the estate tax return has not been finally allowed.

Selecting the Estate's Tax Year

During administration of the estate, the personal representative may be required to file an estate income tax return for income received on the estate assets.

The personal representative may select as the estate's tax year, either a calendar year or a fiscal year that ends within 12 months of the decedent's death. To minimize income taxes, the personal representative should try to spread the estate's income over as many tax years as possible. Tax years should be selected, therefore, to spread income and to avoid higher marginal income tax brackets.

EE and HH Savings Bonds

An executor has the option of reporting accrued interest on EE or HH savings bonds in one amount on the decedent's final income tax return or annually on the estate's income tax returns. If the decedent died early in a tax year (for example, January or February), before the decedent received significant income, the personal representative will probably want to report the accrued interest on the deceased's final income tax return. Moreover, if the accrued interest is not reported on the decedent's final income tax return, the interest is taxable income to the beneficiary who receives the bonds, or it is taxable to the decedent's estate as "income in respect of a decedent."

If, on the other hand, the income from the bonds is reported by the estate as income in respect of a decedent (IRD), rather than as income on the decedent's final Form 1040, then the estate can deduct expenses related to the income. The estate tax attributable to IRD can be deducted by the beneficiary who is the recipient of the IRD and who must include the IRD in his or her gross income.

There is no comparable deduction for income earned in respect of a decedent on the decedent's final income tax return.

Waiver of Executor Commissions

For many estates, the surviving spouse serves as the executor, and an election to waive executor commissions or fees will generally save income taxes. If the surviving spouse will receive the money as a nontaxable bequest, there is no advantage in taking commissions and paying income tax on them. The surviving spouse should follow IRS guidelines for disclaimers in order to avoid this income tax liability.

For some estates, the estate tax rate will be higher than the income tax rate. In these cases, the beneficiary who serves as the executor should take the maximum commission allowed in order to save the difference between the two tax rates. An executor generally is not required to pay self-employment tax on these commissions.

EXHIBIT 72 – 2 **Postmortem Actions to Reduce Income Taxes**	
Medical expense deduction	May be taken on the estate tax return or on the decedent's final income tax return
Estate administration expense deduction	May be taken on the estate tax return or on the estate's income tax return
Waiver of executor commissions	Disclaiming commissions avoids income that will be received as a bequest
Selection of the fiscal year for the estate	Income can be spread over more years
Reporting interest on U.S. savings bonds	Interest can be reported on the decedent's final income tax return or annually on the estate return

S Corporation Election

An executor may either terminate S corporation treatment for a corporation with the consent of a majority of the issued and outstanding stock, or an executor may elect S corporation treatment with the approval of all shareholders.

The decision of the executor and other shareholders will depend upon the relative tax brackets of the corporation and of its shareholders.

Application Questions

1. Jack Dover, who was an accountant, died on August 14 at the age of 60. Dover had accounts receivable from his business in the amount of $55,000. The estate expects to make a large distribution to beneficiaries in July of the following year. What date should the executor select for the close of the estate's fiscal year to reduce income taxes?

   A. September 30
   B. December 31
   C. January 31
   D. March 31
   E. July 31

2. Paul Tussel died with a gross estate of $13 million during 2015. He is survived by his wife and two children. In Paul Tussel's will, his entire estate was left to his wife. Which of the following postmortem techniques will be appropriate to reduce combined estate taxes for Paul and his wife?

   (1) A disclaimer of a portion of all of Paul's assets
   (2) A QTIP election for selected assets
   (3) A disclaimer of the survivorship interest in a joint tenancy
   (4) Elect portability upon Paul's death

     A. (1) only
     B. (2) only
     C. (1) and (3) only
     D. (1), (3), and (4) only

3. Robert and Jane Olson live in California; they have one child and good careers in medical research. Jane's mother died recently, leaving her a gross estate valued at $7 million, including a family farm in Minnesota. Jane's mother had operated the farm for the past 8 years, after her husband died. The farm is valued at $4.7 million, and the land is valued at $2 million. A local real estate broker has contacted Jane about a potential sale of the farmland to a developer for a higher price. Jane, as the only child, has been appointed the executor of her mother's estate. Robert does not want to farm, but Jane is reluctant to sell the family farm.

Which of the following postmortem techniques is most likely appropriate for Jane Olson to pursue, as executor of her mother's estate?

   A. Election of special-use valuation
   B. Election of an installment payment of estate taxes
   C. Creation of a disclaimer trust by Jane
   D. A QTIP election
   E. Election to use the alternate valuation date

4. At the time of her death five months ago, Sandra Carpenter owned a shorefront home in Maine that was valued at $2 million. Her gross estate totals $8 million. Her other assets include $200,000 of personal-use property, $3.8 million of marketable securities and a $2 million landscape business that she owned and operated. Because she developed most of the customers, the business has declined in value since her death and is now worth about $300,000. Sandra left her estate in trust, with income payable to her husband Darrell for life and the remainder to her children. Her husband is retired and receives a pension of $40,000 per year. Darrell is named the executor of Sandra's estate.

Which of the following postmortem elections would reduce the taxes on Sandra's estate?

   (1) A waiver by Darrell of executor commissions for the estate
   (2) Election of an installment payment of estate taxes
   (3) A QTIP election
   (4) Election to use the alternate valuation date

   A. (1) and (2) only
   B. (2) and (3) only
   C. (3) and (4) only
   D. (1), (3), and (4) only
   E. (1), (2), (3), and (4)

5. Which of the following statements concerning the deduction of estate administration expenses are correct assuming there was an estate tax at the time the taxpayer passed away?

   (1) When the beneficiary's income tax bracket is higher than the estate's income tax bracket, administration expenses should be deducted on the estate tax return, Form 706.
   (2) If the estate will be distributed according to an AB trust plan, the administration expenses should be deducted on the estate's income tax return, Form 1041.
   (3) If the estate will be distributed according to an ABC trust plan, the administration expenses should be deducted on the estate tax return, Form 706.
   (4) When the estate tax bracket is higher than both the estate income tax bracket and the beneficiary's income tax bracket, administration expenses should be deducted on the estate tax return, Form 706.

   A. (1) and (2) only
   B. (1) and (3) only
   C. (2) and (4) only
   D. (3) and (4) only
   E. (1), (2), (3), and (4)

6. (Published question released February, 1999; updated)

Mrs. Bailey dies in 2015, leaving her entire $6.8 million estate to her penniless husband Mr. Bailey. Their estate will go to their children at his death. He has terminal cancer and has a life expectancy of 3 years. Using the alternative valuation date, Mrs. Bailey's entire estate equals $6.5 million. Select the postmortem technique Mr. Bailey should utilize to reduce the overall estate tax liability of both estates.

   A. Elect to use date-of-death valuation
   B. Elect to use the alternate valuation method
   C. Disclaim $5.43 million
   D. Disclaim $6.5 million
   E. Disclaim $6.8 million

7. Mr. Perkins recently died this year and left an estate of $8 million. The estate was left in trust to Mrs. Perkins, and she was given a right to all of the income annually. The remainder at her death is to pass to their children. Mrs. Perkins is named the executor. What postmortem techniques might be used to reduce estate taxes on Mr. Perkins' estate?

   A. File a QTIP election for the trust
   B. Elect the alternate valuation date
   C. Disclaim all of the trust
   D. Waiver of executor commissions

8. All the following statements concerning the requirements for a "qualified disclaimer" are correct, EXCEPT:

   A. A refusal must be in writing.
   B. A spouse's refusal must be delivered within 9 months of the date of the decedent's death.
   C. A disclaimer must direct to whom the property is to pass.
   D. A child can wait until after he or she is age 21 to submit a disclaimer.
   E. The person making the disclaimer must not receive any benefit from the property that is disclaimed.

9. All the following statements concerning a disclaimer trust are correct, EXCEPT:

   A. Such a trust provides a haven for disclaimed property.
   B. Lifetime income may be authorized for the trust beneficiary.
   C. The terms of the trust agreement must provide for the ultimate distribution of the disclaimed assets.
   D. The usual purpose of a disclaimer trust is to preserve the federal estate tax marital deduction for the estate of the creator of the trust.
   E. The surviving spouse may not be given a 5-and-5 power.

10. Which of the following statements concerning a disclaimer of an interest held in joint tenancy with right of survivorship at the time of death are correct?

(1) Such a disclaimer is recognized as valid by the laws of some states.
(2) If there is no state law to the contrary, all states will recognize as valid a disclaimer that is recognized as valid for federal tax purposes.
(3) The disclaimer can be used only with regard to joint tenancies created by the testamentary disposition of one of the joint tenants.
(4) A disclaimer of a joint tenancy interest may be made within two years of the event creating the interest.

    A. (1) and (2) only
    B. (1) and (4) only
    C. (2) and (3) only
    D. (2) and (4) only
    E. (3) and (4) only

11. Which of the following is an important purpose of electing QTIP treatment for estate property?

    A. To assure retention of use-valuation of estate assets
    B. To assure qualification of some estate assets for the estate tax marital deduction
    C. To assure availability of the alternate valuation date for estate assets
    D. To assure use of the joint return for federal income tax purposes
    E. To assure that the estate can pay estate tax in installments

12. All the following statements concerning QTIP treatments of estate assets are correct, EXCEPT:

    A. The deceased should elect QTIP treatment in his or her will so it can be implemented at death.
    B. Such an arrangement requires lifetime income from the property for the surviving spouse.
    C. Such an arrangement is actually one of the exceptions to the terminable-interest rule.
    D. QTIP property is irrevocably committed to taxation in the estate of the second spouse to die.
    E. The QTIP election preserves the marital deduction for the estate of the first spouse to die.

13. Which of the following statements concerning the filing of a joint final income tax return following the death of one's spouse is (are) correct?

(1) Usually, a joint return will result in lower income taxes than two separate returns.
(2) A capital loss suffered by the decedent spouse two months before death can be applied against the income of the surviving spouse.
(3) The tax year for a joint return ends on the date either spouse dies.

    A. (1) only
    B. (1) and (2) only
    C. (1) and (3) only
    D. (2) and (3) only
    E. (1), (2), and (3)

14. Which of the following statements concerning the treatment of the deceased's last illness medical expenses for tax purposes are correct?

    (1) The deceased's executor can claim such expenses as deductions on either the decedent's final federal income tax return or as an estate tax deduction.

    (2) Any medical expenses excluded as an income tax deduction because of the 10% rule are deductible on the estate tax return.

    (3) The medical expenses may be claimed as an income tax deduction only if a waiver is filed of any deduction for these expenses on the estate tax return.

    (4) The medical expenses deduction will be most useful in small estates, valued below the exemption equivalent.

    A. (1) and (2) only
    B. (1) and (3) only
    C. (2) and (3) only
    D. (2) and (4) only
    E. (3) and (4) only

15. Which of the following statements concerning the deduction for estate administration expenses are correct?

    (1) Estate administration expenses may be deducted on the federal estate tax return (Form 706).

    (2) Estate administration expenses may be deducted on the estate's federal income tax return (Form 1041).

    (3) If an executor files a waiver of the right to use the deduction on the estate tax return, the waiver can be changed later to take advantage of this deduction.

    (4) The law requires that an executor make use of deductions to favor the life-income beneficiary over a remainderperson.

    A. (1) and (2) only
    B. (1) and (3) only
    C. (2) and (3) only
    D. (2) and (4) only
    E. (1), (2), and (4) only

16. Assume "H" dies on July 1 this year. Most of his estate's income will be spread evenly over the next 12 months, with practically no estate income thereafter. Under these circumstances, which of the following recommendations would you make to "H's" executor?

    A. Select a calendar year as the estate's taxable year.

    B. Select the next 12 months as the estate's taxable year.

    C. Select a fiscal year as the estate's taxable year for the first 12 months, then change to a calendar year.

    D. File a joint return with the widowed sister with whom "H" has been living for the last several months.

    E. Report all of the estate income and deductions at one time.

17. Which of the following statements concerning the tax treatment of the interest accrued at the date of death on Series EE bonds owned by the deceased is (are) correct?

    (1) The executor is required to include any such accrued interest on the deceased's final income tax return.

    (2) Any income taxes paid on the deceased's final return are deductible on the estate tax return assuming an estate tax existed at the time of death.

    (3) Such interest may be treated as "income in respect of a decedent."

    A. (1) only

    B. (1) and (2) only

    C. (1) and (3) only

    D. (2) and (3) only

    E. (1), (2), and (3)

18. Which of the following statements are correct concerning the executor's use of the alternate valuation date for estate assets if there has been a decrease in the overall value of the estate assets in the six months following the decedent's death?

    (1) Estate taxes will be reduced by the selection of the alternate valuation date.

    (2) If some assets appreciated, while others declined, the estate heirs may minimize capital gains taxes on the subsequent sale of the appreciated estate assets.

    (3) The executor may not elect the alternate valuation date if the entire estate will pass to the surviving spouse.

    (4) Assets sold during the six months following death will be valued at the alternate valuation date if these assets have declined in value.

    A. (1) and (2) only

    B. (1) and (3) only

    C. (2) and (3) only

    D. (3) and (4) only

    E. (1), (2), and (3) only

19. All the following statements concerning the qualification for special-use valuation of farm property in the gross estate are correct, EXCEPT:

   A. Only real property qualifies for the special valuation.

   B. The "qualified" property must be equal to at least 35% of the decedent's gross estate.

   C. The "qualified" property must pass to a "qualified" heir.

   D. The "qualified" property must have been owned by a "qualified" person for 5 or more years.

   E. The "qualified" owner must have been a material management participant during 5 or more years.

20. "X's" gross estate is valued at $8 million, of which $2 million is stock in a closely held family corporation whose total stock is valued at $8 million. The estate has debts totaling $4 million. The estate's administrative expenses are estimated to be $200,000. Death taxes are estimated to be approximately $2 million. The executor could not elect special-use valuation for which of the following reasons?

   (1) There is no evidence of real property in the estate.

   (2) The estate fails to meet the 50% rule.

   (3) There is no evidence of a "qualified" heir.

   (4) There is no evidence of use over the last 8 years.

     A. (1) and (2) only
     B. (1) and (4) only
     C. (2) and (3) only
     D. (2) and (4) only
     E. (1), (2), (3), and (4)

21. Based on the information provided in Question 20, which of the following statements concerning a Sec. 303 redemption are correct?

   (1) The estate meets the 35% rule.

   (2) The estate could elect to redeem stock equal to the value of the death taxes and estate administration expenses.

   (3) A Sec. 303 redemption could not be completed if the stock held by "X" is preferred stock, rather than common stock.

   (4) The estate will meet the 35% rule even if "X" owns the stock in joint tenancy with right of survivorship with his or her spouse.

     A. (1) and (2) only
     B. (1) and (3) only
     C. (2) and (3) only
     D. (2) and (4) only
     E. (3) and (4) only

22. All the following statements concerning a Sec. 303 stock redemption are correct, EXCEPT:

   A. The stock to be redeemed must be included in the deceased's gross estate.

   B. All the stock of the corporation owned by the deceased must be more than 35% of his or her adjusted gross estate.

   C. The redeemable amount can be equal to estate administration expenses, death taxes, and debts.

   D. The redeemable amount is taxable as a capital item, rather than as dividend income.

23. All the following statements concerning the installment method of paying federal estate taxes under Sec. 6166 are correct, EXCEPT:

   A. The deceased's interest in the business must be more than 35% of the deceased's adjusted gross estate.

   B. If the business interest represents 51% of the deceased's adjusted gross estate, the full amount of the estate tax may be paid in installments.

   C. The value of the deceased's AGE is the difference between the value of the GE and the sum of the estate's debts and administration expenses.

   D. The business must be "actively carried on" at the time of the decedent's death.

   E. The decedent must have owned an interest in a closely held business.

24. Matt died with a $10 million estate which consisted of his $4 million business, $2 million home and $4 million in stocks and bonds. Which of the following statements concerning the payment of Matt's federal estate taxes in installments under Sec. 6166 are correct?

   (1) The business interest owned by the estate meets the 35% requirement.

   (2) The full amount of the estate tax can be paid under the installment payment arrangement.

   (3) The first installment could be paid three years after the decedent's death.

   (4) The deferred estate tax is interest-free for the first five years after the estate tax return is due.

   A. (1) and (2) only
   B. (1) and (3) only
   C. (2) and (3) only
   D. (2) and (4) only
   E. (3) and (4) only

For practice answering case questions related to Topic 72, please answer the following questions in the cases included in the Appendix at the back of this textbook.

Case	Questions
Bartlett	
Marshall	15
Webster	
Unser	13, 14, and 15
Tingey	
Lytle	
Beals	6
Mocsin	
Young	5
Borelli	25
Cunningham	25
Fred and Mary Ferris	96, 97, 98, 99, and 100

Answers and Explanations

1. E is the answer. The estate will be able to reduce income taxes by making the fiscal year long enough to include the distributions to beneficiaries to occur in July. If these distributions were not going to reduce income, the estate would want a relatively short fiscal year, such as September 30, so that the initial large amount of income would be included in the first year, and the remainder in another year.

2. D is the answer. A disclaimer of a portion of all of Paul's assets will result in assets passing to the children, so the unified credit is not wasted. A disclaimer of a survivorship interest in a joint tenancy will accomplish the same result, using property that was held in joint tenancy WROS. Electing portability on Paul's estate tax return is another way to ensure that his unified credit is not wasted. A QTIP election will not help make use of the unified credit; rather, it is used to qualify property for the marital deduction.

3. B is the answer. The election of an installment payment of estate taxes may enable Jane to hold on to the farm while the estate taxes are paid over 15 years. The estate will qualify for installment payment: the business interest is closely held, it was operated by Jane's mother at her death, and it is more than 35% of the adjusted gross estate. The election of special-use valuation will not help Jane because she does not plan to operate the farm. In general, leasing to others does not qualify an heir for special-use valuation. The alternate valuation date does not seem likely to help because the land is not declining in value. A QTIP election cannot be made here because Jane is not a surviving spouse. A disclaimer trust created by Jane will also not help because the disclaimer will not reduce estate taxes.

4. C is the answer. Sandra's will creates a bypass trust, which will mean the estate takes advantage of her applicable credit amount, but also means there will be estate taxes owed. A waiver of commissions will not help to reduce taxes because the waiver will only mean more assets passing through the estate into the bypass trust. The bypass trust already contains too many assets, so the applicable credit amount will be exceeded. To reduce taxes, the estate needs to qualify more assets for the marital deduction by means of a QTIP election. The assets will then be taxed in Darrell's estate and will take advantage of his applicable credit amount, too. Regardless of the amount of assets in Darrell's estate, the taxes on Sandra's estate will be reduced by the QTIP election. The election of the alternate valuation date will result in a reduced valuation of Sandra's business, which has declined in value. The personal-use assets will also probably decline in value, so the alternate valuation date may reduce taxes on the estate. The estate will not qualify for an installment payment of estate taxes because the closely held business interest is not 35% of the estate.

5. C is the answer. If the estate will be distributed according to an AB or an ABC trust plan, the estate will not pay any estate tax, so administration expenses should be deducted on the estate income tax return. When the estate tax bracket is higher than both the estate income tax bracket and the beneficiary's income tax bracket, administration expenses should be deducted on the estate tax return. The deduction will reduce taxes the most on the estate return, where the marginal rate is higher. When the income tax bracket of the estate beneficiary is higher than the estate tax bracket, administration expenses should be deducted on the estate income tax return, rather than the estate tax return. (1) is not correct because the comparison should be between the estate tax bracket and the income tax bracket of the beneficiary. Comparison with the estate's income tax bracket will not be important if the beneficiary receiving the income will be in a much higher income tax bracket.

6. C is the answer. By disclaiming a portion of the estate, Mr. Bailey can make use of both his and his wife's unified credits. Instead of one estate of $6.8 million, the estates are divided into two estates of lesser amounts. Mrs. Bailey's estate will be able to use the unified credit of $5.43 million in 2015 and a marital deduction of $1.37 million, so nothing will be subject to estate tax. Mr. Bailey will similarly use his unified credit of $5.43 million to reduce estate taxes to zero. The executor cannot use the alterative valuation date as there is no estate tax liability due to the unlimited marital deduction. An estate can only claim alternative valuation date if it decreases the estate tax liability. Disclaiming $6.8 million will only subject the entire estate to the higher tax rates and forfeit using Mr. Bailey's unified credit.

Editor's Note: While it could be argued that he does not need to disclaim anything if Mrs. Bailey's executor elects portability, that option is not offered as an answer choice.

7. A is the answer. The QTIP election can be made for the trust and will mean that the trust assets qualify for the marital deduction. The trust is not a marital trust, so estate taxes will be owed on the trust assets exceeding the unified credit. There is no information suggesting that the alternate valuation date will affect the estate taxes. The disclaimer will only mean that the assets pass to the children and will not qualify for the marital deduction, in that event. The waiver of executor commissions will not reduce estate taxes.

8. C is the answer. The disclaiming person is not permitted to provide directions as to how the interest in the property will pass to an alternate beneficiary. A, B, D, and E are correct statements concerning the requirements for a qualified disclaimer.

9. D is the answer. The usual purpose of a disclaimer trust is to preserve the right to the income from the disclaimed property for the surviving spouse or other heir but place the property outside the gross estate of the disclaimant. Also, by establishing a disclaimer trust under his or her will, the testator would normally provide only income for the spouse. This would not qualify the property for the marital deduction. If the spouse had access to the corpus, he or she would have incidents of ownership, and this would mean an invalid disclaimer. To preserve the MD for the trust creator would mean that the surviving spouse must have control over the property. This is just the opposite of what is actually achieved by the establishment of a disclaimer trust.

10. A is the answer. Both (1) and (2) are correct statements. A disclaimer can be made of a joint tenancy interest held by the joint tenants before one of them died. The disclaimer is valid only within 9 months of the transfer creating the interest.

11. B is the answer. The purpose of electing QTIP treatment for estate property is to assure qualification of that property for the estate tax marital deduction. A, B, D, and E are all nonsense options.

12. A is the answer. The deceased does not make the election of QTIP treatment. The deceased's executor makes the election. B, C, D, and E are correct statements.

13. B is the answer. (1) and (2) are correct statements. (3) is not a correct statement because the surviving spouse's tax year continues to its normal closing date (usually December 31). It does not close on the date of death of the deceased spouse.

14. B is the answer. The executor can claim the medical expenses for the decedent's last illness as deductions either on the final income tax return or on the estate tax return. For income and estate tax purposes, medical expenses are deductible only to the extent they exceed 10% of AGI. The medical expenses may be claimed as an income tax deduction only if a waiver is filed of any deduction for these expenses on the estate tax return. The medical expenses deduction will not be useful if estate tax liability is eliminated through use of the unified credit.

15. A is the answer. Certain estate administration expenses may be deducted either on the estate tax return or the estate's income tax return. If an executor files a waiver of the right to use the deduction on the estate tax return, the executor cannot change it later. The law does not specify that an executor must favor an income beneficiary over a remainderperson, but courts may require some reimbursement of the remainderperson.

16. A is the answer. By selecting a calendar year, "H's" executor can have one-half of the next 12 months of estate income taxed in calendar year one, and the other half of the next 12 months of estate income taxed in calendar year two. B is not as good as A because B means all estate income will be included in one tax year, rather than spread over two years. C is not as good as A because C means all estate income will be included in one tax year. Since there is no more income from estate assets after 12 months, changing to a calendar year after 12 months will do nothing for the tax bill. D is not permitted. Only spouses can file a joint return.

17. D is the answer. Both (2) and (3) are correct statements. (1) is not a correct statement because the executor is not required to include the accrued interest on the deceased's final return. An election can be made to do this, but such an election is not required. The bond interest may be treated as "income in respect of a decedent" and taxed to the person to whom the bonds are bequeathed. This person would report and pay income taxes on all income earned by the decedent prior to death, but not yet received prior to the deceased's death.

18. E is the answer. (2) is a correct statement because the higher value of the assets after six months means a higher cost basis for the estate heirs when they sell the estate assets, and thus a lower capital gain. (1) is correct because the lower value for the estate assets after six months means lower estate taxes. (3) is correct because the alternate valuation date may only be elected when both the gross estate, and the estate tax liabilities will be reduced. If all property passes to the spouse, there is no estate tax liability, so the alternate valuation date may not be elected.

19. B is the answer because it is not a correct statement. There is no 35% rule. However, there is a requirement that at least 50% of the deceased's gross estate must consist of real property and personal property used for agricultural or business purposes. A second requirement mandates that at least 25% of the deceased's AGE must consist exclusively of land that is being used for agricultural or business purposes. A, C, D, and E are correct statements.

20. E is the answer. All four statements are correct. There is no mention of real property, which is required for special-use valuation, so the estate could not have sufficient real estate to meet the 50% requirement. There is also no mention of a qualified heir or of the use of property to qualify for special-use valuation.

21. A is the answer. Statement (1) is correct because the adjusted gross estate is $3,800,000 ($8,000,000 minus $4,000,000 debt, and minus $200,000 in estate administration expenses). The $2 million of stock is more than 35% of the adjusted gross estate. Statement (3) is incorrect because Sec. 303 redemption can apply to any class of stock and any kind of corporation. Statement (4) is incorrect because only one-half of the value of the jointly owned stock will be included in the gross estate, and the adjusted gross estate will not meet the 35% rule.

22. C is the answer. Debt is not one of the items that is used to calculate the amount of stock eligible for a Sec. 303 redemption. The redemption allows capital gain treatment, rather than taxation as a dividend.

23. B is the answer because it is not a correct statement. Under Sec. 6166, only the amount of the estate tax attributable to the inclusion of the business property may be paid in installments and only if the business property is more than 35% of the deceased's AGI. A, C, D, and E are correct statements.

24. B is the answer. (1) is correct, as the business is 40% of the estate. (2) is not correct because only the tax attributable to the closely held business interest may be paid in installments. (3) is correct, but it would be possible to defer the first payment as long as 5 years and 9 months after the decedent's death. Statement (4) is incorrect because only a portion of the deferred tax will bear interest at the preferential rate of 2% for the estates of persons dying after 1997.

Estate Planning for Nontraditional Relationships (Topic 73)

CFP Board Student-Centered Learning Objectives

(a) Identify the impact of divorce and/or remarriage on an estate plan including asset titling and distribution, changes in beneficiary status, and selection of heirs.

(b) Recommend strategies that can be implemented to help ensure the appropriate management and transfer of assets to a same-sex, nontraditional and/or non-married partners.

> ### Estate Planning for Nontraditional Relationships
> A. Children of another relationship
> B. Cohabitation
> C. Adoption
> D. Same-sex relationships

Estate Planning for Divorce and Separation

Persons contemplating divorce have special considerations in estate planning. In some states, divorce revokes a will that names the ex-spouse as a beneficiary; but the beneficiary designations of life insurance, IRAs, and retirement plans are not invalidated by divorce. Changing these beneficiary designations, as well as estate planning documents such as the durable power of attorney, living will, and similar documents, is necessary to protect benefits from passing to a former spouse.

In a divorce, the divorcing parties need to deal with child support, alimony, preserving property for the children of the marriage, and protecting each party's individual benefits, for example, from retirement plans. One technique used in estate planning for divorce and separation is an irrevocable trust for the purpose of guaranteeing payment of alimony and child support. Payment of life insurance premiums can also be made more secure by having assets placed in a life insurance trust, rather than relying on one of the divorcing spouses to pay the premiums.

Remarriage and Children of Another Relationship

When a person remarries, a new will should be executed. One issue to address in the new will is the selection of a guardian for children of the former marriage. If divorced parents cannot agree upon a choice of guardian, a parent should state his or her choice in the will.

While courts are not bound by this choice in appointing a guardian, they try to honor a selection unless it is against the best interests of the child. As a general rule, courts prefer a surviving parent over a decedent's selection of guardian, if different than the parent.

Support Trusts

The financial needs of the children can be protected both by establishing an irrevocable trust for their support and education and by requiring the purchase of disability and life insurance. Management and preservation of assets for children from a former marriage can also be accomplished by means of custodial accounts, irrevocable trusts, and conservatorships.

One concern is the possibility that the children of a former marriage will be disinherited, intentionally or unintentionally. If the estate is left to the new spouse, the children of a former marriage may be overlooked or intentionally disinherited. A pretermitted heir statute may be the basis for a claim if disinheritance appears to have been unintentional. A technique for avoiding disinheritance is to place property in joint tenancy WROS with the children. Various trusts may also be set up to see that the children from a former marriage receive specified property. A sprinkle trust will provide flexibility. Lifetime gifts can also provide for the inheritance.

Cohabitation

Estate planning for unmarried persons is complicated because estate and gift tax marital deductions are only available to married persons. Persons who cohabit are not able to take advantage of the marital deduction to reduce their estate tax obligation when one of them dies. Without the estate tax marital deduction, estate taxes cannot be deferred; consequently, planning for estate liquidity is a primary consideration. Locating assets and heirs may be difficult, too.

While the 2013 Supreme Court ruling on the Defense of Marriage Act changed the federal government's treatment of same-sex marriages (allowing the marriage to be recognized at the federal level if the couple was married in a state that allows same-sex marriages), it did not change the tax treatment of domestic partnerships or civil unions.

Written property settlement agreements, often called domestic partnership agreements, are generally advisable to avoid future lawsuits over property rights and income, i.e., "palimony" suits. The status of unmarried heterosexual and same-sex cohabitants remains uncertain in most states, so property agreements and wills containing specific bequests are important. Naming the other cohabitant as the beneficiary of life insurance is another important strategy. An advantage of this technique is that the beneficiary can be changed if the relationship changes. Lifetime strategies may include a program of gifts, the placement of property in joint tenancy WROS, and the use of trusts.

The revocable trust is another important technique to consider with persons who are cohabiting because these trusts can be changed at any time if the respective relationship should change. The assets in the trust do not need to pass through probate, so they are immediately available to the survivor and may also avoid problems such as a will contest.

An irrevocable life insurance trust might be considered when one of the persons in the relationship has substantial assets. The life insurance death benefit can be removed from the estate and protected for the survivor.

In the circumstance of incompetency, obtaining appointment of a guardian for the individual's person or estate may be a problem for an unmarried cohabitant. A living will and a durable power of attorney are important to ensure that the cohabitant is involved in medical decisions and care. Otherwise, the next of kin will be authorized under most state statutes to make decisions.

Adoption

Under the Uniform Probate Code, an adopted child may inherit from the adopting parent but, depending on state law, the child may or may not from the natural parent who gave the child up for adoption. If an adopting parent dies intestate, the adopted child will receive the same statutory share as a natural child. If a parent wants to change this treatment of an adopted child, a will must be written that explicitly states the child's inheritance. Just as natural children can be disinherited, adopted children can be disinherited.

In situations where a client has adopted foster, or step-children, or may have given a child up for adoption, it is best to avoid class beneficiary designations such as "to all of my children in equal amounts" since it is likely to result in conflicting opinions as to who is, in fact, included in the definition of "my children".

Application Questions

1. Life insurance can be a relatively inexpensive way to resolve which of the following estate planning problems?

  (1) Providing child support for children of a former marriage if the parent dies
  (2) Bequeathing property to a cohabitant to whom the insured is not married
  (3) Preventing a child from a former marriage from being disinherited
  (4) Providing alimony payments for the insured's lifetime

  A. (1) and (2) only
  B (1) and (3) only
  C. (3) and (4) only
  D. (1), (2), and (3) only
  E. (1), (2), (3), and (4)

2. Susan has an estate of about $800,000 and wants some advice on estate planning. Susan has been cohabiting with Lena for two years and wants to provide for Lena after her death. Susan is concerned that her family will raise objections to any inheritance for Lena. Susan has been receptive to suggestions that she delay any plans to confer property permanently on Lena in case they leave the relationship in the future. Which of the following options should be recommended to Susan?

  (1) Joint tenancy WROS
  (2) Revocable trust
  (3) Irrevocable trust
  (4) Life insurance

  A. (1) and (2) only
  B. (1) and (4) only
  C. (2) and (3) only
  D. (2) and (4) only

3. John and Doris have lived together for ten years. They own a house together as tenants in common and also share some joint accounts. Doris suffers from leukemia and recently underwent surgery. Her medical costs are now approaching six figures. Doris does not want John to become responsible for the medical bills should she die. Their state does not recognize common-law marriages, so they have recently discussed marriage. Which of the following estate planning problems exist for John and Doris?

  (1) There may be problems with the passing of the house in the event of death if they are not married and there is no provision in the will or written agreement.
  (2) If they marry, John will be liable for Doris' medical bills.
  (3) The estate tax marital deduction and the gift tax annual exclusion are not available to them if they are not married.
  (4) There may be a problem with joint accounts because Doris is incompetent due to her illness.

  A. (1) and (2)
  B. (2) and (3)
  C. (1), (2), and (3)
  D. (2) and (4)
  E. (3) and (4)

4. Teresa and Kevin are engaged and are planning their wedding for January 27, 2015. If Kevin dies in a car crash the night before the wedding and his will left everything outright to Teresa, which of the following is correct?

    A. Kevin's estate can claim an unlimited marital deduction since they were engaged to be married.

    B. Kevin's estate can exclude $14,000 of assets passing to Teresa due to the annual exclusion.

    C. Kevin's executor can elect to place the assets in a bypass trust.

    D. Kevin's estate can claim the unified credit amount.

5. Troy and Brent met at grad school five years ago and have been in a dedicated relationship ever since. Neither Troy nor Brent has any estate planning documents. If Troy should die today, which of the following assets will pass to Brent?

    A. Life insurance policy with Troy named as the owner and the insured

    B. Retirement account with Troy's sister named as the contingent beneficiary

    C. Condominium held in joint tenancy between Troy and Brent

    D. Brokerage account held as tenants in common between Troy and Brent

For practice answering case questions related to Topic 73, please answer the following questions in the cases included in the Appendix at the back of this textbook.

Case	Questions
Bartlett	
Marshall	
Webster	
Unser	
Tingey	
Lytle	
Beals	7
Mocsin	
Young	
Borelli	
Cunningham	
Fred and Mary Ferris	101, 102, 103, 104, and 105

Answers and Explanations

1. D is the answer. Life insurance may be used to provide alimony payments when the insured dies but will generally not be used for this purpose during the insured's lifetime. The other problems listed in this question can be resolved by means of life insurance.

2. D is the answer. The use of joint tenancy WROS involves a gift of an interest in property, and it is a permanent arrangement. A joint tenancy is not as flexible as a revocable trust, which can be changed at any time before Susan dies. An irrevocable trust also cannot be changed, so it will produce the kind of permanent change Susan wants to avoid. Life insurance is a good option because the beneficiary can be changed at any time.

3. A is the answer. (1) and (2) are correct statements. (3) is incorrect because the gift tax annual exclusion is still available to unmarried persons, even though the estate and gift tax marital deductions are not. (4) is incorrect at the present time because Doris has not been declared totally incompetent. Existing joint accounts will not be rendered useless by incompetence.

4. D is the answer. Kevin's estate can claim the unified credit amount, which will let his estate currently transfer $5.43 million of assets in 2015 before owing an estate tax. A is incorrect, as they would need to actually get married in order to qualify for the marital deduction. B is incorrect, as the annual exclusion applies only to gifts. C is incorrect, as the assets were left outright to Teresa. The executor would not have the power to elect to place the assets in a bypass trust.

5. C is the answer. The condominium will pass automatically to Brent under operation of law since it is held in joint tenancy (with rights of survivorship). The life insurance and brokerage account will pass under the intestacy rules to Troy's blood relatives. The retirement account will pass to Troy's sister under the beneficiary designation form.

APPENDIX

BARTLETT CASE

Hank and Mary Ann Bartlett, ages 64 and 59, respectively, are a married couple with one son Mel, who is the divorced parent of two children: Bobby, age 9, and Amy, age 7. Hank and Mary Ann's only other child was a son, Ben, who died in an auto accident, leaving his wife Sarah and their daughter, Melanie, age 15.

Hank recently retired from a successful business career, during which he and Mary Ann accumulated the following assets:

- Family home, owned by Hank and Mary Ann as tenants by the entirety, currently valued at $850,000.

- Two cars, one owned by Hank, currently valued at $45,000 and one owned by Mary Ann, currently valued at $40,000.

- Household furnishings, owned by Hank and Mary Ann as tenants by the entirety, currently valued at $260,000.

- Clothing and personal belongings owned separately by Hank, currently valued at $25,000; and those owned separately by Mary Ann, currently valued at $80,000.

- Portfolio of stocks, bonds, and certificates of deposit owned solely by Hank, currently valued at $1,700,000.

- Term-to-age-65 life insurance policy, owned solely by Hank, who is the insured and premium payer, with a face amount of $200,000, payable to Hank's estate as the beneficiary.

- Whole life insurance policy, owned by Mary Ann, on which Hank is the insured and the premium payer, and Mary Ann is the beneficiary of the $250,000 face amount.

- Whole life insurance policy owned by Hank, who is the insured and the premium payer, with a $300,000 face amount, payable in equal shares to Hank and Mary Ann's three grandchildren, Bobby, Amy, and Melanie, who are named in the policy as irrevocable beneficiaries.

- Hunting lodge in the mountains, owned entirely by Hank, currently valued at $90,000.

- Collection of antique automobiles, currently valued at $190,000, paid for entirely by Hank but owned on a 50-50 basis by Hank and son Mel as tenants in common.

- Condominium in Florida that was left to Hank by his mother, which is currently valued at $125,000, over which Hank has a general power of appointment.

- Hank and Mary Ann each have very simple wills, as well as living wills. Hank's will leaves the hunting lodge to Hank's former business partner, Don Carter, for the remainder of Don's life, and then to Sarah. Each of the wills provides for a $25,000 charitable cash contribution to St. Jude Children's Research Hospital. Beyond these provisions, each of the wills specifies that all other property of each spouse goes to the other, if living, otherwise in equal shares "... to our children, *per stirpes*."

Assume that Hank died this year in a plane crash. His funeral expenses are $10,000, and legal fees to settle his estate are $30,000. Also, there is a $20,000 mortgage to be paid off on the hunting lodge, and $36,000 of federal and state income taxes are due. The Bartletts live in a state that does not have state death taxes.

Financial Plan Development

CFP® Board has mandated that all CFP® candidates enrolled in a registered education program leading up to satisfying educational requirements and those who could previously challenge the exam take a "capstone course" that teaches individuals how to formulate, draft, and present a financial plan.

Are you a student who needs this course? Keir can help. Visit www.KeirSuccess.com or call 800-795-5347, ext. 101.

Are you an instructor who needs a textbook for this course? Keir can help. Contact Mary Grace Caudill at 800-795-5347, ext. 101.

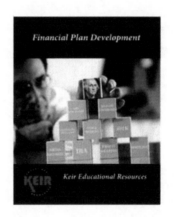

BARTLETT CASE
APPLICATION QUESTIONS

1. How would Hank's gross estate change, if at all, had the collection of antique automobiles been owned by Hank and Mel as joint tenants WROS?

(Topic 53)

A. The gross estate would be unchanged.
B. The gross estate would increase by $95,000.
C. The gross estate would increase by $190,000.
D. The gross estate would decrease by $95,000.
E. The gross estate would decrease by $190,000.

2. Which of the following of Hank's assets will be included in his probate estate?

(Topic 54)

(1) His interest in the family home
(2) The death proceeds of the term-to-age-65 life insurance policy
(3) The death proceeds of the $300,000 whole life policy
(4) The condominium in Florida

A. (1) and (4) only
B. (2) and (3) only
C. (2) and (4) only
D. (2), (3), and (4) only
E. (1), (2), (3), and (4)

3. Which of the following are among the legal characteristics of a tenancy by the entirety, the form under which Hank and Mary Ann's home and household furnishings are owned?

(Topic 54)

(1) It is available only to spouses.
(2) It is a form of joint tenancy WROS.
(3) Hank can bequeath his interest in the home to his son and grandchildren.
(4) Hank's interest in the home and furnishings will be included in his probate estate.

A. (1) and (2) only
B. (2) and (4) only
C. (1), (2), and (4) only
D. (1), (2), (3), and (4)

4. Which of the following are among the legal characteristics of a tenancy in common, the form under which Hank and Mel own the collection of antique automobiles?

(Topic 54)

(1) There is no right of survivorship between the co-owners.
(2) All the property is in the probate estate of the first co-owner to die.
(3) Hank can leave his interest in the collection by will to whomever he chooses.
(4) The entire value of the collection will be includible in Hank's gross estate for federal estate tax purposes because Mel contributed nothing to the purchase price.

A. (1) and (2) only
B. (1) and (3) only
C. (2) and (3) only
D. (2) and (4) only
E. (3) and (4) only

5. What would be the effect on the distribution of Hank's estate if his will were found by a court to be invalid because of a lack of proper witnesses?

(Topic 54)

A. Hank's living will would govern the distribution of Hank's estate.
B. Hank's assets would avoid the probate process before being distributed.
C. The executor of Hank's will would distribute Hank's assets.
D. The state intestacy law would govern the distribution of Hank's estate.
E. The court could use the will to show Hank's donative intent and then give effect to the intent of the instrument.

6. What will be the effect of the phrase "...to our children, *per stirpes*" in Hank's and Mary Ann's wills?

(Topic 55)

A. After Hank and Mary Ann have both died, the estate of the second to die will go to Mel only since he is their only living child.
B. After Hank and Mary Ann have both died, the estate of the second to die will go in equal shares to Mel and Melanie.
C. After Hank and Mary Ann have both died, the estate of the second to die will go entirely to Sarah since she is Melanie's mother.
D. After Hank and Mary Ann have both died, the estate of the second to die will go 50% to Mel immediately and 50% to Melanie when she marries, if ever.
E. After Hank's death, Mary Ann will be prevented from changing her will and leaving the estate entirely to her second husband.

7. If Hank and Mary Ann had decided to jointly make cash gifts to their grandchildren while they were both alive, which of the following is the largest amount they could have given without federal gift tax consequences?

(Topic 56)

A. $14,000 per year to each grandchild
B. $28,000 per year to each grandchild
C. $42,000 per year to each grandchild
D. $3,648,000 as a onetime gift to each grandchild
E. $5,430,000 as a onetime gift to each grandchild

8. Which of the following represents Hank's gross estate for federal estate tax purposes?

(Topic 59)

A. $2,580,000   D. $3,385,000
B. $3,010,000   E. $3,935,000
C. $3,135,000

9. Which of the following represents Hank's adjusted gross estate for federal estate tax purposes?

(Topic 59)

A. $3,039,000   D. $3,095,000
B. $3,050,000   E. $3,125,000
C. $3,075,000

10. Disregarding, for the moment, the matter of the marital deduction, which of the following would be Hank's taxable estate for federal estate tax purposes?

(Topic 59)

A. $3,014,000   D. $3,075,000
B. $3,039,000   E. $3,100,000
C. $3,050,000

11. If, while both were still alive, Hank and Mary Ann had made some taxable gifts to their grandchildren, how would Hank's tentative tax base for federal estate tax purposes be determined?

(Topic 59)

A. The amount of the taxable gifts would be subtracted from the taxable estate to determine the tentative tax base.

B. The gift taxes paid would be added to the estate tax owed to determine the tentative tax base.

C. The amount of the taxable gifts would be subtracted from the adjusted gross estate to determine the tentative tax base.

D. The amount of the adjusted taxable gifts would be added to the taxable estate to determine the tentative tax base.

E. The amount of taxable gifts would have no effect on the calculation of federal estate taxes because they are not includible in the gross estate.

12. Which of the following is the correct term to describe Sarah's interest in Hank's hunting lodge?

(Topic 62)

A. Remainder interest
B. Present interest
C. Life estate
D. Reversionary interest
E. Contingent remainder interest

13. Which of the following statements concerning the marital deduction applicable in Hank's case is correct?

(Topic 66)

A. It applies only to the family home and furnishings since these are the only items that pass to Mary Ann as a tenant by the entirety.

B. It does not apply to the term-to-age-65 life policy proceeds since Hank's estate, not Mary Ann, is the beneficiary.

C. It does not apply to the condominium since Hank has only a general power of appointment over it.

D. It does not apply to the $250,000 whole life insurance policy, owned by Mary Ann and of which she is the beneficiary.

E. It eliminates the usefulness of the state death tax deduction.

BARTLETT CASE
ANSWERS AND EXPLANATIONS

1. B is the answer. 100% of any property held in joint tenancy WROS with someone other than the deceased's spouse is included in the gross estate of the deceased unless it can be shown that the surviving joint tenant paid part of the purchase price of the property.

2. C is the answer. Statement (1) is incorrect because property that passes to another by operation of law is outside the probate estate. (3) is incorrect because property that passes to another by operation of a contract is outside the probate estate. (2) and (4) are both items that are in the probate estate. The death proceeds of the term-to-age policy are included in the probate estate because the policy is made payable to Hank's estate. The condominium is included because Hank had a general power of appointment over it and effectively owns it.

3. A is the answer. Property held in tenancy by the entirety is a form of joint tenancy WROS available only to spouses. Upon the death of one spouse, the property passes by operation of law to the surviving spouse. The decedent cannot bequeath his or her interest in a tenancy by the entirety, and the property is not included in the decedent's probate estate.

4. B is the answer. There is no right of survivorship for property owned in tenancy in common. Each owner's share of the tenancy in common can be disposed of by will and is included in the decedent owner's probate estate. Only the portion owned by the tenant in common is includible in the gross estate.

5. D is the answer. In the absence of a valid will, the applicable state intestacy law determines how the assets are distributed. A is incorrect because a living will is not really a will, but a document expressing the person's wishes with respect to medical treatment and the use of life-support systems when he or she is in a permanent, vegetative state or is near death and is unable to make his or her wishes known. B is incorrect because assets that pass to another by will or intestacy are part of the probate estate. C is incorrect because an executor is one named in the will to manage and distribute the assets; if the will is invalid, the executor has no authority.

6. B is the answer. The effect of the *per stirpes* provision is that children of a deceased child take their deceased parent's share. Therefore, Melanie will receive the portion of the estate that would have gone to her father Ben. After Hank's death, Mary Ann will inherit all of the property in Hank's estate and can leave it entirely to her second husband.

7. D is the answer. Gifts of a present interest, including cash, are eligible for the federal gift tax annual exclusion. The exclusion is $14,000 per year per donee and is double this amount ($28,000) if the donor's spouse joins in the gift. They could also each transfer up to $5.43 million during their lifetimes without having to pay a gift tax, for a total of $10.86 million. Since there are three grandchildren, they could give a one-time gift of $3.62 million to each of them; plus the annual exclusion gift for that year. For answer choice B, it is true that they can gift up to $28,000 per year to each grandchild, but the question asks for the *largest* gift.

8. C is the answer, computed as follows:

Family home	$ 425,000
Hank's automobile	45,000
Household furnishings	130,000
Hank's clothing and personal belongings	25,000
Portfolio of stocks, bonds, and CDs	1,700,000
Term-to-age-65 life policy proceeds	200,000
Hank's whole life policy proceeds	300,000
Hunting lodge	90,000
Antique automobiles	95,000
Condominium	125,000
Gross estate	$3,135,000

Note that the proceeds of the $250,000 whole life policy on which Hank is merely the insured and premium payer are not in Hank's gross estate. Also, one-half of the value of the antique automobiles is included in the gross estate because this property is owned as tenants in common. If the antique automobiles were owned in joint tenancy, their entire value would be included in Hank's gross estate, under the consideration furnished rule of Section 2040.

9. A is the answer, computed as follows:

Gross estate	$3,135,000
– Funeral expenses	(10,000)
– Legal fees	(30,000)
– Hunting lodge mortgage	(20,000)
– Federal and state income taxes	(36,000)
Adjusted gross estate	$3,039,000

Note that the charitable contribution is not deducted in the process of computing the adjusted gross estate.

10. A is the answer. Three items are deducted from the adjusted gross estate to derive the taxable estate: the state death tax deduction, the marital deduction and charitable contributions. The Bartletts live in a state that does not have state death taxes, in this question the marital deduction is disregarded, and the charitable contribution is $25,000, making Hank's taxable estate $3,039,000 – $25,000 = $3,014,000.

11. D is the answer. The adjusted taxable gifts are all taxable gifts made by the deceased after 1976. The adjusted taxable gifts are added to the taxable estate to produce the tentative tax base for estate tax purposes.

12. A is the answer, by definition. B is incorrect because Sarah's interest is a future interest. C is incorrect because Don Carter has a life estate in the lodge. D is incorrect because it describes the right of a donor to receive gifted property back at a later date, such as at the conclusion of a life estate of the donee. E is incorrect. Sarah's interest is not a contingent remainder because it does not depend on her surviving Hank's partner.

13. D is the answer. All property left to Mary Ann qualifies for the marital deduction, including (but not limited to) property passing to her as a tenant by the entirety, so A is incorrect. B is incorrect because these proceeds will go to Mary Ann according to the terms of Hank's will and, therefore, will qualify for the marital deduction. C is incorrect because a general power enables Hank to transfer the property to anyone, and "all other property" of Hank's goes to Mary Ann, so the marital deduction applies to the condominium. E is a nonsense option.

MARSHALL CASE

George Marshall, age 62, owns a successful building supply business called Marshall Depot, Inc. The business is now worth approximately $9,400,000, and George has received an offer from a company that wants to buy the store at that price.

George's wife Sally, age 61, is a homemaker. They have three children: Robert, age 37; Margaret, age 35; and Susan, age 31. Robert is an accountant, Margaret is a teacher, and Susan is a homemaker, married to a doctor.

Sally inherited securities and a vacation home at the shore from her mother. At the time of her mother's death in 2009, the securities were worth $500,000, and they are now worth $675,000. The vacation home was valued at $125,000 when Sally's mother died but is now worth approximately $155,000. Sally's will provides for all of her estate to pass to George, or if he predeceases her, to their children equally.

George's will provides for one-third of his adjusted gross estate to be placed in a marital trust for Sally. The remainder of his estate is to be placed in a residuary trust with income to go to Sally for her life. Sally will have a right to invade corpus, and at her death, any remaining corpus will be distributed to their children *per stirpes*. Estate and inheritance taxes are to be paid out of the funds passing to the residuary trust. George has placed life insurance with a face value of $800,000 in a revocable trust. Under the revocable trust, Sally will receive the income from the trust for life and can direct the disposition of the corpus at her death. George and Sally's estates presently consist of the following property values:

Property Item	Owner	Value
Checking and Savings Account	Joint	$16,000
Money Market Account	Joint	$94,000
Mutual Fund Account	Joint	$660,000
Securities Inherited by Sally	Sally	$675,000
Vacation Home Inherited by Sally	Sally	$155,000
Marshall Depot, Inc.	George	$9,400,000
Vested Profit-Sharing Plan*	George	$795,000
Furniture and Household Goods	Sally	$55,000
Jewelry and Gems	Sally	$75,000
Automobiles	George	$40,000
Life Insurance	Revocable trust	$800,000

*Sally is the designated beneficiary.

George and Sally expect, based on their family history and current health status, that George will live until at least age 80 and Sally will live until at least age 85.

MARSHALL CASE
APPLICATION QUESTIONS

1. All the following are potential problems with George and Sally Marshalls' estate plans, EXCEPT:

(Topic 53)

   A. The securities owned by Sally will be included in George's estate if Sally dies first.

   B. If George sold the business and placed the proceeds in the mutual fund account or money market account, none of these proceeds would pass into the residuary trust for the children.

   C. The vacation home may be taxed in George's estate unless Sally dies first.

   D. If Sally predeceases George, future appreciation on the securities Sally inherited will be added to George's estate and will be subject to estate taxes on George's death.

   E. If George does not sell the business during his lifetime and does not have a buy-sell agreement, this asset may be worth substantially less after his death.

2. All the following statements concerning the estate plans of George and Sally Marshall are correct, EXCEPT:

(Topic 53)

   A. Sally will have complete access to the assets that will be placed in the marital trust under George's will.

   B. George's will should be changed to give personal property to Sally outright.

   C. The full value of jointly owned property at the date of George's death will be included in George's gross estate.

   D. Any death benefits under the insurance policies can be distributed to beneficiaries as directed by the trust document.

   E. Assets passing to the residuary trust for Sally will take advantage of George's unified credit.

3. Assume for this question that the Marshalls live in a community-property state. If George dies today, what will the value of his gross estate be for federal estate tax purposes?

(Topic 53)

   A. $5,967,500   D. $10,667,500

   B. $6,302,500   E. $11,465,000

   C. $6,700,000

4. Assume for this question that George's daughter Susan died after giving birth to a second child, and that George died a year later, leaving the same will as described in the case facts. What portion of the corpus of the residuary trust would each of Susan's children receive at Sally's death?

(Topic 55)

A. 1/8   D. 1/5
B. 1/6   E. 1/2
C. 1/4

5. Which of the following statements concerning the securities inherited by Sally from her parents is correct?

(Topic 57)

A. Sally's basis in the securities is the same as her mother's basis in the securities.
B. If Sally gives the securities to her grandchildren, a generation-skipping transfer tax will be due, regardless of whether the gift is made by will or during Sally's lifetime.
C. If Sally makes gifts of the securities during her lifetime to her children, there will be a step-up in basis for the securities at the time of the gift.
D. If Sally gives the securities to a qualifying charity less than three years before her death, the securities will be includible in her gross estate.
E. If Sally retains the securities until her death, George or her children may be able to sell them and incur little or no capital gain.

6. If George dies today, what will the value of his gross estate be for federal estate tax purposes?

(Topic 59)

A. $10,620,000   D. $12,367,500
B. $11,420,000   E. $12,765,000
C. $11,965,000

7. Which of the following items would be deductible from the gross estate in computing George's adjusted gross estate?

(Topic 59)

(1) A $20,000 car loan
(2) Funeral expenses of $7,500
(3) Medical bills of $8,000 from an appendectomy six months earlier
(4) An unpaid loan of $10,000 from George to his son

A. (2) only
B. (1) and (4) only
C. (2) and (3) only
D. (1), (2), and (3) only
E. (1), (2), (3), and (4)

8. Which of the following statements correctly describes the probable consequences of making the life insurance trust irrevocable?

(Topic 65)

A. George will reduce his income taxes because the future income from the trust policies will not be taxed to him.

B. George will have to pay gift tax, based on the amount of the death benefits of the policies placed in the trust.

C. If George does not live more than three years, the proceeds of the policies will be includible in his gross estate for federal estate tax purposes.

D. Premiums for the life policies will be paid with tax-free dollars.

E. If Sally predeceases George, he can change the beneficiary of the trust to provide for his grandchildren and use his GST exemption.

9. Assume for this question that George transfers income-producing property to the insurance trust and makes the trust irrevocable. Which of the following statements concerning this irrevocable insurance trust is correct?

(Topic 65)

A. The trust income is fully taxable to George.

B. The trust income is not taxable to George and Sally during George's lifetime because no income is paid to George or Sally.

C. The trust will pay taxes on the income, based on the amount of distributable net income.

D. The trust can deduct the amount of premiums paid for life insurance and reduce or eliminate any taxable income.

E. The increase in the cash value of the insurance policies will be taxable to the trust as a tax preference item under the alternative minimum tax rules.

10. Assume for this question that George pays the annual premiums for the life insurance placed in the trust, and that the trust is made irrevocable. Which of the following statements concerning this irrevocable trust is correct?

(Topic 65)

A. The death benefit will not be available to Sally without adverse tax consequences.

B. The death benefit will be included in George's estate whenever George dies.

C. George can borrow from the cash values of the policies without adverse tax consequences.

D. The trust must elect the interest-only settlement option in order to avoid gift tax on the policy proceeds at the time of George's death.

E. If Crummey powers are included in the trust document, the annual payment of premiums by George will qualify for the gift tax annual exclusion.

11. If an estate tax return were filed for George, based upon the case facts, which of the following assets can qualify either partially or entirely for the marital deduction?

(1) Life insurance death proceeds
(2) Mutual fund account
(3) Vested profit-sharing plan
(4) Assets passing to the residuary trust

(Topic 66)

A. (1) and (2) only
B. (1), (2), and (3) only
C. (4) only
D. (1), (2), and (4) only
E. (1), (2), (3), and (4)

12. Which of the following intra-family transfers is LEAST likely to achieve family tax savings for the Marshalls?

(Topic 67)

A. George and Sally transfer the assets in their money market account to a trust that will pay income to them for 15 years and then pass to their daughter Margaret.

B. Ownership of Marshall Depot, Inc. is transferred over several years to a family partnership in which all of the Marshalls are partners.

C. George and Sally transfer securities worth $250,000 to a trust, retaining a right to an annuity income for 15 years, with the remainder to go to their children.

D. Sally sells her vacation home to their son Robert in an installment sale.

E. George and Sally transfer $250,000 of securities to a charitable remainder trust, retaining a life income interest.

13. Assume for this question that Marshall Depot, Inc. operates on a parcel of commercial real estate that has a fair market value of $2,750,000 but has an actual use value of $1,800,000. Which of the following factors would most likely prevent the Marshalls or George Marshall's estate from taking advantage of the special-use valuation for this real estate?

(Topic 68)

A. George took out a $500,000 mortgage on the property.

B. George has operated the business at this location for 10 years.

C. George's son wants to continue the business after George's death.

D. George owns all of the stock of Marshall Depot, Inc.

E. George's wife Sally will inherit the stock and wants to sell it to George's son.

14. Which of the following statements correctly describes an estate freeze technique that George might use in connection with the business interest in Marshall Depot, Inc.?

(Topic 68)

A. In the valuation of gifts of unequal amounts of the voting common stock to George's three children, George's retained common stock will be valued at zero.

B. After recapitalizing, George can give voting common stock to his son and nonvoting preferred stock in the same proportion to his daughters, and George's retained interest will not be valued at zero.

C. If George retains a right to dividend payments that are not qualified payments, the value of his retained stock, as well as any gifts of stock to his children, will be included in his gross estate.

D. The estate freeze rules can be avoided by means of an installment sale to George's son at a substantially discounted price.

E. If George makes an S corporation election, he can then recapitalize and give preferred stock to his children and avoid the estate freeze rules.

15. All the following statements correctly describe problems with George Marshall's current estate plan, EXCEPT:

(Topic 72)

A. George's estate will not qualify for the Sec. 6166 deferral of federal estate taxes.

B. The residuary trust is directed to pay taxes but will have few liquid assets with which to pay them.

C. The assets in the money market and mutual fund accounts will not be available to meet the estate's liquidity needs.

D. The life insurance placed in the revocable trust will increase George's taxable estate for federal estate tax purposes but will not be available to the executor for paying debts and taxes.

E. George could reduce the estate taxes that his executor will pay by leaving Sally more than one-third of the adjusted gross estate.

MARSHALL CASE
ANSWERS AND EXPLANATIONS

1. C is the answer. The vacation home will only be taxed in George's estate if Sally predeceases George. If she dies first, the vacation home and securities inherited from her parents will pass to George and any appreciation on these assets will be taxed in George's estate when he dies. The Marshalls could avoid this estate tax on the appreciation by changing Sally's will to leave the assets in a bypass trust. If Sally predeceases George, her will provides for her entire estate to pass to George. Accordingly, the securities owned by Sally will pass to George and will be included in his estate. In addition, since her entire estate passes to George, the marital deduction reduces her estate to zero, and none of her unified credit will be used. The unified credit will not be lost, however, if Sally's executor makes an election to allow George to apply her unused unified credit to his estate taxes under the portability feature. If George sells his business and places the proceeds in their mutual fund or money market account, he will have converted an asset owned solely by him to a jointly owned asset that passes by operation of law to Sally outside the probate estate and outside the will. As a result, none of the proceeds of the sale of the business will go into the residuary trust for the children. If George were to die after placing the assets in these joint accounts, his probate estate would include only the automobiles and the vested profit-sharing plan.

2. C is the answer. Only one-half of property jointly owned by spouses is includible in the estate of the first to die. Sally will have access to property in the marital trust because she will be given a general power of appointment, and provisions can be included, giving her the right to invade principal and to make gifts. The insurance proceeds can be made payable to the trust, and the distribution will then be made according to the directions and terms of the trust document.

3. A is the answer. The securities and vacation home inherited by Sally are her separate property and are not includible in George's gross estate. The remaining assets are treated as community property, so one-half of the assets are includible in George's gross estate.

4. B is the answer. The *per stirpes* distribution of the corpus in the residuary trust means that each of Susan's children would receive 1/6 of the corpus because the 1/3 interest to which their mother would have been entitled would be divided equally between her two children.

5. E is the answer. The basis for inherited property is the fair market value at the date of death (or later); consequently, a new owner receives a step-up in basis. If the new owner sells the property soon after inheriting it, there will be little or no capital gain, due to the step-up in basis. Thus, when Sally inherited the securities, she received a step-up in basis and did not carry over her mother's basis. If Sally retains the securities until her death (which is anticipated to be when she is at least 85 years old), George and the children would also receive a step-up in basis and could sell the securities without incurring capital gains. While inherited property receives a step-up in basis, a donee's basis is the lesser of the donor's basis or the fair market value at the time the gift is made. Thus, if Sally gives securities to her children, they will carry over Sally's basis. No generation-skipping transfer tax will be owed because the amount of the transfer is less than the $5.43 million GST exemption that will be available in 2015.

6. B is the answer. George's gross estate will include one-half of the jointly owned property and all of the property that is listed as owned by him, including the vested profit-sharing plan. The life insurance in the revocable trust is also included in his gross estate, for a total of $11,420,000.

7. D is the answer. The deductions that may be subtracted from the gross estate to calculate the adjusted gross estate include: (1) funeral expenses, (2) estate administration expenses, (3) debts, and (4) casualty and theft losses during administration of the estate. The loan to George's son is, obviously, not a debt, but the car loan and the unpaid medical bills are deductible debts.

8. C is the answer. If George lives less than three years, the life insurance proceeds are brought back into his gross estate. If George survives three years, the proceeds will not be includible in his gross estate. Making the trust irrevocable does not affect George's income taxes because the accumulating values in the life insurance policies are not currently taxable to George in any event. Since George has not placed any income-producing assets in the trust, the annual premiums will have to be paid by George with after-tax dollars, rather than tax-free dollars. If George is transferring existing policies, the gift is valued in terms of the interpolated terminal reserve, not the death benefit.

9. A is the answer. Under the grantor trust rules, trust income is taxable to the grantor when the trust income is or may be used to purchase life insurance on the life of the grantor or his or her spouse. Premium payments are not deductible. Since the trust income is taxable to George, the trust does not pay taxes on the distributable net income.

10. E is the answer. Crummey powers permit a donor to make an annual contribution which qualifies for the gift tax annual exclusion. The Crummey powers permit the trust beneficiary to withdraw annually the amount of the annual contribution, therefore, the beneficiaries have a present interest. George cannot retain the right to borrow, without running into the adverse tax consequences of the grantor trust rules. If George lives three years after making the trust irrevocable, the death benefit will not be included in his gross estate. The death benefit is not taxable to Sally.

11. B is the answer. The life insurance death proceeds qualify for the marital deduction because they are included in the gross estate, and Sally has a power of appointment over corpus, which makes the trust a marital trust. The residuary trust is a nonmarital trust that provides for the corpus to pass to George's children after Sally dies. The assets passing through this trust do not qualify for the marital deduction. One-half of the jointly owned mutual fund account is included in the gross estate, and these assets pass by operation of law to Sally, so they qualify for the marital deduction. The vested profit-sharing plan can qualify for the marital deduction since Sally is the beneficiary.

12. A is the answer. Use of grantor-retained income trusts has been curtailed because the retained income interest is not a qualified interest for determining gift tax liability. Thus, the entire amount of the Marshall's gift in trust is a taxable gift to their daughter. There is no income tax advantage for the Marshalls from establishing this trust for at least 15 years since the income will be paid to the Marshalls. Since money market funds are placed in the trust, there is not even much estate tax advantage because there is little or no appreciation potential. The tax-favored trust under current law is the grantor annuity trust (GRAT), which is represented in (C). Since the annuity is of equal value to the assets placed in trust, there is no remainder interest, giving rise to gift tax. The assets are removed from the Marshall's estates, and any appreciation will pass to the children in the remainder interest. A family partnership is viable for income shifting; moreover, the capital invested in Marshall Depot, Inc. can be expected to be a material income-producing factor. Since the transfer will be over several years, gift and estate taxes can be reduced by means of lifetime gifts of interests in the business. The installment sale will spread Sally's capital gain over several years and remove that asset from her estate.

13. A is the answer. For special-use valuation, the real estate must be used in a closely held business or farming operation. Since George owns all of the stock of Marshall Depot, Inc., the business is closely held. The real estate must be 25% of the gross estate after deduction of mortgages and secured debt. After deduction of the mortgage of $500,000, the real estate is worth $2,250,000, which is less than 25% of the gross estate. The gross estate was $11,420,000, and the real estate is only about 20% of this amount. The heirs must continue to operate the land in the same closely held business for a period of 10 years to remain eligible for the special valuation and tax benefits. Thus, if George's son were to continue to operate the business, the tax benefits would be retained.

14. B is the answer. Where the retained interests are proportionately the same as the transferred interests, there is no valuation problem under the rules of Secs. 2701-2704. Thus, if George gives the same proportion of voting common stock to his son that he gives nonvoting preferred stock to his daughters, then his retained interests are proportionately the same as the transferred interests. George does not have to give the common and preferred to the same person. The retained interest will not be valued at zero. The installment sale at a discounted price is subject to the rules of Secs. 2701-2704 because such a bargain sale is a gift, and George's right to receive installment payments is a retained interest. The installments may be qualified payments, in which case, George's retained interests will not be valued at zero. In (A), the retained interests and the gift interests are both voting common stock, so there is no valuation problem under Secs. 2701-2704.

15.A is the answer. An executor can elect to defer payment of federal estate taxes for up to 14 years and 9 months under Sec. 6166 if more than 35% of the adjusted gross estate consists of a closely held business interest. George's ownership of Marshall Depot, Inc. will more than meet this 35% requirement. B, C, D, and E correctly describe problems in George's current estate plan. The life insurance in the revocable trust, the jointly owned assets, and the vested profit-sharing plan will increase the adjusted gross estate but will not be available to pay taxes. George could reduce the estate taxes his executor must pay by increasing the portion of his adjusted gross estate that passes to his wife Sally. The assets passing to Sally will qualify for the marital deduction and reduce the taxes owed by George's estate.

WEBSTER CASE

David Webster is 51 years old, and his wife Lucia is 39. They have two children: Laura, age 9, and David, Jr., age 6. David is the vice president of operations for a large chemical company, and Lucia is an urban planner for the city where the Websters live. The Websters live in a 200-year-old home that they have been fixing up for several years. They bought the house as tenants by the entirety for a purchase price of $200,000 and have expended $350,000 in improvements. The house is now worth $850,000. Their mortgage balance is currently $100,000.

David receives a salary of $200,000, and Lucia earns $60,000 annually. David's employer provides group life insurance equal to 2.5 times his annual salary, and Lucia's employer provides $50,000 of group life insurance. David has purchased another $200,000 of whole life insurance, with a cash value of $25,000, and he owns $1 million of term insurance. Lucia is the named beneficiary for all of David's life insurance. Lucia has a whole life policy with a face value of $50,000 and a cash value of $7,000. David is the beneficiary of all of Lucia's life insurance.

The Websters jointly own a vacation condominium in the mountains of a neighboring state, which is worth $430,000, with an $180,000 mortgage. They also own two cars in joint tenancy, which are worth a total of $35,000. The Websters' portfolio of government and municipal securities is worth $350,000. The Websters also own stock that has appreciated from the purchase price of $400,000 to a current value of $550,000. Their checking account contains $35,000, but they owe $3,000 on their joint credit cards.

David is the sole owner of an apartment building that he acquired before his marriage to Lucia. The building is presently valued at approximately $600,000 and has a $150,000 mortgage. Net rental income is about $40,000 annually. David's adjusted basis in the building is $275,000. David is also a tenant in common, with three friends, in a commercial rental property valued at $800,000. The property generates a net income of $20,000, and David is a one-fourth owner. David has recently transferred the apartment building to a revocable trust so that he could have it managed by a trustee and observe the trustee's management skill. The trust will pay income for life to David with the remainder to Lucia.

David's will establishes a trust that will pay income to Lucia for her life and then pay income to the two children until they reach age 21. The trust is to be funded with sufficient assets to take advantage of any unified credit available at his death. The residuary under David's will passes to Lucia. Lucia's will leaves everything to David or to the two children *per stirpes*.

David has made adjusted taxable gifts of $6,000 and has used $1,080 of his unified credit to offset the taxable gifts. If David were to die today, his funeral and estate administration expenses would cost an estimated $30,000.

WEBSTER CASE
APPLICATION QUESTIONS

1. Which of the following statements correctly describes potential problems with David Webster's current estate plan assuming David will live for at least five more years?

(Topic 54)

A. The trust established by David's will qualifies too many assets for the marital deduction.
B. The beneficiary designations for David's life insurance mean the death benefits will be included in his gross estate unnecessarily.
C. David's heirs will not realize much cash from the sale of the apartment building due to capital gains taxes.
D. The testamentary trust for Lucia will fail to qualify for QTIP treatment, even if the executor makes the election.
E. If David dies first, only the commercial property will pass to the trust under his will providing for his children.

2. If David Webster dies today, which of the following property interests will be included in David's probate estate?

(Topic 54)

(1) The vacation condominium
(2) The apartment building
(3) The commercial real estate
(4) The Websters' residence

    A. (3) only
    B. (1) and (4) only
    C. (2) and (3) only
    D. (1), (2), and (3) only
    E. (1), (2), (3), and (4)

3. David and Lucia want to begin to accumulate a fund to pay for the college expenses for their children. The Websters would like to begin by using David's commercial real estate interest. They would like to retain some control over the real estate interest to be able to prevent their children from mismanaging or wasting it. Which of the following techniques is the most appropriate for transferring the real estate interest to the Webster children?

(Topic 56)

A. Uniform Gifts to Minors Act
B. Uniform Transfers to Minors Act
C. Bargain sale
D. Sec. 2503(b) trust
E. Installment sale

4. The Websters have decided that they should consider making gifts to their children of property other than the commercial real estate interest. Which of the following statements concerning the selection of assets for gifts is correct?

(Topic 56)

A. A disadvantage of using life insurance for a gift to the children is its large value for gift tax purposes.

B. An advantage of making a gift of the Websters' stock is that if the children sell it the next year, the appreciation will be taxed at the lower capital gains rate for the children.

C. An advantage of making a gift of the apartment building is that the children will not be subject to a recapture of depreciation when they sell the building.

D. An advantage of making a gift of the vacation condominium is that by giving the condominium away, their estates will avoid ancillary probate.

E. A disadvantage of making a gift in trust of their residence, while retaining a life estate, is that the amount of the gift would be the market value of the house.

5. Assume that David and Lucia have decided to make lifetime gifts to an irrevocable Crummey trust for their children and that they have agreed to gift-splitting. They select the commercial real estate interest to contribute to the trust the first year, and $40,000 of their stock will be given to the children's trust the following year.

(Topic 56)

Which of the following statements correctly describes the advantages to the Websters of the gifts in trust for their children?

A. David and Lucia can use the assets or obtain the income from the trust when they need additional money.

B. Future appreciation of the assets will not be included in either David or Lucia's gross estate.

C. The assets will receive a step-up in basis at the time they are placed in the trust.

D. Gift taxes on the gifts will be included in the gift and are not includible in David's or Lucia's gross estate.

E. Income from the assets will be taxed to the children at their lower rates.

6. Assume for this question that David and Lucia decided to make the gifts of stock to the children under the Uniform Gifts to Minors Act, and they elected to make the gifts net of any gift taxes. Which of the following statements concerning these net gifts is (are) correct?

(Topic 56)

(1) By making net gifts, David and Lucia are preventing any reduction of their unified credits.

(2) Any gift taxes paid by the children will reduce the amount that will be added to David and Lucia's taxable estates as adjusted taxable gifts.

(3) By making net gifts, David and Lucia will increase the basis of the stock in the hands of the children.

    A. (1) only
    B. (2) only
    C. (2) and (3) only
    D. (1), (2), and (3)

7. Assume that David and Lucia have decided to make lifetime gifts to an irrevocable Crummey trust for their children and that they have agreed to gift-splitting. They select the commercial real estate interest to contribute to the trust the first year, and $40,000 of their stock will be given to the children's trust the following year.

(Topic 57)

Which of the following statements concerning these gifts is correct?

    A. David and Lucia will be required to pay some gift tax for these gifts.
    B. The gifts will not qualify for the gift tax annual exclusion.
    C. David and Lucia can avoid reducing their unified credits by use of the Crummey trust.
    D. David and Lucia can elect to split the gift of real estate even though Lucia is not an owner.
    E. While the stock is held by the trust, income from the stock accumulated in the trust will be taxed at David and Lucia's income tax rates.

8. Assume that David and Lucia have decided to make lifetime gifts to an irrevocable Crummey trust for their children and that they have agreed to gift-splitting. They select the commercial real estate interest to contribute to the trust the first year, and $40,000 of their stock will be given to the children's trust the following year.

(Topic 57)

If David dies the year after the gifts have been placed in the trust, what will be the amount of his adjusted taxable gifts?

    A. $6,000   D. $86,000
    B. $52,000   E. $106,000
    C. $78,000

9. If David Webster were to die today, what would be the value of his gross estate?

(Topic 59)

A. $2,825,000   D. $4,225,000
B. $3,050,000   E. $4,325,000
C. $3,625,000

10. If David Webster died at the beginning of 2015 before any of the assets values changed, what would be the value of his taxable estate?

(Topic 59)

A. $618,500   D. $2,318,500
B. $620,000   E. $2,320,000
C. $1,570,000

11. Which of the following statements concerning the computation of the total estate tax for David Webster's estate is (are) correct if David dies during 2015?

(Topic 59)

(1) David's $6,000 adjusted taxable gifts are added to the taxable estate to determine his tentative tax base.
(2) The estate tax rate of 55% is applied to the tentative tax base to determine the tentative tax for David's estate.
(3) A credit for foreign death taxes is subtracted from the amount of the tentative tax.

A. (1) only
B. (2) only
C. (1) and (3) only
D. (2) and (3) only
E. (1), (2), and (3)

12. Which of the following statements correctly describes the advantages or disadvantages of including a sprinkling provision in the trust established by David Webster?

(Topic 62)

A. The trust will no longer be entitled to take the standard deduction generally available to simple trusts for income tax purposes.
B. If one of the children suffers a health impairment, the trustee can direct most of the income and principal to that child, instead of making equal distributions.
C. Creditors will not be able to take trust assets to repay the children's debts.
D. Assets and income can be sprinkled in from other sources and will be supervised by the same trustee for the children's benefit.
E. The assets will be eligible for the marital deduction at David's death and will be subject to estate tax only at the time of Lucia's death.

13. Assume that David and Lucia have decided to make lifetime gifts to an irrevocable Crummey trust for their children and that they have agreed to gift-splitting. They select the commercial real estate interest to contribute to the trust the first year, and $40,000 of their stock will be given to the children's trust the following year.

If David and Lucia established a 2503(b) trust and required the trustee to distribute income annually to their children, which of the following statements would be correct?

(Topic 62)

A. If the stock were sold when Laura enters college, the capital gains on the stock would be taxed to her at her marginal tax rate.
B. Dividends on the stock would be taxed to the trust at the trust's tax rate.
C. If the trustee distributed capital gains from the stock, the trust could not obtain a deduction for such a distribution.
D. Since this trust would be a short-term trust, trust income would be taxed under the grantor trust rules.

14. In which of the following circumstances would the executor of David's estate be able to value the property as of six months after the date of death if David dies during 2015?

(Topic 68)

(1) The commercial property interest declined in value by $50,000 following David's death.
(2) David's entire estate passed to his wife Lucia.
(3) The apartment building increased in value by $50,000, but the stock declined in value by $25,000.
(4) David's executor sold the commercial property interest at $50,000 below its market value two months after David's death.

A. (1) only
B. (1) and (2) only
C. (2) and (3) only
D. (3) and (4) only
E. (1), (3), and (4) only

15. Assume for purposes of this question that, in addition to his other assets, David inherited from his parents a portfolio of securities valued at $550,000 and that he had a child from a previous marriage to whom he would like to leave some assets after Lucia's death. David wants Lucia to have the income from his assets during her life, and he would like to minimize estate and gift taxes. Which of the following techniques would be most appropriate to recommend to David to accomplish these objectives?

(Topic 68)

    A. A deed to the apartment building delivered to an escrow agent

    B. A revocable living trust

    C. Revision of David's will to include a QTIP trust

    D. Revision of David's will to include a power-of-appointment trust

    E. Revision of David's will to give the child by a previous marriage a general power of appointment

WEBSTER CASE
ANSWERS AND EXPLANATIONS

1. **E** is the answer. Although David has provided in his will for enough assets to be placed in a trust to take advantage of the unified credit, only the commercial property will pass to this trust. Moreover, the commercial property does not provide much income for the children. The apartment building has been transferred to a revocable trust and will not pass under David's will. The life insurance will pass directly to Lucia according to the beneficiary designation forms. The remaining assets are owned in joint tenancy and will pass directly to Lucia. If David's heirs sell the apartment building after his death (anticipated to be in at least five years), there will be little or no capital gain because the building will receive a step-up in basis to the date-of-death value.

2. **A** is the answer. The apartment building is held by the revocable trust and will not be subject to probate. The commercial real estate is subject to probate because it is owned by David in tenancy in common and will pass under his will. The property owned jointly or in tenancy by the entirety is not subject to probate, so the residence and vacation condominium will not be subject to probate.

3. **D** is the answer. The Websters cannot give real estate to their minor children under the Uniform Gifts to Minors Act. Real estate can be given to minors under the Uniform Transfers to Minors Act, and if the Websters name themselves as custodians, they will be able to manage the investment until the children reach majority, usually age 18 or 21. With a 2503(b) trust, however, the Websters can name themselves trustees and help manage the asset for any length of time. The Websters could even name a trustee to succeed them and provide continued supervision of the asset for as long as the Webster children live. The bargain sale and installment sale do not provide as much control and management of the asset as does the trust. Moreover, any sale is probably unrealistic since the children would have to be given the money to buy the real estate interest.

4. **D** is the answer. By making a gift of the real estate in another state, an owner can save his or her estate the cost of ancillary probate. Whether Lucia survives David or David survives Lucia, the condominium would be subject to probate in the survivor's estate. Life insurance is a good subject for a gift because the policy has a low gift tax value, in relation to the death benefit that will be paid. Currently, the capital gains rate for David and Lucia would be nearly the same as for their children, so giving appreciated property will not reduce income taxes. Where depreciation has been taken on property, such as the apartment building, the donee takes the adjusted basis of the donor, and the recapture of depreciation is also passed along to the donee. Consequently, the Websters' children would not escape recapture if they sold the building following a gift. If the Websters made a gift of their residence in trust with a retained life estate, the value of the gift would be the remainder interest, not the full market value of the house. Chapter 14 of the Code does not apply.

5. **B** is the answer. One of the main advantages of lifetime giving is that future appreciation will be removed from the donor's gross estate. David and Lucia cannot use the assets or obtain the income when they need additional money because the trust is irrevocable. Irrevocability is the major disadvantage of lifetime gifts. The assets will not receive a step-up in basis at the time they are placed in the trust because a step-up in basis occurs only when the assets pass through an estate. No gift taxes will be paid, so no gift taxes will be includible in David's or Lucia's gross estate.

6. B is the answer. When making net gifts, David and Lucia must still use their unified credits before a donee will have to pay any gift tax. By making net gifts, the amount of David and Lucia's adjusted taxable gifts added to their taxable estates will be reduced.

7. D is the answer. Lucia can consent to split gifts even though she is not an owner of the property. No gift tax will be paid for these gifts to the children's trust because David and Lucia still have most of their unified credits to use to offset any gift tax that would be owed. The unified credit must be used first. The gifts will qualify for annual exclusions due to the Crummey provisions, and the gifts will reduce David and Lucia's unified credits.

8. C is the answer. David already has $6,000 of adjusted taxable gifts. The $200,000 gift of real estate is split between him and his wife, so David's gift is only $100,000. There are two beneficiaries of the trust, so two annual exclusions total $28,000. The taxable gift is, therefore, only $72,000. For the year in which David and Lucia give the stock, there is no taxable gift because the annual exclusions and gift-splitting eliminate any taxable gifts. Thus, the adjusted taxable gifts are $6,000 from previous years, plus the $72,000 from the commercial real estate gift, for a total of $78,000.

9. C is the answer. One-half of the property owned as tenants by the entirety and one-half of all jointly owned property would be included in David's gross estate. The entire value of the separate property including the life insurance would also be included in David's gross estate. As a result, the gross estate consists of the following amounts:

Joint assets and tenants by the entirety property

Home	$850,000
Vacation condo	430,000
Cars	35,000
Government and Muni bonds	350,000
Stock	550,000
Checking account	35,000
Total	$2,250,000
50% included in estate	1,125,000

Plus life insurance

Group term life	500,000
Whole life	200,000
Individual term life	1,000,000

Plus separate assets

Apartment building	600,000
Rental property (25% ownership)	200,000
Total gross estate	$3,625,000

10. A is the answer. The taxable estate would be the gross estate of $3,625,000, less funeral and administration expenses, less debts and mortgages, and less the marital deduction (net value of assets passing to surviving spouse) which is calculated as follows:

Total gross estate	$3,625,000
Less:	
Funeral and estate admin expenses	(30,000)
Debts	
Home mortgage (50%)	(50,000)
Vacation condo (50%)	(90,000)
Credit cards (50%)	(1,500)
Apartment building (100%)	(150,000)
Marital deduction	
Home (50% of FMV – 50% of debt)	(375,000)
Vacation condo (50% of FMV – 50% of debt)	(125,000)
Cars (50%)	(17,500)
Government and Muni bonds (50%)	(175,000)
Stock (50%)	(275,000)
Checking account (50%)	(17,500)
Group term life (100%)	(500,000)
Whole life (100%)	(200,000)
Individual term life (100%)	(1,000,000)
Taxable estate	$618,500

11. C is the answer. Adjusted taxable gifts are added to the taxable estate to determine the tentative tax base. The estate tax rates begin at 18%, and the top marginal estate tax rate is 40% in 2015. The rate is applied to the tentative tax base to determine the tentative tax. The credit for foreign death taxes is subtracted from the tentative tax amount.

12. B is the answer. With a sprinkling provision, the trustee is given flexibility to allocate income and corpus according to the needs of beneficiaries. If one of the children suffers a health impairment, the trustee can direct most of the income and principal to that child, instead of making equal distributions. Trusts are not entitled to the standard deduction, regardless of whether they contain a sprinkling provision. The sprinkling provision is unrelated to the way in which assets and income come <u>into</u> a trust.

13. C is the answer. If the trustee distributed capital gains, the trust could not obtain a deduction for such a distribution. The trust receives deductions only for distributable net income actually distributed to beneficiaries. If the stock were sold when Laura enters college, the capital gains on the stock would be taxed to the trust, not to her. Dividends are taxed to the beneficiaries to whom they are distributed. A 2503(b) trust is not a short-term trust, so the grantor trust rules would not apply.

14. A is the answer. The alternate valuation date is six months after death and may be elected only when the overall estate taxes will be reduced. If the real estate or stock in David's estate decline in value following his death, the executor can elect the alternate valuation date because David's estate taxes will be reduced. Where one asset increases in value and another declines, the alternate valuation date can only be selected if there is a net decrease in value, and estate taxes will be reduced. If an asset is sold, as in (4), the sale price is used for the value. If David's entire estate passes to Lucia, the alternate valuation date cannot be selected because no reduction in estate taxes will result.

15. C is the answer. A deed and a revocable trust would give assets to the child at David's death but would not fulfill David's objective of allowing Lucia to enjoy the income. A power-of-appointment trust would not assure that any assets would pass to the child of a previous marriage because Lucia would be given the power to appoint the property. The QTIP trust would qualify for the marital deduction, provide Lucia with a life income, and still allow David to retain control over the eventual disposition of the asset.

UNSER CASE

Samuel Unser is 67 years of age, and his wife Claudia is 62. Samuel is a founder and one-third owner of Sure Alert Alarm Company, which designs, installs, and monitors security systems for residential and commercial users in several states. The company has been in operation for about 20 years. The company is valued at $7.5 million. All of the stock of Sure Alert Alarm Company is owned by Samuel and two other employees of the company, who own one-third each.

Samuel and Claudia have an annual income of $85,000, and their adjusted gross income is $79,000. Claudia works three days a week without pay at a local orphanage. She and Samuel have been involved with the orphanage for many years and have been frequent contributors to its fund-raising programs.

Samuel and Claudia have one child Bryan, who is 30 years old and unmarried. Samuel and Claudia feel that Bryan is not able to handle large sums of money and cannot manage financial matters responsibly.

Samuel and Claudia are joint owners of a personal residence, valued at $350,000. Samuel owns a sports car, valued at $50,000; and Samuel and Claudia together own two cars, valued at $40,000. The Unsers are joint owners of a portfolio of municipal bonds, valued at $200,000, and stock, valued at $100,000. The Unsers have purchased a joint and survivor annuity that pays Samuel $20,000 per year for life and $10,000 for life to his survivor.

Samuel is the owner of a whole life insurance policy that will pay Claudia a death benefit of $250,000 and has a cash value of $110,000. Samuel also is the owner of a universal life insurance policy that will pay a death benefit of $150,000, and he has group life insurance through his company with a face amount of $100,000. Claudia is the beneficiary of these policies. Samuel also owns a $200,000 universal life policy on Claudia. The policy has a cash value of $89,000, and Samuel is the beneficiary.

Claudia is the owner of a farm in Nebraska that was left to her by her parents. She rents the farm out to tenants, who pay her a portion of the income from their crop each year. The farm is worth $4 million.

Samuel's will provides that all of his stock will be placed in trust, with income payable to Claudia for her life, and at her death, the remainder will be paid to the local orphanage. The will names Claudia as the executor, and in the event of simultaneous death, provides that Claudia will be deemed to have survived him.

Claudia's will provides that the farm will be placed in trust, and income will be paid to Bryan for life. At his death, the trust income will be payable to Bryan's issue for their lives; if Bryan has no children, the income will be paid to the local orphanage in perpetuity.

The intestacy statute in the state where the Unsers live provides that one-half of probate property not distributed by will passes to the surviving spouse, and one-half passes to the decedent's children. The state also has a pretermitted heir statute and a statute providing a spousal elective share of one-half of probate property. The Unsers do not live in a community-property state.

UNSER CASE
APPLICATION QUESTIONS

1. Samuel Unser has fought repeatedly with his son Bryan and would like to see the orphanage receive all of his estate after Claudia's death. Which of the following statements correctly describes a problem with Samuel Unser's current estate plan that will tend to defeat this objective?

(Topic 55)

A. When Samuel dies, the cash value of the universal life insurance policy on Claudia's life will be includible in his gross estate.

B. The pretermitted heir statute may render Samuel's will contestable because Bryan has not been mentioned.

C. Samuel's will lacks a residuary clause.

D. If Samuel and Claudia are killed in a common disaster, Samuel's stock will pass under Claudia's will.

E. The trust for Claudia creates a terminable interest and will not qualify for the marital deduction in Samuel's estate.

2. Assume for purposes of this question that Samuel Unser decided to make a gift of his stock in Sure Alert Alarm Company to an irrevocable trust for his niece Sally, who is 12 years old. Which of the following statements concerning this gift is correct?

(Topic 56)

A. Samuel can retain the right to vote the stock, without the value of the stock being includible in his gross estate at his death.

B. If Samuel establishes a 2503(c) trust for Sally, she will pay tax on all of the accumulated income distributed to her when she reaches age 21.

C. Since Samuel cannot disinherit Bryan by will, Samuel cannot accomplish the same purpose by placing all of his stock in this trust for Sally.

D. If the gift is made within three years of Samuel's death, the value of the stock placed in the trust will be includible in Samuel's gross estate.

E. If the stock pays no dividends and the trustee cannot sell it, the gift will not qualify for the gift tax annual exclusion.

3. Assume for this question that Samuel died today. Which of the following statements concerning the amount attributable to the joint and survivor annuity that would be included in Samuel's gross estate is correct?

(Topic 59)

A. No amount attributable to the annuity is includible in Samuel's gross estate.

B. The includible amount is the number of years of Claudia's life expectancy multiplied by $10,000, plus the number of years of Samuel's life expectancy determined just before he died multiplied by $20,000.

C. The includible amount is the purchase price of the annuity less the two-life remainder factor, using the applicable federal midterm interest rate.

D. The includible amount is the present value of the future payments to Claudia.

E. The includible amount is the purchase price less any payments received.

4. Assume that shortly after Samuel Unser made Claudia a joint owner of his stock in Sure Alert Alarm Company, he suffered a stroke and was hospitalized. Samuel incurred $10,000 of medical bills before he died. His estate administration expenses will be $35,000. Which of the following statements concerning deductions for federal income and estate tax returns is (are) correct?

(Topic 59)

(1) Samuel's executor should deduct the medical expenses on Samuel's individual federal income tax return, rather than on the federal estate tax return.

(2) Administration expenses for Samuel's estate should be deducted on the federal estate tax return, rather than on the estate's federal income tax return.

(3) The executor will be able to redeem stock in Sure Alert Alarm Company under a Sec. 303 redemption in an amount equal to the medical bills and administration expenses.

A. (1) only
B. (2) only
C. (1) and (2) only
D. (2) and (3) only
E. (1), (2), and (3)

5. Samuel is considering a buy-sell agreement with the other two owners of Sure Alert Alarm Company. Which of the following statements concerning the use of a buy-sell agreement by the three owners of this company is correct?

(Topic 60)

A. If the executor is required to sell Samuel's stock under the terms of a buy-sell agreement, the estate will not qualify for a Sec. 303 redemption.

B. If the corporation purchases all of Samuel's stock, the payment to Samuel will be treated as a dividend for federal income tax purposes.

C. A stock-redemption plan would be more equitable than a cross-purchase agreement if there is a substantial difference in ages among Samuel and the other owners.

D. Under a cross-purchase agreement, the insurance purchased by the other owners on Samuel's life must be included in Samuel's gross estate.

E. Samuel's estate will still be able to qualify for the installment payment of estate taxes under Sec. 6166.

6. Assume for purposes of this question that Samuel Unser's will provides that Claudia is to receive all income from the trust, and that she can invade principal to the extent needed for her health, maintenance, and support. Which of the following statements concerning this trust is correct?

(Topic 61)

A. The assets placed in the trust for Claudia will qualify for the marital deduction on Samuel's estate tax return.

B. The power given to Claudia is a general power of appointment.

C. Claudia could file a qualified disclaimer of the power of appointment in favor of Bryan, directing that the income and principal pass to him.

D. At Claudia's death, no amount attributable to the trust or her power of appointment will be includible in her gross estate.

E. Samuel's estate will be entitled to a charitable deduction equal to the remainder interest in the trust.

7. Which of the following statements concerning potential problems with Claudia Unser's estate plan is correct?

(Topic 62)

A. If Claudia dies today, the trust provision for the orphanage will violate the rule against perpetuities.

B. If Claudia dies today, the trust provision concerning income for Bryan's issue will violate the rule against perpetuities.

C. Claudia's will needs a presumption of survivorship clause which states that in case of simultaneous death, Samuel is presumed to survive her.

D. Claudia's will does not have a provision allowing for Samuel's elective share as a surviving spouse.

E. Claudia's will does not make use of any of her unified credit.

8. Samuel is considering establishing a revocable trust for his niece Sally. Which of the following statements correctly describe(s) advantages of the revocable trust?

(Topic 62)

(1) Assets placed in the trust will avoid probate.

(2) Assets in the trust are not subject to the elective share of a surviving spouse.

(3) A will contest will not affect assets placed in the trust.

(4) Samuel will not have to give up any voting rights in the stock placed in the trust.

A. (1) only
B. (4) only
C. (2) and (3) only
D. (3) and (4) only
E. (1), (2), (3), and (4)

9. The Unsers would like to do more to benefit the local orphanage. Samuel would also like to maintain Claudia's lifestyle by providing her with income for life. In addition, Samuel would like to minimize taxes and transfer costs to accomplish these objectives. Given these objectives and constraints, which of the following lifetime gifts by Samuel and Claudia would be the most appropriate?

(Topic 64)

A. Outright gift of stock to the orphanage

B. A gift of stock to a charitable pooled-income fund for the orphanage

C. A gift of stock to a charitable remainder annuity trust for the orphanage

D. A gift of stock to a charitable remainder unitrust for the orphanage

E. A gift of stock to a charitable lead trust for the orphanage

10. Which of the following statements concerning the Unser's planning for lifetime gifts to a qualified charity is correct?

(Topic 64)

A. A gift by the Unsers of the remainder interest in their personal residence would not qualify as a deductible charitable contribution.

B. The income tax advantages to the Unsers of charitable gifts are the same, whether the gift is a lifetime or a testamentary gift.

C. If the Unsers made a bargain sale of appreciated stock from their jointly owned portfolio, they would be required to report some capital gains.

D. If Samuel contributed stock in Sure Alert Alarm Company to a charitable remainder unitrust, and the trust sold the stock the following year, Samuel would have to report substantial capital gains.

E. A gift of stock to the orphanage would be valued for gift tax purposes at the Unsers' adjusted cost basis.

11. Assume that the local orphanage to which the Unsers want to contribute is a qualified public charity, that the Unsers' income is as stated in the case facts, and that the Unsers make no special elections on their income tax returns. What is the maximum charitable deduction available this year to the Unsers on their federal income tax return for gifts of stock in the Sure Alert Alarm Company?

(Topic 64)

A. $20,000   D. $42,500
B. $23,700   E. $79,000
C. $39,500

12. Claudia Unser believes that the farm is too much trouble for her son Bryan or a trustee to manage effectively. She would like to use the farm for making a contribution to the orphanage, but she also wants to provide for Bryan since Samuel may not do so. Claudia does not think that she needs the income from the farm, since she will be provided for by Samuel. In view of these objectives, which of the following techniques would be most appropriate for Claudia Unser?

(Topic 64)

A. An outright charitable gift
B. A wealth replacement trust
C. A charitable lead trust
D. A bargain sale
E. A dynasty trust

13. If Samuel executes a will, leaving his entire estate to the orphanage, which of the following laws could help to protect Bryan from being disinherited by Samuel Unser?

(Topic 72)

(1) A right to elect against the will
(2) A pretermitted heir statute
(3) A family allowance statute
(4) A statute eliminating dower and courtesy

A. (3) only
B. (1) and (2) only
C. (1) and (3) only
D. (2) and (4) only
E. (1), (2), (3), and (4)

14. If Samuel Unser dies without changing his will and before any change in asset values, which of the following postmortem techniques would be most likely to reduce the federal estate taxes for his estate?

(Topic 72)

    A. A qualified disclaimer executed by Bryan

    B. A QTIP election by the executor

    C. A disclaimer trust

    D. Selection of the estate's tax year

    E. Election by the executor of special-use valuation

15. Assume that Samuel Unser decided to make Claudia a joint owner of his stock in Sure Alert Alarm Company shortly before his death. Which of the following postmortem techniques would be the most appropriate to modify Samuel's estate plan to take greater advantage of Samuel's unified credit?

(Topic 72)

    A. A disclaimer trust

    B. A qualified disclaimer of the joint interest in the residence

    C. A QTIP election

    D. An election against the will

    E. Electing the alternate valuation date

UNSER CASE
ANSWERS AND EXPLANATIONS

1. **C** is the answer. Samuel's will lacks a residuary clause, so the property not specifically disposed of in the will passes under the intestacy statute. Bryan will be entitled to one-half of any property not mentioned. While the stock is most of the estate and is specifically mentioned, Bryan will be able to inherit one-half of the sports car and the cash value in the universal life insurance policy on Claudia's life. When Samuel dies, the replacement cost of the universal life insurance policy on Claudia's life will be includible in his gross estate. The pretermitted heir statute does not provide grounds for contesting a will, and omission of Bryan's name from the will does not render Samuel's will contestable. If Samuel and Claudia are killed in a common disaster, Samuel's stock will not pass under Claudia's will. He is the sole owner of the stock, so the stock must still pass through Samuel's estate.

2. **E** is the answer. If the stock pays no dividends and the trustee cannot sell it, the gift will not qualify for the gift tax annual exclusion. By giving the trustee the power to sell the stock, the gift could qualify for the annual exclusion. The income accumulated in the 2503(c) trust is taxed to the trust and not to Sally. Samuel can disinherit Bryan by placing all of his stock in this trust for Sally. Even though the gift is made within three years of Samuel's death, the value of the stock will not be includible in Samuel's gross estate. If Samuel retains a right to vote the stock, it will be includible in his gross estate.

3. **D** is the answer. In computing the gross estate, the present value of the future payments that will be made from an annuity to the decedent's spouse is includible. If the annuity payments end at the decedent's death, nothing is included in the deceased's gross estate.

4. **A** is the answer. Samuel Unser's estate will include one-half of the value of the stock that was placed in joint names with his wife Claudia, and this stock will pass to Claudia by operation of law. The value of the stock, therefore, qualifies for the marital deduction. The additional property in Samuel Unser's estate will pass by intestacy because there is no disposition in the will. This additional property, such as the sports car and the life insurance on Claudia, will pass under the intestacy statute one-half to Claudia and one-half to Bryan. It appears that the property passing to Bryan will not exceed the unified credit, so there is no reason to deduct the medical expenses on the federal estate tax return. The medical expenses are deductible for federal income tax purposes to the extent that they exceed 10% of adjusted gross income. This partial deduction is still better than no deduction on the estate tax return. Similarly, the deduction for administration expenses will be of no value on the estate tax return and should be deducted on the estate's income tax return if it can be used there.

5. **A** is the answer. If the executor is required to sell Samuel's stock under the terms of a buy-sell agreement, the estate will not qualify for a Sec. 303 redemption because the value of the stock included in Samuel's gross estate will no longer exceed the 35% requirement. If the corporation purchases all of Samuel's stock, the payment to Samuel will not be treated as a dividend for federal income tax purposes. A complete redemption avoids dividend treatment. A cross-purchase buy-sell agreement is more equitable than a stock-redemption plan if there is a substantial difference in the

ages among Samuel and the other owners. The reason is that for younger owners, the cost of life insurance on the lives of older owners is much greater. If the corporation pays the premiums, an older owner is, in effect, subsidizing younger owners. Under a cross-purchase agreement, the life insurance purchased by the other two owners on Samuel's life will not be included in Samuel's gross estate because he held no incidents of ownership in those policies.

6. D is the answer. At Claudia's death, no amount attributable to the trust or her power of appointment will be includible in her gross estate because she does not have a general power of appointment. The assets placed in the trust for Claudia do not qualify for the marital deduction on Samuel's estate tax return because Claudia has only a terminable interest. The power given to Claudia is only a limited or special power of appointment because the power can be exercised only according to an ascertainable standard. Claudia could not file a qualified disclaimer of the power of appointment in favor of Bryan, directing that the income and principal pass to him, because a qualified disclaimer cannot have any control over the disposition of the property. If Claudia disclaims, the trust assets will probably pass to the orphanage. Samuel's estate will not be entitled to a charitable deduction for the remainder interest because the value of this interest is unascertainable.

7. B is the answer. The trust that continues in perpetuity for the orphanage does not violate the rule against perpetuities because the trust is established for a charity. However, the trust for Bryan's issue violates the rule against perpetuities because it must end within 21 years and 9 months after the death of a beneficiary who is alive when the trust is created. Bryan is the only beneficiary alive, and the trust for Bryan's issue could continue far past this 21 years and nine months. If Bryan has issue when he dies, the trust will violate the rule against perpetuities. Claudia's will could include a presumption of survivorship clause, but the clause should state that in case of simultaneous death, Claudia is presumed to survive Samuel. Otherwise, Samuel and Claudia have will provisions that are inconsistent and could lead to litigation. Claudia's will cannot provide for Samuel's elective share as a surviving spouse because this elective share is a right that exists, regardless of the will provisions. The trust for Bryan will make use of the unified credit because the farm (worth $4 million) will be placed in the trust.

8. E is the answer. Assets placed in a revocable trust will avoid probate. This advantage is one of the most commonly mentioned reasons for creating a revocable trust. Assets in the trust are also not subject to the elective share of a surviving spouse because the assets pass outside the will. Similarly, a will contest does not affect assets placed in the trust because the assets do not pass under the will, nor under the intestacy laws if the will is overturned. Samuel will not have to give up any voting rights or other ownership rights over stock or other assets in the trust because the trust remains revocable up to the time of his death.

9. B is the answer. By giving the stock to a charitable pooled-income fund, Samuel could provide for a life income to be paid to Claudia, and the orphanage would receive the remainder at her death. Samuel and Claudia would receive the charitable deduction for the value of the remainder interest, which would reduce their income taxes. The transfer costs would be low because the charity establishes the pooled-income fund. With a pooled-income fund, the Unsers would avoid the cost to establish a charitable trust.

Appendix – Unser Case – Answers and Explanations

10. C is the answer. If the Unsers made a bargain sale of appreciated stock from their jointly owned portfolio, they would still have to report some capital gains. Since Samuel Unser was a founder, his basis in the stock is probably low, and the amount of capital gain would depend upon the price at which the stock was sold to the charity. As the owner, Sam would have to assign a portion of his basis to the sale and a portion to the gift. A gift by the Unsers of the remainder interest in their personal residence would qualify as a deductible charitable contribution. The income tax advantages to the Unsers of lifetime charitable gifts are greater than a testamentary gift because testamentary charitable gifts are not deductible against income. If Samuel contributed stock in Sure Alert Alarm Company to a charitable remainder unitrust, and the trust sold the stock the following year, Samuel would not have to report capital gains. The gain would be taxed to the trust.

11. B is the answer. The Sure Alert Alarm Company stock is long-term capital gain property, so the Unser's deduction is limited to 30% of adjusted gross income. Their AGI is $79,000, so 30% is $23,700. The special election to have the gift valued at the taxpayer's adjusted basis would allow them to increase the deduction to 50% of AGI, but if the Unser's adjusted basis is very low, they would not receive much of a deduction for their contribution of the stock.

12. B is the answer. A wealth replacement trust is essentially a life insurance trust with a Crummey power. Claudia can make a gift of the farm and take charitable deductions on her federal income tax returns. The tax savings may be used to make annual contributions to the life insurance trust to pay the premiums on the policy on Claudia's life. The death proceeds will, in effect, replace the value of the farmland donated to charity. The trustee and Bryan will not have to manage the property, and Claudia can make gifts of land over several years to spread out the deductions. A bargain sale will not provide as much to Bryan or to the charity. The outright gift to charity produces only deductions and no replacement of wealth for Bryan. A charitable lead trust provides an income stream to the charity and only a remainder to Bryan. Claudia does not really need the very large charitable deduction that is generated in the year the trust is established.

13. A is the answer. The right to elect against the will is a spousal right allowing a surviving spouse to elect to receive his or her intestate share if the will attempts to disinherit the spouse (or provides for a distribution to the spouse of an amount that is less than the spouse's intestate share). Since Bryan is not Samuel's spouse, a law allowing a spousal right to elect against the will does not protect him. A pretermitted heir statute protects an after-born child but will not protect Bryan. A family allowance statute will protect a surviving spouse and children and should protect Bryan to some extent. A statute eliminating dower and courtesy removes the right of a surviving spouse and will not help Bryan.

14. B is the answer. Samuel Unser's will leaves the Sure Alert Alarm Company stock in trust, with income payable to his wife for life and the remainder to an orphanage. Since Samuel's wife does not have the ability to pass the stock to anyone, the stock is a terminable interest and does not qualify for the marital deduction. The interest given to the trust apparently would not satisfy the requirements for a charitable remainder trust because the will does not require annual payments of at least 5% of the initial value of the trust assets. Consequently, the charitable deduction is also not available. The executor could avoid paying taxes on the assets immediately by making the QTIP election. The marital deduction would then be preserved, and the assets would be includible in Claudia's gross estate.

15. B is the answer. A disclaimer of the joint interest in the residence would mean that Claudia disclaims her interest in the joint tenancy with Samuel, and under the intestacy laws of the state where the Unsers live, one-half of this property would pass to Bryan. The property passing to Bryan would qualify for the unified credit. Since there was no disclaimer trust established in Samuel's will, a disclaimer trust cannot be established after Samuel's death. Under the elective share statute in effect in the Unser's state, an election against the will would mean that Claudia would receive one-half of Samuel's estate outright. The result of such an election would be that more property would probably qualify for the marital deduction, rather than for the unified credit. Similarly, the QTIP election is used to qualify more property for the marital deduction.

TINGEY CASE

Earl Tingey became 58 years of age in March of this year and has $75,000 in his regular IRA (on April 1 of this year, after contributions for last year) and $35,000 in taxable savings accounts. He is the sole owner and president of Tingey Manufacturing, Inc. (an S corporation), which generates between $150,000 and $200,000 in pretax cash flow per year before owner compensation. He would like to leave the business to his two sons (ages 22 and 26), but neither has expressed a current desire to be part of the business, and Earl wonders if they would be willing to put the necessary time into the business to continue its success. He would like some type of supervision of his sons if he left the business to them when he died.

The building that houses the business operations is owned by Earl and his wife (who is age 56) as joint tenants and is free of any liens. The building was recently appraised at $400,000, and the Tingeys believe the value of the building will continue to appreciate as the population of the area increases. The remainder of the Tingeys' estate consists of $250,000 in personal property (home, furniture, cars – all with no debt). Earl has a term life insurance policy with a $250,000 death benefit. Mrs. Tingey has no life insurance coverage. Mrs. Tingey has no interest in continuing the business if Earl should die prematurely. The Tingeys do not live in a community-property state.

TINGEY CASE
APPLICATION QUESTIONS

1. Which of the following strategies will be the best for ensuring continued income for Mrs. Tingey after Earl's death?

(Topic 62)

A. Invest in higher-risk-return assets (individual stocks) to increase growth in the IRA and taxable accounts.

B. Create a QTIP or bypass trust under Earl's will to own the stock of Tingey Manufacturing, Inc and to pay all income to Mrs. Tingey.

C. Have Mrs. Tingey disclaim ownership of the corporation stock left to her in Earl's will.

D. Transfer ownership of the life insurance policy to an irrevocable life insurance trust.

E. Create a GRAT and transfer the building that houses the business to the GRAT during Earl's lifetime.

2. Which of the following statements describes the primary limit on lifetime gifts of the corporation stock and of ownership interests in the building to the sons (assuming they want it)?

(Topic 67)

A. The Tingeys need income from the property and business.

B. The Tingeys will have the expense of gift taxes.

C. Such gifts will not qualify for minority interest discounts.

D. The sons will owe taxes on a sale of the business.

E. The interests held by the sons will prevent a stock redemption.

3. If Earl Tingey passed his stock in Tingey Manufacturing on to his two sons at his death, the value of the stock could be sheltered from federal estate tax under which of the following circumstances?

(Topic 68)

A. The value of the stock does not exceed $3 million.

B. The sons do not also receive interests in the building.

C. The stock makes up at least 35% of Earl Tingey's adjusted gross estate.

D. The building makes up at least 50% of Earl Tingey's adjusted gross estate.

E. There is some remaining applicable credit.

TINGEY CASE
ANSWERS AND EXPLANATIONS

1. B is the answer. The QTIP or bypass trust will allow Mrs. Tingey to receive the benefit of the business income for the remainder of her life, and the business can then pass to Earl's two sons. Higher-risk securities are not appropriate for the Tingeys at this stage of life. The GRAT is used to reduce transfer taxes on an estate through lifetime gifts and will not increase income for Mrs. Tingey. The other two options will not affect Mrs. Tingey's income.

2. A is the answer. With only a small amount in an IRA, the Tingeys need income from the operation/sale of the business and business assets to fund their retirement income. Gift taxes and taxes owed by the sons could be overcome by using the unified credit and corporate distributions. The gifts would qualify for minority discounts.

3. E is the answer. The value of the business will be sheltered from estate taxes to the extent Earl has any remaining applicable credit. The other answer options: A, B, C, and D are incorrect, as they refer to the requirement for the qualified family-owned business exclusion, which expired as of December 31, 2003.

LYTLE CASE

Ann Lytle, age 70, has come to you for help after the recent death of her husband Martin. Martin passed away unexpectedly at the age of 69 just two months earlier. The Lytles did not have any trusts in place, and Martin's will left everything to Ann upon his death. The executor of the will is the Lytle's oldest child Kyle. Kyle is 42, and he has two younger sisters: Cynthia, age 39, and Shannon, age 33. The Lytles have been married for 45 years and owned their home jointly with right of survivorship. The S corporation stock was owned solely by Martin. Ann is listed as the sole beneficiary of Martin's IRA.

Assets		Liabilities	
Checking Accounts	$6,700	Auto Loan (8%)	$5,700
Certificate of Deposit (maturing in 3 months, 5%)	$24,000	2nd Mortgage	$6,200
Martin's IRA	$324,000		
Ann's IRA	$36,000		
Personal Residence	$180,000		
S Corporation Stock (calculated value)	$460,000		
2 Automobiles (Kelly blue book)	$20,000		
Other Personal Assets	$55,000		
Total Assets	$1,105,700	Net Worth	$1,093,800

A review of the Lytles' expenses over the past year shows that they were spending $4,500 per month, after taxes, on food, clothing, travel, and household expenses, excluding payments on the car and mortgage. Ann estimates that her continued living expenses have dropped by 25%, but the drop will be partially offset by $250 per month for Medigap insurance that had been unnecessary while Martin was working because his employer paid the entire cost of health insurance. The company had also paid for group term life insurance (Ann is beneficiary) on its employees equal to 3 times their annual salary, up to $100,000.

Martin had worked at Spectrum, Inc., the company he founded with the two other shareholders 20 years earlier, until he died. Because of his continued employment, he had never applied for Social Security. At his death, Martin's stock amounted to 40% of the outstanding shares. The company had in place an entity redemption agreement, funded with $500,000 of life insurance, with the company as beneficiary. According to the agreement, the redemption is to take place upon the death of a shareholder-officer at a rate calculated, using the average sales of the corporation over the past 24 months. This formula results in a price of $46 for each of Martin's 10,000 shares.

Ann believes that the Lytles' children are well enough off financially that they do not need any inheritance from her. However, she has six grandchildren, ranging in age from 18 down to 2, with the possibility of more to come. She would like to help finance their college education in a fair way. Ann is also very charity-minded and has donated much of her free time to various community causes. She would like to continue her current financial support of these organizations after her death. Ann is very concerned that she not become a burden financially or emotionally on her grown children. Ann's health is excellent, and she foresees living well into her nineties, like both of her parents. Ann's combined federal and state income tax rate is 20%, and she expects it to continue at that rate for the foreseeable future. Ann lives in a non-community-property state. Ann has never had any reason to file a gift tax return in the past. Ann has no experience in investing and wants to have as little involvement as possible.

Inflation rate for the foreseeable future	3%
30-yr. Treasury bond yield	6%
Corporate AAA bond rate	8%
Federal midterm rate	5.83%

LYTLE CASE
APPLICATION QUESTIONS

1. Which of the following assets will be subject to probate after Martin's death?

(Topic 54)

A. Residence
B. IRA
C. Life insurance proceeds
D. Personal assets

2. Which of the following would not be an important provision to consider when revising Ann's will?

(Topic 55)

A. Specific bequests of personal valuables to each of the children
B. The creation of a trust for the benefit of Ann's minor grandchildren, funded by a portion of Ann's assets
C. Specific instructions with regard to funeral arrangements
D. Contingent fiduciary appointments

3. If Ann decides to make gifts to each of her 6 grandchildren, which of the following statements is not true?

(Topic 56)

A. Gifts of up to $70,000 per child may be made to qualified state tuition savings programs, without incurring gift tax.
B. Ann can avoid gift tax on gifts in excess of $14,000 for her oldest grandchildren by the direct payment of tuition to the university where each grandchild is attending.
C. Gifts made under the UTMA, with Ann as custodian, may be included in Ann's estate at her death.
D. Transfers to trusts for the benefit of the grandchildren that will only be available to them upon reaching age 21 will not qualify for the $14,000 exclusion because these are gifts of a future interest.
E. For some of the grandchildren, the kiddie tax rules will apply to income from the gifts if the income is in excess of $2,100 (2015).

4. Which of the following statements concerning planning for the possibility of Ann's incapacity are true?

(Topic 58)

(1) With a living will, Ann appoints family members who can make decisions with regard to Ann's health care in case of any incapacity.

(2) A durable power of attorney will allow Ann's children to reduce her taxable estate by continuing a lifetime gifting program after Ann becomes incapacitated.

(3) A nondurable power of attorney ends in the case of incapacity.

(4) A revocable living trust can provide for contingent trustees who could consummate transactions in case of Ann's incapacity.

    A. (1) and (2) only
    B. (2) and (3) only
    C. (1) and (4) only
    D. (2), (3), and (4) only
    E. (1), (2), (3), and (4)

5. Which of the following statements is true concerning the corporate stock redemption?

(Topic 60)

A. The redemption will be treated as a dividend unless the proceeds are used to pay estate taxes.

B. Ann receives the stock redemption amount tax-free because it is treated as capital gain, and Ann's basis is stepped up at Martin's death.

C. The redemption will result in a reduction in the value of the corporation.

D. Half of the stock will be treated as already owned by Ann and will not receive an adjustment to basis.

E. The stock of the other shareholders will be attributed to Martin's estate under the attribution rules.

6. If Ann transfers her personal residence to a qualified personal residence trust with her three children as beneficiaries and retains a life interest, what are the tax consequences of the transfer? (Assume a $12,000 per year rental value.)

(Topic 63)

A. The home will not be included in Ann's estate at her death.

B. The gift tax before credits will be equal to $7,461.

C. The gift tax before credits will be equal to $14,726.

D. The gift tax before credits will be equal to $38,800.

E. There will be no gift or estate tax consequences.

LYTLE CASE
ANSWERS AND EXPLANATIONS

1. D is the answer. Assets that pass from the decedent to the beneficiary by operation of law are not subject to probate. All assets held jointly with rights of survivorship pass by operation of law and avoid probate. Also, contracts or accounts with designated beneficiaries like the IRA or life insurance pass by operation of law and are not subject to probate. The remainder of the estate must pass through the probate process.

2. C is the answer. Specific funeral arrangements should be left with family members because will provisions may not be available in time for proper planning, and funeral arrangements could be delayed. However, specific bequests of personal property will prevent valuable items from being included in the residuary and sold to pay expenses or cash bequests. The availability of an alternate executor is extremely important in case of the death or refusal of the first designee. Also, funding a trust for minor children protects their interests and allows for some direction in the use of funds. Further, by using a specified percentage of assets rather than a set amount, the executor will not run out of funds before all bequests are satisfied.

3. D is the answer. Gifts made to trusts governed by Sec. 2503(c) of the Code will qualify as present interests rather than future interests if the minor can access the trust corpus at age 21, and the restrictions on that access are no more than allowed by state law. The tax law allows gifts to state tuition savings programs to be averaged over 5 years, thus allowing a gift of $70,000 to be spread over 5 years (using up the exclusion in each of the five years) even though it is all paid in the first year. Gifts directly to education or health care providers for educational or medical expenses can be made in any amount, without affecting the $14,000 annual exclusion or incurring gift tax. If a donor gives gifts to a minor under the UTMA and also acts as the custodian, if the donor-custodian dies before the minor beneficiary reaches the age of majority, the assets in trust are included in the gross estate of the donor-custodian.

4. D is the answer. A durable power of attorney provides the designated attorney-in-fact with the power to consummate transactions that the client cannot consummate due to incapacity. This allows for deathbed gifts that will be excluded from the estate. A contingent trustee may also have the same powers over the trust assets in the case of the primary trustee's (client's) incapacity. A nondurable power of attorney differs from a durable power of attorney because it ceases with the incapacity of the client. A living will can give health care professionals instructions with regard to life support, but it does not appoint a surrogate decision maker. To permit the designation of a family member to make decisions on a variety of health care issues, most states allow for a health care proxy (essentially, a durable power of attorney for health care decisions.) A living will is usually limited to decisions regarding life-sustaining treatment and is, therefore, not useful for other kinds of incapacity.

5. B is the answer. When stock consisting of the entire interest of the decedent is redeemed, it is treated as a capital gain transaction, whether or not the amount is used for estate taxes. Martin's stock would be included entirely in Martin's estate, from which the stock would be transferred through the unlimited marital deduction to Ann, and its basis to Ann would be the stock's FMV. If

$460,000 is considered the FMV of the stock on the date of Martin's death (and is reasonable), then the amount received by Ann would be equal to her basis in the stock. Thus, there would be no capital gain for Ann.

6. C is the answer. The value of this kind of gift is usually the full value of the property because the retained life interest is valued at zero for gifts to a trust for the benefit of family members. However, qualified personal residence trusts are an exception, where the retained life interest is valued using normal methods. The value of the retained interest is the present value of $12,000 received each year for 16 years (Ann's life expectancy), valued at 7.0% (120% of the federal midterm rate), or $113,360. This makes the value of the gift $66,640 ($180,000 personal residence minus $113,360). The gift is not reduced for the annual exclusion because the gifts of remainder interests are future-interest gifts. The tax on the gift from the unified gift and estate tax tables is 26% of the amount over $60,000 plus $13,000, or $14,726. To obtain the gift and estate tax benefits of a qualified personal residence trust, however, Ann needed to make the trust for a specified term of years. Since she retained a life interest, the value of the home will be included in her gross estate for federal estate tax purposes, and it will be included at the date-of-death value. The adjusted taxable gift will be reduced to zero to remove the double tax.

BEALS CASE

James and Anne Beals had been married for 24 years and are now separated. James, who is 55 years of age, is a funeral director and is the owner of two funeral parlors. Anne is 51 years of age and owns and operates a graphic design business. The couple has two children: Ronald, age 16, and Christine, age 13. All of the Beals are in good health. James and Anne have simple wills, leaving their entire estates to each other.

Anne Beals started her graphic design business about 8 years ago. The business is called Beals Designs, and Anne is the sole owner. In order to expand her business, Anne took out a loan about five years ago from the Mellon Bank in the amount of $50,000, and James Beals cosigned the loan. Anne has paid back $5,000 of the original loan amount, leaving a balance of $45,000. Anne makes monthly payments on the loan. The business has done well, and Anne nets about $50,000 annually after paying her expenses.

Anne has three employees. She has adopted a profit-sharing Keogh plan for herself and her employees. Although the plan offers several different investment options, Anne has her account balance invested through the plan in guaranteed investment contracts (GICs). In addition, she has invested IRA money in a balanced mutual fund. She describes herself as a conservative investor. Anne has named James as the beneficiary of her profit-sharing plan and of her IRA.

James Beals has moved out of the home that he owns with Anne as tenants by the entirety. He is currently renting an apartment for $800 per month. Since Anne and James have agreed that she will keep the house in her name, Anne makes the monthly mortgage payment. James and Anne bought the house for $80,000 and have spent $40,000 on capital improvements.

The children will remain with Anne and spend vacations with James. Anne is currently receiving child support and alimony from James. James earns approximately $120,000 annually from his business. He is also the owner of two buildings that are rented to Beals Funeral Home, Inc. One building was purchased 22 years ago for $175,000, and the other was built 12 years ago for a cost of $350,000. Each building is now worth approximately $750,000. James is the sole stockholder and president of Beals Funeral Home, Inc., which is an S corporation.

Beals Funeral Home, Inc. has a 401(k) plan that matches employee contributions at a rate of 50 cents for each dollar contributed by an employee, up to 6% of each employee's compensation. The company has eight employees, in addition to James. The 401(k) plan offers different investment options, and James has invested his 401(k) plan contributions in a balanced mutual fund. James describes himself as a conservative investor. James has named Anne the beneficiary of his 401(k) plan account balance and of his IRA account assets.

James Beals owns a whole life insurance policy with a face amount of $200,000 and term life insurance in the amount of $300,000. Anne Beals owns a universal life insurance policy with a face amount of $200,000. James and Anne have named each other as beneficiaries of these policies. James has a disability income insurance policy that will pay him $1,000 monthly if he is disabled.

<u>Appendix – Beals Case</u>

Since James Beals is a funeral director, he would like to have a lavish funeral. The costs of his funeral will be in the range of $40,000. If he dies today, the administrative expenses for his estate are expected to be $30,000.

JAMES BEALS
Personal Balance Sheet

Assets			Liabilities	
Invested Assets				
Cash/Cash Equivalents	$14,500		Auto Loan	$7,000
Marketable Securities	$250,000		Mortgage*	$200,000
Business Interest	$1,800,000		Lawyers' Fees	$8,000
Life Ins. Cash Value	$35,000			$215,000
	$2,099,500			
Use Assets				
Business Real Estate	$1,500,000			
Personal Property	$45,000		Net Worth	$3,659,500
Automobiles	$30,000			
	$1,575,000			
Retirement Plan Assets				
IRA	$25,000			
401(k)	$175,000			
Total Assets	$200,000		**Total Liabilities and Net Worth**	$3,874,500

* Business real estate: 15-year @ 9%

ANNE BEALS
Personal Balance Sheet

Assets			Liabilities	
Invested Assets				
Cash/Cash Equivalents	$2,500		Auto Loan	$7,500
Marketable Securities	$150,000		Lawyers' Fees	$7,000
Business Interest	$300,000		Business Loan	$45,000
Life Ins. Cash Value	$30,000		Mortgage*	$50,000*
	$482,500			$109,500
Use Assets				
Primary Residence	$200,000			
Personal Property	$52,500		Net Worth	$750,000
Automobiles	$25,000			
	$277,500			
Retirement Plan Assets				
IRA	$24,500			
Profit-Sharing Plan	$75,000			
	$99,500			
Total Assets	$859,500		**Total Liabilities and Net Worth**	$859,500

* Principal residence: originally, 30-year @ 8%

JAMES BEALS
Projected Monthly Cash Flow Statement

Cash Inflows

Salary – S corporation	$8,000
Distribution – S corporation	2,000
Net rental income	5,000
Interest income (tax-exempt)	400
Dividend income	250
Interest income (taxable)	200

Outflows

Rent	$ 800
Food	150
Utilities	125
Transportation (gas, oil, maintenance)	150
Car payment	400
Clothing	250
Entertainment	400
Travel	500
Life insurance	200
Disability insurance	100
Auto insurance	150
Family gifts	500
Charitable gifts	300
Mortgage (business property: PITI)	2,250
Federal income tax	2,800
State income tax	600
Social Security and Medicare taxes	600
401(k) contribution	700
Miscellaneous	100
Alimony	700
Child support	500

ANNE BEALS
Projected Monthly Cash Flow Statement

Cash Inflows

Business income	$4,200
Interest income (tax-exempt)	500
Dividend income	50
Interest income (taxable)	100
Alimony *	700
Child support	500

* Payments cease upon Anne's death or remarriage.

Outflows

Mortgage	$1,100
Food	350
Utilities	175
Transportation (gas, oil, maintenance)	130
Car payment	300
Clothing	350
Entertainment	250
Travel	250
Life insurance	150
Auto insurance	150
Family gifts	300
Charitable gifts	100
Federal income tax	900
State income tax	200
Social Security and Medicare taxes	600
Miscellaneous	100

JAMES BEALS – Investment Portfolio

Common Stock	Fair Market Value
Disney	$ 15,000
DuPont	10,200
Exxon	20,000
Intel	41,400
Lucent	16,200
PepsiCo	12,800
Toys R Us	11,200
Beals Funeral Home, Inc.	1,800,000
Common stock mutual fund	13,200
Balanced fund (401(k))	175,000
Municipal Bonds	
Dreyfus General Municipal Bond Fund	$ 70,000
Bonds	
Vanguard High Yield Corporate Bond Fund	$ 40,000
Income Fund (IRA)	25,000
Cash and Equivalents	
Cash	$ 4,500
Cash equivalents, incl. money markets	10,000
TOTAL	$2,264,500

ANNE BEALS – Investment Portfolio

Common Stock	Fair Market Value
Cisco Systems	$ 40,000
Common stock mutual fund	10,000
Balanced fund (IRA)	24,500
Municipal Bonds	
Merrill Lynch Long Term Municipal Bond Fund	$ 90,000
Bonds	
Scudder High Yield Bond Fund	$ 10,000
Cash and Equivalents	
Cash	$ 2,500
GICs – Profit-sharing plan	75,000
TOTAL	$252,000

BEALS CASE
APPLICATION QUESTIONS

1. Assume that James Beals is named the beneficiary of the assets in Anne Beals' profit-sharing plan account, and their two children are equal contingent beneficiaries. If Anne Beals dies, which of the following statements concerning the disposition of her plan assets are correct?

(Topic 54)

(1) The plan assets will pass through probate.
(2) The plan assets will be includible in her gross estate.
(3) The plan assets will pass to James Beals.
(4) The plan assets will pass to the two children equally.

   A. (1) and (3) only
   B. (2) and (3) only
   C. (1) and (4) only
   D. (1), (2), and (3) only
   E. (1), (2), and (4) only

2. If James Beals dies before transferring his interest in the residence to Anne, what will be the value of his adjusted gross estate?

(Topic 59)

   A. $4,439,500
   B. $4,319,500
   C. $4,129,500
   D. $4,055,500
   E. $3,821,500

3. Assume for this question that James gave his son Ronald a birthday present of a new car that cost $30,000 on June 15, and James and Anne enter a settlement agreement on September 15. The settlement agreement provides for James to pay Anne $5,000 in alimony through the end of the year and then $15,000 per year in alimony for the next three years. A divorce decree is finally entered for James and Anne on April 30 of the following year. Which of the following statements are correct?

(Topic 59)

(1) James and Anne can elect to split gifts on a gift tax return filed after the end of the year in which James gave Ronald the car.
(2) After the divorce, James cannot change the beneficiary designation for his IRA unless he remarries.
(3) Whether Anne and James file a joint income tax return will not affect the amount of alimony income that Anne must report for the year before their divorce.
(4) If James dies before the payments are made under the settlement agreement, his estate can take a deduction for Anne's claims under the agreement.

   A. (1) and (2) only
   B. (1) and (4) only
   C. (2) and (3) only
   D. (2) and (4) only
   E. (3) and (4) only

4. Assume James Beals dies after a divorce decree is issued. Which of the following statements concerning planning issues for his estate are correct?

(Topic 60)

(1) If the value of the business declines after James Beals' death, the executor will not be able to elect the alternate valuation date.

(2) The estate of James Beals will not have a liquidity problem because the life insurance proceeds, marketable securities, and retirement plan assets will be sufficient to pay estate taxes.

(3) In most states, the existing will executed by James is revoked by the divorce, and Anne will not be entitled to a statutory elective share.

(4) If James Beals enters into a buy-sell agreement with a formula price for the sale of the business to another funeral director, the executor of his estate would not need to hire an appraiser to value the business for estate tax purposes.

    A. (1) and (2) only
    B. (1) and (4) only
    C. (2) and (3) only
    D. (2) and (4) only
    E. (3) and (4) only

5. Inadequacies in the current estate plan for Anne Beals can be summarized as follows:

(Topic 60)

(1) Failure to make use of the marital deduction

(2) Failure to avoid ancillary probate

(3) Lack of liquidity

(4) Failure to stabilize and maximize business values

    A. (1) and (3) only
    B. (4) only
    C. (2) and (3) only
    D. (3) and (4) only
    E. (1), (3), and (4) only

6. If James Beals dies before transferring his interest in the residence to Anne, which of the following statements is (are) correct?

(Topic 72)

(1) The estate of James Beals can qualify for special-use valuation for the buildings rented to Beals Funeral Home, Inc.

(2) The estate of James Beals can qualify for a Sec. 303 redemption.

(3) The estate of James Beals can qualify for Sec. 6166 installment payment of federal estate taxes.

(4) The S corporation election for Beals Funeral Home, Inc. will be revoked by failure to establish a Qualified Subchapter S Trust.

    A. (1) only
    B. (2) only
    C. (2) and (3) only
    D. (1), (2), and (3) only
    E. (1), (2), (3), and (4)

7. After the divorce, James Beals wants to change his estate plan to provide for his children to receive everything. Under these circumstances, which of the following actions are recommended for James Beals to take?

(Topic 73)

(1) Change the beneficiary designations for his life insurance
(2) Establish a QTIP trust for his children
(3) Execute a new will to provide a trust for his children
(4) Withdraw the money in his IRA and set up a 2503(c) trust for the children

    A. (1) and (3) only
    B. (1) and (4) only
    C. (2) and (3) only
    D. (2) and (4) only
    E. (1), (2), and (3) only

BEALS CASE
ANSWERS AND EXPLANATIONS

1. B is the answer. Retirement benefits are not subject to probate because the decedent does not hold title to them. The plan trust or fund holds title and has agreed to pay benefits directly to the named beneficiary at the decedent's death. Payments are made according to the option selected by the decedent or beneficiary. Qualified plan assets are generally includible in the decedent-participant's gross estate. In this case, the assets pass to a spouse, so the marital deduction will eliminate any estate tax. As the primary beneficiary of the qualified plan benefits, James Beals would be entitled to receive the plan assets.

2. C is the answer. Since the residence is owned by James and Anne Beals as tenants by the entirety, one-half of the value of the residence will be includible in James Beals' estate. The residence is valued at $200,000, so his gross estate will include $100,000. James Beals' gross estate will include the following assets:

Residence (one-half)	$ 100,000
Life insurance	500,000
Cash	14,500
Marketable securities	250,000
Business interest	1,800,000
Real estate	1,500,000
Personal property	45,000
Automobiles	30,000
Retirement plan assets	200,000
Total	$4,439,500

The adjusted gross estate is the gross estate reduced by debts, funeral and administrative expenses, and casualty and theft losses. Debts total $215,000 on the personal balance sheet, but one-half of the $50,000 mortgage on the residence should be added. James cannot deduct the loan that he cosigned because the estate is not required to pay it. The total debts, therefore, are $240,000. Funeral costs are estimated to be $40,000, and administration expenses will be $30,000. Consequently, the adjusted gross estate is $4,439,500 – $240,000 – 40,000 – $30,000 = $4,129,500.

3. B is the answer. Since James and Anne were married at the time of the gift to their son, they can elect to split gifts on a gift tax return filed after the end of the year. James can change the beneficiary designation for his IRA both before and after his divorce. IRAs are not subject to the ERISA rules protecting a spouse. James and Anne can file a joint income tax return for the year in which they separated because they are still married at the end of that year. If Anne and James file a joint income tax return for that year, the alimony is not reported as income and is not a deduction. If James dies before the payments are made under the settlement agreement, the claims are a deductible debt for the estate. Claims of a former spouse are deductible, based on relinquishment of marital rights if three conditions are met: (1) the spouses entered into a written settlement agreement, (2) the spouses must have been divorced before the decedent's death and within the 3-year period beginning one year before the agreement, and (3) the property interest transferred under the agreement must have been transferred in settlement of the spouse's marital rights. Those conditions are met in this case.

4. E is the answer. Since James and Anne Beals' wills are ordinarily revoked by the divorce, the marital deduction is not available to their estates. The business will be includible in James Beals' estate, and the executor may elect the alternate valuation date if the value of the business declines after his death. If the property had passed entirely to Anne Beals, the marital deduction would have eliminated any estate tax, and the executor would not have been able to elect the alternate valuation date. A liquidity problem is likely because the estate will contain the business interest and the real estate, which are not readily sold. The life insurance is payable to Anne, and the beneficiary designation for the policy is not revoked by the divorce. Similarly, the retirement plan assets will be paid to Anne under a beneficiary designation. The life insurance benefit and retirement money, therefore, are not available to pay estate taxes. A buy-sell agreement entered into at arm's length with another funeral director will provide a valuation for James Beals' business interest, and this value can be used for estate and gift tax purposes. Consequently, if there is a buy-sell agreement, the executor will not need to value the business for estate tax purposes.

5. B is the answer. Anne Beals has a simple will, leaving her estate entirely to James Beals. The assets passing to James Beals will qualify for the marital deduction. Anne will not make use of her unified credit but their assets will not exceed the unified credit available to James Beals if he dies after Anne. There is no problem of ancillary probate because Anne does not own property in another state. Under the current simple wills, Anne's estate will not lack liquidity because her assets will pass to her husband and qualify for the marital deduction. No estate tax will be due at her death. Even if the divorce decree is obtained, the estate tax will be small because Anne does not have an estate that exceeds the applicable exclusion amount ($5.43 million in 2015). Anne has not taken steps to stabilize and maximize values from her business. A buy-sell agreement or similar arrangement would help to ensure that her family realizes the full value from the business at her death.

6. D is the answer. As calculated in Question #2, James Beals' gross estate will total $4,439,500. The first test for special-use valuation is to determine whether the business real and personal property equal at least 50% of the adjusted value of the gross estate. The gross estate must be adjusted for the mortgages and indebtedness, which total $240,000, so the adjusted value of the gross estate is $4,199,500. The real and personal property devoted to the business total $3,300,000, and it must be adjusted for the mortgage of $200,000, so the adjusted value is $3,100,000. This amount is greater than 50% of the adjusted value of the gross estate.

The second test to be met for the special-use valuation is that the real estate must be at least 25% of the adjusted value of the gross estate, which is $4,169,500. The real property is $1,500,000, which is more than 25% of the adjusted value of the gross estate. The business and real property will pass to Anne Beals, who is a qualified heir, so the property will qualify for the special-use valuation if Anne continues to use it for 10 years as a funeral parlor.

To qualify for a Sec. 303 redemption, the stock in Beals Funeral Home, Inc. must be 35% of the adjusted gross estate. The business interest is $1,800,000, which is the value of the stock, and the adjusted gross estate is $4,129,500. The business interest is about 44% of the adjusted gross estate, so the estate will qualify for the Sec. 303 redemption.

Similarly, the estate will qualify for the Sec. 6166 deferral of income tax payment because the value of the decedent's interest in the business is more than 35% of the value of the adjusted gross estate.

The S election is not revoked by the failure to establish a Qualified Subchapter S Trust. An estate can hold S corporation stock for a period of time, without causing revocation of the election. If the stock passes to Anne Beals, there is no automatic revocation from her ownership of the stock.

7. **A** is the answer. The life insurance policies previously named Anne Beals as the beneficiary, so James will need to change the designations. A new will should be executed to reflect the change in James' marital status, and a trust would be appropriate to hold and manage the money for the children. Withdrawing the money from the IRA is not a good idea since it will be taxable income to James. He will also have to pay a 10% penalty for the early withdrawal. The 2503(c) trust can be created with other assets if James wants to make these gifts.

MOCSIN CASE

PERSONAL INFORMATION

Richard Mocsin is 46 years old, and his wife Gloria is 37 years old. Richard and Gloria were married 8 years ago; it was Richard's second marriage and Gloria's first marriage. Richard and Gloria have one child Charles, who is 6 years of age. Richard has two children by his prior marriage: Laura, who is 14 years of age, and Elaine, who is 12. All of the children attend public schools.

Richard is a biology professor at the university and is a partner in Wizard Research Associates, a biotechnology firm that Richard started with three of his associates from the university.

ASSET INFORMATION

The Mocsins own their personal residence in joint tenancy with right of survivorship, and it is currently valued at $250,000. They purchased the home seven years ago for $175,000. They have finished the basement and added a room and bathroom at a cost of $40,000. They have a mortgage balance of $150,000. The Mocsins' household furnishings are valued at $70,000, and Gloria's jewelry and furs are valued at $30,000. Richard and Gloria live in a state that follows the common-law form of property ownership.

Richard and Gloria have a joint checking account that contains $7,000 and a joint savings account that contains $15,000. Interest income on the savings account last year was $450. The Mocsins also have $15,000 in money market mutual funds that paid dividends last year of $515. Richard owns shares in a growth stock mutual fund that he purchased three years ago for $5,000, is now worth $5,750, and paid dividends last year of $100. Dividends on these shares are expected to grow by 8% per year, and Richard believes that a 10% rate of return would be appropriate for these shares, with their degree of risk. Gloria owns shares in a municipal bond fund purchased for $6,300, currently valued at $7,000, and yielding $400 per year tax-free. The Mocsins jointly purchased 500 shares in Power Station, Inc., a public utility company. These shares were acquired at a cost of $6,250, are currently valued at $8,000, and pay annual dividends of $480.

Richard's father died two years ago, and his mother died last year, leaving Richard an inheritance of $150,000 in U.S. Treasury securities, paying 8% interest ($12,000 annually), and a one-half interest in common with his brother in a Florida condominium. The condominium was valued in his mother's estate at $120,000 and was purchased six years ago for $125,000. Real estate taxes on the condominium, half of which Richard includes among his itemized deductions for federal income tax purposes, total $1,000. Both of Gloria's parents are still living.

The Mocsins are also joint owners of a parcel of undeveloped land in the mountains, where they plan to build a vacation home. The parcel of land cost them $75,000 and is currently valued at $70,000. They have a $30,000 mortgage on the property. Interest on the mortgage is $2,700 per year. Real estate taxes are $700.

Richard owns an apartment building near the university that he rents to students. The apartment building was purchased four years ago for $95,000 and is currently valued at $125,000. The annual gross rental income from the property is $11,000. Richard has a mortgage balance of $60,000, and his interest payments total $4,950. His real estate taxes and maintenance expenses are $3,000, and depreciation is $2,850.

The Mocsins are joint owners of two automobiles. The cars are valued at $25,000 and $17,500. Richard owns a sailboat which he bought for $35,000 and is valued now at $40,000.

Richard has a one-fourth interest in the partnership, Wizard Research Associates, which is engaged in research for genetic engineering of various plants. There are no employment contracts for the partners. In addition to the partners, the firm has eight employees, including four research assistants, two secretaries, and two maintenance/hothouse workers. The research assistants are paid $30,000 each, the secretaries are paid $18,000 each, and the other workers are paid $20,000 each.

Richard and his partners believe that the value of Wizard Research Associates is approximately $5 million. There has been no objective valuation, however. The largest asset of the firm is its building and grounds, where the firm has a laboratory, hothouses, and fields for growing experimental plants. The building and land were purchased for $250,000, of which $150,000 was allocated to the building and $100,000 to the land. Additional buildings have been added at a cost of $75,000, and the current value is estimated to be $400,000. The firm has a mortgage balance on the building and land of $150,000. The partnership has been depreciating the building for tax purposes under MACRS.

INCOME TAX INFORMATION

Richard earns $60,000 in annual salary from the university, and he reports another $48,000 of net taxable income from the biotechnology firm. Gloria earns $30,000 working in public relations for a hospital. She also receives $5,000 at the beginning of each year from a trust established by her grandfather, with securities currently valued at $100,000. At Gloria's death, the trust income will be paid to Charles, or if Charles is over age 25, the corpus will be distributed to him. The Mocsins file joint tax returns.

Richard pays child support for his two daughters, in the amount of $400 each per month, and these payments are probably 75% of their support annually. Richard's daughters are in the custody of their mother and live with her for approximately nine months of the year. Richard is required by his divorce decree to maintain a $100,000 life insurance policy to provide child support in the event of his death.

Several years ago, Richard established custodian accounts for Laura and Elaine. Laura's account generates annual income of $900, and Elaine's account has annual income of $850.

Richard and Gloria incur home mortgage interest costs of $12,000 per year. Real estate taxes on their home are $2,500. They will pay $4,500 in state income taxes this year and $150 in personal property taxes. Their contributions to charities totaled $2,000.

RETIREMENT INFORMATION

Gloria owns IRA accounts totaling $17,000. She is now an active participant in a defined-contribution pension plan through the hospital where she works, and her vested account value is $35,000. Eight percent of Richard's gross salary at the university is deducted each year and contributed to a tax-deferred annuity. The university contributes an additional six percent dollar-for-dollar on a tax-deferred basis. The plan is projected to pay Richard $2,500 per month when he retires at age 65 or to Gloria at his death.

One of the partners in Wizard Research Associates is age 65 and about two years away from retirement, and two partners are age 55. The partners would like to prepare for the expected retirement of the 65-year-old partner, as well as the unexpected death or disability of any partner. The partners are also contemplating a retirement program for the firm and would like advice concerning its design.

INSURANCE INFORMATION

The university provides disability income coverage for one-third of Richard's salary, group medical expense insurance covering Richard and his family through a health maintenance organization, and group term life insurance for Richard, with a death benefit of $50,000. Richard owns a whole life insurance policy that will pay a death benefit of $100,000 and has a cash value of $5,500, and he owns a universal life policy with a face value of $150,000 and a cash value of $3,000. The annual premium on the whole life policy is $2,000, and the annual premium on the universal life policy is $800. Gloria has group term life insurance through her employer in a face amount that is equal to her salary.

Property and liability insurance that insures the Mocsins' house for its replacement cost has an annual premium of $1,200. The Mocsins' cars are insured under a personal auto policy providing limits for bodily injury of $100,000/$300,000, property damage of $25,000, uninsured motorists coverage of $10,000/$20,000, no-fault benefits, and a collision deductible of $250. Richard's sailboat is insured under a yacht policy.

ESTATE PLANNING INFORMATION

Richard's will leaves his entire estate to Gloria, but if Gloria predeceases Richard, the estate will be left in trust for Richard's three children equally. Gloria's will leaves her entire estate to Richard or, if he predeceases her, to Charles.

MOCSIN CASE
APPLICATION QUESTIONS

1. Richard would like to accumulate an educational fund for Charles and reduce income taxes on the investment income. He would like to start with $20,000 this year. Which of the following techniques should Richard use this year to achieve these objectives?

(Topic 56)

A. Sec. 2503(b) trust
B. Sec. 2503(c) trust
C. Coverdell Education Savings Account
D. Series EE bonds
E. Sec. 529 plan

2. Assume for purposes of this question that Richard Mocsin decides to establish a 2503(c) trust for the benefit of each of his two daughters and his son. Which of the following statements concerning this arrangement is correct?

(Topic 56)

A. Richard cannot transfer his apartment building to a 2503(c) trust for the children.
B. Richard could place mutual funds in three separate trusts, and the income earned by the trusts would not be subject to the kiddie tax.
C. If Richard and Gloria place their $15,000 in money market mutual funds in a trust for Charles, they will have made a $1,000 taxable gift.
D. Because of the grantor's retained rights under a 2503(c) trust, assets held in trust for the children will be includible in Richard's gross estate if he dies while the children are under age 21.
E. If the children are not given Crummey powers under the trust, the gifts to the trust will not qualify for the gift tax annual exclusion.

3. Richard and Gloria Mocsin are considering the use of UGMA accounts as an alternative to trusts for accumulating an education fund for Charles. Which of the following statements concerning the use of UGMA accounts by the Mocsins is correct? (Topic 56)

A. If Richard is named as the custodian, the account balance will be includible in his gross estate if he dies before the distribution of the account.

B. If Gloria's parents contribute the funds for the UGMA accounts, the annual income on each account will not be subject to the kiddie tax.

C. By using a UGMA account, Richard and Gloria can contribute a maximum of $14,000, without gift tax consequences.

D. Richard can transfer his apartment building to a UGMA account for Charles and use his unified credit to eliminate any gift tax.

E. By naming himself as custodian under the UGMA account, Richard can later make withdrawals from the account for his own use if he needs the money for business reasons.

4. If Richard and Gloria decided to make lifetime gifts, which of the following items of their property would be most financially advantageous for an immediate gift to a Crummey trust for Charles? (Topic 56)

A. Their parcel of undeveloped land
B. One of their cars
C. Their utility company stock
D. Richard's apartment building
E. Richard's whole life insurance policy

5. For his estate plan, Richard's main objective is to provide for Gloria following his death and then after Gloria's death, to provide equal inheritances for his three children. Richard would like to see that these objectives are accomplished with the least amount of estate and income taxes and for the lowest possible transfer costs. Which of the following statements concerning Richard's estate plan correctly describes the most appropriate action for Richard to take? (Topic 68)

A. Richard's current will and estate plan are appropriate for his objectives under the given constraints, so no action is necessary.

B. Richard's current will and estate plan should be modified to include a QTIP trust that will pay income to Gloria for her life, with the corpus distributed to the three children at her death.

C. Richard's current will and estate plan should be changed to provide a credit-bypass trust in the amount that is sheltered by the unified credit and remainder to his two daughters.

D. Richard should execute a deed conveying the apartment building to his two daughters and deliver the deed to an escrow agent for filing at the time of his death.

E. Richard should change the beneficiary designation on his life insurance policies to name the three children equally.

MOCSIN CASE
ANSWERS AND EXPLANATIONS

  1. **E** is the answer. Series EE bonds are only tax-advantaged if used for educational expenses by a taxpayer (married filing jointly) meeting certain age and income restrictions. The Mocsins' have income in excess of the limit already. Although the Mocsins' AGI is below the threshold for the Coverdell Education Savings Account, they can only contribute $2,000 per year in an account for Charles. The 2503(b) and 2503(c) trusts do not provide the tax-free distributions and income-tax-deferral on earnings as would a Sec. 529 plan.

  2. **B** is the answer. Richard could place mutual funds in three separate trusts, and the income earned by the trusts would not be subject to the kiddie tax. Separate trusts are required for the children. The income is not taxed to the children because it is accumulated and taxed to the trust. Richard can transfer his apartment building to a 2503(c) trust. The lack of restrictions on what property can be transferred to a trust is one of the advantages of using these trusts for gifts to minors. If Richard and Gloria place their $15,000 in money market mutual funds in a trust for Charles, they will not have made a taxable gift because they can make tax-free gifts of $28,000 to a single donee annually. The 2503(c) trust is an irrevocable trust, and the grantor has no retained rights; consequently, assets held in trust for the children will not be included in Richard's gross estate.

  3. **A** is the answer. If Richard provides the funds and is named custodian, the account balance will be includible in his gross estate if he dies before the distribution of the account. By naming a third party as the custodian, a parent can prevent the gift from being included in the parent's gross estate. If Gloria's parents contribute the funds for the UGMA accounts, the annual income on each account will still be subject to the kiddie tax. By using a UGMA account, Richard and Gloria can contribute a maximum of $28,000, without gift tax consequences. Richard cannot transfer his apartment building under the UGMA because real estate does not qualify under the UGMA.

  4. **E** is the answer. The value of the gift of the whole life insurance policy is only the cash value, and the death proceeds will not be included in Richard's gross estate if he survives three years after making the gift. The death proceeds are also received income-tax-free. While the policy will require payment of additional premiums, Richard was apparently planning to make these premium payments anyway, and they will not result in any gift tax consequences due to the annual gift tax exclusions. The apartment building is a good subject for a gift, except that there are gift tax consequences because the gift is greater than $28,000. Richard and Gloria may use their unified credits to avoid payment of any gift tax. Another potential drawback to the gift of the building is that the building will not receive a step-up in basis, as it would in Richard's estate, so, eventually, there may be capital gains tax to pay. Moreover, Richard may continue to depreciate the building and use the deductions to offset his income, whereas the trust would not have much use for the deductions. The undeveloped land has declined in value, so the Mocsins could sell it and take a capital loss to offset capital gains income, rather than use it for gifts. Alternatively, if they have no capital gains income, they can offset up to $3,000 per year of ordinary income with this capital loss. The cars are depreciating assets and should not be used for gifts. The utility stock is a good asset for gifts but does not transfer as much value as the life insurance and does not receive the step-up in basis that results from passing through Richard's estate. The income tax advantage of making a gift of the

utility stock is small. While the size of Richard's estate may not currently justify a transfer of the life insurance, future appreciation of the partnership and other assets may make such a gift important to the Mocsins.

5. B is the answer. Richard's current will provides for Gloria to receive all of his estate, and she will leave her entire estate to Charles. Richard can provide for his two daughters to receive a portion of his estate by adding a QTIP trust. This trust will provide income to Gloria for her life and ensures that some of his estate passes to his daughters after Gloria's death. Placing a deed in escrow and changing life insurance to make the children beneficiaries fail to accomplish the objective of providing for Gloria during her lifetime. If Richard funds a by-pass trust in the amount that is sheltered by the unified credit, the remainder will pass to his two daughters, and there will be no assets in Richard's estate to provide an inheritance for Charles.

YOUNG CASE

PERSONAL INFORMATION AND BACKGROUND

Mildred Young has come to consult with you in January this year because her husband Harold has recently died. Harold handled most of the family finances, and Mildred wants some help with arranging her affairs. Harold Young was born on February 24, 1943, and Mildred was born May 15, 1939. The Youngs were married on June 22, 1959. The marriage produced two children: Michael, who is 49 years of age, and Darlene, who is 45.

Mildred worked for a gas company as a home economist until her first child was born. She stayed home to take care of the children until they left for college. She then worked with her husband in his business for 15 years. She stopped working at age 60 to devote herself to church work. She has remained very active in her church work and plans to continue it. Harold worked until his retirement last year.

Family Information

Mildred's son Michael is a lawyer and has two children, ages 12 and 9. Her daughter Darlene is a public school teacher and has three children, ages 17, 15, and 4. Darlene was recently divorced. Darlene's oldest child is planning to start at the state university in the fall of this year. Darlene lives in a community-property state.

ECONOMIC ENVIRONMENT

- Mildred expects inflation to average 4% per year.
- T-bills are currently yielding 2.5%. The 30-year Treasury bond is yielding 5.25%.
- Corporate bonds are yielding 8%. Junk bonds are yielding 9-10%.
- Certificates of deposit are earning 5.5%.
- The expected return on the S&P 500 Index is 10%.
- The expected return on the Russell 2000 Index is 14%.
- The expected return on growth stocks is 12%.
- Mortgage rates are currently 7% on a 30-year mortgage and 6.5% on a 15-year mortgage. Closing costs are 3% of the mortgage amount.

MILDRED YOUNG'S OBJECTIVES

- Increase the amount of her current annual income.
- Arrange her estate plan to minimize transfer taxes and costs and maximize the amounts passing to her children and grandchildren.
- Help Darlene and her family financially.
- Determine her long-term care insurance needs.
- Determine the best method for taking distributions from retirement plans.
- Plan for charitable gifts to her church.

INSURANCE INFORMATION

Homeowners Insurance

Primary Residence - Homeowners Policy Form HO-3

Section I Coverages

A - Dwelling	$275,000
B - Other Structures	$ 27,500
C - Personal Property Coverage	$137,500
D - Loss of Use	$ 55,000
Section I Deductible	$ 250

Section II Coverages

E - Personal Liability	$100,000
F - Medical Payments to Others	$ 1,000

Vacation Home - Homeowners Policy Form HO-3

Section I Coverages

A - Dwelling	$125,000
B - Other Structures	$ 12,500
C - Personal Property Coverage	$ 62,500
D - Loss of Use	$ 25,000
Section I Deductible	$ 250

Section II Coverages

E - Personal Liability	$100,000
F - Medical Payments to Others	$ 1,000

Rental Property - Dwelling Policy Form DP-2

Section I Coverages

A - Dwelling	$150,000
Fire	
Extended Coverage	
Landlord's Liability	

Appendix – Young Case

Automobile Insurance

Personal Auto Policy

Mercedes

| Coverage A | - Liability - Bodily Injury | $300,000 each occurrence |
| | - Liability - Property Damage | $100,000 each occurrence |

| Coverage B | - Medical Payments | $5,000 each person |

| Coverage C | - Uninsured Motorists | $300,000 each occurrence |
| | - Underinsured Motorists | $300,000 each occurrence |

| Coverage D | - Other than collision | Actual cash value less $100 |
| | - Collision | Actual cash value less $100 |

SAAB

| Coverage A | - Liability - Bodily Injury | $300,000 each occurrence |
| | - Liability - Property Damage | $100,000 each occurrence |

| Coverage B | - Medical Payments | $5,000 each person |

| Coverage C | - Uninsured Motorists | $300,000 each occurrence |
| | - Underinsured Motorists | $300,000 each occurrence |

Life Insurance

Insured	Harold Young
Face Amount	$100,000
Type	Whole Life
Cash Value	$72,000
Annual Premium	$3,000
Beneficiary	Mildred Young
Contingent Beneficiary	Michael and Darlene
Owner	Harold Young

Single-Premium Deferred Annuity

Owner	Harold Young
Type of Annuity	Fixed
Current Value	$100,000
Purchase Price	$50,000
Interest Rate	7.5%
Issue Date	4/30/87
Beneficiary	Mildred Young

INCOME TAX INFORMATION

Mildred will file a joint income tax return for herself and Harold for this year. They have been in the 25% federal income tax bracket. The state income tax is 2% of the federal adjusted gross income.

INVESTMENT INFORMATION

Mildred wants to have the same income that she has enjoyed with Harold, but she does not want to take on additional risk. She describes herself as a conservative investor. The Youngs designated their money market fund as an emergency fund and felt that the $50,000 contained in that fund was sufficient.

The rental property was purchased January 1, 1996, for $100,000, of which $15,000 was attributable to the cost of the land.

RETIREMENT INFORMATION

Harold had a pension and profit-sharing plan through his employer. Harold retired in June of last year and had just begun receiving distributions from the company plan before his death. Harold designated Mildred as his beneficiary.

OTHER DATA

- Mildred's will leaves everything to Harold. She would like to make a substantial gift to her church in the most tax-effective way and in a way that will not reduce her income.
- Mildred inherited the vacation home from her mother. The vacation home is located in a different state than Mildred's primary residence.
- Harold's estate is in probate. His will left $600,000 in a trust that will pay income to Mildred annually, and at her death, the remaining assets in the trust will be divided between their two children. The trustee is a bank in the city near where Mildred lives. The remainder of the estate passes to Mildred.
- The Statement of Financial Position and Cash Flow Statement were prepared just before Harold died.

Harold and Mildred Young
Statement of Financial Position
December 31, 20XX

ASSETS

Cash/Cash Equivalents		
JT Checking Account		$ 12,000
JT Money Market Fund (emergency fund)		50,000
H Treasury T-Bills		300,000
JT Certificate of Deposit		150,000
Total Cash/Cash Equivalents		$512,000
Invested Assets		
JT Marketable Securities[1]		$301,400
JT Rental Property		175,000
H Life Ins. Cash Value		72,000
H Annuity[2]		100,000
		$648,400
Use Assets		
JT Principal Residence		$200,000
W Vacation Home		150,000
W Personal Property[3]		80,000
JT Automobiles		42,000
		$472,000
Retirement Plan Assets		
H IRA		$ 75,000
W IRA		40,000
H Money-Purchase Pension		300,000
H Profit-Sharing Plan		100,000
		$515,000
Total Assets		$2,147,400

LIABILITIES

Auto Loan	$ 6,000
Credit Cards	10,000
Mortgage[4]	75,600
Total Liabilities	$91,600

NET WORTH $2,055,800

Total Liabilities and Net Worth	$2,147,400

<u>Appendix – Young Case</u>

W = Wife; H = Husband; JT = Joint Tenancy WROS

[1]See Investment Portfolio.
[2]The single-premium deferred annuity earns a fixed rate of 7.5%.
[3]Mildred's jewelry is valued at $40,000.
[4]Rental property: originally, 30-year @ 9.5%.

Harold and Mildred Young
Statement of Cash Flows
January 1 – December 31, 20XX

Annual Inflows

Salary (Harold)	$ 45,000
Social Security (Harold)	15,900
Interest income (taxable)	22,500
Interest income (tax-exempt)	4,000
Dividend income	4,400
Rental income	15,000
Pension and profit-sharing plans	12,000
IRA distributions	5,000
Total Inflows	$123,800

Annual Outflows

Mortgage (rental – int. $7,227)	$ 8,100
Food	4,800
Car payment	6,200
Utilities (residence)	3,600
Utilities (vacation home)	2,200
Utilities (rental)	1,000
Transportation (gas, oil, maintenance)	2,400
Clothing	3,700
Property taxes (residence)	2,600
Property taxes (vacation home)	2,000
Property taxes (rental)	1,900
Homeowners insurance (residence)	1,000
Homeowners insurance (vacation home)	800
Fire insurance (rental)	900
Auto insurance	1,500
Life insurance	3,000
Hospitalization (Medigap/Medicare)	1,200
Entertainment	8,000
Travel	6,600
Credit cards	18,000
Charitable contributions	7,600
Federal income tax	28,300
State income tax	2,000
Investments	5,000
Miscellaneous	1,400
Total Outflows	$123,800

Harold and Mildred Young
Investment Portfolio

Mutual Funds	Fair Market Value
Growth fund	$ 30,000
Small-cap growth fund	15,000
S&P 500 Index fund	25,000
Total	$ 70,000

Common Stocks

AT&T	$ 3,000
Chase Manhattan	6,500
Chevron	8,000
Coca Cola	7,000
Dell Computer	6,800
Disney	6,500
General Electric	9,000
Verizon	6,500
Home Depot	5,000
IBM	16,500
Lucent Technologies	10,000
Qualcom	5,800
SBC Communications	4,800
United Healthcare	6,000
Total	$111,400

Municipal Bonds

G.O. bonds due in 2023	$ 50,000
Revenue bonds due in 2022	20,000
Total	$ 70,000

Annuities and Insurance

Deferred annuity	$100,000
Life insurance cash value	72,000
Total	$172,000

Bonds

Treasury bonds	$ 50,000
Total	$473,400

YOUNG CASE
APPLICATION QUESTIONS

1. Which of the following weaknesses is (are) present in Mildred's current estate plan assuming she lives for several more years?

(Topic 54)

(1) None of her estate will pass to her church.

(2) None of her estate will pass to her daughter's family.

(3) Her estate will fail to take advantage of the applicable credit amount (unified credit).

(4) Her estate will fail to take advantage of the credit for tax on prior transfers.

  A. (1) only
  B. (1) and (3) only
  C. (1) and (4) only
  D. (2) and (4) only
  E. (3) and (4) only

2. If Mildred wants to help fund the education of Darlene's children and this year contributes $15,000 each to Sec. 529 qualified tuition programs for Darlene's three children, which of the following statements is (are) correct?

(Topic 57)

(1) Mildred cannot make any additional gifts to Darlene's children this year without paying gift tax.

(2) No adverse tax consequences will result from withdrawing money to pay room-and-board expenses at an eligible institution of higher education that the children attend.

(3) Distributions used for private secondary schools for Darlene's children will be excluded from income.

  A. (1) only
  B. (2) only
  C. (2) and (3) only
  D (1), (2), and (3)

3. Assume that Mildred elects the straight life income option for the annuity, and that the pension and profit-sharing plan can be inherited from her after her death. If the asset values shown in the Statement of Financial Position remain unchanged, what will be the value of Mildred's gross estate?

(Topic 59)

  A. $735,200
  B. $1,475,400
  C. $1,775,400
  D. $2,075,400
  E. $2,175,400

4. Which of the following statements are correct concerning Mildred's objectives of helping her daughter's family and of making charitable gifts to her church?

(Topic 64)

(1) A gift to the church of a remainder interest in her residence will provide annual deductions that Mildred can use to reduce income taxes until her death.

(2) Mildred should elect gift-splitting to increase the amount of her lifetime gifts that are not taxable.

(3) For estate planning, a gift to the church of the vacation home is preferable to a gift of an equal amount of T-bills.

(4) Paying the tuition to the university for Darlene's children is preferable to making a gift of the money to Darlene or to Darlene's children.

    A. (1) and (2) only
    B. (1) and (3) only
    C. (2) and (3) only
    D. (2) and (4) only
    E. (3) and (4) only

5. Assume that Mildred will be the executrix for Harold's estate. Which of the following postmortem actions could Mildred take to reduce overall taxes?

(Topic 72)

A. Make a QTIP election

B. Use estate assets to pay off the mortgage on the rental property

C. Deduct the estate administration expenses on the estate's income tax return

D. Select the rental property for the $600,000 of property passing to the trust

YOUNG CASE
ANSWERS AND EXPLANATIONS

1. A is the answer. Since Mildred's will is ineffective for transferring assets, the assets will pass by intestacy. Assets cannot be left to charity without a will, but assets will pass to family members under intestacy distribution. Mildred's daughter will be entitled to a share of the intestate estate. The estate can still take advantage of the unified credit and of the credit for tax on prior transfers.

2. B is the answer. (1) is incorrect. Mildred can elect to have the gifts averaged over 5 years ($3,000 per year per child), which would allow her to make an additional $11,000 in gifts to each child without incurring gift tax. With this election, if Mildred dies within the five years, the amount of the gifts still to be allocated will be includible in her gross estate. (2) is correct. Room-and-board expenses are defined as qualified education expenses as long as they are incurred at an eligible educational institution. Therefore, any withdrawals to pay room-and-board are tax-free. (3) is incorrect. The distributions from a Sec. 529 plan are excluded from income only when used for higher education expenses.

3. B is the answer. Mildred's gross estate will include the cash and cash equivalents, totaling $513,000; the use assets, totaling $472,000; the retirement assets, totaling $515,000; the marketable securities, valued at $301,400; and the rental property, valued at $175,000. The life insurance death benefit of $100,000 will also be included. The annuity is a straight life annuity, so no amount is includible for the annuity. The $600,000 that Harold left in trust will not be included, so this amount must be subtracted. The total is $1,475,400.

4. E is the answer. A gift to the church of a remainder interest will provide a charitable deduction in the year of the gift. If the charitable deduction cannot all be used the first year, it may be carried forward up to five years, but Mildred will not have her income taxes reduced permanently. Mildred cannot elect gift-splitting because she is no longer married. A gift to the church of the vacation home is preferable to the gift of T-bills because the T-bills provide liquidity, and the vacation home will necessitate additional costs of ancillary probate in another state after Mildred's death. Paying tuition to the university is a qualified transfer and has no gift tax consequences.

5. C is the answer. A QTIP election will not reduce estate taxes because Harold's estate will owe no taxes without the election. The $600,000 passing to the trust will be sheltered from estate tax by the unified credit and the remainder of the estate will pass to Mildred and be sheltered by the marital deduction. Since Harold's estate will owe no estate taxes, the administration expenses should be deducted on the estate's income tax return. Otherwise, the deduction is wasted. The rental property cannot be selected for the trust because the rental property was jointly owned and will not pass through probate. Paying off the mortgage would reduce the adjusted gross estate, but there is no benefit to Mildred because the estate owes no tax.

BORELLI CASE

PERSONAL INFORMATION AND BACKGROUND

Louie and Kathleen Borelli have been married for over 50 years and live on a ranch outside of Reno, Nevada. They have enjoyed a comfortable retirement for 20 years, living off the wealth created through Louie's company, Borelli Casinos. Sadly, last month, Louie was diagnosed with a terminal illness and is only expected to live another 12 to 18 months. Louie and Kathleen feel a sense of urgency around planning for the distribution of their estate to ensure that they minimize estate taxes and maximize the value of what will be left to their heirs.

Louie and Kathleen have two children, Jerry and Sal, who have continued their father's legacy by working in the family business. Jerry serves as the CEO of the publicly traded organization, while Sal is a floor manager at the property in Las Vegas. Jerry currently lives with his girlfriend Irene in the penthouse suite at the casino in Reno. He does not have any children. Sal and his wife reside in Las Vegas and have a 22-year old daughter named Emily.

Last year, Louie confessed to Kathleen that about 20 years ago, he had an affair with another woman that resulted in the birth of a daughter named Ava. Ava works as a cocktail waitress in one of the company's casinos, and Louie has been secretly sending money to help with her financial situation.

Name	Relationship	Age	Occupation	Health	Comments
Louie	Husband	78	Retired	Terminally ill	
Kathleen	Wife	75	Retired	Excellent	
Jerry	Son	50	CEO, Borelli Casinos	Excellent	
Sal	Son	47	Casino floor manager	Excellent	Married; one child
Emily	Granddaughter (Sal's child)	22	Just graduated from college	Excellent	Getting married this summer
Ava	Illegitimate child	20	Cocktail waitress	Excellent	Relies on Louie for support

GOALS AND OBJECTIVES

1. Louie and Kathleen want to ensure the efficient transfer of their estate to their heirs.
2. Louie wants to make sure that Ava is not disinherited at his death.
3. Louie and Kathleen would like to give $20,000 in cash to Emily to help fund her wedding.
4. Louie and Kathleen would like to give their shares in XYZ Company to their neighbor whose child was recently killed in a car accident.
5. Louie and Kathleen would like to continue to support the nonprofit research organization that is looking for a cure for Louie's disease, while maximizing their income tax deduction. They have set aside $175,000 in a savings account for this purpose.

INCOME TAX INFORMATION

Louie and Kathleen had an adjusted gross income of $185,000 last year and anticipate it will be the same this year. They made a $100,000 cash charitable contribution this year to the nonprofit research organization trying to find a cure to Louie's disease. They are in the 28% marginal federal tax bracket for the current year.

ESTATE PLANNING INFORMATION

Louie and Kathleen live in a community-property state.

Louie and Kathleen's current wills leave all their assets to each other at their deaths. Jerry is the named executor in both wills.

After Louie was diagnosed as terminally ill, he and Kathleen met with their attorney to discuss drafting new estate planning documents. The attorney has proposed that Louie execute a will in which his entire estate will pass to a testamentary marital trust with a QTIP election. The income from the trust would be paid annually to Kathleen, but she would be restricted to withdrawing principal only for her health, maintenance, and support. At Kathleen's death, the assets would pass equally to Jerry, Sal, and Ava, *per stirpes*. The terms of the trust do not give Kathleen the right to change the beneficiaries, but she can direct a different allocation of assets among the beneficiaries at her death.

The attorney has also recommended that while Louie is still in good mental condition, he and Kathleen both execute advance medical directives and powers of attorney for property and health care.

TRUST INFORMATION

Four years ago, Louie and Kathleen established a trust (called the children and grandchildren's trust) for the benefit of Jerry, Sal, and Emily. The trust must distribute income to Jerry and Sal during their lifetimes, with the remainder to transfer outright to Emily at their deaths. Louie and Kathleen transferred $4 million worth of their shares in Borelli Casinos to the trust. The gift to the trust was considered a split gift for gift tax purposes, and they each elected to allocate their applicable exclusion amount for generation-skipping transfer tax purposes. Louie and Kathleen have no current or future rights with regard to the trust.

Louie and Kathleen elected a representative at the local bank to serve as a corporate trustee over the children and grandchildren's trust. The trustee sold the stock in Borelli Casinos and allocated the proceeds to a portfolio of large-cap growth stocks that do not pay dividends. The selected stocks are well diversified across all major sectors and industries, representing both U.S. and foreign companies. A reasonable administrative fee for the trustee's services is paid directly from the trust. Each month the trustee sends a statement of the trust holdings to Jerry, Sal, and Emily.

To create parity between Ava and his other two children, Louie would like to transfer the remaining $2 million in shares of Borelli Casinos to a grantor trust for Ava's benefit. The trust would pay income to Louie and Kathleen for five years, and then the assets would pass outright to Ava.

INVESTMENT ACCOUNT INFORMATION

Louie and Kathleen have one large brokerage account in which they accumulated assets during Louie's career in the casino business.

While Louie was working, he deferred $500,000 of his salary into his 401(k) plan. After his retirement, he rolled the assets into an IRA account that has since grown to be worth $1,100,000.

Louie and Kathleen allocate the portfolios in both accounts 50% to equities and 50% to bonds.

INSURANCE INFORMATION

Life Insurance

Insured	Owner	Beneficiary	Face Amount	Type	Cash Value	Annual Premium	Notes
Louie	Louie	Kathleen	$2,000,000	Whole life	$750,000	$20,000	Purchased 25 years ago

ANNUITY INFORMATION

Louie inherited a condo in downtown Las Vegas 10 years ago, worth $1,500,000, which he subsequently sold to Sal, in exchange for a single-life $55,000 annual annuity payment made at the beginning of each year. Sal has made 10 payments to date.

Louie and Kathleen Borelli
Projected Cash Flow
for the Current Year

Cash Inflows

Portfolio income	$100,000
Social Security income	$ 32,000
Private annuity income	$ 55,000

Cash Outflows

Taxes (income and real estate)	$ 25,000
Lifestyle expenses	$120,000
Insurance premiums	$ 20,000

Louie and Kathleen save any remaining income into their brokerage account.

Louie and Kathleen Borelli
Statement of Financial Position
as of December 31st Last Year

ASSETS

Cash and Cash Equivalents	
Checking account	$ 75,000
Savings account	$ 175,000
Total Cash and Cash Equivalents	$ 250,000
Invested Assets	
Borelli Casinos company stock[1]	$2,000,000
XYZ Company stock[2]	$ 25,000
Louie's IRA[3]	$1,100,000
Brokerage account[4]	$2,300,000
Annuity[5]	$ 800,000
Total Invested Assets	$6,225,000
Personal-Use Assets	
Nevada ranch[6]	$1,400,000
Cars	$ 75,000
Furniture and household items	$ 250,000
Total Personal-Use Assets	$1,725,000

Total Assets   **$8,200,000**

LIABILITIES AND NET WORTH

Liabilities (None)	
Total Liabilities	$ 0

Total Liabilities   **$ 0**

Net Worth   **$8,200,000**

Notes to the Financial Statements

All assets are considered community property unless otherwise noted.

[1] The basis in the stock is $230,000. This amount represents 20% of all outstanding shares.
[2] XYZ is a publicly traded company. The basis in the stock is $56,000.
[3] Kathleen is the named primary beneficiary. Jerry and Sal are the named contingent beneficiaries.
[4] The basis in the brokerage account is $1,900,000.
[5] See the Annuity Information section for details.
[6] The land is worth $300,000. The basis in the property is $440,000. The mortgage is paid off.

BORELLI CASE
APPLICATION QUESTIONS

1. If Louie died this year, what would be the basis for assets in the brokerage account after his death?

(Topic 53)

A. $1,150,000
B. $1,900,000
C. $2,100,000
D. $2,300,000

2. Which best describes how Louie's interest in the stock of Borelli Casinos will transfer at his death?

(Topic 54)

A. By will
B. By trust
C. By contract
D. By operation of law

3. What is the best way to get the language for the testamentary trust in place prior to Louie's death?

(Topic 55)

A. Execute a new will.
B. Amend the current will through a codicil.
C. Create handwritten instructions.
D. Film a video describing the wishes.

4. If the Borelli's make a gift to their neighbor of the XYZ Company stock and the neighbor immediately sells the stock, what is the neighbor's basis in the shares?

(Topic 56)

A. $0
B. $25,000
C. $31,000
D. $56,000

5. How much of the gift to the neighbor will be taxable to Louie and Kathleen for gift tax purposes?

(Topic 57)

A. $0
B. $11,000
C. $25,000
D. $56,000

6. Which type of tax will be due and payable at the time of the gift to Emily for her wedding?

(Topic 57)

A. No tax will be due.
B. Gift tax only
C. Generation-skipping transfer tax only
D. Both gift and generation-skipping transfer tax

7. What type of power of attorney for health care would be most suitable for Louie?

(Topic 58)

A. Non-springing, durable
B. Non-springing, nondurable
C. Springing, nondurable
D. Springing, durable

8. Which of the following is true with regard to the proposed testamentary trust?

(Topic 59)

A. The assets will be excluded from Louie's gross estate.
B. The income is allowed to accumulate for the benefit of the children.
C. The QTIP treatment will be automatic.
D. The assets in the trust at Kathleen's death will be fully taxable to Kathleen's estate.

9. If Louie dies today, how much of the annuity will be included in his gross estate?

(Topic 59)

A. $0
B. $800,000
C. $950,000
D. $1,500,000

10. What is the biggest risk inherent in the proposed testamentary trust?

(Topic 59)

A. Kathleen will not have enough money to support her lifestyle.
B. Ava could be disinherited.
C. Estate tax will be due at Louie's death.
D. The formation will unnecessarily trigger the GSTT at Louie's death.

11. If Louie died today, how much of the brokerage account would be included in his gross estate?

(Topic 59)

A. $0
B. $1,150,000
C. $1,900,000
D. $2,300,000

12. Which best describes how Louie's gift to the children and grandchildren's trust will be treated in his estate tax calculation?

(Topic 59)

A. It is added to the gross estate in calculating the adjusted gross estate.
B. It is added to the adjusted gross estate in calculating the taxable estate.
C. It is added to the taxable estate in calculating the tentative tax base.
D. It is not added anywhere in the calculation of the estate tax.

13. Which of the following statements concerning the liquidity of Louie's estate is correct?

(Topic 60)

A. The estate will need to borrow from the children and grandchildren's trust for liquidity.
B. The estate can use proceeds from the life insurance policy to satisfy liquidity needs.
C. The estate's best option is to use assets from the IRA for liquidity.
D. Liquidity is not needed at Louie's death.

14. Which of the following is true with regard to the proposed testamentary trust?

(Topic 61)

A. Kathleen would have a Crummey power.
B. Distributions would be subject to an ascertainable standard.
C. Kathleen would hold a general power of appointment.
D. The assets passing to the trust would not qualify for the marital deduction.

15. Which best describes the children and grandchildren's trust?

(Topic 62)

A. A complex, testamentary irrevocable trust
B. A complex, *inter vivos* revocable trust
C. A simple, *inter vivos* irrevocable trust
D. A simple, testamentary revocable trust

16. If Louie transfers the Borelli Casinos stock to the proposed grantor trust, which best describes the valuation of the gift for gift tax purposes?

(Topic 63)

A. The present value of the income stream will reduce the amount subject to tax.
B. The taxable amount is recalculated each year when the income is paid.
C. The entire amount will be taxable.
D. None of the transfer will be taxable.

17. What is the best way for Louie and Kathleen to achieve their goal of giving the money in the savings account to the nonprofit research organization working on a cure for Louie's disease?

(Topic 64)

A. Amend Louie's will to leave the asset to the charity at his death.
B. Complete the gift now.
C. Complete the gift next year.
D. Contribute the assets to a charitable lead unitrust with a term of five years.

18. What would be the best estate planning strategy to recommend for the life insurance policy?

(Topic 65)

A. Gift the policy to an irrevocable life insurance trust (ILIT).
B. Withdraw the cash value and allow the policy to lapse.
C. Continue to pay the premiums and keep the policy.
D. Sell the policy to a viatical settlement company.

19. Which discount to the valuation of Borelli Casinos stock would most likely be available to Louie's estate?

(Topic 68)

A. Minority interest discount
B. Lack-of-marketability discount
C. Blockage discount
D. Key person discount

20. Of the following estate planning techniques, which would be the most effective way to help minimize current and future estate taxes?

(Topic 68)

A. Make annual exclusion gifts to all known relatives.
B. Gift $2 million to the children's and grandchildren's trust.
C. Amend the will to set up a testamentary bypass trust.
D. Transfer all assets into Kathleen's name.

21. If a taxable termination occurred in the children and grandchildren's trust this year, what amount of the trust assets would be subject to the generation-skipping transfer tax (GSTT) assuming no additional contributions to the trust?

(Topic 69)

A. $0
B. $1 million
C. $4 million
D. $5 million

22. If both Jerry and Sal died today, which type of generation-skipping transfer would take place in the children and grandchildren's trust?

(Topic 69)

A. A direct skip
B. A taxable termination
C. A taxable distribution
D. No GST transfer would take place.

23. Which of the following actions taken by the trustee of the children and grandchildren's trust might be considered a breach of his or her fiduciary duties?

(Topic 70)

A. The mailing of monthly statements
B. The payment of administrative fees
C. Investing in a nondiversified portfolio
D. Purchasing stocks that do not pay dividends

24. What would be the basis in Louie's IRA after his death, assuming Kathleen rolls the assets into a new IRA in her name?

(Topic 71)

A. $0
B. $500,000
C. $550,000
D. $1,100,000

25. If Louie died this year, which postmortem planning technique would be available to Kathleen?

(Topic 72)

A. The special-use valuation on the Nevada ranch
B. A qualified disclaimer on the IRA assets
C. A Section 303 stock redemption on the stock in Borelli Casinos
D. A Section 6166 deferral of estate tax election

BORELLI CASE
ANSWERS AND EXPLANATIONS

1. D is the answer. The brokerage account is community property and is eligible for a full step-up in basis (to the fair market value of the entire account) at the first person's death. The basis prior to Louie's death was $1,900,000. The basis step-up will bring the basis up to the $2,300,000 fair market value at the time of death. The community property rules allow for both spouse's basis to be stepped up to fair market value. If they had lived in a separate property state, then the executor would have only been able to increase the basis on Louie's half of the property. This means Louie's basis would have been stepped up to $1,150,000 which would have been added to Kathleen's carryover basis on her 50% of $950,000 for a total basis of $2,100,000.

2. A is the answer. The stock in Borelli Casinos is considered community property, and Louie's one-half interest in this community property passes by will.

3. A is the answer. The best way to add the testamentary trust language is to execute a new will since Louie is making major changes to his current will.

4. B is the answer. Normally, the basis of a gifted asset would carry over to the recipient; however, in this case, the shares in XYZ Company currently contain an unrealized capital loss. The unrealized capital loss cannot be transferred to the recipient, so the neighbor must use the fair market value at the time of the gift ($25,000) as his or her basis. If the neighbor held the stock and later sold it for a gain, he or she would then be allowed to use the higher carryover basis.

5. A is the answer. A gift of community property is automatically considered to be a split gift between the husband and wife. They would each apply their $14,000 annual exclusion amount to the gift, resulting in no taxable gift.

6. A is the answer. The $20,000 cash gift to Emily will presumably come from Louie and Kathleen's community-property assets, so the gift will be a considered a split gift, and Louie and Kathleen will each have a $14,000 annual gift tax exclusion and a $14,000 annual GST tax exclusion. The application of the annual exclusion amounts will shelter the gift from tax.

7. D is the answer. A springing, durable power of attorney would be the best for Louie. Springing means that it will come into effect at the time of his incapacity, and durable means it will survive his incapacity. A non-springing power is not necessary because Louie is still capable of making decisions. A nondurable power of attorney would not serve Louie's purposes because it would not be usable when he becomes unable to make decisions.

8. D is the answer. The assets will be fully taxable to Kathleen's estate. The assets would be included in Louie's gross estate but fully offset by the marital deduction. Income must be paid to the surviving spouse in a QTIP trust. The executor must make a QTIP election in order for the trust to qualify.

9. **A** is the answer. The annuity is a single-life private annuity; therefore, payments are cancelled at death (no survivor benefit), and no value is included in the gross estate.

10. **B** is the answer. Because Kathleen has a limited power of appointment to redirect the assets among the beneficiaries, she could choose to eliminate Ava's interest in the trust. Kathleen should have enough money to support her lifestyle, as half of the community-property assets would transfer to her, and she would have access to the trust assets for health, maintenance, and support. The QTIP trust will maximize the estate tax savings because it will qualify Louie's entire estate for the marital deduction. The transfer will not trigger the GSTT because the beneficiaries of the trust are not skip-beneficiaries.

11. **B** is the answer. The brokerage account is a community-property asset. One-half of the asset will be included in Louie's estate.

12. **C** is the answer. Taxable gifts made after 1976 are added to the taxable estate to calculate the tentative tax base. This treatment ensures that all assets remaining in the estate will be taxed at the highest applicable estate tax rate from the unified gift and estate tax rate table.

13. **D** is the answer. Because all of Louie's assets will pass to Kathleen, there will be no estate taxes due. Liquidity will not be needed.

14. **B** is the answer. Distributions are available to Kathleen for her health, maintenance, and support, which falls within the definition of an ascertainable standard (health, education, maintenance, or support). Kathleen does not have a Crummey power or a general power of appointment (she does have a limited power of appointment, however). The assets transferring to the trust will qualify for the marital deduction due to the QTIP election.

15. **C** is the answer. The trust is simple because it distributes all income attributable to the trust to the income beneficiaries each year. The trust is *inter vivos* because it was established while the grantors were living. The trust is irrevocable because the grantors retained no rights to the trust. A complex trust may accumulate income. A testamentary trust is established at the grantor's death. A revocable trust gives the grantor rights to control the assets or change the provisions of the trust.

16. **C** is the answer. The grantor trust described is a grantor-retained income trust, which is not considered a qualified interest for gift tax purposes. The entire amount will be taxable. If the grantor trust was set up to be a GRAT (annuity trust) or GRUT (unitrust), then the valuation of the gift would be reduced by the present value of the annuity or unitrust amount.

17. **C** is the answer. The Borelli's have already contributed more than 50% of their adjusted gross income to charity for this year and, therefore, are receiving the maximum tax benefit for this year. Any other gifts given this year would carry forward to be used as a deduction in future years, but the time period is limited to five years. Giving the gift next year would extend the time period in which the deductions could be taken by one more year. Naming the charity in Louie's will does not have the most favorable outcome. First, because the asset is a community-property asset, only half of the account would transfer at his death. Second, the estate would receive no tax savings since all assets are receiving the marital deduction at the first death. A CLUT does not ensure that all assets will go

to the charity because it only pays a unitrust amount during the term of the trust, and the remainder would go to some other beneficiary.

18. C is the answer. The best strategy for the life insurance policy is to keep it. The cost of keeping the policy in place is minimal and will secure the $2 million in proceeds for the heirs. A gift to an ILIT would not be advised because if Louie dies within three years, the proceeds will be included in his gross estate. Withdrawing the cash value would not be advisable because income taxes could be due, and the family would not realize the full value of the death benefit. A sale to a viatical settlement company would only be recommended if the family needed the money immediately.

19. C is the answer. The blockage discount would be the best answer. The stock is publicly traded, not closely held. The total amount of the stock represents 20% of outstanding shares (half of which would be included in Louie's estate). The blockage discount is granted when the holding is considered large enough that it might impact the price of the security if it had to be sold all at once.

20. C is the answer. Although Louie and Kathleen have each made taxable gifts in excess of $2 million, the American Taxpayer Relief Act of 2012 allows taxpayers to transfer a total of $5.43 million of assets during lifetime or at death without payment of estate or gift taxes in 2015. Louie and Kathleen, therefore, have not used all of their unified credit. A testamentary bypass trust will take advantage of this additional credit available against the estate tax. Making annual gifts to all known relatives to take advantage of multiple annual exclusion amounts is an effective technique, provided they want their relatives to inherit their assets. However, there is no mention in the fact pattern of this desire. Any gifts in excess of annual exclusion amounts would be currently taxable at the maximum gift tax rate, and gift taxes paid within three years of Louie's death would be pulled back into his estate and be taxed. Transferring assets into Kathleen's name would not remove the community-property characteristics.

21. A is the answer. Because Louie and Kathleen each allocated $2 million of their applicable exclusion amounts for the GSTT at the time of the contribution, the inclusion ratio = 1 – (GST exemption allocated/Taxable transfer) = 0. No assets will be taxable for GSTT purposes at any time unless future contributions are made to the trust.

22. B is the answer. A taxable termination occurs when all non-skip interests terminate in a non-direct-skip trust, leaving only skip-beneficiaries to receive the assets. Jerry and Sal are the only non-skip-beneficiaries of the trust, and Emily is a skip-beneficiary. A direct skip is an outright gift or bequest. A taxable distribution occurs when a payment from a non-direct-skip trust is made to a skip-beneficiary.

23. D is the answer. The trustee has a duty to act in the best interest of the beneficiaries. Purchasing stocks that do not pay dividends means that the likelihood of the trust ever paying out income to the two income beneficiaries is very small. The trustee could be accused of showing favoritism to the remainder beneficiary through his or her choice of investments, which could be considered a breach of fiduciary duty. Mailing statements to all beneficiaries and taking reasonable administrative fees out of the trust assets are appropriate. The facts clearly state that the portfolio is well diversified.

24. A is the answer. The assets in the IRA were the result of deductible contributions to a 401(k), and, therefore, no basis existed in the IRA account at Louie's death. IRA assets are considered income in respect of a decedent (IRD) and are fully taxable upon distribution to the beneficiary. No step-up in basis is allowed for IRD assets.

25. B is the answer. The qualified disclaimer is the only technique available to Kathleen. Section 303 stock redemptions and Section 6166 estate tax deferral elections are only available in cases where a closely held corporation is part of the estate. The special-use valuation is not available, as the ranch would need to be 25% of the gross estate, it would need to be a working ranch, and the heirs would need to continue to operate it as a working ranch for ten years after inheriting the property. These facts are not mentioned in the case fact pattern.

CUNNINGHAM CASE

PERSONAL INFORMATION AND BACKGROUND

Alex has spent most of his life in the outdoors, hiking, rafting, and biking throughout the Appalachian Mountain region in western North Carolina. When he graduated from high school 35 years ago, Alex left his small mountain town in pursuit of glamour and fame as an actor in Los Angeles. After a year of barely making ends meet, Alex realized how much he missed the fresh, clean air and simple life he had left back in North Carolina. He returned home and convinced his younger brother Brent that with their pooled savings and a small loan from the local bank, they could open an outdoor adventure company and spend their lives helping others discover the beauty of the wilderness. Their company, ABC Adventures, proved to be very successful and quickly grew to be the largest and best outdoor adventure company in the region.

Alex also came back to North Carolina to marry his high school sweetheart Beth. They had two children, Graham and Louise, and lived in a small cabin on a hill overlooking the river, only one mile upstream from ABC Adventures. Ten years ago, when their youngest child had just turned 18, Beth was diagnosed with a rare, advanced form of cancer and died only three months later. Alex was devastated but eventually found solace through returning to nature, leading customers of ABC Adventures on expeditions.

Like his parents, Graham married his high school sweetheart Kate. They have three children, ages 7, 5, and 3, and live in a small cottage within walking distance of the local elementary school. Graham has worked in various roles at ABC Adventures since high school and currently serves as the lead rafting guide. Graham loves the outdoors as much as his dad and hopes to continue the legacy that his dad and uncle built. Kate currently stays home to care for the children and plans to continue to do so for the foreseeable future.

Louise is still single. While she does not share the same fondness of the outdoors as her father and brother, she loves managing the retail shop of ABC Adventures. She is currently taking business classes at the local community college in the hope that the coursework will prepare her to take on a bigger role at ABC Adventures. Louise currently rents an apartment just off of Main Street in the quaint downtown area.

Alex was not looking to find love after Beth's death, but three years ago, he met a beautiful woman named Samantha, when she and her daughter Madeline joined one of Alex's educational nature hikes. Alex learned that Samantha also lost a spouse to cancer, and they formed a special bond. Two years later Alex asked Samantha to marry him. They, together with Madeline, now live in Alex's cabin and are planning a small, simple wedding in the fall. Samantha is a Canadian citizen, but Madeline was born in the U.S. and has U.S. citizenship. Educated as a biologist, Samantha is teaching on a temporary work visa at the university in a neighboring town about 35 miles away.

Name	Relationship	Age	Occupation	Health	Comments
Alex		52	Business owner and outdoor enthusiast	Excellent	
Beth	Deceased spouse	40 (at death)	N/A	N/A	
Graham	Son	30	Rafting guide	Excellent	Married; three children
Louise	Daughter	28	Retail store manager; university student	Excellent	Single
Brent	Brother	48	Co-owner in family business	Excellent	Single
Samantha	Fiancée	42	Professor	Excellent	Canadian citizen
Madeline	Samantha's daughter	10	Student	Excellent	U.S. citizen

GOALS AND OBJECTIVES

1. Alex wants to make sure that a new estate plan is in place that will properly protect the inheritance for his children but also help provide for Samantha and Madeline.
2. Alex wants to make sure that Samantha could remain in the cabin if something happens to him.
3. Alex wants to help provide for the American Cancer Society (a 501(c)(3) organization) at his death by leaving them a small minority interest in his business.
4. Alex wants to start transferring some of the ownership of the business to his children now.
5. Alex wants to minimize gift and estate taxes.
6. Alex wants to help provide for Louise's and Madeline's educations.

RETIREMENT INFORMATION

Alex would like to continue working in the company for as long as he can but is committed to beginning gradually to transfer shares of the business to Graham and Louise as they take on more responsibility. Alex would maintain a majority interest in the company until he decides to retire. Samantha would like to continue teaching for another 20 years, and the prospects of extending her work visa are good due to the shortage of biologists in the region.

EDUCATION INFORMATION

Alex would like to help out Louise with her community college tuition payment for the summer and fall semesters, a total of $5,000. Because he and his children never got to attend a traditional four-year college, he would like to set some money aside so Madeline can have the option to attend the institution of her choice. He is planning to open up a 529 plan for her as a birthday gift this year and fund it with $75,000. Her birthday is June 1st.

ESTATE PLANNING INFORMATION

Alex and Samantha never updated their wills after their spouse's deaths. In its current state, Alex's will would leave everything split equally between Graham and Louise, *per stirpes*. Brent is the executor of Alex's will. Samantha's will would leave everything to Madeline, with her attorney Jake Holmes serving as the executor. Her sister Kim is named as Madeline's guardian.

Alex has a revocable living trust that leaves all his assets to Graham and Louise, *per stirpes*.

Alex and Samantha have discussed new estate planning documents with Alex's attorney Kent Long. Kent has proposed that Alex redraft his will to create a testamentary trust that would be funded with enough assets to take advantage of any estate tax exclusion amount available when he dies. The assets would be held in trust for the benefit of Graham and Louise, with Samantha as the trustee. The remaining assets would pass outright to Samantha. Kent also recommends that both Alex and Samantha execute powers of attorney for property and health care.

TRUST INFORMATION

Earlier this year, Alex established a grantor-retained annuity trust (GRAT) and transferred $500,000 worth of stock in a local coffee company called Fourbucks. The term of the trust is five years, and Alex receives an annual annuity payment of $75,000 at the end of each year. The company is planning to issue an initial public offering next year, after which Alex anticipates the assets in the trust could grow to more than $1 million. Graham and Louise are the remainder beneficiaries of the trust.

Over ten years ago, Alex established an irrevocable life insurance trust (ILIT), funded with a $2 million life insurance policy. Alex named his attorney Kent as its trustee. As the trustee, Kent has the power to loan money to Alex's estate and/or purchase assets from Alex's estate at full fair market value. Graham and Louise are the beneficiaries of the trust, and both hold Crummey powers. Alex makes annual gifts to the trust to pay the premium for the life insurance policy.

INVESTMENT ACCOUNT INFORMATION

Alex has one large brokerage account in which he has accumulated most of his earnings. Alex plans to give half of this account to Samantha outright as a wedding gift after they are married.

Alex also has a 401(k) plan through ABC Adventures to which he defers the maximum amount allowed each year. The company matches his deferrals up to 5% of his compensation and makes a 10% profit-sharing contribution each year.

Alex allocates his portfolios in both accounts 50% to equities and 50% to bonds.

BUSINESS INFORMATION

ABC Adventures is a limited liability company owned 65% by Alex and 35% by Brent. A recent valuation estimated the assets of the business to be worth around $4,000,000. The company leases its main property, a lodge, from Alex and Brent for $3,000/month. Other real estate used by the business is owned by ABC Adventures and is valued around $750,000 (basis of $250,000). The company owns equipment (rafts, tents, and other gear) worth $500,000, as well as a large, industrial-strength machine used to clean the equipment, worth $200,000. The equipment is in various stages of its useful life, and accumulated depreciation equals $300,000. The cleaning machine is fully depreciated but is still in excellent condition.

INSURANCE INFORMATION

Life Insurance

Insured	Owner	Beneficiary	Face Amount	Type	Cash Value	Annual Premium	Notes
Alex	ILIT	ILIT	$2,000,000	Whole life	$250,000	$20,000	Bought 12 years ago
Alex	Alex	None	$1,000,000	Group term	None	None	Company-provided

**Alex Cunningham
Projected Cash Flow
for the Current Year**

Cash Inflows

Alex's salary	$225,000
NC lodge rental income	$ 23,400
Investment income	Reinvested
GRAT annuity	$ 75,000

Cash Outflows

Taxes (income, payroll, real estate)	$ 75,000
Retirement plan contributions	$ 17,500
Lifestyle expenses	$ 60,000
Insurance premiums	$ 20,000

Alex saves any remaining income into his brokerage account.

Alex Cunningham
Statement of Financial Position
as of December 31st Last Year

ASSETS

Cash and Cash Equivalents

Checking account	$ 25,000
Savings account	$ 50,000
Total Cash and Cash Equivalents	$ 75,000

Invested Assets

GRAT[1]	$ 500,000
ABC Adventures company stock[2]	$2,600,000
401(k) plan[3]	$ 450,000
Brokerage account[4]	$1,200,000
Total Invested Assets	$4,750,000

Personal-Use Assets

NC cabin[5]	$ 250,000
NC lodge[6]	$ 390,000
Ford truck	$ 15,000
Furniture and household items	$ 50,000
Total Personal-Use Assets	$ 705,000

Total Assets **$5,530,000**

LIABILITIES AND NET WORTH

Liabilities

Mortgage – NC cabin[7]	$ 60,000
Mortgage – NC lodge[8]	$ 80,000
Total Liabilities	$ 140,000

Total Liabilities **$ 140,000**

Net Worth **$5,390,000**

Notes to the Financial Statements

All assets are held in sole ownership by Alex unless otherwise noted.

[1] The Fourbucks Company stock is held in the grantor-retained annuity trust (GRAT) established earlier this year. (See the Trust Information section for details.)

[2] Amount represents Alex's ownership (65% of the total value).

[3] Beth is the named primary beneficiary. No contingent beneficiaries are named.

[4] The brokerage account is owned by Alex's revocable living trust.

[5] The land is worth $45,000. Alex's basis is $200,000.

[6] Amount represents Alex's ownership (65% of the total value). The property is held as Tenants in common with Brent and is leased to ABC Adventures. Alex's basis in his share is $65,000.

[7] There are five years remaining on the mortgage. The interest rate is fixed at 7.0%.

[8] There are 10 years remaining on the mortgage. The interest rate is fixed at 9.5%.

CUNNINGHAM CASE
APPLICATION QUESTIONS

1. Which best describes how Alex's share in the ownership of the NC lodge leased by ABC Adventures will be treated if Alex died today?

(Topic 53)

A. It will be included in his probate estate.

B. It will pass outright to Brent.

C. It will need to be sold by the estate to pay taxes.

D. It will qualify for the special-use valuation.

2. If Alex died today, how would the proceeds of his company-provided group term life insurance policy pass?

(Topic 54)

A. By operation of law

B. By contract

C. By will

D. By trust

3. If Alex died today, which asset would NOT be included in his probate estate?

(Topic 54)

A. NC lodge

B. The term life insurance policy

C. The 401(k) account

D. The brokerage account

4. In addition to the new estate planning documents recommended by his attorney, what document would be MOST important for Alex to implement as part of his estate plan?

(Topic 55)

A. A holographic will

B. A charitable lead trust

C. A prenuptial agreement

D. A power of attorney for health care

5. Which of the following provisions would be of the highest priority in Alex and Samantha's new wills?

(Topic 55)

A. Naming a guardian for Madeline

B. Leaving all assets to each other

C. Creating a revocable living trust

D. Describing their advanced medical directives

6. What is the best way for Alex to help Louise with her education costs and avoid any gift taxes?

(Topic 57)

A. Give the money directly to Louise.

B. Pay the money directly to the school.

C. Place the assets in a 529 plan for Louise's benefit.

D. Place the assets in an irrevocable trust with Louise as beneficiary.

7. If Alex makes a gift to Samantha of assets from the brokerage account as planned, how much of the gift will be taxable?

(Topic 57)

A. None

B. $453,000

C. $586,000

D. All

8. How many annual exclusion amounts can Alex use to reduce the amount of the taxable gift to the trust he created this year?

(Topic 57)

A. None

B. One

C. Two

D. Three

9. What would be the tax consequences of the planned contribution to the 529 plan for Madeline if Alex waited to make the gift on their first wedding anniversary?

(Topic 57)

A. The gift would be subject to gift tax only.
B. The gift would be subject to both gift tax and generation-skipping transfer tax.
C. The gift would be subject to both gift tax and kiddie tax.
D. The gift would not be subject to tax.

10. Which of the following powers would be a reasonable power for Samantha to hold as trustee of the proposed testamentary trust in Alex's will?

(Topic 58)

A. A 5-and-5 power
B. A Crummey power
C. A general power of appointment
D. A special power of appointment

11. Which person in this case is considered to be incapacitated?

(Topic 58)

A. Madeline
B. Alex
C. Beth
D. Louise

12. If Alex died today, which asset would be excluded from his gross estate?

(Topic 59)

A. The 401(k) plan
B. The brokerage account
C. The Fourbucks' stock
D. The proceeds from the whole life insurance policy

13. If Alex executes a new will as recommended by his attorney, how would the assets passing to the testamentary trust be treated in the calculation of the estate tax?

(Topic 59)

A. The assets would be excluded from the gross estate and thus are not taxable.
B. The assets would be sheltered from tax through the use of a marital deduction.
C. The assets would be sheltered from tax through the use of the applicable credit amount.
D. The assets would be included in the taxable estate, and estate tax will be due.

14. If Alex died next year, which asset would be the best source to use to pay estate taxes?

(Topic 60)

A. Assets in the irrevocable life insurance trust
B. Stock in ABC Adventures
C. The North Carolina real estate
D. Assets in the brokerage account

15. Which is the safest and most tax-efficient way for Alex to ensure that Samantha would be able to remain in the house if something happened to him?

(Topic 62)

A. Transfer the house to a revocable living trust that gives Samantha a life estate.
B. Execute a new will, leaving the house to Samantha.
C. Gift the house outright to Samantha today.
D. Place the house in a 10-year QPRT and name Samantha as the remainder beneficiary.

16. Which factor would NOT impact the valuation of the gift to the grantor-retained annuity trust?

(Topic 63)

A. Applicable federal rates
B. The term of the trust
C. The annuity payment amount
D. Graham's life expectancy

17. Which type of charitable trust would be the best to fulfill Alex's goal of providing for the American Cancer Society?

(Topic 64)

A. A charitable lead annuity trust (CLAT)
B. A charitable lead unitrust (CLUT)
C. A charitable remainder annuity trust (CRAT)
D. A charitable remainder unitrust (CRUT)

18. Which of the following statements best describes the gift tax consequences of the premiums paid on Alex's whole life policy?

(Topic 65)

A. The premiums are not considered gifts.
B. The premiums qualify for annual exclusions.
C. The premiums qualify for the marital deduction.
D. The premiums are fully taxable.

19. If Alex executes a new will, as recommended by his attorney, how much of the assets passing to the testamentary trust would qualify for the marital deduction?

(Topic 66)

A. None
B. $14,000
C. $125,000
D. All

20. Which asset of ABC Adventures would be most appropriate for the use of the gift-leaseback transfer technique?

(Topic 67)

A. The stock
B. The real estate
C. The cleaning machine
D. The equipment

21. Which premium or discount would most likely be applied to the gift valuation of stock in ABC Adventures if Alex transfers stock to Graham and Louise next year?

(Topic 68)

A. Control premium
B. Blockage discount
C. Key person discount
D. Lack-of-marketability discount

22. If Alex marries Samantha, which estate planning technique(s) would an attorney most likely recommend to transfer Alex's estate?

(Topic 68)

A. A bypass trust and a QTIP trust
B. A bypass trust and a QDOT trust
C. A bypass trust and a marital trust
D. All assets left outright to the surviving spouse

23. Which individual currently serves in a fiduciary capacity?

(Topic 70)

A. Kent
B. Brent
C. Kim
D. Jake

24. If Alex died today, a portion of the income in respect of a decedent from the 401(k) assets would be reported on which tax return?

(Topic 71)

A. Beth's income tax return
B. Louise's income tax return
C. Alex's estate tax return
D. Alex's income tax return

25. If Alex had died early this year, which postmortem planning technique would be the most effective in reducing or deferring estate taxes?

(Topic 72)

A. Louise makes a qualified disclaimer of her portion of the inheritance.
B. Brent claims a Section 6166 deferral of estate tax.
C. Brent makes a QTIP election on all assets over $5.43 million.
D. Brent elects a Section 2032A special-use valuation on the business real estate.

CUNNINGHAM CASE
ANSWERS AND EXPLANATIONS

1. A is the answer. The lodge is owned as tenants in common by Alex and Brent, which means that Alex's share will not pass automatically to the surviving tenant but, instead, will pass through the will and be included in the probate estate. If Alex died today, his estate would not have the brokerage account to pay estate taxes, but his estate taxes will be low due to the unified credit that will shelter $5.43 million of assets. There is nothing in the case that indicates the lodge would need to be sold to pay the estate tax, especially since the ILIT allows the trustee to loan money to Alex's estate or purchase assets from Alex's estate. The lodge would not qualify for the special-use valuation because it is not worth 25% of the gross estate.

2. C is the answer. Alex's company-provided group term life insurance policy has no beneficiary designated and, therefore, will pass by the terms of his will. Life insurance policies with designated beneficiaries pass by contract.

3. D is the answer. The brokerage account is owned by Alex's revocable living trust and would transfer by the terms of the trust. The 401(k) has his deceased wife as the primary beneficiary, with no contingent beneficiary and would, therefore, pass through the will. The life insurance policy has no beneficiary and would also pass through the will. The NC lodge is owned as tenants in common with Brent, and Alex's share would pass through the will. All items passing through the will are included in the probate estate.

4. C is the answer. Because Alex is planning a second marriage, he should consider executing a prenuptial agreement to protect his assets in the case of death, divorce, or separation. A holographic will is a handwritten will and is not necessary. The power of attorney for health care is one of the documents already recommended by the attorney. The charitable lead trust is not more important than a prenuptial agreement, nor would it satisfy Alex's wishes to leave the charity assets at his death.

5. A is the answer. Once a new will is executed, Samantha's old will that names a guardian would be invalid. She needs to make sure that a guardian for Madeline is named in the new will. Leaving all assets to each other would disinherit Alex's children. A revocable living trust and an advanced medical directive are not provisions detailed in a will; rather, they are separate documents.

6. B is the answer. If education expenses are paid directly to the school, the transfer is considered qualified and, therefore, not a taxable gift. All other methods mentioned would be considered taxable gifts and could trigger a gift tax.

7. B is the answer. Assets exceeding $147,000 in 2015 gifted to a non-U.S.-citizen spouse will be taxable. Alex plans to gift Samantha half of the brokerage account (600,000). $600,000 less the $147,000 exclusion equals $453,000 as a taxable gift.

8. A is the answer. Gifts to grantor-retained annuity trusts are future-interest gifts (a remainder interest after the term of the GRAT) and are, therefore, not eligible to be offset by annual exclusion amounts.

9. A is the answer. Gifts to 529 plans are subject to the gift tax. Since Alex and Samantha would be married at the time of the gift, the gift would not be subject to the generation-skipping transfer tax because Madeline would be Alex's daughter. If Alex and Samantha were not married at the time of the gift, Madeline would be considered a skip-generation for purposes of the gift. The kiddie tax does not apply in this case.

10. D is the answer. A special power of appointment would be the only reasonable power to allow in the testamentary bypass trust. A 5-and-5 power or general power of appointment could trigger the inclusion of some or all of the assets of the trust in Samantha's estate, thereby eliminating the purpose of using the trust to exclude assets from Samantha's estate. A Crummey power is only available to beneficiaries of a trust and does not exist in a bypass trust because the trust is not set up to receive recurring gifts.

11. A is the answer. Madeline, as a minor child, is subject to legal incapacity, regardless of her mental status. Beth is deceased, not incapacitated. There is nothing in the case to indicate that either Alex or Louise would be considered incapacitated.

12. D is the answer. The whole life insurance policy is held by the irrevocable life insurance trust; therefore, the proceeds would be excluded from the gross estate. The Fourbucks' stock is held by the grantor-retained annuity trust and would be included in Alex's estate if he died during the term of the trust. The brokerage account, held by Alex's revocable living trust, and the 401(k) plan assets would both be included in his estate.

13. C is the answer. The testamentary trust in the proposed will is a bypass trust whose purpose is to shelter assets in the amount of the applicable exclusion amount from estate tax. The assets will be included in the taxable estate, but the tax due will be offset by the applicable credit amount.

14. A is the answer. The assets in the irrevocable life insurance trust (proceeds from the $2M life insurance policy) would be the most liquid of the options. The trustee of the trust can lend money to the estate or buy assets from the estate to generate the cash necessary to pay estate taxes.

15. A is the answer. A revocable living trust that gives Samantha a life estate is the best answer of the four choices. If Alex leaves the house to Samantha in the will, there is a risk of a will contest that could take away her rights to stay in the house. If he transfers it outright as a gift or in a QPRT, he runs the risk that something could go wrong later in the marriage, and his children would no longer have rights to the house. The terms of the revocable living trust could be changed at any time if necessary, and Alex could name his children as the remainder beneficiaries for the home after Samantha passes away.

16. D is the answer. The life expectancy of a beneficiary is not a factor in valuing the gift to a grantor-retained annuity trust (GRAT). The value of the transferred asset is bifurcated into a present interest and future interest. The present interest is the present value of the annuity stream and is calculated using inputs such as the life expectancy of the grantor, the term of the trust, the applicable federal rates, and the amount of the annuity payment. The future interest is the remainder interest of the transferred asset left after subtracting the value of the annuity and is equal to the amount of the gift.

17. C is the answer. Alex wishes to leave a minority interest in his business to the charitable organization at his death. Because he wants to give an asset that is difficult to value, he should choose a charitable trust that does not require annual revaluations (annuity trust). The best of the four options is the CRAT because it is an annuity trust that would leave the interest to the charity at his death.

18. B is the answer. The premiums are contributed to an irrevocable life insurance trust, whose beneficiaries hold Crummey powers. This allows the gifts to be considered present-interest gifts and qualify for annual exclusions.

19. A is the answer. The testamentary trust in the proposed will is a bypass trust. Assets passing to this trust would not qualify for the marital deduction.

20. C is the answer. The gift-leaseback technique is most appropriate for fully-depreciated equipment that is in good working condition. The asset can be gifted to a family member and then leased back for business use. Stock cannot be leased. The real estate and equipment are not yet fully depreciated.

21. D is the answer. The lack-of-marketability discount is a commonly used discount in the valuation of transfers of a closely held business. The control premium would not apply because Alex would be gifting minority interests. The blockage discount only applies to companies that are publicly held. The key person discount would only apply if there were a loss of a key person in the business.

22. B is the answer. The typical estate plan for someone with a non-U.S.-citizen spouse and children from a previous marriage would be a bypass trust with a QDOT trust.

23. A is the answer. Kent is the only person serving in a current fiduciary capacity as trustee of the irrevocable life insurance trust. Kim (as a future guardian), Brent (as a future executor), and Jake (as a future executor) will all serve in a fiduciary capacity in the future (after the death of Alex or Samantha, for example) but do not have a current fiduciary duty.

24. B is the answer. Income in respect of a decedent is reported on the beneficiary's tax return. Beth is the primary beneficiary on Alex's 401(k) plan, but she is deceased. No contingent beneficiary is named, so the assets will pass through the will to Graham and Louise, who would each report their share of the distribution on their income tax returns.

25. B is the answer. The Section 6166 deferral of estate tax election is the only option that makes sense – the business is most likely worth more than 35% of the adjusted gross estate, so the estate would qualify. A rough calculation of adjusted gross estate (Net worth + $1M life insurance) = $6.4M. $6.4M x 35% = $2.24M, which is less than the $2.6M value of the business. Louise making a qualified disclaimer would do nothing to reduce or eliminate tax. The real estate assets are not greater than 25% of the gross estate, so the special-use valuation would not apply. No part of the estate would be eligible for a QTIP election because there was no current spouse (they are engaged to be married this fall).

FRED AND MARY FERRIS

PERSONAL INFORMATION

Fred and Mary Ferris have engaged your services for the development of a comprehensive financial plan. Their primary concerns, however, revolve around estate planning objectives.

Fred, age 52, is a one-third owner of an automobile parts supplier in Michigan. The business has survived the cyclical nature of the auto industry through a combination of high-quality parts, just-in-time delivery, and superior cost containment.

Mary, also 52, works part-time at the art institute, mostly to satisfy her aesthetic senses. She expects to continue working until age 60.

This is a second marriage for Fred, whose first wife died at age 32 in a car accident. Fred has one son from that marriage, Ted, age 28, who is happily married but has financial difficulties due to his one child, Ned, age 3, who has special needs.

Together, Fred and Mary have two daughters, both in private high school. Felicity is an honors student in her junior year, and Harmony is a sophomore and has musical talent.

Name	Relationship	Occupation	Notes
Fred	Husband	Business owner	Successful
Mary	Wife	Docent at art institute	Charitably inclined
Ted	Son	Retail sales	Married; special-needs child
Felicity	Daughter	HS junior	Scientifically gifted
Harmony	Daughter	HS sophomore	Musically gifted

Mary has been generous with her time in helping Ted with his special-needs son Ned. Her assistance has solidified her excellent relationship with Ted and his wife Maria, a Canadian citizen. In addition, Mary is quite interested in leaving substantial amounts to the art institute at her death.

Fred's business operates as a C corporation; Fred is an equal one-third owner with Harold Dietz and Gerald Keats. They are seriously contemplating a number of business agreements, including a buy-sell agreement, a non-qualified deferred-compensation plan, and a stock option plan of some kind. All three seek your advice in these matters.

A recent business valuation produced a fair market value of $30 million for the business, with an expectation of 8% annual growth in the next 15 years. As all three owners are in their 50s and want to retire at age 66, they are concerned with successor management.

Fred recently sent a registered letter to Harold and Gerald, indicating his intent that his son Ted should receive his share of the business at Fred's death. At this point, Ted is becoming increasingly interested in his father's business as a career.

The owners each draw an annual salary of $150,000 and take equal bonuses, depending on profitability. Bonuses have averaged $50,000 each in the last five years.

The business has implemented a 401(k) plan with a matching contribution of $.50 per dollar on the first 6% of employee contributions. A dozen well-paid factory workers all participate.

The employees and their families are all covered by an excellent group health insurance plan, as well as group term life insurance equal to their base salary. A separate employer-paid group long-term disability plan also covers all employees for 60% of base pay, with a 90-day elimination period. The group LTD plan is integrated with Social Security and workers' compensation.

ESTATE PLANNING DOCUMENTS

Fred and Mary Ferris each have wills, leaving everything to the survivor. Each will contains a 120-day survivorship clause. In a simultaneous death, the will and state law presume that the wife survives. If there is no surviving spouse, the children of the testator share equally. They each named their surviving spouse as the executor.

Fred executed an unfunded irrevocable trust four years ago for the benefit of his children and grandchildren that he hopes to use in the future. There is no withdrawal right in the trust.

Fred and Mary have made no prior taxable gifts.

At Fred's suggestion, Ted and Maria have created standard revocable living trusts with marital and residuary trusts. Large life insurance policies were also purchased on Ted and Maria ($500,000 each), payable to their respective trusts.

LIFE INSURANCE SUMMARY

Insured	Owner	Type	Face Amount	Premium	Beneficiary
Fred	Fred	Group term	$150,000	Employer-paid	Primary: Mary Secondary: Ted
Fred	Mary	Whole life	$250,000	$4,200/year	Primary: Mary Secondary: None
Fred	Fred	15-year term	$1,000,000	$1,800/year	Primary: Mary Secondary: None

Balance Sheet
Fred and Mary Ferris
December 31, Last Year

Assets			Liabilities

Assets		Liabilities	
Cash and cash equivalents: J	$ 31,000	Car loan: H	$ 17,000
Cash value of life ins.: W	36,000	Mortgage: J	228,000
Short-term fixed-inc. fund: J	40,000		
Value fund: J	83,000	Total Liabilities	$ 245,000
Growth fund: H[1]	110,000		
Global fund: H	31,000		
SPDA: H[2]	160,000		
401(k) plan: H[3]	225,000		
529 plans: H[4]	110,000		
Business: H	10,000,000		
Residence: J	450,000		
Personal property: J	75,000		
Car: H	25,000	Net Worth	$11,131,000
Total Assets	$11,376,000	Total Liabilities and Net Worth	$11,376,000

H = Husband
W = Wife
J = Joint tenancy with right of survivorship

---

[1]Payable on death: Mary

[2]Single-premium deferred annuity, issued 7/1/80; the initial premium was $40,000, and the estate is beneficiary.

[3]Beneficiary: Mary

[4]Mary is the successor-owner at Fred's death; the average annual return has been 0%.

INVESTMENT DETAIL

Asset	Fair Market Value	Basis	Projected Growth Rate	Purchased
Short-term fixed-income fund	$40,000	$41,000	1%	3 years ago
Value fund	$83,000	$50,000	7%	2 years ago
Growth fund	$110,000	$50,000	8%	8 years ago
Global fund	$31,000	$22,000	6%	4 years ago

Fred and Mary Ferris
Cash Flow Projection
Current Year

<u>Inflows</u>

Salary: Fred	$150,000
Bonus: Fred	50,000
Salary: Mary	25,000
Interest/Dividends	<u>Reinvested</u>
Total Inflows	**$225,000**

<u>Outflows</u>

Mortgage: principal and interest	$ 31,200
Real estate tax	6,200
Homeowners insurance (HO-3)	820
Maintenance/Repairs	8,300
Food	7,800
Clothing	4,000
Utilities	5,600
Car loan	7,200
Travel/Vacation/Entertainment	16,000
Life insurance	6,000
Educational funding (daughters' 529 plans)	56,000
401(k) plan contribution: Fred	16,000
Charitable contributions	10,000
Federal income tax	30,000
State income tax	8,000
Federal and state payroll taxes	<u>10,674</u>
Total Outflows	**$223,794**
Surplus	**$1,206**

<u>Goals and Objectives</u> (in order of priority)

1. Provide $120,000 of annual after-tax cash flow to the surviving family members at the death of either spouse.
2. Pay the remaining mortgage balance at the death of either spouse.
3. Provide adequate college funding for their daughters.
4. Provide assistance to Ted for Ned's care.
5. Eliminate the federal estate tax at the first death.
6. Reduce or eliminate the federal estate tax at the second death.
7. Avoid probate at death or incapacity.
8. Secure professional financial assistance for the survivors after either spouse's death.
9. Ensure adequate retirement income from all sources, including the sale of the business interest.

FRED AND MARY FERRIS CASE
APPLICATION QUESTIONS

1. Which of the following is a consequence of the way in which the Ferris' home is titled?

(Topic 53)

A. Either spouse can dispose of his or her interest by will at death.

B. If Mary is the first to die, no portion of the home will be included in her probate estate.

C. At the first death, there is a full step-up in basis for the property.

D. If Fred contributed all of the money to purchase the home, the entire value is included in his gross estate at his death.

2. Which of the following statements describes the effect of the titling of the automobile parts supply business interest?

(Topic 53)

A. Mary must consent to any sale or other disposition of the interest.

B. If Fred is the first to die, no portion of the business interest will pass through probate.

C. At Fred's death, one-half of the value of the business interest will be included in his gross estate.

D. If Fred dies today, there will be a full step-up in basis for the business interest.

3. If Fred and Mary sell the value fund, and the proceeds are invested in the global fund, which of the following statements is correct?

(Topic 53)

A. Fred will have greater control over the disposition of the proceeds at his death.

B. A gift will occur, and a gift tax return will need to be filed.

C. If Fred dies before Mary, the proceeds will not be subject to probate.

D. The proceeds will continue to be owned and titled as when invested in the value fund.

4. Which of the following transfers will result in income tax reduction for Fred and Mary?

(Topic 53)

A. Transferring the growth fund to Fred's trust.

B. Transferring the short-term fixed-income fund to Mary's name.

C. Transferring the business interest to Fred and Mary as joint tenants WROS.

D. Transferring the life insurance to Fred's trust.

5. There are several items of Fred and Mary's personal property that have special meaning to Ted. Which of the following statements concerning the personal property items is correct?

(Topic 53)

A. Ted has a future interest in the items.
B. Ted has a contingent remainder interest in the items if Fred dies before Mary.
C. Ted has a contingent remainder interest in the items if Mary dies before Fred.
D. Ted has no present or future interest in the items.

6. If Fred dies today, what is the amount of his probate estate?

(Topic 54)

A. $160,000
B. $251,000
C. $10,000,000
D. $10,216,000

7. If Mary dies today, how much is her probate estate?

(Topic 54)

A. $0
B. $36,000
C. $110,000
D. $250,000

8. If Mary predeceases Fred, what is the likely disposition of the whole life policy?

(Topic 54)

A. The policy will pass automatically to Fred, outside of probate.
B. The policy will generate a taxable amount to the recipient for the excess over basis.
C. The policy proceeds will pass to Fred's estate at Fred's death.
D. The death benefit will be paid income-tax-free to the beneficiary at Mary's death.

9. Under the current documents, what is the disposition of Fred's business interest at his death?

(Topic 54)

A. The business automatically passes to the surviving owners, who are then required to pay the estate.
B. The business interest goes to Mary and the children, without probate court involvement.
C. The business will pass to Mary, subject to probate.
D. The business will go to Ted under the letter Fred sent to his co-shareholders.

10. Which of the following involves a transfer by contract that avoids probate at the death of both Fred and Mary, regardless of who dies first?

(Topic 54)

A. SPDA
B. Value fund
C. Whole life policy
D. Section 529 plans

11. Which of the following is a correct description of Fred's will?

(Topic 55)

A. Joint will
B. Simple will
C. Pour-over will
D. Mutual will

12. Under the current arrangements, which of the following is Fred able to change without probate court involvement if Mary becomes incapacitated?

(Topic 55)

A. Whole life policy
B. Residence
C. Value fund
D. Cash and cash equivalents

13. If Fred establishes a revocable living trust, which of the following can he freely transfer to the trust?

(Topic 55)

A. Residence
B. Whole life policy
C. Value fund
D. Business interest

14. If Fred dies, and Mary subsequently dies 130 days after Fred's death, which of the following best represents the likely recipients of Mary's wealth?

(Topic 55)

A. Felicity and Harmony
B. Ted, Felicity, and Harmony
C. The estate beneficiaries of Mary and Fred, equally
D. Mary's heirs at law, under the state intestacy statute

15. Under the current arrangements, if Mary were to lapse into an irreversible coma, which of the following is the most likely tool Fred would use to deal with medical issues for her?

(Topic 55)

A. Living will
B. Health care power of attorney
C. Durable power of attorney
D. The courts

16. If Fred gives Ted $8,000 for Ned's benefit, which of the following is correct?

(Topic 56)

A. The gift will adversely affect Ned's eligibility for public benefits.
B. Ted's wife Maria will be entitled to 50%, due to state property laws.
C. Ned will need to cosign any check given to Ted.
D. The gift will qualify for the annual exclusion.

17. Fred and Mary are contemplating a family gifting program of some magnitude. Which of the following is the most legitimate rationale for a gifting pattern?

(Topic 56)

A. Gifts of annual exclusion amounts to the children are inappropriate because the unlimited marital deduction eliminates the federal estate tax.
B. Gifts directly to Ned are suitable, based on need.
C. Gifts to Ted are appropriate to remove the future appreciation for their estates.
D. Gifts to the daughters would serve to enhance their self-motivation.

18. Which of the following gifts is a future-interest gift?

(Topic 56)

A. Fred names Ted as beneficiary of his 401(k) plan.

B. Mary transfers the whole life policy to Fred.

C. Fred changes the beneficiary of his group insurance to his irrevocable trust.

D. Fred transfers $14,000 cash to his irrevocable trust.

19. Which of the following would constitute a generation-skipping transfer if it was made today?

(Topic 56)

A. A direct gift from Fred to Ned's Uniform Transfers to Minors Act account, using the value fund

B. Creation of a special-needs trust for Ned's benefit

C. Designating Ted as the holder of a limited power of appointment over property exclusively for Ned's benefit

D. Nominating Maria as the holder of a general power of appointment over property for Ned's benefit

20. Under the three-year rule, which of the following transfers would be brought back into Fred's gross estate for estate tax purposes?

(Topic 56)

A. A gift of the whole life policy to the irrevocable trust within three years of Fred's death

B. The transfer of Fred's individual term policy to the irrevocable trust within three years of his death

C. The collateral assignment of Fred's group insurance benefit to Ted for Ned's benefit, within two years of Fred's death

D. The purchase of a new policy on Fred's life by the trustee of the irrevocable trust within one year of Fred's death

21. Which of the following, in addition to current arrangements, would generate a taxable gift?

(Topic 57)

A. A gift of $14,000 from the growth fund to Harmony

B. A split gift of $28,000 from Fred and Mary to Ted and Maria from the value fund

C. A gift of Fred's entire interest in the residence to Mary

D. A payment in excess of $14,000 to Felicity's high school for her tuition

22. Seriously contemplating early retirement, Fred wants to know the gift tax payable if he gives Ted 50% of his business interest and sells him the other 50% on a 20-year installment note. Which of the following is correct?

(Topic 57)

    A. Any gift tax is payable ratably over a 20-year period.

    B. No gift tax is payable.

    C. The gift tax due is $1,750,000.

    D. Under this arrangement, Ted would be responsible for the payment of any gift tax.

23. As part of their estate planning, Fred and Mary decide to leave the growth fund to the art institute at Mary's death. To implement the plan, Fred transfers ownership of the growth fund to Mary. Which of the following is correct?

(Topic 57)

    A. The bequest to the art institute will be deferred until Fred's subsequent death.

    B. At Mary's death, the growth fund is included in her gross estate.

    C. The bequest to the art institute will be subject to the 30% AGI limitation.

    D. The growth fund is included in Fred's estate if he dies within three years of the transfer to Mary.

24. This year Mary and Fred each file a Form 709 to elect gift-splitting. What is the maximum amount they can give directly this year to Ted and his family, without gift tax and without resorting to use of the gift tax lifetime exemption?

(Topic 57)

    A. None

    B. $56,000

    C. $84,000

    D. $140,000

25. What is the consequence of a gift directly to the daughters of $28,000 each from Fred and Mary?

(Topic 57)

    A. The gifts are taxable, but no gift tax is due because of the exemption.

    B. The gifts are fully excluded.

    C. The gifts are deductible up to 50% of AGI if made in cash for their education.

    D. The gifts are currently fully taxable because of the daughters' ages.

26. If Fred becomes disabled for 12 consecutive months, which of the following is correct?

(Topic 58)

    A. Benefits from his disability policy are income-tax-free.

    B. The total benefits payable from the disability policy are $67,500.

    C. Benefits payable under the disability policy equal $90,000.

    D. No benefits are payable from the disability policy if Social Security disability benefits are also payable.

27. In the current situation, which of the following is the most serious weakness in terms of the Ferris family's planning for incapacity?

(Topic 58)

    A. Inadequate disability insurance for Fred

    B. Inadvertent disqualification for Ned's government assistance

    C. Lack of a buy-sell agreement, funded with disability buyout insurance

    D. Insufficient protection against long-term nursing care expenses

28. If Mary becomes disabled for more than 90 days, which of the following is correct about her disability benefits?

(Topic 58)

A. She will receive benefits under Fred's long-term disability plan as a qualifying dependent.
B. Benefits from Social Security would be payable as long as her disability is expected to last 12 months or more.
C. Mary would be eligible for 60% income replacement on her own policy.
D. Mary would receive no disability benefits.

29. If Fred becomes disabled, which of the following plans currently provides protection?

(Topic 58)

A. The key person disability insurance of the business
B. Disability buyout insurance
C. Business overhead expense disability plan
D. Group long-term disability plan

30. If Fred became terminally ill, which of the following would provide the most potential benefit?

(Topic 58)

A. A viatical settlement of his whole life policy
B. An accelerated death benefit from his individual term policy
C. An advance on his group term policy
D. The disability income benefits payable under the long-term disability plan

31. If Fred dies, which of the following is not included in his gross estate?

(Topic 59)

A. The funds set aside for Felicity's education
B. The group life insurance
C. The individual term insurance
D. The SPDA

32. If Fred dies today, what is the amount included in his gross estate?

(Topic 59)

A. $10,828,500
B. $10,953,000
C. $12,040,500
D. $12,150,500

33. At Fred's death, which of the following represents the amount deductible from his gross estate in terms of debt?

(Topic 59)

A. $17,000
B. $114,000
C. $131,000
D. $245,000

34. Which of the following represents Fred and Mary's adjusted taxable gifts?

(Topic 59)

A. $0
B. $36,000
C. $110,000
D. $160,000

35. If Fred dies today, which of the following is the amount of the unified credit used in his estate?

(Topic 59)

A. $0
B. $345,800
C. $780,800
D. $2,117,800

36. Considering the current estate plan, which of the following best describes Fred's liquidity position at death?

(Topic 60)

A. Severely impaired
B. Moderately impaired
C. Modestly impaired
D. Adequate

37. For which of the following techniques is Fred's estate currently eligible?

(Topic 60)

A. Sec. 303 partial stock redemption
B. Sec. 6166 installment payment
C. Sec. 2032A special-use valuation
D. Sec. 2703 valuation, due to a bona fide business agreement

38. If Fred completes business succession documents that transfer his business interest at death to Ted, which technique involves the lowest adverse impact on Fred's estate liquidity?

(Topic 60)

A. A funded one-way buyout agreement
B. Sec. 303 partial stock redemption
C. Partial transfer of Fred's individual term policy to Ted
D. Transfer of the whole life policy to Ted

39. Which of the following techniques is most effective in satisfying liquidity needs at Mary's death?

(Topic 60)

A. Transferring ownership of the whole life policy back to Fred
B. Acquiring a new policy on Mary's life, which is owned by Mary
C. Liquidating the growth fund, using a full step-up in basis
D. Arranging for a loan from Fred's business

40. If Fred and Mary are killed simultaneously in an auto accident today, which of the following best describes the liquidity situation?

(Topic 60)

A. Liquidity is sufficient to pay the estate tax.
B. The liquidity in the estate is enough to pay about 50% of the tax due.
C. Since no estate tax will be due, the liquidity position is irrelevant.
D. The conflict between the survivorship clause in the wills and the state law causes the liquidity impairment.

41. Under the current documents, which of the following powers is Mary presumed to have if Fred dies first?

(Topic 61)

A. Five-and-five power
B. Limited power of appointment
C. General power of appointment
D. A power limited by an ascertainable standard

42. At Fred's death, Mary would, in effect, have a general power of appointment over the short-term fixed-income fund to what extent?

(Topic 61)

A. Not at all
B. 50%
C. 100%
D. Her contribution

43. Assuming that Fred funds the existing trust, what is the gift tax treatment of money placed in the trust?

(Topic 61)

A. Gifts to the trust will be future interests.
B. Annual exclusions are available for each trust beneficiary.
C. Each beneficiary has a 5-and-5 power with respect to initial gifts.
D. Trust beneficiaries will have a cumulative right to their respective proportionate share.

44. Which of the following is least likely to be contained in Ted's marital trust for the benefit of Maria?

(Topic 61)

A. General power of appointment
B. Special power of appointment
C. Ability to name her creditors as payees
D. Full withdrawal rights

45. Which of the following is most likely to be contained in Maria's residuary trust?

(Topic 61)

A. General power-of-appointment trust
B. 5-and-5 power
C. Ted's right as the fiduciary to withdraw for his health, education, maintenance, and support
D. Crummey withdrawal rights

46. Fred's current trust can best be described as:

(Topic 62)

A. A funded revocable living trust
B. A simple trust with Crummey provisions
C. An irrevocable trust
D. A complex trust with a general power of appointment

47. Assuming that Fred transfers cash and mutual funds into his existing trust, which of the following is correct?

(Topic 62)

A. The trust assets will not be included in Fred's gross estate at his death.
B. The funding will constitute a transfer for value.
C. Appreciated securities will receive a step-up in basis at the time of transfer.
D. The completed transfer will subject appreciated securities to the recognition of gain.

48. If Ted dies, which of the following best describes his trust?

(Topic 62)

A. The trust retains its revocable character because it is a simple trust.
B. The trust becomes irrevocable.
C. The residuary trust becomes irrevocable, but the marital trust is revocable.
D. The marital trust becomes irrevocable, but the residuary trust is revocable.

49. Fred wants to transfer his group life insurance to his existing trust. Which of the following is correct?

(Topic 62)

A. The transfer is not possible, as he does not own the master group policy.
B. The transfer will violate the rule against perpetuities because it is group insurance.
C. The standard spendthrift provision prevents the transfer.
D. The transfer will constitute a current gift, requiring a gift tax return.

50. To the extent that Fred funds his trust with appreciated securities, which of the following is correct at Fred's death?

(Topic 62)

A. The securities will retain carryover basis due to a lack of a Crummey provision.
B. The transfer will trigger recognition of gain, as it is a completed gift.
C. The appreciation, but not the basis, will be removed from the estate.
D. The securities will not be included in his gross estate if he dies two years after the transfer.

51. Considering the current situation for the extended Ferris family, which of the following is the most viable technique to accomplish one or more of the stated objectives?

(Topic 63)

A. Transferring Fred's business interest to a GRUT, with Fred receiving 6% annual income, and the remainder passing to Ted after 13 years
B. A gift of a present interest from Fred to Ted of the entirety of Fred's fractional business holdings, and Fred and Mary electing gift-splitting to avoid gift tax
C. Placing Fred and Mary's home into a 20-year QPRT, with Ted and Maria as remainder beneficiaries
D. A buy-sell agreement funded with life insurance (premiums paid by Fred), allowing Ted to purchase Fred's shares at his death

52. If Fred were to establish a GRAT, which of the following would be the most suitable asset to transfer?

(Topic 63)

A. SPDA
B. The personal property
C. The whole life policy
D. The growth fund

53. Which of the following transfers would involve the smallest taxable gift?

(Topic 63)

A. Transfer of the growth fund to a 10-year GRAT with a 6% payout
B. Transfer of the value fund to a 15-year GRAT with a 6% payout
C. Transfer of the short-term fixed-income fund to a 15-year GRUT, using an 8% payout
D. Transfer of the home to a 10-year QPRT

54. Which of the following transfers would involve the largest taxable gift?

(Topic 63)

A. Placing the equity mutual funds in a 15-year GRUT with a 7% payout
B. Transferring the short-term fixed-income fund and half the cash equivalents into a 10-year GRUT with a 6% payout
C. Transferring the 15-year term policy to the current irrevocable trust
D. Purchasing a new policy and subsequently transferring it to the irrevocable trust

55. Assuming Fred and Mary plan to retire at age 66 and move to a condominium in Florida, which of the following is correct if they transfer their home to a QPRT for 10 years, and both are killed in an airplane crash two years later?

(Topic 63)

A. The full value of the home is included in Mary's estate.
B. The full value of the home is included in Fred's estate.
C. The value as of the date of transfer is included in Mary's estate.
D. The value as of the date of transfer is included in Fred's estate.

56. Mary is considering a gift to the art institute and has tentatively selected the value fund. If the entire fund is donated, what is the amount of the income tax deduction in the current year?

(Topic 64)

A. $41,500
B. $50,000
C. $62,700
D. $83,000

57. If Fred and Mary decide to leave the value fund to the art institute at Mary's death under her will, which of the following is the amount of the charitable income tax deduction at that time?

(Topic 64)

A. $0
B. $41,500
C. $50,000
D. $83,000

58. If Fred contributes the projected value of the growth fund at his retirement to a single-life CRAT, which of the following is correct?

(Topic 64)

A. The charitable income tax deduction will be approximately $323,000 that year.
B. The charitable gift tax deduction at that time will be $110,000.
C. A subsequent sale of the fund by the CRAT will eliminate capital gains taxes in future years for Fred.
D. The entire amount is removed from his taxable estate at his death.

59. If Fred and Mary want to use a technique that provides funding to the charity affiliated with Ned's disability, while transferring funds to Ted at reduced transfer tax cost, which of the following is most suitable?

(Topic 64)

A. 10-year CRAT, with Ned as the income beneficiary and Ted as custodian
B. 15-year CRUT, with Ted as the income beneficiary, for the benefit of Ned
C. 15-year CLAT, with Ted as the remainder beneficiary
D. Pooled-income fund, with Ned to receive a life income

60. Given Fred and Mary's objectives, which of the following is the most advantageous asset to place into a CRT at Fred's retirement?

(Topic 64)

A. Value fund
B. SPDA
C. Business interest
D. Whole life policy

61. Which of the following is correct regarding the whole life policy at Mary's death?

(Topic 65)

A. The death benefit is payable and is income-tax-free.
B. Any excess premiums paid over the cash value are deductible on Mary's final income tax return.
C. The cash value is included in Mary's gross estate.
D. The excess of the death benefit over the aggregate cost basis is a transfer for value.

62. Which of the following is correct regarding Fred's group life policy?

(Topic 65)

A. Fred can avoid imputed income by allocating the cost of his individual term policy as an offset.
B. If Mary predeceases Fred, the benefit is payable to Ted.
C. The death benefit is not only income-tax-free, but is also excluded from Fred's gross estate.
D. The employer cannot deduct the premium for coverage in excess of $50,000.

63. Which of the following is correct regarding Fred's individual term policy?

(Topic 65)

A. The death benefit is excluded from Fred's gross estate due to the beneficiary designation and ownership.
B. If Mary predeceases Fred, the proceeds will be payable equally to Felicity, Harmony, and Ted.
C. If Fred survives the term, he will receive a refund of premiums paid.
D. If Fred changes the beneficiary to a qualified charity, the premium is deductible.

64. Which of the following is most likely the best strategy for Fred's individual term policy?

(Topic 65)

A. Elect a life-income option with 10-year certain for Mary, to preserve the marital deduction.
B. Transfer the policy to the irrevocable trust to remove the proceeds from Fred's estate and to allow for annual exclusion gifts.
C. Change the beneficiary to a newly created revocable living trust with reduce-to-zero provisions.
D. Gift the policy to Fred's business to effectuate the funding for a cross-purchase buy-sell agreement.

65. Assuming Fred dies today, what amount of insurance is included in his gross estate?

(Topic 65)

A. None
B. $150,000
C. $1,150,000
D. $1,400,000

66. If Fred's death is prior to Mary's, which of the following asset transfers is a potential terminable interest?

(Topic 66)

A. The group term insurance
B. The value fund
C. The 401(k) plan balance
D. The business

67. If Fred dies today, what is the amount of the marital deduction related to the personal residence?

(Topic 66)

A. $0
B. $111,000
C. $222,000
D. $450,000

68. Under the current documents for Fred's son Ted, which of the following is correct?

(Topic 66)

A. Assets passing to Maria qualify for the unlimited marital deduction.
B. Amounts placed in trust for Ted's children will likely escape estate taxation.
C. If Fred dies before Ted, any amounts payable directly to Maria from Fred's estate will require a QDOT.
D. To qualify for the unlimited marital deduction, Maria must elect to become a U.S. citizen prior to Ted's death.

69. In the current situation, if Fred dies today and Mary dies four years later, which of the following represents the amount of the prior transfer credit Mary's estate may take?

(Topic 66)

A. 0%
B. 20%
C. 40%
D. 60%

70. Based on Fred and Mary's objectives, which of the following techniques is most suitable if they assume they will owe an estate tax when they pass away?

(Topic 66)

A. QDOT with reduce-to-zero provisions
B. QTIP with reduce-to-zero provisions
C. Estate equalization, with subsequent exclusive use of a bypass trust for each
D. Estate equalization, with subsequent exclusive use of an unlimited marital deduction trust

71. In order to achieve Fred's objectives regarding his business interest, which of the following techniques is most appropriate?

(Topic 67)

A. Private annuity for Fred's life, exchanging the business to Ted
B. Self-canceling installment note, with Ted as purchaser
C. One-way buy-sell agreement, with Ted as purchaser
D. Placement of the business in the irrevocable trust

72. Assuming that Fred reaches retirement age (66) and that he and Ted contemplate entering into a 20 year installment sale with a SCIN feature at that time using an interest rate equal to the company's growth rate, which of the following is correct?

(Topic 67)

A. Ted would be obligated to pay almost $3 million per year to Fred.
B. If Fred dies 5 years later, Ted would make the remaining 15 payments to Mary.
C. Obligations under the arrangement would cause the inclusion of Fred's business in his estate.
D. An insurance company annuity would be an alternate obligor.

73. Assuming that Fred and his co-shareholders adopt a stock-redemption agreement, which of the following is correct?

(Topic 67)

A. The value of Fred's interest will be pegged for estate tax purposes but may be more than $10 million.

B. $10 million will be the amount included in Fred's estate for the value of his business interest.

C. Up to $30 million in business value could be included in Fred's estate due to the attribution rules.

D. The amount included in Fred's estate will be $10 million plus the requisite life insurance funding.

74. If Fred and his co-shareholders effectuate a trusteed cross-purchase agreement, which of the following is correct?

(Topic 67)

A. An escrow trustee would own the life insurance as a fiduciary on each life.

B. A total of six policies is required.

C. If Gerald dies first, Fred's basis remains the same.

D. If Gerald and Harold die simultaneously, Fred must continue the business with their respective heirs as surviving owners.

75. If a wait-and-see buy-sell agreement is adopted, which of the following is most likely correct if Fred dies first?

(Topic 67)

A. Gerald and Harold have an option to use a cross-purchase of Fred's shares.

B. Fred's estate has the option to ignore the agreement as a postmortem technique.

C. Fred's estate would receive a step-up in basis for the business only if the cross-purchase approach is adopted.

D. Gerald and Harold have the option to void the agreement under the precatory rule.

76. Which of the following is correct regarding debts and expenses paid at Fred's death?

(Topic 68)

A. The mortgage is deductible in full from the gross estate.

B. The car loan is 50% deductible from the gross estate.

C. The mortgage is 50% deductible from the gross estate.

D. The car loan is not deductible from the gross estate.

77. If Fred dies today, which of the following is correct?

(Topic 68)

A. The 401(k) plan balance is included in Fred's probate estate.

B. The group term insurance is included in Fred's gross estate because Fred has incidents of ownership

C. The short-term fixed-income fund is fully included in Fred's estate.

D. Mary will be able to exclude up to $250,000 of the gain on the home from Fred's gross estate.

78. Which of the following techniques will be most appropriate for bypass planning for Fred and Mary?

(Topic 68)

A. Titling of their assets to Fred's irrevocable trust

B. A QTIP trust set up under Fred's will to receive the business interest

C. A pour-over provision in Fred's will, directing the maximum amount available under the unified credit to Fred's irrevocable trust

D. A trust set up by Fred's will to receive the maximum amount available under the unified credit, with income payable to Mary for life and the remainder to their daughters

79. In an effort to reduce the ultimate amount included in Fred's gross estate, which of the following would most likely be an effective technique?

(Topic 68)

A. Corporate recapitalization, using new preferred and common stocks and gifts of stock

B. Transfer of Fred's business interest to a newly created revocable living trust with reduce-to-zero provisions

C. Use of a lack-of-marketability discount to reduce the price in a new corporate stock-redemption agreement

D. Employment of a minority discount in a new cross-purchase agreement

80. Under the current business arrangements, which of the following would be the most likely result at Fred's death if Mary had died the year before?

(Topic 68)

A. There would be a significant risk of a valuation dispute between Fred's estate representatives and the IRS.

B. Fred's letter to his co-shareholders would fix the value of his business interest.

C. Fred's executor would be required to sell Fred's business interest to the corporation.

D. The amount of the minority discount would be assured for Fred's business interest.

81. If Fred funds his irrevocable trust today with a transfer of the growth fund, which of the following is correct regarding the generation-skipping transfer tax (GSTT)?

(Topic 69)

A. Fred should file a Form 709 to claim the GSTT exemption.

B. The transfer will be excluded from gift and GST tax under the annual exclusions.

C. The gift to the trust is considered a taxable distribution for GSTT purposes.

D. The gift to the trust will be deemed a taxable termination, as Fred's ownership rights are terminated.

82. If Fred makes an absolute assignment of his individual term policy to Ted for Ned's special needs, which of the following is correct?

(Topic 69)

A. The transfer qualifies for the GST tax annual exclusion.
B. Fred would use up some of his GST tax exemption to eliminate the GST tax.
C. The action is deemed to be a taxable distribution under the GSTT rules.
D. The transfer is not subject to the GST tax.

83. If Fred and Mary transfer the value fund to the private special education school for Ned's benefit, which of the following is correct?

(Topic 69)

A. The transfer will be fully excluded from the GST tax.
B. Under the GSTT gift-splitting rules, only $55,000 is subject to GSTT.
C. The transaction will constitute a taxable, indirect generation skip.
D. $83,000 is the measurement of the taxable termination of Fred and Mary's ownership rights.

84. If Fred changes the beneficiary of his group life insurance to his irrevocable trust, which of the following is correct?

(Topic 69)

A. The transfer is deemed a taxable distribution at Fred's death for GSTT purposes.
B. There is a possibility for a taxable distribution to Ned.
C. At Ted's later death, the GST tax exemption is unavailable to shelter the taxable termination from GST tax.
D. The proceeds from the insurance will be subject to income tax as a transfer for value.

85. If Fred transfers the growth fund to his irrevocable trust and timely files a Form 709, which of the following is correct?

(Topic 69)

A. The transfer qualifies in full for both gift and the GST tax annual exclusions.
B. He may elect an inclusion fraction of zero for GSTT purposes.
C. The Form 709 would be valid only for gift tax purposes.
D. Ned would become responsible for income tax on trust income after the transfer.

86. At Mary's death, the personal representative (executor) of the will must perform which of the following duties?

(Topic 70)

A. Pay off the car loan.
B. Arrange for the transfer of the whole life policy.
C. Pour over assets at the conclusion of probate to the irrevocable trust.
D. Include the value fund in the probate estate.

87. Based on Fred and Mary's objectives, which of the following is the best selection in terms of a post-death fiduciary for Fred's estate?

(Topic 70)

A. Ted, due to his status as the only adult child
B. Mary, as the surviving spouse
C. Ted and Mary, as co-fiduciaries
D. A bank trust department

88. At Fred's death, the executor of the will must perform which of the following duties?

(Topic 70)

A. Pay off the car loan.
B. Submit the irrevocable trust to the appropriate court jurisdiction.
C. Make a QTIP election as to the residence, to provide Mary with a life estate in the house.
D. Include the growth fund in the probate process.

89. At Ted's death, which of the following best represents the duty of the successor-trustee?

(Topic 70)

A. Arrange to collect the life insurance proceeds.
B. Merge the trust with Maria's trust for ongoing management.
C. Open the probate estate to close off creditors after the statutory period.
D. Admit Fred's letter to Ted in the probate process.

90. At Maria's death, which of the following best represents the duty of the successor-trustee?

(Topic 70)

A. Merge only the jointly held assets with Ted's trust for ongoing management.
B. Coordinate with the executor regarding postmortem elections.
C. Arrange to qualify the trust under the QDOT rules.
D. Open the probate estate to allow for the pour-over of the life insurance proceeds.

91. At Fred's death, which of the following is considered income in respect of a decedent (IRD)?

(Topic 71)

A. Proceeds from the whole life policy
B. The business interest
C. 401(k) plan
D. Growth fund

92. Under the current documents, which of the following best represents the treatment of the SPDA at Fred's death?

(Topic 71)

A. The amount included in Fred's estate is $160,000 less the income tax due on the distribution.
B. An income tax deduction will be available for the proportional estate tax attributed to the SPDA.
C. The full amount of the SPDA qualifies for the marital deduction.
D. The SPDA receives a step-up in basis due to the estate IRD rules.

93. If Fred dies today, what total amount is considered IRD?

(Topic 71)

A. $0
B. $160,000
C. $345,000
D. $385,000

94. If Fred dies today, which of the following is the amount of the income tax deduction the beneficiary of the IRD assets can deduct?

(Topic 71)

A. $0
B. $17,000
C. $228,000
D. $245,000

95. If Mary dies, and Fred subsequently sells the entire value fund, which of the following is the amount of the IRD?

(Topic 71)

A. $0
B. $33,000
C. $41,500
D. $83,000

96. Under the existing documents, if Fred dies first and his estate values are higher six months after his death, which of the following is correct?

(Topic 72)

A. Fred's estate representative should elect to use the alternate valuation date to further elevate the step-up in basis.
B. Fred's estate should use the Section 6166 installment option to pay the increased estate tax due to the increase in value of the assets since date of death.
C. A Section 303 redemption is the logical technique to use in order to avoid dividend treatment for Fred's business.
D. Fred's estate must be valued at his date of death.

97. In the current situation, if Fred dies today, which of the following is likely the most effective technique to reduce the ultimate total tax liability?

(Topic 72)

A. Mary's waiver of executor fee
B. Partial stock redemption under Section 303
C. Special-use valuation under Section 2032A
D. Installment payment under Section 6166

98. In Ted's current trust documents, which election by his personal representative would likely be most important if Ted dies?

(Topic 72)

A. QTIP
B. Sec. 6166
C. Alternate valuation date
D. QDOT

99. If Fred dies today, which of the following statements concerning the use of a Section 303 redemption by Fred's executor is correct?

(Topic 72)

A. Fred's estate will not qualify unless Ted operates the business after Fred's death.
B. The estate can benefit from use of the Section 303 redemption, whether Mary disclaims assets or not.
C. Fred's estate cannot receive any benefit from a Section 303 redemption because the business will receive a step-up in basis at Fred's death.
D. Fred's estate can benefit from the Section 303 redemption only if Fred completes a buy-sell agreement for the business interest.

100. If Fred wishes to add a provision to his will to create flexibility to reduce overall estate costs and taxes for the family, which of the following is most appropriate?

(Topic 72)

A. Qualified disclaimer trust
B. Section 2032A special use valuation
C. QTIP trust
D. Alternate valuation date provision

101. Which of the following techniques should be used to provide for a child of a previous marriage and still provide for Mary?

(Topic 73)

A. Change Fred's will to leave the business interest in a QTIP trust giving Mary income for life and the remainder to Ted.
B. Change Fred's will to leave the house and business interest to his irrevocable trust.
C. Set up a revocable trust for Felicity, Harmony, and Ned and transfer the business interest to the trust.
D. Sell the business interest now to Ted in an installment sale.

102. If Fred is concerned about Mary electing against the will, which of the following actions would avoid that problem and provide for a child of another relationship?

(Topic 73)

A. Transfer the business interest to his irrevocable trust during his lifetime.
B. Transfer the business interest to a revocable trust for Ted.
C. Transfer the mutual funds to a special-needs trust for Ned.
D. Change his will to set up a disclaimer trust for Ned and Mary.

103. If Fred wants to use the business interest for an inheritance for a child of a previous marriage, which of the following statements concerning a buy-sell agreement is correct?

(Topic 73)

A. The buy-sell agreement should provide for a trust for Ted and Ned to buy the stock.
B. The buy-sell agreement should provide for Ted, Felicity, and Harmony to buy the stock.
C. The buy-sell agreement should provide for Harold and Gerald to buy Fred's stock.
D. The buy-sell agreement should not be arranged.

104. Fred wants to consider assets other than the business interest for an inheritance for a child of another relationship. Which of the following statements concerning his other assets is correct?

(Topic 73)

A. Fred could change the beneficiary of his 401(k) plan to the child.
B. Fred could change the beneficiary of the whole life policy to the child.
C. Fred could change the beneficiary of the SPDA to the child.
D. Fred could change his will to leave the value fund to the child.

105. Much to Fred and Mary's dismay, they learned that Felicity has decided to move in with her boyfriend, age 21, as soon as she turns 18. Which of the following is correct?

(Topic 73)

A. Fred can change the beneficiary of Felicity's 529 plan to Harmony.
B. Fred's current will provides for an automatic disinheritance for Felicity.
C. Felicity is entitled to dower rights under Fred's will if Mary dies first.
D. Fred must change his will prior to Felicity's attainment of age 18 in order to disinherit her.

FRED AND MARY FERRIS CASE
ANSWERS AND EXPLANATIONS

1. B is the answer. The home is titled in joint tenancy with right of survivorship, so it will pass outside probate.

2. D is the answer. Fred is the sole owner of the business interest (stock in a C corporation), so at his death, the entire value of his interest will be included in his gross estate and will receive a full step-up in basis.

3. A is the answer. Fred will have greater control over the disposition of the property at his death because he is the sole owner of the global fund. The value fund was owned in joint tenancy, so the investment in the fund passes by operation of law to the survivor, and Fred has no control over the disposition at his death.

4. A is the answer. Transferring the growth fund to the trust will reduce Fred and Mary's income taxes because the income from the fund will be taxed to the trust. Transferring the life insurance to the trust will not reduce income taxes because while Mary owns the policy, the life insurance does not generate taxable income.

5. D is the answer. Ted may inherit under Fred's will, but he has no future interest while Fred is still alive. A will can be changed at any time, and the interest is not even a contingent remainder after Mary's death.

6. D is the answer. Fred's probate estate includes the $10 million business (owned by Fred), the $160,000 SPDA (payable to Fred's estate), $31,000 in the global fund, and the $25,000 car. All other assets pass under operation of law (e.g., joint accounts) or contract (e.g., life insurance, growth fund, and 401(k) accounts).

7. B is the answer. Mary's probate estate includes only the $36,000 cash value of the life insurance policy since Mary is the owner of the policy.

8. C is the answer. The whole life policy will be payable to Fred's estate because Mary did not survive Fred, and there is no contingent beneficiary. Life insurance policies usually require the beneficiary to survive the insured to receive the proceeds. The life insurance proceeds will be paid out tax-free at Fred's death since he is the insured.

9. C is the answer. The business is in Fred's name alone, so it will pass by the probate process, in the absence of a buy-sell agreement.

10. D is the answer. The successor-owner provision of the Section 529 plan avoids probate. A and C are incorrect, as the SPDA and whole life policy will involve probate. B is incorrect, as the value fund will pass under operation of law.

11. B is the answer. It is not a joint will because Fred and Mary each has his/her own document, leaving 100% to the survivor. This is not a pour-over will, as there is no trust executed to capture the assets after probate. It is not a mutual will, as Fred and Mary's wills are two separate, independent documents.

12. D is the answer. The cash and cash equivalents (such as the checking account and cash in a wallet) can likely be used or conveyed without probate court involvement. Mary owns the whole life policy, so Fred cannot act on it. The home and the value fund require two signatures, so Fred cannot change these assets alone.

13. D is the answer. Since Fred owns his share of the business, he can convey it to his revocable living trust. The other choices require action on the part of his wife, as well.

14. A is the answer. Mary's estate will pass to the children of the testator, which are Felicity and Harmony. Ted is not Mary's child.

15. D is the answer. Mary has not executed a living will, a health care power of attorney, or a durable power of attorney. Therefore, a court order would probably be required, and Fred would need to have himself or another person appointed guardian.

16. D is the answer. The gift is a present interest and is not more than $14,000. Ted is not compelled to use the gift for Ned, but likely will do so. A is wrong because Ned is not the donee. B is wrong because Maria is not entitled to any portion of the gift to Ted. C is wrong because Ned is a minor and cannot exercise rights; moreover, the gift is to Ted, not Ned.

17. C is the answer. This will allow for the future appreciation to be removed for their estate. A is wrong because the marital deduction is merely a tax-deferral technique. B is incorrect because Ned is disabled, and he is also a minor. D is wrong because the daughters are already sufficiently motivated.

18. D is the answer. Since there is no Crummey provision, it is a future-interest gift. A is wrong because it is not a completed gift. B is wrong because of the unlimited marital deduction. C is wrong because there is no measurable value, and the beneficiary has a mere expectancy.

19. A is the answer. Although it is a generation-skipping transfer, there would be no tax because of the exemption. B is incorrect because no transfer has yet taken place. C and D are both wrong because there has been no transfer of assets; these are merely document provisions.

20. B is the answer. This transfer would be brought back into the gross estate under the three-year rule. A is wrong because Mary owns the policy; if she transfers it to a trust, the three-year rule does not apply to Fred's estate. C is wrong because the group term insurance will be included in the estate in any event, so it is not brought back into the estate under the three-year rule. D is wrong because the policy was not ever owned by Fred.

21. A is the answer. The gift to Harmony is a taxable gift because it is in excess of the annual exclusion, due to the funding of the 529 plan. B is incorrect because of the annual exclusions and gift-splitting. C is wrong because of the unlimited gift tax marital deduction. D is wrong because of the unlimited exclusion for direct gifts to educational (and medical) donees.

22. B is the answer. No gift tax is payable, as the $5.43 million gift tax exclusion in 2015 covers the entire $5 million gift. A is incorrect because there is no gift tax at this point. D is incorrect because the donor is responsible for the gift tax (unless it is a net gift).

23. B is the answer. Commonly misunderstood, it is included, but fully deductible, under the unlimited charitable estate tax deduction. A is wrong because Fred has already given the asset to Mary. C is wrong because there is no AGI limitation on a charitable bequest for estate or gift taxes. D is wrong because the transfer is not subject to the three-year rule.

24. C is the answer. $14,000 x 2 donors x 3 donees = $84,000. While it may not be advisable to make gifts directly to Ned (so as not to cause him to lose any government assistance that he is receiving), the question did not ask how much they *should* gift to Ted's family, it simply asks how much they *could* gift using annual exclusions and gift-splitting.

25. A is the answer. The gifts would be taxable gifts, due to the 529 plan funding of $28,000 per daughter, also made this year. B is wrong because of the 529 funding. C is wrong because gifts to daughters are not income-tax-deductible. D is wrong because gifts are not income-taxable; also, age is irrelevant.

26. B is the answer. The disability policy has a 90-day limitation period. Thus, Fred will only receive benefits for 9 months. $150,000 base pay x 60%, divided by 12, times nine months equals $67,500. A is wrong because it is employer-paid, resulting in taxable benefits. C is wrong because it ignores the elimination period. D is wrong because there is merely integration with Social Security, not a denial of benefits.

27. C is the answer. This takes some evaluation, and it is a close call. The disability buyout situation is much more immediate and heavy than the potential LTC need that can be solved after the fact, using other techniques.

28. D is the answer. A is wrong because there are no benefits for Mary under Fred's disability insurance. B is wrong because the only available benefit for her is Social Security, and that requires a longer period to qualify than 90 days. C is wrong because she has no coverage.

29. D is the answer. This is the only existing coverage.

30. B is the answer. The insurance company would likely provide a higher amount as an accelerated death benefit than would an independent investor group under a viatical arrangement. C is wrong because a group term policy will not give advances. D is wrong, as the long-term disability payments are 60% of Fred's $150,000 salary, which is only $7,500 per month.

31. A is the answer. 529 plans, although owned by the decedent, are not included in the estate except where the decedent has made an election to treat contributions as though made over 5 years, applied 5 years of annual gift tax annual exclusions, and then died before the five years have ended. The facts do not provide any evidence that the exception applies in this case.

32. C is the answer. $339,500 (One-half of all joint assets = $31,000 + $40,000 + $83,000 + $450,000 + $75,000 = $679,000 x 50% = $339,500) + $110,000 (growth) + $31,000 (global) + $160,000 (SPDA) + $225,000 (401k) + $10,000,000 (business) + $150,000 (group life) + $1,000,000 (individual term) + $25,000 (car) = $12,040,500. The 529 plan is not included in Fred's estate.

33. C is the answer ($131,000 – half the joint debt on the house, plus his entire car loan).

34. A is the answer. No gifts in excess of the annual exclusion have been made.

35. A is the answer. Fred's estate leaves all assets to Mary under the unlimited marital deduction. Since no property is passing to nonspousal beneficiaries, his estate does not use any of his unified credit. If Fred's executor files an estate tax return to elect portability, Mary will be able to transfer property up to $10.86 million at her death, thereby ensuring Fred's unused credit is not wasted. The term "overqualification" is used to describe an estate that passes under the marital deduction and does not utilize the decedent's unified credit. While portability appears to overcome this problem, a credit shelter trust may still be utilized to transfer highly appreciating assets using the decedent's unified credit in order to remove them from the gross estate of the surviving spouse. For example, Fred's $10 million business appreciating at 8% annually would grow quickly in Mary's estate, causing her estate to pay substantial estate taxes in spite of her ability to utilize his unused credit.

36. D is the answer. Liquidity is ample due to the SPDA, life insurance, and the lack of an estate tax (because of the unlimited marital deduction and the $5.43 million exemption amount in 2015).

37. A is the answer. The Sec. 303 partial stock redemption is applicable to the extent of paying administrative expenses, even if estate taxes are not owed. Sec. 6166 and Sec. 2032A require that an estate tax is payable, which is not the case here. There is no buy-sell agreement in effect, so the Sec. 2703 valuation is inapplicable.

38. A is the answer. The "lowest adverse impact" would be the best positive impact. Thus, the funded buy-sell agreement works best.

39. B is the answer. Inclusion in Mary's estate does not matter from an estate tax standpoint (due to the unlimited marital deduction and the $5.43 million exemption), and the policy provides needed liquidity. A is wrong because Fred is the insured. C is wrong because a growth fund is not a proper asset class upon which to rely for liquidity. D is incorrect because a loan, with interest, merely increases the cost.

40. A is the answer. The estate tax due at both of their deaths can be paid from the insurance proceeds. Since Mary is presumed to survive Fred, the life insurance proceeds will be paid to her as the primary beneficiary and then pass into her estate. Fred's estate will pass entirely to Mary, so there will be no tax on his estate. Mary will end up with approximately a $12.4 million estate. However, she can shelter $10.86 million due to her $5.43 million exemption and Fred's $5.43

million exemption which the executor can elect to transfer to Mary under the portability provisions for 2015. This leaves $1.54 million taxed at a rate of 40% which translates to a $616,000 estate tax liability. They have $1.4 million in life insurance which is more than enough to cover the estate tax liability. C is incorrect, as an estate tax will be due since there is no surviving spouse to whom to pass the assets with the unlimited marital deduction. D is incorrect, as the will provisions override state law.

41. C is the answer. Property passing to a surviving spouse who is entitled to the marital deduction is a general power of appointment.

42. C is the answer. As the surviving joint tenant, Mary can do what she wants with the asset.

43. A is the answer. Since there is no Crummey provision, they are gifts of future interests, which do not qualify for the annual gift tax exclusion. C and D are incorrect, as the children have no withdrawal rights.

44. B is the answer. A special (limited) power would be found in the residuary trust. The others constitute general powers included in marital trusts. Typically, a special (limited) power is found in a QTIP trust. However, the fact pattern does not mention that the marital trust is a QTIP trust.

45. B is the answer. The 5-and-5 power is commonly found in the nonmarital residuary trust to give the surviving spouse an opportunity to withdraw principal for any purpose. A is incorrect since a general power of appointment would cause the trust to be a marital trust, rather than a residuary trust. C is wrong, as it would be best to name someone else as trustee. D is wrong, as Crummey withdrawal rights are used for trusts funded with gifts, rather than bequests at death.

46. C is the answer. The irrevocable trust described in the fact pattern has no withdrawal powers or general power of appointment.

47. A is the answer. The value of the assets transferred will not be in Fred's gross estate, although the post-1976 adjusted taxable gifts will be brought back later in the Form 706. B is incorrect because the transfer-for-value rule is an income tax ramification that applies to life insurance. C is wrong because there is carryover basis. D is wrong because the transfer does not involve a sale or other disposition.

48. B is the answer. Ted's entire trust becomes irrevocable as of the date of Ted's death.

49. D is the answer. Even though it is only group insurance, it has value, and because there is no Crummey provision, it is a gift of a future interest that requires a gift tax return from the first dollar. A is incorrect because Fred is able to transfer *his interest* in the policy. B is wrong because the rule against perpetuities, which varies by state, attempts to limit the time during which an irrevocable trust can be in existence. The group insurance is immaterial, as the benefit is paid when the insured dies; then the rule may begin. C is wrong because the spendthrift provision will inhibit a beneficiary's ability to alienate benefits.

50. D is the answer. Neither the securities nor the appreciation is in the gross estate, but taxable gifts will figure later in the estate tax calculation. A is wrong because there is a carryover of basis on all gifts, regardless of whether the trust includes a Crummey provision. B is incorrect because the securities have not been sold. C is wrong because the securities will have been removed from the estate, although adjusted taxable gifts may be brought back later in the Form 706.

51. D is the answer. Fred needs income from his business asset, so a buy-sell agreement is the only feasible solution. All the others involve gifts. A is incorrect because the GRUT will last for only 13 years, after which the business will go to Ted; Fred's objective is that the business should go to Ted at his death. The GRUT is a technique to leverage a transfer at reduced gift tax cost. Fred would get inadequate consideration for the transfer of his business. Similarly, B and C do not provide ample compensation to Fred for his business interest or his and Mary's home.

52. D is the answer. Since it is a growth fund, the appreciation would be out of Fred's estate, and the gift itself would be leveraged. All the other investments would have less appreciation. C is wrong, as Fred is not the owner of the whole life policy.

53. C is the answer. By logic, the more the grantor keeps, the less he or she gives away. Here, Fred would be keeping an income for 15 years, with an 8% payout, all on a smaller amount (the amount transferred into the trust in Answer A is $110,000, Answer B is $83,000, Answer C is $40,000 and Answer D is $450,000). No actual calculations are necessary.

54. A is the answer. An approximate calculation can be made that indicates the rough amount that Fred would be retaining in a GRUT. The sheer size of the amount transferred in A is also a clue. C and D are incorrect, as the value of the 15-year term policy would be the unexpired premiums, and the value of the new policy would be the premium paid.

55. A is the answer. According to the terms of the wills, Mary is presumed to survive, in which case, the home is fully included in her estate.

56. C is the answer. Although it appears that 83,000 is correct, the 30% of AGI limit applies: 30% x $209,000 = $62,700. Note that the $209,000 AGI includes the total inflows of $225,000 less the $16,000 contribution to the 401(k). Technically, the reinvested interest and dividends would increase the AGI allowing a large charitable deduction. However, it would not be a large enough number to increase the deduction from $62,700 all the way to $83,000. As a result, C is the best answer listed.

57. A is the answer. No charitable income tax deduction is available, but an estate tax deduction is available.

58. D is the answer. Although the amount will be in his gross estate, the full amount is deductible as a charitable estate tax deduction. A is incorrect because $323,000 is the approximate total value based on the assumptions in the case; only the present value of the remainder going to the charity is deductible. B is wrong because $110,000 is the current value. (**Editor's Note:** You are not expected to be able to calculate the PV of the remainder interest without additional data supplied.) C is wrong because the four-tier system of taxation from a CRT indicates that the capital gains are distributed to Fred over time.

59. C is the answer. The only technique that satisfies the objective is the CLAT. The charity gets income for 15 years, and Ted gets the principal after 15 years.

60. B is the answer. Given the choices, the best one to donate is the IRD asset because, otherwise, an heir inheriting the SPDA will have to report the distributions as ordinary income. The other choices are less advantageous for the CRT because an heir inheriting the value fund will only report long-term capital gains and will receive a step-up in basis after Fred and Mary's deaths. The life insurance will be received by Mary free of income tax. In addition, the business interest should be subject to a buy-sell agreement with Ted.

61. C is the answer. Fred is the insured, and Mary is the owner. Thus, only the cash value is included in Mary's estate. A is wrong because Fred is the insured. B is wrong because the policy is not being surrendered; moreover, any loss is nondeductible personal loss. D is incorrect because a transfer for value is not involved.

62. B is the answer. If Mary predeceases Fred, Ted will receive the benefits as the secondary beneficiary. A is wrong because Fred can offset imputed income only with his group contributions. C is wrong because the policy is included in Fred's estate. D is wrong because the employer can deduct the cost over $50,000 (but the excess involves imputed income to Fred).

63. B is the answer. Since Fred did not name a secondary beneficiary, it will pass by default to Fred's estate. This means Fred's will controls, which states that the children of the testator share equally. A is wrong because Fred owns the policy. C is wrong because there is no indication of a return-of-premium feature in this policy. D is wrong because the premium would not be deductible.

64. C is the answer. With a large policy like this, it's wise to coordinate the policy with new estate planning documents that optimize the tax benefits, while allowing for post-death control of the distribution of funds. A is wrong because the life-income option invites inflexibility. B is incorrect because the annual exclusion is unavailable due to a lack of Crummey powers. D is wrong because the company owners should purchase new policies, not accept a gift of personal policies, due to the complexity and potential tax problems.

65. C is the answer and is comprised of $1,000,000 of individual term and $150,000 of group. He does not own the whole life policy.

66. D is the answer. This is potentially a terminable interest because Mary will have to survive by at least 120 days to be entitled to receive the business under the will. A, B, and C are all payable directly to the surviving spouse, so there is no chance of a terminable interest.

67. B is the answer. The personal residence is worth $450,000, but there is $228,000 outstanding mortgage. The total net value is $222,000. However, only 50% of the value of the home and the mortgage would be included in Fred's estate. Thus, the marital deduction would be $111,000 which is the 50% net value included in Fred's estate.

68. B is the answer. Because Ted's trust contains reduce-to-zero language, there will be no estate tax at his death. The applicable exemption amount and the maximum marital deduction available to a noncitizen spouse will likely wipe out any tax liability. A is wrong because Maria is not a U.S. citizen. C is incorrect because the QDOT is only for property passing to a noncitizen spouse. D is wrong because other techniques are available to qualify property for the marital deduction.

69. A is the answer. The prior transfer credit is applicable only if there was an estate tax on the death of the first spouse.

70. B is the answer. Due to the second marriage situation and the magnitude of the estate, the QTIP/reduce-to-zero approach works better than the alternatives. The reduce-to-zero provision will place just enough assets in the QTIP trust to reduce the estate tax to zero.

71. C is the answer. Fred's objective is to transfer his interest in the business at his death to Ted. The one-way buy-sell agreement would have Ted purchase Fred's interest at Fred's death. It is a one-way buy-sell agreement as Ted does not have any ownership to sell to Fred if Ted should die first. The private annuity (answer A) and the self-cancelling installment note (answer B) are not correct answers as it would transfer the business today to Ted rather than at Fred's death. Answer D is not correct as the placement of the business in the irrevocable trust would transfer the business to the children and grandchildren.

72. A is the answer. Using $10 million as the present value and 8% as the growth rate, the value at Fred's retirement in 14 years is $29,371,936. A 20 year installment sale at that time would necessitate Ted almost $3 million per year (n = 20, I = 8, PV = 29,371,936, FV = 0 solve for PMT which is $2,991,596). B and C are wrong because nothing is included in the estate of the installment note recipient, as payments stop at death with an installment sale that includes a SCIN feature (self cancelling installment note). D is incorrect because an insurance company is not involved in a private installment sale.

73. A is the answer. A valid stock-redemption agreement would peg the value in a nonfamily situation and would avoid IRS argument if a formula approach is used. Due to the increasing value, a higher amount is likely to be included in Fred's estate. B is wrong because the amount included is likely higher, due to appreciation. C is wrong because attribution is not involved here. D is wrong because the life insurance is not included in Fred's estate, as he does not own it.

74. A is the answer. The idea behind this arrangement is to minimize the number of policies, while retaining the advantages of the cross-purchase approach. B is incorrect because only three policies will be required. C is wrong because Fred gets to increase his basis by virtue of the additional amount he personally pays for the decedent's business interest. D is wrong because the buy-sell agreement takes care of this problem in advance.

75. A is the answer. A wait-and-see approach is normally structured to provide the surviving owners an option to use the cross-purchase first. If they decline, the corporation can step in and effectuate a redemption if that makes sense. B is incorrect because the buy-sell agreement is binding, not optional. C is incorrect because the decedent's estate gets a step-up in basis, irrespective of the type of agreement used. D is wrong because there is no such rule as the precatory rule.

76. C is the answer. Because it is a joint liability, and only half of the asset is included in the estate, only half the liability is deductible.

77. B is the answer. The group term insurance is included in Fred's gross estate because Fred possesses incidents of ownership. The exclusion of $250,000 of gain applies to the income tax laws, not the estate tax laws. A is wrong because the 401(k) is payable directly to Mary. C is wrong because it is jointly owned, and only half is included.

78. D is the answer. The trust that will pay income to Mary for life and the remainder to their daughters will take advantage of Fred's unified credit and provide income for Mary. The titling of assets to the irrevocable trust will not provide for either Mary or Fred if they should need the funds later in life or after the death of the first spouse to die. The pour-over provision to Fred's trust will similarly not provide for Mary and will take most of the estate assets for an irrevocable trust for the daughters. It would not be good bypass planning to leave Mary with so few assets. A QTIP trust will not take advantage of the unified credit and will continue to qualify too many assets for the marital deduction.

79. A is the answer. The recapitalization allows for continuing control of the corporation, while removing the future appreciation from the estate. B, C, and D would result in no reduction in the amount of the estate.

80. A is the answer. Since the letter from Fred (B) to the co-shareholders is not binding, the value is not pegged, and a valuation dispute would be likely with the IRS. C is wrong because there are no documents to require Fred's executor to sell the business. D is incorrect because there is no assurance of a minority discount.

81. A is the answer. It is prudent to anticipate the possibility of a GSTT by filing the Form 709 and allocate the exemption to the transfer. GSTT allocation would probably be automatic, given the terms of the trust, but it would be best to file to formally allocate the GSTT exemption. B is incorrect because the trust does not qualify for either the gift or GST annual exclusions (no withdrawal powers and more than one beneficiary in the trust). C is wrong because a distribution has not occurred. D is wrong because a taxable termination refers to the termination of the child's interest.

82. D is the answer. This transfer would not attract the GST tax, as it does not skip a generation. Thus, A and B are incorrect because it is not a generation-skipping transfer. B is also wrong because the filing of the form now merely allocates the use of the GST tax exemption for a subsequent transfer. C is incorrect because it is not a distribution.

83. A is the answer. A direct payment to the institution will be exempt not only from gift tax, but also GST tax. B, C, and D all incorrectly assume a taxable event has occurred.

84. B is the answer. At some point, when Ted dies, there may be a taxable termination for GSTT purposes. A is wrong because there is not yet a transfer. C is incorrect because the exemption is still available. D is wrong because there is not a transfer for value, but a gratuitous transfer.

85. B is the answer. On the Form, he can make the election to allocate the GSTT exemption. All other responses are incorrect.

86. B is the answer. The only valid response is to transfer the whole life policy, as the car loan is not Mary's, there is not a pour-over provision indicated in the case, and the value fund transfers by title.

87. D is the answer. In this case, the best choice is a bank trust department. As hinted in the objectives, they want professional help. The surviving spouse is named as executor in the document, but Mary can always decline the position.

88. A is the answer. Here, the debt must be paid at Fred's death. B and D are incorrect, as the irrevocable trust and growth fund are not subject to probate. C is wrong, as the house passes automatically to Mary as the surviving joint tenant.

89. A is the answer. In Ted's case, the trustee is the beneficiary and should proceed to collect the life insurance benefit. B is incorrect, as the trust should not be merged together since Ted's assets will need to be placed in a QDOT to qualify for the marital deduction. C is incorrect, as the collection of the life insurance proceeds would be more important than eliminating creditor claims via probate. D is incorrect, as Fred's letter is not binding.

90. B is the answer. The executor technically has the responsibility to make postmortem elections, so the trustee should coordinate activities. A is incorrect, as merging assets is not the top priority. C is wrong, as Ted is a U.S. citizen, so no QDOT is needed. D is wrong, as the life insurance is not subject to probate.

91. C is the answer. Only the 401(k) plan balance is taxable to the recipient. The other will be either tax-free or get a step-up in basis.

92. C is the answer. Because the SPDA goes to Mary through the will, it qualifies for the marital deduction. There will be no estate tax, so no deduction is available on an income tax return for the proportional estate tax. No step-up applies, as it is an IRD asset.

93. C is the answer: $225,000 from the 401(k) plan + $120,000 ($160,000 – $40,000) from the SPDA.

94. A is the answer. No deduction is allowed related to estate taxes paid on IRD assets because there is no estate tax due.

95. A is the answer. There is no IRD because the value fund is not IRD property. Fred inherits Mary's half and gets a partial step-up. His subsequent decision to sell does not constitute a transaction involving IRD.

96. D is the answer. The alternative valuation date (AVD) is available only if the estate and the estate tax are lower as a result of using the date six months after death; thus, A is wrong. B is incorrect because the installment payment of taxes is based on the business included in the gross estate and not the increased value of the assets between date of death and alternative valuation date.

C is wrong because a partial redemption under Sec. 303 is not one of the objectives. A total redemption is desired.

97. A is the answer. Due to the unlimited marital deduction, there is no estate tax liability. As a result, Mary should waive her executor commission in order to avoid having to pick it up into income. B is wrong because the Sec. 303 simply allows for partial stock redemptions for payment of taxes and costs. C is incorrect because there is no indication of real estate owned for the business. D is wrong because the installment payment option only allows for the estate tax to be paid in over a 15 year period. It does not reduce the amount of the estate tax.

98. D is the answer. In order to optimize the use of the marital deduction and the unified credit, a QDOT would be the best alternative because Ted's wife is not a U.S. citizen.

99. B is the answer. If Mary does not disclaim assets under the will, the executor will still be able to make use of the Section 303 redemption to pay funeral and administration costs. There is no requirement that a relative operate the business after the owner's death for a Section 303 redemption. A buy-sell agreement may prevent use of the Section 303 redemption since the stock will no longer be in the estate.

100. A is the answer. The qualified disclaimer trust will help to reduce overall taxes by making it possible to use some of Fred's unified credit to remove highly appreciating assets from Mary's estate. Fred does not own a farm or closely held business that qualifies for Section 2032A special use valuation, nor is this election required to be made within the will. It is elected by the executor of the estate. A QTIP election will maintain the use of the marital deduction. There is no alternate valuation date provision in the will. The alternate valuation date is elected by executor of the estate if appropriate.

101. A is the answer. Ted is the child of a previous marriage, and Fred would like Ted to have the business interest after his death. A QTIP trust will allow Mary to receive income from the trust, and the business will pass to Ted at her death. The installment sale is not likely to work now because Ted is having financial difficulty, so making a down payment would probably be a problem for him. In addition, Fred has several years before retirement.

102. B is the answer. A revocable trust is not subject to Mary's right to elect against the will, so the business interest would pass to Ted. A disclaimer trust does not avoid a wife's election against the will.

103. D is the answer. If the business interest will be used as an inheritance for Ted, it should not be sold under a buy-sell agreement. The sale will liquidate the asset and may result in the loss of the inheritance to Ted.

104. C is the answer. Fred can change the beneficiary of the SPDA to Ted, instead of to his estate. Fred cannot change the beneficiary of the 401(k) plan because federal law requires the spouse as beneficiary. Fred cannot change the beneficiary of the whole life policy because Mary is the owner. The value fund is jointly owned, so Fred cannot leave it by will to Ted.

105. **A** is the answer. Only this choice reflects what Fred is able to do. B is wrong because Fred's will has no such provision. C is wrong because dower rights apply only to a spouse. D is wrong because Fred can change his will any time prior to death to disinherit someone or to make other changes.

WYATT ESTATE PLAN

William Wyatt has consulted you for financial planning and wants you to develop proposals for an estate plan. From meetings with Wyatt, you have gathered the following information:

William Wyatt

- Bill is 58 years old and in good health.
- Bill's wife June is 55 years old and is also in good health. They have been married 32 years.
- Bill and June own their home as tenants by the entirety, and the house is currently valued at $750,000. The Wyatts purchased the home ten years ago for $110,000.
- Bill is an officer and 25% shareholder of a plastics company he started with three associates 20 years ago. All of the stock is owned by the four founders. Bill is in charge of marketing and brings in most of the large contracts for the company. If Bill became disabled or died, the business would probably decline significantly, but the remaining shareholders would likely want to continue the business.
- Bill files a joint return with his wife, and they are in the highest marginal income tax bracket.
- Bill and June have two children, a son James Wyatt, age 30, and a daughter Grace Wyatt, age 28.
- Bill and June have adequate homeowners, automobile, and medical insurance and also umbrella liability insurance.
- Bill has $500,000 in universal life insurance policies. Bill owns the policies and has named June as the beneficiary. The total cash value of the policies is $37,000.
- Bill is a partner in a French restaurant that he bought with a friend about five years ago. The restaurant earns him about $10,000 per year.
- Bill is the sole owner of a commercial property valued at $1,575,000. The property is rented out as a store and two apartments and has an outstanding mortgage balance of $150,000. The property provides Bill with a net income of about $28,000 per year.
- Bill's wife works two or three days a week as an interior designer.
- Bill's will, executed ten years ago, leaves his entire estate to June.
- Bill would like to make some large contributions to his college.
- Bill is concerned because his wife and daughter have had a falling out, and his wife recently changed her will to disinherit their daughter. Bill wants to see that his daughter receives an inheritance.

James Wyatt

- Jim is a trained chef and works at Bill's French restaurant, where he is also the manager. Jim would like to continue the restaurant, and Bill wants Jim to have the restaurant.
- Jim is not married and has an apartment near the restaurant.
- Jim is currently in the 15% marginal tax bracket.

Grace Wyatt

- Grace was recently divorced for the second time and has three children: Joshua, age 8, from the first marriage; and Amber, age 5, and Heather, age 4, from the second marriage.
- Grace works as a veterinary assistant and receives some child support from her second husband.
- Grace is in the 25% marginal tax bracket.

Bill's Estate Planning Objectives

Bill Wyatt's main estate planning objectives are as follows:

- To provide June with an adequate annual income from the assets included in Bill's gross estate if he predeceases her
- To provide Jim and Grace with the maximum amount of Bill's estate after June's death
- To avoid estate taxes being imposed on assets not needed to provide adequate income for June

ADDITIONAL INFORMATION

- Property ownership (title) is described in the following statement of financial position:

STATEMENT OF FINANCIAL POSITION
as of December 31, last year
William and June Wyatt

ASSETS (1)

Cash/Cash Equivalents

Checking Account (JT)	$ 2,000
Money Market Fund (JT)	55,000
Total	$57,000

Invested Assets

Certificate of Deposit from First Savings (JT)	$100,000
U.S. Treasury Notes (2) (H)	175,000
Municipal Bonds (H)	310,000
Growth Stock Portfolio (H)	285,000
Commercial Real Estate (H)	1,575,000
French Restaurant (H)	55,000
Stock in Plastics Company (H)	380,000
Total	$2,880,000

Use Assets

Residence (TE)	$750,000
Personal Property (JT)	150,000
Automobile (H)	35,000
Automobile (W)	30,000
Vacation Condo (TE)	165,000
Total	$1,130,000

TOTAL ASSETS	$4,067,000

LIABILITIES AND NET WORTH

Liabilities (3)

Credit Card Balance (W)	$ 4,200
Auto Loan (H)	19,000
Auto Loan (W)	15,000
Mortgage Balance on Residence (TE)	85,000
Mortgage Balance on Condo (TE)	35,000
Mortgage Balance on Commercial Property (H)	150,000
Total	$ 308,200

NET WORTH	$3,758,800

TOTAL LIABILITIES AND NET WORTH	$4,067,000

(1) Listed at fair market value
(2) Matures August 30, 2019
(3) Only principal debts listed
(H) Owned solely by husband
(W) Owned solely by wife
(JT) Owned by husband and wife in joint tenancy with right of survivorship
(TE) Owned by husband and wife in tenancy by the entireties

1.   **FEDERAL ESTATE TAX ANALYSIS**

From the information presented in the statement of financial position and the preceding narrative, complete the following lists for William Wyatt's current gross estate and for the property that will be eligible for the marital deduction. The lists should be completed as though Bill dies on July 1, 2015 and there has been no change in the value of his assets and he has not amended his will. Assume that Bill's assets are valued as described in the financial statement and that there will be no reduction for death taxes. Bill and June live in a common-law property state. Assume that June will not remarry.

For each item listed, indicate the total dollar value that will be included in Bill's gross estate. If no amount will be included, write "Zero."

   A.   The Gross Estate

Property Interest	Included Amount
Checking Account	$
Money Market Fund	$
Certificate of Deposit	$
U.S. Treasury Notes	$
Municipal Bonds	$
Growth Stock Portfolio	$
Commercial Real Estate	$
French Restaurant	$
Stock in Plastics Company	$
Residence	$
Personal Property	$
Automobile (H)	$
Automobile (W)	$
Vacation Condominium	$
Life Insurance	$

For each item listed, indicate the total dollar value that will be eligible for the marital deduction on Bill's estate tax return. If no amount is eligible, write "Zero."

B.   The Marital Deduction

Property Interest	Deductible Amount
Checking Account	$
Money Market Fund	$
Certificate of Deposit	$
U.S. Treasury Notes	$
Municipal Bonds	$
Growth Stock Portfolio	$
Commercial Real Estate	$
French Restaurant	$
Stock in Plastics Company	$
Residence	$
Personal Property	$
Automobile (H)	$
Automobile (W)	$
Vacation Condominium	$
Life Insurance	$

C.   Estate Tax Calculation

Assume for purposes of this calculation that Bill made adjusted taxable gifts of $80,000 and used $18,200 of his unified credit to offset these taxable gifts. Assume also administrative expenses will be $35,300 but they will be deducted on the estate income tax return. Assume that there will be no charitable bequests.

Calculate the following for 2015:

(1)   The gross estate $

(2)   The taxable estate $

(3)   The tentative tax base $

(4)   The tentative tax (see Tax Table) $

(5)   Total estate tax payable $

2.   **ESTATE PLAN ANALYSIS**

Identify four significant weaknesses in William Wyatt's current estate plan and make specific recommendations to correct these weaknesses.

Weakness 1:

Recommendation:

Weakness 2:

Recommendation:

Weakness 3:

Recommendation:

Weakness 4:

Recommendation:

3.   **LIFETIME GIFTS**

A.   Bill is considering making lifetime gifts to Jim and Grace. Bill would like to see what gift taxes would be required and what the advantages are of making lifetime gifts. Assume for this analysis that Bill and June will file timely elections to split gifts. Assume that gifts are made equally to Jim and Grace and that the annual exclusion remains at $14,000.

Complete the blanks for the following projected program of lifetime gifts:

Year	Total Annual Gifts	Bill's Annual Taxable Gifts	Bill's Cumulative Taxable Gifts	Cumulative Gift Tax Prior to Unified Credit	After Unified Credit
Pre-2015			$80,000	$18,200	$ 0
2015	$116,000	____	_____	_____	
2016	96,000	____	_____	_____	
2017	66,000	____	_____	_____	
2018	56,000	____	_____	_____	

B.   Describe for Bill Wyatt the effect of lifetime gifts on the following items:

(1)   The value of Bill's gross estate

(2)   The estate tax that will be payable by Bill's estate

C.   If Bill gives his interest in the French restaurant to Jim, and the restaurant business grows rapidly and increases significantly in value, explain whether the gift has been more or less beneficial in reducing estate taxes than gifts of other property.

D.   If the vacation condominium is located in a state different from Bill's and June's residence, explain why a lifetime gift of the condominium by Bill and June may be advantageous.

4.   **ESTATE PLANNING RECOMMENDATION**

William Wyatt's main estate planning objectives are as follows:

(a)   To provide June with an adequate annual income from the assets included in Bill's gross estate if he predeceases her

(b)   To provide Jim and Grace with the maximum amount of Bill's estate after June's death

(c)   To avoid estate taxes being imposed on assets not needed to provide adequate income for June

A.   Select which of the following techniques is most likely to achieve Bill's objectives. Place a check mark next to the technique you select.

_____ Estate trust

_____ Family bypass (B trust)

_____ Power-of-appointment trust (A trust)

_____ QTIP trust (C trust or Q trust)

B.   Discuss how the estate planning technique you selected will accomplish each of Bill Wyatt's objectives.

Objective (a):

Objective (b):

Objective (c):

5.   ESTATE PLANNING RECOMMENDATION

A.   From the following choices, select which estate planning technique would be the most appropriate to recommend to Bill Wyatt to reduce his gross estate, save estate and gift taxes, and provide for Bill's family:

_____ Revocable trust   _____ Irrevocable life insurance trust

_____ 2503(b) trust   _____ Power-of-appointment trust

B.   Describe how the technique you selected will accomplish the following objectives:

(1)   Reduce Bill Wyatt's gross estate

(2)   Save estate and gift taxes

(3)   Provide for Bill Wyatt's family

2015 UNIFIED FEDERAL ESTATE AND GIFT TAX RATES

If the amount is:	The tentative tax is:
Not over $10,000	18% of the amount
Over $10,000 but not over $20,000	$1,800, plus 20% of the excess over $10,000
Over $20,000 but not over $40,000	$3,800, plus 22% of the excess over $20,000
Over $40,000 but not over $60,000	$8,200, plus 24% of the excess over $40,000
Over $60,000 but not over $80,000	$13,000, plus 26% of the excess over $60,000
Over $80,000 but not over $100,000	$18,200, plus 28% of the excess over $80,000
Over $100,000 but not over $150,000	$23,800, plus 30% of the excess over $100,000
Over $150,000 but not over $250,000	$38,800, plus 32% of the excess over $150,000
Over $250,000 but not over $500,000	$70,800, plus 34% of the excess over $250,000
Over $500,000 but not over $750,000	$155,800, plus 37% of the excess over $500,000
Over $750,000 but not over $1,000,000	$248,300, plus 39% of the excess over $750,000
Over $1,000,000	$345,800, plus 40% of the excess over $1,000,000

SUGGESTED ANSWERS

1. **FEDERAL ESTATE TAX ANALYSIS**

   A. The Gross Estate

Property Interest	Included Amount
Checking Account	$ 1,000
Money Market Fund	$ 27,500
Certificate of Deposit	$ 50,000
U.S. Treasury Notes	$ 175,000
Municipal Bonds	$ 310,000
Growth Stock Portfolio	$ 285,000
Commercial Real Estate	$1,575,000
French Restaurant	$ 55,000
Stock in Plastics Company	$ 380,000
Residence	$ 375,000
Personal Property	$ 75,000
Automobile (H)	$ 35,000
Automobile (W)	$ none
Vacation Condo	$ 82,500
Life Insurance	$ 500,000

   B. The Marital Deduction

Property Interest	Deductible Amount
Checking Account	$ 1,000
Money Market Fund	$ 27,500
Certificate of Deposit	$ 50,000
U.S. Treasury Notes	$ 175,000
Municipal Bonds	$ 310,000
Growth Stock Portfolio	$ 285,000
Commercial Real Estate	$1,425,000 (1,575,000 – 150,000 of related debt)
French Restaurant	$ 55,000
Stock in Plastics Company	$ 380,000
Residence	$ 332,500 (375,000 – 42,500 of related debt)
Personal Property	$ 75,000
Automobile (H)	$ 16,000 (35,000 – 19,000 of related debt)
Automobile (W)	$ none
Vacation Condo	$ 65,000 (82,500 – 17,500 of related debt)
Life Insurance	$ 500,000

C.   Estate Tax Calculation

(1)		The gross estate	$3,926,000
		– Funeral and administrative expenses	(0)
		– Debts, mortgages, and liens*	(229,000)
		= Adjusted gross estate	3,697,000
		– Marital deduction	(3,697,000)
(2)		The taxable estate	$ 0
		+ Adjusted taxable gifts	80,000
(3)		The tentative tax base	$ 80,000
(4)		The tentative tax (see Tax Table)	$ 18,200
		– Unified credit (2015)	2,117,800
(5)		Total estate tax payable	$ 0

* The debts, mortgages, and liens consists of $19,000 of debt on the credit card, $42,500 of debt on the home, $17,500 of debt on the condo and 150,000 of debt on the commercial property which totals $229,000.

2.   ESTATE PLAN ANALYSIS

Weakness 1: Bill Wyatt's current will leaves all the property in his estate to his wife.

Recommendation: Bill should leave property to the children to take advantage of the unified credit. The unified credit in 2015 allows Bill to leave up to $5.43 million to his children free of estate tax. Since Bill's gross estate is less than $4 million, he could make maximum use of the unified credit by leaving all of this estate in a bypass trust paying income to his wife and remainder to the children. Even if Bill does not want to leave all of his estate in a bypass trust, he will probably be well-advised to place at least a portion of his assets in a bypass trust to use some of his unified credit. In 2015, the portability provision allows a surviving spouse to add any unified credit not used by the deceased spouse to the surviving spouse's unified credit. Thus, if Bill does not use all of his unified credit, the remaining portion of his unified credit is available for June's estate to use at her death. Nonetheless, it may make sense for Bill to provide in his estate plan to use some of his unified credit to remove appreciation from June's estate and to ensure that both children receive a portion of his estate should June's disagreement with their daughter continue.

Weakness 2: Bill Wyatt's current will leaves no assets to his daughter, and she is likely to be disinherited by Bill's wife. Bill wants to see that she is not completely disinherited.

Recommendation: Bill can make lifetime gifts to his daughter or make use of various will substitutes, such as a deed in escrow or joint tenancy with right of survivorship. Bill has ample property in sole ownership, so he could make a bequest for his daughter in his will; but, to ensure that matters are carried out according to his wishes, Bill might be better served by using lifetime gifts or will substitutes.

Weakness 3: Bill Wyatt's current will does not provide for any charitable bequest, and Bill would like to make some large contributions to his college.

Recommendation: Bill can make use of various charitable trust arrangements, such as a CRAT, CRUT, pooled-income fund, or charitable lead trust. One or more of these arrangements could meet Bill's objectives.

Weakness 4: Bill Wyatt and his plastics company probably need a buy-sell agreement to arrange for the transfer of stock, in the event of an owner's death or disability. When Bill dies, his estate will have limited marketability for the shares, and his family is not likely to enter the plastics business.

Recommendation: Bill should persuade the other owners of the need for a buy-sell agreement to ensure an orderly transition in the event of an owner's disability or death. Either a cross-purchase plan or a stock-redemption plan would work in this situation.

The above answers are only some of the weaknesses that may be found in this estate plan. Other apparent weaknesses may be important and acceptable for purposes of this case analysis question.

3.   **LIFETIME GIFTS**

   A.

Year	Total Annual Gifts	Bill's Annual Taxable Gifts	Bill's Cumulative Taxable Gifts	Cumulative Gift Tax Prior to Unified Credit	After Unified Credit
Pre-2015			$ 80,000	$18,200	$ 0
2015	$116,000	$30,000	110,000	26,800	0
2016	96,000	20,000	130,000	32,800	0
2017	66,000	5,000	135,000	34,300	0
2018	56,000	0	135,000	34,300	0

Note: This chart reflects the taxable gifts made only by Bill, and all gifts are split. The annual exclusion was assumed to remain at $14,000, even though it is subject to indexing.

   B.   (1)   By making lifetime gifts, Bill Wyatt will be able to reduce the value of his gross estate. If Bill's wife consents to gift-splitting, they can make gifts of $28,000 per donee, tax-free. With gifts of $28,000 to Jim and $28,000 to Grace, the annual gift tax exclusion will permit tax-free transfers of $56,000 per year. The taxable gifts (totaling $135,000 in the previous chart) will be added to Bill's taxable estate to establish the tentative tax base for the calculation of the estate tax due at Bill's death.

(2)   The reduction in Bill's gross estate will actually not result in much change in the estate tax payable upon his death because most of the assets are passing to his wife and thus will be eligible for the marital deduction. Those assets, however, will be subject to tax in his wife's estate if she survives Bill. Overall estate taxes will be reduced if the lifetime gifts are made. The lifetime gifts will reduce the asset values that otherwise would be included in June's estate at her death.

C.   A gift of appreciating assets is particularly recommended because the appreciation escapes both gift and estate taxes. After the French restaurant is given to Jim, any appreciation in the value of the business will belong to Jim and will not be included in Bill's gross estate.

In 2015, Bill will be able to leave $5.43 million of assets to heirs without payment of estate tax. Since Bill's gross estate is estimated to be less than $5.43 million, there is likely to be an advantage to Bill in not making the gift and leaving it to Jim in his estate. The asset would then receive a step-up in basis to date of death value. If Jim sold the restaurant later, the capital gains tax would be substantially lower due to the stepped-up basis.

Since there is no guarantee that Congress will continue to allow estates a unified credit sheltering $5.43 million of assets, Bill may want to proceed with a gift to Jim to take advantage of the unified credit that can be used against the gift tax and that can shelter up to $5.43 million of assets in 2015.

D.   A lifetime gift of the vacation condominium may be advantageous to avoid the necessity of ancillary probate. Because the condominium is located in a different state, ancillary probate will likely be necessary to transfer the property to heirs. The condominium is titled in both Bill and June's names as tenants by the entireties, so the property will not pass through probate until the death of the second spouse. A lifetime transfer of the condominium might be delayed until after the first spouse dies, but disposition should be considered at that time to avoid ancillary probate.

4.   ESTATE PLANNING RECOMMENDATION

A.   The technique that should be recommended to achieve William Wyatt's objectives is the family bypass trust (B trust).

B.   Objective (1): The assets placed in the family bypass trust will eventually pass to the children, but the trust can be set up to pay income to Bill's wife for her life, to ensure that she has adequate income. The will can provide for a portion of the assets in Bill's estate to pass directly to June, for her use and enjoyment. As noted above, the family bypass trust could receive up to $5.43 million of assets from Bill's estate and still not result in estate taxes for Bill's estate.

Objective (2): The family bypass trust will result in Jim and Grace receiving the remainder interest in the trust after June's death. The trust will have taken advantage of the unified credit, so no estate taxes will be owed at either Bill's or June's deaths. Consequently, more of the estate will pass to the children.

Objective (3): Since the family bypass trust will take advantage of the unified credit, the estate taxes that would be owed at June's death after 2015 will be reduced. Instead of overqualifying property for the marital deduction, property is placed in the bypass trust to use the unified credit available to Bill. Bill's estate will include sufficient assets so that some assets could pass to June, in addition to the assets placed in the bypass trust. The income from the bypass trust is also payable to June for her life.

5. ESTATE PLANNING RECOMMENDATION

A. The technique that should be recommended to achieve the stated objectives is the irrevocable life insurance trust.

B. Objective (1): The death proceeds of the life insurance policies owned by Bill at the time of his death will be included in his gross estate. If Bill transfers the policies irrevocably to the trust, giving up all incidents of ownership, and then lives more than three years, the proceeds will not be included in his gross estate.

Objective (2): The life insurance policies can be transferred with little or no payment of gift taxes. The cash values are only $37,000. If June is the beneficiary of the trust, no gift tax will be due because of the gift tax marital deduction. If the children are beneficiaries, Bill can use split gifts to place the policies in trust, without incurring any gift tax. By gift-splitting, Bill can use the gift tax annual exclusion to make tax-free gifts of $28,000 to each of his children. No estate tax will be due on the property at the time of Bill's death. The trust can also be structured to transfer the property to Bill's children at June's death and thus avoid estate taxes in her estate.

The irrevocable life insurance trust may not be required if Bill dies in 2015 because the $5.43 million exclusion amount would shelter his estate assets even if the life insurance death benefit were included in the gross estate. However, many states impose death taxes after just a $1 million exemption amount so the ILIT may still be useful to provide liquidity for the estate.

Objective (3): The irrevocable life insurance trust can be drafted to provide June with a life income, and the trust can provide the children with a life income, or the remainder interest can be left to the children at June's death. The trust can provide for the needs of Bill's family, using the income from the assets, and they may be given a limited right to invade corpus.

WILLIAMS – HYPOTHETICAL ESTATE TAX RETURN

At the time of his death on March 21, 2015, Efrem Williams owned a home in joint tenancy with his wife Wilma. The house was valued at $300,000 and had a mortgage balance of $100,000. Efrem also owned an apartment building, valued at $3 million, with a mortgage balance of $500,000. Efrem owned a portfolio of stocks, valued at $2,750,000, and he owned some U.S. Treasury bonds worth $250,000. Efrem had a bank account in his own name with a $25,000 balance and another joint bank account with his son Ralph that had a balance of $15,000. Efrem contributed all of the money to the joint account. Efrem owned two life insurance policies that had face amounts totaling $200,000, and the $200,000 death proceeds were paid to his wife. His wife owned another policy on Efrem's life that paid her $50,000. Efrem also owned a vacation condominium with a value at his date of death of $150,000. At Efrem's death, he was receiving payments from a pension annuity that will continue to pay a survivorship benefit monthly to Wilma. This pension benefit has a present value of $325,000.

Efrem left a will in which he bequeathed $100,000 to his alma mater and placed the residue in trust. The trust will pay only income to Wilma, and, at her death, the remainder will be paid to Efrem's son Ralph. Assume that no QTIP election will be made by the executor. Efrem made taxable gifts in 2000 of $200,000. These gifts were made outright and in cash. Efrem's estate is not entitled to any credit for prior transfers, for foreign death taxes, or for pre-1977 gift taxes. The state death taxes for Efrem's estate were $30,000.

Efrem's debts paid by his executor totaled $25,000. The expenses of his funeral were $8,000, and the expenses for administering his estate were $20,000.

Editor's Note: The hypothetical case uses a 2013 Form 706 as the IRS has not yet released the 2015 estate tax returns. We were able to modify the 2013 form to use the 2015 unified credit amount.

Calculate Efrem Williams' Federal Estate Tax

The U.S. Estate Tax Return, Form 706, found at the end of the chapter, has been completed for the hypothetical estate of Efrem Williams. Preparation of the Form 706 logically begins with the entry of information in the Schedules A through I (the schedules are omitted here for simplification), and this information is then summarized in Part 5, entitled "Recapitulation," which appears at the bottom of Page 3 of Form 706. In the Recapitulation, Item 1 is the value of the real estate owned by Efrem Williams at the time of his death. The entry of $3,150,000 is the total value of the apartment building ($3 million) and the vacation condominium ($150,000). The home that Efrem owned jointly with his wife is not listed in Item 1, but is in Item 5, for jointly owned property.

Item 2 is the value of all stocks and bonds owned by Efrem at the time of his death. The stocks and bonds totaled $3 million. Item 3 is for mortgages, notes, and cash owned by the decedent, that is, owing to the decedent, not for mortgages owed by the decedent. Thus, this line contains the entry of $25,000, which is the amount of cash in the bank account in Efrem's name. The joint bank account is listed in Item 5, as joint property.

Item 4 is insurance on the decedent's life and contains the $200,000 from the policies owned by Efrem. The $50,000 life policy owned by Efrem's wife is not included in Efrem's gross estate. Item 5 is the value of the jointly owned property, including one-half of the value of the home ($150,000) and all of the joint bank account with his son ($15,000). Because the home is jointly owned with a spouse, only one-half is includible in the gross estate; but, all of the bank account with a nonspousal joint tenant is included because Efrem contributed all of the money. Item 9 is the value of the survivorship benefit under Efrem's pension annuity. The total gross estate is $6,865,000.

The Recapitulation also contains the deductions from the gross estate, beginning at Item 14. The amount of the funeral expenses is shown at Item 14 and is $8,000. Item 15 is the decedent's debts, which are $25,000. Item 16 is the total amount of the mortgages owed by the decedent and includes the mortgage on the apartment building of $500,000 and one-half of the $100,000 mortgage on the home, for a total of $550,000. (Note: Since only one-half of the home is includible in Efrem's gross estate, usually, only one-half of the mortgage balance is deducted. By paying off the mortgage, the estate could deduct the full amount.) Item 20 shows the administration expenses for the estate, in the amount of $20,000. Item 21 is the value of all property passing to the spouse which qualifies for the marital deduction. The property passing to Efrem's wife includes the pension annuity ($325,000), one-half of the value of the home ($150,000), and the life insurance death proceeds paid to her ($200,000), for a total of $675,000. The marital deduction does not apply to the $50,000 insurance death proceeds paid to Efrem's wife because these proceeds were not included in the gross estate. The marital deduction also does not apply to the assets placed in the testamentary trust under Efrem's will because Efrem's wife receives only a terminable interest under the will. Item 22 is the charitable bequest of $100,000 to Efrem's alma mater. The total deductions are $1,378,000. Notice that on the estate tax return, there is no separate calculation of the adjusted gross estate; rather, all deductions are subtracted together. The value of the adjusted gross estate is important, however, for determining the eligibility of the estate for deferred payment of the federal estate tax, under IRC Sec. 6166.

The estate tax is calculated in Part 2 – Tax Computation, which appears on Page 1 of Form 706. Line 1 of Part 2 is the total gross estate – previously calculated in the Recapitulation Sec., Item 13 – which is $6,865,000. The total allowable deductions are entered at line 2 from the Recapitulation, Item 24, and are $1,378,000. The state death tax deduction is entered on line 3b. When the deductions are subtracted from the total gross estate, the taxable estate is $5,457,000.

Line 4 is the amount of the adjusted taxable gifts to be added, to arrive at the tentative tax base. In this case, Efrem had made $200,000 of taxable gifts in 2000. Note that no gift taxes were paid because the unified credit offset any gift tax liability. Consequently, no amount was added to the gross estate for gift taxes paid within 3 years of death under the gross-up rule. In addition, no amount will be shown as a credit for tax on prior transfers at line 14 later in the return. Line 5 is the total of the taxable estate and adjusted taxable gifts, which is $5,657,000.

The tentative tax is calculated from the Tax Table. The tentative tax on $5,657,000 from the Table is $345,800 plus 40% of the amount over $1,000,000 (.40 x $4,657,000 = $1,862,800). The tentative tax, therefore, is $2,208,600, as shown on line 6. Line 7 is not applicable to this estate, so the next step is to apply the credits.

In the calculation for the estate of Efrem Williams, the entire unified credit is used, so $2,17,800 is subtracted from the tentative tax of $2,208,600, leaving a tax of $90,800. There are no additional credits. The tax due to the IRS – as shown on the bottom of Form 706, Page 1 – therefore, is $90,800.

Form **706**	United States Estate (and Generation-Skipping Transfer) Tax Return		OMB No. 1545-0015

(Rev. August 2013)

Department of the Treasury
Internal Revenue Service

▶ **Estate of a citizen or resident of the United States (see instructions). To be filed for decedents dying after December 31, 2012.**
▶ Information about Form 706 and its separate instructions is at *www.irs.gov/form706.*

Part 1—Decedent and Executor

1a Decedent's first name and middle initial (and maiden name, if any)	1b Decedent's last name	2 Decedent's social security no.
Efram	Williams	777 88 9999

3a City, town, or post office; county; state or province; country; and ZIP or foreign postal code.	3b Year domicile established	4 Date of birth	5 Date of death
1234 Main Street Anytown, Anystate 12345	1926	12-19-26	03-21-15

6b Executor's address (number and street including apartment or suite no.; city, town, or post office; state or province; country; and ZIP or foreign postal code) and phone no.

6a Name of executor (see instructions)

Bob Smith

5678 Main Street
Anytown, Anystate 12345

6c Executor's social security number (see instructions)

123   45   6789

Phone no.   555-666-7777

6d If there are multiple executors, check here ☐ and attach a list showing the names, addresses, telephone numbers, and SSNs of the additional executors.

7a Name and location of court where will was probated or estate administered	7b Case number
Anytown, Anystate	C-9876

8 If decedent died testate, check here ▶ ☑ and attach a certified copy of the will. **9** If you extended the time to file this Form 706, check here ▶ ☐

10 If Schedule R-1 is attached, check here ▶ ☐ **11** If you are estimating the value of assets included in the gross estate on line 1 pursuant to the special rule of Reg. section 20.2010-2T(a) (7)(ii), check here ▶ ☐

Part 2—Tax Computation

1	Total gross estate less exclusion (from Part 5—Recapitulation, item 13)	1	6,865,000
2	Tentative total allowable deductions (from Part 5—Recapitulation, item 24)	2	1,378,000
3a	Tentative taxable estate (subtract line 2 from line 1)	3a	5,487,000
b	State death tax deduction	3b	30,000
c	Taxable estate (subtract line 3b from line 3a)	3c	5,457,000
4	Adjusted taxable gifts (see instructions)	4	200,000
5	Add lines 3c and 4	5	5,657,000
6	Tentative tax on the amount on line 5 from Table A in the instructions	6	2,208,600
7	Total gift tax paid or payable (see instructions)	7	0
8	Gross estate tax (subtract line 7 from line 6)	8	2,208,600
9a	Basic exclusion amount	9a	5,430,000
9b	Deceased spousal unused exclusion (DSUE) amount from predeceased spouse(s), if any (from Section D, Part 6—Portability of Deceased Spousal Unused Exclusion).	9b	0
9c	Applicable exclusion amount (add lines 9a and 9b)	9c	5,430,000
9d	Applicable credit amount (tentative tax on the amount in 9c from Table A in the instructions)	9d	2,117,800
10	Adjustment to applicable credit amount (May not exceed $6,000. See instructions.)	10	0
11	Allowable applicable credit amount (subtract line 10 from line 9d)	11	2,117,800
12	Subtract line 11 from line 8 (but do not enter less than zero)	12	90,800
13	Credit for foreign death taxes (from Schedule P). (Attach Form(s) 706-CE.)	13	0
14	Credit for tax on prior transfers (from Schedule Q)	14	0
15	Total credits (add lines 13 and 14)	15	0
16	Net estate tax (subtract line 15 from line 12)	16	90,800
17	Generation-skipping transfer (GST) taxes payable (from Schedule R, Part 2, line 10)	17	0
18	Total transfer taxes (add lines 16 and 17)	18	90,800
19	Prior payments (explain in an attached statement)	19	0
20	Balance due (or overpayment) (subtract line 19 from line 18)	20	90,800

Under penalties of perjury, I declare that I have examined this return, including accompanying schedules and statements, and to the best of my knowledge and belief, it is true, correct, and complete. Declaration of preparer other than the executor is based on all information of which preparer has any knowledge.

Sign Here

▶ _____ Signature of executor   ▶ Date

▶ _____ Signature of executor   ▶ Date

Paid Preparer Use Only

Print/Type preparer's name	Preparer's signature	Date	Check ☐ if self-employed	PTIN
Firm's name ▶			Firm's EIN ▶	
Firm's address ▶			Phone no.	

For Privacy Act and Paperwork Reduction Act Notice, see instructions.   Cat. No. 20548R   Form **706** (Rev. 8-2013)

Form 706 (Rev. 8-2013)

Estate of:	Decedent's social security number		
	777	88	9999

Part 4—General Information *(continued)*

If you answer "Yes" to any of the following questions, you must attach additional information as described.	Yes	No
10 Did the decedent at the time of death own any property as a joint tenant with right of survivorship in which **(a)** one or more of the other joint tenants was someone other than the decedent's spouse, and **(b)** less than the full value of the property is included on the return as part of the gross estate? If "Yes," you must complete and attach Schedule E		✓
11a Did the decedent, at the time of death, own any interest in a partnership (for example, a family limited partnership), an unincorporated business, or a limited liability company; or own any stock in an inactive or closely held corporation?		✓
b If "Yes," was the value of **any** interest owned (from above) discounted on this estate tax return? If "Yes," see the instructions on reporting the total accumulated or effective discounts taken on Schedule F or G		✓
12 Did the decedent make any transfer described in sections 2035, 2036, 2037, or 2038? (see instructions) If "Yes," you must complete and attach Schedule G		✓
13a Were there in existence at the time of the decedent's death any trusts created by the decedent during his or her lifetime? . .		✓
b Were there in existence at the time of the decedent's death any trusts not created by the decedent under which the decedent possessed any power, beneficial interest, or trusteeship?		✓
c Was the decedent receiving income from a trust created after October 22, 1986, by a parent or grandparent?		✓
If "Yes," was there a GST taxable termination (under section 2612) on the death of the decedent?		✓
d If there was a GST taxable termination (under section 2612), attach a statement to explain. Provide a copy of the trust or will creating the trust, and give the name, address, and phone number of the current trustee(s).		
e Did the decedent at any time during his or her lifetime transfer or sell an interest in a partnership, limited liability company, or closely held corporation to a trust described in lines 13a or 13b?		✓
If "Yes," provide the EIN for this transferred/sold item. ▶		
14 Did the decedent ever possess, exercise, or release any general power of appointment? If "Yes," you must complete and attach Schedule H		✓
15 Did the decedent have an interest in or a signature or other authority over a financial account in a foreign country, such as a bank account, securities account, or other financial account?		✓
16 Was the decedent, immediately before death, receiving an annuity described in the "General" paragraph of the instructions for Schedule I or a private annuity? If "Yes," you must complete and attach Schedule I	✓	
17 Was the decedent ever the beneficiary of a trust for which a deduction was claimed by the estate of a predeceased spouse under section 2056(b)(7) and which is not reported on this return? If "Yes," attach an explanation		✓

Part 5—Recapitulation. Note. If estimating the value of one or more assets pursuant to the special rule of Reg. section 20.2010-2T(a)(7)(ii), enter on both lines 10 and 23 the amount noted in the instructions for the corresponding range of values. (See instructions for details.)

Item no.	Gross estate		Alternate value	Value at date of death
1	Schedule A—Real Estate	1		3,150,000
2	Schedule B—Stocks and Bonds	2		3,000,000
3	Schedule C—Mortgages, Notes, and Cash	3		25,000
4	Schedule D—Insurance on the Decedent's Life (attach Form(s) 712)	4		200,000
5	Schedule E—Jointly Owned Property (attach Form(s) 712 for life insurance) .	5		165,000
6	Schedule F—Other Miscellaneous Property (attach Form(s) 712 for life insurance)	6		0
7	Schedule G—Transfers During Decedent's Life (att. Form(s) 712 for life insurance)	7		0
8	Schedule H—Powers of Appointment	8		0
9	Schedule I—Annuities	9		325,000
10	Estimated value of assets subject to the special rule of Reg. section 20.2010-2T(a)(7)(ii)	10		0
11	Total gross estate (add items 1 through 10)	11		6,865,000
12	Schedule U—Qualified Conservation Easement Exclusion	12		0
13	Total gross estate less exclusion (subtract item 12 from item 11). Enter here and on line 1 of Part 2—Tax Computation	13		6,865,000

Item no.	Deductions		Amount
14	Schedule J—Funeral Expenses and Expenses Incurred in Administering Property Subject to Claims	14	8,000
15	Schedule K—Debts of the Decedent	15	25,000
16	Schedule K—Mortgages and Liens	16	550,000
17	Total of items 14 through 16	17	583,000
18	Allowable amount of deductions from item 17 (see the instructions for item 18 of the Recapitulation)	18	0
19	Schedule L—Net Losses During Administration	19	0
20	Schedule L—Expenses Incurred in Administering Property Not Subject to Claims	20	20,000
21	Schedule M—Bequests, etc., to Surviving Spouse	21	675,000
22	Schedule O—Charitable, Public, and Similar Gifts and Bequests	22	100,000
23	Estimated value of deductible assets subject to the special rule of Reg. section 20.2010-2T(a)(7)(ii) . . .	23	0
24	Tentative total allowable deductions (add items 18 through 23). Enter here and on line 2 of the Tax Computation	24	1,378,000

Page 3

 www.keirsuccess.com

GANTRY – HYPOTHETICAL GIFT TAX RETURN

In 2015, Elmer Gantry gave the First Baptist Church $100,000 for its missionary campaign. Elmer paid for his mother's medical bills in the amount of $17,000, and he gave his mother Rosie a new house that he purchased for $200,000. Elmer gave his wife Essie a diamond necklace, valued at $125,000. Elmer also established a trust that would pay income to Essie for her life, with the remainder payable to their son Philip at Essie's death. The life-income interest is valued at $300,000, and Philip's remainder interest is valued at $75,000. Elmer paid for Philip's college tuition in the amount of $15,000. Elmer made taxable gifts in 1988 of $150,000 and in 1989, of $350,000. Elmer's wife has agreed to split gifts with him. Essie also gave their son Gerald a $15,000 motorboat.

Editor's Note: The hypothetical case uses a 2014 Form 709 as the IRS has not yet released the 2015 gift tax forms. We were able to modify the form to use the 2015 unified credit amount.

Calculate Elmer Gantry's Federal Gift Tax Obligation

The United States Gift Tax Return, Form 709, found at the end of the chapter, has been completed for Elmer Gantry for 2015, using the case facts. The first step in determining Elmer Gantry's gift tax is to list the gifts subject to gift tax on Schedule A, on Page 2 of the return. When completing Schedule A, it is important to remember that the medical and educational exclusions apply to the payment of medical bills for Elmer's mother and the payment of college tuition for Philip. Therefore, these payments are not considered gifts and are not listed on Schedule A.

Elmer Gantry made a total of five gifts to four different parties, including the First Baptist Church. The five gifts are recorded in Schedule A, Part 1. The gifts are split, and the net transfer is listed in Column H. The gift that Essie made to Gerald is also listed because Elmer and Essie must split all gifts for the year, so Elmer must report half of this gift. The total value of the gifts is added from Column H and entered in Part 4, line 1, where the total is $620,000. This total is calculated before deducting any amounts qualifying for the annual exclusion, the marital deduction, or the charitable deduction.

For each gift of a qualifying present interest, the annual exclusion for 2015 of $14,000 is subtracted, including marital and charitable gifts. No annual exclusion applies to gifts of a future interest, so no deduction will apply to the gift to Philip of the remainder interest in the trust. The annual exclusion will apply to each of the other parties, including Essie ($14,000), Rosie ($14,000), Gerald ($7,500), and the First Baptist Church ($14,000). The total annual exclusions, therefore, are $49,500. This amount is entered on line 2 of Part 4.

The amount claimed for the marital deduction is entered on line 4. The life-income interest in trust for Essie is a terminable interest. Therefore, the marital deduction does not apply to this gift. Only the gift of the necklace valued at $125,000 will qualify for the marital deduction. On line 5, the annual exclusion applicable to the gift to Essie, which was previously deducted, is eliminated from the marital deduction in the amount of $14,000. On line 7, the amount of the charitable deduction for the gift to the First Baptist Church – after gift-splitting and the reduction for the annual exclusion – is $36,000.

Elmer Gantry's taxable gifts, as shown on Schedule A, Part 4, line 11, are $423,500. This amount is also entered on the first page of Form 709, in Part 2 – Tax Computation, on line 1. On line 2, enter the amount of Elmer Gantry's gifts in prior years, or $500,000. This total of taxable gifts is taken from Schedule B, line 3, on page 3 of Form 709. After adding the gifts from Schedule A and Schedule B, enter the total taxable gifts on line 3, which is $923,500. Next, calculate the gift tax on the total, using the table of Unified Federal Estate and Gift Tax Rates. Also calculate the gift tax for prior gifts, entered on line 2. Now, subtract the gift tax for line 2 from the total gift tax for line 3, to find the amount of gift tax owed on gifts in the current year. Finally, complete lines 8-14 and deduct Elmer Gantry's allowable unified credit, to find the amount of gift tax he owes. In this case, no gift tax is owed.

Form **709**	United States Gift (and Generation-Skipping Transfer) Tax Return	OMB No. 1545-0020

Form **709**

Department of the Treasury
Internal Revenue Service

United States Gift (and Generation-Skipping Transfer) Tax Return

▶ Information about Form 709 and its separate instructions is at *www.irs.gov/form709.*

(For gifts made during calendar year 2014)
▶ See instructions.

OMB No. 1545-0020

20**14**

1 Donor's first name and middle initial	2 Donor's last name	3 Donor's social security number
Elmer	Gantry	111-22-3333

4 Address (number, street, and apartment number)	5 Legal residence (domicile)
1234 Main Street	Anytown, Anystate

6 City or town, state or province, country, and ZIP or foreign postal code	7 Citizenship (see instructions)
Anytown, Anystate. 12345	USA

Part 1—General Information

		Yes	No
8	If the donor died during the year, check here ▶ ☐ and enter date of death _____ , _____ .		
9	If you extended the time to file this Form 709, check here ▶ ☐		
10	Enter the total number of donees listed on Schedule A. Count each person only once ▶ 4		
11a	Have you (the donor) previously filed a Form 709 (or 709-A) for any other year? If "No," skip line 11b	✓	
b	Has your address changed since you last filed Form 709 (or 709-A)?		✓
12	**Gifts by husband or wife to third parties.** Do you consent to have the gifts (including generation-skipping transfers) made by you and by your spouse to third parties during the calendar year considered as made one-half by each of you? (see instructions.) (If the answer is "Yes," the following information must be furnished and your spouse must sign the consent shown below. **If the answer is "No," skip lines 13–18.**)	✓	
13	Name of consenting spouse Essie Gantry 14 SSN 444-55-6666		
15	Were you married to one another during the entire calendar year? (see instructions)	✓	
16	If 15 is "No," check whether ☐ married ☐ divorced or ☐ widowed/deceased, and give date (see instructions) ▶		
17	Will a gift tax return for this year be filed by your spouse? (If "Yes," mail both returns in the same envelope.)	✓	
18	**Consent of Spouse.** I consent to have the gifts (and generation-skipping transfers) made by me and by my spouse to third parties during the calendar year considered as made one-half by each of us. We are both aware of the joint and several liability for tax created by the execution of this consent.		

Consenting spouse's signature ▶   Date ▶

19	Have you applied a DSUE amount received from a predeceased spouse to a gift or gifts reported on this or a previous Form 709? If "Yes," complete Schedule C		✓

Part 2—Tax Computation

1	Enter the amount from Schedule A, Part 4, line 11	1	423,500
2	Enter the amount from Schedule B, line 3	2	500,000
3	Total taxable gifts. Add lines 1 and 2	3	923,500
4	Tax computed on amount on line 3 (see *Table for Computing Gift Tax* in instructions)	4	315,965
5	Tax computed on amount on line 2 (see *Table for Computing Gift Tax* in instructions)	5	155,800
6	Balance. Subtract line 5 from line 4	6	160,165
7	Applicable credit amount. If donor has DSUE amount from predeceased spouse(s), enter amount from Schedule C, line 4; otherwise, see instructions	7	2,117,800
8	Enter the applicable credit against tax allowable for all prior periods (from Sch. B, line 1, col. C)	8	155,800
9	Balance. Subtract line 8 from line 7. Do not enter less than zero	9	1,962,000
10	Enter 20% (.20) of the amount allowed as a specific exemption for gifts made after September 8, 1976, and before January 1, 1977 (see instructions)	10	0
11	Balance. Subtract line 10 from line 9. Do not enter less than zero	11	1,962.000
12	Applicable credit. Enter the smaller of line 6 or line 11	12	160,165
13	Credit for foreign gift taxes (see instructions)	13	0
14	Total credits. Add lines 12 and 13	14	160,165
15	Balance. Subtract line 14 from line 6. Do not enter less than zero	15	0
16	Generation-skipping transfer taxes (from Schedule D, Part 3, col. H, Total)	16	0
17	Total tax. Add lines 15 and 16	17	0
18	Gift and generation-skipping transfer taxes prepaid with extension of time to file	18	0
19	If line 18 is less than line 17, enter **balance due** (see instructions)	19	0
20	If line 18 is greater than line 17, enter **amount to be refunded**	20	0

Sign Here

Under penalties of perjury, I declare that I have examined this return, including any accompanying schedules and statements, and to the best of my knowledge and belief, it is true, correct, and complete. Declaration of preparer (other than donor) is based on all information of which preparer has any knowledge.

May the IRS discuss this return with the preparer shown below (see instructions)? ☐ Yes ☐ No

▶ _____   _____
Signature of donor   Date

Paid Preparer Use Only

Print/Type preparer's name	Preparer's signature	Date	Check ☐ if self-employed	PTIN

Firm's name ▶   Firm's EIN ▶

Firm's address ▶   Phone no.

Attach check or money order here.

For Disclosure, Privacy Act, and Paperwork Reduction Act Notice, see the instructions for this form.   Cat. No. 16783M   Form **709** (2014)

Form 709 (2014)   Page **2**

SCHEDULE A | **Computation of Taxable Gifts** (Including transfers in trust) (see instructions)

A   Does the value of any item listed on Schedule A reflect any valuation discount? If "Yes," attach explanation . . . . . . Yes ☐ No ☑

B   ☐ ◄ Check here if you elect under section 529(c)(2)(B) to treat any transfers made this year to a qualified tuition program as made ratably over a 5-year period beginning this year. See instructions. Attach explanation.

Part 1—Gifts Subject Only to Gift Tax. Gifts less political organization, medical, and educational exclusions. (see instructions)

A Item number	B • Donee's name and address • Relationship to donor (if any) • Description of gift • If the gift was of securities, give CUSIP no. • If closely held entity, give EIN	C	D Donor's adjusted basis of gift	E Date of gift	F Value at date of gift	G For split gifts, enter 1/2 of column F	H Net transfer (subtract col. G from col. F)
1	See Statement 1 attached		800,000	various	800,000	187,500	612,500

Gifts made by spouse —*complete **only** if you are splitting gifts with your spouse and he/she also made gifts.*

	Gerald Gantry, son, motorboat		15,000	6-12-15	15,000	7,500	7,500

Total of Part 1. Add amounts from Part 1, column H . . . . ► | 620,000

Part 2—Direct Skips. Gifts that are direct skips and are subject to both gift tax and generation-skipping transfer tax. You must list the gifts in chronological order.

A Item number	B • Donee's name and address • Relationship to donor (if any) • Description of gift • If the gift was of securities, give CUSIP no. • If closely held entity, give EIN	C 2632(b) election out	D Donor's adjusted basis of gift	E Date of gift	F Value at date of gift	G For split gifts, enter 1/2 of column F	H Net transfer (subtract col. G from col. F)
1							

Gifts made by spouse —*complete **only** if you are splitting gifts with your spouse and he/she also made gifts.*

Total of Part 2. Add amounts from Part 2, column H . . . . ►

Part 3—Indirect Skips. Gifts to trusts that are currently subject to gift tax and may later be subject to generation-skipping transfer tax. You must list these gifts in chronological order.

A Item number	B • Donee's name and address • Relationship to donor (if any) • Description of gift • If the gift was of securities, give CUSIP no. • If closely held entity, give EIN	C 2632(c) election	D Donor's adjusted basis of gift	E Date of gift	F Value at date of gift	G For split gifts, enter 1/2 of column F	H Net transfer (subtract col. G from col. F)
1							

Gifts made by spouse —*complete **only** if you are splitting gifts with your spouse and he/she also made gifts.*

Total of Part 3. Add amounts from Part 3, column H . . . . ►

(If more space is needed, attach additional statements.)   Form **709** (2014)

Form 709 (2014)   Page 3

Part 4—Taxable Gift Reconciliation

1	Total value of gifts of donor. Add totals from column H of Parts 1, 2, and 3	1	620,000
2	Total annual exclusions for gifts listed on line 1 (see instructions)	2	49,500
3	Total included amount of gifts. Subtract line 2 from line 1	3	570,500

Deductions (see instructions)

4	Gifts of interests to spouse for which a marital deduction will be claimed, based on item numbers _____3_____ of Schedule A . .	4	125,000		
5	Exclusions attributable to gifts on line 4	5	14,000		
6	Marital deduction. Subtract line 5 from line 4	6	111,000		
7	Charitable deduction, based on item nos. ___1___ less exclusions .	7	36,000		
8	Total deductions. Add lines 6 and 7			8	147,000
9	Subtract line 8 from line 3			9	423,500
10	Generation-skipping transfer taxes payable with this Form 709 (from Schedule D, Part 3, col. H, Total) . .			10	0
11	**Taxable gifts.** Add lines 9 and 10. Enter here and on page 1, Part 2—Tax Computation, line 1			11	423,500

Terminable Interest (QTIP) Marital Deduction. (see instructions for Schedule A, Part 4, line 4)

If a trust (or other property) meets the requirements of qualified terminable interest property under section 2523(f), and:

    a. The trust (or other property) is listed on Schedule A, and

    b. The value of the trust (or other property) is entered in whole or in part as a deduction on Schedule A, Part 4, line 4,
then the donor shall be deemed to have made an election to have such trust (or other property) treated as qualified terminable interest property under section 2523(f).

If less than the entire value of the trust (or other property) that the donor has included in Parts 1 and 3 of Schedule A is entered as a deduction on line 4, the donor shall be considered to have made an election only as to a fraction of the trust (or other property). The numerator of this fraction is equal to the amount of the trust (or other property) deducted on Schedule A, Part 4, line 6. The denominator is equal to the total value of the trust (or other property) listed in Parts 1 and 3 of Schedule A.

If you make the QTIP election, the terminable interest property involved will be included in your spouse's gross estate upon his or her death (section 2044). See instructions for line 4 of Schedule A. If your spouse disposes (by gift or otherwise) of all or part of the qualifying life income interest, he or she will be considered to have made a transfer of the entire property that is subject to the gift tax. See *Transfer of Certain Life Estates Received From Spouse* in the instructions.

12 Election Out of QTIP Treatment of Annuities

☐ ◄ Check here if you elect under section 2523(f)(6) **not** to treat as qualified terminable interest property any joint and survivor annuities that are reported on Schedule A and would otherwise be treated as qualified terminable interest property under section 2523(f). See instructions. Enter the item numbers from Schedule A for the annuities for which you are making this election ► -

SCHEDULE B   Gifts From Prior Periods

If you answered "Yes," on line 11a of page 1, Part 1, see the instructions for completing Schedule B. If you answered "No," skip to the Tax Computation on page 1 (or Schedules C or D, if applicable). Complete Schedule A before beginning Schedule B. See instructions for recalculation of the column C amounts. Attach calculations.

A Calendar year or calendar quarter (see instructions)	B Internal Revenue office where prior return was filed	C Amount of applicable credit (unified credit) against gift tax for periods after December 31, 1976	D Amount of specific exemption for prior periods ending before January 1, 1977	E Amount of taxable gifts
1988	Ogden, Utah	38,800	0	150,000
1989	Ogden, Utah	117,000	0	350,000

1	Totals for prior periods	1	155,800	0	500,000
2	Amount, if any, by which total specific exemption, line 1, column D is more than $30,000			2	0
3	Total amount of taxable gifts for prior periods. Add amount on line 1, column E and amount, if any, on line 2. Enter here and on page 1, Part 2—Tax Computation, line 2			3	500,000

(If more space is needed, attach additional statements.)   Form **709** (2014)

Elmer Gantry
Form 709 for the Year Ending 12/31/15
111-22-3333

Statement 1 – Schedule A, Part 1

Item number	Donee's name, relationship, and description of gift	Donor's adjusted basis of gift	Date of gift	Value at date of gift	For split gifts, enter 50%	Net transfer
1	First Baptist Church, cash	$100,000	4-1-15	$100,000	$50,000	$50,000
2	Rosie Gantry, mother, house	$200,000	5-6-15	$200,000	$100,000	$100,000
3	Essie Gantry, spouse, necklace	$125,000	6-17-15	$125,000	N/A	$125,000
4	Essie Gantry, spouse, life interest in Elmer's trust	$300,000	7-22-15	$300,000	N/A	$300,000
5	Philip Gantry, son, remainder interest in Elmer's trust	$75,000	7-22-15	$75,000	$37,500	$37,500
Total		$800,000		$800,000	$187,500	$612,500

WORTHINGTON – HYPOTHETICAL GIFT TAX RETURN WITH GST TAX

Sondra Worthington gave her grandson $6,014,000 in cash during 2015. She had already given this grandson $1,513,000 in cash in 2011. After deducting the annual GST exclusion, Sondra used up $1.5 million of her exemption under the generation-skipping transfer tax. Sondra has made no other taxable gifts. (Note: the annual exclusion in 2011 was $13,000)

Editor's Note: The hypothetical case uses a 2014 Form 709 as the IRS has not yet released the 2015 gift tax forms. We were able to modify the form to use the 2015 unified credit amount.

Calculate the Generation-Skipping Transfer Tax

This lifetime direct-skip transfer is reported on the U.S. Gift Tax Return, Form 709. The Form 709 at the end of this chapter was prepared for this hypothetical case. The first step in completing Form 709 is to enter the donee's name and relationship to the donor, a description of the gift, and the value of the gift on Schedule A, Part 2, which appears on page 2 of Form 709. The value of the gift shown on Schedule A is then entered in Schedule D, Part I, which appears on page 4 of Form 709. The amount of any gift-splitting and the annual exclusion are then subtracted. In this case, there is no gift-splitting, so the gift is only reduced by the $14,000 annual exclusion available in 2015. The net transfer is, therefore, $6,000,000.

In Part 2 of Schedule D, the amount of available exemption is computed. Part 2 is on page 5 of Form 709. Sondra Worthington used $1.5 million of the exemption available in 2011, but there is additional exemption available in 2015. For 2015, the GST exemption is $5.43 million. Accordingly, Sondra Worthington allocated an additional exemption amount of $3.93 million. The net transfer of $6 million is entered in Part 3, Column B. The inclusion ratio is calculated in Columns C, D, and E. The inclusion ratio in Column E is then multiplied by the 40% tax rate, and the result is multiplied by the net transfer of $6 million. The GST tax is $828,000. This amount is reported on line 16 of page 1 of Form 709. Note that this tax will be in addition to the gift tax owed on the transfer. For completeness, the gift tax on the Form 709 is also included at the end of this computation. Since the tax rate for gifts above $1,000,000 is 40%, the combined gift and GST taxes due are $1,987,200, as shown on the bottom of page 1 of Form 709.

Form **709**	**United States Gift (and Generation-Skipping Transfer) Tax Return**	OMB No. 1545-0020
Department of the Treasury Internal Revenue Service	▶ Information about Form 709 and its separate instructions is at *www.irs.gov/form709*. (For gifts made during calendar year 2014) ▶ See instructions.	2014

Part 1—General Information

1 Donor's first name and middle initial	2 Donor's last name	3 Donor's social security number
Sondra	Worthington	222-33-4444

4 Address (number, street, and apartment number)	5 Legal residence (domicile)
5678 Main Street	Anytown, Anystate

6 City or town, state or province, country, and ZIP or foreign postal code	7 Citizenship (see instructions)
Anytown, Anystate 12345	USA

		Yes	No
8	If the donor died during the year, check here ▶ ☐ and enter date of death _____ , _____ .		
9	If you extended the time to file this Form 709, check here ▶ ☐		
10	Enter the total number of donees listed on Schedule A. Count each person only once ▶ 1		
11a	Have you (the donor) previously filed a Form 709 (or 709-A) for any other year? If "No," skip line 11b	✓	
b	Has your address changed since you last filed Form 709 (or 709-A)?		✓
12	**Gifts by husband or wife to third parties.** Do you consent to have the gifts (including generation-skipping transfers) made by you and by your spouse to third parties during the calendar year considered as made one-half by each of you? (see instructions.) (If the answer is "Yes," the following information must be furnished and your spouse must sign the consent shown below. **If the answer is "No," skip lines 13–18.**)		

13	Name of consenting spouse	14 SSN	
15	Were you married to one another during the entire calendar year? (see instructions)		
16	If 15 is "No," check whether ☐ married ☐ divorced or ☐ widowed/deceased, and give date (see instructions) ▶		
17	Will a gift tax return for this year be filed by your spouse? (If "Yes," mail both returns in the same envelope.)		
18	**Consent of Spouse.** I consent to have the gifts (and generation-skipping transfers) made by me and by my spouse to third parties during the calendar year considered as made one-half by each of us. We are both aware of the joint and several liability for tax created by the execution of this consent.		

Consenting spouse's signature ▶   Date ▶

19	Have you applied a DSUE amount received from a predeceased spouse to a gift or gifts reported on this or a previous Form 709? If "Yes," complete Schedule C		

Part 2—Tax Computation

1	Enter the amount from Schedule A, Part 4, line 11	1	6,828,000
2	Enter the amount from Schedule B, line 3	2	1,500,000
3	Total taxable gifts. Add lines 1 and 2	3	8,328,000
4	Tax computed on amount on line 3 (see *Table for Computing Gift Tax* in instructions)	4	3,277,000
5	Tax computed on amount on line 2 (see *Table for Computing Gift Tax* in instructions)	5	545,800
6	Balance. Subtract line 5 from line 4	6	2,731,200
7	Applicable credit amount. If donor has DSUE amount from predeceased spouse(s), enter amount from Schedule C, line 4; otherwise, see instructions	7	2,117,800
8	Enter the applicable credit against tax allowable for all prior periods (from Sch. B, line 1, col. C)	8	545,800
9	Balance. Subtract line 8 from line 7. Do not enter less than zero	9	1,572,000
10	Enter 20% (.20) of the amount allowed as a specific exemption for gifts made after September 8, 1976, and before January 1, 1977 (see instructions)	10	0
11	Balance. Subtract line 10 from line 9. Do not enter less than zero	11	1,572,000
12	Applicable credit. Enter the smaller of line 6 or line 11	12	1,572,000
13	Credit for foreign gift taxes (see instructions)	13	0
14	Total credits. Add lines 12 and 13	14	1,572,000
15	Balance. Subtract line 14 from line 6. Do not enter less than zero	15	1,159,200
16	Generation-skipping transfer taxes (from Schedule D, Part 3, col. H, Total)	16	828,000
17	Total tax. Add lines 15 and 16	17	1,987,200
18	Gift and generation-skipping transfer taxes prepaid with extension of time to file	18	0
19	If line 18 is less than line 17, enter **balance due** (see instructions)	19	1,987,200
20	If line 18 is greater than line 17, enter **amount to be refunded**	20	0

Attach check or money order here.

Sign Here

Under penalties of perjury, I declare that I have examined this return, including any accompanying schedules and statements, and to the best of my knowledge and belief, it is true, correct, and complete. Declaration of preparer (other than donor) is based on all information of which preparer has any knowledge.

May the IRS discuss this return with the preparer shown below (see instructions)? ☐ Yes ☐ No

▶ _____   _____
Signature of donor   Date

Paid Preparer Use Only

Print/Type preparer's name	Preparer's signature	Date	Check ☐ if self-employed	PTIN
Firm's name ▶			Firm's EIN ▶	
Firm's address ▶			Phone no.	

For Disclosure, Privacy Act, and Paperwork Reduction Act Notice, see the instructions for this form.   Cat. No. 16783M   Form **709** (2014)

Appendix – Worthington Case

Form 709 (2014)
Page 2

SCHEDULE A   Computation of Taxable Gifts (Including transfers in trust) (see instructions)

A   Does the value of any item listed on Schedule A reflect any valuation discount? If "Yes," attach explanation . . . . . . Yes ☐   No ☐

B   ☐ ◄ Check here if you elect under section 529(c)(2)(B) to treat any transfers made this year to a qualified tuition program as made ratably over a 5-year period beginning this year. See instructions. Attach explanation.

Part 1—Gifts Subject Only to Gift Tax. Gifts less political organization, medical, and educational exclusions. (see instructions)

A Item number	B • Donee's name and address • Relationship to donor (if any) • Description of gift • If the gift was of securities, give CUSIP no. • If closely held entity, give EIN	C	D Donor's adjusted basis of gift	E Date of gift	F Value at date of gift	G For split gifts, enter ½ of column F	H Net transfer (subtract col. G from col. F)
1							

Gifts made by spouse —*complete **only** if you are splitting gifts with your spouse and he/she also made gifts.*

Total of Part 1. Add amounts from Part 1, column H . . . . ► | |

Part 2—Direct Skips. Gifts that are direct skips and are subject to both gift tax and generation-skipping transfer tax. You must list the gifts in chronological order.

A Item number	B • Donee's name and address • Relationship to donor (if any) • Description of gift • If the gift was of securities, give CUSIP no. • If closely held entity, give EIN	C 2632(b) election out	D Donor's adjusted basis of gift	E Date of gift	F Value at date of gift	G For split gifts, enter ½ of column F	H Net transfer (subtract col. G from col. F)
1	Michael Worthington, grandson, cash		6,014,000	04-28-15	6,014,000		6,014,000

Gifts made by spouse —*complete **only** if you are splitting gifts with your spouse and he/she also made gifts.*

Total of Part 2. Add amounts from Part 2, column H . . . . ► | 6,014,000 |

Part 3—Indirect Skips. Gifts to trusts that are currently subject to gift tax and may later be subject to generation-skipping transfer tax. You must list these gifts in chronological order.

A Item number	B • Donee's name and address • Relationship to donor (if any) • Description of gift • If the gift was of securities, give CUSIP no. • If closely held entity, give EIN	C 2632(c) election	D Donor's adjusted basis of gift	E Date of gift	F Value at date of gift	G For split gifts, enter ½ of column F	H Net transfer (subtract col. G from col. F)
1							

Gifts made by spouse —*complete **only** if you are splitting gifts with your spouse and he/she also made gifts.*

Total of Part 3. Add amounts from Part 3, column H . . . . ► | |

(If more space is needed, attach additional statements.)   Form **709** (2014)

© 2015 Keir Educational Resources   Appendix – 171   800-795-5347

Part 4—Taxable Gift Reconciliation

1	Total value of gifts of donor. Add totals from column H of Parts 1, 2, and 3	1	6,014,000
2	Total annual exclusions for gifts listed on line 1 (see instructions)	2	14,000
3	Total included amount of gifts. Subtract line 2 from line 1	3	6,000,000

Deductions (see instructions)

4	Gifts of interests to spouse for which a marital deduction will be claimed, based on item numbers _____ of Schedule A	4				
5	Exclusions attributable to gifts on line 4	5				
6	Marital deduction. Subtract line 5 from line 4	6				
7	Charitable deduction, based on item nos. _____ less exclusions	7				
8	Total deductions. Add lines 6 and 7				8	0
9	Subtract line 8 from line 3				9	6,000,000
10	Generation-skipping transfer taxes payable with this Form 709 (from Schedule D, Part 3, col. H, Total)				10	828,000
11	**Taxable gifts.** Add lines 9 and 10. Enter here and on page 1, Part 2—Tax Computation, line 1				11	6,828,000

Terminable Interest (QTIP) Marital Deduction. (see instructions for Schedule A, Part 4, line 4)

If a trust (or other property) meets the requirements of qualified terminable interest property under section 2523(f), and:

a. The trust (or other property) is listed on Schedule A, and

b. The value of the trust (or other property) is entered in whole or in part as a deduction on Schedule A, Part 4, line 4, then the donor shall be deemed to have made an election to have such trust (or other property) treated as qualified terminable interest property under section 2523(f).

If less than the entire value of the trust (or other property) that the donor has included in Parts 1 and 3 of Schedule A is entered as a deduction on line 4, the donor shall be considered to have made an election only as to a fraction of the trust (or other property). The numerator of this fraction is equal to the amount of the trust (or other property) deducted on Schedule A, Part 4, line 6. The denominator is equal to the total value of the trust (or other property) listed in Parts 1 and 3 of Schedule A.

If you make the QTIP election, the terminable interest property involved will be included in your spouse's gross estate upon his or her death (section 2044). See instructions for line 4 of Schedule A. If your spouse disposes (by gift or otherwise) of all or part of the qualifying life income interest, he or she will be considered to have made a transfer of the entire property that is subject to the gift tax. See *Transfer of Certain Life Estates Received From Spouse* in the instructions.

12 Election Out of QTIP Treatment of Annuities

☐ ◄ Check here if you elect under section 2523(f)(6) **not** to treat as qualified terminable interest property any joint and survivor annuities that are reported on Schedule A and would otherwise be treated as qualified terminable interest property under section 2523(f). See instructions. Enter the item numbers from Schedule A for the annuities for which you are making this election ► _____

SCHEDULE B   Gifts From Prior Periods

If you answered "Yes," on line 11a of page 1, Part 1, see the instructions for completing Schedule B. If you answered "No," skip to the Tax Computation on page 1 (or Schedules C or D, if applicable). Complete Schedule A before beginning Schedule B. See instructions for recalculation of the column C amounts. Attach calculations.

A Calendar year or calendar quarter (see instructions)	B Internal Revenue office where prior return was filed	C Amount of applicable credit (unified credit) against gift tax for periods after December 31, 1976	D Amount of specific exemption for prior periods ending before January 1, 1977	E Amount of taxable gifts
2011	Cincinnati, OH	545,800		1,500,000

1	Totals for prior periods	1	545,800		1,500,000
2	Amount, if any, by which total specific exemption, line 1, column D is more than $30,000			2	0
3	Total amount of taxable gifts for prior periods. Add amount on line 1, column E and amount, if any, on line 2. Enter here and on page 1, Part 2—Tax Computation, line 2			3	1,500,000

(If more space is needed, attach additional statements.)   Form **709** (2014)

Form 709 (2014)   Page **4**

SCHEDULE C Deceased Spousal Unused Exclusion (DSUE) Amount

Provide the following information to determine the DSUE amount and applicable credit received from prior spouses. Complete Schedule A before beginning Schedule C.

A Name of Deceased Spouse (dates of death after December 31, 2010 only)	B Date of Death	C Portability Election Made?		D If "Yes," DSUE Amount Received from Spouse	E DSUE Amount Applied by Donor to Lifetime Gifts (list current and prior gifts)	F Date of Gift(s) (enter as mm/dd/yy for Part 1 and as yyyy for Part 2)
		Yes	No			
Part 1—DSUE RECEIVED FROM LAST DECEASED SPOUSE						
Part 2—DSUE RECEIVED FROM PREDECEASED SPOUSE(S)						

TOTAL (for all DSUE amounts applied from column E for Part 1 and Part 2)

1	Donor's basic exclusion amount (see instructions)	**1**	
2	Total from column E, Parts 1 and 2	**2**	
3	Add lines 1 and 2	**3**	
4	Applicable credit on amount in line 3 (See *Table for Computing Gift Tax* in the instructions). Enter here and on line 7, Part 2—Tax Computation	**4**	

SCHEDULE D Computation of Generation-Skipping Transfer Tax

Note. Inter vivos direct skips that are completely excluded by the GST exemption must still be fully reported (including value and exemptions claimed) on Schedule D.

Part 1—Generation-Skipping Transfers

A Item No. (from Schedule A, Part 2, col. A)	B Value (from Schedule A, Part 2, col. H)	C Nontaxable Portion of Transfer	D Net Transfer (subtract col. C from col. B)
1	6,014,000	14,000	6,000,000
Gifts made by spouse (for gift splitting only)			

(If more space is needed, attach additional statements.)   Form **709** (2014)

Form 709 (2014)   Page **5**

Part 2—GST Exemption Reconciliation (Section 2631) and Section 2652(a)(3) Election

Check here ▶ ☐ if you are making a section 2652(a)(3) (special QTIP) election (see instructions)

Enter the item numbers from Schedule A of the gifts for which you are making this election ▶ ---------------------------

1	Maximum allowable exemption (see instructions)	1	5,430,000
2	Total exemption used for periods before filing this return	2	1,500,000
3	Exemption available for this return. Subtract line 2 from line 1	3	3,930,000
4	Exemption claimed on this return from Part 3, column C total, below	4	3,930,000
5	Automatic allocation of exemption to transfers reported on Schedule A, Part 3. To opt out of the automatic allocation rules, you must attach an **"Election Out"** statement. (see instructions)	5	0
6	Exemption allocated to transfers not shown on line 4 or 5, above. **You must attach a "Notice of Allocation."** (see instructions)	6	0
7	Add lines 4, 5, and 6	7	3,930,000
8	Exemption available for future transfers. Subtract line 7 from line 3	8	0

Part 3—Tax Computation

A Item No. (from Schedule D, Part 1)	B Net Transfer (from Schedule D, Part 1, col. D)	C GST Exemption Allocated	D Divide col. C by col. B	E Inclusion Ratio (Subtract col. D from 1.000)	F Maximum Estate Tax Rate	G Applicable Rate (multiply col. E by col. F)	H Generation-Skipping Transfer Tax (multiply col. B by col. G)
1	6,000,000	3,930,000	.655	.345	40% (.40)	.138	828,000
					40% (.40)		
					40% (.40)		
					40% (.40)		
					40% (.40)		
					40% (.40)		
Gifts made by spouse (for gift splitting only)							
					40% (.40)		
					40% (.40)		
					40% (.40)		
					40% (.40)		
					40% (.40)		
					40% (.40)		
Total exemption claimed. Enter here and on Part 2, line 4, above. May not exceed Part 2, line 3, above		**Total generation-skipping transfer tax.** Enter here; on page 3, Schedule A, Part 4, line 10; and on page 1, Part 2—Tax Computation, line 16					828,000

(If more space is needed, attach additional statements.)   Form **709** (2014)

JOHNS – HYPOTHETICAL ESTATE TAX RETURN
WITH GST TAX

During his lifetime, Charles Johns made extensive gifts to his grandchildren, using $5,3300,000 of his $5,430,000 exemption under the generation-skipping transfer tax rules. However, he also made another $100,000 gift during his lifetime to his best friend that used up his remaining exemption amount available for estate taxes. Charles Johns died in 2015, leaving his granddaughter Janice a bequest of $200,000. He also left his grandson James a bequest of $200,000 but specified that the bequest to James must bear the burden of the GST tax. For simplicity, assume that these are the only assets Charles had at death and that his estate incurred no expenses.

Editor's Note: The hypothetical case uses a 2013 Form 706 as the IRS has not yet released the 2015 estate tax returns. We were able to modify the 2013 form to use the 2015 unified credit amount.

Calculate the Generation-Skipping Transfer Tax for Each of these Testamentary Gifts

These testamentary direct-skips are reported on the U.S. Estate Tax Return, Form 706, for the estate of Charles Johns. The Form 706 at the end of this chapter was prepared for this hypothetical case. The first step is to determine the amount of GST exemption available. In Schedule R, Part 1, page 23 of Form 706, the entries reflect that Charles had used $5,330,000 of his exemption and had only $100,000 of GST exemption available.

In Part 3 of Schedule R, page 25 of Form 706, the direct-skip transfer to Janice Johns that does not bear the GST tax is entered. The GST tax is computed in lines 1 through 8. The amount of the generation-skipping transfer is $120,000 after the $80,000 payment of estate taxes (see line 2). The $100,000 of remaining GST exemption is allocated to this transfer and then the 40% tax rate applied at line 8 to generate a GST tax due of $8,000. In Part 2 of Schedule R, page 24 of Form 706, the direct-skip transfer to James Johns that bears the GST tax is entered. The tax is computed in lines 1 through 8. The amount of the generation-skipping transfer is $120,000 after the $80,000 payment of estate taxes, and because the gift must bear the GST tax, the tax is computed by dividing by 3.500000. The tax is $34,286. The tax on the generation-skipping transfer to Janice, calculated in Part 3, is added at line 9, so the total GST tax due on both gifts is shown on line 10 and is $42,286. This amount is entered on line 17 of Part 2 – Tax computation, on page 1 of Form 706. This is then added to the $160,000 estate tax liability for a combined estate and GST tax due of $202,286.

Form **706** (Rev. August 2013) Department of the Treasury Internal Revenue Service	**United States Estate (and Generation-Skipping Transfer) Tax Return** ▶ Estate of a citizen or resident of the United States (see instructions). To be filed for decedents dying after December 31, 2012. ▶ Information about Form 706 and its separate instructions is at *www.irs.gov/form706*.	OMB No. 1545-0015

Part 1—Decedent and Executor

1a Decedent's first name and middle initial (and maiden name, if any) Charles	1b Decedent's last name Johns	2 Decedent's social security no. 555 66 7777

3a City, town, or post office; county; state or province; country; and ZIP or foreign postal code.	3b Year domicile established 1934	4 Date of birth 01-12-34	5 Date of death 04-15-15

7890 Main Street
Anytown, Anystate 12345

6b Executor's address (number and street including apartment or suite no.; city, town, or post office; state or province; country; and ZIP or foreign postal code) and phone no.

6a Name of executor (see instructions)

Diana Williams

1234 Main Street
Anytown, Anystate

6c Executor's social security number (see instructions)

888 99 0000

Phone no. 555-123-4567

6d If there are multiple executors, check here ☐ and attach a list showing the names, addresses, telephone numbers, and SSNs of the additional executors.

7a Name and location of court where will was probated or estate administered

Anytown, Anystate

7b Case number

B-2345

8 If decedent died testate, check here ▶ ☑ and attach a certified copy of the will. **9** If you extended the time to file this Form 706, check here ▶ ☐

10 If Schedule R-1 is attached, check here ▶ ☐ **11** If you are estimating the value of assets included in the gross estate on line 1 pursuant to the special rule of Reg. section 20.2010-2T(a) (7)(ii), check here ▶ ☐

Part 2—Tax Computation

1	Total gross estate less exclusion (from Part 5—Recapitulation, item 13)		**1**	400,000
2	Tentative total allowable deductions (from Part 5—Recapitulation, item 24)		**2**	0
3a	Tentative taxable estate (subtract line 2 from line 1)		**3a**	400,000
b	State death tax deduction		**3b**	0
c	Taxable estate (subtract line 3b from line 3a)		**3c**	400,000
4	Adjusted taxable gifts (see instructions)		**4**	5,430,000
5	Add lines 3c and 4		**5**	5,830,000
6	Tentative tax on the amount on line 5 from Table A in the instructions		**6**	2,277,800
7	Total gift tax paid or payable (see instructions)		**7**	0
8	Gross estate tax (subtract line 7 from line 6)		**8**	2,277,800
9a	Basic exclusion amount	**9a** 5,430,000		
9b	Deceased spousal unused exclusion (DSUE) amount from predeceased spouse(s), if any (from Section D, Part 6—Portability of Deceased Spousal Unused Exclusion).	**9b** 0		
9c	Applicable exclusion amount (add lines 9a and 9b)	**9c** 5,430,000		
9d	Applicable credit amount (tentative tax on the amount in 9c from Table A in the instructions)	**9d** 2,117,800		
10	Adjustment to applicable credit amount (May not exceed $6,000. See instructions.)	**10** 0		
11	Allowable applicable credit amount (subtract line 10 from line 9d)		**11**	2,117,800
12	Subtract line 11 from line 8 (but do not enter less than zero)		**12**	160,000
13	Credit for foreign death taxes (from Schedule P). (Attach Form(s) 706-CE.)	**13** 0		
14	Credit for tax on prior transfers (from Schedule Q)	**14** 0		
15	Total credits (add lines 13 and 14)		**15**	0
16	Net estate tax (subtract line 15 from line 12)		**16**	160,000
17	Generation-skipping transfer (GST) taxes payable (from Schedule R, Part 2, line 10)		**17**	42,286
18	Total transfer taxes (add lines 16 and 17)		**18**	202,286
19	Prior payments (explain in an attached statement)		**19**	0
20	Balance due (or overpayment) (subtract line 19 from line 18)		**20**	202,286

Under penalties of perjury, I declare that I have examined this return, including accompanying schedules and statements, and to the best of my knowledge and belief, it is true, correct, and complete. Declaration of preparer other than the executor is based on all information of which preparer has any knowledge.

Sign Here

▶ Signature of executor ▶ Date

▶ Signature of executor ▶ Date

Paid Preparer Use Only

Print/Type preparer's name	Preparer's signature	Date	Check ☐ if self-employed	PTIN
Firm's name ▶			Firm's EIN ▶	
Firm's address ▶			Phone no.	

For Privacy Act and Paperwork Reduction Act Notice, see instructions. Cat. No. 20548R Form **706** (Rev. 8-2013)

Form 706 (Rev. 8-2013)

Estate of:	Decedent's social security number		
	555	66	7777

Part 4—General Information (continued)

	If you answer "Yes" to any of the following questions, you must attach additional information as described.	Yes	No
10	Did the decedent at the time of death own any property as a joint tenant with right of survivorship in which (a) one or more of the other joint tenants was someone other than the decedent's spouse, and (b) less than the full value of the property is included on the return as part of the gross estate? If "Yes," you must complete and attach Schedule E		✓
11a	Did the decedent, at the time of death, own any interest in a partnership (for example, a family limited partnership), an unincorporated business, or a limited liability company; or own any stock in an inactive or closely held corporation?		✓
b	If "Yes," was the value of any interest owned (from above) discounted on this estate tax return? If "Yes," see the instructions on reporting the total accumulated or effective discounts taken on Schedule F or G		✓
12	Did the decedent make any transfer described in sections 2035, 2036, 2037, or 2038? (see instructions) If "Yes," you must complete and attach Schedule G		✓
13a	Were there in existence at the time of the decedent's death any trusts created by the decedent during his or her lifetime? . .		✓
b	Were there in existence at the time of the decedent's death any trusts not created by the decedent under which the decedent possessed any power, beneficial interest, or trusteeship?		✓
c	Was the decedent receiving income from a trust created after October 22, 1986, by a parent or grandparent?		✓
	If "Yes," was there a GST taxable termination (under section 2612) on the death of the decedent?		✓
d	If there was a GST taxable termination (under section 2612), attach a statement to explain. Provide a copy of the trust or will creating the trust, and give the name, address, and phone number of the current trustee(s).		
e	Did the decedent at any time during his or her lifetime transfer or sell an interest in a partnership, limited liability company, or closely held corporation to a trust described in lines 13a or 13b?		✓
	If "Yes," provide the EIN for this transferred/sold item. ▶		
14	Did the decedent ever possess, exercise, or release any general power of appointment? If "Yes," you must complete and attach Schedule H		✓
15	Did the decedent have an interest in or a signature or other authority over a financial account in a foreign country, such as a bank account, securities account, or other financial account?		✓
16	Was the decedent, immediately before death, receiving an annuity described in the "General" paragraph of the instructions for Schedule I or a private annuity? If "Yes," you must complete and attach Schedule I		✓
17	Was the decedent ever the beneficiary of a trust for which a deduction was claimed by the estate of a predeceased spouse under section 2056(b)(7) and which is not reported on this return? If "Yes," attach an explanation		✓

Part 5—Recapitulation.

Note. If estimating the value of one or more assets pursuant to the special rule of Reg. section 20.2010-2T(a)(7)(ii), enter on both lines 10 and 23 the amount noted in the instructions for the corresponding range of values. (See instructions for details.)

Item no.	Gross estate		Alternate value	Value at date of death
1	Schedule A—Real Estate	1		0
2	Schedule B—Stocks and Bonds	2		0
3	Schedule C—Mortgages, Notes, and Cash	3		400,000
4	Schedule D—Insurance on the Decedent's Life (attach Form(s) 712)	4		0
5	Schedule E—Jointly Owned Property (attach Form(s) 712 for life insurance) .	5		0
6	Schedule F—Other Miscellaneous Property (attach Form(s) 712 for life insurance)	6		0
7	Schedule G—Transfers During Decedent's Life (att. Form(s) 712 for life insurance)	7		0
8	Schedule H—Powers of Appointment	8		0
9	Schedule I—Annuities	9		0
10	Estimated value of assets subject to the special rule of Reg. section 20.2010-2T(a)(7)(ii)	10		0
11	Total gross estate (add items 1 through 10)	11		400,000
12	Schedule U—Qualified Conservation Easement Exclusion	12		0
13	Total gross estate less exclusion (subtract item 12 from item 11). Enter here and on line 1 of Part 2—Tax Computation	13		400,000

Item no.	Deductions		Amount
14	Schedule J—Funeral Expenses and Expenses Incurred in Administering Property Subject to Claims	14	
15	Schedule K—Debts of the Decedent	15	
16	Schedule K—Mortgages and Liens	16	
17	Total of items 14 through 16	17	
18	Allowable amount of deductions from item 17 (see the instructions for item 18 of the Recapitulation)	18	
19	Schedule L—Net Losses During Administration	19	
20	Schedule L—Expenses Incurred in Administering Property Not Subject to Claims	20	
21	Schedule M—Bequests, etc., to Surviving Spouse	21	
22	Schedule O—Charitable, Public, and Similar Gifts and Bequests	22	
23	Estimated value of deductible assets subject to the special rule of Reg. section 20.2010-2T(a)(7)(ii) . . .	23	
24	Tentative total allowable deductions (add items 18 through 23). Enter here and on line 2 of the Tax Computation	24	

Page 3

Form 706 (Rev. 8-2013)

SCHEDULE R—Generation-Skipping Transfer Tax

Note. To avoid application of the deemed allocation rules, Form 706 and Schedule R should be filed to allocate the GST exemption to trusts that may later have taxable terminations or distributions under section 2612 even if the form is not required to be filed to report estate or GST tax.

The GST tax is imposed on taxable transfers of interests in property located outside the United States as well as property located inside the United States. (see instructions)

Part 1. GST Exemption Reconciliation (Section 2631) and Special QTIP Election (Section 2652(a)(3))

You no longer need to check a box to make a section 2652(a)(3) (special QTIP) election. If you list qualifying property in Part 1, line 9 below, you will be considered to have made this election. See instructions for details.

1	Maximum allowable GST exemption	1	5,430,000
2	Total GST exemption allocated by the decedent against decedent's lifetime transfers	2	5,330,000
3	Total GST exemption allocated by the executor, using Form 709, against decedent's lifetime transfers	3	0
4	GST exemption allocated on line 6 of Schedule R, Part 2	4	0
5	GST exemption allocated on line 6 of Schedule R, Part 3	5	100,000
6	Total GST exemption allocated on line 4 of Schedule(s) R-1	6	0
7	Total GST exemption allocated to *inter vivos* transfers and direct skips (add lines 2–6)	7	5,430,000
8	GST exemption available to allocate to trusts and section 2032A interests (subtract line 7 from line 1)	8	0

9 Allocation of GST exemption to trusts (as defined for GST tax purposes):

A Name of trust	B Trust's EIN (if any)	C GST exemption allocated on lines 2–6, above (see instructions)	D Additional GST exemption allocated (see instructions)	E Trust's inclusion ratio (optional—see instructions)

9D	**Total.** May not exceed line 8, above	9D	
10	GST exemption available to allocate to section 2032A interests received by individual beneficiaries (subtract line 9D from line 8). You must attach special-use allocation statement (see instructions)	10	

Schedule R—Page 23

Form 706 (Rev. 8-2013)

Estate of:	Decedent's social security number
	555 66 7777

Part 2. Direct Skips Where the Property Interests Transferred Bear the GST Tax on the Direct Skips

Name of skip person	Description of property interest transferred	Estate tax value
John James	Cash	200,000

1	Total estate tax values of all property interests listed above	1	200,000
2	Estate taxes, state death taxes, and other charges borne by the property interests listed above . .	2	80,000
3	GST taxes borne by the property interests listed above but imposed on direct skips other than those shown on this Part 2 (see instructions)	3	0
4	Total fixed taxes and other charges (add lines 2 and 3)	4	80,000
5	Total tentative maximum direct skips (subtract line 4 from line 1)	5	120,000
6	GST exemption allocated	6	0
7	Subtract line 6 from line 5	7	120,000
8	GST tax due (divide line 7 by 3.5)	8	34,286
9	Enter the amount from line 8 of Schedule R, Part 3	9	8,000
10	**Total GST taxes payable by the estate** (add lines 8 and 9). Enter here and on line 17 of Part 2— Tax Computation	10	42,286

Schedule R—Page 24

Form 706 (Rev. 8-2013)

Estate of:	Decedent's social security number		
	555	66	7777

Part 3. Direct Skips Where the Property Interests Transferred Do Not Bear the GST Tax on the Direct Skips

Name of skip person	Description of property interest transferred	Estate tax value
Janice Johns	Cash	200,000

1	Total estate tax values of all property interests listed above	1	200,000
2	Estate taxes, state death taxes, and other charges borne by the property interests listed above . .	2	80,000
3	GST taxes borne by the property interests listed above but imposed on direct skips other than those shown on this Part 3 (see instructions)	3	0
4	Total fixed taxes and other charges (add lines 2 and 3)	4	80,000
5	Total tentative maximum direct skips (subtract line 4 from line 1)	5	120,000
6	GST exemption allocated	6	100,000
7	Subtract line 6 from line 5	7	20,000
8	GST tax due (multiply line 7 by .40). Enter here and on Schedule R, Part 2, line 9	8	8,000

Schedule R—Page 25

2015 Key Facts and Figures

Keir Educational Resources compiled the following key facts and figures for the CFP® Certification Examination to assist you with your preparation for this comprehensive exam.

Please note the following items:

1. This list is not intended to be an all-inclusive listing of facts and figures tested on the CFP® Certification Examination.

2. Very few of the figures included in this list will be provided in your CFP® Certification Examination booklet. **Only the items underlined will be provided**. For example, all of the underlined Personal Exemption, Standard Deductions and Itemized Deductions information listed on the next page are provided. However, the exam booklet does not include information about the self employment taxes or kiddie taxes. As a result, you will need to know how to calculate both taxes. Likewise, you will need to memorize all the other items that are not underlined.

Personal Exemption	**2015**
Personal exemption amount per person	4,000

Phaseout of 2% for every $2,500 ($1,250 MFS) or fraction thereof that AGI exceeds the following amounts

Single	$258,250
Married filing jointly or surviving spouse	$309,900
Married filing separately	$154,950
Head of household	$284,050

Standard Deductions	**2015**
Single	6,300
Married filing jointly or surviving spouse	12,600
Married filing separately	6,300
Head of household	9,250

Additional standard deduction amount if age 65 or older or blind

Married (per person)	1,250
Unmarried	1,550

Taxpayer is claimed as a dependent

No earned income	1,050
Earned income (earned income plus amount)	350
Maximum deduction using earned income	6,300

Phaseout of Itemized Deductions

Phaseout of 3% of the amount by which AGI exceeds the threshold:

Single	$258,250
Married filing jointly or surviving spouse	$309,900
Married filing separately	$154,950
Head of household	$284,050

Employment Taxes   **2015**

Social Security tax rate

Employer's portion	6.2%
Employee's portion	6.2%
Total for self-employed individual	12.4%

Maximum amount of earnings subject to Social Security taxes	118,500

Medicare tax rate

Employer's portion	1.45%
Employee's portion (on all net self-employment income)	1.45%
Total for self-employed individual (on all net self-employment income)	2.9%
Employee's additional Medicare surtax on earnings above $200,000 ($250,000 MFJ, $125,000 MFS)	.9%

Maximum amount of earnings subject to Medicare taxes	Unlimited

Total employment taxes

Employer's portion	7.65%
Employee's portion	7.65%
Total for self-employed individual	15.3%

Percentage of self-employed earnings subject to SE taxes	92.35%

Percentage of SE taxes deducted above-the-line	50%

Kiddie Tax   **2015**

Amount not subject to tax due to personal exemption	$1,050
Amount taxed at child's rate of 10%	1,050
Unearned income above these amounts taxed at parents' marginal tax rate	Unlimited

Child Tax Credit	**2015**
Child tax credit per child	1,000

Phaseout of $50 for every $1,000 or fraction thereof that AGI exceeds the following amounts (completely phased out if AGI exceeds threshold by $20,000 per child):

Single	75,000
Married filing jointly or surviving spouse	110,000
Married filing separately	55,000
Head of household	75,000

Child or Dependent Care Credit	**2015**

Maximum amount of qualifying expenses

One child or dependent	3,000
Two or more children or dependents	6,000
AGI amount when credit reduced to 20% level	43,000

Maximum credit, assuming taxpayer's AGI at 20% level

One child or dependent	600
Two or more children or dependents	1,200

American Opportunity Tax Credit (formerly called Hope Credit)	**2015**

Credit percentage amounts

First $2,000	100%
Second $2,000	25%
Maximum credit	$2,500

Phaseout starts at the following AGI amounts:

Single	80,000
Married filing jointly or surviving spouse	160,000
Married filing separately	0
Head of household	80,000

Credit completely phased out at the following AGI amounts:

Single	90,000
Married filing jointly or surviving spouse	180,000
Married filing separately	0
Head of household	90,000

Lifetime Learning Credit	**2015**

Credit percentage amounts

First $10,000	20%

Maximum credit	$2,000

Phaseout starts at the following AGI amounts:

Single	55,000
Married filing jointly or surviving spouse	110,000
Married filing separately	0
Head of household	55,000

Credit completely phased out at the following AGI amounts:

Single	65,000
Married filing jointly or surviving spouse	130,000
Married filing separately	0
Head of household	65,000

Education Expenses	**2015**

Above-the-line deduction for educational loan interest payments	2,500

Phaseout of educational loan interest deduction starts at the following AGI amounts:

Single	65,000
Married filing jointly or surviving spouse	130,000
Married filing separately	0
Head of household	65,000

Educational loan interest deduction completely phased out at the following AGI amounts:

Single	80,000
Married filing jointly or surviving spouse	160,000
Married filing separately	0
Head of household	80,000

Education Expenses   **2015**

Above-the-line deduction for tuition and related expenses   expired

AGI limitations to claim up to the full $4,000 above-the-line deduction

Single   expired
Married filing jointly or surviving spouse   expired
Married filing separately   expired
Head of household   expired

AGI limitation to claim up to $2,000 above-the-line deduction if AGI exceeds the limits above for the $4,000 deduction

Single   expired
Married filing jointly or surviving spouse   expired
Married filing separately   expired
Head of household   expired

Tax-free treatment on Series EE bonds

Phaseout of tax-free treatment on Series EE bonds starts at the following AGI amounts:

Single   77,200
Married filing jointly or surviving spouse   115,750
Married filing separately   77,200
Head of household   77,200

Tax-free treatment on Series EE bonds completely phased out at the following AGI amounts:

Single   92,200
Married filing jointly or surviving spouse   145,750
Married filing separately   92,200
Head of household   92,200

Coverdell Education Savings Accounts	**2015**
Coverdell Education Savings Account (ESA) contribution limit	2,000

Phaseout of ESA contribution starts at the following AGI amounts:

Single	95,000
Married filing jointly or surviving spouse	190,000
Married filing separately	95,000
Head of household	95,000

ESA contribution completely phased out at the following AGI amounts:

Single	110,000
Married filing jointly or surviving spouse	220,000
Married filing separately	110,000
Head of household	110,000

Section 179 Deduction	**2015**
Section 179 deduction amount	25,000
Limit on property placed in service	200,000

Income Tax Rates   **2015**

Marginal tax rate ends at the following income levels:

Single

10%	9,225
15%	37,450
25%	90,750
28%	189,300
33%	411,500
35%	413,200
39.6%	Unlimited

Married filing jointly or surviving spouse

10%	18,450
15%	74,900
25%	151,200
28%	230,450
33%	411,500
35%	464,850
39.6%	Unlimited

Married filing separately

10%	9,225
15%	37,450
25%	75,600
28%	115,225
33%	205,750
35%	232,425
39.6%	Unlimited

Head of household

10%	13,150
15%	50,200
25%	129,600
28%	209,850
33%	411,500
35%	439,000
39.6%	Unlimited

Income Tax Rates	**2015**
Trusts	
15%	2,500
25%	5,900
28%	9,050
33%	12,300
39.6%	Unlimited

Tax rates for capital gains and dividends	**2015**
Taxpayers in the 39.6%	20%*
Taxpayers in the 25%, 28%, 33%, and 35% tax brackets	15%*
Taxpayers in the 10% or 15% tax bracket	0%

*For single taxpayers with AGI over $200,000 ($250,000 MFJ; $125,000 MFS) an additional 3.8% Medicare Contribution tax will apply to capital gains to the extent that Net Investment Income exceeds the threshold level.

Alternative Minimum Taxes (AMT)	**2015**
AMT exemption amounts	
Single	53,600
Married filing jointly or surviving spouse	83,400
Married filing separately	41,700
Head of household	53,600

Phaseout of AMT exemption of 25% of AMTI that exceeds the following amounts:	
Single	119,200
Married filing jointly or surviving spouse	158,900
Married filing separately	79,450
Head of household	119,200

AMT tax rates

On the first $185,400 of AMT taxable income (2015)	26%
On income above $185,400 (2015)	28%
On capital gains and dividends	20%**

**The maximum tax rates on capital gains and dividends used in computing the regular tax are used in computing the tentative minimum tax as well (15% for most taxpayers, 20% for high-income taxpayers)

Estate and Gift Taxes   **2015**

Annual gift tax exclusions
Gifts to any person	14,000
Gifts to a U.S. citizen spouse	unlimited
Gifts to a noncitizen spouse	147,000

Lifetime gifts
Applicable exclusion amount	5,430,000
Applicable credit amount	2,117,800

Bequests at death
Applicable exclusion amount	5,430,000
Applicable credit amount	2,117,800

Top estate tax rate	40%
Top gift tax rate	40%

Generation-skipping transfer (GST) tax
Annual GST exclusion	14,000
Lifetime GST exemption amount	5,430,000
Flat GST tax rate	40%

Special-use valuation limit	1,100,000
Section 6166 special 2% interest rate	1,470,000

Retirement Plans   **2015**

Taxpayer or employee contribution limits
IRA (combined traditional and Roth IRA limit)	5,500
401(k) plans	18,000
403(b) plans	18,000
457 plans	18,000
SIMPLE plans	12,500

Catch-up contribution limits
IRA (combined traditional and Roth IRA limit)	1,000
401(k) plans	6,000
403(b) plans	6,000
457 plans	6,000
SIMPLE plans	3,000

Retirement Plans	**2015**
Defined-contribution plan limitations	
Participating payroll	25%
Maximum percentage of employee's compensation	100%
Participant's contribution not to exceed	53,000
Maximum compensation to be considered	265,000
Defined-benefit plan limitations	
Maximum annual benefit	210,000
Maximum compensation to be considered	265,000
SEP plan limitations	
Maximum percentage of employee's compensation	25%
Participant's contribution not to exceed	53,000
Minimum compensation needed to participate	600
Maximum compensation to be considered	265,000

Qualified plan definitions

Highly-compensated employee
Any employee who owns 5% or more of the company
Any employee among the top 20% highest-paid and paid more than — 120,000

Key employee

Any officer earning	170,000
Any employee who owns 5% or more of the company	
Any employee who owns 1% or more of the company and makes	150,000

Phaseout of IRA deduction starts at the following amounts:	
Single	61,000
Married filing jointly or surviving spouse	98,000
Married filing separately	0
Head of household	61,000

IRA deduction completely phased out at the following amounts:	
Single	71,000
Married filing jointly or surviving spouse	118,000
Married filing separately	10,000
Head of household	71,000

Phaseout of IRA deduction with an active participant spouse	
AGI limit when phaseout starts	183,000
AGI limit when completely phased out	193,000

Retirement Plans   **2015**

Phaseout of Roth IRA contributions starts at the following amounts:
Single   116,000
Married filing jointly or surviving spouse   183,000
Married filing separately   0
Head of household   116,000

Roth IRA contribution completely phased out at the following amounts:
Single   131,000
Married filing jointly or surviving spouse   193,000
Married filing separately   10,000
Head of household   131,000

Social Security Benefits   **2015**

Limit on earnings before the reduction of benefits of $1 for every $2 earnings above limitation
Under full retirement age   15,720
Over full retirement age   n/a
Amount needed to earn one Social Security credit   1,220

Medicare   **2015**

Part A deductibles for hospital stays
Days 1-60 (total deductible for all 60 days)   1,260
Days 61-90 (deductible per day)   315
Days 91-150 (deductible per day)   630

Part A deductibles for skilled nursing facility
Days 1-20   0
Days 21-100 (deductible per day)   157.50

Part B monthly premium (monthly premiums will be higher if AGI   104.90
exceeds $85,000 for single taxpayers or $170,000 MFJ taxpayers)

Part B annual deductible   147

Selected Facts and Figures

Editor's Note: A sheet of formulas such as those presented below accompanies the CFP®Certification Examination as an aid to the person taking the test. However, the formulas are not labeled. For your information in preparing for the test, we have indicated what the formulas may be used for.

Value: Constant Dividend Growth Model

$$V = \frac{D_1}{r - g}$$

Req. Rate of Return (CDGM)

$$r = \frac{D_1}{P} + g$$

Covariance

$$COV._{ij} = \rho_{ij}\, \sigma_i\, \sigma_j$$

Two-Asset Portfolio Standard Deviation

$$\sigma_p = \sqrt{W_i^2\, \sigma_i^2 + W_j^2\, \sigma_j^2 + 2W_iW_jCOV._{ij}}$$

Beta

$$\beta_i = \frac{COV._{im}}{\sigma_m^2} = \frac{\rho_{im}\sigma_i}{\sigma_m}$$

Population Standard Deviation

$$\sigma_r = \sqrt{\frac{\sum\limits_{t=1}^{n} (r_t - \bar{r})^2}{n}}$$

Sample Standard Deviation

$$S_r = \sqrt{\frac{\sum\limits_{t=1}^{n} (r_t - \bar{r})^2}{n - 1}}$$

Conversion Value of a Bond

$$CV = \frac{Par}{CP} \times P_s$$

Req. Rate of Return:
Security Market Line (CAPM)

$$r_i = r_f + (r_m - r_f)\, \beta_i$$

Req. Rate of Return: Capital Market Line

$$r_p = r_f + \sigma_p \left[\frac{r_m - r_f}{\sigma_m}\right]$$

Sharpe Performance Index

$$S_p = \frac{\bar{r}_p - \bar{r}_f}{\sigma_p}$$

Jensen Performance Index

$$a_p = \bar{r}_p - [\bar{r}_f + (\bar{r}_m - \bar{r}_f)\beta_p]$$

Treynor Performance Index

$$T_p = \frac{\bar{r}_p - \bar{r}_f}{\beta_p}$$

Duration

$$D = \frac{\sum\limits_{t=1}^{n} \dfrac{C_t\,(t)}{(1 + i)^t}}{\sum\limits_{t=1}^{n} \dfrac{C_t}{(1 + i)^t}}$$

OR,

$$D = \frac{1 + y}{y} - \frac{(1 + y) + t(c - y)}{c[(1 + y)^t - 1] + y}$$

Percentage Change in a Bond's Price, Given a Change in its YTM

$$\frac{\Delta P}{P} = -D \left[\frac{\Delta y}{1 + y}\right]$$

Information Ratio

$$IR = \frac{R_P - R_B}{\sigma_A}$$

TAX TABLES PROVIDED ON CFP® CERTIFICATION EXAMINATION

SCHEDULE X: Single
2015

Taxable Income Over	But Not Over	Pay	+	% on Excess	of the amount over
$ 0 –	9,225	$ 0		10%	$ 0
9,225 –	37,450	922.50		15	9,225
37,450 –	90,750	5,156.25		25	37,450
90,750 –	189,300	18,481.25		28	90,750
189,300 –	411,500	46,075.25		33	189,300
411,500 –	413,200	119,401.25		35	411,500
Over 413,200		119,996.25		39.6	413,200

SCHEDULE Y-1: Married Filing Jointly and Surviving Spouse
2015

Taxable Income Over	But Not Over	Pay	+	% on Excess	of the amount over
$ 0 –	18,450	$ 0		10%	$ 0
18,450 –	74,900	1,845.00		15	18,450
74,900 –	151,200	10,312.50		25	74,900
151,200 –	230,450	29,387.50		28	151,200
230,450 –	411,500	51,577.50		33	230,450
411,500 –	464,850	111,324.00		35	411,500
Over 464,850		129,996.50		39.6	464,850

SCHEDULE Y-2: Married Filing Separately
2015

Taxable Income Over	But Not Over	Pay	+	% on Excess	of the amount over
$ 0 –	9,225	$ 0		10%	$ 0
9,225 –	37,450	922.50		15	9,225
37,450 –	75,600	5,156.25		25	37,450
75,600 –	115,225	14,693.75		28	75,600
115,225 –	205,750	25,788.75		33	115,225
205,750 –	232,425	55,662.00		35	205,750
Over 232,425		64,989.25		39.6	232,425

SCHEDULE Z: Head of Household
2015

Taxable Income Over	But Not Over	Pay	+	% on Excess	of the amount over
$ 0 –	13,150	$ 0		10%	$ 0
13,150 –	50,200	1,315.00		15	13,150
50,200 –	129,600	6,872.50		25	50,200
129,600 –	209,850	26,722.50		28	129,600
209,850 –	411,500	49,192.50		33	209,850
411,500 –	439,000	115,737.00		35	411,500
Over 439,000		125,362.00		39.6	439,000

Married filing jointly with income over $250,000 and singles over $200,000 who have net investment income will be subject to an additional 3.8% tax on the lesser of net investment income or the excess of MAGI over the threshold amount, whichever is less.

High income individuals are subject to increased payroll taxes. All wages, bonuses, commissions, and self-employment income are subject to an additional Medicare tax of 0.9% above the thresholds of $200,000 for single filers, $250,000 for joint filers, and $125,000 for spouses filing separately.

CORPORATE INCOME TAX RATES
2015

Taxable Income Over	But Not Over	Pay	+	% on Excess	of the amount over
$ 0 –	50,000	$ 0		15%	$ 0
50,000 –	75,000	7,500		25	50,000
75,000 –	100,000	13,750		34	75,000
100,000 –	335,000	22,250		39	100,000
335,000 –	10,000,000	113,900		34	335,000
10,000,000 –	15,000,000	3,400,000		35	10,000,000
15,000,000 –	18,333,333	5,150,000		38	15,000,000
18,333,333 –	…………			35	0

Note: Taxable income of certain personal service corporations is taxed at a flat rate of 35%.

ESTATES AND NONGRANTOR TRUSTS INCOME TAX RATES
2015

Taxable Income Over	But Not Over	Pay	+	% on Excess	of the amount over
$ 0 –	2,500	$ 0		15%	$ 0
2,500 –	5,900	375.00		25	2,500
5,900 –	9,050	1,225.00		28	5,900
9,050 –	12,300	2,107.00		33	9,050
12,300 –	………	3,179.50		39.6	12,300

STANDARD DEDUCTION AND PERSONAL EXEMPTIONS

	2015
Standard Deduction*:	
Single	$6,300
Married filing jointly/	
Qualifying widow(er)	12,600
Married filing separately	6,300
Head of household	9,250
Dependent	1,050**

* increased by $1,250 for a married taxpayer age 65 or older or blind ($2,500 if both 65 and blind); by $1,550 for a single taxpayer age 65 or older or blind ($3,100 if both 65 and blind)

** or $350 plus earned income, if greater

Personal Exemption: $4,000

COVERDELL EDUCATION SAVINGS ACCOUNTS
(Education IRAs)

Modified AGI Phase-Out Range for Contributions to Coverdell Education Savings Accounts:

Married Filing Jointly	$190,000 – $220,000
Single	$95,000 – $110,000

AMERICAN OPPORTUNITY CREDIT AND LIFETIME LEARNING CREDIT

American Opportunity Credit – Up to 100% of first $2,000 and 25% of the next $2,000 of qualified education expenses paid for a maximum of $2,500 total, subject to MAGI phase-out beginning at $80,000 if Single, $160,000 if Married Filing Jointly.

Lifetime Learning Credit – Up to 20% of the first $10,000 of qualified education expenses paid, subject to MAGI phase-outs beginning at $55,000 if Single, $110,000 if Married Filing Jointly.

Modified AGI Phase-Outs for American Opportunity Credit:
<u>2015</u>

Married Filing Jointly	$160,000 – $180,000
Others	$80,000 – $90,000

Modified AGI Phase-Outs for Lifetime Learning Credit:
<u>2015</u>

Married Filing Jointly	$110,000 – $130,000
Others	$55,000 – $65,000

CHILD TAX CREDIT

Modified AGI Beginning Phase-Out Range for Child Tax Credit (Phase-out complete when MAGI exceeds applicable threshold by $20,000 per child):

Married Filing Jointly	$110,000
Single/Head of Household	$ 75,000
Married Filing Separately	$ 55,000

2015 ESTATE AND GIFT TAX RATE SCHEDULE

Column A	Column B	Column C	Column D
			Rate of tax on excess over amount in Column A
Taxable amount over	Taxable amount not over	Tax on amount in Column A	Column A Percent
$ 0	$ 10,000	$ 0	18
10,000	20,000	1,800	20
20,000	40,000	3,800	22
40,000	60,000	8,200	24
60,000	80,000	13,000	26
80,000	100,000	18,200	28
100,000	150,000	23,800	30
150,000	250,000	38,800	32
250,000	500,000	70,800	34
500,000	750,000	155,800	37
750,000	1,000,000	248,300	39
Over 1,000,000		345,800	40

Applicable Exclusion/Credit Amount for Estate Tax

Year	Applicable Exclusion	Applicable Credit
2006-2008	2,000,000	780,000
2009	3,500,000	1,455,800
2010	5,000,000	1,730,800
2011	5,000,000	1,730,800
2012	5,120,000	1,772,800
2013	5,250,000	2,045,800
2014	5,340,000	2,081,800
2015	5,430,000	2,117,800

Applicable Exclusion/Credit Amount (Gift Tax)

Year	Applicable Exclusion	Applicable Credit
2006-2009	1,000,000	345,800
2010	1,000,000	330,800
2011	5,000,000	1,730,800
2012	5,120,000	1,772,800
2013	5,250,000	2,045,800
2014	5,340,000	2,081,800
2015	5,430,000	2,117,800

Alternate Minimum Tax Exemption for 2015

Single	53,600
Married Filing Jointly	83,400

Table VI – Ordinary Joint Life and Last Survivor Annuities;
Two Lives – Expected Return Multiples

Ages	65	66	67	68	69	70	71	72	73	74
65	25.0	24.6	24.2	23.8	23.4	23.1	22.8	22.5	22.2	22.0
66	24.6	24.1	23.7	23.3	22.9	22.5	22.2	21.9	21.6	21.4
67	24.2	23.7	23.2	22.8	22.4	22.0	21.7	21.3	21.0	20.8
68	23.8	23.3	22.8	22.3	21.9	21.5	21.2	20.8	20.5	20.2
69	23.4	22.9	22.4	21.9	21.5	21.1	20.7	20.3	20.0	19.6
70	23.1	22.5	22.0	21.5	21.1	20.6	20.2	19.8	19.4	19.1
71	22.8	22.2	21.7	21.2	20.7	20.2	19.8	19.4	19.0	18.6
72	22.5	21.9	21.3	20.8	20.3	19.8	19.4	18.9	18.5	18.2
73	22.2	21.6	21.0	20.5	20.0	19.4	19.0	18.5	18.1	17.7
74	22.0	21.4	20.8	20.2	19.6	19.1	18.6	18.2	17.7	17.3
75	21.8	21.1	20.5	19.9	19.3	18.8	18.3	17.8	17.3	16.9
76	21.6	20.9	20.3	19.7	19.1	18.5	18.0	17.5	17.0	16.5
77	21.4	20.7	20.1	19.4	18.8	18.3	17.7	17.2	16.7	16.2
78	21.2	20.5	19.9	19.2	18.6	18.0	17.5	16.9	16.4	15.9

from Reg. Sec. 1.72-9

One-Life-Expected Return Multiples

Age	Multiples Life Expectancy	Age	Multiples (Life Expectancy)	Age	Multiples (Life Expectancy)
5	76.6	42	40.6	79	10.0
6	75.6	43	39.6	80	9.5
7	74.7	44	38.7	81	8.9
8	73.7	45	37.7	82	8.4
9	72.7	46	36.8	83	7.9
10	71.7	47	35.9	84	7.4
11	70.7	48	34.9	85	6.9
12	69.7	49	34.0	86	6.5
13	68.8	50	33.1	87	6.1
14	67.8	51	32.2	88	5.7
15	66.8	52	31.3	89	5.3
16	65.8	53	30.4	90	5.0
17	64.8	54	29.5	91	4.7
18	63.9	55	28.6	92	4.4
19	62.9	56	27.7	93	4.1
20	61.9	57	26.8	94	3.9
21	60.9	58	25.9	95	3.7
22	59.9	59	25.0	96	3.4
23	59.0	60	24.2	97	3.2
24	58.0	61	23.3	98	3.0
25	57.0	62	22.5	99	2.8
26	56.0	63	21.6	100	2.7
27	55.1	64	20.8	101	2.5
28	54.1	65	20.0	102	2.3
29	53.1	66	19.2	103	2.1
30	52.2	67	18.4	104	1.9
31	51.2	68	17.6	105	1.8
32	50.2	69	16.8	106	1.6
33	49.3	70	16.0	107	1.4
34	48.3	71	15.3	108	1.3
35	47.3	72	14.6	109	1.1
36	46.4	73	13.9	110	1.0
37	45.4	74	13.2	111	0.9
38	44.4	75	12.5	112	0.8
39	43.5	76	11.9	113	0.7
40	42.5	77	11.2	114	0.6
41	41.5	78	10.6	115	0.5

Uniform Table of Applicable Distribution Periods
for Required Minimum Distributions

Age of the Employee	Applicable Divisor	Age of the Employee	Applicable Divisor
70	27.4	93	9.6
71	26.5	94	9.1
72	25.6	95	8.6
73	24.7	96	8.1
74	23.8	97	7.6
75	22.9	98	7.1
76	22.0	99	6.7
77	21.2	100	6.3
78	20.3	101	5.9
79	19.5	102	5.5
80	18.7	103	5.2
81	17.9	104	4.9
82	17.1	105	4.5
83	16.3	106	4.2
84	15.5	107	3.9
85	14.8	108	3.7
86	14.1	109	3.4
87	13.4	110	3.1
88	12.7	111	2.9
89	12.0	112	2.6
90	11.4	113	2.4
91	10.8	114	2.1
92	10.2	115 and older	1.9

CFP Board's Topic List for CFP® Certification Examination

78 Principal Topics

For Exams Given March 2012 or later

General Principles of Financial Planning

1. Financial planning process
2. Financial statements
3. Cash flow management
4. Financing strategies
5. Function, purpose, and regulation of financial institutions
6. Education planning
7. Financial planning for special circumstances
8. Economic concepts
9. Time value of money concepts and calculations
10. Financial services regulations and requirements
11. Business law
12. Consumer protection laws

Insurance Planning

13. Principles of risk and insurance
14. Analysis and evaluation of risk exposures
15. Health insurance and health care cost management (individual)
16. Disability income insurance (individual)
17. Long-term care insurance (individual)
18. Annuities
19. Life insurance (individual)
20. Income taxation of life insurance
21. Business uses of insurance
22. Insurance needs analysis
23. Insurance policy and company selection

Investment Planning

24. Characteristics, uses and taxation of investment vehicles
25. Types of investment risk
26. Quantitative investment concepts
27. Measures of investment returns
28. Asset allocation and portfolio diversification
29. Bond and stock valuation concepts
30. Portfolio development and analysis
31. Investment strategies

Income Tax Planning

    32. Income tax law fundamentals

    33. Tax compliance

    34. Income tax fundamentals and calculations

    35. Characteristics and income taxation of business entities

    36. Income taxation of trusts and estates

    37. Basis

    38. Tax consequences of the disposition of property

    39. Alternative minimum tax (AMT)

    40. Tax reduction/management techniques

    41. Passive activity and at-risk rules

    42. Tax implications of special circumstances

    43. Charitable contributions and deductions

Retirement Planning

    44. Retirement needs analysis

    45. Social Security (Old Age, Survivor, and Disability Insurance, OASDI)

    46. Types of retirement plans

    47. Qualified plan rules and options

    48. Other tax-advantaged retirement plans

    49. Regulatory considerations

    50. Key factors affecting plan selection for businesses

    51. Investment considerations for retirement plans

    52. Distribution rules, alternatives, and taxation

Estate Planning
53. Characteristics and consequences of property titling
54. Methods of property transfer at death
55. Estate planning documents
56. Gifting strategies
57. Gift tax compliance and tax calculation
58. Incapacity planning
59. Estate tax compliance and tax calculation
60. Sources for estate liquidity
61. Powers of appointment
62. Types, features, and taxation of trusts
63. Qualified interest trusts
64. Charitable transfers
65. Use of life insurance in estate planning
66. Marital deduction
67. Intra-family and other business transfer techniques
68. Deferral and minimization of estate taxes
69. Generation-skipping transfer tax (GSTT)
70. Fiduciaries
71. Income in respect of a decedent (IRD)
72. Postmortem estate planning techniques
73. Estate planning for non-traditional relationships

Interpersonal Communication
74. Client and planner attitudes, values, biases and behavioral characteristics and the impact on financial planning
75. Principles of communication and counseling

Professional Conduct and Fiduciary Responsibility
76. CFP Board's *Code of Ethics and Professional Responsibility* and *Rules of Conduct*
77. CFP Board's *Financial Planning Practice Standards*
78. CFP Board's *Disciplinary Rules and Procedures*

GLOSSARY

ESTATE PLANNING

2503(b) trust. A 2503(b) trust must specify that income will be distributed annually to the beneficiary. This kind of trust is frequently used for minors and does not require distribution of principal when the beneficiary reaches majority.

2503(c) trust. A 2503(c) trust allows the trustee to accumulate income or to expend income and principal on behalf of the minor beneficiary. When the beneficiary reaches age 21, the unexpended income and principal must be made available to him or her. The beneficiary need not exercise the right to receive this distribution, and the trust can continue for an additional period of time.

5-and-5 power. The income beneficiary of a trust may be given a general power of appointment annually over the greater of: (1) $5,000, or (2) 5% of the trust assets. When the income beneficiary dies, only that year's potential withdrawal will be included in the gross estate. The failure to exercise the 5% power in prior years will have no federal estate tax significance. But, any amount above 5% that could have been appointed in the year of death (but was not) must be included in the gross estate of the possessor of the power of appointment.

Abatement. Abatement is the reduction of bequests when the assets of an estate are not sufficient to pay estate debts, costs, and all bequests. In the absence of an "abatement clause" in the will, specifying how reductions shall be made in such an event, the legally established order of priority in cutting bequests is followed.

Ademption. Ademption is the loss by a beneficiary of a specific bequest when the property has been disposed of prior to the testator's death. In such case, the beneficiary receives nothing.

Adjusted taxable gift. Adjusted taxable gifts are the value of all lifetime gifts made by the deceased after 1976. This amount must be added to the taxable estate to determine the tentative tax base.

Alternate valuation date. The alternate valuation date is six months after the decedent's date of death.

Alternate valuation election. The executor may elect to value estate assets at the date of death or six months later, if the estate tax will be reduced.

Ancillary probate procedure. If a decedent owned real estate located in a state other than his or her state of residence, probate proceedings must be conducted, not only in the state of residence, but also in each state where real estate is owned.

Annual exclusion. Federal tax law permits a donor to make present-interest gifts up to a maximum of $14,000 annually to any number of donees, without gift taxes being assessed. If the donor's spouse consents to the gift, the annual exclusion is $28,000 for each donee. The annual exclusion will be indexed for inflation and will increase in multiples of $1,000.

Ascertainable standard. A power is not general if the benefit is limited by an "ascertainable standard" relating to the health, education, support, or maintenance of a person or persons in whose favor the power may be exercised.

Available unified credit. The unified credit is generally referred to as the applicable credit amount. After subtracting the taxpayer's federal gift tax liability for the current calendar year from the amount of remaining unified credit, the difference is the available unified credit at the beginning of the next year.

Bargain sale. A bargain sale means that the transfer of property is for consideration that is less than fair market value.

Blockage discount. Blockage discount is a valuation technique. The theory behind the blockage discount is that a sizeable amount of stock contained in the decedent's gross estate cannot be readily sold at one time without decreasing the stock's market price. Thus, for valuation purposes, the value of the whole block of stock will be something less than the market price per share multiplied by the number of shares.

Buy-sell agreement. This is a contractual agreement among the stockholders of a close corporation (or between partners). The purposes of the agreement are to guarantee a market for the sale of the stock when a shareholder dies or becomes disabled at a guaranteed price (or a price formula) and to guarantee the surviving owners or business entity the right to buy the stock of the deceased at a stipulated price. When the agreement is structured properly, the stipulated price may be used to fix the value of the deceased's stock for federal estate tax purposes. Usually, the buy-sell agreement is funded with life insurance and disability income insurance policies.

Bypass trust. Known also as the "B" trust or credit-shelter trust, the bypass trust is designed to receive property that will take advantage of the individual's unified credit by not qualifying for the marital deduction. The trustee may be directed to distribute the net income of this trust to the surviving spouse during his or her lifetime, or the income may be accumulated or directed to other persons in order to reduce the overall income tax effect on the family.

Charitable deduction (estate). For federal estate tax purposes, a deduction from the adjusted gross estate is permitted to the extent of 100% of the value of any property conveyed to a qualified charity (provided the deceased had such rights over the property at death, so that the property is includible in the gross estate).

Charitable deduction (gift). The gift tax charitable deduction is a deduction for gift tax purposes, available to a donor who transfers property to a qualified charity (to the extent not already excluded by the annual exclusion).

Charitable lead trust. A charitable lead trust enables a taxpayer to obtain an income tax deduction for a charitable contribution, while retaining a reversionary right to the trust corpus. The income from the trust assets is paid to a charity for a specified number of years, and the remainder passes to noncharitable beneficiaries.

Charitable remainder. If assets are placed in trust with income payable to a noncharitable beneficiary, and the assets are to be given to a qualified charity at the beneficiary's death, the interest passing to charity is called a charitable remainder.

Charitable remainder annuity trust. Under the charitable remainder annuity trust, the income stream to the donor or other noncharitable beneficiary is a fixed dollar amount each year for life. The charity receives the remaining assets in the trust after the death of the life annuitant.

Charitable remainder unitrust. The charitable remainder unitrust is essentially the same as the charitable remainder annuity trust, differing only in that the income stream is variable and is a specified percentage (5% minimum) of the trust's assets, determined annually. If desired, the interest stream can be either the lesser of the aforementioned percentage of assets or the total trust income.

Charitable stock bailout. This arrangement provides for the gift of closely held stock to a qualified charitable organization, with the understanding that if the stock is put up for sale, it must first be offered to the corporation for redemption. In this fashion, the donor can avoid losing control of the corporation. The charitable bailout provides a donor with a current tax deduction and, ultimately, with a lower federal estate tax liability because of the transfer of closely held stock to a qualified charity.

Codicil. A codicil is a testamentary document executed with the same formality as a will, which modifies or changes part of a previously executed will.

Community property. Community property is any property acquired by a husband or wife during their marriage while they have a domicile in a state having community-property laws. Community-property states are Alaska, Arizona, California, Idaho, Louisiana, Nevada, New Mexico, Texas, Washington, and Wisconsin. The property is owned by each of the spouses, share and share alike.

Completed gift. A completed gift occurs only when property (the subject of the gift) has been placed beyond the donor's recall. Incomplete transfers may exist because of incomplete delivery or revocable transfers to trusts.

Complex trust. A complex trust is any trust that accumulates income, makes charitable contributions, or distributes corpus.

Conduit principle. For federal income tax purposes, an estate or trust is a conduit for income which is distributed to beneficiaries and is taxable to them. Any income accumulated is not taxed to the beneficiaries, but, instead, is taxed to the trust or estate. The general principle is that beneficiaries are taxed on the income currently distributed or credited, and the estate or trust is taxed on the portion it accumulates.

Contractual designation. This refers to specialized contracts that designate a beneficiary to receive property or income from property after the death of the person who initiated the contract. Annuities and distributions under qualified pension plans are two examples of contractual designations of beneficiaries.

Crummey power. A Crummey power is the noncumulative right of a trust beneficiary to withdraw some or all of the grantor's annual contribution to a trust. Crummey powers are often limited by a "five-and-five" power to avoid having assets includible in the beneficiary's gross estate due to a lapse of the power. A Revenue Ruling requires that the beneficiary have reasonable time and reasonable notice of the existence of the withdrawal right.

Crummey trust. A Crummey trust is a trust designed to permit a gift of a present interest that is eligible for the annual gift tax exclusion. This is accomplished by giving the beneficiary a Crummey power.

Cumulative gift tax. The government applies the gift tax rates to total lifetime taxable gifts, rather than only to taxable gifts made in the current year. Thus, in any given year, the taxpayer computes the gift tax on all cumulative gifts, regardless of when made. The taxpayer computes the tax on all gifts and then subtracts the amount of tax paid in prior years.

Custodianship. A custodianship involves supervision of a minor's property by an adult fiduciary. Custodianships are usually under the Uniform Gifts to Minors Act or the Uniform Transfers to Minors Act.

Deed of title. A deed of title conveys legal title to a property to a named person. Such an instrument transfers title when the deed is executed and delivered to the grantee or to an escrow agent. The deed is irrevocable, so the transfer may be a completed gift.

Disclaimer. A disclaimer is an absolute, unqualified renunciation of any beneficial interest, enjoyment, or ownership of property.

Disclaimer trust. The disclaimer trust is an irrevocable trust created under a testator's will to hold any estate assets that are disclaimed by a surviving spouse. The disclaimer trust agreement should authorize the distribution of a lifetime income to the surviving spouse but provide for the ultimate distribution of the trust assets to a beneficiary other than the surviving spouse at his or her subsequent death. Since the surviving spouse has only an income interest for life, the trust corpus is not included in his or her gross estate.

Discretionary trust. A discretionary trust gives the trustee authority to distribute or not to distribute income or corpus. The advantage of the discretionary trust is the flexibility given to the trustee.

Distributable net income (DNI). Distributable net income is, essentially, taxable income, as opposed to accounting income, which determines the ceiling on the amount taxable to the beneficiary of a trust, as opposed to the amount actually distributed by the trust. The trust beneficiaries are given the benefit of all trust deductions, including any deductions arising from expenses associated with the trust corpus. DNI also establishes the limit on the deduction which can be taken by the trust when calculating income tax liability for the distributions made to the beneficiaries.

Domicile. An individual's permanent residence in a particular jurisdiction, where he or she intends to return. The domicile determines in which location the estate is probated and what state can assess inheritance or estate tax.

Donee. The donee is the person who receives and accepts the gift of property.

Donor. The donor is the person making a gift of property to another person or to a qualified charity.

Double deduction rule. Most administrative expenses cannot be deducted on both the federal estate tax return (Form 706) and the estate's income tax return (Form 1041). Code Sec. 642(g) requires the executor to elect on which return he or she will use the deduction for administration expenses. Requiring such election prevents a double deduction.

Election against the will. An election against the deceased spouse's will by the surviving spouse is permitted under the laws of most states. The surviving spouse is thus protected against the possibility of being disinherited by the provisions of the decedent's will. Only a spouse may elect against the decedent's will. All other family members may *contest* a will that provides less than what they believe to be their rightful share of the deceased's estate.

Election to defeat conveyance of entire community-property interest. In a community-property state, if a decedent-spouse bequeaths the entire community-property interest to a third party, the surviving spouse has the right to file a statutory election to defeat the decedent-spouse's action. Thus, by filing a statutory election, the surviving spouse can protect his or her one-half interest in the community property.

Elective share statute. A surviving spouse cannot be totally disinherited in most states because such a spouse is protected against a vengeful or improvident decedent by "right of election" or "elective share" statutes. These statutes provide the surviving spouse with a specified percentage of the estate if the share devised in the will is less than the statutory share.

Endowment life insurance. Endowment insurance provides for the payment of the policy's face amount upon the death of the insured within a specified period and for payment of the face amount of the policy at the end of the specified period if the insured survives.

Estate trust. An estate trust qualifies for the marital deduction, even though income accumulates and is payable to the surviving spouse only by the discretion of the trustee. The trust ends upon the death of the surviving spouse, and the assets of the trust and accumulated income are paid to his or her estate at that time.

Executor commission. The executor commission is a fee paid for administering the estate and is often a percentage of the probate estate.

Exemption equivalent. The exemption equivalent, also called the applicable exclusion amount, is the dollar value of the deceased's taxable estate that is exempt from federal estate taxes because of the availability of the unified tax credit. The exemption equivalent for 2015 is $5.43 million for estate taxes.

Fair market valuation. Fair market value is the most frequently used technique for valuing assets contained in the gross estate. Fair market value is commonly regarded as the price agreed upon by a willing seller and a willing buyer when neither party is under any pressure to agree to a price.

Family-limited partnership. In a family-limited partnership, the parents are typically the general partners, and the children have received gifts of limited partnership interests. As general partners, the parents retain management control over the partnership business. Gifts of limited partnership interests will be entitled to discounts for lack-of-marketability and minority interests, so the parents will save substantially on gift taxes. There may be some shifting of income from higher-bracket parents to lower-bracket children, and there is some asset protection from creditors.

Family settlement agreement. A family settlement agreement resolves any disputes over a decedent's estate and is arranged by the family members outside of the court. However, for such an agreement to be valid, it must be approved by the court. Such agreements are labeled as "favorites of the law" because they are economical in the use of the court's time.

Fiduciary is a person in a position of trust and confidence who is required to act for the benefit and best interests of another person. An executor or administrator of an estate and a trustee for a trust are fiduciaries. The executor and administrator have a duty to act in the best interests of the beneficiaries of the estate. The trustee must act in the best interests of the trust beneficiaries. Attorneys-in-fact, guardians, and custodians are also fiduciaries.

Five-and-five power. The income beneficiary of a trust may be given a general power of appointment annually over the greater of: (1) $5,000, or (2) 5% of the trust assets. When the income beneficiary dies, only that year's potential withdrawal will be included in the gross estate. The failure to exercise the 5% power in prior years will have no federal estate tax significance. But, any amount above 5% that could have been appointed in the year of death (but was not) must be included in the gross estate of the possessor of the power of appointment.

Flower bonds. Flower bonds are United States Treasury obligations traditionally redeemed at a discount, but if owned by a decedent at death, these bonds can be redeemed at par value (plus accrued interest) in payment of federal estate taxes.

Fractional interest rule. The fractional interest rule applies to property owned jointly by persons who are not married. The rule requires that a fractional part of the full value of jointly owned property be excluded, based on the contribution of the survivor. The numerator of the fraction is the amount contributed, and the denominator is the full value of the property at the time the contribution was made. If "A" contributes $20,000, and "B" contributes $10,000 to buy a property valued at $30,000, then "A's" estate could exclude 1/3 of the value of the property at his or her death.

Freeze. A freeze is any technique that prevents appreciation of an asset from remaining in the estate of the owner.

Funded life insurance trust. A funded life insurance trust contains assets that will be sufficient to pay the annual premiums on the life insurance policies placed in the trust. Income from the assets placed in the trust will be taxed to the grantor to the extent it is used to pay premiums for policies on the grantor's life or on the life of the grantor's spouse.

General power of appointment. A general power permits the holder to transfer the property subject to the power of the holder, the holder's estate, the holder's creditors, or the creditors of the holder's estate. Such property will be included in a decedent's gross estate, regardless of whether the power could be exercised at death or only during the decedent's lifetime.

Generation-skipping transfer tax (GSTT). The GSTT is tax on transfers to beneficiaries two or more generations below the transferor. The tax is imposed on skips that take place by means of lifetime gifts or testamentary disposition. The tax is imposed on the transferor or his or her estate.

Generation-skipping trust (GST). A generation-skipping trust has beneficiaries who belong to generations which are two or more generations younger than the grantor of the trust. In years past, the generation-skipping trust was widely used to avoid estate taxes as property passed through succeeding generations. The mechanism was to convey, via an irrevocable trust, a life interest in property from one generation to the next with, generally, an ultimate time limit of "lives in being at the time of creation of the trust plus 21 years." The beneficial effect of the old-time generation-skipping trust has been eliminated by establishment of the generation-skipping transfer tax (GSTT).

Gift of a future interest. If the right to use, possess, or enjoy property is delayed, the gift is of a future interest.

Gift of a present interest. For a gift of a present interest, the donee must have the immediate right to use, possess, or enjoy the gift.

Gift tax charitable deduction. A person may make gifts of any amount to qualified charities tax-free.

Gift tax marital deduction. A person who makes a gift to his or her spouse is permitted an unlimited gift tax marital deduction. To qualify for the deduction, the gift must meet the following requirements: (1) it must be given by a donor who is a U.S. citizen, (2) it must be given to one's spouse, and (3) the interest in the property given must not be a terminable interest. A gift that qualifies for the marital deduction is made free of any federal gift tax.

Gift-leaseback. A gift-leaseback usually involves family members. A parent in a high tax bracket may give property to a child and then lease the property back from the child. The transaction might be partially a gift and partially a sale. The parent will continue to use the property as before but will now make lease payments to the child.

Grantor. The grantor of a trust is the person who creates it by placing the assets under the supervision of a trustee. The grantor is also called the settlor.

Grantor annuity trust. A grantor annuity trust is an irrevocable trust wherein money or property is transferred to the trust in exchange for an annuity of a specified dollar amount for a specified period of time. The value of the annuity is calculated using the IRS interest rate factors, and the value of the property transferred is deemed to have a fair market value comparable to the value of the annuity. The principal amount in the trust at the end of the annuity period can be distributed or can remain in the trust for the beneficiaries.

Grantor-retained income trust (GRIT). Under the grantor-retained income trust, the grantor irrevocably transfers assets to a trust for a specific number of years. The grantor retains the right to receive a specific dollar amount of income or a specific percentage of the principal sum in the trust annually. At the end of the specified number of years, the assets remaining in the trust are transferred to one or more named beneficiaries.

Gross estate. A person's gross estate is the total value of all property owned or over which a power of appointment is held at the time of death. The deceased's proportionate ownership in a property as a tenant in common is includible in the gross estate. Special rules apply to joint tenancies with rights of survivorship.

Gross-up rule. The gross-up rule refers to the inclusion in the decedent's gross estate of all gift taxes paid on gifts made within three years of the decedent's death. The value of the gifts is excluded, but the taxes paid on such gifts must be included in the decedent's gross estate.

Guardianship. A guardian is appointed by a court to manage the property of an incapacitated or incompetent person and to take care of such person's needs.

Income in respect of a decedent is income earned by a decedent; but at the time of the decedent's death, the money was not actually paid to the decedent. For example, dividends may be declared before death, but not paid until after death. Rent may be owed, but not paid until after death.

Incomplete gift. An incomplete gift is any gift over which the donor retains rights in a property or a right to revoke it. Incomplete delivery and revocable transfer to a trust are examples of incomplete gifts.

Inheritance tax. Some states impose an inheritance tax on the beneficiary's right to receive property from the decedent's estate. The level of tax may vary based on the degree of blood relationship between the decedent and the beneficiary.

Installment payments of estate tax. Under Sec. 6166 of the Internal Revenue Code, an executor may elect to pay the estate tax attributable to a closely held business in annual installments if the business is at least 35% of the decedent's adjusted gross estate.

Installment sale. An installment sale involves payments over a period of years. The seller can spread the receipt of capital gain over several tax years and thus defer the tax payments assessed against the gain. The seller usually retains a lien against the property sold, so the unpaid installments are secured by the property. An installment sale may be advantageous to the purchaser because he or she can pay the principal balance of the debt over a period of time.

Interest-only option. An interest-only option is a settlement option under which life insurance death proceeds are held by the insurance company, and the beneficiary receives only the interest on those proceeds. The interest payments are taxable as ordinary income. The beneficiary usually has the right to elect any of the other options.

Interpolated terminal reserve. The interpolated terminal reserve for a life insurance policy is the value of the reserve on a given date. Reserve values are shown by insurance companies as of the end of a given year. The reserve value at the end of six months, for example, would be the value at the end of the preceding year, plus one-half the difference between that year's value and the next year's terminal value.

Intestacy. Intestacy occurs when an individual dies without executing a valid will disposing of his or her property. The decedent's property is then distributed according to a statutory scheme.

Intestate estate. The intestate estate is all of an individual's property subject to distribution according to intestate laws.

Irrevocable living trust. An irrevocable living trust is created during one's lifetime and requires the creator to give up the trust property forever. In addition to eliminating probate, it may reduce the family's income tax liability and the grantor's estate tax liability. The principal negative features of this type of trust are the irrevocable nature of the property transfer, the limitations placed on the grantor's control of the trust assets, and the possibility of gift tax liability.

Issue are biological offspring of a person. Issue can include children, grandchildren, and great-grandchildren. Issue usually does not include adopted children.

Joint and survivor annuity. A joint and survivor annuity provides periodic payments as long as either of two annuitants, usually a husband and wife, remains alive. While the payments continue until the second death, the amount may be reduced after the first death.

Joint and survivor life insurance. See survivorship life insurance.

Joint tenancy bank account. Joint tenancy bank accounts can be set up by entering into an agreement with a financial institution that the proceeds of the account will pass to the survivor. Both joint tenants sign the signature cards and can make deposits and withdrawals. Since the proceeds belong to the survivor under the agreement with the bank, these accounts have been held to pass outside probate and, therefore, are an effective will substitute.

Joint tenancy with right of survivorship. A joint tenancy in real or personal property is a substitute for a will because the property passes by operation of law to the surviving joint tenant, without having to pass through probate administration. Usually, this type of ownership is described as joint tenancy with right of survivorship to distinguish it from a tenancy in common. Joint tenancy with right of survivorship permits property to pass automatically to the survivor without probate proceedings, while property held in a tenancy in common usually will not pass automatically to co-tenants.

Joint will. A joint will is a single will executed by two or more individuals, generally a husband and wife.

Key individual life insurance. Key individual life insurance refers to a policy purchased by a business on the life of an important or key employee, where the business owns and pays for the policy and is named as the beneficiary. The proceeds at death are received free of income tax and can be used to offset lower profits and/or to help pay for a replacement. Premiums are not tax-deductible by the business firm.

Key personnel discount. The key personnel discount is a common technique used in valuing closely held stock. If the closely held business is headed and operated by one member of the family, for example, the founder, and if the founder also has a controlling interest in the stock, the value of the stock will probably diminish when the founder dies. Thus, a discount is appropriate in valuing the stock for estate tax purposes.

Kiddie tax. For minors under the age of 19 (24 if a student), any unearned income above $2,100 (in 2015) is taxed at the minor's parents' top marginal income tax rate.

Lack-of-marketability discount. When the executor of a deceased stockholder's estate attempts to sell the deceased's stock in a closely held corporation, a discount is sometimes allowed, based on the stock's lack of marketability.

Lapse. A lapse is the termination of a power without exercise.

Legacy. A legacy is a gift of personal property made by will.

Legatee. A legatee is a person who receives a gift of personal property under another's will.

Life insurance trust. Life insurance trust can refer to a variety of trust arrangements – both living and testamentary – designed to receive, hold, and/or distribute life insurance policies and/or proceeds.

Living will. A living will is a signed written statement setting forth an individual's wishes that life-support technology or artificial means not be used to prolong life if the person ever becomes a terminal patient or permanently unconscious.

Marital deduction. There is an unlimited marital deduction available for federal gift and estate tax purposes. This means that one spouse can transfer to the other spouse an unlimited amount of property, either during lifetime or at death, without the imposition of either federal gift or estate taxes. To qualify for the marital deduction, the transferee spouse must be given control over the property.

Minority interest discount. Stock held by a minority shareholder in a closely held corporation is sometimes given a discount for estate tax purposes. This discount is premised upon the minority shareholder's inability to influence corporate policy, compel dividend distributions, or force corporate liquidation, merger, consolidation, or sale.

Mutual will. A mutual will is a will made pursuant to an agreement between two or more individuals to dispose of their property in a certain way. Mutual wills can be a joint will or separate wills.

Net gift. A net gift is made conditionally. The condition is that the donee must pay the amount of the gift tax. The value of a net gift is the fair market value of the gifted property minus the amount of the gift tax payable.

Net gift technique. A net gift requires the donee to pay the federal gift tax. The Supreme Court has held that for net gifts, the donor has taxable income to the extent that the gift tax paid is in excess of the donor's cost basis. Any gift tax the donor or the donee pays will increase the donee's cost basis only to the extent that the gift tax is on the net appreciation of the property while the property was held by the donor. This means the gift tax must be apportioned between the appreciated and unappreciated parts of the total value of the property.

Noncharitable beneficiaries. Noncharitable beneficiaries are usually the taxable individuals who are the income beneficiaries of charitable remainder trusts and pooled-income funds and who are the corpus beneficiaries of charitable lead trusts.

Objective. An objective is a measurable target that a client plans to achieve.

Partial-interest gift. In a partial-interest gift, the donor transfers the remainder interest in a property but retains the right to use the property, such as the right to live in his or her personal residence or use his or her farm until death. A deduction is available for the gift of less than all of the taxpayer's interest in a property, where the interest given is a qualified conservation easement in perpetuity.

Partnership capital freeze. A partnership capital freeze permits the value of a partner's interest to be "frozen" at its present value during life, for estate tax purposes, with all or any part of later increases in value going to other members of the family partnership. A parent will retain a so-called "preferred" interest. This means the parent will have a preferred right to any income distribution and also will have a preferred position in case of liquidation of the partnership. The children will have a "regular" interest. This means that they participate in any distribution of income after the parent receives his or her preferred share. However, all future appreciation in the value of the business is assigned exclusively to the "regular" partners (usually, the children). Thus, if the business prospers, the parent avoids increased estate taxes.

Payable-on-death (POD) account. Payable-on-death accounts can be set up at financial institutions by depositing funds in an account for the benefit of another, payable on the death of the depositor. Whether this kind of account will be an effective will substitute depends upon controlling state law. Some states exempt POD accounts from the formalities of will execution, but other states do not honor the exemption and may impose post-death taxes, as well as administration expenses.

Personal holding company. A personal holding company is a corporation created for the purpose of owning selected assets of the family. Typically, the assets selected are highly-appreciated assets the creator of the corporation wishes to exclude from his or her gross estate for federal estate tax purposes. The stock of the new personal holding company issued to the creator of the corporation may be given by the creator to the family members so as to make maximum use of the gift tax annual exclusion and the unified tax credit to reduce the value of his or her gross estate.

Pooled-income fund. A pooled-income fund is virtually the same as a charitable remainder trust but is created and maintained by a public charity, rather than a private donor. Property given to the fund is commingled with that of other donors, and each donor (or other named income beneficiary) receives a pro rata share of the trust income annually.

Pourover trust. A pourover trust permits assets to be "poured in" from another source or sources. A pourover trust can be particularly useful for receiving, containing, and distributing employee benefits, Keogh plan funds, life insurance proceeds, IRA benefits, and bequests from wills. The trust may be revocable or irrevocable. The latter type avoids probate. A pourover trust can provide that the primary beneficiary has only a life interest, with the remainder going to another beneficiary or beneficiaries upon the death of the primary beneficiary.

Power of appointment. A power of appointment confers a right to determine who will receive certain property. A power of appointment may be a general power or a limited power. Thus, a testator can give a child the right to determine how the testator's residual estate will be distributed among the testator's grandchildren. This power of appointment is limited (not a general power) because the child can only allocate property among a limited class of beneficiaries. The holder of a limited power cannot take title to any of the property in his or her own name.

Power-of-appointment trust. A power-of-appointment trust, also called an "A" trust, grants the surviving spouse a general power of appointment over the principal and income, and the power is exercisable by the surviving spouse alone. This trust is used to hold those funds that qualify for the marital deduction. Assets in the trust avoid probate upon the death of the surviving spouse.

Precatory language. Precatory language is an expression of a hope or a wish in a testator's will, instead of a direction or command. Firm and clear language of intent should always be used in a will, rather than vague, precatory language. The court may refuse to give any effect to unclear language in a will.

Preferred stock recapitalization. In a preferred stock recapitalization, the capital structure of a corporation is rearranged so that preferred stock is issued in exchange for some of a stockholder's common stock. The recapitalization removes some future appreciation of the common stock from the owner's estate. The use of such recapitalizations has been restricted by tax laws.

Prenuptial, or premarital, agreement is an agreement entered into before marriage to plan for the events of separation, divorce, or death of the parties. The agreement may deal with issues such as custody of children, disposition of the parties' property, and waiver of the spousal right to an elective share.

Pretermitted heir is an heir omitted from the decedent's will. Pretermitted heirs are usually children born after the making of the will. In some states, a pretermitted heir is entitled to an intestate share of the decedent's estate. Pretermitted heir statutes are also called after-born child statutes.

Private annuity. A private annuity is an annuity between two entities, neither of whom is an insurance company. The terms of the typical arrangement provide for the sale of property or a business interest by the annuitant to a second entity, which agrees to make periodic payments, usually for the lifetime of the annuitant. In the past, the annuitant could spread out the capital gain in much the same way as under an installment sale. For income tax purposes, the annuitant treated each payment as partially a tax-free return of capital (return of cost basis), partially as a capital gain, and partially as ordinary income (annual interest element). Proposed regulations require the seller to recognize all of the capital gain in the year of the sale instead of as annuity payments are received. The obligor cannot deduct any part of the payments made to the annuitant.

Private nonoperating foundation. Private nonoperating foundation is the general term for nonprofit organizations such as private charities (religious, educational, scientific, etc.), domestic fraternal societies, war veterans' associations, and nonprofit cemeteries. The maximum deduction available for gifts to a private nonoperating foundation is the lesser of 30% of the donor's AGI or 50% of the donor's AGI, minus the value of any charitable deductions the donor has taken for gifts to public charities.

Probate. Probate is an orderly procedure for submitting and paying creditors' claims, for documenting and transferring title to the decedent's property, for proving the validity of the decedent's will, for providing a specific person(s) with the necessary authority to collect and to distribute the decedent's assets on behalf of the estate, for providing a systematic administration (inventory, appraisal, and accounting) of the decedent's estate, and for providing notice of the decedent's death and estate proceedings to all interested parties, so they may act in a timely fashion or be barred from further rights. Judicial supervision and approval minimize the possibility of future claims against the estate by heirs and creditors.

Public charities. Public charities are the educational, scientific, religious, medical, and related nonprofit organizations which are publicly supported. Examples of public charities include the Red Cross, the United Way, universities, hospitals, churches, synagogues, etc. Groups that aid or prevent cruelty to children or animals and governmental units that use donations solely for public purposes are included in this category. The maximum deduction available for gifts to qualified public charities (50% organizations) is 50% of the donor's adjusted gross income (AGI).

QTIP. QTIP means "qualifying terminable-interest property." A QTIP interest provides a life income with a power to invade during the lifetime of the surviving spouse and qualifies for the marital deduction. The value of the property at the death of the donee-spouse (life-income beneficiary) is includible in the gross estate of the donee-spouse. The grantor-spouse specifies how remaining assets are to be disposed of at the death of the donee-spouse. The executor for the deceased's estate (first spouse to die) must elect the extent to take the marital deduction.

QTIP election. To qualify estate property for the estate tax marital deduction, the property must be left to the surviving spouse under conditions that avoid the terminable-interest rule. However, qualifying life-income property (known as QTIP property) is an exception to the terminable-interest rule. Such property will be treated as QTIP property only if the executor so elects. The executor's election statement must promise that the property's value at the date of death of the surviving spouse will be included in his or her gross estate. Thus, by electing QTIP treatment, the executor preserves the marital deduction for the estate of the first spouse to die, even though the surviving spouse has a terminable interest in the property that provides the life income.

Qualified disclaimer. By satisfying the Code requirements for a qualified disclaimer, an estate beneficiary may avoid receipt of property bequeathed to him or her. To be a qualified disclaimer, the refusal to accept the property must be in writing and must be delivered within nine months of either the date of transfer or the date the disclaimant becomes twenty-one years of age. The disclaimed property must pass to someone else, without the disclaimant giving any direction as to how the disclaimed property is to be used or disposed of. Failure to meet these requirements will mean the disclaimant is making a taxable gift.

Qualified disclaimer of power. A disclaimer is a refusal by a donee of a power of appointment to accept the power. The refusal must be an irrevocable written statement. There are no gift tax consequences for the person who executes a qualified disclaimer. In filing a qualified disclaimer, the named holder of the power of appointment must be careful to conform to the formal requirements of the IRC.

Qualified heir. A qualified heir is defined by the Internal Revenue Code to include ancestors, lineal descendants, spouses, cousins, daughters-in-law and sons-in-law, and other members of the immediate family.

Qualified personal residence trust (QPRT). The QPRT allows a taxpayer to transfer his or her personal residence to a trust and retain the right to live in the home for a period of years. For gift tax purposes, the retained right by the taxpayer is not valued at zero. The gift of the remainder interest does not qualify for the annual gift tax exclusion, as it is a future-interest gift.

Qualified organization. For a charitable contribution to be deductible, it must be made to a qualified organization as determined by the Internal Revenue Service. IRS Publication 78 presents a detailed listing of qualified organizations.

Qualifying property. The word "qualifying" is typically used to mean the property qualifies for the marital deduction. Qualifying property is an interest in property, or a specific portion of property, passing from the decedent-spouse to the surviving spouse, of which the surviving spouse receives a qualifying interest. (The value of the property at the death of the donee-spouse is includible in her or his gross estate.)

Quasi-community property. This is property that was originally acquired by spouses in a non-community-property state which, upon the family's subsequent move to California, Idaho, or Arizona, is treated as community property.

Reciprocal will. A reciprocal will is a will in which each testator names the other as his or her beneficiary. This reciprocity can also be accomplished by a joint will or separate wills.

Related-use asset. A gift of long-term, appreciated tangible personal property provides a deduction equal to its fair market value if the asset is donated to an organization whose purpose is related to the nature of the gift, e.g., a painting or a sculpture given to a public art gallery. In this case, it is a related-use asset. The same gift made to the Boy Scouts or the Red Cross is use-unrelated, and the deduction for the gift is limited to the taxpayer's adjusted basis. The deduction for use-related tangible personal property is the same as it is for long-term capital-gain property.

Remainder interest transactions (RITs). In a remainder interest transaction, the parent sells a remainder interest in property to a child, and the parent retains the right to possess and enjoy the property for his or her lifetime. The child pays the present value of the remainder interest. If the parent is age 58, the child would pay approximately 23% of the property's value. The parent removes the property from his or her gross estate for federal estate tax purposes, and the child receives the property at the death of the parent.

Remainderperson is any person who holds a remainder interest in property, such as the right to trust assets after a life estate ends.

Residuary clause. A residuary clause in a will provides a method for disposal of any portion of the estate remaining after payment of all debts, administration expenses, taxes, and specific bequests.

Retained interest. A retained interest in property is any interest that the prior owner retains for himself or herself in a transaction. For example, a mother gives her home to her daughter but retains the right to live in the house for her lifetime. The mother holds a retained life estate.

<u>Retained life interest</u>. The retention of the right to the possession or enjoyment of trust income by the grantor for the period of his or her life constitutes a retained life interest.

<u>Reversionary interest</u>. A reversionary interest in property arises when a possibility exists that at a future date, the transferred property either may return to the decedent or to his or her estate or may be subject to the decedent's power of disposition.

<u>Revocable trust</u>. A revocable trust or revocable living trust is created during one's lifetime (as distinguished from a testamentary trust that becomes operative at the death of the testator) and can be revoked or terminated by the grantor (creator) at any time prior to death.

<u>Revocation power</u>. The power to revoke is the right retained by the grantor to change the terms of a trust or to cancel it entirely.

<u>Rule against perpetuities</u>. The rule against perpetuities in many states permits the creator of a trust to extend the life of a trust only for the lifetime of any persons alive at the time the trust is created plus 21 years and nine months. The rule against perpetuities does not apply to trusts created for charitable beneficiaries. A testator may establish a perpetual trust for a charitable beneficiary.

<u>Sale-leaseback</u>. A sale-leaseback occurs when one party sells property to another and then leases it back from the purchaser. A business entity may be short of cash, so it sells a warehouse and immediately leases it back. The business firm can deduct the monthly lease payments as an expense for income tax purposes. Another purpose is to reduce income for a family member in a high marginal tax bracket. However, such a transaction must be arranged carefully because the IRS will scrutinize a transfer "designed solely and merely to shift income taxes."

<u>Second disposition</u>. A second disposition typically refers to a sale of property recently acquired by an installment purchaser. The first seller has obtained the tax advantages of an installment sale with the capital gain spread over several years. The buyer now arranges a second disposition with little or no capital gain. If the second disposition is within two years of the installment sale, the IRS now requires the first seller to realize all capital gains at the time of the second disposition.

<u>Sec. 303 redemption</u>. Under Sec. 303 of the Internal Revenue Code, a decedent's stock may be redeemed from the estate, and such a redemption will not be treated as a dividend if all the stock of the corporation owned by the deceased is more than 35% of the decedent's adjusted gross estate. The estate will receive this special treatment for redeemed stock up to the total of federal estate taxes, state death taxes, and funeral and administrative expenses.

<u>Security</u>. Security is the protection provided for a loan to give the lender the right to take property belonging to the borrower in the event of a default in making payments. Security is often also provided in other transactions, such as installment sales.

<u>Short-term (Clifford) trust</u>. A Clifford trust is a limited irrevocable trust was been helpful in family financial planning situations. Prior to March 1, 1986, its primary purpose was to effect

income-shifting and, thereby, provide family income tax savings, while still providing for the return of the corpus to the grantor after a minimum period of ten years and one day.

Simple trust. Income from a simple trust must be distributed fully in the year the income is earned, but the trustee is not permitted to distribute any corpus. For federal income tax purposes, capital gains are not treated as part of the distributable net income of a simple trust. If the trust ceases to meet the previous requirements, the trust will be treated for tax purposes as a complex trust.

Single-life annuity. Under a single-life annuity, periodic payments are made for the annuitant's life and cease when the annuitant dies. At the death of a single-life annuitant, there is no value in the annuity that is includible in the deceased's estate.

Sole ownership. Sole ownership exists when property is held in an individual's name and is owned entirely by that individual.

Special power of appointment. A special power of appointment places restrictions on the donee's choice of appointees. It enables the holder of the power to appoint property to others designated by the donor of the power, but not to the donee, his or her creditors, his or her estate, or the creditors of his or her estate.

Special-use valuation. Special-use valuation is a method for valuing real estate used in a closely held business or for farming purposes. Special-use valuation, if elected by the decedent's executor, may result in significant estate tax savings.

Spendthrift trust. A spendthrift trust is designed to protect the trust assets from the "spendthrift" propensities of the trust's beneficiaries. Thus, a trust provision may prohibit a trust beneficiary from assigning his or her interest in the trust corpus. Such a provision also prevents creditors from reaching the trust assets by any legal or equitable process.

Split gift. Gift-splitting means that a married donor may treat a gift to a third party as if his or her spouse made one-half of the gift. The non-donor-spouse must consent to the splitting. The donor is required to file a federal gift tax return, indicating that the gift is a split gift. If either spouse elects to implement gift-splitting, and the second spouse consents, all gifts made by the spouses during that current reporting period (calendar year) must be treated as split gifts.

Split-dollar life insurance. Split-dollar life insurance provides for a company and an employee to split the premium cost for a policy on the insured employee. An agreement is also made as to dividing the death proceeds between the employee's beneficiaries and the company.

Split interest purchases (SPLITS). A split interest purchase is typically arranged so that a parent acquires a life-income interest in newly purchased property, and a child acquires a remainder interest in the property. The purchase price might be divided on approximately a 75%/25% basis, depending on the parent's age and expectation of survivorship. At the parent's death, the child would acquire absolute title to the property, with no federal estate tax consequences for the parent.

Standby trust. A standby trust is designed to become operational if the grantor becomes temporarily or permanently disabled. A person might arrange for such a trust in anticipation of a temporary absence from the U.S. The trustee is authorized to use the trust assets to provide for the needs of the disabled grantor of the trust. There are no tax advantages associated with the standby trust. Its primary benefit is the professional management of the grantor's property in case of the grantor's disability.

Support trust. A support trust is designed to provide continuing income to the named beneficiaries in discharge of the grantor's legal obligation to provide for their support. A support trust has achieved considerable popularity as a device used by a parent, pursuant to the terms of a dissolution of marriage. The trustee is instructed to make periodic income payments to the custodial parent to fulfill the grantor's support obligation for minor children. Such trusts typically terminate when the youngest child reaches majority.

Survivorship life insurance. A survivorship life insurance policy, also called joint and survivor life insurance, pays the death benefit at the death of the last of two or more insured individuals. The policy may be term, whole life, or universal. The policy can insure two or more persons when there is an insurable interest, such as husband and wife, parent and child, business owners, or key employees.

Survivorship presumption. Married persons may provide in their wills that in the event of simultaneous death in a common disaster such as a plane crash, one of the married persons will be presumed to be the survivor. Such a provision is helpful in avoiding litigation among heirs and estates.

Taxable estate. The taxable estate is the adjusted gross estate minus: (1) the amount of any charitable bequests, and (2) the amount of the marital deduction. The adjusted gross estate is the gross estate minus the expense deductions.

Taxable gift. A taxable gift is the value of a gift subject to federal gift taxes after the allowance for gift-splitting, annual exclusions, the marital deduction, and charitable deductions.

Tenancy by the entirety. Tenancy by the entirety exists when spouses own property jointly with right of survivorship. Each spouse is said to own the entire property, so that no part can be taken by the creditors of one spouse.

Tenancy in common. Tenancy in common exists when property is owned by two or more persons, each owning an undivided interest in the property, but the size of the interest is a fraction of the whole. Each owner or tenant owns his or her portion separately and can pass it to his or her heirs because the survivor does not become the owner of the whole.

Tentative tax and tentative tax base. The tentative tax base is determined by adding to the taxable estate the amount of all adjusted taxable gifts, i.e., the value of all gifts made after 1976 that required the deceased to file a federal gift tax return. The estate Tax Tables are then applied to the tentative tax base to arrive at the tentative tax.

Term insurance. Term insurance provides protection for a definite but limited period of time. If death occurs during the term for which the policy is written, the death proceeds are payable. If the insured survives the term, the policy expires.

Terminable interest. A terminable interest terminates or fails after the passage of time, upon the happening of some contingency, or upon the failure of some event to occur. Property in which a surviving spouse has a terminable interest normally does not qualify for the marital deduction.

Testamentary trust. A testamentary trust is created in accordance with the instructions contained in a person's will. Testamentary trusts are used primarily when an individual wants complete control over property until death but wants the property to be used for the benefit of the trust beneficiaries according to the testator's instructions.

Testate estate. The testate estate includes all property that passes under the terms of a valid will executed by the owner before death.

Total gift. The full net value of the gift of property before subtracting the allowed reductions. The allowed reductions are: (1) gift-splitting, (2) annual exclusions, (3) the marital deduction, and (4) the charitable deduction.

Totten trust. Totten trusts are created when deposits are made to a bank or savings account for another person's benefit, and the depositor names himself or herself as trustee of the account. The depositor retains the right to withdraw any funds, and the beneficiary has no right to the funds until the depositor dies. Since payment of the account is dependent upon the death of the depositor, some states hold that the testamentary rules apply to Totten trusts. The Totten trust, therefore, is not viable as a will substitute in all states.

Transfer-for-value rule. The life insurance transfer-for-value rule requires that a purchaser of a policy must recognize taxable income to the extent the death proceeds exceed the purchaser's cost basis. The purchaser's cost basis is composed of the original purchase price plus subsequent net premiums paid. The following transfers for value are not subject to the transfer-for-value rule: (1) transfer to the insured, (2) transfer to a partner of an insured, (3) transfer to a partnership in which the insured is a partner, (4) transfer to a corporation in which the insured is an officer or stockholder, and (5) transfers by gift, between spouses, or incidental to a divorce.

Transferor is a person who transfers property, either during life or at death, to another person, called the transferee. A transfer may be a gift or a sale.

Unfunded life insurance trust. If one or more life insurance policies are placed in a trust, but the trust does not have assets sufficient to pay the premiums as they come due, the life insurance trust is unfunded. The grantor (or other person) must then make additional contributions in order to provide the funds to pay premiums.

Unified estate and gift tax system. A unified estate and gift tax system has been in effect since 1977. Under this system, lifetime gifts and bequests at death are now taxable at the same rate.

As indicated previously, any part of the unified tax credit not used for lifetime taxable gifts may be used to reduce the federal estate tax.

Unified tax credit. This credit may be used against either the federal gift tax or the federal estate tax. To the extent the credit is not used against the federal gift tax, it is available to be used against the federal estate tax. The credit from 1987 to 1997 was $192,800, which is the estate tax that would be due on a taxable estate of $600,000. Over the last few years, the unified tax credit has been increased, and in 2015, it is $2,117,800, which is the estate tax on a taxable estate of $5.43 million.

Uniform Gifts to Minors Act (UGMA). The Uniform Gifts to Minors Act allows lifetime gifts to minors. Title is placed in the name of a custodian on behalf of the minor. The custodian has limited powers of investment.

Uniform Transfers to Minors Act (UTMA). The Uniform Transfers to Minors Act allows lifetime gifts and testamentary transfers to minors. Title is placed in the name of a custodian on behalf of the minor.

Universal life insurance. In universal life insurance, a fixed percentage of the gross premium is allocated to the insurer's expenses. The remainder is credited to the policy's cash value, which appreciates monthly at market rates of interest.

Unlimited marital deduction. The estate of a decedent who dies after December 31, 1981, may deduct (for federal estate tax purposes) the full value of all qualifying property passing to the surviving spouse, including community property, without limitation as to the amount.

Unrelated-use asset. See also "related-use asset." The limit on the deduction for use-unrelated tangible personal property is the lower of the taxpayer's cost basis or 50% of adjusted gross income.

Variable life insurance. The term "variable life insurance" usually refers to a policy for which the death benefit and the policy's cash value vary with the investment experience of a segregated investment account maintained by the insurer. The rationale behind the variable life insurance policy is that during a period of inflation, the family needs additional protection, and, second, this additional protection can be paid for through the increased value of the segregated investment account. The funds in the segregated account are invested primarily in common stocks and other equities. These investments are expected to appreciate in value as inflation increases the family's need for more life insurance protection. Neither the death benefit nor the policy's cash value is guaranteed, but a minimum death benefit is guaranteed.

Whole life insurance. A whole life insurance policy commits the insurer to paying the face amount of the policy when the insured dies, and the policyholder pays a fixed periodic premium which remains the same for the duration of the policy. Most whole life policies mature as endowments at age 100 (age 120 for newer policies).

Will contest. A will contest is litigation conducted under the supervision of the appropriate court. Family members and relatives who believe the deceased's will is invalid for some reason must present their arguments in court. If the will is held to be invalid because of lack of testamentary capacity or for other reasons, the will provisions will be set aside, and the estate assets will be distributed in accordance with the state's intestate laws.

Will substitute. A will substitute is any means of property ownership or disposition of property that avoids a state's laws of intestacy and obviates the need for a will and probate administration. Will substitutes are often referred to as "poor man's wills."

Willing buyer-willing seller rule. See "fair market valuation."

INDEX

Adjusted Gross Estate –
    Secs. 2053, 2054, and 2058 ....59.9
Adjusted Taxable Gifts..59.11
Adoption..73.3
Advance Medical Directives – Living Wills 58.6
Advantages of Probate...54.9
Alternate Valuation Date – Sec. 2032 ....72.1
Ancillary Probate...54.4
Annual Exclusion – Sec. 2503............................57.5
Annuities...68.11
Appreciated Property 56.4
Appropriate Gift Property 56.4
Ascertainable Standard 61.2
Asset Protection Trust 62.4
Assets Subject to Probate.....................................54.5
Attribution Rules 60.4
Avoiding Probate, Techniques for........................54.7
Avoiding Will Contests 55.4
Bargain Sale – Sec. 1011 ....64.8
Bargain Sales 56.2, 67.7
Beneficiary Designations.....................................65.6
Blockage Discount..68.8
Bond Valuation..68.11
Business Agreements 55.6
Buy-Sell Agreements.................................60.3, 67.1
Buy-Sell Agreements; Types of............................60.3
Bypass or Credit –
    Shelter Trusts ("B" or Family Trust)............68.2
Bypass Planning – Formula Approach 68.3
Bypass Planning – Unified Credit:
    Now Portable To Surviving Spouse 68.2
Bypass Trust 62.3
"C" or "Q" Trust..66.4
Calculation and Analysis of the
    Effect of a Lifetime Gift Program 56.13
Calculation of Gift Tax – Sec. 2502 ....57.9
Calculation of the GSTT – Sec. 2642 ....69.5
Cash Flow Plan for Estate Liquidity...................60.10
Chapter 14 Rules for RITs and SPLITs 67.9
Chapter 14 Valuation –
    Retained Interests Valued at Zero –
    Secs. 2701-2704 ....68.15
Characteristics and Consequences of
    Property Titling 53.1

Charitable Deduction...64.4
Charitable Deduction – Sec. 2055 ....59.10
Charitable Deduction – Sec. 2522 ....57.8
Charitable Deduction – Secs. 2055 and 2522 ....64.1
Charitable Deduction Planning.............................64.3
Charitable Gift Annuity 64.8
Charitable Gift Techniques....................................56.3
Charitable Lead Trusts (CLATs and CLUTs) 64.7
Charitable Remainder Trusts 64.7
CLATs and CLUTs 64.7
Closely Held Business Interests...........................60.2
Closely Held Stock 68.8
Closely Held Stock –Use Caution 56.7
Cohabitation 73.2
Common Will Provisions 55.2
Community Property 53.6
Community Property and Probate 54.6
Community Property vs. Non-Community Property .53.1
Comparison of Agreements 60.5
Competency..56.2
Complex Trusts 62.10
Compliance, the cost of 59.14
Conservation Easement – Sec. 170......................64.10
Contribution Rule 59.5
Control Interests 68.16
Control is Maintained 54.12
Co-Ownership Discount 68.12
Corporate vs. Individual Trustee 70.3
CRAT – Sec. 664...64.3
CRATs and CRUTs; Comparison of 64.5
Credit for Tax on Prior Transfers – Sec. 2013....59.13
Credit for Tax Paid on Gifts before 1977 ....59.11
Cross-Purchase Agreement...................................60.4
Crummey Powers 57.5-57.7
Crummey Trusts 56.15
CRUT –Sec. 664...64.4
Current Gift and Estate Tax System –
    Prior Taxable Gifts 57.3
Date of Death and Alternate Valuation Date –
    Sec. 2032 ....68.7
Date of Transfer..68.7
Deduction of Estate Administration Expenses 72.7
Depreciated Property May Be Advantageous
    for Gifts 56.7

Differences between Gift and Estate Taxes 57.3

Direct Skip – Two or More Generations
    Below the Donor – Sec. 2612 ....69.2

Disadvantages of Intestacy 54.3

Disadvantages of Probate 54.10

Disclaimer of Joint Interest....................................72.4

Disclaimer Trusts..72.3

Discretionary and Sprinkling Provisions 62.6

Distributable Net Income (DNI) 62.11

Dividend Treatment – Sec. 302; Avoiding 60.4

Domestic Partnership Agreements..........................55.6

Donee's Basis 56.10

Donor-Advised Fund 64.9

Dower and Curtesy – Sec. 2034 ....59.6

Durable Power...58.4

Durable Power for Health Care 58.5

Durable Power for Property.....................................58.4

Dynasty Trust 62.5

EE and HH Savings Bonds 72.8

Election Against the Will..72.5

Entity-Purchase Agreement 60.3

Estate and Gift Tax Consequences 61.4

Estate and Gift Taxation 64.10

Estate Equalization with Nonmarital Trusts 68.5

Estate Freezes 68.14

Estate Liquidity 60.1

Estate Liquidity – Improving 60.2

Estate Liquidity, Cash Flow Plan 60.10

Estate Planning Documents 55.1

Estate Planning for Divorce and Separation 73.1

Estate Planning for Nontraditional Relationships.73.1

Estate Planning Weaknesses and Pitfalls............54.14

Estate Tax Calculation..59.15

Estate Tax Compliance and Tax Calculation........59.1

Estate Tax Filing Requirements – Sec. 6018 ....59.2

Estate Tax Impact of Joint Tenancy 54.11

Estate Tax Situation..56.2

Estate Taxation of Trusts..62.7

Estate Taxes, Deferral and Minimization 68.1

Estate Taxes, Disclaimer to Reduce 72.3

Estate Trusts 66.5

Estate Valuation Agreements 60.3

Estates of Nonresidents, Not Citizens –
    Secs. 2101 and 2108 ....66.7

Exception for Gift Taxes Paid on Appreciation..56.11

Exclusion of Property from the Gross Estate........68.1

Executor, Duties of the 70.2

Exempt Gifts...69.2

Exempt Property Award 72.6

Exemptions: (1) Tuition Payments
    (2) Medical Care Payments – Sec. 2503........57.4

Fair Market Value...68.7

Family Limited Liability Company (LLC).........67.12

Family Limited Partnership (FLP)......................67.10

Family Settlement Agreements............................72.6

Federal Gross Estate – Sec. 2031 ....59.3

Fees..70.3

Fiduciaries 70.1

Fiduciary Duties 70.1

Fiduciary Duties – Breach of.................................70.3

"50-50 Rule" – Sec. 2040 ....59.5

50% Rule 64.5

Filing Form 709 ....57.1

Filing the Return – Sec. 2603 ....69.4

First-Offer Provision..60.5

First-to-Die Insurance..65.2

"5-and-5 Power" 59.4, 61.3

FLP 67.10

Full Step-Up in Basis for Community Property ...53.8

Funded Revocable Trusts 58.6

Future Interests 64.3

General Nondurable Power.....................................58.3

General Power 61.2

General Power of Appointment – Sec. 2041 ....59.4

Generation-Skipping Transfer Tax (GSTT) –
    Secs. 2601 and 2641 ....69.1

Generation-Skipping Transfer Tax (GSTT)........56.16

Gift and Estate Taxation of Life Insurance...........65.6

Gift Tax – Net Gifts; Paying the...........................57.10

Gift Tax Compliance and Tax Calculation 57.1

Gift Tax Filing Requirements...............................57.1

Gift Tax Marital Deduction – Sec. 2523(i)...........66.7

Gift Tax Rules for Trusts.......................................62.6

Gift Tax Value of Life Insurance..........................56.6

Gift Tax; Calculation of – Sec. 2502 ....57.10

Gift Taxes Payable for Gifts after 1976.............59.11

Gifting Strategies...56.1

Gift-Leaseback 67.8

Gifts 67.11

Gifts Causa Mortis 59.8

Gifts of Community Property 53.7

Gifts of Non-Income-Producing Property 57.7

Gifts of Partnership Interests at
    Discounted Values..67.10

Gifts of Present and Future Interests.....................56.8
Gifts Subject to Debts...56.3
Gifts Subject to Tax..57.4
Gifts to Minors 57.6
Gifts to Noncitizen Spouses..................................56.9
Gift-Splitting – Sec. 2513 ....57.4
Gift-Splitting – Sec. 2652 ....69.2
Grantor-Retained Income Trust (GRIT) 63.1
Grantor Trusts – Secs. 671-678 ....62.9
AT – Sec. 2702(b).....................................63.4
ATs and GRUTs – Not Surviving the Term....63.5
RATs and GRUTs – Surviving the Term 63.5
RATs vs. GRUTs...63.5
GRIT 63.1
Gross-Up Rule 59.6
Group Term Life Insurance 65.3
GRUT – Sec. 2702(b)..63.5
GSTT 56.16
GSTT Annual Exclusion – Sec. 2642(c) 69.2
GSTT Exemption – Sec. 2631 ....69.1
GSTT Exemption, Automatic Allocation 69.5
Guardian, Duties of the.......................................70.2
Guardianship...58.2
Homestead Allowance 72.6
Improving Estate Liquidity..................................60.2
Inadvertent Intestacy..54.3
Incapacity Planning 58.1
Incapacity, cost of..58.2
Inclusion of Gifts in the Gross Estate 56.12
Income in Respect of a Decedent – Sec. 691........71.1
Income Shifting 56.9, 67.10
Income Shifting with Joint Tenancy....................54.10
Income Tax Bracket..56.2
Income Tax Consequences of
    Forgiveness of Note......................................67.2
Income Tax Deduction and Public Charities –
    Sec. 170 ....64.2
Income Tax Deductions with Private Charities 64.2
Income Tax Treatment - Private Annuity 67.5
Income Taxation of Lifetime Transfers 56.9
Income Taxation of Trusts...................................62.8
Income-Producing Property.................................56.4
Incorporation 67.13
Indirect Gift 57.5
Inflation Protection with CRUTs.........................64.5
Installment Payment – Sec. 6166.........................60.6
Installment Payment of Estate Taxes....................72.4

Installment Sales – Sec. 453 ....67.2
Insured Cross-Purchase Agreement......................60.4
Intentionally Defective Grantor Trust...................67.6
Inter Vivos and Testamentary Charitable Gifts.....68.7
Inter Vivos and Testamentary Trusts 62.2
Inter Vivos Gifts 56.1
Intestacy..54.2
Intestate Distribution – If No Children Survive....54.3
Intestate Distribution – If Only Children Survive 54.3
Intra-Family and Other Business Transfer............67.1
Intra-Family Loan..67.7
IRD, Assets Qualifying as 71.1
IRD, Calculation..71.1
IRD, Income Tax Treatment................................71.1
IRD, Retirement Assets 71.1
Irrevocable Life Insurance Trust..........................65.5
Joint and Survivor Annuity – Sec. 2039 ....59.5
Joint and Survivor Annuity vs. Single Life 67.6
Joint Ownership Convenience Account.................58.8
Joint Return, Filing 72.7
Joint Tenancy Property.......................................66.2
Joint Tenancy WROS 53.2
Joint, Mutual, and Reciprocal Wills 55.2
Key Person Life 65.3
Key Personnel Discount 68.9
Lack-of-Marketability Discount 68.9
Life Estates 66.3
Life Insurance.................60.9, 64.3, 65.1, 65.3, 66.2
Life Insurance – Gifts of.....................................57.5
Life Insurance – Sec. 2042 ....59.4
Life Insurance as Ideal Gifts...............................56.5
Life Insurance in Community-Property States 53.7
Life Insurance Policies 68.11
Life Insurance Techniques..................................65.6
Lifetime Gift Strategies 68.1
Lifetime Gift-Giving Techniques 56.4
Living Wills..55.5
Living Wills – Advance Medical Directives 58.6
LLC 67.12
Loan..60.9
Long-Term Care Insurance.................................58.8
Loss of Control 54.11, 65.5
Management Can Be Observed 54.13
Marital Agreements 55.6
Marital Deduction..66.5
Marital Deduction – Sec. 2056 ....59.10
Marital Deduction – Sec. 2523 ....57.8

Marital Deduction and Bypass Trust Planning 68.2
Marital Deduction is Unlimited in Amount 66.2
Marital Deduction Lost for Noncitizens 66.6
Marital Deduction Requirements –
    Secs. 2056, 2523, and 2106 ....66.1
Marital Trusts 62.4, 66.3
Medicaid Trust...58.7
Medical and Personal Decisions.........................58.5
Medical Expense Deduction 72.7
Minority Discount...68.9
Modifying or Revoking a Will 55.4
Mutual Funds...68.11
Net Gifts 56.4
No Income or Transfer Tax Advantages.............54.13
Noncitizen Residents – Estate Planning for.........66.6
Nonfamily GRITs..63.2
Omitted Dividends Added to Estate or Gift........68.16
One-Half of Community Property Is Included
    in the Gross Estate 53.8
Outright Bequests 66.2
Outright Gifts...64.1
Overqualification of Property for the Marital
    Deduction 54.11
Owned Property – Sec. 2033 ....59.3
Ownership and Beneficiary Considerations 65.2
Ownership...65.1, 65.5
Partial Intestacy 54.3
Partnership Capital Freeze.................................67.12
Pegging Value with Buy-Sell Agreements 68.10
Per Capita 55.3
Per Stirpes...55.3
Personal Holding Company Rules.......................67.14
Planning for Gifts 56.1
Policies on Another Person.................................59.5
Political Contributions..57.4
Pooled-Income Fund...64.6
Postmortem Planning Defined............................72.1
Pour-Over Trust...62.4
Power of Attorney 55.5, 58.3
Power to Amend, Alter, or Revoke – Sec. 2038...59.8
Power-of-Appointment Trust
    (Marital or "A" Trust) 66.3
Powers of Appointment – Sec. 2514 ....61.1, 61.3
Powers of Guardians..58.3
Predeceased Parent Exception – Sec. 2651..........69.4
Preferred Stock Recapitalization 67.13, 68.14
Present and Future Interests...............................53.10

Private Annuity..67.4
Private Foundation...64.2
Probate Process...54.4
Proceeds Payable to the Executor or Estate Is
    Included 59.5
Property Below Basis Should Not Be Used
    for Gifts 56.7
Property in Other States Is Good for Gifts 56.8
Property Interests Included in the Gross Estate 59.3
Protection from Creditors ....54.1(
Provide for Incapacity ....54.
Publicly Held Stock..68.
QDOT...66.7
QPRT...63.2
QTIP 66.6
QTIP Election – Sec. 2056 ....72.5
QTIP Trust 62.4
QTIP Trust ("C" or "Q" Trust)............................66.4
Qualified Conservation Easement 68.12
Qualified Disclaimer – Sec. 2518 ....72.2
Qualified Domestic Trust (QDOT) – Sec. 2056A....66.7
Qualified Interest Trusts 63.1
Qualified Personal Residence Trust (QPRT) –
    Sec. 2702 ....63.2
Qualifying Transfers...66.2
Quasi-Community Property..................................53.8
Rate Structure..62.8
Real Estate 68.12
Reciprocal Trusts..59.7
Recommendation of Appropriate Trust 62.7
Recommendations for the Form of
    Property Interest 53.9
Reducing Gifts to Taxable Gifts 57.4
Relationship..56.2
Release or Lapse of a Power – Sec. 2514(e)........61.3
Remainder Interests 64.7
Remainder Interest Transaction (RIT)..................67.8
Remainderpersons and Income Beneficiaries.....53.10
Remarriage and Children of Another Relationship ..73.1
Resale Rules – Sec. 453(e) 67.3
Retained Life Interests – Sec. 2036 ....59.7
Reverse Gifts – Sec. 1014(e) 56.5
Reverse QTIP Election 69.2
Reversionary Interests – Sec. 2037......................59.8
Reversions and Remainders................................53.10
Revocable and Irrevocable Trusts...............62.2, 62.3
Revocable Living Trusts.....................................54.12

Right of Survivorship 55.5
RIT 67.8
Rule Against Perpetuities 62.5
S Corporation 67.14
S Corporation Election 72.9
Sale of Assets 60.1
Sale-Leaseback 67.7
SCIN 67.3
Sec. 2503(b) Trust and Sec. 2503(c) Trust 62.5
Sec. 303 Redemption 60.7, 72.4
Section 2503(b) Trusts 56.14
Section 2503(c) Trusts 56.14
Selecting Gifts 56.8
Selecting Gifts for Donees 56.2
Selecting Property for Outright Gifts to Charity ...64.3
Selecting the Estate's Tax Year 72.8
Selecting the Executor 70.2
Self-Canceling Installment Note (SCIN) 67.3
Separate Property 53.6
Settlement Options 65.6
Simple Trusts – Secs. 642(b) 62.10
Sole Ownership 53.1
Special or Limited Power 61.2
Special Power 58.3
Special-Needs Trusts 58.7
Special-Use Valuation – Sec. 2032A 60.8, 68.12, 72.4
Spendthrift Trust 62.4
SPLIT 67.9
Split-Dollar Life Insurance 65.3
Split-Interest Purchase (SPLIT) 67.9
Springing Power 58.5
Standby Trust 62.5
Standby Trusts – Unfunded Revocable Trusts 58.7
State Death Taxes 59.14
State Death Taxes Deduction – Sec. 2058 ....59.10
Subtraction Method 68.15
Support Trusts 62.5, 73.2
Survivorship Life 65.2
Tangible Personal Property Trusts 63.4
Tax Act Changes – 2001 and 2010 ....57.2
Tax Liability 57.10
Tax Treatment of Distributions to Beneficiaries ..62.8
Taxable Distribution 69.3
Taxable Estate 59.9
Taxable Termination 69.3
Techniques for Gift Giving 56.2
10% Minimum Value for Common Stock 68.16
10% Rule 64.5

Tenancy by the Entirety 53.4
Tenancy in Common 53.5
Tentative Tax Base – Sec. 2001 ....59.11
Tentative Tax Calculation 59.11
Term Interests, Life Estates, and Remainders 68.12
Terminable Interests 59.10, 66.5
Testamentary Distribution 54.2
Titling Assets to the Trust is Often Forgotten 54.13
Totten Trust 62.3
Transfer at Death 54.1
Transfers (Large) to Trusts – Planning For 69.6
Transfers in Trust 67.6
Transfers in Trust with Retained Interests –
    Sec. 2702 ....68.16
Transfers within Three Years of Death –
    Sec. 2035 ....59.6
Trust Accounting Income 62.11
Trust Beneficiaries: Income and Remainder 62.6
Trust Features 62.1
Trust Ownership 53.9
Trust Taxable Income 62.11
Trustee, Duties of the 70.2
Trusts 55.5, 58.6
2010 Tax Act Retroactively Reinstated the
    Estate Tax As of 2010 ....59.1
2014 Applicable Exclusion, Gift and Estate Tax 57.2
UGMA 56.2
Unfunded Revocable Trusts – Standby Trusts 58.7
Unified Credit – Sec. 2010 ....59.11
Unified Credit or Applicable Credit Amount –
    Sec. 2505 ....57.8
Unified System 57.2
Uniform Fiduciary Access to Digital Assets
    Act (UFADAA) 70.4
Unpaid Installments at the Owner's Death 67.3
Uses of Irrevocable Trusts 62.3
Uses of Probate Avoidance Techniques:
    Joint Tenancy – Inexpensive and
    Easy to Set Up 54.10
Uses of Revocable Trusts 62.3
UTMA 56.3
Valuation Date 69.4
Waiver of Executor Commissions 72.9
Wealth Replacement Trust 64.9
Will Contest 72.6
Wills 55.1
Wills, Types of 55.2